William McKinley
and His America

Other books by

H. WAYNE MORGAN

Eugene V. Debs: Socialist for President (1962)
Writers in Transition: Seven Americans (1963)
The Gilded Age: A Reappraisal (1963) (Ed.)

William McKinley and His America

H. WAYNE MORGAN

SYRACUSE UNIVERSITY PRESS 1963

This work has been published
with the assistance of a
Ford Foundation grant.

Composition in Linotype Old Style No. 7
with display in Monotype Caslon Old Style

DESIGNED BY FREEMAN CHAMPNEY
JACKET DESIGN BY FRANK MAHOOD

Manufactured in the United States of America
by The Vail-Ballou Press, Inc., Binghamton, New York

To
George E. Mowry
and to
Brainerd Dyer

Acknowledgments

My travels in writing this book carried me from coast to coast and introduced me to some of the finest libraries and librarians in the country. It is a pleasure to repay my great debt to them here in the small way of printed thanks.

Mrs. Clara Beatty of the Nevada Historical Society resurrected long-lost materials on the silver question which were of prime importance. Mrs. Laura Ekstrom of the State Historical Society of Colorado did likewise, and was of great help. Mrs. Alice P. Hook of the Historical and Philosophical Society of Ohio gave me many hours of her time. Mr. Watt Marchman and his very cordial and helpful assistants, Mrs. Ruth Ballenger and Mrs. Rose Sberna, at the Hayes Memorial Library, gave me every benefit of their splendid library and made my stay in Fremont a great pleasure as well as a profit. Mrs. Alene Lowe White was of great assistance at the Western Reserve Historical Society. I am grateful to Mr. Edward Heald and his staff at the Stark County Historical Society in President McKinley's home town, Canton, for reminiscence as well as information.

At the Ohio Historical Society Mr. James Rodabaugh was his usual amiable and helpful self, and Miss Frances Goudy, Mrs. Elizabeth Martin, Mrs. Marion Bates, and Mr. George Kirk gave unstintingly of their help and cordiality during a long stay. Mr. Jack Musgrove, Mr. Fleming Fraker, and Mrs. Opal Williamson at the Iowa State Department of History and Archives were very helpful. Michigan's William L. Clements Library afforded much useful information, and Mr. Howard Peckham, its director, and Mr. Roger Barry, then his assistant, showed me every courtesy. Miss Josephine Harper and her staff at the State Historical Society of Wisconsin were of great help.

At the Library of Congress, I wish especially to thank Mr. Edwin A. Thompson, who not only gave me superb service, but enlivened many months of research work. At the New York Public Library, Mr. Paul Rugen and Mr. Robert Genett helped a great deal. Mr. Stephen T. Riley and his staff at the Massachusetts Historical Society were very helpful. Mrs. Russell Tobey was kind and efficient at the New Hampshire Historical Society. The late Professor Oscar D. Lambert and Mrs. Pauline Kissler at the West Virginia University Library gave freely of their time and cordiality.

I am grateful to Mr. and Mrs. Luther Day for welcoming me into their home in Cleveland and for giving me free access to the papers of William R. Day. Mrs. Sarah D. Winslow of Santa Monica, California, a niece of President McKinley, kindly divulged her memories to me in several happy afternoons. I wish to thank Hon. George Cabot Lodge for permission to use the papers of Henry Cabot Lodge; Winthrop W. Aldrich for permission to use the Nelson Aldrich papers; and Miss Helen Bawsel for permission to use her father's papers for the period when he was a secretary to Congressman McKinley. I was unable to use the papers of George P. Cortelyou since they are in the possession of a scholar writing his life. From what I have seen of them, and from portions already published, they seem unlikely to add anything important to the story of McKinley's life.

I am especially grateful to several colleagues who helped in this project. Mr. Thomas E. Felt of the College of Wooster very generously shared with me the results of his prodigious research on the life and times of Marcus A. Hanna. He has at all times been not merely helpful, but also cheerful and kind. Professor Donald H. Breese of Whittier College, Professor George E. Mowry of the University of California at Los Angeles, Professor Stanley Jones of the University of Illinois at Chicago, and Professor Thomas A. Bailey of Stanford University have all read very carefully certain portions of the book. They saved me from many errors, and added a great deal to the study. Needless to say, they are not responsible for whatever shortcomings remain.

I must thank the Haynes Foundation of Los Angeles for the grant which made this work possible. The Research Committee of the University of California at Los Angeles gave me funds for a tour of Western archives that was most productive. The University of Texas provided substantial funds for secretarial work.

Portions of this book have appeared in *Ohio Historical Quarterly*, *The Historian*, and *The New Mexico Historical Review*, and I am grateful for permission to reprint that material here. I wish also to thank the following firms for the use of copyrighted materials: The Ohio Historical Society for *The Diary and Letters of Rutherford B. Hayes* (Columbus: 1922–1926); Harper and Row for Julia B. Foraker, *I Would Live It Again* (New York: 1932), and Margaret Leech, *In The Days of McKinley* (New York: 1959); Houghton-Mifflin Company for Charles S. Olcott, *Life of William McKinley*, 2 vols. (Boston: 1916), and William Roscoe Thayer, *Life and Letters of John Hay*, 2 vols. (Boston: 1929); Exposition Press for B. H. Bristow, *Fraud and Politics at the Turn of the Century* (New York: 1952); Harvard University Press, and the President and Fellows of Harvard College for Elting Morison *et al.* (eds.), *Letters of Theodore Roosevelt* (Cambridge: 1951); G. P. Putnam's for A. W. Dunn, *From Harrison to Harding*, 2 vols. (New York: 1922); Charles Scribner's Sons for H. C. Lodge (ed.), *Selections from the Correspondence of Theodore Roosevelt and Henry Cabot Lodge*, 2 vols. (New York: 1925), and H. H. Kohlsaat, *From McKinley to Harding* (New York: 1923).

H. WAYNE MORGAN

University of Texas
Spring, 1963

Contents

Acknowledgments vii

I Origins and Ancestors 1

II The Volunteer Soldier 15

III Ohio Lawyer 33

IV Raising the Standard of Protection . . . 55

V Congressman William McKinley . . . 81

VI Serpents, Sharks, and Cooing Doves:
   Ohio Politics, 1880–1890 92

VII A National Figure 105

VIII The McKinley Tariff: Victory and Defeat . . 123

IX Governor of Ohio 152

X The McKinley Boom 183

XI The Front-Porch Campaign 209

XII Cabinetmaking 249

XIII The New Administration 272

XIV Presidential Profile 303

XV Cuba Libre! 326

XVI From Peace to War 351

XVII Commander-in-Chief 379

XVIII Making Peace 400

XIX Problems of Empire 424

XX The Diplomacy of Power 450

XXI President of All the People . . . 475

XXII Journey to Buffalo 509

XXIII Epilogue 526

Notes to Chapters 531

Index 589

Origins and Ancestors

THE OHIO RIVER crosses the land in a great fertile valley, giving wealth and beauty to six states. It carries the commerce of a nation's heartland, and its great cities are port cities, rich with the splendor and vitality of the inland seas. Throughout most of the nation's early history it was a cultural as well as geographic boundary. To its south gentle hills and hidden valleys fell away to a land marked by slavery and an old agricultural way of life. To its north lay a land equally rich, if not richer, in earth, mineral wealth, and a heterogeneous population. In the autumn and summer the Ohio's waters move languidly past the beauty on its banks; in spring and winter its languor becomes power, and ice and mud often swirl upon man's works as though the river still prizes its independence. A century after slavery and its institutions fell, the Beautiful Ohio is still a boundary between old and new, North and South, though in its waters and along its banks all of these meet and mingle.

The great river carries water to the Mississippi. In the eighteenth and early nineteenth centuries it also carried people from East to West. Of those who came to its valley in the eighteenth century none were more diverse, more numerous, more influential than the Scotch-Irish. Their first homes were in Virginia, Pennsylvania, and the entrepôts of the East Coast; from there they moved to Kentucky, West Virginia, Ohio, all the fertile and beckoning lands of the Ohio Valley which were the West in the eighteenth century.

Few national groups have given more to the American heritage than the prolific Scotch-Irish. Physically strong, they turned much of their strength to the basic crafts that sustain life. Their physical stamina carried with it a fierce independence in the face of government, coupled with respect for the law and individual rights, that placed them on the side of the Revolution in America. Not averse to good living and high spirits, they combined sport with work. Most

I

important, they brought with them to a strange new land the customs of an old civilization, and respect and demand for education and learning that made them carriers of culture on the frontier.

William McKinley drew strength and will from a long line of hard working, God-fearing Scotch-Irishmen, the same hardy stock that populated and subdued the frontier. The McKinley tree had deep roots, reaching back into the soil of its native country as well as that of its adopted America. The family had its black sheep who grazed in the same pastures with the white, and its early achievements in America were not extraordinary in any historical sense, but the very solidness of its heritage and the basic nature of its accomplishments marked it as good stock.

William McKinley's ancestors came from the Scotch highlands, where they were famous for their independence.[1] The Caledonian mountains bred a race of men as hardy as their habitat. Few wars passed them by; few hesitated to fight for their beliefs; and unless they faced an unusual opponent, they won their fight. Legend records that in the Battle of Pinkie in 1547 a stalwart highlander named "Findla Morh," or the Great Findla, was killed. In Gaelic his name read Fionn-Laidh, and was pronounced "I-on-lay." His four sons took the name MacIanla, meaning "sons of I-on-lay." Their descendants shortened and simplified the name to MacKinlay.

The MacKinlays, restless as well as hardy, eventually settled near Calender, in Perthshire. In 1690, James MacKinlay, "James the Trooper," joined the army of William III, en route to Ireland, as a guide, and stayed after the Battle of the Boyne, July 1, 1690, to found the Irish branch of the family tree.

The story of their ultimate migration to the new world is clouded in history. Why they came, who was involved, where they first settled, and the path of their westward movement is uncertain. That they came to better themselves is undoubtedly true; they may also have come, like the ancestors of William McKinley's mother, for religious freedom. The earliest MacKinlay immigrant to the New World was David McKinley, who at the age of twelve settled in York County, Pennsylvania, early in the eighteenth century. "David the Weaver," as he was called, adopted the "McKinley" spelling.

About 1743, David McKinley purchased a tract of land in York County, on the Susquehanna River, where his descendants farmed many years after his death.[2] The family was not prominent in politics, but accepted their share of the burdens of local government by serving on juries, occasionally holding law enforcement offices, attending to tax affairs, and in general fulfilling their ideals of social and personal responsibility.[3]

Those ideals rested on a strong sense of individualism and independence of character. When the American Revolution came, the McKinley men joined the colonial frontier ranks. David McKinley, born in 1755, great-grandfather of the President, enlisted as a recruit from Pennsylvania and saw a total of twenty-one months service between 1776 and 1778. He participated in the usual local skirmishes against the British and their Indian allies. After the war he lived in Westmoreland County, Pennsylvania, for fifteen years, and then moved to New Lisbon, Columbiana County, Ohio.[4]

Ancestors on both sides of President McKinley's family were iron workers and tinkers. His maternal great-grandfather, Andrew Rose, Jr., left the Continental army in order to cast lead bullets and cannon, an occupation more crucial to the ragged patriot armies than wielding a gun.[5] The small forge that he and other McKinley ancestors worked impressed many things on their descendants. Work with the hands, creativity, independence—all were reflected in their occupation.

David McKinley, the Revolutionary War veteran, fathered ten children, one of whom was James Stevenson McKinley, the President's grandfather, born in 1783. He married Mary Rose, whose ancestors had emigrated with William Penn to the New World. James and Mary McKinley settled in Mercer County, Pennsylvania, where he worked in the iron-foundry business. A son, christened William, was born to them on November 15, 1807, in New Lisbon, Ohio, where the family had moved seeking better prospects.[6]

This man who was to father a president was not extraordinary except in the force of his character. Strong of physique, he was true to his heritage in his taciturnity. Like his father and grandfather, he knew many trades; the life to which he was born required ready adaptability to hardship. He could forge iron, mend fence, paint, plow, tend animals, build houses, work wood, and occasionally invent things. At sixteen he worked full days, rising early and retiring early. His later pictures show a strong jaw, large nose, and keen eyes,

3

which reflect the determination and ability of the inner man. His education was limited to grammar school, scattered reading, and a small talent at figuring. He read Dante, the Bible, and Shakespeare; his neighbors later recalled that he wore the pages thin on all his books.

William McKinley, Sr., as he was called when his own son rose to national prominence, travelled a great deal during his youth in Ohio, tending to his furnace business.[7] But his travels did not prevent him from desiring and acquiring a family. Nancy Allison, whom he married in 1829, was a perfect companion for the pious, industrious, and independent McKinley. Old Mr. McKinley in after years fondly remembered that his wedding present to his new wife was a trip to a nearby spring where in mid-January the newlyweds took a mutual drink of icy water from a gourd dipper.[8]

The hardihood symbolized by that chill journey was evident in everything Nancy Allison McKinley undertook. Like her husband, she was descended from early immigrants, though her stock was English rather than Scotch-Irish. Her ancestors had fled England to live in Holland, where they could better practice their Puritanism. Her family originally came with Penn to Pennsylvania; one of her forebears owned a sizable tract of fertile land in that colonial breadbasket.[9]

Nancy Allison McKinley was later to exert a profound influence on all her children, and especially upon William, Jr. Her husband was often absent overseeing his foundries and on other business, and the duties of raising their large family fell mainly upon her. She accepted the burden without comment. If she felt her lot hard she never said so. The family formed the center of her life, and she was a devoted, if often stern, mother. Her fondness never became weakness, nor did her love for the children prevent her from raising them with the strict discipline that turned love into the deeper sense of responsibility that motivated her family.

Like her husband, Mother McKinley, as she was affectionately called, lived to see her son successful. Her lifetime of good works and solid if prosaic living gave her the perspective of common sense. "Mother McKinley was the leader in Niles of much that was good," a childhood friend of her son remembered.[10] "I recall her quiet dignity of manner," another noted. "She was just the same in the

4

midst of common-place duties as in a palace if she had been reigning there." [11]

Rural isolation and the need for self-help sharpened Mrs. McKinley's sense of responsibility to her family and neighbors. She tended sick friends, helped with welfare cases, bore her share of the community's problems, and acted as peacemaker, for she detested strife. She boarded visiting ministers and teachers. She and her sister had charge of the Methodist church in Niles, and swept, scrubbed, painted, and tended it with the same efficient thoroughness they applied to their own hearths and homes. According to one recollection, they "ran the church, all but the preaching."

When she visited relatives in other towns, she thought nothing of the necessary horseback ride, or of perching the youngest child on her lap so that he too might see distant cousins and aunts. No amount of worldly fame could offset in her eyes any man's failure to use all his talents. Nor was she ever over-impressed by William's political achievements. When he was governor of Ohio, she took the train to see him, and when a fellow passenger asked if she had relatives in Columbus, she replied only: "Yes, I have a son there." [12] Few who knew her at any stage in her life would have suspected her of producing a president, least of all herself. "After all, I don't believe I did raise the boy to be President," she said simply in her later years. "I tried to bring up the boy to be a good man, and that is the best that any mother can do. The first thing I knew, my son turned around and began to raise me to be the mother of a President." [13]

In the 1840's, Niles resembled scores of other country hamlets in Ohio. It boasted little more than a tree-shaded, unpaved street, lined by clapboard houses, a country store, a small church, and a bridge across the creek. It was laid out in the 1830's, but as early as the first decade of the century, discoveries of coal and iron ore in the adjacent hills promised it a future as a manufacturing town. By the 1830's, a local foundry was turning out regular consignments of andirons, stove castings, pipe, and household utensils, and the plant boasted a smokestack thirty feet high, little short of a man-made wonder for the area. In this factory the elder William McKinley entered into a brief partnership in the iron business. He made little money as manager and foreman, and he owed any success to his diligence and common sense rather than to any innate business

5

acumen. But he was never in debt beyond his ability to pay, and happily for him, his household expenses were few, for the older children helped their thrifty mother with her work.[14]

In this tiny hamlet, on January 29, 1843, Nancy McKinley bore a son, promptly christened after his father, William McKinley, Jr. He used this signature until his father's death in 1892. The area in which this future president was born produced a number of famous politicians with whom McKinley was later associated. James A. Garfield; William B. Allison, later a favorite son of Iowa; Matthew S. Quay, later boss of Pennsylvania politics; Thomas C. Platt, later boss of New York politics; and the two Shermans, William and John, were among those who either were born or spent the early part of their lives in this general area.

If it be true that successful politicians and statesmen spring from humble circumstances, William McKinley had a good beginning. The town of Niles, whose closest large neighbor was fledgling Youngstown, offered nothing extraordinary. "There wasn't much of a town there then, hardly anything but the furnace I was managing," the President's father later recalled. "Strange times those were, so different from now. No railroads, no canals and terribly poor, wild country roads." [15] The house in which this seventh of nine children was born fitted his later success story. It was a long, low, clapboarded and whitewashed two-storied structure, one part of which was a village grocery store. There was a chimney at one end of a steeply gabled roof, and the windows were carefully draped. Luxurious lengths of beautiful woodbine plant grew from the roof.[16]

Though he did not often reminisce about his childhood, President McKinley did remember the general sense of peace and isolation of his childhood in Niles. "I need not tell you that many very cherished memories crowd my mind as I stand in this presence," he said to well-wishers in Niles in 1899. "The old frame school-house and the church have disappeared, and in their places splendid structures have been built." [17] Beneath his strong reserve there was a deep craving for affection and a strong streak of sentimentality in William McKinley, and he expressed much of this in recollections of his youth. Time could not erase the nostalgia he felt not only for the simple town of Niles and its charming surroundings, but for the uncomplicated life it represented. As time increased the burden of his responsibilities, there arose in his mind's eye a vision of those un-tarnished days of boyhood's splendor. He remembered Niles and Youngstown as villages, before their peaceful rural environment was rudely shattered by the surge of power machinery, or lighted at night by the glare of massive steel furnaces. Progress came, sweeping all this away. Men travelled faster when William McKinley was president, but in his memories the old stage still rattled its way be-tween Poland and Massilon and all the other little towns that became cities.[18]

Like most uneducated men, William McKinley, Sr., longed that his children rise above his own station through education. Though lacking diplomas and degrees, the elder McKinley was not ignorant. Both he and his wife tried hard to maintain adequate intellectual standards in the midst of the arduous duties of child-raising. Hume's *History of England,* Gibbon's *Decline and Fall,* and the early works of Dickens graced the scant library shelves alongside the Bible in their household. The better monthly magazines were read carefully by every member of the family old enough, and saved to be passed on to the less fortunate. Horace Greeley's *Weekly Tribune* came into the home to fortify an anti-slavery bias that reflected the McKinleys' humble origins and Northern sympathies.[19] Though the family lacked intellectual pretensions, they encouraged study.

The stern but loving mother permitted no straggling in her chil-dren. They rose and retired early, and in between they quickly learned the basic responsibilities of life while living normal and happy childhoods. William got his share of attention but his mother did not dote on him. "I had six children [at that time], and I had all my own work to do," she remembered. "I did the best I could, of course, but I could not devote all my time to him." [20]

She did not have to, for he learned to care for himself. Though he had his bouts of sickness, William was usually healthy and anxious to join in games with his playmates. He early exhibited two traits that he carried through manhood— a reluctance to talk, and acute powers of observation. "He began to take notice of things when very young," his mother recalled.[21]

Mother McKinley enrolled her children in Sunday school before regular school, for she was a devout church-goer. The strong desire for education and learning appeared early. "My ideas of an educa-

7

tion were wholly practical, not theoretical," she said later in phrases worthy of her ancestry. "I put my children in school just as early as they could go alone to the teacher, and kept them at it. I did not allow them to stay away." [22] Though she herself was too busy to help them with their studies, they did not lack parental appreciation for their efforts, or parental prodding when they lagged.

Unlike most small boys, William was intrigued by school. It challenged him, and he enjoyed even the arduous tasks of copying and memorizing for recitation. He seldom fell behind in his work and was adept at accomplishing the tasks assigned him. "In talking with him as a boy and as a man," a childhood friend remembered, "I found that he reached his conclusions almost by intuition." [23] This was a key trait in McKinley's character, and one that helped him greatly in his later career: from the first he had an uncanny ability to judge men in conversation, and to see the simplest solution to a problem through reflection and insight. His real education never came from books, however much he liked study, but from observation. His personal charm and willingness to work were tempered by a common sense that sharpened his insight into the men and events around him.

The little school in Niles was no different from hundreds of similar rooms all over the United States in the mid-nineteenth century. The girls sat on one side of the room and the boys on the other. The benches and desks were made together in rows that extended the length of the room, with a cast-iron stove in the center. The teacher's desk often boasted a substantial rod, but the usual punishment was being forced to stand in the center of the room amid the jeers and snickers of fellow students, who also carried on the punishment after school.[24]

William entered school as the war with Mexico drew to a close. The small folk were aflame with patriotism, and the McKinley children did their share of parade-ground drills in paper hats and wooden swords. The school teacher, for whom the children had some affection despite his hard demands, was named Alva Sanford, and bore what his students fancied was a resemblance to Santa Anna, the Mexican dictator. He was promptly dubbed "Santa Anna," and became the secret object of many skilfully planned assaults.[25] William's taste for reading, his desire to please his family, and his own

8

interests made him a good if not brilliant student. "Billy had a head on his shoulders," as one former teacher put it.[26]

The elder McKinley was not satisfied with Niles' educational facilities and wished to send his youngest children elsewhere for a more substantial education. The nearest place was Poland, Ohio, which boasted an academy, or high school, founded by New Englanders. In 1852 the family moved there so the children could attend the academy. It meant considerable inconvenience for the father, whose business took him elsewhere, but he rode on horseback to see his family on weekends.

Although a step above Niles, Poland was no metropolis. It lay in the center of a rich farming area whose fringes were already being eaten by industry and mining. A part of the original Western Reserve, it was supposedly called Poland because that name could not easily be misspelled. Not always a sleepy town, in the years before the Civil War it would be a station on the Underground Railroad. When the future President was a mere boy, "Bluff Ben" Wade came over from Ashtabula to deliver a rousing speech against the hated Fugitive Slave Law of 1850.[27] Inevitably, the McKinleys came to hate slavery and its system.

The McKinley home in Poland was a large white frame dwelling with green blinds, and had a rising sun painted over the gable window. Maple trees stood in the yard, which was surrounded by a neat white picket fence. Mother McKinley had ample room in her new kitchen.

In recollection long years afterward, when boyhood and its surroundings had taken on the flavor of nostalgia and the charm of distance, McKinley fondly remembered Poland. It was "the trim, neat little village on the yellow creek with its tasty white frame dwellings, its dear old academy and the village store from which we got our political inspiration, and . . . the old churches, which, as boys, we attended under the careful and devoted guidance of our friends and guardians."[28]

Schooling did not interrupt childhood's greater joys, for William participated in sports and games with zest. As a boy he played a game called "Old Sow," in which a block of wood was maneuvered into a hole with a stick, a childish version of golf. He fished occasionally though he never liked it, swam with friends, and once al-

9

most drowned.[29] "William was a great hand for marbles," his mother recalled, "and he was very fond of his bows and arrows. He got so that he was a very good shot with the arrow and could hit almost anything that he aimed at. The thing he loved best of all was a kite. It seems to me I never went into the kitchen without seeing a paste pot or a ball of string waiting to be made into a kite. He never cared much for pets. I don't believe he ever had one. We did not own a horse, so he never rode or drove. . . . He loved to go barefoot. In going barefoot when he stubbed a toe or bruised his foot, he was proud as a king in showing the injury to the other boys. When summer came he always had a stone bruise. His shoes came off before the snow had left the ground." [30]

He had a serious side to him that neither friends nor family failed to see. Someone once stole his sweetheart, according to legend, and it disturbed him but did not keep him from his chores and studies.[31] They, after all, were more important. The shell of reserve and armor of dignity that so impressed the men he met later in public life were already building up in his youth. "He was just like other boys, except that he was of a more serious turn of mind," his mother said.[32]

He had his duties as well as his games. He often hurried home from school to help his mother. When his father was home, he helped cut wood, clear the yard, or tend cows. In Niles, as a small boy, he had learned to handle cattle, and his major chore then was driving the milk cows into the lot morning and evening. His freezing feet hurried over the winter ground. He stopped periodically to warm them in the places where the cows had lain, and remembered even as President that he had never known a more delicious feeling of luxury.[33]

The academy which he attended was not pretentious. It boasted no elegant campus or dazzling faculty, but it was adequate. Adversity dogged its early history, but the same spirit that moved the frontier west kept its doors open. Founded by Presbyterians, the institution passed under the control of members of the Methodist Episcopal Church, to which the McKinleys adhered. The energetic faculty devoted evenings and Saturdays to fund raising and what a later age would call public relations, and their zeal offset in part the earlier lack of money, soon making possible the erection of a three-story brick building to house the academy. Miss E. M. Blakelee was preceptress from 1849 to 1880, and influenced young William McKinley. A friend of his sister Anne, she vowed that she would teach longer than the McKinley girl, and the two made a game as well as a profession of teaching.[34]

McKinley was as diligent in Poland as he had been earlier in school. "He was always studying, studying, studying all the time," an acquaintance remembered.[35] "It was seldom that his head was not in a book," another recalled.[36] He still managed to attend parties, outings, and picnics, however, and doubtless arranged some of his own. There is no record of the subjects he studied at the academy, but they were most certainly standard fare: arithmetic, English grammar and literature, rhetoric, American history and government, Latin, and perhaps a touch of Greek.

The school debating society intrigued him more. Named after Edward Everett, the famous Massachusetts educator and orator, the "Everett Literary and Debating Society of Poland" was a combination debating club and lyceum. The students even outfitted a special room for its meetings. A collection was taken up, rugs bought and laid down, curtains hung, pictures procured for the walls, and the whole room painted. On the first meeting in the new quarters the boys appeared with muddy shoes, and when the girls protested, they removed them and debated in stocking feet until slippers were procured for future meetings.[37]

McKinley took a genuine interest in the society's affairs and was a leading member. He studied after school and devoted much of his spare time to preparing material for society debates. He read in the academy library, and developed a fondness for Longfellow, Whittier, and Byron. No longer did he participate in many games, except for occasional baseball matches, but he swam irregularly in summer and skated in winter.[38]

He had an aptitude for the practical; toward theoretical things his attitude was indifferent. His mind was always essentially retentive rather than creative. His ideas of education, like his mother's, were twofold: education should rest on facts and the tools of everyday life, and it should enable every man to fulfill his talents. No one was surprised when in after years he told a crowd of school children that their education, properly pursued, was the key to their dreams, and that he who worked hardest learned the most. "Avoid the dangerous tendency of the times toward superficial knowledge, which accepts shallow show rather than real acquirement. . . . Exact knowledge is the requirement of the hour. Luck will not last. It may help you once, but you cannot count on it. It is not permanent. Labor is the only key to opportunity. You are all here to do something, to work out a destiny, to discover the forces of nature and make them serve man's uses and God's purposes." [39]

His own efforts to discover God's design produced a devout piety in William McKinley. His sincere lifelong adherence to Methodism in part reflected his deep attachment to his mother, for whom the church was a center of existence. She longed to give one of her sons to the ministry, and William's diligence and aptitude for study seemed to mark him for the cloth. She often said that she was sorry he had only become president when he could have had such a useful and brilliant career in the church.

The church at Poland, then in charge of the scholarly and kindly Reverend W. F. Day, held many vigorous camp meetings and revivals. Like the academy, it was a center of fellowship, fraternization, and cultural interest, as well as an institution for saving souls. At sixteen, with his older sister Sarah, William came forward to the mourner's bench to "profess" his religion. His studious attention to Sunday school lessons and his long talks with teachers and prominent laymen had already marked him as a prize addition to the church.[40]

As the nation drifted into sharpened sectionalism and toward civil war, the McKinleys, like most people in Ohio, became more and more aware of the proximity of a peculiar institution. Across the Ohio River lay another land with strange customs. The Underground Railroad, travelling ministers, and local politicians all sharpened interest in the slavery question. "Practically, the McKinleys were very strong abolitionists, and William early imbibed very radical views regarding the enslavement of the colored race," his mother recalled. Young William often visited the local tannery, staffed largely by Democrats, and argued on the slavery question. His eloquence and knowledge were put to good use, but he converted no one. Yet he remained on friendly terms with the men involved, so skilful and kindly was his personal manner. He often stayed home to entertain

12

his sisters, to whom he was always devoted, but he preferred the more robust company of young men his own age, with whom he discussed the topics of the day, as well as horses, trade, and weather.[41]

This "strong abolitionism," fortified by a belief in the sanctity of the Union, prompted the young McKinley's enlistment in the Civil War. The desire for unity, the wish to preserve the Union, and the determination to make nationalism triumphant in all spheres of national life later translated themselves into his political philosophy of nationalism. It was not accidental that on the eve of the Civil War he took the negative side of the question: "Resolved, that it would be [good] policy on the part of the Federal Union to evacuate Fort Sumter," which the Athenian Literary Society of Poland debated on March 12, 1861.[42]

In 1860, at age seventeen, McKinley enrolled in Allegheny College in Meadville, Pennsylvania. A noted school of its day, the small institution afforded the best nearby facilities for higher education. Mother McKinley and Sister Helen loaned him their savings, for his mother still had secret ambitions to see him in the clergy. The young student and his cousin, William M. Osborne, journeyed to college by stage in September, 1860, and lived frugally together in a rooming house not far from the campus.

Diligence and hard work rather than cleverness or brilliance eased McKinley's path and made him respected and relatively successful. He displayed his retentive memory by learning his fellow students' names, home towns, and fields of study. Yet his bookishness did not keep him from social affairs, and his genial nature was in demand at such functions, particularly parties. His interest in politics sharpened at college, and when a Southern classmate toasted Jefferson Davis, McKinley told him hotly that he would fight on Southern soil before he would accept treason. Though he was a skilful debater he made no enemies, for as his Latin teacher said, he had "a winsome personality." [43]

Illness of an undetermined nature, coupled perhaps with a lack of finances, forced him to quit college later in the winter of 1860, and return home. The only degree he ever received from Allegheny was an Ll.D. in 1895.[44] Financial troubles overtook the family; William, Sr., was left responsible for a brother's debts, and other events tightened the household's already severe economy.[45]

13

It was not in young William to stay idly home while hard times pressed the family. All the bent of his training prompted him to make his own way. As one elder resident remarked: "He was a good steady young fellow, as I remember." [46] As a boy he had worked on farms and in neighbors' woodlots and cow pastures to earn pocket money and to help his family, but he never showed any desire to make money as an end in itself. Thus, while the doctrine of work was deeply ingrained in him, its chief satisfaction was not monetary gain but a sense of accomplishment. He was not a "go-getter," that species of man-on-the-make so admired in many frontier environments.

A clerk's job in the post office in Poland [47] served as a stopgap, but McKinley had neither liking nor talent, if any was required, for the work. When a teaching position opened in the old Kerr school district, he applied. In days when teaching, like the law, required no special study, it was not hard to "find a school." It was a logical choice for him: he liked youngsters, they respected him, he was well-read, and his sisters had already started in the profession.

The school was some three miles from town and the teacher walked. Neighbors later remembered seeing his slim figure leap over fences and cut across lots and fields.[48] At eighteen, he was a handsome boy, with ample dark hair, a somewhat slight but muscular build, and penetrating eyes. His courtesy and kindness enhanced his physical attractiveness, and more than one young lady's heart doubtless fluttered as he opened his books and assigned lessons. "My wages were, I think, $25 a month, and I boarded around," he recalled in 1895. "My parents, however, lived only three miles from the schoolhouse, and the most of the time I stayed with them and walked to school and back every day. Six miles would be a big walk for me now, I suppose, but it did not seem much then." [49]

This uncomplicated life, with the attendant studies, was rudely interrupted. The winter of 1860–61 was not a pleasant time in many American towns, for the embers of sectional hatred flared into the flames of civil war. Prepared in childhood for life in a rural society, McKinley soon found himself in the midst of men and forces he had not created or mastered. He who had prized the years of youth and who had done his best to fulfill his talents was now ready to emerge into manhood.

II

The Volunteer Soldier

THE CIVIL WAR came to Poland as it did to many other small towns throughout the North. The tensions that followed Lincoln's election, Southern bellicosity, and the gradually crystallizing Northern determination to defend the Union culminated in the bombardment of Fort Sumter on April 12, 1861. McKinley's cousin and confidant since boyhood, William Osborne, remembered working in a rolling mill one spring day when an elderly man rushed in and shouted: "They've fired on her! They've fired on her!" [1]

One day in June, 1861, Poland's main street came alive with flags and bunting, and the verandas jutting out over the dusty thoroughfare were lined with crying women and cheering men and boys. Here and there a small group of young ladies did not follow their mothers' examples; instead of crying, they fanned nervously and watched every movement. Charles Glidden, leading local attorney, mounted the steps of the tavern and made an earnest and eloquent appeal for volunteers. As he spoke, man after man left his companions and lined up to join the military contingent. Poland did not lack enthusiasm for the cause; no man was ever drafted from her precincts.

One of the watchers kept his head. Though already noted for his seriousness, McKinley felt the occasion's emotions. But he was still only eighteen, needed at home, and was accustomed to deliberation and consultation before acting. However much he wished to fight, he must think it over. Caught in the excitement of the moment between conflicting duties, McKinley and Will Osborne were in doubt. The Poland Guards, as the local contingent was called, later assembled with due pomp on the village green and marched to Youngstown where they entrained for Columbus and basic training. [2]

Osborne and McKinley saw their friends off, still undecided. On the buggy trip home they talked it over carefully and decided to enlist. It was their duty, any man who stayed behind would be ridiculed, it was their chance to get away from home and see the world. "Bill, we can't stay out of this war," McKinley said seriously. "We must get in." Osborne agreed but insisted that they tell their parents. McKinley thought a moment, then nodded.[3] Reaching home, McKinley told his mother what he had decided to do. If she felt any undue emotion, she hid it. She replied: "Well, boys, if you think it is your duty to fight for your country, I think you ought to go."[4] Neither of the boys was hot with emotion at the prospect before him. "Our enlistment was in cold blood, and not through the enthusiasm of the moment," Osborne insisted. "It was done as McKinley has done the most things of his life, as the logical offspring of careful conclusion."[5]

McKinley and Osborne went to Cleveland and then to Columbus, where they were sworn in by General John C. Fremont at Camp Jackson, the big basic training center near Columbus. "General Fremont, I remember, seemed a great man to me, a boy of seventeen, whose mind had been thrilled with the story of his wonderful adventures in the West," McKinley recalled in 1895. "I remember he pounded my chest and looked square into my eyes, and finally pronounced me fit for a soldier."[6]

The enthusiastic young recruits thought war would provide a holiday; it was, in fact, a four-year nightmare of pain and destruction. McKinley, who could not bear as a child to inflict pain on an animal, and who all of his life hated disorder and destruction, was thrown into some of the grimmest battles of the war. "We knew little of the great sacrifices which were to come or the scope and extent of that great war," he told an audience years later, "we only knew that the Union was threatened with overthrow; we only knew that the Nation of our fathers was in danger by the hand of treason."[7] The earnest young soldier wrote home: "Our boys are all determined to stand by the stars and stripes, and never give up until their lives are sacrificed, or the Government placed upon a firm and solid foundation."[8] His slavery-hating ancestry and his own sense of responsibility dictated no other course.

The Poland Guards originally intended to enlist for only three months in the federal service, but on arriving at Camp Jackson, now Camp Chase, they discovered that only three-year enlistments were available. They talked it over and when the vote was taken all but two enlisted for the full three years. One was rejected by the doctors, and the other was a divinity student who felt that three years would be too much out of his education. In the end, both men joined the regiment for the full term. On June 11, 1861, the Twenty-third Ohio Volunteer Infantry Regiment was sworn into federal service, with the Poland Guards comprising Company E. McKinley was fortunate to be in the Twenty-third OVI, for it was staffed by some of the future's most famous and influential men. The first colonel was William S. Rosecrans, who shortly left as a brigadier general. The first lieutenant colonel was Stanley Matthews, later a prominent Ohio Republican, U.S. senator, and member of the United States Supreme Court. Most important for McKinley was Major Rutherford B. Hayes, later the regimental commander, who instantly liked the young soldier.

Life at Camp Chase was new and different for the country boys who composed most of the regiment. Its tent city, subjected to a strange new discipline, held about 3,000 men by late July, quartered in some 300 tents. The Poland Guards formed a committee to answer mail and packages from home. McKinley was a member of it and wrote several letters to his home town newspaper, thanking the home front for clothing, food, tobacco, and money, all of which bolstered sagging spirits in a strange environment.[9]

Fortunately, the war started slowly, for the new Federal forces were in poor condition to fight a battle. Drilling and waiting occupied most of the days for the new recruits. Occasional visits from home folk highlighted the routine, but camp life was generally dull. Prayer meetings, which the young McKinley attended regularly, were a welcome stimulant and relief, for they afforded opportunities for fraternization as well as spiritual comfort. "The prayer meetings which we have been holding semi-weekly seem to have a good effect upon our brother soldiers, and are exerting a salutary influence, not only among our own company, but upon adjoining companies," he reassured the home folks.[10]

Those who enlisted for the sake of fancy uniforms were sorely disappointed. "Our eyes have also grown dim looking for our coats with brass buttons," McKinley wrote home late in June.[11] When weapons came, a day eagerly awaited by the young recruits, they were chagrined, for their muskets dated from the War of 1812. Their disappointment turned to resentment and flared into a minor rebellion, which the eloquent Hayes quelled with promises and soothing words. "The officers spent most of the day in trying to persuade us to receive the guns for a few weeks, if only for the purposes of drill," McKinley recalled. "None of us knew how to use any kind of musket at that time, but we thought we knew our rights and we were all conscious of our importance." Hayes finally persuaded the men to take the guns. "From that very moment he had our respect and admiration, which never weakened but ever increased during the four eventful years that followed." [12]

The young McKinley was undoubtedly morally strict in comparison to many of his fellows. He did not drink, was chaste, and did not yet swear. To some of his fellows he may have seemed prudish, but most of them were from similar family backgrounds. Had his moral rigor not been offset by his youth and rather charming seriousness, he might have been merely a bore. "It seems to be the determination of most, if not all, of our company, to preserve the good morals they brought with them, by avoiding the many temptations which necessarily surround them in Camp," he wrote home. "It is by no means essential that an individual who has enlisted to defend his country should forget his early teachings and bury his parents' instruction in oblivion. No—he can continually keep them before his mind, even remembering that they are like 'burning glasses, whose collected rays point with warmth and quickness to the heart.' " [13]

Late in July uniforms arrived, replete with overcoats which "give us the appearance of our Revolutionary fathers," and the final outfitting provoked a burst of patriotism: "May we be as bold soldiers as they were, and stand up for our God given rights as they did. May we never forget that we owe to them the support of the government they so nobly fought to establish. May we never become oblivious to the fact that it is ours to hand down to posterity this government as free, as pure, and as spotless as our sires transmitted it to us." [14]

McKinley did his share of guard duty, and routine camp policing. "I enjoyed sleeping on a rough board much better than I expected, with naught but an overcoat and a blanket to cover me," he noted in his brief diary after a stint of night guard duty.[15] He and friends left camp on brief passes, even enjoying one trip to Columbus, but his indulgences in spirits did not exceed lemonade. His chief transgression was an occasional cigar. Sometimes he read poetry from the works of Byron, revealing a slightly romantic vein which he never overcame. All too many days were summed up briefly: "All passed off as usual." [16] The Fourth of July, with speeches by Hayes and others and daytime balloons and night-time fireworks, was a welcome break.

The order and routine of camp life ended in the last week of July, when the Twenty-third OVI marched hastily into western Virginia after guerrillas.[17] Travelling partly by wagon but largely by foot, they reached the rugged area "where it is said 'seceshers' are thick." Sleeping on the hard ground in the cold night air, they rose the following morning to continue their march, and camped at the small settlement of Glenville, Virginia. The scenery impressed McKinley, the country boy used to Ohio's rolling hills. "Around me on the right and left are hills, high, such as I never witnessed before." [18]

Though he had not tasted battle, and in fact had not yet seen an enemy, thoughts of death ran through his mind. He recorded in his diary the testament he wished to leave behind, punctuated with all the boyish doubts and serious mien that reflected his age:

> Tomorrow's sun will undoubtedly find me on a march. It may be I will never see the light of another day. Should this be my fate I fall in a good cause and hope to fall in the arms of my blessed redeemer. This record I want to be left behind, that I not only fell as a soldier for my Country, but also as a Soldier of Jesus. I may never be permitted to tread the pleasant soil of Ohio, or see and converse with my friends again. In this emergency let . . . my parents, brothers and sisters, and friends have their anxiety removed by the thought that I am in the discharge of my duty, that I am doing nothing but [that which] my revolutionary fathers before me have done, and also let them be consoled with the solacing thought that if we never meet again on earth, we will meet around God's throne in Heaven. Let my fate be what it may, I want to be ready and prepared.[19]

Such thoughts run through nearly every man's mind on the eve of battle; few commit them to paper, and fewer still with such honesty. There was a certain compelling naiveté about McKinley throughout his life, but nowhere was it more evident, or more sincere, than during the Civil War. He seemed motivated throughout that conflict by a serene, often exalted belief that he would emerge safely. The stoicism that carried him through the rest of his life began to build in the war.

There were not many guerrillas. It all seemed like a game of hide-and-seek played at rapid march. The men grew weary and testy. McKinley did his share of grumbling about the harsh marching, bad food, and lack of evident purpose.[20] False alarms were hourly occurrences, and were not without occasional humor. Fellow pickets returned one evening, he wrote home, to tell a "scary story" of enemy infiltration. While guarding a bridge they heard footfalls and the rattle of sabers. Hunched in expectation, they never saw their adversaries, but were sure they wore gray:

> On the following night, four of us volunteered to go out and catch the 'seceshers' if possible. Accordingly we started out about dusk led by a certain lieutenant of our regiment. It would have done your heart good to have seen the above lieutenant prodding the thick bushes with his gilded sword, fancying to himself that he saw the hideous monster in the shape of a rebel. Ah,—the ambitious officer was disappointed; instead of sticking a secesh, he without doubt stuck a skunk. We came to this conclusion from the fact that a strong smell issued from the bushes. We imagined a great many strange things to appear before us, but all proved to be shadows instead of realities. We at last arrived at the hitherto 'scary' spot, stationed ourselves, and it was my lot to be placed in a cornfield by the roadside. I stayed there until morning, cocked my old musket, and was almost in the act of shooting a number of times, when the strange vision would disappear and on examination I would discover a piece of foxfire, an itinerant 'hog,' or a lost calf, which undoubtedly wandered from its mother in infantile days. We returned in the morning, sleepy, tired, and not as full of romance as the night before.[21]

Dispelling romance was a major business in the long war that followed, but the soldier who could laugh at himself was a better fighter.

The army resumed its desultory marches, on call for foraging and reconnaissance patrols, passing the scenes of former battles, slowly hardening into a fighting unit physically and mentally fit for the rugged terrain and its adversary. The simplest pleasures, like adequate rest and occasional breakfasts of wild blackberries, took on monumental proportions. The towns it camped near afforded little in the way of entertainment, but many of the people were pro-Unionists, and entertained the boys in blue when their scant stores permitted.

Neither side, blue or gray, was prepared for a real test of strength, and the skirmishing in western Virginia was only a minor series of probes. But by September enough forces had concentrated to make a battle inevitable, and on September 10, McKinley went into his first real action. If he had any doubts about the hardships of war or any illusions of the glories of battle, they vanished that day. The men captured an advance guard of Confederates and then came upon smoldering camp fires. The order to load was given and the men advanced. Shortly after three in the afternoon, "the firing commenced, and for over three hours the booming of cannon, the report of muskets could be distinctly heard, and the smoke could be seen rising to the Heavens." After a bombardment the men of the Twenty-third OVI deployed toward the Confederate lines at a dog-trot. Through meadows, cornfields, and thick laurel that tore at their hands and clothing, they advanced to cover flanking attacks. They clambered over sharp stones, climbing steep precipices, and along trails often so steep that they had to crawl on hands and knees and hold each other's belts to keep from falling. Arriving at the river crossing that led to enemy earthworks and gun emplacements, they found it impossible to cross. Pinned under enemy fire, they sat in water and mud listening to the cannonballs whiz past and occasionally fall with a dull thud into the morass around them. "We returned in the darkness of the night. I need not mention the difficulties we had in returning," McKinley noted tersely. Re-forming their lines, the tired and famished men found straw and cold rations and lay down for a fitful night's sleep, not knowing what the next day would bring.[22]

Happily for them, the Confederates under General John B. Floyd withdrew from their positions, leaving behind a large quantity of stores and personal booty, including Floyd's trunks, most of which the green young soldiers curiously inspected.[23] The Confederate withdrawal and the lateness of the season signaled winter quarters, and later in the month, after more minor skirmishing, the Twenty-third OVI marched to the damp environs of Camp Ewing, Virginia, to spend the winter in fitful bouts with fevers, colds, and rainy discomforts before fighting again in the spring. The last item in McKinley's hastily kept diary was a happy one; the men were paid "all flush," and he himself pocketed thirty-one dollars.[24]

Life's slow pace in winter quarters gave the men a chance to discuss their prowess and reminisce about their recent battle experience, which took on greater dimensions with every telling. The evening camp fires summoned up the shadows of imagination as well as experience among the new soldiers. Their engagement, known in the official reports as the Battle of Carnifex Ferry, was certainly not crucial in the war effort, but it was important to them. "This was our first real fight," McKinley recalled later, "and the effect of the victory was of far more consequence to us than the battle itself. It gave us confidence in ourselves and faith in our commander. We learned that we could fight and whip the rebels on their own ground." [25]

The winter of 1861–62 was one of doubt for the Federal forces, but it was also a time of hardening and new determination to mold an army to defeat the threat to the Union. The government and people alike settled to the task they had not fully anticipated. For the army in damp quarters in Virginia, the boredom was broken by the usual drills, letters from home, occasional visits from friends, and talk and speculation of coming struggles.

The long inaction ended in April, 1862, when the Twenty-third OVI moved with its unit toward Princeton, Virginia, still searching for guerrillas. Princeton was evacuated and the Federals moved to East River, to Camp Piatt, and to the Kanawha River area. Forced marches, small rations, and bad weather made the struggle harder. In three days they marched a hundred miles. From Parkersburg they were happy to ride the railroad to Washington, yelling and cheering at the damsels in the country depots and waving to farmers in the fields, or talking, playing cards, and sleeping in their seats. In the capital they joined fresh forces under General George B. McClellan who, it was rumored, planned an offensive into northern Virginia.[26]

McKinley had been promoted in April to commissary sergeant

and was assigned the onerous task of distributing rations, checking on fodder for horses, and attending to the endless stream of paper work necessary in the quartermaster division. He signed his name a thousand times, pondered columns of figures, checked addition, and personally supervised loading and unloading of supplies and rations. His compassion for animals eased the task somewhat, and he gave as much attention to the horses' wants as to those of his comrades.[27] McKinley's diligence caught Hayes' attention, and the latter looked upon the taciturn young man almost as a son. ". . . I came to know him like a book, and love him like a brother," Hayes remembered in 1891.[28] Impressed by his unflagging attention to details, Hayes quietly supported McKinley's career. ". . . We soon found that in business, in executive ability, young McKinley was a man of rare capacity, especially for a boy of his age . . . ," Hayes said in praise.[29]

Application, not brilliance, carried him; it was the same in military as in civil life. He remembered thirty years later what an old veteran told him when he entered the army: "Now, William, let me give you a word of advice. You can get along in your new place in such a way that it will be a bad rather than a good thing for you. On the other hand, you can easily make yourself so valuable to your superior that he cannot get along without you. Do little things not exactly under your supervision. Be conscientious in all your duties, and be faithful, and it will not be long until your superior officer will consider you an indispensable assistant." [30]

In after years he repeated this advice without guile, for while he was consciously ambitious he was also consciously dutiful; he lacked the imagination and the talent to scheme. Nor would he ever have violated a relationship for promotion. But assigned a duty, he performed it thoroughly. He later bespoke much of his own philosophy of success in letters to his nephew serving in the Philippines in 1899. Counselling him to exactness in his paper work, and respect toward his superiors, he also indulged in some revealing advice. "Keep your nerve always; never lose your courage nor your level head. Nerve and level-headedness are indispensable to a good soldier. Do your whole duty; obey all the orders of your superior; be kind to those who are subordinate to you." [31] How much it all said of the uncle,

23

rather than of the young nephew. Life, like education and duty, McKinley might have added, is basically a matter of substance and routine rather than dash and brilliance.

The Union defeat in August at Cedar Mountain and Second Manassas imperilled the Federal forces in northern Virginia, and even threatened the national capital itself. General George McClellan grouped his forces for a defensive action in Maryland to prevent the Southern army from reaching Washington, and the Ohioans were among the spearhead.[32] Advancing into Frederick, Maryland, they drove the Confederates from the city and then moved toward Middleton. Standing for a fight, the Confederates prepared for the Battle of South Mountain on September 14, 1862, the first serious engagement leading to the major Battle of Antietam.

Years afterward, in one of his few reminiscences about the war, McKinley remembered the beauty of that fall day. "It was a lovely September day—an ideal Sunday morning." As part of General Ambrose Burnside's corps, the Ohioans quickly formed their lines and prepared to move on the Confederate positions. "Our regiment was quickly formed in the woods and charged over rocks and broken ground, through deep underbrush, under heavy fire of the enemy at short range, and, after one of the hottest fights of the war, we drove them out of the woods into an open field near the hilltop." [33]

The area around Sharpsburg, Maryland, was the scene of fierce fighting for several days, culminating in the Battle of Antietam. Flushed by partial success, and eager to prevent Lee's withdrawal, McClellan moved his forces across the rugged terrain against the main enemy positions. The fight began early on the morning of September 17, 1862, the Union forces attempting at several points to cross creeks and fields to crush the Confederates. Time had not permitted the men adequate food or rest, and many reeled from exhaustion. The day wore grimly on into what Hayes later called "the bloodiest day of the war, the day on which more men were killed or wounded than on any other day of the war. . . ." [34]

Commissary Sergeant McKinley felt stranded and isolated behind the lines. He was only too conscious of his comrades' plight. Looking around, he saw a number of stragglers and an inspiration passed quickly through his mind. Hastily hitching mules to two wagons, he filled them with supplies, enlisted the aid of the first

24

privates he saw to help drive, and began a dash that made him famous in his regiment. He mounted the wagon seat and whipped up the mules for a furious dash toward the front lines. One wagon lost its team, but McKinley kept his own mules charging toward the front. It was almost dusk, but when the men saw that he was trying to bring them supplies, they raised a tremendous shout. The noise was such that other units sent scouts to investigate. They returned with the astonishing story that Sergeant McKinley had driven his commissary wagon into the front lines and was serving hot coffee and rations to his exhausted men.[35]

It was one of those exploits so surprising that it remained vivid to spectators years afterward, many of whom dropped their guns to watch McKinley's progress. One eye witness reported thirty-five years later:

> Our Regiment had gone into the fight at daylight, without breakfast or rations of food of any kind, and was the first command to receive the fire of that memorable day. Our regiment became almost completely exhausted from fighting, fatigue, and lack of food and water. While in this condition we saw a wagon, drawn by army mules, coming towards us from the rear at breakneck speed, through a terrific fire of musketry and artillery that seemed to threaten annihilation to everything within its range.
>
> I have many times since thought it a miracle that it and its escort was not utterly destroyed. The wagon, when it arrived, proved to be in charge of Comrade McKinley, and contained a supply of cooked rations, meat, coffee, and hardtack, and was heartily welcomed by our tired and half famished boys.

Though not present himself, Hayes later often commended McKinley's daring and novel action.[36] McKinley's own immediate superiors did not overlook it. "He showed spirit and energy of the first class, in not only keeping us *fully supplied* with rations, throughout the fight, but in having them fully prepared for eating also," Lieutenant Colonel Comly noted. "We had *plenty* when everybody else was short. He delivered them to us . . . with perfect coolness."[37]

McKinley's disregard for personal danger and his quick thinking marked him for promotion. Sergeant McKinley let it be known that officer's bars would be welcome.[38] "Our young friend, William McKinley, commissary sergeant, would be pleased of promotion, and would not object to your recommendations for same," the regimental surgeon wrote Colonel Hayes. "Without wishing to interfere in this matter, it strikes me he is about the brightest chap spoken of for the place." [39] Hayes, convalescing in Ohio from a wound at South Mountain, saw Governor David Tod and recommended McKinley's promotion. Accordingly, McKinley was cited for bravery on the field and given a battlefield promotion dating from September 24, 1862, on November 3, 1862. Thereafter he was Lieutenant McKinley.[40] A long-lasting movement to secure the Congressional Medal of Honor for him eventually came to nothing.

Furloughs were now available, and McKinley took his only wartime leave. Arriving at Columbus for a quick visit with Colonel and Mrs. Hayes, he was gratified to receive his new promotion. "If I may indulge a moment in reminiscence, let me tell you, General, that the proudest and happiest moment of my life was when in 1862 I was sent from the regiment on recruiting service with other sergeants, and upon arriving at Columbus found that you had my commission as 2nd lieutenant, and that it had been issued upon your personal recommendation, for what as a boy, I had done at Antietam." [41]

He went to Poland from Columbus. It was good to be home, to have decent food and the companionship of his sisters and brothers and friends. He sported his new lieutenant's bars with all the relish of a new officer. His sister Sarah noted happily that he was "bubbling over with enthusiasm." [42] His serious mien always hid a bantering nature, but he reserved his sense of humor for private occasions when it did the most good. Given to teasing, he delighted in embellishing the accounts upon which his eager sisters doted.

His recruiting work did not prevent him from enjoying his leave, for the task was not arduous. Staying at first class hotels rather than the poorer ones that hosted his comrades, he and the Twenty-third OVI boys "splurged," and cut a large figure in Ohio hotel society behind the lines. Or at least they thought they did. "Very proper," Hayes noted with fatherly indulgence. "They are the generals of the next war." [43]

Though grateful for his promotion and ambitious to rise from the ranks, McKinley left his comrades with regret. "I always look back with pleasure upon those fourteen months in which I served in the ranks," he said later. "They taught me a great deal. I was but a school-boy when I went into the army, and that first year was a formative period of my life, during which I learned much of men and facts. I have always been glad that I entered the service as a private, and served those months in that capacity." [44]

Though winter suspended fighting on many fronts, the Twenty-third OVI was ordered into Pennsylvania early in October, 1862, to check reports of raids from Confederate cavalry. Marching double quick and with little rest, they ate breakfast, lunch, and dinner in three different states.[45] This stint entitled them to time for rest and recuperation that stretched into weeks of dreary inactivity in winter quarters. It gave McKinley and his comrades the chance to write home and to attend to personal details between drills and inspections. McKinley's correspondence was limited and ordinary. After all, what could one say to one's mother and brothers and sisters except that all was as well as could be expected? "There is nothing new in Camp, all being quiet," he wrote home in the spring of 1863. "This is Sunday, and consequently have more time than usual, as I suspend all unnecessary business on that day. We had a fine dinner today, Roast Chicken, Mashed Potatoes, Custard Pudding, Green Apple and Cherry pies, Bread and Butter, &c. What do you think of that dinner? . . . My health is good and spirits fine. Love to all." [46] If the chicken came surreptitiously from a nearby farm, he did not say so; that was one aspect of war that the home front need not understand in detail.

Though he suffered from the usual camp ailments and discomforts of marching and life in the open, McKinley's robust constitution carried him through the entire war without major illness. By 1863 he was a hardened veteran, his slim, muscular build highlighting a handsome, boyish face, most prominent for its piercing eyes. He temporarily enhanced his appearance, doubtless trying to look older and more manly, with a scraggly beard and thin mustache that did not outlast the war. Conscious of his inferior height, which he listed meticulously at five feet, six and a half inches, he carried himself straight as a ramrod and walked at a rapid pace. By now an excellent horseman, he inspired Colonel John J. McCook of the "Fighting McCooks" to recollect that he was "the keen-cut specimen of the volunteer soldier." [47]

He read newspapers avidly and eagerly pored over the books and magazines that fell into his hands. His reading was primarily

27

for information, and he followed the conflict closely through official reports and from talks with others. He cultivated further his habit of careful listening. His powers of synthesis then gave him the answers he wished. He and Hayes and other regimental officers, often with visiting guests, cantered through the woods near camp. Winter snow later afforded time and chance for sleigh rides.[48]

Late spring and early summer of 1863 broke the regiment's rest. The colorful rebel cavalryman, John Hunt Morgan, dashed for Ohio in July, 1863, and Hayes' troops cut him off. Then the Ohioans were hurriedly attached to General George Crook's corps and sent in pursuit of guerrillas between Richmond and the southwestern part of Virginia. The terrain was rugged and the forced marches exhausting, but the nature of the combat was fiercest of all. "Daily we were brought into contact with the enemy," McKinley remembered. "We penetrated a country where guerrillas were abundant and where it was not an unusual thing for our men to be shot from underbrush—murdered in cold blood." [49]

In March, 1863, McKinley had been promoted to first lieutenant. In the spring of 1864, back with Company E of the Twenty-third OVI, his old Poland company, he took part in a severe test. Assaulting Confederate lines of communication and supply, Crook's corps raided the Virginia and Tennessee Railroad and participated in minor engagements that culminated in the Battle of Cloyd's Mountain, May 9, 1864. About noon of that day the regiment prepared to advance through thick brush and across open meadows under a withering fire. Forcing the Confederates back, they engaged the enemy, who attempted to load their artillery when the Federals were a scant ten feet away. Casualties were heavy and the action fierce.[50] Following their assault, the Federals marched over the bad terrain, short of food, exhausted and worn. "Two days and two nights, without sleep or rest, part of the time wholly without food; fighting and marching and suffering; it seems to me, as I recall it, almost unreal and incredible that men could or would suffer such discomforts and hardships, . . ." McKinley remembered.[51] When rest came most men followed Hayes' suit, who reported tersely: "Stopped and ate; marched and ate; camped about dark, *and ate all night.*" [52]

The command halted near Charleston, West Virginia, on July 1, 1864, in hope of rest and recuperation. But Hayes' forces were detached to the area around Harpers Ferry to stop threatened raids into the North. Thrown against superior numbers, they were once surrounded but cut their way out and joined the main body of Crook's forces near Winchester on July 22, 1864. The exhausted Federals greeted with relief and gratitude the news that Early had been ordered to retire to Richmond.

Their idyll was short-lived; the report was false, and on a bright Sunday morning, July 24, 1864, a Confederate attack rudely shattered the stillness of late sleep. Early's forces fell on the exhausted Union army, aware that many of the Federals had been sent into the Shenandoah Valley. The surprise was complete and devastating, but the Ohioans rallied. The troops quartered near Kernstown, some ten miles south of Winchester, were driven back steadily and badly demoralized as the Confederates pushed their advantage. One battalion was isolated in an orchard, and the harassed Hayes sent McKinley to lead them to safety. "None of us expected to see him again, as we watched him push his horse through the open fields, over fences, through ditches, while a well-directed fire from the enemy was poured upon him, with shells exploding around, about and over him." Obscured by shell bursts, McKinley's little chestnut mare emerged safely and he led the isolated men to safety. "I never expected to see you in life again," Hayes said gratefully when McKinley returned without a scratch. As darkness fell, the command came upon a group of artillery pieces. McKinley offered to save them from enemy hands, but Hayes was doubtful. Pressed, he finally agreed, and McKinley's group of volunteers wheeled the guns to safety.[53]

The next few weeks were a confusion of march and countermarch as the desperate Confederates tried to stay the Union advance into Virginia. In September, McKinley, now a captain on General Crook's staff, fought in the Battle of Opequhan. Carrying verbal orders to General Duval, commander of the Second Division, to move his men to a new flank position, he was asked by the commander: "By what route shall I move my column?" The orders were vague and McKinley thought rapidly, quickly looking over the terrain before raising his arm and pointing up a ravine. "I would move up this creek," he answered. Duval declined to be advised by a junior officer. "I will not budge without definite orders." McKinley looked him squarely in the eyes and said: "This is a case of great emergency, General. I order you, by command of General Crook, to move your command up this ravine to a position on the right of the army." Disaster could have ruined McKinley and cost many lives, but his judgment was sound and the division made the maneuver without incident. His superiors later laconically assured him that since the movement was successful, he had been right.[54]

The Battle of Opequhan ended in Union victory but the badly depleted forces retired for rest and replacements. Once again the Confederates used the element of surprise, this time on October 19, 1864, at Cedar Creek. General Philip Sheridan, the Union Commander, was in Washington for conferences, and the command itself was spread thinly at several points. Attacking in the morning, Early's forces drove the Federals from position to position until demoralization spread through Union ranks. McKinley worked furiously, carrying messages and orders and attending to gun emplacements. Hearing the sound of firing, Sheridan, who had spent the night in Winchester, hurried toward his lines to encounter a scene of confusion and apparent defeat. Spying McKinley tending an artillery piece, Sheridan reined in and asked where Crook was, and the Captain pointed the way. Sheridan, in conference with fellow officers, decided to re-form his men, and someone suggested that he ride down the lines. Affixing shining new gold epaulettes, the General did so and rallied his men from defeat.[55]

Hayes watched McKinley's work on Crook's staff with pride and noted with satisfaction that "he has not been wounded but everyone admires him as one of the bravest and finest young officers in the army." [56] General Crook himself wrote appreciatively that McKinley had done excellent work and "amidst the thickest of the fight cheered the men onward and encouraged them by example to do their whole duty. . . ." [57] For his "gallant and meritorious services" at Opequhan, Fisher's Hill, and Cedar Creek, President Lincoln made McKinley a brevet major of volunteers on March 13, 1865.[58] He and his comrades did their small share to sustain the President when they voted for Lincoln in November, 1864, using a battered army ambulance for an election booth, and writing their ballots by the flame of a guttering candle.[59]

While visiting a hospital late in the war, McKinley was struck by the good feeling shown among certain of the prisoners, whose blue and gray uniforms denoted allegiances at odds with their friendliness. He discovered that they were Masons, and further inquiry into an organization that commanded such loyalty convinced him that he should join. In May, 1865, in Winchester, he joined the Masonic Lodge, and retained his allegiance to the end of his life.[60]

For him the rest of the war was anticlimactic. When not on duty, he amused himself by reading letters from home and friends. His sisters kept him posted on Ohio news and tried their best to equal his own teasing. "Don't you wish some of your sisters could get married?" his sister Helen wrote puckishly.[61] "We all want to see you very much but must submit to military law," sister Anne wrote.[62] His parents followed their usual ways during the war, though his father's iron works prospered more regularly.

The men of the Twenty-third OVI awaited the end of the war, holding parties, mock drills, anxious to get home.[63] The orders came at last, and the regiment was mustered out at Cumberland, Maryland, on July 26, 1865, after participating in a grand review of federal troops in Washington. Travelling by rail to Camp Taylor near Cleveland, they were paid and discharged.[64]

McKinley did not often reminisce about his war service. He attended his share of GAR reunions and addressed more than his share of veterans' rallies, but he spoke little of his own service. He more often referred to the general war effort and the sacrifice involved for the whole country. He best stated his whole attitude when he was president: ". . . the memories of war are sweeter than service in the war."[65] Detesting all strife and disorder, he saw no allure in the horrors, devastation, and discomforts of war. Sentimental in many things, he was too hardheaded ever to cast a patina of sentiment over so cruel a thing as war. The conflict inclined him "to reflect on the destruction and misery caused by civil war."[66]

Though his record was outstanding, he never felt that he had done anything extraordinary. "My experiences did not differ from those of a million young men who went into that great war," he said. "There was nothing uncommon about it. It was simply the incidents of camp and march and battle common to the soldier in general. We carried our muskets and marched along together. We all of us felt our importance, I suppose."[67] He was doubtless sincere, but he was also too modest. His steadiness, judgment, discerning attitude toward men, and willingness to make personal sacrifices set him apart from his fellows. He might also have said more often what he later tersely noted: "We of today but faintly comprehend what our soldiers then endured." [68]

Perhaps, after all, the war was not a crucible of fire for him. His basic values were not really tested or reshaped, for they were largely fixed when he entered the Army. Army service only hardened his convictions, gave him a sense of proper conduct, and enlarged his world view. He learned much of the cruelty as well as the kindness of men. He had been brave, had risked his life, but he had acted with the deep conviction that no harm would come to him. The stoicism of his later years is evident in his military career. His apparent heedlessness rested on assurance. Behind the façade of tact, charm, and reserve he presented to the world, there are unfathomable depths that seem to say he knew what history held for him.

At twenty-two, a brevet major, wearing a title that would cling to him the rest of his life as a personal and political trademark, he emerged from the Civil War. His future was uncertain. His first task was simply to return to civil life, to seek a profession, marriage, and a family. If he looked back with particular regret or joy on his military career, he told few people of it. Late in life, however, he must often have reflected that war was singularly influential on him. Many events of his youth flowed from one great war. The central events of his later life clustered around another, but smaller, war. How ironic that he who hated war should thus twice be a child of Mars.

~ III ~

Ohio Lawyer

OR ALL his quiet demeanor and rural charm, Rutherford B.
Hayes was a shrewd man. His pleasant exterior hid an inner
talent for good judgment that rested on wide experience and
a sound education. A pampered, over-protected childhood, during
which he was surrounded by women, produced in him a youthful in-
security that did not prevent his becoming a successful lawyer, or
dampen his genuine bravery in the Civil War. His desire to live the
quiet life of a country squire, surrounded by friends and books, in
his beautiful home in Fremont, Ohio, did not forbid his entering
that least secure of all professions, politics. Nor did his effacing personality lessen his success at the game; ambition was the key to his
life. Hayes knew his men, and he knew that young William McKinley was a man with a future.

McKinley was uncertain about that future. He thought briefly
of a military career, assuming that peacetime service would have
stability and challenge; happily his father dissuaded him.[1] His
mother's hopes that he might join the ministry did not appeal to
him, for already beneath the surface of his charm, ambition demanded more challenging outlets than the church. His mind made
up, he wrote Hayes for advice, and his old commander recommended a business career. "My notion of the place for a young man
is a fine large growing town *anywhere*, but would prefer a town in
the West. St. Louis, Kansas City, Leavenworth, Omaha, Chicago,
etc., are my favorites," Hayes wrote. "With your business capacity
and experience I would have preferred railroading or some commercial business. A man in any of our western towns with half your
wit ought to be independent at forty in business. As a lawyer, a man
sacrifices independence to ambition which is a bad bargain at best.
However, you have decided for the present your profession, so I
must hush."[2] McKinley, already studying law, thought enough of
the advice to file it carefully among his papers, but did not follow it.

33

For all its good intentions, it was poor counsel for McKinley. He had no real aptitude for business. Never in his life did he desire to make money. The only business affair he ever entered into resulted in near disaster to his political fortunes, and his later law practice was comfortable but not lucrative. He was ambitious, but he longed for eminence rather than riches. He wanted the prestige, power, and sense of accomplishment which he thought the law and politics would give him. He liked people and he also wanted them to love him; that may have been the real hidden reason for his entering politics.

The William McKinley who emerged from the war was an attractive but curious man. Charming and courtly as he already was, his associates noted his taciturnity and the impassive view he often had of life. Clearly there were depths to the man which no one sounded. The major outlines of his personality had already focused; the future only sharpened them in bold relief.

The fibers that form a man's personality and the inner foundations upon which his most personal attitudes rest are formed in his youth. There the lasting impressions, influences, the first contacts with life sharpen heredity and cast the molds for later growth. Mark Hanna once said that he and his friend were both Scotch-Irish, but that McKinley got the Scotch and he got the Irish. It was more than a flippant remark. Perhaps the key to McKinley's whole enigmatic personality lies in that simple observation.

There seemed to be little of the Irish in him. His deliberation and reflection subverted any irrational tendencies in his make-up. His temper was sure but slow. His relations with people rested on insight rather than on emotion. His decisions came from careful deliberation, never from quick or thoughtless action. Caution was the keynote of all his life. He respected deeds more than words; tasks were challenges to be overcome. The tragedies of his personal life and the necessities of his profession veneered his whole life with a layer of charm and personal kindness so sincere that he thought first of others even as he lay dying. That basic sense of kindness merged in him with a deep sense of responsibility and duty that was never a pose, but a way of life.

His most striking personality trait was a pronounced streak of fortitude. He seems to have sensed from youth, through some inner

34

intuition, that his path would be hard, that caution must be his key-note, and that his lot would perhaps be tragic. If there was a central design in McKinley's life, it was epitomized by a belief in getting things done and in an almost brooding sense of destiny.

McKinley inherited much of his patience and industry from his parents. Some deep strains in his ancestry focused in him as an overpowering desire for order and unity, which in his later political life translated itself into his idea of economic nationalism. He needed love, as all men do, but the yearning became in him a part of his central need for order. He saw the chaos of life and determined to build against it in his own world. His religion buttressed this deter-mination, teaching that life was transitory but that every man had a talent to fulfill while on earth.

Coupled with this was a degree of self-effacement that was re-freshing in a public figure. Elihu Root, John Hay, Theodore Roose-velt, and scores of other people who worked with McKinley re-marked on this aspect of his character, magnified by his personal kindness. Hating chaos, he cared for results. Who got the credit was secondary to him. Conscious of his position and duly ambitious, he never enhanced his power at the price of other men's reputations; nor did he take credit where it was not his due.

His command of self and taciturnity in public did not reflect a basically insecure man. Rather, they reflected a determined and pur-poseful man. Nor was his bent toward quietness the mark of any bitterness or deep frustration, for he genuinely loved people, and his even temper and kind disposition gave the lie to those who thought him merely an actor. He did not parade his emotions, for he did not need to; he preferred dignity to display. He did not feel the need to impress men with anything but his sincerity and ability. His lack of humor was always more ostensible than genuine, for in pri-vate he was often funny and delightful.

To him the basic reward of public life was working with people, for mankind and the problems of personality fascinated him. Most of the charm of the theater, to which he was devoted, lay in the actor's dissection of character, and in the compelling lights and shadows of the diverse characters and personalities portrayed. The good politician is a good actor, and McKinley consciously fulfilled this role in later life. The face he presented to the world did not always reflect the inner man. But his kindness and courtesy rested on a deep-seated respect for people. There was nothing of the misanthrope about him.

With these complex strains fortified by his enlarged view of life acquired in the war, he was inevitably restless in Poland. For a time he corresponded with old army friends, but was anxious to begin some kind of work. "You know, I am at times in imagination somewhat flighty, [but] I have gotten over all that," he wrote his friend Russell Hastings in a remarkably personal letter. "[I] am now once more a 'rustic youth,' wrapped in the mysteries of law. The 'solemnities' of the 'marriage contract,' the old customs of the Saxons and Danes, are constantly flitting through my brain. I dream of lands, tenements and hereditaments, and wake up [to] think I am an heir. Isn't that strange! I am getting along much better than I expected; Poland is very tame, but I have banished myself. I often feel I would like to have Hastings and Webb stop in and talk over old matters or new ones. Whenever you can make it convenient, stop and see me. We have a small house, but the doors are high." [3]

He began studying law in the office of Charles Glidden, the area's most prominent attorney.[4] Glidden's patience, courtesy, and gentle demeanor offset the dullness of the dusty law books which the studious McKinley read hour after hour, day after day. In after years, the very recollection made him thirsty, but it was the way to success.

Glidden realized that McKinley's powers of application and sense of judgment would make him a good attorney, and urged him to attend law school. The deficiencies of study in a country lawyer's office in rural Ohio were all too obvious. In September, 1866, McKinley packed his books and clothes, put a small amount of borrowed money into his wallet, bade his friends and family goodbye, and left for Albany, New York, to attend the fall term of the Albany Law School, then a famous legal institution. He roomed there with George Arrel, later an attorney in Youngstown, who remembered vividly that McKinley studied long and hard, but also loved the social life. He seldom missed a theater production, and attended parties, teas, and receptions. Though convivial, he disliked vulgarity.

36

"He never quarreled but he had a mind of his own and was very determined," Arrel said. "Even at that time he had made up his mind to enter public life, and clearly showed an ambition to go to Congress. He worked very hard, often reading until one or two o'clock in the morning. It was his very great industry rather than genius, that paved the way for his success." [5]

Popular with girls and well-liked among his fellows, McKinley knew many people but had few really close friends. His pleasant demeanor and easy charm only made his lapses into naiveté more appealing. When he went to Albany he had never eaten ice cream. At the annual reception for the law students given by Judge Amasa Parker, the Judge's lovely daughter Grace handed him a dish of ice cream, which he dutifully tasted. "Poor Mrs. Parker," he said, eyeing the plate, "do not tell her the custard got frozen." Grace patiently explained ice cream to him, and he was not the least embarrassed. "You know, I was a simple country boy," he said years later when recounting the incident. [6]

Perhaps bored with the routine of legal learning, and doubtless anxious to return home to friends and family, McKinley left Albany in the spring of 1867. [7] He felt that he had prepared enough and was anxious to establish a practice. In March, 1867, he was admitted to the bar in Warren, Ohio.

Little Poland was hardly the place to practice. The nearest logical choice was Canton, where his sister Anne was already teaching school. [8] Canton, to which he moved later in 1867, was not an unwise choice. It was a county seat, in the center of a prosperous agricultural district, with the promise of an industrial boom. It was also, he must have noted, an excellent center from which to work in politics.

McKinley risked his meager capital in a small office in the new bank building, center of the town's commercial and legal fraternities. [9] He received clients and callers in a cluttered office, generally seated behind an overflowing pigeon-hole desk, in striking contrast to his immaculate figure. He affected the fashionable black frock coat of the day, a boiled shirt, and carefully arranged purple tie that nestled in majesty under the invariably hard collar. His clothes highlighted his dark handsomeness, and his muscular frame made him an impressive figure. His practice consisted largely of the routine court and probate cases that befall a country lawyer. His taste for the law was not consuming, but he enjoyed it.[10]

Judge George W. Belden, prominent attorney, had an office in the same building. Belden was a Union Democrat, who before the war, as a U.S. attorney, prosecuted eighty professors and students from Oberlin College for assisting runaway slaves. The Republican community forgave this, for the Judge was never a copperhead. Attracted to the pleasant McKinley and impressed by his thoroughness, Belden kept his eye on the young man. One evening he idly strolled into McKinley's office and dropped a sheaf of papers on the desk. He did not feel well, he said, but had to appear in court the following morning. Would McKinley take over the case? The latter protested that he was not prepared on such short notice. Belden turned to leave and said, "If you don't try this case, it won't be tried." McKinley reluctantly agreed and spent the night over the documents, dutifully appearing in court the following morning. "I can see him now, as he stood before the court for the first time, young, eager, ambitious, well-prepared, self-poised but not over-confident; how he impressed me as he arose and told the court, 'What we contend for in this lawsuit'—I recall the very words of his opening," William A. Lynch, a prominent Canton attorney, remembered.

As he began his argument, McKinley glanced to the rear of the courtroom, where to his astonishment Judge Belden sat placid as a schoolgirl, a slight smile around his mouth. Without pausing, McKinley faced the court and continued his argument, successfully, as it turned out. Several days later, Belden stopped by McKinley's office, and before the latter could either laugh or protest at the trick, the Judge dropped twenty-five dollars on his desk. McKinley rose to protest that the fee was too large, and Belden followed him around the room pressing the money on him, chuckling, "It's all right, Mac, I got a hundred." That was not all. Belden's partner had been elected to the bench, and he needed a new associate; would McKinley join him? He would indeed, and the two entered a partnership that was prosperous for McKinley, as Belden gradually withdrew from practice.[11]

McKinley did not neglect his social duties. He was happy to

38

spend evenings with his sister, and enjoyed visiting the Beldens and various men friends, with whom he discussed horses, law, and farming. "We have tried a number of cases this term, and have generally been successful," he wrote his sister Sarah, and could not forego the postscript: "The sleighing is fine. . . ." [12] He kept in close touch with his father and mother, whose pride at his success found an outlet in words of encouragement. "I am pleased to hear that your business is good," his father wrote in quiet praise.[13] McKinley's success in the law could have been considerable had he not ventured into politics; his associates thought that he could have led the Ohio bar. His methodical dissection and study of every case, his courtesy toward the bench, and his ability to impress people could have made him wealthy and prominent.[14]

It was comforting and helpful to have some of his family near, for because of his court duties, he corresponded infrequently with relatives not living nearby. "He is very lazy about writing and depends upon me to do all the correspondence," Anne noted.[15] On quiet afternoons and Sundays, he stretched out for a nap while his sister dutifully brushed his clothes or wrote friends about his career. In lax seasons, when he had more free time than usual, he read, or walked and talked with friends, but his leisure seldom lasted long; Hayes was right about the law and ambition. "Court begins the first of June, then will come his harvest," Anne wrote.[16] His younger brother Abner, so different from William in his joviality and glad-handing, moved to Canton with his bride, augmenting further the already substantial McKinley family resident there, for his father and mother had presumably moved there too.[17]

McKinley's assets as a fledgling lawyer consisted of diligence, personal contacts, and a pleasant personality that attracted attention. But something deeper and even more rewarding drew his fellow townsmen to him. His sense of tolerance, which made him many friends among Canton's Catholic element, and his genuine unwillingness to quarrel or engage in strife, made him popular and respected long before he entered politics. It is a rare gift in any man to reconcile disparate views and warring forces, but this was the relish in McKinley's life, the center of his grand design. His absence of bigotry in a provincial society was all the more remarkable. He worked with the Masons, the YMCA, of which he was president for a time, and with the Methodist Church, in which he and Mother McKinley were especially active. Many Sundays the McKinley home was open to visiting ministers, and several times it served as headquarters for delegates to a local conference. As in Poland, old Mrs. McKinley was a pillar of the church.[18]

With Abner's support and not a little prodding, McKinley entered the Canton Building Association as secretary in 1869, but dropped out after a time. His interest in business somewhat aroused, he later borrowed enough money to build a small block of office space on Market Street, which provided a semblance of financial security and a small income most of his life.[19]

Law practice kept him busy during the day, and his convivial nature made him a ready guest in the evenings, but his work load was not oppressive and his willingness to speak appealed to local Republicans. Politics was a natural adjunct to the law, and the hustings were often more familiar than the bar to young lawyers. When and where he first spoke was a mystery; the veils of twenty years cloud any man's memory. One oldster recalled that the young Major spoke eloquently from the tavern steps for his friend Hayes, running for governor in 1867.[20] Some remembered that the Major's first stump speech was as a substitute for an ailing Republican regular; one stated that he made his first speech earlier to returning troops in Poland; McKinley himself remembered that he made his first political speech during the Hayes campaign of 1867.[21] Whenever it was, he made one speech early in his career that he did not forget, and which was often recounted later by Senator Charles Manderson of Nebraska, who once lived in Canton.

Manderson and McKinley were scheduled to speak from the same platform one evening, and knowing the Major's penchant for fact-gathering and careful preparation, Manderson sought him out before the appointed hour. Accustomed himself to extemporaneous speaking, he did not want the younger man to steal his thunder. Walking casually toward the meeting hall, Manderson asked: "By the way, Major, I'm not prepared for this affair. Would you mind telling me what you are going to talk about?" McKinley outlined his remarks, after which Manderson nodded and said easily: "Major, you've got this in pretty good shape, and I'm only going to speak

offhand. Don't you think you'd better let me be the 'curtain-raiser?' "
McKinley deferred to the older man, not thinking of the advantage
of speaking first. When Manderson began his speech, McKinley sat
bolt upright in astonishment as he heard every one of his own points
roll easily off Manderson's tongue. With supreme cordiality, the
speaker turned at the conclusion of his remarks and said coolly,
"And now, gentlemen, in proof of all I have told you, we have taken
pains to collect some interesting figures and other documentary
evidence, and if my distinguished colleague will kindly hand me the
papers which he has in his pocket, I will read them to you." Mc-
Kinley handed over the papers, later laughed at the joke on himself,
and never let it happen again.[22]

The presidential election of 1868 was a clarion call to all true
Republicans. Ohio Republicans, anxious to see the South punished,
supported Grant, the "Hero of Appomattox." In Canton, McKinley
began organizing Grant clubs in August, and accepted the post of
chairman of the Republican Central Committee for Stark County,
directing the organization in the area. It was not an easy job, for the
district was divided between the Democrats and Republicans, and
required a great deal of speaking and paper work.[23]

In Canton itself, the Grant club welcomed him enthusiastically.
"Major McKinley elicited the cheers of the audience by a stirring
address. . . ."[24] In the fall he was busier than ever, political affairs
alternating with law business. "Major McKinley followed with an
address filled with his usual fire," his home town paper reported of
one meeting. At the campaign's close, he addressed veterans' groups,
and on election night he read out the returns as they ticked in over
the telegraph wires. His friends prophesied a bright political future
for him.[25]

His devoted labors called for a suitable reward, and Christmas
found him ready for a vacation. He and a group of friends joined
hands and glasses for a convivial Christmas celebration, and the
Repository noted slyly: "Friend McKinley has been making merry
with his friends this Christmas and new year. Notices on his slate
about Christmas said 'Back January 2.' He is now back looking all
the better for the span of rest."[26] The span of rest did not preclude
further political work, for his own ambitions were now aroused, and

by spring he was organizing for Republican victory in local contests.[27] And he never hesitated to make himself useful to friends when asked for patronage recommendations.[28]

This careful building bore fruit in 1869, when he announced his candidacy for prosecuting attorney of Stark County. The Canton newspaper supported him as "a good lawyer and a fine orator." The office was not a choice one, offering more routine detail than excitement, but it was a logical beginning. It was difficult to win because of Democratic strength in local contests, and defeat would be a setback to McKinley's future plans. He early learned that in politics, as in love, if nothing were ventured, nothing was gained. To no one's surprise he easily won the Republican nomination in July, and to everyone's surprise but his own he defeated his Democratic opponent in the fall. The *Repository* remarked as McKinley assumed office on January 1, 1870: "Let Republicans see to it that the shortcomings of others are not charged to his account, and that, in the performance of his duties he is sustained by all who desire to see the laws sustained and enforced." [29]

The duties during his term were not arduous, but they gave him a wider audience and more experience with the public and the political fraternity. He was still chairman of the local Republican Central Committee, and was accordingly renominated without opposition in the summer of 1871. The *Repository* supported him for work well done and suggested a victory couplet:

> No rogue e'er felt the halter draw
> With good opinion of the law.

This time the Democrats were ready, nominating the prominent William A. Lynch, and campaigned vigorously to nip McKinley's budding career. The Major spoke extensively, accompanied several times by a brass band and hearty cheers, but he fell before the normal Democratic trend, though defeated by only 143 votes.[30]

Other affairs intruded on McKinley's mind, and defeat did not sting as much as it might have. Politics now gave way to romance, and the charms of the drawing room matched those of the meeting hall. Bachelorhood ill suited him, and his natural desire for a home and family was sharpened by his own reserved emotional life. His good looks and local prominence, as well as his promising career, made him an easy mark for local belles, but none struck his fancy, though he escorted many and his name was linked often with many others behind discreet fans and over clattering teacups.

By 1870, everyone knew where his heart was headed, most of all its object, Ida Saxton. Miss Saxton was a daughter of Canton's most prominent family. Old John Saxton, Ida's grandfather, was a pioneer Ohio editor who founded the Canton *Repository* in 1815 and who edited it until 1871, having the privilege of noting in its pages the downfall of two Napoleons. He brought in his first press by ox-team and composed the newspaper as he set up the type. His shrewd judgment and sharp tongue earned him the reputation of a Nestor of Ohio editors, and the whole northeast corner of the state knew his opinions.

Many of these attributes had shaped Ida's father, James Saxton, though he had a more forgiving nature. He had his father's stubbornness, set opinions, and independent views. He maintained a charming home and solid business connections as he branched out into banking and investments.[31] Saxton discouraged Ida's suitors, for he secretly wished her to keep his home for him, but he also had strong beliefs on women's place in society. In the end he let Ida make up her own mind, something the strong-willed girl would have done anyway. Educated at Brook Hall Seminary in Medea, Pennsylvania, and pampered by her well-to-do family, Ida was indeed her father's daughter. She early showed a streak of stubborn independence and flighty irrationality that later deepened into tragic illness.

Like most young girls, she was given to pretty things, fine clothes, fancy parties, and since she knew little of the world, these were the center of her life. In 1869 she and her sister and a party of friends followed current fashion by touring Europe as a fitting climax to their finishing-school education. Writing home glowing reports of their travels, the girls prepared all of Canton for their elaborate homecoming in 1870. Laden with fancy furs, jewelled music boxes, clothes, false hair pieces, and assorted tourist items, Ida and her sister "Pina" returned to Canton supposedly to reign as belles until the proper beaux appeared.

Ida seems to have met McKinley first on a summer picnic, but he made little impression on her. She was restless; her nervousness already showed in her photographs. Her mouth set downward, her eyes were firm, almost hard, she seemed tense and nervous. Her own unsettled affairs and tensions in her family heightened her loneliness as she cast about for a suitable young man.[32] With her father's approval she began working at his bank as a cashier and attracted the younger male depositors, many of whom included bouquets with their deposits.[33] But she still met none who pleased her. She would not settle for the dullness of a rural Ohio town, and her lack of emotional balance demanded someone far more sound and reserved than the average man.

The Major was soon attracted to her. His trips to the bank came more and more frequently, though he had little enough money either to deposit or withdraw. The chance of even a casual conversation was worth the agonies of uncertainty. His charm and urbanity carried him over the rough spots of initial introduction. Ida was strongly attracted to him for his silent strength, his smooth manners, and unfailing charm, not to mention his good looks. All Canton soon knew that the two were in love, though they both continued their appointed duties. Somewhat coquettish, already possessive and jealous, Ida was tense when he was not with her. When McKinley was late to a party she rushed from guest to guest demanding: "Have you seen the Major? Do you imagine the Major is sick? Has the Major been called to the city?" Yet when he appeared, she was as demure, almost cool, as ever.[34] It was always thus with young love, and even more so in an age that demanded propriety in courtship.

The Major made no secret of his love for Ida. Her natural beauty attracted him, and he sensed in her a deep need for him that blinded him to her nervousness or made him ignore it. "Oh, if you could have seen what a beauty Ida was as a girl," he often said later. "Ida was the most beautiful girl you ever saw," he once told Mrs. Joseph B. Foraker.[35]

A moonlight night, quietly clopping horses, and the crest of a certain hill near Canton prompted him to ask the question, and Ida readily accepted.[36] The preparations went forward rapidly, for James Saxton approved his daughter's choice and shrewdly marked his new son-in-law for a brilliant career. For McKinley himself, there were two guests who must be there, Mr. and Mrs. Hayes, and he accordingly wrote in his awkward hand:

> I have a mind to get married—time 24th of next month—place
> Canton. It is now settled that Miss Saxton and I will write our
> fortunes at the above time and place. I of course am happy and
> want my friends to know it and therefore hasten to tell *you*.
>
> Away down at Camp opposite Charleston, in that scolding
> widow's house, I promised Mrs. Hayes I would give her long notice
> of my marriage and she in turn promised she would be present and
> the General, if not in direct terms, by his silence consented to the
> arrangement—thereby agreeing he would be present. I have performed
> my part of the agreement and I do hope you will find it convenient
> to perform yours. I think I am doing a good thing. Miss S. is every-
> thing I could hope for. She is good, &c.[37]

It was, to say the least, a reserved statement, but it fitted his modesty and showed his belief that his marriage would bring him the love and companionship he sought. The couple were united on January 24, 1871, in the Presbyterian church in Canton, despite an absent-minded minister who almost forgot to attend. Ministers of two faiths performed the ceremony, though Ida later joined her husband's congregation.[38]

A secret honeymoon journey carried them to New York. Their return to Canton signalled a celebration by a host of friends, and they lived briefly at the old St. Cloud Hotel while deciding on a house. Mr. Saxton came to their rescue and gave them the house on Market Street that was the scene of the 1896 campaign. When he went to Congress in 1877, McKinley sold the house. Leasing it back after 1896, he finally bought it in 1899, hoping to refurnish it and use it for his declining years. While in politics, he and Ida stayed at the Saxton home in which Ida's family lived, and which also had resounded to the footsteps and voices of such notables as James G. Blaine, Grant, the Shermans, John A. Logan, and even the noted actor Joseph Jefferson.[39] Neither house was large, but both were comfortable, equipped with ample reading space for McKinley, room for entertainment, and a yard for relaxation.

Marriage brought added responsibilities in founding a home and participating in all the details that go with the first years of union. McKinley was happy; his whole constitution lent itself to the marital state that satisfied his need for love, as well as his desire to make Ida happy.

Ida was interested in temperance, and the young lawyer required but a minimum of prodding from her to begin his short career as a temperance reformer. The local ladies were zealous in their crusade against Demon Rum, and Canton's substantial German element frowned upon their invasions. One Henry Balser operated a brewery near North Market Street, around which a group of women congregated to ask him to cease serving Satan. The sturdy German declined the invitation, whereupon the ladies knelt upon the sidewalk to pray for him, obstructing business at the same time. The brewer and his wife promptly washed down the sidewalk and the ladies' dresses in a suds of beer, and were hauled into court for disorderly conduct. McKinley and Lynch secured a hung jury, which was a victory of sorts for the temperance group, for the law ordinarily would have been with Balser. The city council later passed an ordinance forbidding liquor sales on Sunday and election days.[40]

McKinley sandwiched temperance meetings in between legal work and politics. His adherence to the cause was not really strong, but it reflected his moral and religious bias toward regulated conduct. An early speech outlined this belief: "It is poor logic indeed to say that because men drink and always have we will therefore license and protect dealers in the wicked traffic. Because there is sin and crime and wrong abroad in the land therefore we will legalize them. Enunciate such a principle and you may bid a long farewell to social, moral and political reform." [41]

McKinley's most prominent action in the temperance movement was his effort as prosecuting attorney to prevent the illicit sale of liquor to students at Mount Union College in nearby Alliance. Assiduously gathering evidence and witnesses for his case, he prosecuted with such thoroughness that the illegal sales stopped. One student took the stand and told such a frank story that the jury was duly convinced. His name was Philander Knox, and he was later attorney-general in William McKinley's cabinet.[42] McKinley was also instrumental in bringing Elizabeth Cady Stanton and Victoria Woodhull to Canton, where they talked on temperance and women's suffrage. If the men of the community thought less of him for it, they did not say so. He also opposed laxer licensing laws for liquor dealers,

46

and his work was rewarded after 1876 with political support from local temperance groups and journals.[43] He probably would have settled for local option, with carefully enforced age limits, rather than outright prohibition.

Ida's quick temper settled during the first year of her marriage, and she openly adored "the Major," as she called him publicly, and "Dearest," as she called him privately. He was attentive to her every want, spending long evenings at home listening to her idle conversation, entertaining other young couples, helping her with the details of the new home. His happiness and gratitude increased in the spring of 1871 when Ida became pregnant. Children would enrich his life more than ever, and the wall of reserve around him began to mellow before the chill Christmas Day, 1871, when his first child, a daughter named Katherine, was born.

Katie, as he called her, was the apple of her father's eye as she grew into a sprightly and often impudent little girl, walking uneasily to impress proud grandparents, hanging on the gate to see her father come down the walk, or sitting on his lap to hear his stories and recount her own childish day's adventures. Her mother was apprehensive about her welfare, and grew irritable if she did not obey; Ida transferred her possessiveness from her husband to the child, though it was not as selfish as it seemed to many. Her compulsive love was showing through the surface. Ida had the child photographed; she even commissioned an oil painting of her favorite pose. She supervised every detail of the little girl's life, forbidding her to go out alone and fussing when her father wanted to take her for a ride.

This possessiveness abated somewhat on April 1, 1873, when a sister, named after her mother, was born. But the child was sickly, and when she died on August 22, 1873, Ida was distraught. Her nervousness and irrationality were more and more evident. She became short-tempered; she was jealous of the Major's time; he did not dare be seen with another woman. Her strength failed and she spent days in bed, morosely poring over her misfortune, scarcely able to rise. Friends and family attributed her despondency to her illness, but there were darker shadows in her mind. Had she done something wrong? Was this a punishment from God? Was she still in jeopardy? Where would her tragedy end?

In anguish Ida turned more and more to Katie, admonishing her to take care, fearful lest she too should be taken. The Major's attentions to the child increased as he tried to offset the mother's nerves. Uncle Abner found Katie swinging on the garden gate one sunny afternoon and asked her to come for a walk. Thinking a moment, she said pertly, "No, I mustn't go out of the yard or God'll punish Mama some more. . . ." [44]

The mother's fears emerged from the shadows and assumed reality when little Katie succumbed to typhoid fever and died on June 25, 1875. Ida's whole world seemed shattered. She had Katie's portrait set upon her dressing table every day; few days passed in the remainder of her life when she did not discuss the tragedy of her children. The sudden deaths of other members of her family prostrated her, and she lay abed behind closed doors while silent-footed neighbors and relatives attended to the household duties. God actually seemed to punish her in her manifold losses. Out of everything in life she had salvaged only her husband, and her obsessive love for him now became a fixation as she jealously and pitifully forbade him to leave her side. She even had his portrait painted and hung on the wall opposite her bed so that his face was the first thing she saw upon awaking in the morning. He gave up walking and riding, his only exercise, and dutifully complied with her every whim and wish. He cut his business to a minimum to spend his time with her. In the fires of mutual grief they forged bonds that lasted their remaining twenty-six years of wedded life.

Ida McKinley never really understood her complex husband's full needs, but she genuinely and deeply loved him. Her affection was not born of desperation or tragedy, but of real love for him. Her illness was such a constant and daily occurrence, and of such a compelling nature, that McKinley deliberately denied any shortcomings she may have had. Her utter dependence on him fulfilled his basic need to be loved, and that mattered most.

His reserve and command of self saved him from a similar melancholy, for, having so dearly loved his daughters, his grief, too, was great. He seldom spoke openly thereafter of the tragedy, though many understood that it left profound marks upon him.[45] Many years later he touched obliquely upon his sorrow when writing a friend who had lost a child: "Only those who have suffered in a similar way can appreciate the keenness of such affliction." [46] Thereafter he delighted in the company of young people, and was a doting and watchful uncle to his nieces and nephews and their young friends. In Canton he was a special mark for children, and often as not he had, besides a cheery smile and wave of the hand, a present for them in his pocket.

Ida tried her very best to rally. She rose from her sickbed and commanded her relatives to leave. She insisted that her husband continue his law work and politics. She opened her house and entertained, and if she knew that her neighbors whispered that she had "fits," that she was prostrated much of the time, that her temper and irritability reflected a deeper mental illness, she did not appear to notice. She took bromides to sleep, and compounds to maintain her strength. She went to various doctors all over the state and in the East. Though in later years many thought her a burden upon her husband, her agonizing fight against illness actually reflected her determination to sustain him. However difficult she may have been at times to her husband and the people around him, her struggle was a brave attempt to overcome her tragedy and to support her husband who needed her now more than ever.

Before Katie's death, early in June, McKinley had been a county delegate to the state Republican convention that nominated Rutherford B. Hayes for the governorship for an unprecedented third time. Hayes' success would require the labor and sacrifice of all true Republicans, and especially of his friends like McKinley.[47] Perhaps to escape personal tragedy, and also through a strong desire to elect Hayes, McKinley threw himself into the campaign, arguing for traditional Republican principles—sound money, tariff protection, enfranchisement of the Negro. He conferred with Hayes and organized Hayes clubs, speaking when asked, always on call for party business, ever trying to crowd to the back of his mind the pall of gloom that hung over the silent house in Canton.[48]

Fall brought cooler weather and the Major took the stump in many towns, speaking to the accompaniment of brass bands, bonfires, and torchlight parades. Hayes' election was the signal for triumph and helped put the Ohio leader on the road to the White House. None rejoiced more than his former commissary sergeant. And the latter, already wise beyond his years in the ways of politics, built political fences with patronage letters and recommendations for friends. He had already laid plans for a congressional race the following year.[49]

In the spring of 1876, with Hayes emerging as a contender for the Republican presidential nomination and with McKinley himself ready for a congressional race, labor troubles offered a godsend to the young Canton lawyer. In March, coal miners in the Tuscarawas Valley struck for higher pay and better working conditions. Their plight was genuine, and merited the vivid descriptions in the Democratic press. Reductions in wages over the last year were the strikers' major grievance, but the whole system under which they worked for long hours and low pay enraged them. The management's argument that the hard times after the Panic of 1873 forced cutbacks and wage reductions was not accepted by the miners. They pointed out that corporation profits had not decreased and insisted that management wished to break an incipient labor movement. There was no compunction about recruiting strikebreakers in Cleveland, nor was there any dearth of "scabs" to fight the strikers. In April, strikebreakers at the mines provoked a violent clash with the armed strikers. One company official was nearly killed, and a number on both sides were severely injured. Local authorities were unable to stop the violence and wired Governor Hayes for militia.[50]

Hayes was placed in a dilemma. He sympathized with the miners and was acutely aware of the political repercussions of strikebreaking in an election year. It would be folly to identify the Republican state administration with the mine operators. But the disorder was a threat to law, and property had been destroyed; clearly he must send troops. The soldiers quelled the rioting and one miner was wounded trying to escape arrest. The owners, backed by state authority, reduced wages and forced the men back to work.

The surest way to blacken labor's eye in that era was to identify it with violence. Public opinion ran strongly against the group of miners arrested for disorderly conduct, and no local attorneys would defend them. Hearing of their plight, McKinley took their case. He sensed the injustice of their being without counsel and doubtless also saw the political advantage of being on their side in a congressional district that seesawed between Democratic and Republican control.[51]

The mine owners, one of whose members was Marcus Alonzo

Hanna, were represented by distinguished counsel, his old acquaintances from Canton, Lynch and William R. Day, when the trial opened late in June. McKinley had gathered facts, witnesses, and information about the defendants, and even talked with Hayes about the problem.[52] His quiet and dignified demeanor and his thoroughness impressed Mark Hanna, who liked efficiency in business and politics. He knew nothing of the law, but he was a keen judge of men. He marked McKinley well, though they were technically opponents.[53]

At the trial, McKinley used all his carefully prepared evidence. He eloquently outlined the miners' poverty, their bad living and working conditions, the economic desperation that drove them to strike. He did not justify their violence, but maintained that had the operators been more reasonable there would have been no strike and no violence. Deftly and shrewdly he put each member of the jury in the miners' place. The jury convicted only one man, who received a three-year prison term. Realizing the miners' plight, McKinley would not accept a fee.

The case was relatively unimportant but it convinced much of the labor element of both parties that McKinley would be a good man to have in Congress, and it brought McKinley and Hanna together to begin one of the most famous and successful partnerships in American political history. Oddly enough, in after years neither man could remember exactly when they first met. In 1904, Hanna remembered that he had met McKinley about thirty years before. McKinley himself alluded to his friendship of "more than twenty years" in 1896 when offering Hanna a cabinet post. Straining his memory in 1903, Hanna recalled that he had met McKinley prior to the trial in 1876. They probably met casually and without notable impression on each other as early as 1871.[54]

Mark Hanna was a good friend for any man to have. Six years older than McKinley, he was already successful in business, dabbling in politics, and civic affairs. His stout, fast-walking figure was a familiar sight in Cleveland, and his varied interests and endless energy made him a collector of coal mines, slag pits, theaters, and fine homes. His real love was management, and politics afforded a fertile field for that energy. An ardent Republican, high protectionist, gold-standard advocate, he was not a snob in any sense of the word. Admired by his workers, fair to men who were fair to him, he established a reputation for equitable dealing with labor that put him far in advance of his fellow entrepreneurs. He never lost the touch of earth and the sweat of labor that first made him successful, and to the end, his humanity and personal common sense tempered a drive that in other men would merely have been ruthlessness. In politics he strove for efficiency. Believing as he did that economic prosperity meant political stability and prosperity for everyone, he strove to implement these doctrines through the Republican party. He instilled in the men around him a devotion and loyalty that rested on his basic humanity. He could be ruthless when all else failed, but his charm was legendary. He wore a velvet glove, but the touch of steel lay beneath it.

Though the years of intimate friendship and cooperation lay in the future, Hanna undoubtedly gauged McKinley well from the first. He saw in him the moderation, the personal deftness, the political insight, the balance and order, the smoothness and tact that he himself sometimes lacked. The one's weaknesses complemented the other's strengths; they were in almost every way an ideal working team. "I became intimate with him soon after he entered Congress, and our friendship ripened with each succeeding year," Hanna remembered.[55]

Meanwhile, McKinley began his strenuous campaign for the district congressional nomination. To his credit, he frankly admitted that he wanted the position; he claimed to have heard no oracular call from the "people." He was a relative newcomer to politics, and there were three other contenders for the nomination, all pillars of their communities and difficult candidates to face. The Democrats rejoiced that "the Majah," as they called him with tongues in cheeks, faced divisions in his own ranks, for they saw a formidable candidate in him; his appeal to labor might effectively cut into the Democratic votes. Opponents indulged in a vicious whispering campaign, floating rumors that he had been a drunkard in the army, a story that Hayes and former comrades promptly scotched.[56]

Columbiana County led the way, giving him its delegation to the district convention in June; his defeat of the other candidates in that county's race paved the way for a clean sweep. Stark County was the key: if he could carry it, the nomination was his. He learned at once that hard work wins more votes than mere charm, and he visited out-of-the-way villages and country farms in his search for support. By August he could write his brother-in-law confidently: "Things look well for me at home here." Still, he took no chances. A friendly doctor took him on his rounds, where he shook hands with sick and well patients, smiled at babies, and ate his share of country cooking, meanwhile chatting easily with farm wives starved for the sight of city company. He spoke amid flying sawdust to grime-covered workers in a sawmill. A business friend introduced him around the barbershops, where he shook innumerable hands and smiled unnumbered times in a routine that became the pattern of his life.[57]

By the first week in August, Judge Frease sensed defeat and withdrew. The bandwagon was clearly rolling and the cheering delegates to the district convention nominated McKinley after the other candidates withdrew on August 15, 1876. "Comparatively young, vigorous, educated, well-posted, a fine orator, and with a personal magnetism that ever secures friends, he will make a canvass such as this district has rarely if ever had," the *Repository* boasted.[58]

McKinley had already sent his congratulations to Hayes, now the Republican presidential nominee. "I am highly gratified with your nomination and feel that the Republican party did the very *wisest* and best thing in placing you at the head of its ticket," he wrote on July 1.[59] Throughout the campaign he worked for Hayes and the national ticket. His reward was support from Hayes and private assurances to party notables that the young candidate deserved to be watched and helped.[60]

Despite the *Repository*'s cheery injunction that it was a Republican year, and that "Major McKinley is holding a splendid series of meetings in this district, and is everywhere making a fine impression, and hosts of friends," the candidate worked hard. He already knew enough of Ohio's cutthroat politics to realize that nothing was certain until the ballots were counted. All the wearying campaign details passed through his hands, and he spoke so often that his throat nearly gave out. At a major address in Youngstown he read off Samuel J. Tilden's supposed reform record in such a tone that good Republicans were convinced that the Democratic standard-bearer was a fraud. "Would you have such a man for President?"

McKinley called out. "YES!" yelled a leather-lunged Democrat in the back row, and the smiling Major rang back: "There is a fellow who says yes. He must need reformation." [61]

McKinley preferred to run his campaign on the tariff issue, for it cut across party lines, and he admonished workers to vote for him and protection to insure their jobs. The touchiest issue on which he dwelled, and the haziest in his own speaking, was the currency question. The Democrats charged that when with Democrats he was for silver, and when with Republicans he was for gold. In truth, he was for "honest money," and then as later was a sincere bimetallist, faithfully reflecting his constituents' wishes.[62]

When the ballots were in, McKinley defeated Leslie Sanborn by 3,300 votes against the bets placed by older politicians, many of whom were wary of the upstart Canton lawyer. Hayes, who had followed the contest while enmeshed in his own, was pleased at his protégé's success, and was doubly happy to have him in Congress. His own election hinged on a doubtful arrangement that deprived him of control of Congress. Late in January, 1877, convinced that Hayes and the Republicans had won honestly, and anticipating an early session of Congress, McKinley went to Washington to engage housing for himself and his wife, and to familiarize himself with the city.[63]

At thirty-four he stood on the threshold of a brilliant career, a beginning which would take him to the summit of American politics and to international fame and power. In ten years he would be a leading Republican; in fifteen he would be a contender for the presidency; in twenty he would be president. It is doubtful that he sensed this in 1876; he was, after all, only a beginner in Ohio politics, a country lawyer just elected to Congress. And yet, maybe that sense of destiny told him more than he revealed. Perhaps he felt then that his future would be bright. And perhaps also tragic.

IV

Raising the Standard of Protection

PRESIDENT Rutherford B. Hayes had had enough trouble reaching the White House without facing Congress, but he summoned the Forty-fifth Congress into special session on October 15, 1877. As he sat in his new seat for the first time, William McKinley saw around him faces that were famous or to be famous. Some distance from the Ohioan, the hulking figure of Thomas Brackett Reed, of Maine, filled a desk to overflowing. There was also Joseph G. Cannon, of Illinois; Eugene Hale and William P. Frye, of Maine, both later to have long senatorial careers. Ohio herself sent a distinguished delegation; in addition to McKinley there was J. Warren Keifer, later speaker of the House, and James A. Garfield, Hayes' floor leader in the House and president in 1881. On the Democratic side McKinley saw the cherubic face of Roger Q. Mills, of Texas, and the granite profile of John G. Carlisle, of Kentucky, both formidable adversaries.

At the other end of the Capitol, through marbled and statued corridors, sat the members of the "Cave of the Winds," the United States Senate. Many were freshmen destined to fame, many were veterans, savoring the power and prestige that flowed from their position: William B. Allison, of Iowa; Justin Smith Morrill, of Vermont; James G. Blaine, of Maine; Roscoe Conkling, of New York; L. Q. C. Lamar, of Mississippi. The clear Republican majorities in Congress ended with Reconstruction, and the pendulum of congressional power alternated between Democrats and Republicans for most of the rest of the century. Only twice, however, in 1884 and 1892, did the Democrats elect a President. The Senate became the stronghold of Republican power and often offset a Democratic House. Staffed with Republicans of long tenure, wise in the ways of obstruction as well as legislation, it was a major party fortress.

The House differed from the staid upper chamber. As pressures for change mounted in the late 1870's and 1880's, especially as Western discontent focused in Granger movements and free silver, the lower house became a cross section of the interests in both major parties. Debate was free, often heated, and rules were less sacred than in the Senate.

The 1870's and 1880's were transitional times for the America which the Republican party represented. The party clung to the old issues and rhetoric of its birth, by which it consolidated its power during and after the Civil War. Its program reflected the groups that composed it. It was a coalition of interests, appealing with many programs to various sections and interests in the country. Eastern elements supported its stand on protection and "sound money." Western interests accepted tariff protection and internal improvements, liberal homestead laws and government subsidies to the railroads, and pressured through the party for varying degrees of monetary inflation.

Whatever its faults, and they were many and manifest in practice, the Republican party was at least the great national party of its day. To the politicians it was a machine for winning elections; to the theorist it symbolized a kind of progress for the whole country; to the man above both it was a vision of unity. In some respects, William McKinley was all three. McKinley accepted this party and its issues wholeheartedly. Yet he was not allied with the elements of it that came in time to speak only for triumphant business interests; in his mind there was a difference between wholesome economic development and mere business. He was now a "liberal" in the sense that he favored legislation designed to control business influence in the national government, to provide civil service reform, and to advance the cause of labor in state and nation. His opposition to the influence of corporations in government and his lack of connection with the reactionary elements of the party revealed his Ohio origins and showed him more responsible to the will of the people at large than many older Republicans who enjoyed the insulation and security of assured re-election in New England and elsewhere. Significantly, he was a recognized Republican labor spokesman in the 1880's. And he opposed all efforts to abandon the historic moral principles on which the party first rose to power.

McKinley had a keen ear for his laboring constituents. His precarious political district, his own origins, his personal background of self-made success all committed him to further the cause of labor. He supported immigration restriction to help labor; he believed in protection largely because it insured prosperity for the worker; he favored some form of monetary inflation because he believed that it helped the masses; and he favored regulating corporate influence in government because he feared that it boded ill for balanced national development if one interest outstripped the others.

He was, of course, cautious. Ohio politics taught him to be that first and foremost. But he also sincerely believed that the voice of the people was a proper yardstick of leadership, and was always reluctant to take a new stand without consulting public opinion. His principles rarely differed from those of the party as he knew it in Ohio and the Middlewest. Fortunately for him, his rise to national fame rested on the issue on which his party was most united, tariff protection.

The House was shortly called to order, organized, and began its business under the gravel of the protectionist Democrat, Samuel Jones Randall, of Pennsylvania. The Democrats controlled the lower house with 153 members to 140 for their opponents. In the Senate the division stood at 39 Republicans, 36 Democrats, and 1 Independent. Thus the pattern of congressional politics for the next twenty-odd years was spelled out.

With his usual industry, McKinley quickly settled to his task. He was assigned to the relatively unimportant Committee on Revision of the Laws, and later filled a vacancy on the innocuous Committee on Expenditures in the Post Office Department.[1] Newcomers could hardly be choosers. He presented petitions, saw callers, answered mail, and attended to the duties that often make flunkies of statesmen. He found time for occasional social calls on President Hayes and the James A. Garfields, but otherwise went out little because of his wife's health.

This routine was broken in October, when Richard P. "Silver Dick" Bland of Missouri, the most prominent silverite in the House, introduced a free-coinage measure. McKinley faced his first dilemma: his sympathies were with silver, but his party was committed to gold and the resumption of specie payments on January 1, 1879. His fellow Ohioan, John Sherman, had been selected as Hayes'

Secretary of the Treasury to carry out this policy. To whom should he turn for advice? Garfield, the floor leader and also an Ohioan, stood by gold and the President, and so advised his young friend. But it was not that simple. The Ohio legislature had declared for the restoration of the silver dollar. His own home town newspaper, operated by his wife's family, favored silver. There was no mistaking the tone of his mail. Reluctant to differ from his party, but with genuine conviction, McKinley voted for the Bland measure on November 5, 1877. The bill went to the Senate; silver was distasteful to the upper house, but compromise was a political necessity. The final agreement added the name of William B. Allison to the measure and provided for the monthly purchase of not less than $2,000,000 and not more than $4,000,000 worth of silver by the government. McKinley voted with the House majority to concur in the amendments.[2] As expected, President Hayes vetoed the measure. On February 28, 1878, McKinley voted to override the veto, thereby again opposing his friend in the White House and choosing the silver which his conscience and constituents favored.

In later years he covered his early pro-silver stand with discreet silence, but this voting record was to prove highly embarrassing in the charged atmosphere of 1896. Unquestionably, he favored silver during his early congressional career. Though he never again voted for free coinage, he was "on the ragged edge of free silver."[3] He favored what he called "sound money," and opposed greenbacks and other inflationist schemes. He believed that gold and silver could be held at par and circulated at equal value by government support. He was only too aware of the intense pressures brought to bear, especially in the Mississippi Valley, in favor of inflation; he later recalled the dark days of the early 1870's, punctuated by hard times and financial deflation. His stand won laurels at home. "Major McKinley voted for the re-monetization of silver the other day, like a man who has the courage of his convictions," his home town newspaper reported.[4]

Garfield's forceful stand against silver deeply impressed McKinley, and for a time he was uncertain. "If there were any temper in Congress or in the country which would tolerate or listen to discussion I should be glad to debate the case fully," Garfield wrote. "But it is an epoch of madness." When the veto was overridden he noted sadly: "I again voted alone among the Ohio delegation—and almost alone in the Mississippi Valley." [5]

The new congressman did not doubt the wisdom of his course. "I voted against the veto," he wrote his brother Abner. "You are wrong in adhering to a single standard." [6] He was sorry to diverge from the Hayes administration, but his action did not cost him any friendship or support in that quarter. In truth, the currency question was a secondary issue to him and he never understood its full economic ramifications. Stronger heads than his were turned by the silver siren; his district favored inflation; he was inexperienced. He himself also favored regulated inflation as a partial cure for the financial and economic distress that affected his section and the West.

Charges that he favored "cheap money" were false, for he campaigned vigorously against unrestricted inflation. He later freely admitted his early ignorance. ". . . he did not pretend to be a doctor of finance and had followed the popular trend of that time," Mark Hanna later said. He strongly favored the resumption of specie payments in 1879; he had campaigned in Ohio in 1875 for Hayes and sound money; he even worked for friends in other states against the greenback craze; he believed that no currency should be issued not backed by gold.[7] In accepting renomination in 1878, he defended greenbacks when backed by gold and pointed to the coming resumption of specie payments as proof that the Republican party favored honest money.[8] In his judgment on silver he was ill-informed and hasty; time proved his action unwise. But in 1877, in view of the pressures and the advice available, he saw no alternative.

It was not to silver but to tariff protection that the young congressman turned his attention. The tariff had ceased to be an issue after the Civil War because of economic prosperity and because it was superseded in the public mind by the controversial issues of Reconstruction. The Panic of 1873, and later the government surplus, revived controversy over both protection and free trade, and the issue remained in the forefront of American politics for the rest of the century.[9] McKinley arrived in Congress at the moment when the tariff question acquired new life; in time it became synonymous with his name.

Opinion on the tariff question fell into three broad categories:

free trade, tariff for revenue only, and protection. Like the silver question, the tariff issue crossed party lines and geographic sections, but it was in one form or another a dividing principle between the two parties. Free trade—the absence of tariff regulation—had few adherents except academics and theorists. "Tariff for revenue only," taxing products not produced in the United States, with only modest duties on manufactured goods, was the principle for which the Democratic party stood. But the party was divided, for Southern congressmen eagerly protected their agricultural interests while voting against duties on manufactured goods. In the North, Democratic protectionists spoke for industrial sections like Pennsylvania, New York, and New England, leaving their party in order to vote with the Republicans on the issue.

Tariff reform was popular because it savored of change, but protection had its friends. As capital accumulated and investment expanded, business interests were unwilling to relinquish tariff protection. Efforts at reduction in the early 1870's failed. McKinley himself always held that no substantial element of the population desired reduction.[10] Just how much the tariff actually helped industry was a mystery, but business *thought* it helped and thus made it a party issue.

It was not surprising that McKinley adhered to tariff protection. Hayes supposedly first advised the young lawyer to study the tariff in preparation for his political career. The story is doubtless true, but the roots of his belief ran back to the dimness of childhood, when he heard his ironmaster father complain before the evening fire that foreign competition made honest men close their forges. The child in this case was the father of the man, and McKinley entered Congress with much study of the question behind him.[11]

Few questioned the sincerity of his belief in protection. The great protected industries which he saw from his train window in travelling from Ohio to Washington assured him that he was right. Trips through the industrialized Northeast solidified his belief. "It was a deep conviction, almost a religion, with him. No one who worked with him could doubt it," Robert La Follette remembered.[12] He admitted being a high protectionist. "Why, they call me a high protectionist," he told a Virginia audience in 1885. "I am a high protectionist; I do not deny it, and I would not be seriously disturbed in mind if the tariff were a little higher." [13] His policy was a national one, with exceptions for none; he sharply criticized the Democrats for their inconsistency. "We ask nothing for northern labor which we do not freely accord to southern labor; nor for northern industries that we do not cheerfully extend to southern industries." [14]

His whole tariff theory rested on two assumptions: that the tariff produced high wages, and that the American system of his day was not ready to face foreign competition. The home market must be closed to sustain both American labor and industry. He himself had no connections with any industry that might have benefited from the tariff. His constituents were the laborers of northeastern Ohio's iron factories, and he watched their interests zealously. "Reduce the tariff and labor is the first to suffer," he said in his first major address on the subject. "He who would break down the manufactures of this country strikes a fatal blow at labor. It is labor I would protect," he reiterated in 1883. He scorned those who felt that wages should seek their own level. "We do not want fifty-cent labor," he retorted on being told that it would be available were it not for protection. The security afforded to labor by tariff protection buttressed the American ideal to which he clung. "Here the mechanic of today is the manufacturer of a few years hence." But he was no mere materialist; none decried more than he the money-getting of the age. He prized the homely virtues of honesty, diligence, thrift, and individualism, all of which were symbolized for him by economic wealth protected by the tariff. These virtues had made him successful; they could do the same for others.[15]

He quickly made his position clear: his first act as a representative was to submit a petition from steelworkers in his district opposing reduction of the tariff. It was the first of many such documents. His campaign tours brought him into contact with thousands of workers, and he never failed to explain patiently why he stood for protection. More than one grimy head nodded in agreement as he toured factories and mines. It was said that he could make a tariff schedule read like poetry, and he developed an effectively simple manner of presentation that impressed even hostile audiences. His stand with the labor element in his district alone accounts for his repeated re-election in the face of gerrymanders and the hostile Democrats.

World trade did not lure him. "The 'markets of the world' in our present condition are a snare and a delusion. We will reach them whenever we can undersell competing nations, and no sooner. Our tariffs do not keep us out, and free trade will not make it easier to enter them." [16] Closing the home market to foreign competition allowed free trade within the United States, and free competition among manufacturers in the separate states insured fair prices and good wages.

He was deaf to the old cry that the tariff raised prices, for to him any such rise was more than offset by higher wages. He rested his whole theory on the assumption that cheap goods meant hard times. "When prices were the lowest did you not have the least money to buy with?" he asked an audience in 1889.[17] He argued that prices of finished goods had declined under protection as production expanded and methods of distribution improved, while at the same time, wages rose. "Less duty might cheapen the peanut for a time," he told a southern audience in 1885, "but it would only be temporary; when the foreign article had broken down our production the price would go up and be higher than ever." [18] He nevor forgot the lesson of his childhood—cheap foreign iron ruined domestic production, then raised prices.

He insisted that the tariff was not paid by the consumer but by the foreign producer.[19] Revenue must be raised and so the selective tariff was most effective, since it both produced funds and protected home industry. He opposed tariff reformers who insisted that taxes ought to be levied on products not produced in this country, such as tea and coffee, arguing that in that case the domestic consumer would pay the maximum tax, with no compensating factor of protection to home industry.

He understood the opposition engendered by party platforms, but the academic doctrines of free trade exasperated him. Every college in the country seemed to produce tariff reformers. He often aimed a shaft at the academics by insisting that "actual results outweigh an idle philosophy." Protection might not be "favored in the colleges, [but] it is taught in the school of experience, in the workshop, where honest men perform an honest day's labor, and where capital seeks the development of national wealth." [20]

Trusts were not identified with protection until late in the great tariff debate of the 1880's and 1890's, but McKinley never conceded a connection between the two. He consistently favored anti-trust legislation while in Congress and sincerely opposed trusts. "They are, however, in no wise related to the tariff, and the tariff is in no way responsible for them," he stated flatly in 1888. As early as 1882 he insisted that "we have few, if any, manufacturing monopolies in the United States today. They can not long exist with an unrestricted home competition such as we have. They feel the spur of competition from thirty-seven states, and extortion and monopoly can not survive the sharp contest among our own capitalists and enterprising citizens." In similar vein, he insisted repeatedly that no princely fortunes grew from the tariff; the genuine businessman put his wealth in his works, not his vaults.[21]

These were the basic tenets to which he held fast in his discussion of the tariff. He grounded his theory of protection in the simplicity of his own life. He knew little formal economic theory, nothing of finance. The speculation and stockjobbing of his day repelled him. He believed in labor freed from the competition of cheap foreign goods. It was his gift to simplify a complex subject, and in his enthusiasm he often oversimplified. National progress came from more than the tariff. Natural wealth, enterprise, capital, geographical location, markets—all of these, as he knew, had raised the American standard of living far above that of Europe. Yet to his way of thinking the tariff protected it all and thus made it all possible. He knew the revolution that protected industry had wrought in Ohio, and he interpreted it as a national transformation.

But to him there was something more to protection, something more easily felt than explained. "It encourages the development of skill, and inventive genius as part of the great productive forces," he said early in his career.[22] He identified the tariff with prosperity and national development, which to him represented the highest form of patriotism. The tariff was a historic policy, dating from the founding of the government, inculcating and encouraging all the homely virtues that had made the nation great. Of all the economic forces in the nation's history, none was so potent, none so real, none so influential as the tariff. Through the dull tax schedules that bored other men he found the romance of history in the unfolding development of the nation's wealth.

Who is to say that he was not merely sincere but also justified? That protection had fostered industry was accepted by everyone; the division lay in the need for its continuation. He never denied that there were inequalities in the tariff, or that some reform was necessary, or that slow change might be beneficial. He objected to the continual agitation of the subject as a political issue, because he felt this was bad for the nation's economy. Indeed, the fault of protection lay not so much in the theory itself as in the method of its enactment. Tariff schedules were made by congressmen, pressured by protected interests—weak vessels with eyes on election dates, open to bribery, doubts, and fears. No scientific management of the tariff was possible in the welter and confusion that surrounded every effort to change a jot or tittle of any schedule.

All men have their dreams. McKinley's in time came to be that of an all-inclusive nationalism that might fail to blot out party divisions on the great national issue of the day, but would at least rise above them. To him the basis of that nationalism was the protective system that worked for all sections of the country and for all of the people. His great personal desire for order and unity became in his public life a demand for national unity and cohesion. His frequent references to the Founding Fathers in his speeches, his admiration for the nationalism of Henry Clay and the old Whig party, and his efforts to make that nationalism the basis of the Republican program stamp him as a leading nationalist in American politics at the end of the nineteenth century. He worked for a new American System.

As it developed over the years, McKinley's stand on the tariff reflected the era's dominant economic trends. He became a national leader because he spoke for national interests; the most important of these was the economic expansion symbolized by protection. He wisely decided at the beginning of his career to identify himself with a national issue; it was his good fortune to believe in that issue and what it represented.

With all this in mind, McKinley appeared for the regular session of Congress in December, 1877. He had not yet had time or opportunity to identify himself with any party leaders, but he was ready for the first chance to display his mettle in debate. His chance came in the spring of 1878, when Fernando Wood of New York,

64

Democratic chairman of the House Ways and Means Committee, introduced a tariff-reform bill. It aimed at a reduction of the articles dutied; free entry for all goods not dutied; simplification of customs collection; free raw materials for shipbuilding; and the abolition of compound duties.[23] On April 15, 1878, McKinley rose to lead the attack on the bill with a carefully prepared speech. One of the visitors at this night session noted that "he had a somewhat youthful appearance, was short in stature, and with a clear complexion indicating health and vigor." Ordinarily, he had little to say in Congress and made few speeches not dealing with the tariff, preferring to concentrate on his main interest, to master it in every detail, to be an expert in one thing rather than a dilettante in many things. Speaking slowly without notes and with few oratorical flourishes, he told the minimum number of jokes and indulged in few fanciful flights with the American eagle. His impressive appearance, his deep-set flashing eyes, his gestures, his calm, mellifluous voice all conveyed a sense of deep conviction.[24]

Fully conscious that the eyes of influential men were upon him, McKinley presented a calm, reasoned argument. He opposed Wood's bill because it reduced the revenue at a time when it was needed; it further unsettled business, which was just recovering from the panic; it was the product of theory, not experience; and it ignored popular opinion, which was against reduction. The bill was "a piece of patchwork, and abounds in inconsistencies. It is neither free trade, tariff reform, nor protective tariff. It has none of the virtues of either, but the glaring faults of all systems. It is an attempt to change a law which does not improve the old one. It is an experiment opposed by all experience."[25] When he sat down he was roundly applauded. The Democrats realized that a formidable opponent was in the making.

It was not to impress the Democrats that McKinley had worked so hard; he was more concerned with the reaction from his own side. and he was shortly welcomed into the councils of party protectionists. Impressed by the young man's ability and willingness to work, William D. "Pig Iron" Kelley of Pennsylvania, the leading protectionist of his day, nicknamed for his solicitous affection for his state's iron interests, took a fancy to him. The subsequent death of one of Kelley's proteges drew him closer to McKinley, and he began to prepare the Ohioan for his mantle. Visitors to the galleries who inquired about the striking young figure were often told: "Oh, that's Pig-Iron Kelley's lieutenant, Major McKinley of Ohio." [26] For his own part, the Major respected Kelley, whose influence was powerful in party councils, and who always had a kind word for those around him. Respect ripened into affection, and Kelley's death in 1890, while McKinley was fashioning his own famous tariff bill, inspired the Major's best brief eulogy.

Reprints from the *Congressional Record* of his attack on Wood's tariff-reform bill were shortly on their way to Ohio and elsewhere. "Mr. McKinley's constituents may well be proud of him and his efforts to save the industries of his district from the ruin that threatened them in this wicked tariff scheme," his home town newspaper reported with masterful overstatement.[27] The bill languished, a victim of congressional delay and debate. When Congress moved to adjourn three months later, its author asked permission to have the Ways and Means Committee sit during the summer to take testimony. "The Committee of Ways and Means have been here six months without an opportunity to report anything," Wood said. McKinley shifted in his seat and rejoined amid general laughter, "They reported a bill on the tariff." Wood turned on the Ohioan and snapped, "I know they did, and you were one of the men who were very industrious in slaughtering it." Unruffled, McKinley replied, "I must say that I am very much delighted with the result of our action." [28] In naming him a chief offender, Wood paid him a high compliment that did not go unnoticed on either side of the aisle.

It was not all silver and tariff in the early days of McKinley's congressional career. The election of 1876 supposedly ended Reconstruction, but the thorny problem of the South would not die. McKinley entered Congress when all but the minor problems of Reconstruction had passed, though the South and the Negro were still uppermost in many Northern minds. In time, he mellowed in his attitude toward the residual problems of the Civil War. As president he was praised as a bringer of peace to the sections, and he died secure in the knowledge that he, the last Civil War veteran to occupy the White House, had done much to "heal the wounds of sectional strife." But at the opening of his career he handled the bloody shirt as deftly as any political matador of his day.

It never occurred to him that the Democrats might run the government as well as the Republicans. He lived in an era that took its politics seriously, when campaigns combined all the virtues and defects of politics, religion, and entertainment. Mere flag-waving did not prompt McKinley and the orators of the day to identify their party with progress and the best in national life. As Mrs. Foraker said, "The Republican Party had saved the Union. It was the Union." [29] McKinley could have agreed with John Sherman when he said, "In these times a bad Republican is better than an average Democrat." [30]

McKinley was quick and acid in his condemnation of Southern injustices toward the Negro. The old cry that the South ought to be left along to deal with its problems angered him. "The war is over, the flag of the lost and wicked cause went down at Appomattox more than twenty years ago," he told an Ohio audience in 1885, "but that does not prevent us from insisting that all that was gained in war shall not be lost in peace . . . the struggle cost too much human life and public treasure to be apologized for, or frittered away, under any pretext. The results admit of no compromise." [31] He and many others favored enforcement of the Fourteenth Amendment by reducing Southern representation in Congress until the Negroes were enfranchised.

Southern stubbornness and opposition to "Yankee meddling" took a concrete form. The Democratic-dominated Congresses of the Hayes administration attached riders to the Army appropriations bills requiring that no federal officials might regulate elections. All violators, including the president, were to be subjected to severe penalties.[32] Republican opposition to these measures was instant and violent. As Hayes' floor leader in the House, Garfield led the attack and McKinley was a valuable lieutenant in the word battles that occupied much of every day's session.

To McKinley the Southern obstruction was "a bold and wanton attempt to wipe from the law all protection of the ballot box and surrender its purity to the unholy hand of the hired repeater and its control to the ballot box stuffers of the great cities of the north and the tissue ballot party of the south." [33] He supported federal control of elections while attacking the Southerners for withholding vital appropriations for the army. The funds were ultimately passed, but not without the generation of much congressional heat.

He fell into a heated exchange with J. C. S. Blackburn of Kentucky when debate opened on a proposition to permit former Confederates to enter the Army and to receive pensions. "The first fruits of their dominion are not assuring to the country, and will not, I am certain, incline the people to clothe them with still greater power. Threatened revolutions will not hasten it, extra sessions, useless and expensive, will not accelerate it." [34] In such word battles as these the patience which he displayed at other times vanished, and he exhibited all the Scottish stubbornness and quickness of tongue that impressed everyone who debated with him.

A congressman's term is short and McKinley soon faced the election of 1878. The Democratic legislature gerrymandered his district in a transparent effort to defeat him.[35] In accepting the Republican nomination at Massillon in August, he lashed out at the gerrymander. "The redistricting was not in the interest of fairness, but to increase Democratic representation, in violation of every principle of fairness." [36] Though it added an extra burden to his campaign and his already taxed resources, it was to be a familiar story. In his acceptance speech he attacked the Democrats for their conduct in Congress, called for sound money, praised the tariff, and bestowed laurels on President Hayes. The campaign that followed was rough and tumble, for he faced a formidable majority in the new district. He worked day and night, speaking, shaking hands, appearing at endless functions. His meetings were generally successful, and a surprising degree of enthusiasm welcomed him even in doubtful areas, largely because of his stand on silver and the tariff. But he remained vigilant. "I intend making a very close, active canvass and if appearances are not altogether deceptive, I ought to get through," he wrote Hayes. "I mean to deserve success, *anyhow*." [37] When the ballots were counted he won by more than 1,200 plurality, and Hayes jubilantly wrote a friend: "Oh, the good luck of McKinley. He was gerrymandered out and then beat the gerrymander! We enjoyed it as much as he did." [38] McKinley himself was justly happy. "I fought my campaign for honest money and protection to American industry. I fought it straight . . . and the good people acquiesced." [39]

Enjoying the security of re-election, he resumed his work. Much of it was petty, the presentation of endless petitions, checking on private pension bills, looking after patronage. Pressure came from the Grand Army of the Republic to remove postmasters who were not veterans, but McKinley did not heed the call.[40] He was very conscious of patronage, the oil that ran the political machine, and spent weary hours checking the progress of recommendations for appointments in his district. In distributing his favors and using his influence he did his best to avoid local factionalism. "Personally I would be on your side," he wrote an office seeker, "officially I must consult the public sentiment of your community and take into account other proper considerations."[41] Many an afternoon he wearily mounted the steps of the White House or some government bureau to check on appointments with the harried officials within.[42] He was involved in a momentary controversy over his efforts to secure a federal job in California for his brother Abner; the opposition press cried "Nepotism!" but the tempest quickly died in the teapot and he emerged unscathed. He scrupulously avoided conflict with fellow party members in appointments; thus he declined to give advice on appointments not in his district.[43]

It was all very pleasant being a congressman, but he did tire of checking to see if memorial cannon had been delivered to a club; if this or that widow had received her pension; if some federal appropriation would help the district. He introduced a flood of anti-liquor and anti-polygamy petitions, and even a petition to exempt wild animals from tariff duties when imported by zoos. He favored the proposed Reagan Interstate Commerce Act and introduced petitions from Grange organizations supporting railroad regulations. He was a tireless committee worker, solicitous of details others avoided, present at meetings others shunned.[44]

Early in 1880, the Ohio legislature elected his friend James A. Garfield to the United States Senate, creating a vacancy on the House Ways and Means Committee. McKinley wished to sit there, since the committee dealt with tariff legislation. Speaker Randall told Garfield that he would appoint whomever he chose, and Garfield chose McKinley. Thus after only three years in Congress he sat on the most important committee of the House.

As the Hayes administration closed, McKinley congratulated his old chief on his record. Hayes did not seek a second term, and the nomination went to Garfield. McKinley did not move in the councils that chose presidential candidates, but he heartily endorsed Garfield. He was at the party's disposal and toured the state. At one parade he appeared as a marcher clad in a yellow oilcloth cape and carrying a spluttering torch through a rainstorm.

McKinley was up for re-election and his own canvass was as hectic as usual. "I will have a hard fight—am in the minority, but things look very hopeful. I have a large dist., hard to canvass," he hurriedly wrote an admirer. "But I will get through with good health I think." [45] Garfield helped him, not only because of friendship but because he needed McKinley in Congress.[46] Visiting Canton as his guest, the presidential candidate made a short speech to an enthusiastic crowd.[47]

Perhaps Garfield's support explained it, but more likely it was hard work that gave McKinley a third victory. "My majority is 3,572, the largest since 1868 anyhow and I don't know what it was then," he wrote Garfield after the victory, with a touch of pride that erased the memory of all the stump meetings and campaign dust he endured to win.[48] The Ohio election was held early and he had yet to fill speaking engagements farther east. Garfield's narrow victory in November was still a victory, and McKinley rejoiced with all good Republicans, the more so because the Democratic candidate, General Winfield Scott Hancock, had dared to call the tariff "a local issue." [49]

The ink on his letter of congratulation to Garfield was hardly dry before he was recommending office seekers to the harried President-elect. "Am I the first?" he asked puckishly in a letter of introduction written for a friend.[50] As the new President fashioned his cabinet he asked McKinley's advice, and the latter, with several other Ohio men, called in Mentor to approve Senator Allison as secretary of the Treasury.[51] Though the appointment did not materialize, the fact that McKinley had been consulted reflected his growing stature.

Overworked and tired of the freezing eastern weather, McKinley decided to visit San Francisco in the spring of 1881, as soon as the short session was over. With President Garfield safely inaugurated and with his patronage recommendations on file, he risked a rumored extra session and crossed the country. He was anxious to place his brother Abner in a federal appointment in California, and his trip may have been an effort to survey the situation there, as well as a pleasure outing.[52] The long arm of favor seeking reached back to Washington, however, as McKinley kept up the pressure for appointments; patronage never took a holiday.

Garfield was tragically shot in July and lingered on the verge of death in the summer heat. Returning from California, McKinley hastily sought the latest news of the President's condition. "The public suspense is awful," he reported.[53] With Garfield's death in September, McKinley lost a friend and counselor. It was only fitting that he planned the memorial services on behalf of the dead President in the House of Representatives—fitting and ironic, for someone else would perform the same service for him twenty years later. He persuaded the reluctant James G. Blaine to deliver the principal eulogy. A former rival of Garfield, and then his secretary of State, Blaine had been present at the assassination, and hesitated to deliver the eulogy because of his emotions, but finally agreed. On February 27, 1882, McKinley and John Sherman escorted the new President, Chester A. Arthur, to his seat, and Blaine delivered his celebrated address to Congress.

The Forty-seventh Congress, which met in regular session on December 5, 1881, was Republican by a slender majority in the House. J. Warren Keifer of Ohio was elected speaker. The chairmanship of the Ways and Means Committee passed to William D. Kelley, and McKinley was duly appointed a member. He also served on the Committee on the Revision of the Laws, but devoted his time to the tariff. His work was intensified by rumors that the new President favored tariff revision and wished to crown his unexpected administration with a successful reform measure.

McKinley was a consistent supporter of the Arthur administration, though he never knew the President well. His familiar consultation with Hayes and Garfield was no more. He supported Arthur's demands for civil service reform and voted for the Pendleton Act of 1883, characterizing civil service reform as "the only good thing proposed by a Democrat for twenty-five years . . ."[54] Congress passed a bill excluding Chinese immigrants for twenty years; Arthur vetoed it but hinted that more lenient legislation would meet his approval. McKinley voted for the final bill that outlawed Chinese immigration for a period of ten years.[55] His vote reflected the labor sentiment of his district; though the threat was far away, on the West Coast, labor everywhere was opposed.

Storm clouds now rose on the political horizon in Ohio. Early in 1882 he learned that his renomination would be contested, and hurried home to mend fences.[56] He had won three successive contests, two from the same district; Columbiana County's spokesmen claimed that he had no right to a third term from his old district, which had been restored. Historically the seat had rotated among the counties composing the district, and it was now his turn to defer. He had no such intention; having risen so far in six years, he was ready to contend with Republicans as well as Democrats for the chance to rise further. He was in constant contact with his brother Abner, who forwarded all relevant information to Washington.[57] Hopeful contestants approached him in the spring, anxious to discover his course. He greeted them with the courtesy that made him famous, but let it be known that he intended to run again. "I was disposed to be a little caustic," he wrote home concerning one such interview, "but my better judgment advised me against it." [58]

As he manipulated to solidify his position within the district, more and more of his time and energy went to the game of survival. "This constant struggle all the time is anything but agreeable, but it seems necessary to any success in life in anything," he wrote sadly. "In politics it is a little more irritating than in other things, but I can stand it. There must be in our vocabulary no such word as 'fail.' " [59] As the district convention assembled he still worried about gerrymanderers. In the end he won renomination after a hard fight. "A desperate fight was made against me which gives my victory more than ordinary significance," he wrote Hayes.[60]

But the struggle had only begun. The Democratic nomination went to Jonathan Wallace, a former Union supporter during the Civil War, who had supposedly then followed Clement Vallandigham, leader of the Peace Democrats opposing the war, who had been especially active in Ohio. Associated with the greenback element, Wallace, who had already failed in several contests, stood also for "Free beer and a circus on Sunday"—or so said McKinley's press.[61] Wallace and his followers were determined to win, shrewdly playing on some Republican dissatisfaction with McKinley's renomination, and a general Democratic trend. When the votes were counted, McKinley received eight votes more than Wallace, many of whose ballots were invalidated because they were not marked with his proper name.

Wallace contested the case. In December the state canvassing board certified McKinley, and he returned to Washington, where he later cheerily said he would remain "until they put me out of Congress." [62] Wallace proposed to do just that, and immediately began collecting evidence, visiting Washington for talks with prominent Democrats, and organizing his case for presentation before the congressional committee appointed to investigate the election.[63]

The expense of the contest worried McKinley, since he could ill afford it. A few friends offered to help, but he was reluctant to accept money even though the case cost him four thousand dollars, only half of which was paid by Congress.[64] The case was placed on the House calendar when the new Congress met, and the contestants could only wait and work. Having been admitted to the House, McKinley continued in his full capacity as a member of the House Ways and Means Committee and the Committee on Revision of the Laws. "I am busying myself getting ready for my contest in the House next winter," he wrote a year after the election. "I have got a good case— strong and I think can't be overturned." [65] If he had doubts he kept them to himself, but an Ohio friend put his finger on the heart of the matter when he said that the case might be good, but "whether it will be strong enough for a Democratic congress is another question." [66]

While enduring the suspense of his contest, McKinley was busy, for the tariff pot was again boiling. True to rumors of change, President Arthur proposed fiscal reform. The chief problem this time was a rare one, a surplus in the Treasury. The return of prosperity and careful management of expenditures kept the Treasury sound. The tariff reformers had roused public opinion. Even beneficiaries of protection realized that some rates would have to be lowered. With this in mind, Arthur recommended in his first annual message of December, 1881, that a commission be appointed to study the tariff question, empowered to make recommendations to Congress. It was a novel procedure, for Congress was jealous of its prerogative in financial legislation. The plan appealed to many in both parties as a way of adjusting the tariff scientifically, and of appeasing public opinion.

On April 6, 1882, McKinley delivered a lengthy set speech on the subject, which met with close attention, since he spoke for the high tariff wing of the party. He opened by making it clear that he favored the bill, then proceeded with his usual exposition of tariff history, concluding with a veiled warning: "I will vote for the bill now under consideration, because, among other reasons, I have no fear of an intelligent and businesslike examination and revision of the tariff by competent civilians who shall be known Americans and favorable to the American system." [67] In other words, he favored a commission composed of protectionists; he pointed out that it could merely recommend, not legislate, and that Congress could ignore it if it were radical. His acceptance of the idea of scientific management set him apart from the more hidebound Republicans who considered even this a dangerous precedent, and was the first step down from high protection in his long descent to ultimate free reciprocity. The speech aroused some enthusiasm; other representatives ordered thirty thousand copies and the iron manufacturers of Pittsburgh asked for five thousand. "It was no great effort, but seems to have struck a popular chord," he wrote home.[68]

After it was formed in May, 1882, the commission toured the country, taking testimony for the report which it submitted to Congress the following December. Its recommendations were surprisingly liberal: it suggested cuts in many rates, proposed a court of customs, and advised a general simplification of revenue collection. The protectionists rallied as if Fort Sumter had been fired on again. An acrimonious debate followed, complicated for McKinley by his election contest.

The "Mongrel Tariff" that resulted from the debate justly deserved its name, for it was a hodgepodge of conflicting ideas and inconsistencies. The Senate drafted its own bill, calling for lower rates and reduction of internal taxes. The House draft included more modest reductions in the rates than those suggested by the commission. In the end, legislation was passed only by parliamentary struggle and maneuver.

On January 27, 1883, McKinley contributed his mite to the confusion. He agreed that revenues should be reduced but argued that lowering the rates would increase imports and swell revenues. He proposed modifying the internal revenue taxes instead. He reminded the House that "it is much easier to reduce duties than it is to impose them . . ." and insisted that no one really wanted a drastic reduction. He was interrupted by Democrats, anxious to blunt the edge of his attack, and for once lost his temper. When a heckler cited English precedent, he snapped out, "I do not care what they do in England."

He proceeded to show the effects of the tariff on labor and said in passing, "I speak for the workingmen of my district, the workingmen of Ohio, and of the country." Congressman Springer of Illinois, seated across the aisle, suddenly roused himself and rapped out, "They did not speak for you very largely at the last election!" An ominous silence fell on the House. It was a painful reminder of his uncertain status. McKinley turned to Springer, bowed slightly, and said gently but firmly, "Ah, my friend, my fidelity to my constituents is not measured by the support they give me!" Applause broke the charged silence and McKinley faced his adversary for several minutes before he could continue. "I have convictions upon this subject which I would not surrender or refrain from advocating if 10,000 majority had been entered against me last October." A fresh burst of applause swept the chamber and McKinley, unquestionably the victor in the sally, proceeded with his speech. The outcome of the debate was the final passage of a confused measure drafted by neither house but by a conference committee. McKinley voted against it because it reduced rates on wool and steel, the two great interests for which he spoke.[69]

McKinley was not the only one with troubles in 1882; the congressional elections that year were bad for the Republicans. Talking with Secretary of the Treasury Charles Folger one day about his contest, he remarked that he had won by a mere eight votes. Folger looked at him and said, "Young man, let me tell you that eight votes is a mighty big Republican majority this fall."[70] Fortified by this Republican defeat, and with an eye on the coming presidential election of 1884, the Democrats pushed the matter to a conclusion. "I do not believe you can well hope for any remedy by this congress," McKinley wrote a friend concerned over the steel schedules. "They [the Democrats] are determined to reduce and I doubt if a single thing in the whole schedule of the tariff will be advanced." [71]

True to this expectation, Congressman Morrison of Illinois introduced legislation providing for a horizontal reduction of 20 per cent in the tariff. Despite McKinley's uncertain status, he again led the opposition. He opposed a horizontal cut as unscientific and indiscriminate, characterizing the measure as "the invention of indolence. . . ." Smiling, he turned to Morrison and said, "Take twenty inches off the leg of the distinguished chairman of the Committee of Ways and Means and you would still have a stump, but take twenty inches off of one of the smallest persons to be found about this House and you would leave him without any stump at all." A sepulchral voice intoned from a back seat, "That is a good stump speech, Major," and the House dissolved in laughter. Warming to his subject and pleased by his reception, he could not forbear further humor. Asserting that the only supporters of the bill were featherbrained reformers and men with private incomes, he said that "that class of gentlemen 'neither reap nor sow, and do not gather into barns.' " Pleased with the Biblical sally, Kasson of Iowa interjected, "And the lilies?" McKinley took the cue: "Yes, the lilies. They are like 'the lilies of the field . . . ; they toil not, neither do they spin.' " He was ill at ease when he started but the speech ended as one of his best efforts. He had announced that he would move to strike the enacting clause of the bill, thus killing it, on May 6, but on that day he sat silent in his seat while George Converse of Ohio, one of Randall's followers, made the motion. The vote carried, 156–151, ending any hope of tariff legislation at that session and vividly illustrating the division on the question among the Democrats. [72]

His speech on the Morrison bill was his last major effort at that session, for his contest now came to the floor. The House committee assigned to the case worked with a will at the boring details. [73] Wallace's claim rested on the assumption that erroneously marked ballots were intended for him and gave him a majority. McKinley consistently offered to give Wallace these votes, since they were obviously intended for him, but insisted that enough fraudulent votes had been counted to make any such majority meaningless. "My contest goes slowly along. It will however be reached at no great distant day," he wrote as the day of reckoning approached. "I have an excellent case." On May 14, 1884, the Committee on Elections returned an adverse report, and on May 27 he was unseated by a strict party vote. Roger Mills refused to vote with his party, as did five other Democrats, believing that McKinley had been honestly elected. But the opposition's attitude was best summed up by the member who said: "A Democrat should vote for a Democrat on general principles. McKinley is a good man to turn out anyway." Friends who stopped by his desk to console him after the result met a stolid silence; only after the sting wore off could he resume the banter of conversation.[74]

Somone asked him if he thought politics a good career and he answered sadly, "Before I went to Congress I had $10,000 and a practice worth $10,000 a year. Now I haven't either." [75] For the moment the glittering prize was made of fool's gold. But the tarnish quickly faded and he returned to Canton late in May to a hero's welcome. After scoring his opposition, he announced that he would run again to vindicate his principles.[76]

The gerrymanderers were at work and he was given a new district with a Democratic majority of over a thousand. "The new district is not a *bad one*," he wrote a friend, with doubtful consolation. "We can carry it with work and union." [77] Friends canvassed the new district, working for his nomination, while he was in Washington. He simply did not have time to return to Ohio to seek the nomination while important legislation was debated in Congress. "I should like the nomination," he said frankly, "and if it were offered I should feel grateful for it, pull off my coat and do my best. But I am not going to scramble for it." [78] He did not have to scramble for it. "The outlook in the new district . . . seems very good," he wrote in March, and when the district convention assembled he was duly nominated on a high tariff platform.[79]

Once out of Congress, McKinley returned to Ohio to participate in the coming national election. The state Republican convention, at which he served as temporary chairman, named him a delegate-at-large to the national convention, and he served as Ohio's representative on the Resolutions Committee, which promptly elected him chairman. It was a mark of distinction, and he undertook the task with satisfaction. The delegates to Chicago in June, 1884, divided their sympathies among James G. Blaine, John Sherman, President

Arthur, and assorted dark horses. McKinley supported Blaine; the peculiar web of charm and magnetism cast by the "Man from Maine" ensnared him despite Ohio's support of John Sherman. For a while he thought that the ticket would be Blaine and Robert Todd Lincoln as vice-presidential candidate.[80]

On the third day of the convention McKinley was accorded a priceless opportunity. A report from the Rules Committee on the selection of delegates to the next national convention caused tremendous commotion. Delegates rose on their chairs to shout at the chairman; fights broke out on the floor; the galleries were in an uproar. Chairman John B. Henderson, venerable statesman from Missouri, could not be heard over the tumult and cast about for a substitute. His eye fell on McKinley; he motioned, pointing to his gavel. McKinley nodded, threaded his way through the crowd, took the gavel amid great confusion, and faced the angry sea of faces. His gavel fell with a vengeance; the delegates watched the new chairman and quieted on seeing his determined look.[81]

McKinley had worked hard on the platform, determined to make it an expression of sound Republican doctrine. He was well known to the delegates because of his recent work on behalf of the tariff. A flurry of excitement greeted the announcement that he would now read the platform, and ladies' hearts as well as fans fluttered as the darkly clad, handsome "Napoleon of Protection" rose to read the document in a loud clear voice. The statement endorsed the Arthur administration, called for high protection but favored reducing the surplus through "scientific" reform, straddled the currency question by endorsing bimetallism, favored regulation of the railroads, the eight-hour day, civil service reform, and veterans' pensions.[82] With McKinley in the chair the resolutions passed without dissent.

On June 6, with balloting on candidates under way, the Blaine boom fast became a steamroller. Sherman's supporters were bitter against the Man from Maine, and J. B. Foraker, Sherman's manager, suddenly moved for adjournment in an effort to halt the stampede. Confusion reigned in the Blaine ranks, but McKinley called for recognition. His appearance was the more dramatic because of his position in Ohio. When he could be heard he announced: "I hope no friend of James G. Blaine will object to having the roll call of the States made . . . as a friend of James G. Blaine, I insist that all his friends shall unite in having the roll of the States called, and then vote that proposition down." [83] Foraker's motion was defeated and Blaine was nominated on the fourth ballot. He faced a newcomer to the national political arena, the Democratic governor of New York, Grover Cleveland. Though the New Yorker was a less colorful figure than Blaine, it later proved that his appearance was deceiving and that his stolid figure cloaked a winner.

McKinley left the dust and heat of the convention with a national reputation, based largely on his tariff stand, but also on his efficient work at the convention. "Ohio was in front as usual," a friend wrote Hayes. "Her McKinley and Foraker won golden opinions. The former's platform was a model of construction, and he always displayed ability and good judgment. How he has grown during the last six years! I rejoice in his success." [84]

The turmoil of politics proceeded apace through the summer. McKinley undertook an extensive campaign in his district, anxious to vindicate his principles and to regain whatever strength and prestige he had lost by being unseated. Though he was mellowing, his tongue still had a sharp edge. At one debate an opponent asserted that the Republicans had rigged the economic structure so that any fool could get rich. "Permit me to inquire further, Doctor," McKinley asked blandly, "why you are not a wealthy man?" [85]

Blaine himself spoke for him in Ohio during a western tour, and McKinley accompanied the presidential candidate at several stops. When Blaine spoke in Massillon he received an enthusiastic reception, but the voters had ears only for McKinley: "The people would scarcely listen to anyone except Mr. McKinley." In mid-October, the Major was triumphantly re-elected by a comfortable majority, amid the jubilant celebration of his Canton neighbors, who gave him a torchlight parade and an all-night celebration. [86]

Cleveland's election the following November was a bitter blow to good Republicans. Some counted it revolution that the party of sedition should triumph in a presidential contest; heads shook everywhere at the thought that "Rum, Romanism and Rebellion" had won at the polls.

For McKinley himself, 1884 was the high point of his early career: he was vindicated by his constituents; his tariff principles had been approved; his name had figured prominently in the

House of Representatives; he was a leading figure at the Republican national convention; and he had favorably caught the eyes and ears of many leading politicians. Cleveland's victory foreshadowed continued tariff controversy, and now fortified by support at home and by national reputation, McKinley could enter the fray with high expectations. Victory was sweet in 1884, but the uses to which it could be put in the years ahead seemed even sweeter.

V

Congressman William McKinley

IFE IN WASHINGTON in the 1880's was pleasant. Even then the "City of Magnificent Distances" impressed natives and visitors alike, though many of the distances lacked magnificence. One did not have to travel far to see the jerry-built slums of the city's poorer element, and then, as now, poverty existed within the shadow of wealth. But for the senators and congressmen, whether they lived in private homes or in the numerous boarding houses of varying taste and cost that lined Capitol Hill, private life as well as public life had its compensations. The city's surroundings were charming and impressive. There was an ease of life and flow of hospitality that made Washington seem almost a southern city. Few forgot that the South lay but a stone's throw across the lazy Potomac.

It was a time of formality in manners that disappeared as Washington and the nation it represented grew to world power. But the eyes that watched the city in the 1880's did not see the changes that lay ahead. It was also an era of horse-drawn trolleys, gaslight, frock coats, and twelve-course dinners; the whole pattern of living was geared to a tempo that would bore rather than charm a later generation, intent on speed. Congressmen, cabinet officers, foreign dignitaries, visiting statesmen, even the President casually strolled through the tree-lined walks and parks, admiring the statuary and architecture that their grandchildren would abhor, or taking in the city's other sights. If heat overcame them they simply sat on cool verandas, talking as little as possible.

The McKinleys did not enter into the city's glittering social whirl. Ida's illness prevented more than a minimum of such affairs, but in any event, they had no taste for the lavish. Both preferred the quiet solitude that rounded out a strenuous day, and they spent most of their evenings alone together, or with a small group of friends. Often as not, McKinley sat with his wife, reading a newspaper, half-listening to her talk as she plied the knitting or crochet needles that marked her progress through rugs and slippers.

It would have strained their meager resources and burdened Ida physically to buy or rent a house in expensive Washington fashion. Instead, they took a small suite of two rooms at the comfortable old Ebbitt House, where McKinley rubbed elbows and exchanged stories with the numerous other congressmen, military officers, and government officials who made the hotel their home. One room served as McKinley's workroom and the other as a bedroom. When guests arrived they either sat with the young couple in the workroom or went downstairs to the parlor. Such quarters at first seemed cramped and somewhat uncomfortable, and it was irritating to be unable to afford the quiet comfort they enjoyed in Canton. Leisure time, personal wealth, the settled habits of family life were the hostages which McKinley gave to his political fortune; in his case they were never returned.

Ida was his chief concern and he did few things without first reflecting on how she would react. She was a curious figure, this frail woman who was the center of his life. Of the love between them there was no doubt. Charming, beautiful, and cultured when well, she seemed to be the ideal wife. But an attack of nervous illness, however slight, made her pathetic and irritable, and at such times she was demandingly dependent on her husband. She took great pride in his accomplishments and growing reputation and in her limited social contacts, zealously guarded his position. She had few friends and passed long hours of solitude busy only with her needles and yarn. One of her favorite occupations was making slippers; ultimately she made five thousand pairs, many of which she gave to friends or to charity.[1] Though she had little social life, she never felt that her husband sacrificed her to his career. Pictures of him covered the walls, and when a little boy asked her why, she took him on her knee and said, "Because he's a dear good man and I love him."[2]

For greeting guests Ida chose the customary dark dresses from which she seldom varied. Occasionally she wore a small diamond or emerald. She preferred simplicity, within the limits of the age, but it was an expensive simplicity. Her tastes and her medical bills were a burden on her husband's small salary, though a small personal income of her own later alleviated this problem.

Her health preyed on McKinley's mind continually. Her recov-

ery from a bout of illness lightened his load and brightened his outlook, though he knew that another siege would doubtless follow.
"Ida is growing stronger and better. She was four days without any
fainting attacks, and they have been less frequent than on other
days," he wrote his family hopefully.[3] Solicitous friends inquired
about her progress, and he was usually willing to discuss her well
being with a smile.

When he was away from Washington and she was unable to
accompany him, as was often the case during election campaigns,
he wrote at least once a day. Though he could say little, the thought
counted. "He can say he loves me," Ida once told a friend. If he
stayed long he expected her to write him, and never trusted the un-
certainties of the telephone when keeping in touch.[4]

When marooned on Capitol Hill he always sent a note to the
hotel, recounting his day's work and telling her when to expect him.
"Don't worry about me, for if I feel badly I will come home," he
wrote during one exhausting night session.[5] To please her he ate
well, generally at the House restaurant, and on cold evenings was
likely to send home for his overcoat if he had forgotten it rather
than to face her censure by returning without it. Whatever the
reason for delay in seeing her, his message to her was always the
same: "Receive my evening benediction of love."[6]

His days generally followed a fixed routine. He rose early, a
habit ingrained from childhood, breakfasted simply but heartily,
and read portions of his correspondence before setting out for his
office or the House. In fair weather he often walked or rode the
horsecar, though he liked to drive. Those who watched him walk
up Pennsylvania Avenue saw a darkly clad figure, somewhat short,
well-proportioned, crowned by an impressive head that won him
the nickname the Napoleon of Protection because of a fancied resemblance to the prisoner of Elba. He carried himself well to compensate for his short stature and walked briskly with an observant
eye on the details he passed. He moved with a natural dignity that
seemed to add height. He habitually wore a dark frock coat or Prince
Albert, generally buttoned in both winter and summer. In his button-
hole gleamed his favorite flower, a red carnation, that he might
transfer to the lapel of a visiting friend during the course of the
day.[7]

His courtesy was legendary. When others, harried by official worries, turned callers away, the visitors could almost always pour their troubles into McKinley's sympathetic ear. He did not promise them much, but he listened. The patience he developed in dealing with his wife carried over into his political career. His benign expression was not a mere habit but the reflection of genuine kindliness. "He had an innate dignity and at the same time a warm sympathetic nature," La Follette noted.[8] A willingness to listen, an infinite patience, a kind gift of flowers, a thoughtful turn of the pen— in these and countless other ways he revealed the charm and courtesy that endeared him even to political opponents. He was never a backslapper; his friendliness was covered with a cloak of dignity and a certain courtly air that indicated his awareness of his position and his respect for those with whom he talked. In his committee work he was willing to listen to the arguments of the opposition. "He had a rare tact as a manager of men. Back of his courteous and affable manner was a firmness that never yielded conviction, and while scarcely seeming to force issues he usually achieved exactly what he sought," La Follette again remembered.[9] While he was patient he was no man's tool, and he had a mind of his own which he did not fail to express. "He had the conservatism of his Scotch-Irish ancestry, overlaid with a deep veneer of kindliness which many mistook for weakness," an observer wrote. "You could go far with McKinley where essentials were not involved, but you hit hardpan when integrity or principle was at stake."[10]

He was a tireless worker in committee and in his office. He answered all of his mail and tended to every request sent him, not forgetting to send reprints of speeches to constituents. If folks at home complained he checked the matter, and if he could not help them he told them why. It took time and energy, and the days often passed in swift succession, leaving little impression on him. "I have not written you because first I have been up to my eyes with work. . . ." he explained to his family in Ohio, who wondered about his silence.[11]

Then there were the speeches that increased as his career prospered. Always cautious in utterance, he prepared every speech carefully and spoke either from notes or memory. He had an excellent memory for figures and amazed many audiences with columns of statistics. His diligence was matched only by his patience, and absorption in his work brought him great satisfaction. It was a rare day when he admitted: "I feel very much out of sorts today. My speech of two hours yesterday tired me out some." [12] If friends scolded him for overwork, he laughed and said: "A good soldier must always be ready for his duty." [13] Fortunately he enjoyed good health, though it was perhaps lack of exercise that made him susceptible to colds.

He was promptly in his seat at almost every day's session, smiling, shaking hands, talking to fellow members on the floor, or else he was surrounded in the hall or cloakroom by friends and supplicants. He impressed one as "a clean shaven, sweet-faced, approachable man who seemed to have as many friends on one side of the House as on the other." [14] When he attacked a point raised on the Democratic side, he did so as gracefully as possible, and his opponents usually returned the favor. "My opponents in Congress go at me tooth and nail," sighed the acid Tom Reed, "but they always apologize to William when they are going to call him names. . . ." [15] When debate waxed hot he was likely to stop at a desk and drop a kind word, caution a new member, or smooth ruffled feelings. "McKinley was a great peace-maker. He discouraged all kinds of acrimony in the debates," one remembered.[16] A prominent Democrat recalled that "he was one of the most pleasing and delightful of associates and my acquaintance with him was of the most agreeable character." [17]

Those differences not settled on the floor could be talked out in the House barbershop, which he enjoyed patronizing. The barbers vied with each other to serve him, and he sat placidly in the chair, smoking, repeating the best of his endless fund of anecdotes, chaffing with other congressmen, joking with the bootblack. He was an eminent tease. "When he once had a joke on me he rang all the changes; and no one enjoyed a joke on himself more thoroughly than he did," Mark Hanna recalled. Cautious at other times, he was often voluble under the lather, a trait shared by Tom Reed.[18]

His standing with the newspaper fraternity was high, doubtless because of his patience with their impertinence and because he seldom spoke unless he had something to say.[19] McKinley's speaking manner was effective in an age that savored political oratory. His words carried greater meaning and conviction because they lacked embellishment. Others strove for ornamentation in speech; he worked for simplicity. "He was, in common-sense manner, in diction, in intellect, and in effectiveness, a model," a noted rival said. "I have never known any popular orator able to accomplish more than he with the masses, their desires and ambitions, their methods of thought and how to put himself *en rapport* with them." [20]

Nevertheless, every speech was an ordeal. If he had no secretary, he wrote out his notes and drafts in his crabbed, irregular hand. With hundreds of speeches behind him, he was still nervous before an audience. "My heart goes down into my boots whenever I get up before an audience," he confessed in after years, "and I tremble until I have begun to talk." [21] Robert La Follette left a vivid impression of McKinley's speaking style:

> McKinley was a magnetic speaker; he had a clear, bell-like quality of voice, with a thrill in it. He spoke with dignity, but with freedom of action. The pupils of his eyes would dilate until they were almost black, and his face, naturally without much color, would become almost like marble—a strong face, and a noble head. When interrupted in a speech or debate, instead of seeking to put his man at a disadvantage, as Reed did, he sought to win him. [22]

He gave freely of his time to the Republican cause, and every campaign found him in distant areas in support of friends up for re-election. On such trips he travelled well—for who could forego the sumptuous Pullman fare of the day—but then, as later, he always listened more than he talked. As his reputation grew so did the demands on his time, and he often simply declined speaking engagements and appearances. [23] These campaign speeches and tours introduced him to audiences far and wide and acquainted him with the problems, politics, and leaders of many sections. They did much to make him a national leader long before he was president.

He was a good listener, drawing men out, gathering their ideas, weaving their beliefs into his own when he could, attempting to understand them when he could not. "His manner was that of a gleaner—the sympathetic drawer-out," a prominent acquaintance remembered. [24] He understood men's actions by understanding men, and the human personality fascinated him as if it were some complex and absorbing game. If he developed a theory of democracy it was simply that the people were right, and while he was willing to stand for his principles and to lead opinion in that sense, he never

86

risked losing control of his followers by outstripping them. He had a keen sense of public opinion and an innate shrewdness told him that it paid little to take popular stands if there was no means of enacting them.

The McKinleys spent some of their time going out socially. He was "a very frequent visitor" to the White House during the Hayes administration, spending Sunday evenings reading aloud or singing hymns with the family, joining them for dinner, or even standing in the receiving line to welcome guests, a task which Ida always enjoyed when well. The White House fare was not sumptuous—"Lemonade Lucy" Hayes banned alcohol, and her husband subsisted on plain fare—but it was at least familiar and wholesome. The President often let down his bewhiskered dignity and "promenaded" with Ida. The Hayeses were lonely in the White House, for he had few friends in either party, or anywhere for that matter, and so they welcomed the McKinleys as if they were children. The Hayes's sons were about McKinley's age, and they had much in common. McKinley often took Mrs. Hayes to a missionary society meeting or lyceum lecture if her sons were busy, and such pleasant tasks and visits alleviated the monotony and drudgery of patronage matters and public affairs.[25]

For all of this attention the McKinleys were truly grateful. "We are very glad to be permitted to be in Washington during your term of office," McKinley wrote his old commander. "We are indebted to yourself and Mrs. Hayes for much pleasure while in Washington." When at home in Canton he often invited the Hayeses, who vacationed in Fremont, to run over for a visit. "No contest to interfere with our pleasure . . . , and no politics shall intrude upon us. . . . No interviewer shall be permitted to enter," he promised. McKinley was sad and nostalgic when Hayes left the presidency in 1881. "[Ida] misses Mrs. Hayes and yourself every day, and so do I. We wish you [would] come here again." Curious to see the White House as redecorated by President Arthur, the young couple surveyed the steamboat-palace splendor of that epicure's rearrangement, but their eyes were caught by a new painting of Mrs. Hayes. It was "simply superb, and in the new frame beggars description. We are proud of it. Ida and I went up to inspect it and the above are our final sentiments."[26]

McKinley was also close to James and Lucretia Garfield. Though he did not know Garfield well on first arriving in Washington, both were drawn together by common origins and sympathies. McKinley himself remembered that Garfield had been "my counselor and friend in manhood. . . ." [27] He and Ida were often at the Garfield home for simple but pleasant dinner parties, and the two men played cards together with other politicians. They were mutual advisors and confided in each other, for both, veterans of Ohio politics, could keep a secret. [28]

The McKinleys reciprocated this hospitality as best they could, but while Ida's poor health was a valid excuse, they also had little money for entertaining. McKinley's only income aside from his salary was the small rental from the Canton property and occasional law fees when Congress was out of session. Many congressmen frankly lobbied for corporations, but he refused all such chances. He took only modest campaign contributions and charged, if anything, only expenses for out-of-town speeches. His assets during this period never exceeded $20,000, representing mostly his Canton property, which was mortgaged. He had little ready cash between pay checks, but was always an easy mark for those in straitened circumstances. [29]

Washington was impressive and the heat of legislative battle was invigorating, for McKinley liked work, but it did get tiresome. The McKinleys managed to leave town when Congress adjourned and spent as much time as possible in Canton. Even this was a mixed blessing, however, for every year was election year in Ohio, and the coming of fall intensified the canvass. In addition to politics, there were many public affairs—picnics, commencements, reunions; the Major even blacked his face and sang in a minstrel show to entertain the young people of Canton, though not without some visible embarrassment. There were also more formal functions, such as the dedication of the Garfield monument in Cleveland, where he spoke with other distinguished statesmen. If he had time and weather permitted, he and Ida might picnic with other young couples. A lawyers' outing found him placing bets on a boat race, with ice cream and strawberries as the stakes. [30]

When in Canton, they stayed at the old Saxton house on Market Street. It was substantial, with all the filigree and latticework characteristic of the age. Evenings usually found him on the veranda, rocking and fanning, nodding to passers-by, calling helloes to neighbors, or chatting with Ida and visitors. He entertained more in Canton than in Washington because of the better facilities, and many evenings were punctuated by conversation and cigars among the men and talk of home and family among the women.

Community service also called, and he served as a trustee of the Methodist church most of his life. His work with the local YMCA and on behalf of temperance won gratitude from many families. He also worked with his Masonic lodge.[31]

He himself was not seen on a high-wheeled bicycle, but he enjoyed as a spectator the sport of cycling, participating to that vicarious extent in the greatest rage—next to the bustle—of his day. He attended one long-distance contest that lasted so far into the night that he gave up and went home, thoughtfully leaving some remarks with the toastmaster. If bicycling was not the sport for his physique or station in life, driving a team was. His passion for horseflesh dated from his Army service, when he developed a practised eye for the fine horses for which he was noted, together with his elegant carriage, and he enjoyed driving whenever possible. He and Ida sometimes drove in the country in good summer or autumn weather, for this was one of her few diversions, and she enjoyed it as much as he did. Likely as not, he would drive the team to the blacksmith shop to have it checked, talking easily with the smith through the haze of cigar smoke that usually surrounded him. He also enjoyed walking through town, stopping frequently to talk with friends about crops or business.

Whether in Canton or Washington, McKinley was always conscious of his appearance and wore only the most becoming clothes. Throughout his mature years he was clean-shaven. Later he would be the only president between Johnson and Wilson not to sport some hairy adornment as evidence of manly pride. He shaved himself most mornings, in an ambidextrous fashion, using one hand for one side of his face, the other hand for the other side. He often read the newspaper or correspondence during the process and walked around freely talking to anyone present, for army life had taught him how to live without mirrors.[32]

Vanity forbade being seen with spectacles, which he used for reading only, but he came at regular intervals to the Canton optometrist's to buy a new pair, testing them by reading a newspaper with them balanced on his nose.[33] As president, he used glasses on a black string that ran around his neck, but was almost never photographed wearing them.

His duties and his solicitude for Ida kept him from proper exercise; besides, his generation did not believe in it. During his congressional career he gained considerable weight, always carefully minimized by his clothes. His boyish face filled out, and the slender handsomeness of youth fell before the onslaught of middle age. Long hours of indoor work and little activity accounted for his expanding girth, but if it alarmed him he did nothing about it. His generation did not believe in diets either.

Man cannot live by virtue alone, and McKinley permitted himself a few vices. His daily routine was not always one of sweetness and light, or of good composure and stolid patience. "Uncle Joe" Cannon once banged the table and told "Mac" that a little vice was a good thing. His listener was not willing to go that far, but characteristically, said he would consider the principle if not the practice. McKinley was irritated at newspaper reports that he drank and played cards, complaining in the cloister with Cannon that he couldn't sip a wine glass or touch a casino deck without offending some constituent.[34] He was abstemious of liquor, but did not deny the pleasures of either the table or the sideboard.

His chief vice was smoking cigars. Though he tried to quit swearing when mustered out of the Army, he could not give up this other bad habit which he had acquired there. When in Washington he spent evenings in the Hotel Ebbitt parlor, smoking profusely, talking with friends, perhaps even tasting a little Scotch whiskey, teasing the newsmen with whom he was so friendly. In deference to Ida he smoked downstairs and never complained of his ostracism from the household.[35] He was a steady customer of the newsstand in front of the Ebbitt, where he ordered boxes of cigars. He generally left the box under the counter after scrawling his name on it, and filled his pockets each morning as he went to the House. The newsboy estimated that he smoked at least fifty cigars a week, and often more if the session was tiresome or the weather bad. Friends, knowing of his taste, sent many gift boxes, and every successful speech brought fine cigars from sympathizers and acquaintances.[36]

The first years of his service in Congress were pleasurable as well as profitable, and he never forgot the friendships he made. In after years he was given to easy reminiscence, and the pleasant Canton and charming Washington of those days occupied a special niche in his memory. As his duties increased and as he followed his ambitions he had less and less time for personal diversions and pleasures, but the kindness, thoughtfulness, patience, and industry which he displayed in his private and public affairs smoothed the paths of politics for himself and others. In these years he developed the tact, charm, courtesy, and easy intercourse that enabled him to manage men so successfully in his later years. None of the politician's wiles escaped him. The political process became for him a way of life, an attitude of mind, an art, and in the end no one better mastered its principles and practices. He understood people because he was a person; he knew their fears and weaknesses because he was prey to them too. He was willing to mix with them to learn their attitudes and secrets, to understand their minds, to penetrate their personalities and thus broaden and deepen his own understanding of the human nature that so fascinated him.

He enjoyed his public life, savored his private life; each in its way was rewarding. He liked the plaudits of the crowd, but there was more to it than simple egotism. There was also a sense of accomplishment and a belief in what he stood for. He tended to his duties and worked always for the future. What had he said to Abner? "This constant struggle all the time is anything but agreeable, but it seems necessary to any success in life in anything. In politics it is a little more irritating than in other things." Maybe so, but for him it proved to be worthwhile.

∽∾∾ VI ∽∾∾

Serpents, Sharks, and Cooing Doves:
Ohio Politics, 1880-1890

HE ASTUTE William Allen White was never more correct than
when he said that Ohio politics of the late nineteenth century "combined the virtues of the serpent, the shark, and
the cooing dove." [1] Ohio was a key state in late nineteenth century
politics. She furnished presidents in 1876, 1880, and 1896. Many
national political figures, Republicans and Democrats alike, rose
from Ohio to national power. The state was a battleground for the
forces that shaped America in the decades after the Civil War, and
the confusion and ferocity of her political quarrels are a microcosm
of the same events on a national scale. Industrialization, immigration, sectionalism, economic expansion, and Western restlessness all
flavored her politics. In a general sense the state was Republican,
for her electoral vote always went to the Republican presidential
candidate. But she also sent a large Democratic delegation to Congress, and one of her senators was almost always a Democrat.[2]

Because they appealed to so many divergent groups and interests,
the "Ohio men" developed the art of compromise. Protestants and
Catholics, wets and drys, farmers and workers, hard and soft-money
men, Northerners and Southerners—these and many other groups
tugged insistently at the coattails of the Shermans, Garfields,
Hayeses, and McKinleys.[3]

The Ohio Republicans were far from unified. Not content to war
against the Democrats, various forces and leaders caused factional
alliances within the party, so that safe majorities were never sure at
any election and were usually bought with a heavy price in work and
campaigning. Ambitious leaders seized upon local issues to affect
state campaigns and to bargain for power and influence in the name
of party unity.

The cast of characters on the stage of Ohio Republicanism was

92

large, but by the mid-1880's four men dominated the scene. The most prominent of these was Ohio's elder statesman, John Sherman. Few men boasted such a career as his. He was a congressman, U.S. senator, secretary of the Treasury, a founder of the Republican party, and a presidential candidate at every Republican national convention between 1880 and 1888. His name was attached to some of the most important legislation of the late nineteenth century. A "sound-money" man, he was not above compromise with silver to save his position. A high protectionist, he spoke well for the wool growers and manufacturers of Ohio. A senior senator, he was reckoned with in every important bill of his day.

"Uncle Jawn" may have been a great statesman and a financial expert, but he lacked the color of personality and the seasoning of humor. He seemed never to have been young. The frost of his severely bearded face reflected to many the inner man. "The Ohio Icicle," as he was unkindly called,[4] had a large and faithful following, built on party service and national position, the prestige of regularity and soundness, buttressed by a talent for compromise and vast legislative experience. If few of his constituents loved him, they respected and admired him for his service to Republicanism.

Since he spent most of his time in Washington, Sherman delegated his state affairs to able lieutenants. By the mid-1880's the foremost of these was Marcus Alonzo Hanna, businessman and politician of Cleveland. The same energy which he poured into business sparked his activities in politics, which he first undertook as a diversion and to help certain friends. His alliance with Sherman rested upon respect for the elder statesman and belief in the Republican principles for which he stood. His ambition to back a presidential candidate crystallized around Sherman, and when that idol failed, around his friend William McKinley. Astute, willing to work, a genius at getting what he wanted, he rapidly became Sherman's chief spokesman and managed the Senator's presidential boom in 1888.[5]

The brightest light and most promising threat to the Sherman-Hanna group arose after 1883 in the form of Joseph Benson Foraker, lawyer and judge, of Cincinnati. His entry into state politics was meteoric. A party stalwart, fired with ambition for high office, Foraker had executive ability and political effectiveness; he rose on the conflicts that threatened others. A stubborn fighter, colorful, deft at employing popular issues, he appealed to the masses of Ohio Republicans with all the color and charm that Sherman lacked. Not that he lacked principles; but they were even in his own time old fashioned. He used the bloody shirt, worked for corporate interests, waxed eloquent at soldiers' picnics, and in the end went down, somewhat unjustly, under political reform.[6]

More successfully than any of these men, William McKinley rose above the conflicts of state politics. His gift for silence and evasion, his personal charm and deftness, his status as a national figure after 1884, and above all his identification with a great national issue important to Ohio, the tariff, combined to hold him more aloof from party battles than his equally prominent and ambitious contemporaries. There was a McKinley faction, but the Major did not seem to be in it. He cast his lot unquestioningly with the Sherman group because he believed in the Senator's principles. His standing with that group made him a figure in a well-established machine and further identified him with the oldest wing of the party. In this as in everything else he was never an outsider; that role was left to Foraker.

To McKinley and his fellow Ohioans of the Gilded Age, every year was election year. Torchlight parades and picnics punctuated almost every week of the year as someone ran for something. Federal offices were filled in even-numbered years, state offices in odd-numbered years. When a United States senatorship was at stake, fierce contests raged in every legislative district so that a Republican legislature could elect a Republican senator. These purely local contests generated more heat than they deserved and contributed to party factionalism.

The young congressman knew of these forces and of his stake in the game, but he touched them relatively little in his early career. Insuring his hold on his peripatetic constituency was hard enough, and he did well to avoid the sharks and shoals around Canton, to say nothing of those in Columbus. Yet no state campaign passed him by and when his services on the stump were needed he gave freely.[7] When national figures visited Ohio he entertained them, and in national election years gave unstintingly of his time despite his own contest. He could always be counted on for "a spirited speech." But most of his work was confined to northeastern Ohio, and he

94

was not well known in the rest of the state until the early 1880's.[8]

He did his share of routine party work, serving on the Resolutions Committee in every state convention between 1875 and 1889, except 1881. In 1880, he was temporary chairman of the state convention held at Columbus late in April. In that capacity he delivered a forceful keynote speech. His declaration that Ohio would support Sherman in the national convention brought a storm of applause, but when it subsided he could not forbear mentioning duties to Grant and above all to his idol, that "peerless debater, the fearless statesman, James G. Blaine." [9] His work at Columbus won him a position as Ohio's representative on the Republican National Committee for 1880.

He rose rapidly during the state campaign of 1883. In that year the question of liquor regulation loomed large, threatening the Republican hold on the German vote, so crucial in the southern part of the state. Charles "Calico Charlie" Foster, so named because of his dry-goods business, shrank from defeat as governor and wished to save any prominent Republican from disaster. His eye fell on the ambitious Foraker, who was an orthodox Republican, sufficiently ambitious to risk defeat. He was also a native of Cincinnati who would thus offset ill feeling in that area, and was of no moment to the state machine. Foraker snapped at the chance and won the support of prominent Republicans, including McKinley, in his race for the nomination and later for the governorship.[10]

McKinley was chairman of the Resolutions Committee at the state convention held in June, reporting a strong platform favoring protection, restoration of the wool duties cut by the Mongrel Tariff, and regulation of the liquor traffic. Foraker's nomination went smoothly, and the Major escorted him to the rostrum through the tumultuous delegates. The crowd was not disappointed, for "Fire Alarm Joe" delivered a typical speech, attempting to infuse life into the coming campaign that seemed overwhelmingly against him.[11]

Returning to Canton, McKinley took the stump for Foraker and the whole state ticket. He predicted that the Democratic candidate, George Hoadly, "will be one of the worst beaten men that ever ran for office in Ohio." [12] It all sounded like whistling in the dark, which it was. Foraker was soundly beaten in the election, failing to triumph over a Democratic trend, the liquor question, and the Mongrel Tariff.

McKinley was genuinely distressed. "Nobody in the State regrets your defeat more than I do," he wrote after the election. "You deserved a different result and could have had it if the fight could be had over again. We are all proud of you anyhow. No candidate for Governor ever made a more brilliant canvass, and the friends you made will stick to you through life. I hope the great tax upon you physically will not prove to have been too much for you. I shall want to continue our friendship and hope to see you and hear from you often." [13] He must have remembered the letter and its protestations later when he withdrew his support from Foraker, though his break with him was never as sharp as was Hanna's. At the outset he genuinely liked Foraker, and their relations in public and private were cordial though never intimate.

The following year was a presidential election year and the heat of state politics glowed warmer than ever. Because of his stand on the tariff question, McKinley went to the state convention that year with added prestige. The delegates cheered as he smiled his way to the platform, stopping now and then in the crush to shake hands or say hello. He delivered a brief, typical speech as permanent chairman, calling for party unity and principles.[14]

The real struggle came when delegates-at-large to the national convention were chosen. Though McKinley presided over the convention with impartial dignity, he was a prominent Blaine follower and Ohio was pledged to Sherman. Amid great confusion, he declined to entertain the motion that he be chosen by acclamation as one of the delegates. Like Peter, he thrice denied the call, overruling contrary motions. Perhaps he was being coy, though he spoke with force and sincerity. More likely, he sincerely did not wish the post because he was committed to Blaine and disliked opposing Sherman. In any event, the delegates would not take no for an answer. The confusion mounted; flowers were scattered over the delegates to cries of "McKinley! McKinley!" At last he was duly elected along with Foraker, Hanna, and William West, another Blaine supporter. Foraker praised McKinley for "the handsome compliment the convention paid you," and McKinley reciprocated in kind.[15]

Things were not so cheerful at the national convention itself, for it was quickly apparent that McKinley would stick with Blaine to the end; Ohio had sent a divided delegation. Hanna remembered the

Major's active work and that "we contested the delegation vigorously for our men." [16] Blaine's nomination brought joy to McKinley, but not to Foraker and Hanna. There was talk that Foraker would be named for vice-president and McKinley suggested that he present his fellow Ohioan's name. Foraker demurred without Sherman's support so the Major promised to keep silent unless called upon. Outwardly harmony reigned, but privately Sherman blamed McKinley for not helping him more. "The unexpected defection of McKinley, and the overwhelming popular demand for Blaine made your task difficult and impossible," the Senator wrote his manager. Foraker himself blamed McKinley, and Hanna was not so sure; the convention drew Hanna closer to Foraker in a friendship that grew in the next three years.[17]

The fight loomed between Blaine and Cleveland, and everyone went to work. McKinley talked, Foraker stumped, Hanna raised money, and Ohio had no rest until Cleveland's election in November, which prostrated the trio. "I have not had the heart to write to any of my partners in misery since the election, for I was completely used up over it," Hanna wrote. "Not especially at being defeated, but in such a senseless way." [18]

There was no time for rest, for the close of one campaign announced the advent of another. In the spring of 1885, there was talk that McKinley would stand for the governorship, which he promptly denied. He refused to participate in the pre-convention footwork and felt that if Foraker wanted the nomination he could have it. A fresh rumor was manufactured that Hanna, emerging as a state leader, wanted the governorship, which he too flatly denied, pledging himself to Foraker. Foraker quickly secured promises of support from Sherman, Hanna, and other Republican leaders.[19]

At the state convention in June, McKinley again presented an orthodox platform and his customary ringing speech. Foraker was duly nominated and a campaign of revenge against the Democrats ensued which called forth the best efforts of every veteran. McKinley stumped his section, speaking to farmers, workers, towns-people, anyone who would listen. His speeches were successful and audiences cheered his partisan attacks on the new Cleveland administration. His loyalty to Foraker was unquestioned.

All rejoiced in Foraker's election that October. The promise of friendship between the two men had matured, and many agreed with former President Hayes when he wrote: "McKinley is a friend worth having." [20] But the seers predicted that a new force had arrived on the scene. Foraker's election marked his arrival as a power in state politics. Inevitably he would build his own organization, drawing followers from Sherman.

On the surface all was calm; Foraker had not been inaugurated before the canny McKinley, never one to pass a pie counter, was at hand recommending appointments. The chief plum at stake was the state oil inspectorship, a lucrative post whose salary was paid by fees collected from the firms investigated. Hanna wished W. M. Bayne appointed as a reward for his services and to help his own position in Cleveland. But McKinley too had a candidate, the incumbent Louis Smithnight, and talked to Hanna. "I had a call from Major McKinley and his O.I. candidate. The Major is never behind with his claims," Hanna grumbled. "I tell him he 'wants the earth' and it looks as if I was getting about where I generally do in politics —left with only the reputation of being a good fellow, always accommodating, etc. etc. However, I told McKinley that I only cared for *you* in this matter." [21] The Major's charm moved the mountain and Hanna stepped aside. "I hope you will be able to satisfy McKinley in the matter, for you two should have no differences," he said in offering to withdraw his man.[22] The position fell vacant after Foraker's re-election in 1887, and the two men again presented different candidates. This time, Foraker chose his own man, the later notorious George Cox, a close supporter who had done yeoman work during the campaign.[23]

Throughout Foraker's first term in the statehouse the three men consulted each other frequently on party affairs and patronage.[24] Foraker aspired for more than the governorship, and his gift for oratory took him far afield for speeches and appearances. In 1887 he gained national attention by refusing to comply with President Cleveland's order to return captured Confederate battle flags to the Southern states. "No rebel flags will be returned while I am governor," he tersely informed a friend. Hearts fluttered in veterans' homes from sea to sea, and when Cleveland withdrew the order for other reasons, Foraker was in the national limelight. McKinley was said to remark that he "was a great deal more concerned about the enforcement of constitutional provisions than he was about what should be done with rebel flags," which nettled Foraker.[25] Lines were dividing Ohio Republicans. As the state convention of 1887 approached it was apparent that the Hanna–McKinley–Sherman group would oppose the Foraker group and attempt to prevent the popular Governor's further rise. Sherman was concerned because he was unsure of Foraker's loyalty to his cause and because he suspected the Governor of having senatorial ambitions.[26]

A conference of Sherman men at Canton on June 24, 1887, foreshadowed the coming break. McKinley arranged for Sherman, Hanna, and others to meet to discuss the Senator's prospects in the coming national contest of 1888. Foraker was not invited and secrecy was observed until a newspaper leak broke the story. The members of the conference agreed to demand Sherman's endorsement for the presidential nomination at the coming state convention and stood ready to prevent Foraker's further rise in state politics. Hanna blithely told Foraker that he was going to Canton to talk politics with Sherman and then, after the conference, asked Foraker what he thought about endorsing Sherman for the presidency a year early. Foraker was opposed because it would divide the state convention and was premature.[27] He was deeply angered at being excluded from the conference at Canton. He directed his anger chiefly at Hanna, but he recognized only too well that the original invitation had been McKinley's and that the conference had been held at the latter's home. These facts alone pointed to McKinley's position within the Sherman group. The Sherman men were irritated at Foraker's lukewarm support of the Senator. Though piqued at the treatment accorded him by "The Combination," Foraker smothered his resentment and finally agreed to endorse Sherman in the name of party unity and to insure his own renomination and re-election.[28]

McKinley quietly opposed Foraker's continued rise; he recognized a rival when he saw one and disliked the popular Governor's attitude toward Sherman. His own friendship with Hanna was growing closer and he was anxious that a determined fight be made for Sherman at the coming national convention. But whatever he may have wished, there was to be little party unity in the four years ahead.

Though Foraker tried to oil the troubled waters, his triumphant

99

re-election in 1887 foreshadowed further factional fights, for the Sherman group now saw the direction of his sail—the Senate.[29] Hanna's friendship with Foraker was showing strain, and McKinley's position was well known; neither would sit idly by while the Governor built a machine. It was rumored that certain party leaders had fixed the succession in the hierarchy of state offices after the election of 1887. McKinley's response was instant. "I do not quite understand what you mean by the political possibilities being marked out for the next six or seven years. I do not think that any attempt to mortgage the future will meet with favor among our people and I should be sorry to believe that any attempt of that sort should be made," he wrote with unaccustomed emphasis.[30] It was a blunt warning to the Forakerites.

As the state convention approached and throughout the spring of 1888, the Sherman men dickered for position and consulted on the Senator's presidential boom. Hanna took the lead, but McKinley was generally at hand with ready advice. Amenities with Foraker were observed, but the events of the past year still rankled; his advice was generally asked after the course had been plotted. The Shermanites still distrusted him, and he still felt that Sherman's chances were poor.[31]

At the state convention in 1888, McKinley consorted closely with Sherman, and the two were observed in a lengthy conversation during which Sherman uncharacteristically smiled while McKinley uncharacteristically talked.[32] Whispers of intrigue permeated the sessions, but one thing was now certain: McKinley had abandoned Blaine for Sherman altogether.

At the national convention, Foraker drew brickbats and no roses from Sherman's followers, especially Hanna, who freely charged him with lack of faith in the Senator's cause. As head of the Ohio delegation he had not, according to the Shermanites, displayed proper loyalty to the Senator; instead he advanced his own cause through treachery, and when that failed, had turned to Blaine. Foraker's dislike of McKinley and his jealousy of his growing prestige moved him to say harsh things during the convention.[33] His protestations that he had been loyal to Sherman fell on deaf ears, and the convention ended his friendship with Hanna.

After Benjamin Harrison's nomination and the destruction of

Sherman's last chance at the presidency, Foraker broke with the Senator's group and determined to pursue an independent course no matter what the cost. "From Toledo to Chicago my neck was under a yoke, but now I am free," he wrote a friend. Late in 1888, talk of a post for Ohio in the new President's cabinet further divided Foraker, Sherman, and McKinley, all of whom were mentioned.[34]

But the real prize was the senatorship, and Foraker was prepared to seek it even by openly attacking Sherman.[35] His motive was compounded of ambition, stubbornness, and revenge. "If they had not made up a combination to prevent me from going to the senate, then I would not want the position," he wrote bitterly after the national convention. "Now I have made up my mind to go after it."[36] The Combination was Sherman, Hanna, and McKinley. Foraker's senatorial ambition cost him whatever support he had left in the Sherman camp and divided the Ohio party into warring factions. Hanna shelved Foraker. Sherman's defeat turned him to McKinley, and he was convinced that if Ohio could not make Sherman president, she could make McKinley.

Foraker's second term drew to a close and he eyed a third, but Ohio precedent denied third terms to chief executives. Hanna opposed a third term for Foraker because he was anxious to prevent his rise as a national leader and presidential possibility, preferring to groom McKinley for that role. Feeling between the once friendly Foraker and Hanna families was now bitter. McKinley made no secret of his own views, and when the state convention met late in June, 1889, he nominated A. W. Jones for governor against Foraker.[37] Foraker was easily the strongest candidate and his strength was augmented by failure of the anti-third termers to unite on anyone. Sensing the trend among the delegates, at a crucial moment McKinley leaped upon a table and seconded a call for Foraker's unanimous renomination. The table went down under the Major's weight, but Foraker was renominated to face tradition, most Democrats, and some Republicans.

Though disliking Foraker, McKinley campaigned for him for the sake of party unity, calling on his audiences to vote for "our splendid candidate for Governor, Joseph Benson Foraker."[30] What it cost him to do so was his secret, but the Governor was, after all, a Republican. No such appeasing attitude emanated from others in the Sherman–Hanna group. The Major might face an audience and call for unity—switching discreetly to the wool schedule, sit in silence while men stabbed one another, talk of the weather when reputations were being blasted, make friends while others made enemies, but many of Hanna's and Sherman's lieutenants were bitter at Foraker. "I have never been unfriendly to Gov. Foraker," wrote Ben Butterworth, a staunch Hanna man and friend of McKinley in Congress. "I have been a vastly better friend to him than he has been to himself, although he may doubt it. Unfortunately he does not permit anybody to come near him unless to burn incense in his nose. He seems not to have learned that the wounds of a friend are faithful while the kisses of an enemy are deceitful." [39]

As if he did not have enough troubles, Foraker stumbled into the greatest blunder of the campaign, one which cost him dearly in terms of disaffection within the party. Early in the fall, a Cincinnati lawyer told Foraker that he would probably face opposition from prominent Republicans as well as Democrats in the campaign. Intrigued, Foraker asked why. The lawyer then told him that while in Congress, James E. Campbell, the Democratic gubernatorial nominee, had introduced a bill providing for the use of a standardized patented ballot box at all federal elections. The company to manufacture these boxes was owned by Campbell and certain other prominent politicians who stood to make a fortune from such a monopoly. After much dickering, Foraker procured the papers concerning the transaction and was astonished to find the names of Sherman, McKinley, Ben Butterworth, and other prominent Republicans on the papers. Consultation with friends and careful examination convinced him that the signatures were genuine. Discretion was necessary, for discrediting Campbell might also destroy his own party if the entire list of names was published.

In mid-September he met Murat Halstead on the train and showed him the papers. Halstead immediately demanded that Foraker either make the affair public or he himself would print it in his newspaper, the powerful Cincinnati *Commercial-Gazette*. Foraker hesitated but furnished copies to Halstead. In a speech later in the month he mentioned Campbell's connection with the affair. To his astonishment, Halstead printed a facsimile of the document bearing Campbell's signature on October 4. Campbell, displaying a wisdom that Foraker might well have adopted, discreetly refused to discuss the matter at all and watched the Republicans flounder deeper and deeper in the mire.

Foraker had discovered in the meantime that the documents were forgeries, the signatures having been cleverly transcribed from congressional franks. He moved to quash the matter, apologizing to Campbell. But the Democrats were not done. Shortly before the election, in a clever move designed to prevent Foraker from answering the charges, Campbell published the documents with the complete list of names attached. Illness and a sense of defeat kept Foraker from rallying and he lost the election.[40]

The reaction in the Republican camp was instant and violent. McKinley felt the blade between his shoulders and Hanna's followers denounced Foraker roundly. Sherman spoke for them all when he said, "It has always seemed strange to me that Foraker, having in his possession a paper which implicated Butterworth, McKinley and myself, in what all men would regard as a dishonorable transaction, did not inform us and give us an opportunity to deny, affirm or explain our alleged signatures." [41] Clearly Foraker had acted hastily and unwisely, goaded by his desperate fight against Campbell and his bitterness toward the Shermanites.

Badly shaken, McKinley and Butterworth at once introduced a resolution in the new session of Congress for an investigation of the charges. Hearings were held in Washington at which McKinley testified that he knew absolutely nothing of the entire affair. The upshot was a decision that Foraker had been honestly deceived, but it also served as a reproof for his having been so unwitting a tool. Charles Grosvenor, representing McKinley and Butterworth, was so agitated that he could hardly speak coherently at times and lost no opportunity to blast Foraker. He saw to it that the committee investigated thoroughly in the search for evidence against the Governor.[42]

Foraker now openly cast his eyes on the Senate seats which would fall vacant in 1890 and 1892. It was rumored that McKinley would leave the lower house for the Senate, and Foraker demanded that the Major announce his intentions one way or the other. McKinley had no intention of standing for the Senate seat and early in 1890 formally denied the rumors.[43]

If nothing else, Foraker had been defeated—so thought the Sherman–Hanna–McKinley group. But they were wrong. With the resiliency of determination, the ex-Governor returned to fight another day and was elected to the Senate in 1896. Ironically he served with Hanna between 1897 and 1904.

McKinley emerged from the ballot-box investigation without spot or rancor, which is the story of his career in Ohio politics. Men marvelled at the dexterity and deftness with which he avoided party conflicts and emerged victorious from encounters that killed lesser men. His personality accounts for some of his success, his caution for much more. He had a splendid eye for bandwagons and never mounted one until he was sure of its direction. His national standing gave him added prestige and position.

It was an eventful decade in Ohio politics. A re-alignment had taken place that made McKinley a front runner for Ohio's favors in the national arena. Most important of all, he was firmly allied with Mark Hanna. Two men could hardly have been less alike, yet their affection and cooperation was legendary. Like opposite poles they attracted each other's qualities. McKinley's charm and urbanity, his ease and dignity, compensated for Hanna's bluffness and rough amenities. McKinley had patience to temper Hanna's impetuosity; Hanna had drive to temper McKinley's caution.

Ohio politics taught McKinley lessons he never forgot and brought into play all the qualities of management that he used to such effect in his affairs. It taught him that politics could be cruel, that men were ambitious, that reputations would be sacrificed in a moment, that no one was to be trusted until tested. It was all part of the larger game, with the same fascinations and challenges, the same rewards and compensations. He knew his share of serpents and sharks, and even perhaps an occasional cooing dove.

A National Figure

WASHINGTON had not seen anything like it in twenty-five years; the capital was overrun by Southern Democrats. Explosions, rebel yells, a Virginia reel accomplished with the aid of whiskey, the sound of drums and rattle of carriages announced the arrival of the advance guard of "Confederate Brigadiers" who led their host to Washington for the inauguration of Grover Cleveland, the first Democrat to occupy the White House since 1861. It was March, 1885, and the city was in an uproar of confetti, oratory, and strong drink. Gray uniforms dotted the expectant crowds which came early for the spectacle. Republicans shook their heads grimly, prophesying that this was but the hors d'oeuvre preceding the main course of license, corruption, and incompetence under a Democratic administration.[1]

Happily, the Democrats and ex-Confederates were throwing firecrackers instead of bombs, and a glance at the stolid and unimaginative figure of the new president dispelled fears of revolution and mob violence. But the scent of change *was* in the air, no Republican denied that, and it was not a meaningless spectacle, this inauguration of the first Democratic President in a generation.

The first session of the House to which McKinley reported in December, 1885, was Democratic by a substantial margin and apparently prepared to sustain Cleveland's rumored plans for reform. But he moved cautiously, temporarily more concerned with patronage than reform. His colleagues had wandered in the desert without manna for a generation and they did not propose to go home empty-handed.

On December 5, 1885, the Republican members of the House caucused and McKinley supported Thomas B. Reed for the speakership. Reed was duly nominated but defeated, as expected, by the Democrat, John G. Carlisle. McKinley and Reed were easily among the most outstanding men on the Republican side, and the Major's home town paper reported with pardonable pride that he was the deftest committee worker and manager of men in the House.[2]

There was little question, however, that the Democratic administration would press for tariff reform. Party doctrine, the mounting Treasury surplus, and an apparent popular mandate supported it. But the Democrats walked softly on the issue, for their unity was more apparent than real. Randall and the Easterners would never support drastic reform. The President's penchant for reform, if indeed he had one, must wait. His annual message of 1885 was vague on the subject, inclined to moderation.

McKinley rallied protectionist support. Early in 1886 he corresponded with his friends and drew up sample petitions for workmen and manufacturers to sign, from which he could quote in the anticipated tariff debate. He made it clear that there was no hope for any increase in the tariff rates and that a substantial decrease was a decided danger as long as the Democrats were in power.[3]

McKinley was right. The prominent Democrat revenue-reformer, William R. Morrison of Illinois, was chairman of the House Ways and Means Committee and shortly drafted and reported a bill reducing rates. On April 14, 1886, the bill came to the House, strongly opposed by McKinley, Reed, and the other Republican members of the committee. The measure was a test vote, designed to warn the protectionist Democrats that reform was in the offing and to gauge their reaction. The President did not wait long to see how divided his following was. On June 17, 1886, Morrison moved that the House resolve itself into a committee of the whole to discuss the tariff bill; the motion failed to carry, to applause on the Republican side. Randall and the protectionist Democrats had voted with the Republicans; the split in the party was still there.[4]

Other issues also occupied the new administration. Western protest and railroad corruption created a demand for regulation. McKinley supported the Interstate Commerce Act of 1887, which regulated interstate common carriers. "In any view there is no harm in trying this experiment; and in this effort, small and inconsequential as it may seem to be, I am confident we are moving in the right direction, and that nothing but good can result," he said.[5] The death of Vice-President Hendricks late in 1885 prompted Congress to remedy the defective presidential succession law. McKinley supported the old plan whereby the vice-president was succeeded by the president pro tem of the Senate and speaker of the House, since he felt that elected officials should be in the line of succession. But his plan failed and cabinet succession was adopted.[6]

Cleveland, justly concerned over expenditures for pensions, vetoed the Dependent Pensions Bill, passed by heavy majorities in the Democratic House and Republican Senate. McKinley voted to override the veto, which was sustained. He was not above waving a slightly crimson shirt in defense of the men who saved the Union, and helped keep Cleveland at his desk writing veto messages for pension bills by feeding the hopper with private bills as often as called upon.[7]

While tending to his national affairs, McKinley kept in touch with the situation at home. For once he seemed to face an easy contest in 1886, for his regular district was restored.[8] "The question of my return to Congress from the 20th District I shall leave entirely with the Republicans of the several counties," he wrote. "I have served them so long that they know whether they want me further." [9] Early in June, fortified by his recent stand against tariff revision, he made a flying visit home and announced that he was a candidate; he faced no real opposition for the nomination. He was duly nominated early in the fall and was besieged in his hotel room by hundreds of well-wishers, many bearing floral bouquets.[10] His re-election made him one of the ranking Republicans in the House.

The regular session of the Fiftieth Congress assembled in December, 1887, to face an astonishing message from the President. Never before had a chief executive devoted his entire annual message to a single topic, but Cleveland chose to do so, and that topic was the tariff. The new Congress was Democratic, and the President risked party division in opening the subject, but he believed that popular opinion as well as party principle demanded action. In his message, he noted that the Treasury surplus was unfair to the taxpayers and recommended reduction of the revenues; the fairest method was reduction of the tariff. Expenditure of the surplus was wasteful and unwise; purchase of outstanding government bonds was extravagant; reduction of the excise taxes on liquor and tobacco was offensive to many. He sincerely hoped that every member of Congress would rise above party, for after all, "It is a condition which confronts us, not a theory." [11]

Cleveland had clearly sounded a call; the first answer came from across the seas, where James G. Blaine was vacationing. With an eye on the presidential contest of 1888, Blaine denounced Cleveland's stand, outlining in a famous interview the standard protectionist arguments. Further thunder came from the right, as McKinley told the sympathetic Boston Home Market Club in February, 1888, that the Democrats were dangerous on the tariff question. He quickly perceived that he who picked up the gauntlet thrown down by Cleveland could make a reputation.[12]

The Democrats pushed their plans forward. The chairman of the House Ways and Means Committee was Roger Q. Mills of Texas, whose appointment by Speaker Carlisle had enraged the protectionist Democrats. Mills was an avowed and energetic free trader. The issue was squarely drawn and Mills's appointment reflected the stubborn determination of congressional Democrats, especially the Southerners, back by the administration, to cut tariff rates and fulfill the promise of reform. Randall had made it abundantly clear that he would not follow the President's lead in tariff reform, but Mills now decided to ignore the Easterners and write a real reform measure. He cloistered himself with his tables, charts, and midnight oil. When he came to Washington in December, he had already drafted and printed a bill that met his demands. No hearings were held; minority members of the committee spoke their protests but they went no further; threats and charm did not move the Texan; he was determined that the tariff be revised and saw no need for lengthy and time-consuming hearings.[13] He was sincere, but it was bad politics, for his methods not only angered the Republicans but the Eastern Democrats.

On April 2, 1888, Mills's closet opened and he presented his bill to the House. It was indeed a reform measure, providing general reduction of the rates; free raw materials, including wool; and the substitution of ad valorem for specific rates in many schedules.[14]

The bill carried a minority report written by McKinley which mercilessly attacked the measure. He attacked the secrecy of the bill's composition; charged that ad valorem rates were antiquated and corrupt; said that the bill was sectional, which it was; insisted that the changes would increase rather than diminish the revenues by increasing importations; attacked the administration for not distributing the surplus through the purchase of government bonds; and asserted that abolition of the excise taxes was the proper method of reducing the surplus.[15] It was a strong, well-written report that went straight to the heart of the matter, showed the weaknesses of the Democratic stand, shrewdly capitalized on the division in the administration ranks, and offered a plausible protectionist substitute for radical reform.

On April 17, 1888, general debate on the bill began. This was McKinley's chance to make himself a national figure by leading the attack on tariff reform. He waited for the proper psychological moment, determined to make his speech a summation of the protectionist argument. He did not speak until May 18, a month after general debate began. On that day he rose to deliver the ablest, lengthiest, best-reasoned speech of his career to that date.

His argument contained nothing new, but he stated it simply and effectively. He insisted that the low rates provided on several items in the new bill would extinguish home industries. He lashed out at Cleveland for "dispensing special favors" to secure passage of the bill; it was well known that the President had tightened every screw in sight and oiled many a recalcitrant wheel with patronage. McKinley scored the Democrats for forgetting the farmer, pointing out amid general laughter that all he got under the bill was free sheep-dip. With a fine mixture of humor and sarcasm he flayed the academic free traders who had helped frame the bill, and dismissed their work as woolgathering. "I would rather have my political economy founded upon the every-day experience of the puddler or the potter than the learning of the professor, or the farmer and factory hand than the college faculty." He ridiculed the theory that lower duties meant lower prices, insisting that they also meant lower wages and production. The bill would not diminish the surplus: only higher rates, shutting off imports, would do that.

The high point of the speech came when he refuted Mills's contention that the tariff increased the price of workingmen's clothing. McKinley paused a moment in his speech, glanced around, and fumbled in his desk before producing a bulky bundle. Applause and laughter greeted his display of a full suit of men's clothing. Leopold Morse, Democratic representative and clothier from Boston, sat near McKinley and had querulously questioned his figures. Now the Major glanced toward Morse, "an imposing looking little man with a big round head and short legs." [16] Morse petulantly asked where McKinley had bought the suit. Smiling, the Major replied amid general laughter: "Come now, will the gentleman from Massachusetts know his own goods?" When the laughter subsided, McKinley read the sales slip to Morse's satisfaction, announcing that the suit had cost ten dollars and that a similar suit was within the reach of every workingman anywhere in the United States because of protection. Morse looked over the slip carefully and shook his head while McKinley proceeded to show that prices had actually declined under tariff protection and that goods were available to more workers because the tariff kept their wages high.[17]

He sat down amid great applause, and members crowded around his desk to congratulate him. He had made his mark; none now denied that he was the foremost protectionist. "With the exception of Mr. McKinley we do not recall any Republican speaker who has contributed anything to the discussion of the important [tariff] question," noted one paper, weary of the interminable debate.[18]

There was an unhappy sequel to McKinley's play with the suit of clothes. Mills quietly checked on his own and concluded that the Major had oversimplified the issue. As he made his final summation on the last day of debate, his mind a welter of facts and figures, Mills forgot the suit. But his son, sitting in the gallery, passed down a scribbled note: "Don't forget McKinley's suit of clothes." Mills smiled and remembered. He displayed proof of his own that the manufacturer had sold the ten-dollar suit for that price because it was slightly under the figure allowed him by the tariff, while it actually cost him only half that figure.[19] It proved, if nothing else, that you could do anything with tariff statistics, but it did not change McKinley's argument. The important thing was not the price of clothing as such but that it was easily within reach of every workingman because protection guaranteed higher wages; remove that protection and the price of clothing, however cheap, was irrelevant if fewer people could buy. The tariff debate was far from finished.

After the bill passed in the House, it went to the Republican Senate, where Fabian tactics prevailed throughout the summer.

Attention now turned from the floors of Congress to the national party conventions. Cleveland's renomination by the Democrats was assured, but a fierce fight loomed in the Republican arena. There was no dearth of candidates in the GOP. Michigan supported Russell Alger; Iowa put forward William B. Allison; Indiana divided her affections between Walter Q. Gresham and Benjamin Harrison; New York spoke for Chauncey Depew, despite that punster's claim that the only presidency he wanted was that of the New York Central Railroad. Everywhere the name of Blaine charged the atmosphere. Although defeated in 1894, the Plumed Knight was still a magnet for a large segment of the party.

Ohio and McKinley had a candidate, John Sherman. On paper, Senator Sherman's chances were excellent. An active pre-convention canvass secured him a large block of Southern votes, with scattered support in the East. Ohio stood behind her favorite son, though not without some hesitation. Yet the Senator's strength was his weakness, for he stood against the field. His support came largely from the South and was a token only, since it promised him no electoral votes as a candidate. Despite his longevity and ability, Senator Sherman was simply not popular. It was no secret that he had "the presidential fever in the severest form. . . ."[20] It was a crucial year for John Sherman; his presidential aspirations would mature now or never, for his strength was at its apogee and his age would prevent future contests. He had come at last to the major bend in the road; would he take the turn to the White House or continue in his path to the Senate? He himself politicked in the South and elsewhere, but stirred little enthusiasm. The magnetism he lacked was focused in the Man from Maine. Blaine's friends were suspiciously active despite the Plumed Knight's avowed withdrawal from the race.[21]

McKinley played a leading part in the preconvention shadow-boxing, committed wholeheartedly to Sherman. Yet he was disquieted to see his own name mentioned as a prominent dark horse. His speech against the Mills bill produced a flurry of predictions that he would cut a large figure at the Chicago convention. His name was linked with many prominent leaders: it was to be a Blaine–McKinley ticket, someone said; no, it was to be a Depew–McKinley ticket, someone else whispered; no, it would be a Harrison–McKinley ticket. Of all the potential dark horses, McKinley stood in the best position; youth, geography, principles, and party service pushed him forward.[22]

Even Foraker, an erstwhile opponent, saw McKinley's position. "He is not so popularly known, but he is well enough known to the men who make men acquainted with the people, viz., the newspapermen and the politicians of the country to make amends for that," he wrote privately. "His record on the tariff makes him among the foremost exponents of that doctrine, while [his] splendid record as a soldier identifies him with the patriotic sentiment of the country. It is in this respect that I think he would do even better than Sherman. I do not mention this because I have any idea of turning away from Sherman, but only as something to be thought of should the time come when the last button is gone from Sherman's coat." [23] But the two were, after all, rivals, and Foraker suspected a deliberate McKinley boom, quietly manufactured by Hanna. McKinley publicly denounced all such efforts, but privately was pleased and flattered. Pleased and flattered, perhaps, yet troubled, despite Foraker's suspicions, for his loyalty to Sherman was above question.[24]

With Charles Grosvenor, Ben Butterworth, Hanna, and other Sherman men, McKinley did his share of buttonholing, flattering, pressuring, and promising with politicians in positions to help the Sherman cause. Associates praised his work.[25]

Ohio, as usual, was divided, and Sherman's hold on the state delegation was shaky. Blaine feeling was evident even there, and many delegates frankly inclined toward Foraker or McKinley. Foraker's position was a difficult one. He was openly irritated and angered by the discourtesy and suspicion with which the Sherman men treated him, but he headed the Ohio delegation in an effort to heal the party wounds.[26] Anxious to have Foraker's public support, Sherman was not so anxious to entrust his fate to the popular and ambitious Governor. That responsibility he assigned to Hanna, which also angered Foraker. The Governor was not even permitted to nominate Sherman, lest he "Garfield" the convention; that card had been played against Sherman before. Instead, Foraker seconded General Daniel Hastings, of Pennsylvania. Foraker was willing to abide by his pledge to support Sherman as long as there was hope for his cause, but he did indeed have a roving eye.[27]

Amid heat and confusion, and with the delegates anticipating an open fight, the Republican National Convention met in Chicago on June 19, 1888. McKinley hastened to tell the first reporter in sight that rumors of a split in the Ohio delegation were false. "We are all for Senator Sherman, and feel well satisfied with the outlook." Blaine was out of it, he said, and predicted that Sherman would receive 360 votes on the first ballot. Asked about a second choice for Ohio, he smiled and artfully parried the thrust: "An Ohio man has no second choice. If Sherman is not nominated it will be for this convention to choose the candidate." So saying, he donned his best white suit and departed with friends for a tour of the city.[28]

Still the rumors persisted, and he later told a reporter somewhat angrily that stories of his own candidacy were pure fabrications. "I would rather have my right arm cut off" than desert Sherman, he told one newsman.[29] But popular approval sparked the rumors, and his first appearance on the convention floor caused a "prolonged hum of applause" among the delegates. Once more hearts and fans fluttered in the galleries as the darkly clad Napoleon of Protection made his way to his seat. Admirers mobbed him, shaking hands, asking questions, offering advice and congratulations.[30]

While delegates sweltered and politicians dickered, McKinley and the Resolutions Committee wrote a platform. As in 1884, he was chosen to present it, and his hand was evident in every phrase. The long sessions did not tire him, for he realized the work's importance and felt the sense of history at his elbow. Here was another chance to vindicate his great principle. On Thursday, June 21, he rose to read the platform. His progress to the rostrum was a continuous ovation. "It was plain that Mr. McKinley was very near the hearts of a great many delegates."[31]

He faced his audience with a firm glance; never did he resemble Napoleon more. He looked fresh and rested despite his arduous labors. He wore his customary dark, tightly buttoned Prince Albert, vividly adorned with a large red, white, and blue Sherman badge.[32] Finally his reception subsided and he read the platform in a loud clear voice. Applause punctuated some of the sentences. Now he was at the tariff plank; his voice became clearer and firmer. "We are uncompromisingly in favor of the American system of protection," he said.

> We protest against its destruction as proposed by the President and his party. They serve the interests of Europe; we will support the interests of America. We accept the issue, and confidently appeal to the people for their judgement. Its abandonment has always been followed by general disaster to all interests, except those of the userer and the sheriff. We denounce the Mills bill as destructive to the general business, the labor and the farming interests of the country, and we heartily endorse the constructive and patriotic activity of the Republican Representatives in Congress in opposing its passage.

Applause carried him to the peroration of the plank. "If there shall remain a larger revenue than is requisite for the wants of the government we favor the entire repeal of internal revenue taxes rather than the surrender of any part of our protective system at the joint behest of the whiskey trust and the agents of foreign manufacturers." The line was drawn; Cleveland took his stand and so did the Republicans. The tariff was the issue. McKinley's hand was evident in planks dealing with civil service reform, anti-Chinese legislation, an isthmian canal, and pensions, all of which he favored. Great applause greeted his finished report and favorable comment flooded the Republican press.[33]

After adoption of the platform, nominations were in order. Foraker, as nominal chairman of the Ohio delegation, seconded Sherman's nomination. As he made his way to the platform through the expectant delegates, a large floral wreath bearing his name was placed at the rostrum. An excited hum filled the huge hall; Sherman's managers frowned. They knew that the Governor's support was lukewarm, that his name was mentioned frequently for the vice-presidency and even the presidency, that there was even a Foraker marching club in Chicago. Was he disloyal? Irritated by the gesture, Foraker waited until the wreath was removed, explaining later that it was only a gift from admirers and had nothing to do with his suspected candidacy. His eloquent speech for Sherman further troubled the Senator's managers, for it sounded more like an echo for Foraker than a second for Sherman.

The first ballot followed on Friday and illustrated Sherman's true position; he received 229 votes, largely from the South, while the remainder were scattered among several potentially strong candidates: Allison, Harrison, Alger, Gresham—and Blaine. Sherman was far from the top, 416 votes being necessary for the nomination; could he make the ascent? A second and a third ballot followed, bringing him slight gains but leaving the general situation unchanged. The convention adjourned so that the managers might maneuver, and Sherman's stock fell.

After the first day's balloting, Hanna wired full details to Sherman on his private line. Ohio's position was vital; obviously Foraker was lukewarm; [34] furthermore, other Ohio men were weak. Most disquieting of all, McKinley had received several votes during the balloting. This was a surprise. McKinley himself was disturbed, for he was in a real dilemma; the memory of Garfield was in everyone's mind. Would McKinley now follow that Ohioan's footsteps and capture the prize from Sherman a second time? If he sat silent, delegates would assume that he was a tacit candidate and his following would grow if the major candidates deadlocked. If he denied his candidacy he might attract more attention, as Garfield had done, and further his own cause. What to do? Sherman's managers hastened to assure him of McKinley's loyalty. "He wants to do what will promote your nomination without leaving him under suspicion that he has been dealing in bad faith with you," Butterworth telegraphed. "He would without an if or but demand of the Convention that his name should not be used and that to persist in it would reflect upon his integrity, and be an assault upon his honor. The danger is that the exhibition of the quality that prompts him would increase his vote. He has been and is thoroughly loyal and has worked like a Trojan to promote your nomination." [35]

After the preliminary ballots, McKinley returned to Sherman's headquarters for a talk with Hanna and Butterworth. All agreed that it would be best to deny his candidacy, for his own sake and Sherman's. Listening intently, McKinley put down his cigar, reached for a telegraph blank, and wrote out a statement. "If this thing is repeated tomorrow, that is what I am going to say," he told Hanna as he shoved the paper toward him. [36] Hanna read the statement and agreed.

On Saturday, June 23, the balloting continued. Connecticut cast a vote for McKinley. Looking about, he quickly climbed upon a rickety chair and signalled for recognition. Pale, somewhat nervous, he waited as the excitement mounted. The buzz of conversation and scattered cheering gradually died and he faced the chairman. He denied anyone's right to vote for him since he was not a candidate. He came pledged to Sherman; he would not desert him now, certainly not to promote his own interests. Every eye was upon him; the galleries were hushed; the very air was charged as he continued:

> It has pleased certain delegates to cast their votes for me for President. I am not insensible to the honor they would do me, but in the presence of the duty resting upon me I can not remain silent with honor. I can not, consistently with the wish of the State whose credentials I bear, and which has trusted me; I can not with honorable fidelity to John Sherman, who has trusted me in his cause and with his confidence; I can not, consistently with my own views of personal integrity, consent or seem to consent, to permit my name to be used as a candidate before this convention. I would not respect myself if I could find it in my heart to do so, or permit to be done that which could even be ground for anyone to suspect that I wavered in my loyalty to Ohio, or my devotion to the chief of her choice and the chief of mine. I do not request—I demand, that no delegate who would not cast reflection upon me shall cast a ballot for me.[37]

The pregnant silence was broken by waves of applause and cheering as he sat down, still pale and suddenly tired from the strain. "McKinley's speech was very strong," a Shermanite instantly wired Washington.[38] Had it been wrong? Would his statement, despite its strength, rally rather than weaken the incipient sentiment for him? The clerk's voice droned the call of states as men crowded around him to congratulate him on his stand and gained the impression that he was very emphatically sincere and would not enter any race so long as Sherman stood. Mark Hanna watched and listened, shrewdly gauging his man, impressed by the sincerity that animated him, and eventually he arrived at a lasting conclusion: "I felt [that his speech] destined him as a marked man for President." [39]

The ballots showed Sherman's strength to be stationary. Depew withdrew, and most of his support drifted to Harrison. The latter was suddenly second, only shortly behind Sherman. In the early afternoon the convention was electrified by a rumor that Blaine

William McKinley as a young man before the Civil War (upper left), at 18 when he enlisted in the 23rd Ohio Volunteers (upper right), and late in the Civil War (below).

Representative
McKinley in
the 1880's.

McKinley with the House Ways and Means Committee.

Mr. and Mrs. William McKinley at home in
Canton, Ohio, during the first campaign.

McKinley's
front-porch
campaign
of 1896
attracted
hordes of
well-wishers.

William Jennings Bryan, Democratic candidate
for the presidency in 1896.

Garrett A. Hobart,
vice-president during
McKinley's first term.

Cartoon in
Harper's Weekly,
July 25, 1896,
bearing caption,
"Farmer McKinley
takes off
his coat."

IN 1861
WILLIAM MCKINLEY
WAS UPHOLDING HIS
COUNTRY'S HONOR,—
AND HE'S DOING
IT YET!

IN 1861
THIS IS WHAT
WILLIAM J. BRYAN
WAS DOING,—
AND HE'S DOING
IT YET!

Bearing the caption, "The deadly parallel," the above sketch appeared in *Harper's Weekly* of August 29, 1896.

Depicting Cuba as a forlorn waif knocking at President McKinley's door, a cartoon in *Judge*, December 5, 1896, queries, "What kind of an answer will he get at this house?"

Marcus Alonzo Hanna,
McKinley's
campaign manager.

President McKinley dictating to his secretary, John Addison Porter.

President McKinley and his secretary, George B. Cortelyou, at Brooklyn Navy Yard.

Recruitment poster during the Spanish-American war.

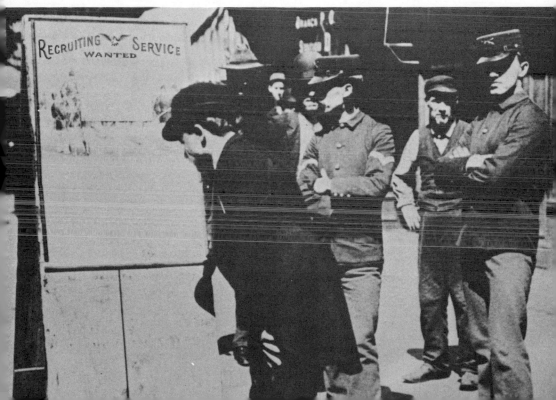

Speaker of the House,
Thomas B. Reed

The President and his cabinet in 1899. Left to right:
McKinley, Lyman Gage, John Griggs, John D. Long, John Hay,
James Wilson, Elihu Root, Ethan A. Hitchcock, Charles E. Smith.

President McKinley on the stump, *circa* 1898-99.

The second campaign:
the full dinner pail
and cartoon parody.

The irrepressible Theodore Roosevelt, McKinley's
running mate, threatened to overshadow the
President during the second campaign.

McKinley during
his second term.

McKinley's last
public address at
the Pan American
Exposition in
Buffalo, New York,
September 5, 1901.

Brown Brothers

Artist's conception of the assassination of President McKinley.

would shortly announce his candidacy; the break was imminent. And now Foraker showed his hand. Asserting that he had been faithful to Sherman but that the Ohioan no longer had a chance, he announced his support of Blaine if the Plumed Knight was a candidate. Ohio had broken. Foraker was prompted in his action by a dislike of McKinley and Hanna, and a strong desire to deflate the McKinley boom. He had also been approached by Blaine backers with flattering offers.[40] The McKinley trend was evident everywhere on Saturday, and talk of his candidacy as a dark horse irritated Foraker, who envisioned that role for himself.

As Sherman declined and the major candidates settled into grooves, the pressure for a dark horse mounted; McKinley was a logical choice. Sherman's fate was obvious now, and the Ohio men, led by Hanna, rallied to McKinley as their best hope. His party service, popularity, and ability drew them to him, as well as his consistent identification with Sherman's cause; who better to inherit the Senator's mantle? Did Hanna now dare fail to capitalize on McKinley's popularity, losing Ohio's chance to name the candidate? In view of Foraker's past record toward Sherman, he could hardly turn to him in preference to McKinley; it would be well to halt any Foraker boom that might be manufactured elsewhere.

Foraker bitterly insisted that Hanna had pushed the Major all along, awaiting his opportunity; now it was at hand and the delegates would be stampeded.[41] Caucuses, meetings, deals punctuated Saturday afternoon and evening as delegates and managers made their weary rounds. Eastern groups, it was hinted, openly hoped that "lightning will strike McKinley." [42] McKinley himself was busily dissuading supporters and trying to rally support to Sherman, anxious that his position not be misinterpreted. Some of his supporters were as stubborn as he, but if strong words were necessary he had them; eloquent profanity moved recalcitrant followers.[43] All evening the shadowboxing continued. Exhausted, he retired, only to be awakened by conversation in an adjoining room. It was later said that he overheard men planning to use his name and rose to confront them in his night shirt, like Banquo's ghost, demanding that they desist.[44]

Hanna and Butterworth hung over the private wire, nervously smoking cigar after cigar while McKinley, when not canvassing other delegations, relaxed briefly on a horsehair sofa whose contours did not match his own and which seemed to exhaust, rather than to rest, occupants. By late Saturday afternoon, reluctantly, knowing how much victory meant to Sherman, and genuinely sad over the task at hand, friends telegraphed him in Washington: "Our delegation is breaking up. Your friends are standing by you yet the fight on Monday will be McKinley against Blaine. I know whereof I speak."

Prominent men now urged Sherman to withdraw in McKinley's favor, begin a stampede, and beat Blaine, thus salvaging something from his candidacy. Hanna was blunt: "The Blaine move is to be made on the next ballot. We think McKinley the only man who can defeat him. Who do you advise? Can Ohio afford to lose the opportunity? I regret the situation but fear I am right." Murat Halstead seconded the motion: "Can we afford to lose the opportunity of securing a nomination for the State? Give us the word and we believe we can pull McKinley through." [45]

McKinley reaffirmed his support of Sherman. "There is nothing I will not do or say and demand with all the earnestness of my nature to promote your nomination," he telegraphed. "The Major has earnestly protested against action in his favor," a friend wired. "If all our friends had been as true as McKinley we should be much nearer a solution of the contest," another reported.[46]

The Senator was adamant. He would never again be so near the mountain top. With a pride born of position, buttressed by ambition and a dislike of Blaine, he refused to withdraw in favor of McKinley or anyone else.[47] He committed himself to the end of the race. "Let my name stand. I prefer defeat to retreat. Each delegate should act as he deems best for his country . . . I like McKinley, but such a movement would be unjust to others, and as I view it, a breach of implicit faith . . . ," he wired. "I will be true and frank. Stand to our position and fall, if need be, with honor." He thanked the Ohio men, but blamed his failure on Blaine's deception.[48]

The managers now turned not to Blaine but to the colorless Indianan, Benjamin Harrison. If they wanted glamor it was a strange choice. "Sherman won't do; he is too cold," a delegate said. "Why, he is a red hot stove compared to Harrison," answered the nearest Sherman supporter.[49] But glamor was not the yardstick; Harrison was safe, reliable, well known, and from doubtful Indiana.

On Sunday, June 24, Andrew Carnegie, Blaine's host in Scotland, cabled the Blaine managers that their leader was not a candidate and favored Harrison. Men hurried to Indianapolis where, after pious church services, Harrison answered their questions. He answered well, and the managers returned to Chicago with a candidate in their pockets. Sherman was impossible; Blaine was out; Depew had withdrawn; McKinley, the most logical dark horse, was too weak; Harrison was the man.

Sherman's managers made a last frantic effort to shore up the walls. Blaine's refusal brought Foraker back to the fold. Missionaries canvassed other delegations for Sherman. On Monday morning, shortly before the convention reassembled, Hanna and the Ohioans offered cabinet posts to L. T. Michener and W. W. Dudley, Harrison's managers, if they would switch to Sherman. They declined and set about their business, which was Harrison's nomination.[50] Later in the day the Indianan was nominated, with Levi P. Morton of New York as his running mate. There was nothing more to say except what Sherman wired his friends: "I certainly am not disheartened or dishonored. We have made a gallant fight if we have not won the battle." [51]

The convention left a bitter taste in many mouths. Foraker's disloyalty cost him dearly in Ohio politics and prompted his final break with Hanna. The applause that greeted McKinley's appearance on the last day of the convention was salt in the Governor's wounds. Though Foraker hotly denied that he had ever been unfaithful to Sherman, he now belonged to a different camp.[52]

McKinley's conduct was lauded everywhere; once again he emerged safely from a sordid fight. Hanna could not forbear pointing to him with pride: "I cannot refrain from again mentioning the heroic conduct of Major McKinley under the most trying circumstances." [53] Sherman was alive to his debts: "I will certainly recognize in some fitting way the heroic conduct of Major McKinley referred to in your last telegram." [54] Once again, McKinley attracted the notice and praise of prominent men. "High praise must be accorded to Major McKinley for the firmness with which he withstood all temptations. If he had been a weak vessel like Garfield, he might have been tempted to his destruction." [55] McKinley himself felt entirely free from blame. "I was sent by the Republicans of Ohio to vote and work for John Sherman and I did so," he told the Canton crowd that welcomed him home. "Not one moment did I falter nor allow any other interest to interfere with the cause in which I labored." [56]

Political conventions are erratic bodies, unpredictable in general, and that of 1888 might well have chosen McKinley; his popularity with the galleries and delegates was evident throughout the proceedings. But galleries and even delegates do not always choose presidential nominees, and it is difficult to see how he could actually have been nominated barring hysteria and an unpredictable stampede. McKinley was popular, but he was a weak candidate despite his identification with the great issue of the campaign. Harrison was by far the most logical candidate, given his party status, age, name, and residence in doubtful Indiana.[57]

In any event, it was fortunate that McKinley was not nominated, for Republican victory that fall was another matter. Hanna was not yet in the position he graced in 1896, and it is unlikely that McKinley could have won over Cleveland. Republican prospects were at best doubtful. "I have little confidence that whoever is now nominated can be elected," a prominent Republican wrote.[58] McKinley was flattered by his reception and grateful for his growing reputation, but he wisely followed a straight course, looking toward the future. He exhibited an ability that grew with time and that became invaluable to his cause—winning applause *after* defeat. Without risking anything he had won the confidence and support of many men who could help him in the future. Furthermore, he genuinely respected the prize at stake, a presidential nomination; he would not stoop to bargain or to conquer. Now as on other occasions, McKinley's old friend Rutherford Hayes summed it up: "You gained gloriously," the former President wrote from the shady groves of Fremont, far from the battle's din. "The test was a severe one, but you stood it manfully. It was finely done. A better crown than to have been nominated." Then he shrewdly added: "There were ambitious men near you at Chicago . . . of course, men in political life must be ambitious. But the surest path to the White House is his who never allows his ambition to get there to stand in the way of any duty, large or small." [59]

A dual struggle now loomed; the Republicans must elect Harrison and also defeat the Mills bill, which was still pending and which the House had passed on July 21. A sub-committee of the Senate Finance Committee, led by Allison and Aldrich, promptly took the bill into safe hands. Allison assured Harrison that a substitute would be drafted on which the party could stand. "There is no danger of passing the Mills bill," Sherman wrote. "We can defeat that. . . ." And so they did.[60]

A substantial element of the party favored some downward revision of the bill as the only way to meet the Democratic challenge. But the protectionists saw that delay was a better weapon. Hearings were held, and a new measure known as the "Senate substitute," protectionist in tone, was fictitiously put forward as an amendment. It was debated and debated, and the inevitable pamphlet war ensued as congressmen flooded constituents with talk and print. On October 20, Congress adjourned without action on the bill, which was killed in the short session after the election for lack of a conference committee.[61]

Speakers crowded country as well as city rostrums in an intensive campaign, and money flowed freely in many precarious districts. McKinley spoke widely in Ohio, which must be held for Harrison, and in the South. His own canvass blended with the national effort and for once he faced little opposition; his reputation was too strong to overcome.[62]

Election day came and the Republicans won; though Cleveland received more popular votes, Harrison carried New York and Indiana to win in the electoral count. Hard work and the liberal use of money had done it: the frightened protected interests raised a large campaign fund which party strategists used to carry doubtful areas with "blocks of five." [63] Whatever the means of victory, McKinley was exultant. "Wasn't it a great victory?" he asked a Pittsburgh audience. "I worked so hard stumping during the fight that I haven't got over it yet. If the Republicans shape their policy properly, the election of Harrison means another long lease of power. If we hadn't won this time I don't know when we should have succeeded." [64]

The flurry of election excitement subsided, but speculation on the new cabinet took its place. McKinley was mentioned in the newspapers but warily told reporters only that he expected Harrison to choose "first class men." If the talk was serious, nothing came of it, though he was a possible choice from Ohio due to his tariff record, stature in Congress and the party, and his campaign work.[65]

As 1888 closed, McKinley took comfort from his greatly enhanced reputation. Harrison's victory seemed to him to be a popular mandate on the principle to which he devoted his career. Tariff legislation was inevitable in the new Congress. He had visions of his name attached to a great protective measure. The materials of history were at hand; he need only apply himself to the task.

The McKinley Tariff: Victory and Defeat

WASHINGTON'S cold was chilly indeed to the newly elected members of the Fifty-first Congress who straggled into the nation's capital in late November and early December, 1889. But the warmth radiating from the friends and spirituous beverages of the various contenders for the House speakership took the chill off many evenings, as members were wined and dined, asked and begged for their support. For the first time since 1875, all three branches of the federal government were Republican; there was a slender majority in the House, and the speakership would be no empty honor. The right man, with prudence and wisdom, might use his gavel to build a ladder to greater things.

The Fifty-first Congress promised to be one of the most important in recent history. It took no seer to predict that battles would rage over the tariff, the silver question, trust regulation, and federal control of elections—not to mention pensions, patronage, and all the incidentals of politics. Elected by a narrow margin, the Harrison administration must work fast to retain power.

McKinley was a candidate for the speakership, but he did not enter the sweepstakes without reflection. He faced powerful opposition—Thomas B. Reed, Joseph G. Cannon, and others figured in the race—and he risked antagonism and friction. Yet the post was worth the fight. Next to the presidency itself, the speakership was the most important office in Washington. Not only was the Speaker a ranking official, but he controlled legislation through committee appointments, had influence in the party, and wielded parliamentary power in the House.

McKinley's name was mentioned for the office after his re-election in 1888, but he did not commit himself. "Little can be known about the speakership until near the time when Congress meets," he wrote Hayes. "If we should have an extra session (which I doubt) it would soon be settled. I am doing no soliciting. If I am successful the selection will come in an honorable and self respecting way." [1] But between the short session in March and the assembly of the new Congress in December, 1889, he decided to make a determined race for the post. Not only did he himself "solicit" support; he enlisted the aid of friends. By early fall he departed for Washington to confer with supporters. "I think we will get to Washington early on account of the speakership," his secretary wrote. But caution was still the watchword. *"Never mention his candidacy."* [2]

Out of habit and respect for his opponents, McKinley preferred a calm contest and declined to use derogatory information about Reed, his foremost rival. He might well have hesitated to taunt that sharp-tongued statesman, for in the picturesque world of politics none stood out in bolder relief than Thomas Brackett Reed. Tall of stature and wide of girth, his genuine intellect and parliamentary ability matched his wit and acid sarcasm. Where McKinley was soft, he was harsh; where the Major was kind, he was rough; where the Ohioan was conciliatory, he was outspoken. Reed's caustic wit levelled many an idol, Democrat and Republican alike, and he had a keen ear for cant and small patience for self-righteousness. A strict party man, his mind never grasped the idea that the Democrats could be right, and they suffered mercilessly from his chanting taunts, delivered in a highpitched Maine drawl that made his words and figure even funnier. He once opened a speech, at which a large contingent of Democrats appeared, with the remark that "if a photographic snapshot could be taken of the Democracy at any time or any place it would reveal them in the act of doing some mean, low-lived and contemptible thing." A chorus of hisses and boos greeted this dictum, while Reed stood, placid as a Buddha, waiting for the tumult to subside, after which he said calmly: "There, I told you so." [3]

McKinley himself was not on the biting end of Reed's lash, though Reed had little respect for him; but he knew how many other men had squirmed in their seats while Tom Reed pilloried them. "Everybody enjoys Reed's sarcastic comments and keen wit," he once said, "except the fellow who is the subject of his satire." Reed disliked hecklers, especially Democrats, and once said after answering one: "Having embedded that fly in the liquid amber of my remarks, I will proceed." [4] He had no illusions about the political game, and his sarcasm reflected a profound cynicism.

For once Reed bridled his tongue and followed the advice of managers who feared that he would alienate support by talking too much. He longed to deflate McKinley and asked his chief manager, Henry Cabot Lodge, hopefully: "Mayn't I say anything about Napoleon?" obviously referring to McKinley. "No, that is just what you must not say," was the answer, and Reed abided by it. [5] Reed came to Washington in mid-November to confer with his backers and solidify his lines. He had the support of the New England delegations, and Lodge assiduously garnered more; Theodore Roosevelt bustled down to the capital for Reed and set up headquarters in the backroom of a hotel. Lodge accused McKinley's friends of making promises for support, while doing the same thing himself. Reed's dislike for McKinley deepened as the deadline neared. "I think the campaign will be much assisted by McKinley's pronunciamentoes which show how little he knows about it." [6]

In point of fact, McKinley said little, preferring as always to work quietly. His tariff record gained support from many protectionists. He hoped for help from such Southern Republicans as seasoned the House, and worked vigorously during the last two weeks of November. Mark Hanna, alive to the possibilities of such a victory, hurried to Washington and settled next door to McKinley in the Ebbitt. [7]

Yet for all his friends and past record, McKinley's cause was hopeless. Reed was too well known as a strong-handed parliamentarian. The Major's abilities had other and better uses than those afforded by the Speaker's chair, and many who liked and respected him nevertheless supported Reed because they felt that the unruly House needed his strong hand. As the Republican caucus approached, McKinley's followers were still hopeful. On the eve of the gathering the New York delegation voted for Reed, and on November 30 the caucus endorsed him, with 85 votes to McKinley's 38. No rancor animated the Ohioan as he moved to make the nomination unanimous. [8]

Congress convened on December 2, and Reed promptly defeated John G. Carlisle, the Democratic nominee. Carlisle and McKinley escorted the man-mountain to the chair, both hidden by the new Speaker's figure during the short procession. If the physical size of the presiding officer counted, the House was in for great things.[9] As the congressional pageant unfolded in the next few months, McKinley must have thanked his lucky stars that he did not hold Reed's place, for the Speaker became one of the most maligned figures in recent politics. McKinley lacked the determination and willingness to incur enmity, and had he been elected it is doubtful that the Fifty-first Congress would have worked with as much speed as it did. Furthermore, he was accorded the priceless chance to draft a tariff bearing his name that later helped him to the White House. Had he been Speaker, none of this might have happened.

With the initial pageantry of opening Congress over, the members pushed aside floral gifts and prepared for work. Reed labored on committee assignments for some time. Judge Kelley's ill health forbade his service as chairman of the Ways and Means Committee, and that plum fell to McKinley; the archpriest of protection would be in charge of tariff legislation.

McKinley's talents were much in demand, for Reed asked his advice in making committee appointments and in drawing up new rules. His knowledge of rules and his talent for compromise supplemented Reed's harshness. Though they disagreed at many points, they worked well together in harness. Reed's strong arm and tongue whipped members into line, and McKinley's smooth touch soothed their feelings. "He never had a harsh word for a harsh word," La Follette recalled especially of this stormy session, "but rather a kindly appeal: 'Come now, let us put the personal element aside and consider the principle involved.'" [10]

As administration floor leader, McKinley disliked the rough-and-tumble debate and delegated much of his work to Cannon, who learned his lessons well. The Major's ability and personality won him party plaudits. "The Republicans are loud in their praise of Major McKinley's leadership," a Washington newspaper reported. "They say he is cool, level headed and courageous, quick to see a point and alert in pressing it home." Work consumed his time, to Ida's disappointment. "My good husband's time is all occupied so that I see but little of him," she wrote home to Ohio.[11]

Reed had no taste for debate in the Rules Committee and merely informed the Democratic members of his decision. He would call in Benton McMillin, Democratic member of the committee, hand him a slip of paper containing a new decision, and drawl laconically: "Mack, here is an outrage McKinley, Cannon and myself are about to perpetrate. You will have time to prepare your screams and usual denunciations." [12]

Reed at once prepared a new set of rules that provoked ample Democratic screams and denunciations. The most troublesome problem he faced was the so-called "disappearing quorum." Previous Speakers had not recognized as present those members who refused to answer their names in a roll call; an obstructionist minority could refuse to answer, make the point of no quorum, and stall the House procedures. Reed decided to do something about it. The Republican majority was so slender that the party could not tolerate dilatory Democratic tactics if it was to dispatch the vital business at hand.

The House adjourned for Christmas on December 21 and reassembled on January 6, 1890. An ominous atmosphere greeted the members, for rumors that new rules were in the offing permeated the cloakrooms. McKinley refused to be interviewed on the subject, though he knew of Reed's plans. The Speaker had warned his lieutenants that he would attack the problem at the first opportunity, but could not name a date. On January 29, 1890, the explosion came.

A contested election case was announced, the roll was called, and the Democrats, who sat silent in their seats, jubilantly shouted, "No quorum." Undaunted, Reed calmly directed the clerk to record as present enough seated Democrats to make a quorum. There was a moment's silence, then pandemonium engulfed the chamber. Reed made no effort to quell the rioting Democrats but proceeded to intone the names of members to be recorded as present. To one taunt that he had no power to count a member present Reed replied: "The Chair is making a statement of fact that the gentleman from Kentucky is present. Does he deny it?" [13]

McKinley strongly supported the Speaker. In the House he vigorously opposed that Democrats and outside the House he made it clear that the Republicans backed Reed's demand for new rules.

The Speaker continued to count quorums, facing shaking fists with characteristic calm. "Say, Tom, did you count a hat?" one wag asked after he read off a list of names.[14]

The following day, January 30, McKinley defended the new rulings before packed galleries. The matter came in the end to dispatch; to do business or not to do business. It mattered not that Democrats and Republicans had in the past done things that they now condemned. "I am not saying that you gentlemen on the other side are doing differently from what we have done for fifteen or twenty years past," he told the Democrats with disarming candor. "I have sat here and filibustered day after day in silence, refusing to vote, but I can not now recall that I ever did it for a high or a noble or a worthy purpose." Good natured jeers and laughter greeted him. "There was never a time I did it that I now remember when I did not feel ashamed of myself." It was not fair that a minority could stall a democratic government. "Talk about the 'tyranny of the majority'; the tyranny of a minority is infinitely more odious and intolerable and more to be feared than that of the majority. The position of the gentlemen on the other side means that they will either rule or ruin, although they are in the minority. We insist that while we are in the majority they shall do neither." [15]

The confusion continued, but Reed pursued his course, impervious to cries of "Czar!" and "Tyrant!" Democratic hysteria amused him, and his efforts for order were so severe that he broke his gavel. But order he would have, and on February 14, 1890, the new rules were adopted, after acrimonious debate, by a strict party vote. They did away with the disappearing quorum and dilatory motions. Legislation could now proceed with the House firmly under Republican control. McKinley publicly supported Reed's stand but privately disliked his harshness, though he admitted that perhaps it was necessary in view of the Democrats' willingness to obstruct the hated Speaker.

McKinley announced in December that he would hold extensive hearings on a new tariff measure and that unlike Mills, he would present no "dark lantern bill." The Ways and Means Committee settled to its task, in time producing 1,400 pages of testimony. Democrats charged that only protectionists appeared and that others were barred from testimony. McKinley hotly answered that he,

Reed, and Carlisle, the committee's ranking Democrat, chose the committee room and that no one was denied admission. "In this connection I want to say there has not been a single interest in this country that asked for a hearing before the Ways and Means Committee that has not been heard." [16] Day after day he sat in patient, attentive attitude, digesting information, asking questions, smoking cigars, as the parade of witnesses passed before him. Day sessions were cut short by other business, and there was no peace even at home, as the committee members worked over their assigned schedules at night in McKinley's rooms at the Ebbitt. As April approached, after months of testimony and hectic work, the committee announced that the end was in sight.

At that point Secretary of State Blaine appeared on the scene with a remarkable plan, designed to win markets and influence voters in the fall elections. He was enamored with the Pan-American Congress, in session in Washington during the tariff hearings, and saw the possibilities of free trade within the hemisphere. He took his idea to President Harrison, who approved, and then approached the Ways and Means Committee. His initial plan permitted the president to admit duty-free certain agricultural products from South American countries that admitted American goods duty-free; the arrangement would work through executive agreements. The committee members listened while the Secretary talked. They were doubtful, though some public opinion supported Blaine. The Republican members of the committee went to the State Department, where Blaine, though ill, delivered a spirited statement in favor of his idea. Suggestions that he be calm were vain. "No, no, I can't talk when I sit down," he said, his brilliant eyes flashing. McKinley was impressed, partly by Blaine, more by the idea's possibilities. But the other Republicans were not; protection was a dogma to them. [17]

While the Pan-American Congress was still in session, Blaine learned that hides, hitherto on the free list and a large item in the South American trade, would be dutied in the new bill. He protested that no one would benefit and that it would be "a slap in the face" of the South Americans. "Pray stop it before it sees the light. Such movements as this for protection will protect the Republican Party into speedy retirement." [18] McKinley read the letter and agreed; hides were placed on the free list in the bill as reported to the House. But still the majority of the committee opposed the reciprocity program, and the bill went to the House without it. Blaine bided his time; he would return to fight another day, for in the tangled Senate debate he could surely accomplish something.

McKinley's first step in revising the tariff was the passage of an act simplifying the customs service. The measure, sincerely designed to remedy defects in existing regulations, provided a board of examiners to appraise disputed goods, defined contested terms, relieved the customs courts, and rooted out abuses and corruption in the general administration of customs collections.[19] With this enacted, he moved to the main business at hand, the new tariff bill.

McKinley reported the measure to the House on April 16, 1890; he opened general debate on May 7, with the most extended tariff speech of his career. Though he did not know it, it was his last major congressional address. Crowded galleries greeted him as he rose; splashes of color enlivened the spectacle; a hush fell upon the House. The drama of the moment was impressed upon them all, for he had come at last to the pinnacle of his career, the presentation of a tariff bearing his name.

He began by stating that the party now fulfilled the mandate accorded it in 1888 and had saved the protective system without abolishing the excise taxes. He denied the assertion of the accompanying minority report, written largely by Mills, that the bill would increase rather than decrease revenues; importations and revenues would decline under the new higher rates. The bill presented many innovations in tariff making, not the least of which was a complete schedule of duties on farm products, designed to prevent importations of wheat and other foodstuffs from Canada and Europe. It was a frank bid for Western support and an answer to the claim that the tariff was devised only for Eastern manufacturing interests.

Passing to reciprocity, McKinley admitted that he sympathized at times with opponents of reciprocity. "We have been beaten in every instance" of reciprocity, he said. But he left the problem to Blaine and other experts. Thus he kept the door ajar for future developments.

In the important metal schedule the rates were substantially those accorded by the Mills bill, in some cases lower. Only on tin did the bill offer any radical departure. In that schedule McKinley proposed to protect not an infant but an embryo interest—tin-plate milling. Tin plate, sheet steel covered with tin, was not manufactured in the United States, though the canning industry imported large quantities. Previous attempts to develop a home industry failed when the English killed the domestic industry by underselling. He would now raise the rates on tin so that foreign importations would be cut and adequate protection be given a nascent domestic industry. "It may add a little temporarily to the cost of tin plate to the consumer," he admitted, "but will eventuate in steadier and more satisfactory prices." Asserting that the country had the resources and the market, he insisted that here was a model experiment for protection. Could an industry be created, not merely fostered?

In the woolen schedules he admitted frankly that the rates were slightly above those of the act of 1883, thus recognizing the enormous pressures brought to bear by the woolgrowers. The wool industry had been depressed for some time; this was McKinley's answer. He labored for a time over other schedules, pointing out that the committee had attempted to compensate for some high rates by lowering others.

Despite the subject's complexity, he held his audience. He closed with a general call for protection and recited his own fidelity to the doctrine. He paused, savored the hush of expectant attention, turned slightly to face the galleries, and then summed up:

> With me this position is a deep conviction, not a theory. I believe in it and thus warmly advocate it because enveloped in it are my country's highest development and greatest prosperity; out of it come the greatest gains to the people, the greatest comforts to the masses, the widest encouragement for manly aspirations, with the largest rewards, dignifying and elevating our citizenship, upon which the safety and purity and permanency of our political system depend.

He stood for a hushed moment, as if to register the effect on his audience, then slowly sat down. A crash of applause, punctuated by cries of "Vote! Vote!" greeted his effort.[20]

Reed's rules were in full effect and the party stood behind him, ready to avoid any repetition of the endless Mills debate. A mere four days were set aside at first for general debate. Bound by time limits and watched over by Czar Reed, House members were more concerned with brevity than were senators, more eager to impress galleries with a shining pun or dazzling thrust.

The tin schedule bore the brunt of the short House debate. The thought of protecting something that did not exist was a torch to the powdermill of Southern rhetoric. The Republicans remembered Judge Kelley's cry: "In God's name do not let the gentlemen lead us to declare that the people of this country shall never manufacture tin plate!" The industry was a symbol of sorts to the protectionists; the Allison substitute for the Mills bill contained a duty on tin plate, and several economists had recommended adequate protection.[21] Even Democrats admitted that the tin ores of the Black Hills could be mined if a market were assured. Letters from manufacturers favored protection by more than two to one. The acrid charges of collusion with the trusts, hurled at Republicans, failed to move the House, and the rate was duly provided in the bill after a narrow victory.

When the debaters were not flaying or defending the tin schedule they were busy with sugar. That item was counted on to sweeten the bill for many doubtful voters. Widespread dislike of the sugar trust prevailed; McKinley himself had tangled with its agents.[22] He and other protectionists saw a double-edged sword in sugar: by placing raw sugar on the free list they could break the monopoly's control over refined sugar. They could also go to the people with the plea that they had freed sugar and the poor man's table of a tax. The appeal of such a measure in the Midwest was great. Yet it would be unfair to domestic sugar producers to withdraw protection, so the committee recommended a bounty of two cents a pound for domestic sugar, an idea to which McKinley himself came with reluctance and which he accepted as the only fair way out. Since nearly seven-eighths of our sugar was imported and taxed, free sugar would reduce the excess revenue.

But opposition was instantaneous and fierce. It was amusing to see the Southern Democrats writhe on their own petard; free traders elsewhere, when sugar was touched they out-protected the Pennsylvanians. They would not have a bounty; it was unfair, unconstitutional, uncertain; they *demanded* protection. Beet producers from California and other areas joined the chorus. Prominent Southern Republicans, such as could be found, opposed the idea. Free traders thought it a wild scheme.[23]

Others, of course, disagreed. Ranking Republicans such as John Sherman and Joseph Cannon had long recommended free sugar with a compensating bounty. Other countries had tried a bounty system successfully. Many felt that, as in the case of tin, it was a chance to develop an industry through protection. McKenna, a Republican from California, introduced an amendment placing sugar on the dutied list but was voted down, and free sugar remained in the bill.

Such gall and wormwood as the tin and sugar schedules, not to mention the general rate increases, choked the Democrats, but restrictions on debate added insult to injury. The Republicans had the votes, the rules, and in Reed the will to restrict dilatory tactics, and they did not scruple to silence opposition. The Major was deaf to all pleas for consideration of private bills out of order. Supplicants trailed him to the cigar stand, knowing that he smoked profusely, or pleadingly followed him down the corridor, only to have him smile maddeningly and disappear into the chamber. Speed was of the essence; both realized that Senate action would be slow and that the measure must be placed before the voters in time to be explained before the fall elections.

It was a golden opportunity for the Democrats and they promptly cried "Gag!" levelling lurid charges at the Speaker. One member accused McKinley of abetting "the triumph of the caucus system." [24] On one such occasion, the Major replied with unaccustomed heat: "When you were in control of this House you 'considered,' and did nothing. We 'consider' and we do something. What we want and what the country wants is results, not speeches." [25]

But the Democrats used their time to good party advantage. Accusations filled the chamber. ". . . The present radical increase in many of the duties smacks more of a desire to reward contributors of 'fat' than a desire to frame a broad, statesmanlike, and patriotic bill," said one Democrat, referring to Harrison's campaign funds. Richard Bland decried the whole scheme as a conspiracy of the trusts, which fitted admirably with his other belief that all other evil was a conspiracy of "The Money Power." Yet from a party viewpoint, the soundest advice came from Grover Cleveland. "I have thought as I have seen the Republicans getting deeper and deeper into the mire that our policy should be to let them flounder." [26]

The debates had a humorous side; they were not all imprecations and shouting. Since Reed disliked lobbyists, having encountered so many himself, he ordered ex-members off the floor and otherwise crimped their operations. He even forbade the sale of liquor in the

House restaurant. Private arrangements were made, however, and party lines crossed in the basement if not on the floor.

The bill ground to a vote and McKinley was everywhere, urging its speedy passage. His smiling countenance was familiar to visitors in the galleries, fellow members in the cloakrooms, and the reporters who tugged his coattails. And over all presided Reed's calm and immovable bulk. After regulating debate and amendments, the bill passed by a strict party vote of 164 to 142, and went to the Senate.

Other lesser problems intruded. The "everlasting clatter for office," as Cleveland called it, occupied much of President Harrison's time and was a real problem. Four years of Democratic rule had displaced many Republican officeholders, and now the spoilsmen like James Clarkson, W. W. Dudley, and "Corporal" Tanner rewarded their friends. Cries of pain emanated from the civil service reformers.

President Harrison stood squarely in the center of the patronage fight. The best of politicians found the presidency a burden, but he more than other men suffered in its grasp. Cool, aloof, aristocratic in his tastes, a brilliant lawyer with a legalist's mind, he could not shed the cloak of dignity to descend into the political arena. Frosty in appearance, he chilled the very air about him. He could entrance large crowds, but he froze men when he talked to them alone. He could do a man a favor and make an enemy, it was said, while McKinley could refuse a man a favor and make a friend. "He was gifted beyond comparison with a capacity to be disagreeable," said one contemporary.[27] Yet he was a good executive; he lacked political technique, not ability.

As his lieutenants worked in the Pension Bureau rewarding the old soldiers for their votes in 1888, and in the Post Office Department, where Democrats were turned out wholesale, pressure for civil service reform mounted. McKinley recognized its need; during his career he had tramped many weary miles, seeking jobs and favors for constituents. "I wish we had a good civil service law," he lamented early in 1889. "It would be a wonderful help." [28]

The more flagrant activities of Harrison's followers disgusted him, especially in the Post Office Department. Many Republicans began to question the civil service law, and it was rumored that funds for the law's operation would be withheld. McKinley at once attacked opponents of the appropriation, using his position and prestige to assist the reformers. When the House delayed approving the measure, he rose and condemned the bill's opponents. If the party thought that it could evade its pledges it was mistaken; the people demanded reform and it was necessary to the needs of growing government. "The merit system is here and it is here to stay, and we may as well understand and accept it now," he told his colleagues with a forceful bluntness that surprised many.[29] His effective language helped pass the measure and insure the law's immediate future.

Though the tariff and silver questions occupied most of the session's time, agitation for trust regulation produced the famous Sherman Anti-Trust Act, which McKinley supported. The bill attracted little public opposition; the pressures for its passage were too strong. McKinley was sincere in his condemnation of trusts, anxious that they be regulated by a moderate and wisely administered law, especially since he knew the charges that the tariff mothered the trusts. He also supported a bill to grant federal employees the eight-hour day.

The measure that generated the most heat if not the most light during the spring was the Federal Elections bill, quickly nicknamed the "Force Bill" by Southern opponents. It was designed to provide federal supervision of federal elections in the states and was fathered by Henry Cabot Lodge. It reflected Northern concern over disfranchisement of Negroes in the South. Divided motives produced it: genuine distress at disfranchisement, and equally genuine distress at loss of Republican votes in the border states. Southern reaction to federal supervision of elections was as violent in 1890 as it had been in the 1870's, and the Southerners threatened to stall the whole legislative process rather than permit passage of the bill. In June, Lodge and other Northerners supported the measure with vehement speeches. McKinley was blunt in his arraignment of the Southerners and informed them that "the people of the North would not continue to permit two votes in the South to count as much as five votes in the North."[30] The bill duly passed the House on July 2 and was sent to the Senate, where a different and unkinder fate awaited it.

Though he himself disliked many aspects of the Harrison administration, McKinley remained a loyal party man, supporting administration measures like the outrageous Dependent Pensions bill. However questionable some Republicans might be to him, they were generally more palatable than the Democrats. Harrison often cooled even McKinley's kindness, and the Major muttered more than once that the President might at least thaw if not warm his listeners. He chaffed at what he thought was uneven distribution of patronage in Ohio. "I do not think he [Harrison] is doing right in the matter," he wrote Hanna after a conference with the President, "but he is the man who has the last say, and I suppose we will have to submit." [31] Submission did not breed liking, however, and before long Washington knew that he and Harrison had fallen out. As a favor to the President, who wished to pick a better time for the appointment, McKinley had kept hands off a federal judgeship which Harrison had promised him. Pressured into a corner, McKinley asked a final time and met a chill refusal. "Mr. President," he said in rising to go, "if you were in my place and I in yours, and you had made the sacrifice for me that I have made for you, you wouldn't leave this room without that appointment. Good-day." So saying, he left, not to return to the White House during Harrison's tenure.[32]

Once through the House, the tariff bill went to the Senate Finance Committee. That committee, staffed by prominent and influential men of both parties, was presided over by the venerable Justin Smith Morrill, of Vermont. Veteran of many a tariff war and father of much significant financial legislation, Morrill was chairman in name only. His age—he was born in 1810—and poor health made him delegate the management of legislation to other members. He asked William B. Allison to manage the McKinley bill, but the experienced Iowan begged off and recommended Nelson Aldrich, of Rhode Island.[33] Morrill then assigned the task to Aldrich.

The bill could hardly have passed into more willing hands. Aldrich entered the Senate in 1881 and quickly mastered financial legislation. A businessman in politics, with firm connections on the highest levels of society, industry, and politics, he hungered for results. He managed his affairs with an iron hand, clothed always in the velvet glove of a legendary charm. Though he could be hard or yielding, as the occasion demanded, results counted, and he never hesitated to force his way, if necessary, toward the goal in sight.

The deft, tactful Allison, who was thought able to traverse the Senate floor wearing wooden shoes and make no more noise than a a fly on the ceiling, lacked the iron drive required to push legislation, but he was an astute manager of men and a skilful compromiser. His talents complemented those of Aldrich, and the two, like Reed and McKinley in the House, were an admirable team.

The McKinley bill was no stranger to Aldrich and Allison, for it was in essence the "Senate substitute" for the Mills bill, a substitute which they themselves drafted late in 1888. The agitation against raising the rates had already taken effect; Allison publicly stated that he was not happy with some of the increases, and other senators felt likewise. To discover the extent of this feeling and to bargain for time while other legislation was worked out, Aldrich held private hearings on the bill, attended largely by representatives of protected interests. Though assailed by the Democrats, he denied that any important interest was refused admission.[34] On June 18, 1890, he reported the bill to the Senate with more than four hundred amendments; some were verbal and technical, some raised and some lowered rates. Clearly an endless debate was in the offing.

But there was no debate just yet, for in the early summer all issues faded before the silver question. Those who believed that the Bland–Allison Act of 1878 had settled the silver question were in for a surprise. By 1890, the beginning of the stormy years that brought the issue to national dominance, Western discontent demanded further remedial action. Angered by the refusal of every administration to buy more than the minimum amount of silver under the Bland–Allison Act, pressed on by unwavering belief in their cause, reflecting genuine economic distress, the Westerners came to the Fifty-first Congress to obtain results.

Like the tariff, the issue crossed party lines; no stronger gold-standard advocate than Grover Cleveland lived, yet his party favored silver. The Western Republican senators led the van of inflation sentiment, while their Eastern counterparts sustained the gold standard. To the Westerners it was a sectional and a class issue; Eastern creditors were robbing Western debtors by demanding payment in appreciating dollars. The simplest answer was easy money, depreciated currency, some form of inflation. Mine owners, alarmed at the fall in silver prices, wanted a subsidy and monthly purchases, and claimed that this, in turn, would benefit everyone by placing more money in circulation.

Whatever the economics of the question, it appealed to those in power as a political problem, to be dealt with by legislative compromise. The silver men supported Harrison in 1888 because they believed he favored free silver. Secretary of the Treasury Windom's annual report in 1889 suggested remedial legislation, and it was agreed that "something must be done for silver." Early in the year, Westerners were sure that a free-silver bill would be passed.[35]

The Senate was now the stronghold of silver sentiment, where numbers and unlimited debate helped the Westerners, but the situation differed in the House. Political necessity dictated action, but Reed bitterly opposed the silver men and threatened to block any measure. Asserting that the sentiment was temporary and that prosperity would return and shortly bring the West to its senses, he counselled caution and strongly opposed any further compromise with the silverites. But he misjudged his men; he was unaccustomed to dealing with real fanatics. "Speaker Reed is mistaken; the excitement of the West is not temporary," wrote Senator William M. Stewart of Nevada, the most voluble of the Senate silverites. "It will last as long as contraction continues, and the people will have relief or know the reason why." [36]

As heat descended on Washington, so did rumors of deals and compromise; something would definitely be done to help the silver men; the tariff could not be delayed. It was said that Reed and McKinley, under enormous pressure, hurried to the White House and finally agreed to sustain a measure providing for the free coinage of American silver in order to gain speedy action on the tariff and other legislation. Reed later replied to the story with characteristic bluntness. "No such interview ever occurred or the equivalent or the like of it. I will add that I never at any time heard even a rumor of such a proposition, nor of anything that could give rise to such a remarkable story." McKinley himself answered with equal vigor, ". . . The whole story is without substance or truth. . . ." [37]

Other members of the House were more receptive and despite Reed's opposition, passed a silver-purchase measure. House members were pressured to compromise lest a free-silver measure be passed; only the belief that Harrison would veto free silver prevented its passage. McKinley, as in 1878, advocated bimetallism and the use of silver. Once again he reflected his constituency as well as his principles, for Ohio was still "soft money" country. He supported the original House bill not because he liked it but because he recognized it as the best that could be obtained, and he honestly favored some kind of remedial legislation.

But another story unfolded in the Senate, where on June 17, Western Silver Republicans joined with Democrats and voted for free and unlimited coinage of silver. The Houses were at loggerheads; compromise was in order. Legislation ground slowly to a halt as the silverites filibustered and threatened to talk until they got their way. McKinley urged a conference on the two measures. A meeting followed, but accomplished nothing. McKinley, however, strongly opposed free coinage, and in an emotional speech, on June 25, condemned the Senate's recalcitrance and taste for free coinage in a classic statement of bimetallism:

> To tell me that the free and unlimited coinage of the silver of the world, in the absence of cooperation on the part of other commercial nations, will not bring gold to a premium, is to deny all history and the weight of all financial experience. The very instant that you have opened up our mints to the silver bullion of the world independently of international action, you have sent gold to a premium; and when you have sent gold to a premium, then you have put it in great measure into disuse, and we are remitted to the single standard, that of silver alone; we have deprived ourselves of the use of both metals.

He and many others still hoped that government action could hold the metals at parity; hence his support of a monthly-purchase plan, in effect a government subsidy.[88]

The tariff bill now stood in the center of the controversy, for the silverites quickly saw its importance to their Eastern brethren; unsettled business conditions, loss of money, uncertain investments followed tariff debate. If the bill were threatened, they might turn a suitable compromise. The tariff was delayed when the Westerners in the Senate voted with the Democrats to finish the silver debate before proceeding; the meaning was clear—no silver, no tariff.[39]

The silver senators were in an excellent position. Led by able men like Henry Moore Teller of Colorado, John P. Jones, and Senator Stewart of Nevada, they were a power to be reckoned with in debate. The shaky Republican hold in the Senate gave them the balance of power and they did not hesitate to vote with the Democrats.

They were united in a bloc for the first time, grimly determined to obtain action for silver. As Senator Sherman said, they "had a very decided advantage in tariff legislation" due to their numbers and cohesion. The genuine fear of a free coinage measure among Eastern politicians compounded this. Senators and party leaders from this area recognized the necessity of compromise to avoid intraparty disunity and the defeat of the tariff and other legislation.[40]

Would the Westerners defy their party and President, risk political ostracism, wreck the tariff and perhaps silver legislation as well, all for fanaticism? Admittedly they were caught between two fires. It was said then and later that the West cared nothing for the tariff, but that was not true. It was a party principle, a historic policy, and they thought it was of genuine benefit to their section. The underdeveloped economies of Western states depended on protection from foreign wool, hides, and ores. "I do not believe that the country is suffering from protection," Stewart wrote a critic, "on the contrary I believe that our protective tariff, though defective in many respects, is all that saves the productive industries in this country from ruin." Stewart and Teller were staunch protectionists and defended the policy as beneficial to their section. But this same Stewart said bluntly that "there will be no tariff legislation this session unless a silver bill is passed." [41]

Yet by June they too were ready for compromise. Harrison's definite refusal to accept a free-silver bill blunted the edge of their attack, for they could not override a veto. They shrank from disrupting the party. They faced weakness in their own ranks; many Westerners were new in Congress and were hungry for the patronage and administration support which was denied them until they accepted compromise. Stewart and Teller, with long tenure and assured re-election, might be radical, but other silverites in both Houses tended toward compromise.[42]

Aldrich bided his time, sheltering his tariff bill while the compromisers worked. By late June the Westerners, defeated in free coinage, accepted compromise rather than defeat of the tariff; the rates accorded them on many products meant the difference between prosperity and poverty to their underdeveloped states. Their lengthy efforts for compromise silver legislation reflected in large measure their unwillingness to abandon their party and protection. Their final decision to bolt and follow silver came only after soul-searching that reduced Teller to tears in the national convention of 1896, and their failure in that election proved to many that they could not survive outside the party, free silver or not.

The compromisers, led by Sherman, who disavowed the bill bearing his name, set to work, and by July 14 the necessary legislation was passed.[43] Only with success in their hands did the Westerners agree to take up the tariff bill. But they were under no illusions; the fight had opened wounds that would not heal for years, and they knew that their party favored free silver no more than it ever had.

If the tariff supporters thought that they could proceed once silver was out of the way, they were disappointed. The Federal Elections bill, having been committed to the Senate, provided the Southern Democrats with an endless topic of debate, and they threatened to filibuster the session to death unless it was withdrawn. Though anxious to proceed with legislation, many Republicans felt as strongly on the measure as the Democrats. They were placed in a true dilemma: aside from the political advantages to be gained from a free and fair count in Southern elections, supervised by federal officials, they were genuinely angered by disfranchisement of the Negroes. It was the central issue of the Civil War, the theme of Reconstruction, the cardinal party policy which they had defended through thick and thin; could they now surrender it so lightly in favor of expediency?

McKinley needed no inspiration on the subject. He had already suggested that the army might be used to insure free elections and fair counts in the South. Rumors that the Southerners would permit passage of the tariff if the Elections bill were withdrawn provoked him. "No such agreement exists to my knowledge. More than that, I have never heard of such a proposition. I don't see how it could be seriously considered. The Republican Senators, who are in the majority, will not place themselves in the position of trading one bill for the other." But the Republican senators were not in the majority: silver entered the picture again. Some of the Far Western Republicans were States' rights followers, antagonistic to a strong federal elections bill.[44]

Mr. Aldrich's troubles did not come singly that dreary, humid summer. What to do? Must the tariff be held up or die in the committee room? With characteristic vigor he quietly investigated the possibilities of invoking cloture on Senate debate. It was a daring scheme, even for him, for unlimited debate was the chief senatorial shibboleth. He organized a committee consisting of himself, Senators George F. Hoar and John C. Spooner, constitutional lawyers William P. Frye, John Sherman, and John J. Ingalls. A Republican caucus empowered them to investigate the subject and report back for further action. But tradition, dignity, and sensitivity thwarted Aldrich, for a large bloc of his Republican colleagues boycotted the caucus indicating that they did not like the scheme. Vice-President Levi Parsons Morton suddenly became dedicated to duty and seldom left the chair; he refused flatly to cooperate in the movement for cloture, regardless of party principles involved.[45]

What force could not accomplish, indirection might, and the Republicans decided to see how talkative the Democrats were by prolonging the daily sessions to wear them out. Nothing wore out the Southerners; there was no cloture. Instead, upon Senator Quay's motion in August, a gentleman's agreement was reached whereby the Elections bill was delayed until the short session so that the tariff might be taken up.

In the midst of all this confusion, Secretary Blaine was not idle. He had withdrawn to stronger lines in his battle for reciprocity, and now returned to the fight, hoping to win from the Senate what the House denied him. He wanted a provision attached to the pending tariff bill to permit the president to admit duty free certain South American products when those countries agreed to admit certain American goods duty free. Here was a way to maintain protectionist sentiment in the United States, win friends in Latin America, develop foreign markets, and gather plaudits for himself and the Harrison administration.

Several members of the Finance Committee supposedly favored reciprocity of some kind. To test and develop this sentiment in the upper house, Blaine corresponded with senators and carefully exercised his famous charm in laying his lines. Harrison warmed to the proposal. Both men saw that free sugar robbed the United States of a potent weapon in reciprocity negotiations, for it was a major product imported from Latin America. If it were admitted free without similar concessions from south of the border, they lost a bargaining point.

Blaine was a curious mixture of charm and candor—he boycotted most of Harrison's dinners because both the President and his friends bored him—but he talked earnestly and well to the duly attentive members of the Senate Finance Committee. For two hours he wove all the old spell of charm that surrounded his name. Some members nodded; others were silent. At the end of the tiring session they announced that they disliked the idea. Shaking with excitement and frustration, Blaine rose to go and in the process of saying a few final words became so agitated that he smashed his new silk hat. He fired a parting shot: "Pass this bill, and in 1892 there will not be a man in the party so beggared as to accept your nomination for the presidency." [46]

Washington soon buzzed with the story that Blaine had smashed his elegant new silk hat in rage at the committee's shortsightedness, but the members were no less skeptical. Allison disliked the idea, fearing that it was a bad precedent. Many questioned the constitutionality of Blaine's proposal. The Old Guard Republicans united against the measure because it smelled of tariff reform. [47]

The more McKinley looked at Blaine's proposal the better he liked it. Just why and at what point he began this change is unknown. Perhaps he was sickened by the greed the protected interests displayed during the debate. Perhaps he also saw that the "infant industries" that clamored for more protection were no longer infants. He realized that some national interests were being sacrificed in tariff making to placate local interests, and his long-held belief in the unity of the nation as a whole was sorely tested.

He was alive to reciprocity's political possibilities. It was obvious even now that the bill's high rates were unpopular; this was a way to sweeten the measure, especially for the Midwest. If reciprocity were adopted, passage of the bill might be speeded up, and the elections loomed nearer every day. He saw the virtues of his friend Ben Butterworth's position when he said: "If the Senate passes the bill as it left the House, in five years there won't be enough left of the Protective System to put into bankruptcy. It is to preserve the system and not destroy it that I ask for revision." [48]

Though disappoined by the slowness of his progress, Blaine pressed on. On June 4 he wrote Harrison that the Pan-American Congress favored reciprocity, asserting that American agricultural goods would find a market in South America if admitted free. Harrison forwarded the letter to the Senate and pressured for reciprocity. Senator Hale of Maine introduced a plan drawn up by Blaine. On July 11 Blaine wrote Senator Frye of Maine an open letter asking for reciprocity. A second stronger one followed on July 25, demanding compensations for free sugar.[49]

The talk and propaganda had its effect; reciprocity appealed to the Midwest. Interests there saw potential South American markets for farm goods. Easterners were likewise swayed. "It captivates the businessman with the appearance of shrewd Trade in it. It appears to employ the duties not merely as a means of protection, but a means of bargain for the extension of our own trade," a businessman wrote. By late July reciprocity was assured.[50]

The reciprocity section adopted by the Senate under special rules late in the debate did not satisfy Blaine, but that was unavoidable. His original plan would have given reciprocity with Canada and Mexico, admitting wool and raw ores free, an arrangement which the protectionists would not accept. The final plan allowed the President to *impose* duties as penalties on Latin American products entering the United States if those countries did not accord free entry to certain American products within a certain time. Revised as it was, the final reciprocity provision was an outstanding feature of the McKinley Act, for the protectionists had at least set a precedent. It was in fact a means of modifying the tariff whose great possibilities for the future McKinley used later as president. Much of the credit for the treaties subsequently negotiated belongs to Blaine, but McKinley's own support of the measure assisted greatly in its final adoption.

By mid-July, with other business finally attended to, the Senate turned to the tariff bill. Though the public was disinterested and the bill's passage now inevitable, learned dissertations and three-hour speeches on ammonia, iron sulphate and nails bored the upper house. As in the House, the brunt of the discussion fell upon the sugar and tin schedules. The Louisianans' demands for protection were humorous indeed, "audacious," as one protectionist said. Senator Gibson failed to win protection for sugar with a special amendment, and Aldrich defended the proposed bounty scheme. Sentiment on the tin schedule divided between the manufacturers who wanted to start tin works and thus desired protection, and the users of finished tin who feared increased prices. In the end the tin duty remained with modifications.

As the summer wore on, businessmen became alarmed and demanded final action. "I am a life-long Republican but I voice the sentiments of many leading Republicans when I say such lethargy as is displayed by your august body will give the election in 1892 to the Democrats," one wrote.[51] Hanna bluntly told Sherman that unless action came fast "I don't know where we will get our 'aid and comfort' for the future," obviously referring to campaign funds.[52]

While the Senate worried over tariff schedules, heat descended on Washington. The House went about its business, though not without discomfort. Reed was a startling figure in the chair when he shed his boiled shirt for a flannel one and decorated the ensemble with a black waist sash. He looked "like an honest rutabaga wound in a black ribbon." In an effort to keep cool, Democratic members crowded around a lemonade bowl in the basement, into which some thoughtful soul poured three quarts of Kentucky rye. Even the elegant McKinley, fastidious to the end, finally shed his waistcoat and appeared, thumbs in galluses, as "a veritable Napoleon in undress."[53]

Finally, on September 10, the Senate passed the tariff bill by a strict party vote, amid denunciations and predictions of political calamity from the Democrats. But still the ordeal was not over, for a conference was necessary to make the bill presentable to both Houses. For ten days the two groups of conferees labored over their differences, struggling through the 4,000 items and 450 amendments. Sherman, a Senate conferee, said in weary disgust: "I have been hard at work for a week or more on this tariff conference committee. I trust I will not live long enough to have any connection with another."[54]

At last, on September 27, McKinley faced the House to justify and explain the conference report which he asked it to approve. His tone was tired and disillusioned. He pointed out the reductions in the metal schedules, but insisted that steel was adequately protected.

The tin duty was set at 2.2 cents a pound and he predicted the creation of a great industry. Wool rates were raised "to correct the inequalities" of the law of 1883, and in their new form they gained endorsement from the National Wool Growers' Association. The complex sugar schedule was compromised to satisfy conferees, and he was happy to report that raw sugar was free. He concurred in the reciprocity amendment and gave it his blessing. He pointed out that the revenue tax on tobacco was slightly lowered. He need hardly have bothered; friend and foe alike were anxious to dispose of the report and return home. The House accepted the conference report by a strict party vote; the Senate agreed on September 30, and on October 1, as the session died, Harrison signed the bill into law. Protectionists were pleased with their handiwork, but few people were ever as wrong as Senator Morrill when he wrote, "I think it is good enough to stand for a decade." [55] In fact it did not stand half that long.

Long before its passage a flood of rhetoric engulfed it, and no tariff was subjected to such malignancy and falsehood as that of 1890. McKinley himself was dissatisfied. "Many of the changes I do not like, but you see there is no time to specify," he said when the Senate bill was reported. "I scarcely know what will be the end of it." [56] In after years he told a member of his cabinet: "You misapprehend my attitude as to the protective tariff. I was chairman of the committee in the House which advocated the tariff rates under a bill known as the McKinley Bill, but I thought then, and think now [1897], that it is for our best interests to return gradually to a much less drastic system of tariff." [57] Many Republicans, fearful for their political lives, begged the tariff managers to lower or at least not to increase the rates. McKinley himself, sensing the futility of fighting the current, simply surrendered to the inevitable at the end of the fight. When asked later why he had accepted such high rates, he replied: "For the best reason in the world, to get my bill passed. My idea was to get the act through Congress, and to make necessary reductions later. I realized that some things were too high, but I couldn't get my bill through without it." [58]

It was at best a poor method, this surrendering to pressure, but as the Democrats discovered in 1894, it seemed inevitable in tariff making. "No tariff bill was ever framed that was not largely made up by compromises, . . ." McKinley honestly admitted.[59] If he had been left to himself in an ideal situation he no doubt could have framed a justifiable measure, but the interplay of forces and rush of greed overwhelmed the best intentions. There was little justification beyond political expediency for raising the tariff rates. Cuts in the steel schedules were fictitious, for the industry was beyond protection. Raises in the wool rates reflected the belief that the depression in that industry could be raised by protection, when in fact the tariff probably had little to do with it. Other rate increases, averaging 4 per cent, while they did not greatly affect business, were difficult to justify. Charges that the increased rates were exorbitant were false, for no schedule was raised drastically; the central point is that no schedule deserved raising at all.

The tariff makers of 1890 confronted two distinct problems, both of which they solved—the Treasury surplus and the demand from business interests for higher rates. Due to cuts in revenue, the Sherman Silver Purchase Act, and expenditures by the "Billion Dollar Congress," the surplus quickly disappeared, and the Cleveland administration inherited a close Treasury balance in 1893. The demand for protection was fulfilled, though even at that many cried for more, like children at a candy counter.

The tariff of 1890 came in the midst of industrial expansion and great economic development and reflected the Republican party's willingness to sustain business interests. The act presented four features that marked the outer reaches of protection: a bounty to compensate free sugar, a full agricultural schedule, a rate for a non-existent tin industry, and an extended reciprocity. This last and most important feature marked the final stages of ultra-protection, for it was a warning that no further increases could be adopted without some compensating feature.

In much of what he set out to do McKinley succeeded: he helped foster a tin-fabricating industry that in time fulfilled many of his hopes, he reduced the surplus, he granted protection, he entered upon moderate reform with reciprocity. But the over-all judgment of his work is harsh. The bill was not as bad as its opponents claimed; it was not operative long enough to produce either disaster or happiness. Yet it is important chiefly as a symptom of the times, a reflection of the economic expansion of the day.

Early in the spring, the Democratic Ohio legislature redistricted the state. What sweeter vengeance than to gerrymander out of Congress the author of the odious tariff bill? McKinley and other Ohio men hung over telegraph wires to Washington, awaiting news of their fate, turning glum when they heard it. McKinley's new district was Democratic by a margin of 3,000; it seemed that even he could not overcome that, and visiting Democrats from Ohio predicted his Waterloo.

Late in August, with Congress still in session, he hurried home to accept renomination. Brass bands, parades, flowers, and bunting greeted him, and he was nominated by acclamation after the minimum procedure. He presented a spirited defense of the Fifty-first Congress and prepared for the gruelling campaign that lay ahead. In July the Democrats nominated John G. Warwick to oppose him.[60]

Few congressional campaigns ever witnessed such an outpouring of effort. Democrats and Republicans both organized speaking bureaus and literary brigades, filling cities and towns with propaganda. The Democrats predicted that high prices would follow the tariff bill. Peddlers toured the countryside selling nickel tin cups for a quarter; pie pans brought a dollar—all due, they said, to the new tin schedule. Farmers were warned that they would shortly drink from gourds since they could not afford tin cups. The one great boon, free sugar, failed the Republicans, for it did not go into effect for six months.

The storm center was McKinley's own district. His national reputation, anger at the gerrymander, protectionist Democrats, and hard work counted in his favor. "The outlook is surprisingly favorable," he himself wrote Hanna, with his accustomed good cheer. "I can win." [61] Knowing how much the distortions of the new tariff would affect the farm vote, he supported other Ohio congressional candidates in rural areas, urging Hanna and his friends to intervene in close contests elsewhere to help him in his own area. Many of these aspirants were Grange candidates, and McKinley again showed his sympathy with the growing movement for change. Harrison, Blaine, Reed—everyone he could command spoke or wrote for him. Hope rose as October waned; yet notes of pessimism surrounded him. "It is thought here by some that he will be re-elected," a secretary wrote. "I however am not sanguine." [62]

As election day dawned, bets were placed that the Major would win despite the obstacles. All day the people of the district went to the polls amid great tension and excitement. Many Democrats conceded defeat; many Republicans sensed victory. The Major would do it again. First returns that evening fed the flames of McKinley victory bonfires and it seemed that he had won. But the trend broke when outlying areas reported. The columns filled and added: it was a Democratic year. McKinley, who went to the special hall hired by his Canton neighbors to hear the returns, fell silent and left early, anxious that no one else break the bad news to his wife.

Late in the evening, George Frease of the Canton *Repository* found him sitting in the shadows of his library, lost in thought. All the years of sacrifice and work seemed to have brought this reward. Frease looked at his old friend and said: "It's all over. What am I to say in the paper?" McKinley laid aside his cigar, looked at the editor absently, thought a while, then grew suddenly firm. "In the time of defeat victory may be nearest," he said, and reached for a piece of paper. He started to write an editorial for the *Repository*. He slowly spelled out the first sentence: "Protection was never stronger than it is at this hour." [63]

The full result was a Democratic landslide; 236 Democrats would face a mere 88 Republicans in the new House. The tariff and its author seemingly had been repudiated. But there were other issues: the Reed rules, the extravagant appropriations, the silver question, the whole Harrison administration. The country was angry at the "Billion Dollar Congress," and Reed's remark that this was "a Billion Dollar Country" was not good enough. "Corporal" Tanner's raid on the Treasury for "the boys in blue," to the cry of "God help the surplus!" nettled many. Reed, who weathered the storm, was bitter. "It looks for the moment as if this was a world made mostly for cowards and laggards and sneaks . . . ," he wrote Lodge.[64]

McKinley ran a sensational race, cutting the 3,000 adverse majority to 300. It was simply a Democratic year; the issues were distorted; neither he nor his tariff had a chance. "Insofar as the result is a condemnation of the McKinley law it is a condemnation without trial." [65] Shortly after the defeat, McKinley met Hanna and discussed the results. He condemned the misuse of the bill by his opponents: "But wait and see, Mark—wait and see. The principles and policies of that bill will yet win a greater victory for our party than we have ever had before. The misunderstanding will yet contribute to overwhelming Republican success." [66] He took the defeat in stride. "Met McKinley; brave and cheerful over his defeat," Hayes noted.[67] But others told a different and doubtless true story. After the election, McKinley, Cannon, and other lame ducks sat talking amid cigar smoke, commiserating over their hard luck. McKinley said wearily that he was glad it was all over and that he wouldn't mind private life for a while. "That's what I always tell the boys," Cannon growled, "but, Mack, let's don't lie to one another." [68]

Once again McKinley displayed his uncanny ability to rise phoenix-like from the ashes of defeat. The shouting had not died before a McKinley boom for governor was launched. "Governor Campbell might as well make his will now. His mantle will be given to Governor McKinley next year." [69] Plans were launched immediately for his race; newspapers beat the drum; he would go from defeat to victory on the state and national stage.

Only the short session of Congress, lasting from December to March, remained. He returned to Washington with brave countenance but heavy heart to face the taunts of Democrats and the sympathy of Republicans, scarcely knowing which was worse. Routine business occupied his time and that of the House. He sponsored a bill to untangle problems arising from the tariff in relation to Hawaii. A motion to repeal the McKinley Act drew a gentle reply from him. The silver axe still hung over Congress' head, for the Westerners would not leave without one final assertion of their will. There was talk that a new plan for reorganization of the national banks would be introduced. But it was a touchy subject; skins were thin and memories long after the recent fight over the Sherman Act. McKinley himself preferred inaction, fearing that any move toward fiscal legislation would result in unforeseen calamity. "The danger of any financial legislation that might be proposed is that the Free Coinage people would use it to pass a free coinage bill," he wrote Hanna.[70] He was right; the free silverites needed no excuse to pass a bill. In mid-January, 1891, the Western Republicans in the Senate combined with Southerners to displace the Federal Elections bill from the calendar in order to put through a free-coinage measure that never passed the House. They proved their point; it could be done in the Senate, at least. By March it was all over. The exultant Democrats jeered Reed's closing remarks, and friend and foe alike packed for long journeys home.

McKinley was sorry to go but realized fully that his hard work and astute observations had taken him far since 1877. He held an important place in the party and was strong in Ohio, whose geography was important in any future larger contest. He was a national figure, identified closely with a great national issue and with many friends who would gladly help him upward. The tariff would shortly dominate politics again, and hard times after 1894 would give the defunct McKinley Act a glamor that it never had when operative. Its author would soon be called "The Advance Agent of Prosperity."

Prestige, political skill, stature, contacts—all these his congressional years gave to him. He could have had no better training for the greater career that now awaited him. Already there was talk that he would be president—if not in 1892 then in 1896. In the meantime, the road to the statehouse in Columbus seemed open, his for the taking. And beyond that, who could tell?

∽∾ IX ∽∾

Governor of Ohio

T HE GOVERNOR of Ohio in 1891 was a substantial Democrat
named James E. Campbell. To the average man his office
seemed a formidable responsibility: Ohio was a key state in
national politics, a rich commonwealth, with a varied population
and an economy that required careful supervision. But the casual observer was wrong if he thought the governor of Ohio in those days
was powerful. Unhappy experience with early governors who took
themselves too seriously brought changes to the state constitution
that made the executive all but impotent. He might recommend legislation but not veto it; his appointments were carefully watched; and
his individual appointments in many areas of the state government
were superseded by controlling boards, which meant overlapping
authority, conflicting aims, and cumbersome delay.

But the office had its rewards. If not powerful as an administrator, the incumbent was potent as a politician, for few posts afforded a better steppingstone to greater things in national affairs.
The cabinet, the Senate, the presidency itself were closer to the governor of Ohio than to many stronger state leaders. Ohio's governor
was automatically a party leader, a national figure, an advisor in
political strategy, a perpetual candidate for something else by virtue
of his position.

The gubernatorial nomination seemed McKinley's for the asking.
He was a brilliant campaigner with a long record of party service in
both state and nation, an expert manager, an able politician, and a
national figure. Yet nothing was ever sure in Ohio politics, and
doubts crossed McKinley's mind. What if he failed to win the election? Would that not end his promising national career? He might
better let the tariff issue cool and then seek re-election to the House,
where he could resume his national leadership and work toward the
White House. For however publicly silent he was on that subject, the
White House was already much in his mind.

152

In the spring of 1891, shortly before Congress adjourned, a group of Ohio friends quietly visited McKinley in Washington and talked firmly and long about the coming state convention. It would be foolish, they said, to turn aside a sure thing; his candidacy would unite the party, for only he could rally the dissident Forakerites to the regular standard. His election, and they were sure that he could win, would give him the presidential nomination in 1892 or 1896.[1] McKinley was publicly silent, but he realized that retirement after a defeat would be almost as bad as another defeat: nothing dulls the politician's appeal like absence from the limelight.

The Ohio friends made their points and returned home. Senator Sherman already supported McKinley; he himself faced a ferocious fight against both Foraker and the Democrats for re-election in 1892, and he would give aid for aid.[2] Still McKinley hesitated, sounding out friends and testing the ground. "So far as I am concerned, I should be quite content to look after my personal affairs, which have suffered of course by my long absence from my business and my clients," he told reporters. "If the path of duty seems to lead me to the gubernatorial candidacy, I shall take it, and if it doesn't I shall try to pick up the threads of my long neglected law practice and shall be quite as happy in professional as in political life."[3]

To those with an experienced ear it was a fancy way of saying, "Yes." But first McKinley quietly assured himself of united party support and even contacted the Foraker crowd.[4] Would Foraker support him in a show of unity? It appeared that he would, despite his readiness to challenge Sherman and despite the fact that Hanna was Sherman's manager and an implacable foe. As early as 1890, cautious overtures had emanated from both camps for a "love feast" which failed to materialize because Hanna and McKinley felt that the Forakerites should be taught a lesson.[5] Yet Asa Bushnell and others around Foraker now seemed receptive.

The state convention was scheduled for June, but some weeks prior to that date, McKinley paid an unadvertised call on the Forakers in the seclusion of their home. He was frank. Would Foraker nominate him at the convention and support his ticket? Foraker agreed. In the back of his mind, and perhaps McKinley's too, he knew that Sherman would not live forever; if he himself failed in his Senate race this year, there was always 1898, when McKinley's support might be crucial.[6]

The doubts faded from McKinley's mind. The day before the convention met he arrived in Columbus with the delegation from Stark County, and arm-in-arm with members of Cleveland's Tippecanoe Club, went to his hotel. The coaches were covered with streamers and placards proclaiming: "Tippecanoe and McKinley too!" A brass band accompanied the retinue to the Neill House and serenaded the Major.[7]

The rest of the affair went off like clockwork. Foraker gave one of his fire-eating speeches, after which the delegates uproariously chose the Major by acclamation. He did not disappoint them in his acceptance speech, delivered in his usual effective manner. He accepted their platform, promised a hard fight, and pointed out that they would all have to work to insure the election of a Republican senator. He touched briefly on a major campaign issue, free silver, and concluded. "Experience at home and throughout the world has demonstrated that a fluctuating, irredeemable currency falls most injuriously upon the laborer and agriculturalist of the country." [8]

The Democrats renominated Campbell on a free-silver, low-tariff platform. They admitted that McKinley was a formidable adversary. Nor were the Republicans overconfident. "We are to have a hard fight and the enemy are already at work," the trusted William M. Hahn wrote.[9]

As soon as the convention closed, each side prepared strategy. The Democrats would score McKinley's record on silver, and the Republicans would blast free trade. It would have been an old story, had not both issues been so nationally prominent. McKinley was frankly in an ambiguous position on silver. As in 1877, the currency question did not interest him. His politics and personal convictions caused him to abandon free silver after 1878; he was now nationally known as a bimetallist. He shrewdly perceived that the Democrats were more openly divided on this issue than the Republicans, and candidly admitted: "I am in favor of the double standard, but I am not in favor of the free and unlimited coinage of silver in the United States until the nations of the world shall join us in guaranteeing to silver a status which their laws accord to gold." Pointing out that Eastern Democrats were closer to the Republicans on the currency issue, he appealed for support from all followers of "sound money" and then deftly switched to the tariff.[10]

The man most conspicuous for his absence was Mark Hanna. Absorbed in his management of Sherman's fierce contest against both Democrats and Republicans, he spent little time with the Major. His chief contribution was campaign funds, which he effectively solicited as far away as Iowa and New York, for both Sherman and McKinley had been friends of protected interests and ranking Republicans. Hanna carefully forwarded some funds to McKinley for his own use and sent the rest to the state committee. He himself spent thousands of dollars on the campaign. Late in August, McKinley wrote his friend: "I am a thousand times obliged for your letter with enclosure. I will forward it at once to the State Committee. I beg you will give all of my friends who participated my sincere thanks. It was most generous of you and others and I have to thank you most of all." Two weeks later he wrote that his personal needs were satisfied, and sent all further funds to the state chairman.[11]

The tariff was central in any McKinley campaign, and the Democrats invited Roger Q. Mills to face his old adversary in the campaign. The McKinley forces responded by calling in prominent Republicans. Foraker redeemed his promise and spoke for McKinley, and McKinley in turn agreed not to appoint to the new State Committee anyone of whom Foraker disapproved. James G. Blaine, who was too busy to respond, wrote a strong letter endorsing McKinley. "The election of Campbell means Free Trade and corruption of the currency," the Man from Maine insisted. "I believe Ohio will stand by McKinley." [12]

The real campaigning fell on McKinley. His whole life seems in a sense to have transpired on the stump, so constantly did he campaign for himself or someone else. He began the campaign in Niles, his birthplace, and a seat of the steel industry. The little hamlet brushed the grease and coal dust from its buildings long enough to welcome the conquering hero late in August. A tin arch traversed its main street, bearing an immense sign: "Protection is Prosperity," and one reporter noted that the whole town seemed to be tin-plated as it advertised the budding tin industry fostered by the McKinley Tariff.[13]

Elsewhere, his reception was much the same. The workers

cheered him to the echo when he toured an iron foundry and ate dinner off utensils made exclusively from American tin. In Cleveland the faithful packed the Music Hall for an elaborate reception. Wherever he went, his hotel room was always open to the public, and he often retired late at night after an arduous day of speechmaking and handshaking. His approachability, geniality, and sympathetic charm made him popular with almost everyone he met.[14]

By accident he met his opponent at Lakeside and chatted pleasantly while photographers fussed with their cumbersome equipment. The two candidates promised a joint debate at Ada, Ohio. Early in October, the debate was carried off in great dignity in that little town, to the satisfaction of all concerned. Excursion trains brought loads of the curious and the faithful from all over the state, and McKinley's followers flooded the area with tin goods, while Campbell's appeared marching to the tune "The Campbells Are Coming." No one was surprised by the subject matter or the delivery; Campbell attacked the tariff and McKinley lashed free silver. McKinley supported labor and promised the farmer prosperity under Republican rule.[15]

By October the McKinley organization was running so smoothly and the Major's reception was so heartening that victory seemed assured. "Everything out here looks encouraging," his secretary wrote. "We anticipate a good sound majority . . . nothing short of a grave mistake on our part can beat us." [16] McKinley's caution and smooth organization forbade any such mistake.

McKinley ended his campaign on November 1 with a speech to his neighbors in Canton. It had been a gruelling campaign. "Indeed, I can recall no campaign wherein the real issues involved have been so squarely put before the voters of the State . . . ," he said. On election day he voted, ate supper early with friends and family, and then retired to his study to await the returns. Downtown Canton was not so calm. The square was alive with torches, firecrackers kept many a good citizen from an early slumber, and more than one of the sober Major's neighbors went through town on rubber legs.[17]

As Canton gave itself over to celebration, the returns carried her favorite son to victory. A comfortable margin of 20,000 separated him from Campbell, and the state legislature was Republican by nearly 50 votes. "The result is a great victory for the protective and financial policy of the Republican party," he wrote Russell Alger. The victory had other significance. "Won't McKinley be an important factor in the Presidential election?" Blaine inquired privately of Alger. "He is ambitious for it, and if you will notice Ohio has always had a Presidential candidate." [18] This aspect of McKinley's victory did not elude the victor as he noted with satisfaction his impression on the public at large.

The time for celebration passed quickly. "Need rest," he wired Hanna who invited him to Cleveland for a celebration. "Think therefore better not have jollification." He and Ida entrained for New York to visit friends, buy clothes, and rest, and also, as he said to reporters when stepping into his car, "to prepare a grist of appointments, thereby ending the agony." Though a minor illness kept him in bed later in December, he worked steadily on his inaugural address, legislative proposals, and the ubiquitous appointments.[19]

Severe weather did not deter the faithful at inauguration time, and when the Governor-elect mounted the capitol steps on January 11, he looked out over an impressive array. Party notables, many friends, and a host of supporters peopled the steps, plaza, and snowy lawns of the capitol grounds. His voice was clear and strong as he repeated the oath of office and accepted congratulations from his predecessor. The rotunda, in which he took the oath, was crowded by over three thousand guests, who stirred amid banks of flowers and bunting.[20]

In his address McKinley breathed the spirit of conciliation that had made him famous. Turning to members of the legislature in attendance, he said, "It is my desire to cooperate with you in every endeavor to secure a wise, economical and honorable administration, and so far as can be done the improvement and elevation of the public service." From generalities he passed to specifics: an appropriation for the Ohio exhibit at the Columbian Exposition, creation of a state tax commission to study the state's revenue problem, protection of workers in industry, a report on the Ohio canal system, revision of the voting laws, and redistricting of the state.[21]

The cheers that greeted him on emerging from the capitol were but a preview of a grand celebration. Nine infantry regiments and one of artillery paraded in their finest uniforms. Flags waved, supporters shouted greetings, and a citizens' parade marked his advent as a state leader. Canton and Stark County held places of honor in the lines of bands, YMCA groups, men's clubs, ladies' associations, fraternal groups, and political organizations that added color and excitement to the parade.

The new Governor liked the plaudits of the crowd and was his usual charming self to all comers, but he made it clear that while he recognized the limitations of his office, he would be more than a figurehead.[22] His chief concern was labor. His interest reflected his career as a labor lawyer, his understanding of labor's growing strength and changing status, and his sympathy with the working man's problems.

He immediately asked for legislation requiring the use of safety devices in dangerous industries. The hazards of railroading recommended immediate action. He seconded the demand of the state railroad commissioner that railroad companies be required to use automatic couplers and other safety devices. The Governor also recommended laws requiring railroads to furnish heated vestibules on their cars to protect conductors and brakemen from the freezing weather in which they often worked. This, he insisted, would prevent many bad accidents.[23]

A cause far closer to his heart, and one which reflected his concern for conciliation, was an abritration system to prevent and settle labor disputes. The scheme he outlined rested on four points: voluntary and free arbitration for parties involved; public interest in arbitration negotiations; just awards carried out by proper means; and impartial investigation into the causes of strikes, with full publicity. He used public opinion in the scheme because he knew from past experience how effective it could be, and he knew also that recalcitrant parties in labor disputes could be brought to conciliation much quicker by public opinion than by force.

Under his quiet direction a law embodying these principles rapidly passed the legislature. McKinley knew that many in his own party opposed recognition of labor's rights, and his tact and personal influence were effective in steering such legislation. Legislator after legislator emerged from the Governor's office convinced that such a system was necessary; yet he nowhere risked his prestige or influence by undue pressure or publicity.

The legislature followed the pioneering act of Massachusetts, and

Ohio became the second state to have a general arbitration board. It had its weak points, but it was a hopeful and, as it turned out, a good beginning. The board dealt with strikes involving at least twenty-five persons in the same industry in single counties or cities; it could not regulate railroads and was most effective in dealing with strikes in the coal and metal industries. In January, 1896, when McKinley left office, this board had successfully settled fifteen of the twenty-eight strikes and lockouts it dealt with.[24] It owed much of its success to McKinley's wise refusal to use the legislation for politics.

In April, 1892, again with McKinley's support, the legislature fixed $1,000 fines and six-month jail sentences for employers who refused to permit employees to join unions.[25] To a later generation such laws are antiquated, but to the 1890's even recognition of the rights of labor was unusual, and Ohio and the McKinley administration were thus in front of the van.

With these and other acts and public statements the Governor solidified his labor support. He did all this with little publicity and was loath to play to the labor grandstand. Faced with a threatened strike, he usually quietly asked labor leaders and employers to confer and arbitrate their differences; if this failed, he used his prestige with equal quietness. His tact, charm, courtesy, and the soundness and impartiality of his motives impressed everyone he met in these situations and made him a highly effective arbitrator. In July, 1894, he presided over one meeting of employees and employers of the Hocking Valley Railroad; by nightfall the strike was over, and traffic moved normally the following morning.

On at least one occasion he was irritated by those who accused him of courting labor's favor. He denied that he had advised employers to keep their factories running during election months to help his cause. "My whole public life has been devoted to the advocacy of a system which gave men employment and kept the shops running," he noted tersely.[26] He confided to one correspondent that he had figured prominently in several arbitration decisions but did not publicize his role because he did not want "to indulge in any pyrotechnics."[27] He also did not wish to jeopardize his neutral standing with too much publicity.

His second immediate problem was taxation. The wealthy state of Ohio suffered from an unequal distribution of the tax burden; real estate bore heavy levies while investments went almost untaxed. Despite some opposition within his own party, McKinley recommended the creation of a nonpartisan commission of experts to study the problem and make suggestions for new tax laws. The commission established reported to the legislature in December, 1893, recommending levies on corporations, franchise and use taxes, and a general levy on intangible wealth.[28]

The Governor had touched a sensitive nerve, for many of his backers were men of wealth and corporate influence. Hanna and Foraker found a temporary common meeting ground in opposing the legislation that ultimately taxed corporations and franchise holders.[29] McKinley deftly stood above the strife, though all concerned knew that his sympathies lay against the corporations. Again he refused to use the issue for partisan purposes, wisely seeing that he would crystallize opposition to the new tax program if he did. He remained silent, using private pressure to enact laws while making no enemies and losing no support. The laws finally passed during his second administration taxed railroads, foreign corporations doing business in Ohio, and telegraph, telephone, and express operators.[30]

The Ohio Canal Commission worked in obscurity and under many handicaps, for though the dilapidated and antiquated canal system was a financial responsibility to the state, the public knew little of and cared less for the problem. The McKinley administration could not offset this indifference, though it sponsored studies and proposals to renovate, sell, or close the canals.[31]

In the state institutions Governor McKinley followed a vigorous policy of efficient nonpartisan control. He appointed Republicans to the staffs of state asylums, orphanages, and prisons, but he did not remove deserving and efficient Democrats even when pressured to do so. When there were rumors of an asylum scandal, he immediately warned the officers involved to expect a full investigation and prosecution of any guilty parties.[32]

The ladies even got the vote in a small wave of ballot reform when in 1894 they were permitted to vote in school elections. Suffragettes hailed it as a victory, even though the law provided separate but equal ballot boxes for the sexes.[33]

When he faced the legislature in January, 1893, McKinley could point with pride to things accomplished and outline more things to come. Enjoining economy on that body, he also promised reduced expenditures in his department. He asked further appropriations for the state reform schools and a penal system for younger inmates designed to rehabilitate rather than punish them. He also repeated his demands for labor legislation.

He worked well with the legislature. His sense of dignity and consciousness of legislative prerogative earned the respect of the legislators and made him an effective if unspectacular executive. Many of his recommendations were uninspired, but others, such as his labor proposals, were sound beginnings. "Regarding the legislature, I think all fair-minded people will agree that it has been conservative, free from scandals, and has made a record that will be of strength to us in the next campaign," he said early in 1894 in an epitaph he could have applied to all his dealings with the state lawmakers.[34]

The political strategy behind his close attention to the state's affairs bore fruit exactly as he planned. His sense of duty compelled him to carry out his responsibilities, but he never forgot the road he was travelling to the presidency. By concentrating on state affairs he appealed to the people and politicians as an executive. He permitted the tariff issue to slumber until hard times after 1893 made him the prophet of prosperity. Once he had demonstrated his capacity for state leadership he could return stronger than ever to his familiar role of a national leader.

Despite the heavy work load he found time for a private life. His financial situation was sounder than ever before. Though the Governor's salary was only $8,000, without an executive mansion, living costs were lower in Ohio than in Washington. He and Ida lived in a small but comfortable suite of rooms in the old Chittenden House just across the street from the capitol. When the hotel burned, they moved to a new suite in the Neil House, with an ample apartment consisting of office, parlor, bedroom, dining room, storeroom, and maid's quarters. As in Washington, they rarely entertained because of Ida's illness.

Like most busy politicians, he got his information from people rather than books; after all, as he told his secretary, people wrote the books. His great gift for rapid assimilation enabled him to draw ideas from many people as if they were his own. His temper was as even as ever, though the Scottish stubbornness sometimes came through the surface. Opha Moore recalled his being irritated only once, when a visiting politician told him a dirty story. "I wish that fellow would stay away from here," McKinley said sourly.[35]

He did not devote all his time to politics and ceremonies. He often rode horseback with his staff and sometimes tempted fate and his silk hat by dashing ahead of them when they cantered in the countryside. Football was new to him and Mark Hanna, and when they attended the Princeton–Yale game, both were in a quandary. McKinley kept asking Hanna what was going on, and the latter had to admit that he didn't know. McKinley finally said that he felt like the country boy who said, "They didn't have no game; they got into a scrap and kept fightin' all the time when they ought to have been playin' ball." [36]

His chief duties were political, however. His "plain and practical style of putting things on the platform" appealed to a great many, and he was in constant demand as a speaker. In dealing with the crowds that came constantly to see him, he developed a special handshake known as the "McKinley grip" that saved him pain and discomfort. In greeting a man, he smiled and never attempted to overbear or impress his caller. The caller never got to him first, however, for the Governor seized his guest's fingertips and squeezed warmly before his own hand was caught in a vise-like grip. In the receiving line he took the caller's right hand in his own first, held him by the elbow with his left hand, and deftly pulled him by, smiling as the guest passed.[37]

Though he showed little humor in public, he was still a private tease. Young people had no rest from his wit, and he often chided fellow politicians about their calling. He told a visitor the story of the politician who declined baptism by immersion because he didn't want to be out of public view that long.[38]

McKinley's days were full, beginning early, for he was still an early riser. After a sound sleep he rose, shaved himself, breakfasted with Ida, and walked across the street to his office, carrying the morning papers under his arm and a supply of fresh cigars in his pocket. Thus fortified, he made an imposing appearance as he greeted passers-by. At the spot where his statue stands today, he always turned and waved to his wife, who watched from her bedroom window.

His large airy office, its windows opening onto the High Street frontage, its floors deeply carpeted, and its walls hung with paintings, was easily accessible to all callers. Answering letters was his first task. He had already developed the handy ability to answer a letter while reading it, and he dictated while walking up and down, the letter in his hand. He worked through his correspondence rapidly, for most of his replies were perfunctory. Occasionally he laid a sheet aside to be answered later in his own hand.

A system of electric bells summoned his secretaries, and he always had a cheerful greeting for them. Piles of carefully sorted newspaper clippings laid out by one secretary kept him abreast of world events. He interviewed private callers in a sedate anteroom, whose walls had no ears. His staff soon adopted their chief's habits of silence and dispatch, and eased his work load greatly.[39]

His chief concern, as always, was Ida, and no matter what transpired at 3 P.M. every day he opened his window to wave a white handkerchief toward the Neil House. Shortly an answering flutter would reply, indicating that she had seen his signal, an event that buoyed up her afternoon and proved that her "dearest" thought of her even in the midst of state business.

For the first time in many years, Ida's health seemed greatly improved. Perhaps the Ohio air agreed with her, or perhaps she was in the hands of better doctors. Whatever the reason, she seemed more tranquil, less subject to her erratic tempers, and better physically. McKinley's attentions to her still surprised friends and callers. Her slightest discomfort was a signal for swift action. "A thousand times I have seen him spring from his chair with an almost startling speed of movement to those not accustomed to his ever watchful care," one man remembered.[40] Her maid and her daily female callers, as well as her youthful nieces, eased much of her burden, as did her pride in her husband's position. The Major himself attended to many of her minor affairs, largely to please her and to show his devotion.

His own pleasures were much the same. A cigar, a substantial but simple meal followed by a glass of Apolinaris water, and good conversation was enough when he was home. He might take a short walk in the cool evening or read before the fire in winter, but his sedentary nature did not demand the strenuous life. Such occasional luxuries as oranges for breakfast were rare for him, and came only when he was a guest of wealthy friends such as the Myron Herricks.[41]

In 1892 the presidential contest brought him back into the national limelight. Frosty old Benjamin Harrison was still president and determined to be party leader as well. Those who opposed him would have their chance in the national convention of 1892; more than one party leader was anxious to see another man carry the Republican standard, for Harrison was not popular. Would McKinley's magnetism and standing with the people now make him a threat to leaders in his own party? As 1892 approached many wondered if he would sharpen his presidential ambitions or bide his time. Many favored him over Harrison. As early as January, 1892 his secretary wrote that "people around here are talking McKinley for president." [42]

The man causing the most immediate speculation was not McKinley but secretary of State Blaine. Would he oppose Harrison? Days before the convention met, Blaine resigned in a huff, and Harrison accepted the resignation with even more curtness than usual. Aging and ill, Blaine was not publicly a candidate, but his name still opened divisions in the party that boded ill for Harrison's forces. All the while, McKinley was lavish in his praise of the President and did not indicate his own aspirations. Senator Sherman declined to be a candidate, releasing Mark Hanna to work for McKinley.[43]

McKinley's precise position on the presidential nomination of 1892 was hard to define. He was even more silent than usual on this touchy issue. Would he be a reluctant candidate? Or would he merely let events take their course, honestly supporting Harrison? On the other hand, as Harrison's followers believed, did he play false to the President, with Hanna backing an active boom all the way? The young Republicans favored McKinley, and he could count on much Midwestern support if he chose to fight for the nomination. Thomas B. Reed's followers supposedly offered him a cabinet post if he would join their boom, an offer Hanna wisely declined.[44]

James S. Clarkson and Louis T. Michener, Harrison's adept managers, who could match coins with Hanna any day, watched the Ohioans suspiciously. Reports filtered in steadily that McKinley was an active candidate, but Harrison himself refused to believe it. "I cannot believe he will oppose me in any way," the President insisted, though McKinley's silence and shadowy movements irritated him. The Harrison strategy was to isolate McKinley as permanent chairman of the convention, where he could be watched on the platform.[45]

Late in April, the Ohio convention chose McKinley, W. M. Hahn, Foraker, and Bushnell as delegates-at-large to the national convention. McKinley's arrival in Minneapolis early in June prompted a boomlet that showed amazing vitality; his name was often mentioned as a dark horse and his mere appearance brought applause. "McKinley is the favorite of the dark brigade," a supporter wired Harrison. And Hanna insisted privately on June 9 that "Mr. McKinley can be nominated easily." Reports circulated that a McKinley boom would be built around Southern support. Earlier in the year, Hanna had done preliminary work in New York and elsewhere, testing sentiment for his friend. Privately he was saying that McKinley himself "has had a feeling that the lightning might strike him," and admitted candidly that he, Hanna, "had done a little work in that direction." [46]

Hanna even swallowed his gorge and spoke to Foraker, suggesting that they present a solid front for McKinley. Foraker was receptive, for he disliked Harrison and did not believe he could win.[47] Hanna talked with Platt of New York and Quay of Pennsylvania. Among Western delegates he found strength for McKinley, but warned the Governor's friends that his name would be considered only in case of a deadlock. In Kansas and Nebraska "the choice was almost unanimous for McKinley," and Hanna found many Midwestern delegates who would vote for McKinley after they fulfilled their instructions to vote for Harrison on the first ballot. Hanna was sure that "a word" from Allison or Gear of Iowa would bring the Corn Belt to McKinley's bandwagon. Hanna kept all this in mind, carefully noting McKinley's appeal in the Midwest, for he would use this information in 1895 and 1896.

By Thursday afternoon, Hanna was sure that the Blaine men would switch to McKinley; they were bitter at Harrison and remembered that Blaine had spoken kindly of McKinley in the past. He spent all night before the convention assembled trying to gather enough votes to prevent a first ballot victory for Harrison, as New

York and Pennsylvania "friends" assured him that if he could do so, they would follow into Ohio's camp.[48]

But the President's faithful "Twelve Apostles," headed by Michener and Clarkson, rapidly formed their lines and closed the breach. When the conclave gathered in the steaming heat, some fifteen thousand spectators knew in their hearts that they would choose Harrison again. It was so hot that resin from the green lumber in the roof showered down on the delegates, gumming their hair and ruining their clothes. But the heat did not dampen all the ardor, and frenzied demonstrations greeted each nomination. Blaine's name drew such a thundering response that Chairman McKinley restored order only by warning the delegates that their stamping feet would literally bring the house down. When Harrison's name was presented, the delegates rushed into the aisles again, and a lithesome girl in gray grabbed a banner with a war whoop to snake dance her way among the delegates for "Old Ben." [49]

McKinley presided with impressive dignity while the Harrison men worried about his reception. "The peculiar McKinley applause" broke out whenever he spoke or appeared, and many delegates saw in him their nominee for 1896.[50] He paid no apparent attention to the demonstrations, though the frantic reception accorded his keynote speech on the tariff heartened him. Even the Harrison men grumbled some faint praise for his impartiality in the chair.

When the balloting began, McKinley sat on the rostrum fanning himself. When votes were cast for him he looked down at H. H. Kohlsaat and shook his head, his face still impassive, and fanned faster.[51] When Ohio's turn came, Foraker cast 2 votes for Harrison and 44 for McKinley. Cheers and boos mingled in the confusion that followed, and McKinley gavelled the chamber into order before challenging the vote. Foraker calmly replied that since the chairman was not acting as a delegate he could not contest the vote, but McKinley ruled him out of order and ordered the delegation polled. The new tally revealed 1 for Harrison and 44 for McKinley; only McKinley's proxy voted for the President under instructions.[52]

When Texas voted for Harrison and gave him the nomination, McKinley left the rostrum and moved that the choice be made unanimous. Protests greeted this because the remaining states wanted their votes recorded. McKinley relented and the final tally gave

Harrison 535 votes to 182½ for Blaine and 182 for McKinley, with others scattered. Harrison had won, but not all his prestige and power had secured a unified nomination.

McKinley later adjourned the convention and hurried outside through a crush of admirers toward his hotel. The milling throng would not let him walk or ride, but carried him in acute embarrassment to his suite. Looks of agony flashed across his face as he realized while in transit that an exposed and gartered leg dangled helplessly in public view. Safely in his room, accompanied by Kohlsaat, he stripped down to his underwear to cool off. Hanna shortly joined them, exclaiming, "My God, William, that was a damned close squeak!" and promptly imitated their sartorial condition.[53]

The rest was anticlimax, but the air was full of recriminations, and even the Republicans sensed defeat. As Platt said, his New York delegates wrapped themselves in furs to ward off the chill of Harrison's nomination and returned home to face defeat. The President's managers were angry with McKinley and Hanna; they noted sourly that neither had tried to stop the McKinley boom as they had in 1888 when Sherman was threatened. Some even hinted that McKinley's attitude had cost him much support in the party. Harrison himself had only formal and congratulatory words for McKinley.[54]

The whole affair indelibly impressed Mark Hanna. Vivid recollections of the McKinley boom of 1888 rose in his mind as he watched the Governor and carefully noted the enthusiasm that his name inspired in delegations from all parts of the country. Everyone acknowledged him as McKinley's spokesman. He had indeed found the man with whom he might enjoy the vicarious power and pleasures of great national office. "The demonstration at Minneapolis convinced me that, although it was an impolitic thing for his interests to nominate him there, in the next national convention the popular demand for his candidacy would over-ride all opposition."[55] To focus and sharpen that "popular demand," and to give it endurance and impetus with a superb political organization became Hanna's driving purpose in the next few years.

Hanna saw no truth in charges that he and McKinley had been unfair to Harrison. "I do not consider that Governor McKinley was placed in any false position by what was done," he wrote Sherman.

"I do not consider that the administration have any right to criticize his actions because his friends—and I was at the head of it—took the responsibility of doing just what we did do. Governor McKinley's position today as the result of all that transpired at Minneapolis is in the best possible shape for his future. His bearing and conduct and personal magnetism won the hearts and respect of everybody." [56]

Hanna was sincere, but a touch of false innocence flavored his remarks. He knew how angry the Harrison men were over the profusion of McKinley buttons, placards, and streamers that littered their path to victory. Ears as keen as his had heard revolt in the cheers for McKinley. What exactly did Hanna and McKinley hope to gain by their little play at Minneapolis? It seems unlikely that McKinley would have sought the nomination against Harrison. On the other hand, he had no great love for Harrison, though he respected his Republicanism. He knew everything that Hanna did and surely gave him his blessing. Like Hanna, he secretly must have hoped for a deadlock, but at the same time he was undoubtedly not overanxious, for 1892 was not a Republican year and he could ill afford defeat. He was more anxious to have his name before the delegates and the country, serving notice that he was henceforth the leading contender for the nomination in 1896, when it would be far safer.[57]

Chosen to head the formal delegation of notification that called on Harrison in the White House on June 20, McKinley was obviously embarrassed by Harrison's coldly formal greeting; the group made their pronouncements and then dispersed into the state dining room for a frigid luncheon. Though McKinley had already publicly and privately praised the ticket, clearly there were those whose memories would be long.[58]

But whatever the frictions, he was a Republican of national prominence and he was eager to begin the campaign, even though Republican preparations were tinged with gloom. On June 21, 1892, he spoke on protection to a large crowd in Carnegie Hall. In the campaign that followed, states as far away as Maine and Colorado asked his services on the stump. At one time his secretary reported that he had 1,500 invitations to speak.[59] When election day brought its inevitable Republican defeat and installed Grover Cleveland in the White House a second time, McKinley had little to regret. As usual, he emerged from the fray with an enhanced reputation. "He is bound to be the nominee for the presidency [in 1896], and the very fact of the defeat this year will elect him the next time," his secretary noted.[60]

Resuming his duties as governor in the chilly winter of 1892–1893, McKinley had no premonition of the personal disaster that lay just ahead. One balmy spring-like day in February, 1893, he boarded a train for New York. The tang of spring in the air was matched by the bright carnation in his lapel and the genial smile he gave the well-wishers who saw him off. In his pocket was a speech for the Ohio Society of New York.[61] Fate intervened that day in Buffalo just as it intervened in the same city later in his career. The train stopped; there was an urgent telegram for the Governor. He excused himself from the conversation to read it. It told a simple story: Robert Walker, an old friend in Youngstown, had failed in business; his notes were being called; many were countersigned by Governor McKinley and he would be called upon to meet them.

Walker, a boyhood friend, had needed money for his business. In gratitude for loans as a young law student and later for small campaign contributions, McKinley signed notes believing that they amounted to only a few thousand dollars. When new notes were presented to him for countersignature, he took Walker's word that they were renewals. He believed that his indebtedness was limited; this, plus Walker's known integrity and apparent wealth, reassured him. Now the Panic of 1893 was upon the land, its shadow filling the threshold of every business house, and Walker was among the countless businessmen who were failing.

McKinley's face hardened as he read the message. The easy lines of geniality vanished and his eyes seemed dazed. In an instant the possibilities of the situation appeared to him. All his hard work, the years of sacrifice in politics, all the bright future with the great prize itself seeming within his grasp might be swept away. He cancelled his speech and sped to Youngstown. As the train raced over the rails, for once he lost his composure. He resolved to give Walker "such a talking to as he would remember the rest of his life." He spent the early morning hours with friends in Youngstown and in hasty conference with his brother Abner. He would not rest. "I cannot sleep; I must see Walker," he exclaimed. "I must understand the situation before I can rest for my whole future, politically and financially, is involved in this." Upon seeing his old friend his anger melted, and his harsh reproof became the gentle admonition: "Have courage, Robert, have courage! Everything will come out all right." [62]

The story broke in the newspapers, and after his talk with Walker, McKinley issued a statement denying that he was connected with Walker's business. "I was not interested with Mr. Walker to the extent of a dollar in any of his enterprises and only endorsed for him as a friend, believing that he was wealthy and that I would not be called upon to pay," he said bluntly. He had never known that Walker's liabilities exceeded $20,000.[63]

By now offers of help poured in. "My purse is open," H. H. Kohlsaat, part owner of the Chicago *Daily Inter-Ocean* and a strong Midwestern Republican, wired from Chicago. Haggard from anxiety and lack of rest, McKinley went to Cleveland to meet his friends. Kohlsaat, Myron Herrick, William R. Day, and others gathered to help. The Governor was obviously strained; black rings bordered his eyes and his voice shook. Asked the extent of his liabilities, he shook his head and answered honestly, "I don't know—it may be $100,000, $200,000, or $500,000." Time was of the essence and McKinley's friends moved rapidly. While they talked, the Governor's weary footsteps echoed as he paced up and down an upstairs bedroom. Finally he came downstairs and said despondently, "I have kept clear of entanglements all of my life. Oh, that this should come to me now!" Looking around he said: "I wish Mark was here." [64]

The newspapers retailed conjecture and speculation but generally sympathized with McKinley. "The financial troubles of Governor McKinley will be learned with deep regret not only in Ohio but all over the country. He has been a liberal, kind hearted man and has always done more for others than for himself," a Columbus paper noted.[65]

McKinley at once made it clear that he was liable for the debts. If necessary he would retire from public life and practice law to raise the money. Mrs. McKinley was visiting in Boston at the time but hurried home on hearing the bad news, to place her property at her husband's disposal. His friends protested that this was not necessary and that she must not impoverish herself. A native stubbornness repelled such suggestions. "My husband has done everything for me all my life," she snapped. "Do you mean to deny me the privilege of doing as I please with my own property to help him now?"[66]

When the initial shock passed, McKinley quickly regained his composure and soon acted as a stabilizing force on the others; his native caution and emotional detachment enabled him to see the problem as a whole. His friends set quietly to work, while he himself stayed briefly with Herrick, "sweating blood," as he tried to learn the full extent of his indebtedness.[67] Hanna finished the business that had detained him in the East and hurried to Cleveland. Walker's affairs were tangled. When assured that the sum involved was $20,000, Herrick breathed a sigh of relief. Then the figure rose to $50,000; in a few days' time it was over $100,000, far more than McKinley could possibly pay.[68]

With McKinley's approval, Hanna, Herrick, Day, and Kohlsaat constituted themselves his trustees and began acquiring the outstanding notes and undertook to manage the McKinleys' property. Attempts to dissuade Mrs. McKinley were fruitless, as the pair assigned all assets to the trustees. Finally Hanna agreed to accept Mrs. McKinley's property with the private understanding that it would not be used.[69]

McKinley and his friends had feared the inevitable publicity. Would it not be said that a man who foolishly signed blank checks and who could not manage his own finances was not fit to be governor of Ohio, much less president of the United States? Surprisingly, this was not so; instead, a wave of sympathetic understanding surged toward McKinley from all parts of the country and all classes of people. His kindly nature and great popularity among the people, the fact that men in similar situations welcomed so august a personage as the Governor of Ohio to their ranks, and the refreshing spectacle of an honest politician publicly going broke produced sympathy rather than disfavor. "I am receiving an excessive mail and so full of comfort," McKinley wrote Herrick shortly after the disaster.[70]

Many correspondents feared that Mrs. McKinley might be left penniless. "My mail [is] overflowing with sympathy and the most earnest protest against Mrs. McKinley turning over her property," he wrote the trustees. A mutual friend said bluntly, "Because McKinley has made a fool of himself, why should Mrs. McKinley be a pauper?"[71]

The McKinleys acted wisely from the first, in good faith and with full publicity. "He and Mrs. McKinley have of course acted nobly in determining to pay all," noted a member of the Governor's staff. "I am inclined to think, however, that his many and wealthy friends will look after his interests fully." [72] McKinley's "many and wealthy friends" were even then hard at work raising a private fund to save his political future. The four trustees worked quietly and efficiently to avoid speculation in the outstanding debts. McKinley handled public relations, though he was unaware of the full scope of the trustees' project. Herrick remained in Cleveland and directed the whole affair. Day looked after the legal details, and Hanna and Kohlsaat shouldered the onerous task of seeking funds.

McKinley returned to his duties in Columbus and left all details to the trustees, with whom he was in constant contact.[73] Nevertheless, through devious channels news concerning their proposed fund reached him. Though surprised and gratified, his deep sense of integrity and Scottish pride would not permit it. He penned a lengthy statement disclaiming such a fund. "While appreciating this noble generosity on their part, I cannot consent to the use of this fund for the cancellation of my debts." He instructed the trustees to acquire the debt, paying "dollar for dollar, but I insist that they hold it, as an obligation against me to be paid off as fast as I can do it. I cannot for a moment entertain the suggestion of having my debts paid in the way proposed or in any other way than I have herein indicated, so long as I have health to earn money." He was deeply moved by his friends' generosity. "But you and other of my friends must know that, feeling as I do, I must respectfully and gratefully decline the application of the contributions from my fellow citizens to the payment of my debts." [74] And so the matter rested as far as he was concerned; he assumed that the trustees would buy up notes to be held until he could pay them in the future.

But that was not the plan of the trustees. Oblivious to the Governor's stubbornness, they went about their business. Field agents visited prominent men and talked with much tact and caution of McKinley's predicament; after all, McKinley was not a "beggar," as Herrick pointed out.[75] Many wealthy men were willing to donate, but they did not know how long it would be before they joined the Governor in bankruptcy.

Of all the men who engaged in the affair, none went with heavier heart than Mark Hanna. His genuine affection for McKinley and his belief in him were well known, and it was no secret that he longed to see his friend in the White House. The whole affair hit him as hard as it did McKinley, and at times this and his own worries dragged him down into depression. "I have no heart for any other work until McKinley is relieved from this awful strain," he wrote.[76]

A public subscription materialized despite McKinley's protests. Contributions addressed to him or to "the McKinley fund," ranging from nickels to dollars, poured in on the trustees and the Governor. Though these contributions would have paid the debts, McKinley announced publicly that he would not accept them; his pride was still inflamed. Judge Day did not see how they could keep people from sending their money if they wanted to.[77] Strange things happened. Many former comrades from the Civil War repaid old debts and made additional gifts. After reading about his troubles, one man whom he had helped years before returned the loan with interest. Strangers offered to lend or give substantial sums.[78]

McKinley kept only those contributions he considered legitimate and returned the rest.

Satisfying as it was to know that the public sympathized, McKinley also realized that he could not risk political entanglements in accepting funds. "There are lots of well-meaning people in this world that want to give a dollar to raise the Governor's debts, and in doing it would raise his hair at the same time," Kohlsaat noted with the shrewdness of a born reporter.[79] Hanna was especially alive to the political complications and insisted that "we are doing this in a semi-confidential way and will not receive any money from persons except those who give from *proper motives*." [80] He was not one to wipe out financial debts with political liens. Several large contributions were refused when it became apparent that they would later entail demands for patronage. As Herrick put it, "That fund had to be as free as human foresight could make it of any implied obligation." [81] If favors were promised there is no known record of it.

By early March, McKinley rested easier as light penetrated the financial gloom. Hanna's circle of industrialist friends gave generously and he was ruthless in his search for funds. He exchanged no promises for cash, but he reminded them of how much McKinley had helped them in the past. It would be folly to end his career now when he and his principles stood so near a national success that would benefit them all. Hanna's many friendships and his force of character loosened more than one pocketbook.[82]

Some fellow politicians were wary, though most faithfully followed Hanna's and McKinley's lead, reflecting the loyalty which both men drew from subordinates. Senator Sherman was, as usual, cautious. He offered to help, but his lifetime in Ohio's cut-throat politics showed him the heart of the matter. "If his liabilities are [too] . . . great it is hardly worthwhile for us to help." [83] In the end the politicians recognized a threat to McKinley as a threat to themselves; they could not afford to lose their best vote-getter.

Hanna suffered no doubts as he contacted friends. John Hay sent a check for $2,000 together with kind words. Hanna invaded Pennsylvania, where Philander Knox gave $500, while promising more; he moved to the Carnegie works, where he drew $2,000 from Henry Clay Frick; in Ohio, Charles P. Taft gave another $1,000.[84] In Illinois, Kohlsaat discreetly lunched and dined with a variety of businessmen. Nobody could help a bankrupt, he was told; times were hard and money scarce. But the talkative editor was as relentless as Hanna, and sessions over brandy and cigars generally loosened checkbooks. The Illinois Steel Company chipped in $10,000; George Pullman was asked for $5,000; and Philip Armour gave $5,000. Under Herrick's blandishments, Ohio banks holding McKinley's notes discounted them 10 per cent as a donation to the fund. By June the fund seemed large enough to insure the Governor's future.[85]

Neither national catastrophe nor personal misfortune could stay election days. When the crisis calmed, the McKinleys vacationed briefly in the South. In Washington, he parried all political questions with a combination of deft charm and guile. "Matters political are now out of season, too early, and wouldn't be timely," he told reporters with a smile.[86] He continued on his way, sure of renomination, knowing that the financial disaster had not dimmed his public popularity. Hard times only added luster to his name, and he was shortly boomed as "The Advance Agent of Prosperity," an odd title for a bankrupt.

By late May, two weeks before the state convention, there was no doubt of his renomination. The delegates to the convention greeted his name with cheers. He treated them to a thumping stump speech on the tariff, discussed Democracy's hard times, and paid passing attention to the currency question that daily assumed more and more national prominence. Condemning the Cleveland administration's lack of action, he shrewdly saw its chief weakness: "With a gold president and a silver congress what can be done?" [87]

He mapped out a campaign that took him into 86 of the state's 88 counties to deliver 130 speeches and shake thousands of hands. Warning of overconfidence, while grateful for the popularity of his name, he did not rest until election day. In September he began campaigning in earnest in Akron, where huge labor delegations greeted him. He donned a white plug hat, given him by a delegation 3,000 strong from Canton, and spoke on the tariff and prosperity. Six hundred kilted Scotch steel workers led the booming parade that followed, and flowers decorated his progress. Calls for out-of-state speakers went unanswered, for as D. B. Henderson of Iowa said, "in your state you have this year a walk away." Tom Reed did come to help McKinley, and indulged in his usual sarcasm. In Cleveland, when a Democrat heckled his speech and was about to be put out, Reed called, "For heaven's sake, don't put him out. It would be an insult to such a night to put the fellow outside." [88]

While McKinley campaigned his trustees continued their duller work. By September they reported that collections and pledges exceeded liabilities, and by November they closed their books with a stern admonition that the Governor watch his affairs more closely. McKinley arranged for Herrick to manage his finances, a task which the Ohio banker fulfilled admirably until his friend's death eight years later.

As his financial problems faded, the people of Ohio gave McKinley a plurality of 80,000 at the polls, the greatest gubernatorial victory since the Civil War. In the moment of victory, he must have reflected on what his friends had done for him. From potential tragedy they had wrought a miracle; they administered over $130,000 worth of notes and left his property intact. Over 5,000 people, high and low, contributed to the McKinley fund, and the trustees' efficiency was such that no claim was ever filed against the McKinley estate. Absorbed in politics and trusting his friends' judgment, McKinley had not known until after his re-election that his debts were paid. When he demanded the subscription list that he might repay the donors, the trustees refused. There is no evidence that any of the donors ever asked to be repaid, or were repaid, or that any political favors were ever given in return for funds.[89]

The most amazing aspect of the affair was the attitude of the people at large. Poor men as well as rich donated to the fund. McKinley had patently been negligent; he may have been a tariff expert but he obviously could not keep his own checkbook. This very disinterest in money redounded to his favor with the people, and they felt him more than ever to be one of them. Some deep chord of understanding was struck between him and the many who also felt the pinch of hard times. "The estimation in which you and your noble wife are held today by all good men is worth many times more than all the wealth of the Vanderbilts and Goulds," wrote one hitherto unknown admirer.[90] The affair did not dim his presidential aspirations. As he looked toward 1894 and a second inauguration as governor of Ohio, McKinley's future seemed brighter than ever.

Grover Cleveland used to call 1894 his year of troubles, as well he might, surrounded as he was by economic depression and social unrest, and facing formidable Republican opposition at his front while fellow Democrats sniped behind him. In the nation's long agony in the grip of the darkest depression of the century, social discontent flared forth. The quack, the honest but misguided man, the desperate radical all waxed strong and grew eloquent on the tragedies of that unhappy year.

As it was for Cleveland, so it was to be for the Governor of Ohio. Ohio bore her share of depression's bitter fruit. Things were so bad that McKinley suggested that the national guard forego appearing at the inaugural ceremonies; most of them were young men who had been out of work, and the ceremony would be a hardship for them. But an impressive array of uniforms and well-wishers greeted his inauguration on January 7, 1894. His address was brief. "A short session and but little legislation would be appreciated at a time like this," he told the legislators. In closing he stated his own view of government: "The best government always is that one which best looks after its own, and which is in closest heart-touch with the highest aspirations of the people." [91] William McKinley understood the kind of democracy that reflected the will of the people.

The depression hit Ohio's coal miners and railroad workers with special severity; layoffs, lockouts, and the tensions of chronic unemployment sharpened tempers on all sides. Governor McKinley's ties with labor were strong; labor leaders befriended and advised him, and he sympathized with much of organized labor's goals, a sympathy which the workers returned at the polls. It would presumably be politically dangerous to move against labor. Yet McKinley never hesitated to fulfill what he considered to be his larger duty to Ohio even if it meant antagonizing labor and using force. In the great strikes of the spring of 1894, when warned that the national guard might lose him many votes, he turned in irritation upon his counsellors. "I do not care if my political career is not twenty-four hours long, these outrages must stop if it takes every soldier in Ohio." [92]

McKinley had little to lose in using force to halt strike violence. Refusing to use the national guard as strike breakers, he dispatched no troops until all local resources had been exhausted. He conferred privately with labor leaders, who understood his situation and who were impressed by his firmness and sense of duty to the state. They knew that he was not a "company man" but a harassed state executive trying to preserve order.

In March, 1894, coal miners growled with discontent, and McKinley told local authorities that he would furnish troops if necessary. But the break in the labor problem came late in April, when the United Mine Workers ordered an estimated 200,000 men out of coal mines to protest against wage cuts and bad working conditions. McKinley, a friend of the UMW's John McBride, supposedly called McBride to his office and warned against violence. "John, you have gone too far," the Governor said. "If you do not stop it before evening, I'll order out the entire National Guard." [93]

Late in May angry miners attacked strikebreakers and attempted to halt nonstriking railroaders. In Cincinnati for Decoration Day, McKinley received a telegram announcing that Glouster, Corning, and Athens were in the hands of mobs, and local authorities were powerless. He immediately dispatched troops, who were roughly handled at Glouster. To allay public fears of a general labor war and to stiffen resistance to violence, the Governor made it clear that he would use troops as often as necessary. When striking miners stopped trains, national guardsmen rode the cars through the mobs, despite showers of rocks and glass.[94]

While negotiators talked, the Governor stated that he would withdraw troops from any area that became pacified; he was conscious not only of the political disadvantages, but also the expense to the state. As a sign of confidence, Ohio banks loaned money to the state to pay the national guard. By mid-June, McKinley could write: "We have really been in a most critical situation the last week or ten days, but happily, I think the worst is over. I am glad to know that my course has had the approval of the people. . . ." Ohio newspapers of both parties by and large supported him.[95]

Even the labor troubles of Illinois intruded on him, and the famous Pullman strike brought him wakeful hours. He sent Abner on a discreet mission to George Pullman in Chicago. The workers had just grievances, Abner said; it would be wise to compromise; public opinion would turn against the party in this election year; conciliation was the spirit of the times. Pullman listened and then politely but firmly told Abner to mind his own business. The little encounter said much of Pullman and more of McKinley. True, the latter was alive to the politics involved, but he interceded mainly on behalf of the workers.[96]

McKinley often stayed up late at night following reports, and he sometimes watched the guardsmen depart for troubled spots. He displayed his usual calm firmness during all the crises. He preferred, as he had said, to work through arbitration without any "pyrotechnics." He much preferred to meet with the parties involved and settle their dispute quietly without publicity. He was firm but kind with strikers in a year and in circumstances when other people advocated severe repressions. The inevitable reaction after strike violence turned public opinion against the workers. "Bridge burners, train wreckers and highwaymen are usually shot on sight," one out-of-state newspaper fumed in criticizing McKinley's "softness" on the strikers. If he paid any attention to such things, he said nothing, but his home town newspaper probably spoke for him when it said quietly, "If some coal operators in the craze of competition did not forget that coal miners are human beings, the expensive coal strike might have been averted." [97]

Social unrest added to McKinley's problems. In Ohio the demand for relief from the depression culminated in "General" Jacob S. Coxey's "army" of unemployed, who began their march on Washington from Massillon, Ohio, the visionary Coxey's home. Asking for public works financed with long-term federal bonds and the issuance of paper money, the army travelled through Ohio into Pennsylvania. Passive resistance and sheer numbers won over many towns as the men foraged across the countryside, bumming food and free train rides in what one newspaper called "the longest free lunch on record. . . ." The railroads naturally resented nonpaying fares, and when the army swarmed into empty boxcars and refused to budge, local authorities called for militia. Troops evicted the men without violence or ill feelings, gave them a day's uncooked rations, and moved the trains in a normal manner.[98]

In the ugliness of social strife, race hatred also broke out. In Washington Court House, Ohio, a Negro was convicted of raping a white woman and jailed for transport to the state penitentiary. Mobs formed and milled about the courthouse, threatening lynching. Tempers flared and liquor did the rest. The sheriff wired the governor for troops, which came under the command of Colonel A. B. Coit. Coit warned the crowd to disperse and then barricaded his men in the courthouse. When the crowd attacked the jail, Coit's men fired, killing two and wounding a dozen men. Indicted for manslaughter, Coit was involved in a long and expensive trial that resulted in his acquittal in 1896. McKinley sent his congratulations and asked the legislature to pay the trial's full costs. "We want to remember that the freedom to make laws does not give the freedom to break them," McKinley reminded his constituents later in the year. By 1895 the violence had all but disappeared, and there were only two calls for the militia that year.[99]

Meanwhile, McKinley showed his human sympathy in a striking way. Early in 1895 he received reports that many miners' families were on the verge of starvation in the hard-hit Hocking Valley. A committee of citizens from Nelsonville called on him to ask for immediate action. Appalled, he acted swiftly. He contacted leading merchants and bankers in Columbus, and by five o'clock the next morning a relief train was on its way; arriving four hours later, its supplies averted real hardship and possible famine. A group of citizens and the state's chambers of commerce organized a fund that paid for the supplies and kept them circulating to needy areas. In the end, some 10,000 people received such relief at a cost of nearly $50,000.[100]

Even labor violence and social discontent did not stay the hand of politics; 1894 was a crucial election year for the Republicans, for hard times and the inflexibly conservative image of Cleveland's national administration would bring them victory. In the Democrats' disaster lay McKinley's opportunity; a year of Democratic rule had fulfilled all his dire predictions, and the tariff and prosperity issues identified with his name gained tremendous force. He now went forth as the spokesman of prosperity and Republicanism.

Despite pressing duties at home, McKinley was on call for Republicans everywhere, and the demands on his time now far exceeded those of 1892. He spoke in Maine for protection; in St. Louis he filled an immense hall with cheering faithful; and a train tour brought him in contact with the leading politicians of the Midwest. He spoke 371 times in 16 states, making 23 speeches in one day as his train crossed Nebraska. State committees and local groups vied for his presence, and school children, farmers, workers, young ladies bearing flowers, and everyone who was curious or concerned crowded around him. His dignified figure and clear voice impressed many, while his right hand sawed through the air to strike the open fingers of his left hand when he made a telling point. His voice rose to an almost evangelical pitch over many crowds, who agreed that although he lacked the barrel-organ qualities of many contemporary orators, he was indeed effective.[101]

He displayed at a whistle stop in Kansas much of the understanding of people that made him successful. At Hutchinson the train was scheduled to stop in the depot, but the crowd was so large that the engineer stopped some distance away so that the official party could make a safer exit. As he alighted from his car, chatting amiably with Governor Morrill of Kansas, McKinley immediately noted the discrepancy in distance. Quickly asking why they stopped so far away from the crowd, he was told that it was to spare him discomfort. "Oh, you should not have done this," he answered. "A man in public life cannot afford to avoid the people." He then walked through the crowd to make amends. Later in the afternoon a dense crush of people confronted him in the town square where he was to speak, and it seemed that the official party could not even reach the platform. Turning to Governor Morrill, McKinley said, "Now, Major, you follow me and I will take care of this crowd. Don't be uneasy, I won't get hurt." So saying, he approached the edge of the crowd and began shaking hands. As he did so, the people respectfully fell back and cleared a path for him and his party.[102]

The election results satisfied McKinley's best expectations. The Democratic Congress was swept out by a lopsided Republican majority in both houses; the tariff and gold standard were safe for the time being. He himself had gained the ears and respect of countless people in the Midwest and East, and more importantly, he gained the allegiance of local party officials and workers. At the same time he deftly entwined his name with prosperity and protection, the two issues which he hoped would be the backbone of the campaign of 1896.[103]

With that election won, he moved inexorably into Ohio politics. He did not desire a third term. As a show of unity he publicly endorsed Asa Bushnell, Foraker's lieutenant, and privately agreed that Foraker should have his Senate seat in 1896 in return for support in the presidential contest. Campaigning for Bushnell in the fall of 1895, McKinley had the satisfaction of seeing him elected by a slightly larger margin than he himself had received in 1893. The trend was Republican everywhere.[104]

As his term drew to a close, Ohio paid McKinley a final accolade. He shared honors at the inauguration with Bushnell, and every effort was made to show him the respect and affection due him. In a valedictory to the legislature he spoke fond words of his state and fellow citizens:

> I shall always cherish these evidences of their confidence and regard. I wish for them, one and all, happiness in their homes and prosperity in their several fields of labor . . . May this good old state, with all its proud achievements and precious memories, be preserved under a wise Providence for still grander achievements in all that constitutes a free, happy and prosperous commonwealth.

Arriving in Canton as private citizens, the McKinleys faced the inevitable parade. There were roses for Ida and accolades for the Major, followed by an evening serenade. When these were over, McKinley disappeared into the quietness of his study and began work on the already pressing problems attending his campaign for the presidential nomination. In his life there were few moments of rest and almost no time when politics did not claim his attention. There was to be no role of private citizen for him now or ever again. "It is just plain Mr. McKinley of Canton, now; but wait a little while," the *Repository* said.[105]

The governorship of Ohio was not an empty office for McKinley. True, he was not a great governor, but perhaps the office did not permit executive greatness. It gave him executive experience. It taught him how to work with legislators. It gave him a national platform from which to speak. It enabled him to weld his stand on protection into a national call, gave him Ohio's convention votes, took him far and wide across the country in an endless chain of publicity that made him the leading contender for the Republican nomination of 1896. The social and economic crises of his tenure enabled him to demonstrate his methods of acting and gained him further respect in responsible circles. Whatever else it had been, the Ohio governorship had not been a hollow honor. And now, as the spring of 1896 emerged gradually from the snows of discontent, he intensified his own political work. As the *Repository* said, "wait a little while."

X

The McKinley Boom

LIFE IN CANTON as an ex-governor had its compensations. The Major and Ida spent more time together and with old friends. Long evenings before the fire became more important to them than the hectic grind of daily politics, and McKinley walked the streets of his home town with a greater freedom than he had known in years. He was always a familiar figure there, but he was now a famous man, next in line, his neighbors were sure, for the presidency itself. People smiled and congratulated him, stopped him on the streets, pointed him out to visitors when he stopped in the drugstore for Ida's medicine or talked horses with the blacksmith.

The McKinleys redecorated their old house on Market Street, and in the flush of their first real home life in over twenty years, he and Ida recalled their youth. "We have got back our old home in Canton, keeping house for the first time in twenty-two years, and in the house [in] which twenty-five years ago we took up our house-keeping as newly married people," he wrote Whitelaw Reid with a touch of almost boyish pride.[1] In the midst of his retirement he celebrated his twenty-fifth wedding anniversary, and gifts from friends and admirers all over the country heightened the occasion.[2]

But both William and Ida knew that their seclusion was short-lived; in fact, it was not real at all. The long-distance telephone called the Major back to the demands of politics hourly, and a steady stream of important visitors and floods of mail reminded him that he was in the midst of a complex, crucial, and difficult struggle for the Republican presidential nomination. Reporters shadowed his home, and servants set the table nightly for twelve, always assuming that some important guest would stay for dinner after political talk.

McKinley was busier than ever in 1895 and especially after leaving the governorship in 1896, gathering delegations and swaying public opinion to his side. A dry fatalism hung over his work; he believed that destiny had secured this role for him. As early as 1892, he told a Boston host that he would be elected president. Recalling his wartime experiences, he remembered that he had told his mother no harm would come to him. He felt the same about political battles.[3]

Destiny or not, McKinley was in a pre-eminent position in the Republican party. His national reputation, the product of years of party work, his personality, which had influenced literally millions of people, his lack of real enemies, his geographical location, and above all his political and economic nationalism made him "available" in every sense of the word. His widespread political contacts now paid him well. Prominent men from coast to coast boosted his chances and joined his cause, reflecting a steadily growing belief that in the midst of depression he was best qualified to restore prosperity. His standing with the people was unquestioned. "McKinley has a great diffused strength all over the country, and is, in his own mind, almost certain of the nomination," John Hay wrote in the spring of 1895.[4] Mark Hanna himself, whose belief in the people's desire for McKinley was sincere and unflagging, wrote: "He is undoubtedly the popular choice of the Republicans of the country, and would . . . prove the most available and safest candidate." [5]

He knew the dangers of running too early. As John Hay put it, "A year is a good while in American politics," and Whitelaw Reid was even more blunt: "A boom for '96 which starts in '93 is in danger of withering before harvest time." [6] Nonetheless, McKinley and his advisors decided upon a quiet and efficient campaign to keep him in the public eye, and his tours during the campaigns of 1892 and 1894 amply justified their contention that he was the Republican front-runner.

The organization that carried him to victory rested chiefly on the labor of Marcus Alonzo Hanna, who had dreamed since 1888 of putting his friend in the White House. There is remarkably little written evidence of their friendship. Few letters passed between them, for each preferred face-to-face conference and private emissaries. They were undoubtedly close; in effect their minds functioned as one. Intuition dictated much of their affairs. While McKinley could shake hands, make speeches, write courteous and thoughtful notes, and smile his way through conferences and receptions, he had a curious lack of talent for party organizational work. He needed someone who understood him and his appeal to organize his cause for victory. That man was Mark Hanna. Hanna's chief genius was an understanding of men. As he began to organize the McKinley boom he too knew few details of political organization. But he learned quickly that politics are men; who knows one knows the other.

Hanna's relations with McKinley were widely misunderstood in his own time. Cruel caricatures lampooned Hanna, among the first to treat with organized labor, as a huge bloated creature feeding off workingmen. McKinley, who had proved his integrity and ability during twenty-five years in public life, was the monkey on Hanna's string. Many—and not only Democrats—imagined that Hanna was the master, when in fact he was the loyal lieutenant; that McKinley was the tool, when in fact he planned and approved the strategy that brought him victory. But those who watched them closely saw that Hanna was the subordinate. William Allen White noted that Hanna was "just a shade obsequious in McKinley's presence . . ."; Charles G. Dawes knew that the Major gave the orders; and the shrewd Kohlsaat said that Hanna's attitude toward McKinley was "always that of a big, bashful boy toward the girl he loves," a story that Hanna liked and repeated.[7] He was seldom informal and never familiar with McKinley, treating him with respect and deference in private as well as in public. Hanna often said that his association with McKinley, whose inflexible morality he admired, made a better man of him; without McKinley's steadying influence, Hanna might have become merely another party boss, like his Eastern contemporaries.

Hanna deeply loved his great friend. As early as 1892 he wrote:

> You are not mistaken in your opinion and standard of McKinley. He is all you believe him to be and as true as steel. Nothing short of a miracle or death will prevent his being the nominee of the party in '96, and to that end I have enlisted, to accomplish which I am prepared to be politic and patient, but if to secure it sharper weapons are required I shall not hesitate to fight with the same sword I have often used in the interests of our mutual friend, John Sherman.[8]

He worked for the Major out of affection and respect. "I acted out of love for my friend and devotion to my country," he said simply in 1896, after he had succeeded in his mission to elect McKinley president.[9]

McKinley's essential objectivity, which enabled him to master so many crucial situations, governed this relationship too. But he admired Hanna sincerely, respected his talents, and appreciated his efforts. Acutely conscious of his own reputation, he knew what other men said of his relationship to Hanna; he saw daily in 1896 the cruel cartoons and knew the malicious whispers of men who often smiled at him, though not once did he ever acknowledge them.

Hanna came to his work with a philosophy that complemented McKinley's. His directness and essentially unintellectual attitude gave him the basic clue to American society in his day: material wealth was the key to power. Spreading it evenly in some form of national prosperity was the great mission of the American system. The Republican party was the implement of that mission. He did not fear the power of business in politics, for he assumed that this meant greater wealth for all. And yet he never trusted the political judgment of businessmen, for their thoughts ran too easily in the narrow, complementary grooves of mere economics and class consciousness. They were too apt to panic, with a lack of insight that belied their failure to understand the complexities and needs of the total American social and political system. In the dark days of 1894, labor unrest had provoked his wealthy friends to talk of revolution, a view which Hanna dismissed with a snort. Years later he argued with Roosevelt that the Grangers had been useful citizens; Roosevelt thought them maniacs. Government must function as the clearing house of nationalism, as the go-between for all the elements of the nation—labor, capital, farmer—to preserve the critical balance of disparate forces that made the amazing American system work, he felt. He was a Hamiltonian in believing that those who owned should also rule, but he tempered and expanded this belief with a genuine respect for people and an understanding of the system's needs that made him far more than another big businessman or a mere political boss.

McKinley's attitude was essentially the same, though he was more alive to the subtle political and social complexities of the problem. He was less interested in gaining political power for business than in making the nation prosperous. If the one went with the other, he did not question it. His deep belief in the people's judgment and his abiding understanding of their wants and needs told him that they would correct whatever abuses the system produced. As the great nationalist of his day, he rose above sectionalism on the force of the tariff issue, seeing in the economic system it protected the secret of American greatness and success. The people at large, with all their diverse and conflicting interests, concerned him; their wealth and prosperity were his party's trust. Balance was the key to success. His Whiggery came of age in 1896, and he won his battle because he spoke from a national platform, on national issues, and offered national solutions. The Republican party, which had triumphed after the Civil War on the force of its coalition of sectional interests into a national framework, found in him the ideal statesman to protect its golden age in the late nineteenth century.

McKinley's patient waiting and long attention to nationalism paid rich dividends in the years after 1893, when the shadows of poverty and social strife blotted out Democratic arguments and added fresh luster to Republicanism, and especially to his name. The fiasco of tariff reform in the Wilson-Gorman Act of 1894, which became a hiss and a byword, the Democrats' inability to solve the currency question, and the Cleveland administration's failure to answer social discontent with anything but repression worked directly in McKinley's favor, for he was widely recognized as the chief spokesman of the opposite policies. In the Democrats' disaster lay his great opportunity.

Throughout McKinley's terms as governor, Hanna carefully fostered his interests, awaiting the time when he could begin a full-fledged movement to make him president. In January, 1895, Hanna formally retired from his business to devote his full time to McKinley's cause, sensing that the time had come to form an organization. With customary directness and a certain naivete he went to New York to consult with the Eastern Republican bosses. Tom Platt, Matt Quay, Nelson Aldrich, Joe Manley and others conferred with him behind walls that revealed no secrets.

Returning to Cleveland, Hanna, elated by his success, described the powwow to his chief. McKinley and Myron Herrick listened attentively one evening, after a leisurely dinner, as Hanna outlined his success. "I don't suppose you saw anything about that meeting yesterday in the newspapers, did you?" he asked as he lit a cigar; he was proud that the newsmen had not caught him. He smoked a moment and turned to McKinley. "Now, Major, it's all over but the shouting. Quay wants the patronage of Pennsylvania; Aldrich, of New England; Manley, of Maine. Platt wants New York, but he wants it in writing; you remember he was fooled on Harrison." He paused and then said innocently, "I think they are willing to leave this region to me."

McKinley listened silently as Hanna outlined what he thought was the easiest and surest way to gain the nomination. He thought a moment after Hanna finished, watching his cigar smoke curl its way toward the ceiling, then his face grew serious. "Mark, some things come too high. If I were to accept the nomination on those terms, the place would be worth nothing to me and less to the people. If those are the terms, I am out of it." Hanna looked surprised, but quickly raised his hand. "Oh, no, not so fast. I mean that on those terms the nomination would be settled immediately, but that does not mean that their terms have got to be accepted. There is a strong sentiment for you all over the country and while it would be hard to lick those fellows if they oppose against you, damned hard, I believe we can do it." In his heart, Hanna must have known that McKinley would never agree to any such "easy" arrangement; his moral probity rejected it at once.

McKinley's features softened and he sat quietly for a while looking into the distance. His intuitive contact with Hanna seemed almost to materialize. Finally he turned and asked, "How would this do for a slogan: 'The Bosses Against the People'? How would that sound?" Hanna slapped his thigh and agreed; it became the McKinley movement's official slogan.[10] McKinley saw at once the essential flaw in Hanna's scheme: it worked against public opinion. Far wiser in the ways of the public mind than the average politician, he knew that people could no longer simply be manipulated; the days of easy bossing were over.

It would be foolish and naive to hold that Hanna and McKinley did not bargain for support in building their boom. Both were realists and experienced at the game. But they were practical as well as moral: why promise anything before arriving at the position of demanding something in return? McKinley saw immediately that once he were nominated, if he carried public opinion he could demand

188

party loyalty from the bosses; he could always gain more by working with public opinion than by avoiding it.

The organization which Hanna now swiftly whipped to perfection rested first on McKinley's personality and public record, but a host of devoted subordinates labored for victory. Joseph P. Smith, the Ohio state librarian; Charles Dick, Hanna's most trusted aide and ultimate successor in the Senate; William McKinley Osborne; Abner McKinley; and others travelled discreetly to distant areas, sounding public opinion and conferring for their leader. McKinley himself remained silent throughout 1895 while he was governor; it would be unbecoming and perhaps dangerous to campaign openly. He preferred to lay the organizational groundwork while other politicians slept. Hanna's home was headquarters for meetings, and he hosted numerous powerful politicians. Congressman Charles Grosvenor kept a close eye on prospective delegates to the national convention. Issues of friendly newspapers found their way into the homes of delegates and alternates and influential Republicans. Copies of McKinley's speeches, printed at Hanna's expense, went across the land. McKinley badges, posters, and buttons flooded through the mails until one opponent exclaimed with the voice of experience: "McKinley has plastered the land with his literary bureau." [11] While other candidates and managers waited on fate, McKinley insured his own with hard work. "If Mr. Hanna has covered every district in the United States in the same manner that he did those in Alabama, McKinley will be nominated, . . ." Senator Chandler of New Hampshire noted.[12]

While Hanna and his agents took to the field in 1895, McKinley worked steadily at home in Columbus and then in Canton. By early 1896, with his machine in high gear, he suffered writer's cramp from signing his name to nearly three hundred letters a day. Working fourteen hours a day, he permitted himself little relaxation except his incessant smoking. His whole political life had prepared him for this gruelling task.[13]

And always there were the calls for speeches. "No man in this country is in such demand," his secretary noted.[14] His every appearance signalled demonstrations. In Pittsburgh his speech on the tariff in 1894 was so successful that the audience passed him over their heads to the door when he finished.[15] Conscious of the powers of the press and with an unusual reputation among newsmen, he freely granted interviews, though he seldom said much. "He can be both communicative and guarded and not mix the two efforts," one man noted.[16] In 1894 and 1895 he travelled on tour in a private railroad car and conversed with politicians in public so that the people could see that he made no deals. When he was receiving visitors in the car, the curtains were always open and his large wicker chair faced the door, whose knob banged against the backs of fluent politicians, reminding them when it was time to go. He missed few tricks in convincing the people that he was not a machine politician.[17]

His tact and charm as well as his caution were evident in dealing with favor seekers from other states. Declining to express an opinion on rival factions lest he seem to meddle, he informed one correspondent, "I do not 'swing delegations.' That is out of my line." But he did not hesitate to give professional advice. "Look over the ground carefully; make a quiet but strong canvass of the delegates; be sure you have the strength, and if you have, then instruct," he wrote a cohort.[18]

Everywhere he went, McKinley boomed the tariff issue, anxious to avoid silver and to capitalize on his long record of economic nationalism. He freely attacked the Democratic administration. "It set out to reduce the cost of living and instead has reduced living itself." [19] Readers who opened their Cleveland *Leader* in mid-November, 1893, saw McKinley's face rising like the sun over the dawn of prosperity; he was henceforth the Advance Agent of Prosperity.[20] So intensely did his organization center on protection that one opponent noted bitterly: "McKinley is making his whole capital on the theory that he is the only protectionist." [21] And a correspondent told Matt Quay that "McKinley's whole point seemed to be to keep the tariff question to the front and to ignore the financial question." [22] The policy paid off in support from businessmen, labor, and Republicans in general, for as Whitelaw Reid noted, they were far more united on the tariff than anything else.[23]

McKinley now claimed the support from labor that he had built so carefully over the years. "I am proud to say that among my warmest and closest personal friends are some of the leaders in the great labor organizations of the country," he wrote.[24] Labor delegations called on both him and Hanna to pledge support.

McKinley's discreet refusal to answer all queries on the currency question drew acid fire. Platt accused Hanna's agents of talking gold to gold men and silver to silver men. The long-winded free silverite, Senator Stewart of Nevada, demanded that the Major declare his stand but got no answer for his pains. And acerb Tom Reed was reminded of the circus where "there was always at least one first class acrobat who could ride two horses at once." Elsewhere, opponents dubbed McKinley a "political trimmer" and a "prince of straddlers" on the currency question.[25] McKinley knew political dynamite when he saw it. Aspiring to run on the tariff, he would not add momentum to the silver question by explaining his stand on it; nor would he risk alienating support by doing so. Caution triumphed over a courageous declaration that might have cost him strength.

Hanna in turn accused his opponents of using McKinley's silence on the silver question as a needle to further their own interests. McKinley stated flatly that he would not run on a free-silver platform; he was a bimetallist, but beyond that he would not go. He preferred to meet the challenge after the nomination. "I think our people will re-enact the currency platform of 1892, and then stop," McKinley wrote privately, illustrating how badly he misjudged the sweep of silver sentiment. Little did he know that mere bimetalism would not do for either party in 1896; or perhaps he did know and preferred not to admit it.[26]

As the McKinley boom gained steam late in 1895 and early in 1896, it gained enemies. Fellow politicians awoke to their danger; rival newspapers sent reporters to manufacture scandals. McKinley's financial integrity was assailed; his loyalty and principles questioned; his subservience to Hanna stated. "Hanna will shuffle and deal him like a pack of cards," the vicious Hearst press said. But there were no hidden scandals, and the men around McKinley were so proper that all the venom settled on the long-suffering Hanna who, though he had grounds for libel suits, never yielded to the temptation.[27]

The most curious muckraking came from the anti-Catholic American Protective Association, which had tangled with McKinley before for refusing to exclude Catholics from his state appointments as governor. Now the APA publicly stated that McKinley, Hanna, and their followers were the Pope's agents. Publicly McKinley remained silent, stating his indignation only to those who came to see him, while he privately assured men like Russell Alger that such "stories told about me are base fabrications or else the veriest kind of twaddle." [28] One more given to publicity would have rallied Catholics by denouncing the propaganda, but McKinley was unwilling to touch the issue. To answer it would give it prominence.

Erratic Ohio was a key to the McKinley boom. She must back her favorite son without division. Hanna and McKinley once again assured Foraker of their desire for unity. Early in 1895, McKinley denied that he was a senatorial candidate, clearing the doubts from Foraker's mind. When Foraker was duly elected to succeed Calvin Brice early in 1896, McKinley congratulated him, and "Fire Alarm Joe" agreed not only to support him but to nominate him at the national convention. On March 10, 1896, the Ohio state convention endorsed McKinley, repeating an action it had taken the previous year. Ohio was safe.[29]

Hanna began his national campaign in earnest in the South, for it was the weakest link in the national Republican chain and an area whose capture would automatically place McKinley in the lead. The Southerners were really "an immense dress parade," as one man noted, for they cast no Republican electoral votes; but they sent delegates to the national convention. They had been the core of Sherman's support in 1888, though they broke for Harrison that year, a mistake that Hanna would not allow in 1896.[30] McKinley was no stranger to the South. His speeches there in 1892 and 1894 were sellouts. Hanna bought a pleasant cottage in Thomasville, Georgia, ostensibly for winter vacations, but actually to enable McKinley to meet leading Southern Republicans in quiet and gracious surroundings. To this charming retreat the McKinleys bestirred themselves in March, 1895, for what the Major stoutly insisted was only "a little rest and outing"; after all, he was not an announced candidate. He had already expressed indignation at the "ridiculous" construction placed on one of his meetings with Hanna.[31] The little pantomime fooled no one, and Southerners knew that he came to "discuss the condition of little Miss Boomlet. . . ." [32] For some days the visiting statesmen came and went through Mrs. Hanna's delightful sun parlor. Oranges and lemonade were the order of the day as McKinley charmed even the Southerners. He treated all as friends and confined himself to generalities interspersed with talk of the tariff and Democratic mistakes.

Leaving Thomasville, the Major and "Colonel" Hanna, with their small but loyal force, undertook a march to the sea that carried them through Florida and thence to Washington for talks with John Sherman. The Major was still publicly silent on politics and gave exhaustive dissertations on the weather when badgered by reporters.[33] His charm, dignity, and sense of responsibility impressed many Southern delegates. His deft stand in favor of Negro suffrage without force skirted a dangerous issue; Louisiana loved him for the tariff on sugar; Florida appreciated protection for citrus; Texas, West Virginia, and Kentucky were impressed by his statesmanlike temper. Clearly he had the edge over Republican opponents in the South.[34] Hanna's careful work in that section paid rich dividends. He needed 453½ votes to nominate McKinley, and nearly half that number came from the South and border states.

All this travelling, the posters and buttons, the printing and newspaper subscriptions, cost money, and opponents hinted that it came from "improper sources." Hanna hotly denied that he bought anyone or anything, or that he used funds improperly. "I say that charge is absolutely false," he said in a red flash of temper. ". . . I have never found it necessary to create sentiment for McKinley. In every state of the Union the movement has been entirely spontaneous."[35] Smiles played around the mouths of reporters and politicos. Spontaneous indeed!

Doubtless Hanna did not bribe anyone outright but he used funds liberally to establish organizations and buy materials. He wrote a friend that McKinley's associates had not contributed to his campaign "because he is very much averse to that method," and said flatly that "the use of money to influence votes is not a method that I favor at all. This campaign must not be one in which money is used for other than necessary expenses."[36] McKinley himself returned many fees advanced for speeches and sought no funds, though friends like John Hay, Philander Knox, and Russell Alger donated from time to time. Hanna himself bore almost the whole cost of the boom. "I am putting up the money needed thus far for McKinley because I did not want to ask assistance until I knew more about who his friends were to be." [37] The most obvious source was dry, for national protectionist groups would donate no money for the very good reason that all the leading Republicans were protectionists; they would support no one until he was safely nominated.[38] Local protectionists in New England, Illinois, and parts of the South did, however, provide both funds and a focus for McKinley's boom in their areas. Hanna spent some $100,000 of his own funds on the McKinley boom.

Not until late 1895 and early 1896 did fellow politicos awake, and then they found the Hanna organization far in front. They saw at once that Hanna's strategy was to secure the Southern bloc, appeal to labor, industry, and the middle class on prosperity, and to avoid the currency question in favor of drubbing the Democrats with the prosperity theme. The McKinley organization, well staffed and with ample funds, was in high gear, ready to carry the Major's cause into any state. McKinley aimed to secure state delegations pledged to vote for him, and if that failed, to secure endorsements for him on the second ballot. McKinley men everywhere were careful not to offend fellow Republicans publicly; party harmony was, after all, their chieftain's watchword.

The most obvious Republican contender was former President Harrison. Fully as close-mouthed as McKinley, Harrison kept his own counsel. Business interests eyed his past record, his geographical influence, and his prestige. Though Platt hoped he was not a candidate, one watcher reported a "strong undercurrent for Harrison," and Hanna himself said bluntly, "I consider Harrison as much of a candidate as anyone and I know the 'little game' his managers are trying to play." [39]

Privately Harrison assured everyone that he was "only taking a citizen's interest in politics. . . ." [40] Yet he knew that his name counted in political circles and he was undecided about a draft. "I do not like to appear to be in the attitude of the little boy that followed the apple-cart up the hill, hoping the tail-board might fall out," he wrote Senator Elkins.[41] Finally, Charles W. Fairbanks, a loyal Indianan, approached the chilly old General and said frankly: "If you, General, wish to be a candidate, I shall help you. If not,

I am for Major McKinley." [42] Harrison assured Fairbanks that he was not a candidate and early in February, 1896, he publicly announced that he would not seek the nomination.

Harrison's withdrawal sparked a scramble for Indiana's votes, for she was an important weather vane in the crucial Midwest. McKinley was clearly in the lead. "There is no use trying to disguise the fact that McKinley has a very strong pull in the state . . ." a Harrison advisor wrote.[43] Anti-McKinley attempts to secure an uninstructed delegation that might be swung to someone else at the convention failed as Indiana Republicans repaid the Major for his many campaign forays into their state.[44] Hanna's strenuous efforts rested on his belief that Harrison's withdrawal was sincere.[45] Indiana's endorsement of McKinley was a long step toward securing the Midwest.

The former President's withdrawal posed another problem. His supporters had hoped to rally sentiment around him to halt the McKinley boom; had they been able to do so, Hanna's organization might have failed before Harrison's prestige. The Eastern bosses, defeated in Indiana, had chosen another tactic: they would establish favorite sons in every state, scattering delegate strength until the convention, forcing McKinley to face the field, hoping that they could control a compromise candidate. Seasoned veterans thought that "they cannot otherwise control against McKinley," for as John Hay noted, "The McKinley boom shows curious and increasing vitality. . . . If he holds on till June he will be nominated, unless a combination of all other elements takes place against him—and such a combination will be extremely difficult." [46]

Undoubtedly, Platt, Quay, and other Eastern bosses did have a tacit "combine," the term that Hanna used against them, to stop McKinley. Their power was clearly threatened, they wished to control the final choice, and they wished that choice to come from farther East than Ohio. Chauncey Depew quite candidly stated that except for the favorite sons, McKinley would sweep all before him.[47] The scheme had its dangers, of course, and Governor Morton of New York perceived its adverse effects on public opinion, counselling his backers to avoid the appearance of all evil.[48] As the combine emerged and the bosses obviously set their faces against McKinley, his stock rose with the public. As Senator Mason of Illinois said drily, "Nobody seemed to be for McKinley except the people." [49]

McKinley himself happily surveyed his progress in February, 1896. "Things are looking well all along the line," he wrote. "Indeed, they could not well look better. Every new entry in the field, it seems to me, has a tendency to weaken the Eastern friends." [50] The bosses' inability to control all their entrants also worked to his advantage. But the chief danger was overconfidence. "Don't let Mr. Hanna underrate the desperation of the combined opposition, or forget that they have all the money they want," Reid cautioned. [51]

As McKinley surveyed the field in the Midwest he saw a real potential threat in the form of the senator from Iowa, William B. Allison. Ideally suited to speak for his section, possessing an impressive record on silver, and eminently safe to the business interests, the experienced Iowan posed a substantial potential threat. His caution, smooth political ability, and power and prestige in the Senate gave him a reputation for effective legislative ability. He was always a greater threat than the more public Speaker Reed, for he was exactly the kind of noncontroversial, pliable man the bosses could use to break up the McKinley boom in a deadlocked convention.

Harrison's withdrawal sent many of his followers to the Allison camp, though ultimately most of them came over to the Major. Publicly Harrison endorsed no one, but privately he favored Allison. [52] Through 1895, Allison steadily refused to announce his candidacy and protested that his friends loved him too much, protestations that McKinley and Hanna took with more than a grain of salt. [53] The Senator's bimetallist record appealed to many, especially in the crucial West and Midwest, and his supporters sent out printed material boosting him. [54] The talk over coffee and cigars in many private dens was that the combine would turn to Allison when everyone else died on the vine; he was clearly the second choice after McKinley in the Midwest. [55] Nor were his supporters idle. Touring the Midwest in a private railroad car dubbed the "Davy Crockett," they drummed support with farmers and businessmen. A McKinley follower wrote presciently that "the activity of the Allison people in parts of the West is a little disquieting." [56]

McKinley approached the Allison boom with great care, for he could not afford to alienate any Midwestern support. Warning his lieutenants not to step on the Senator's toes, he publicly praised Allison and granted him every right to be a favorite son; after all, he had never interfered in other states' politics, he said.[57] McKinley chose silence and behind-the-scenes work, counting on his own organization and prestige to carry him through.[58] Allison's chief weakness was his personality. His grayness fitted him for compromise and manipulation but not for presidential leadership. He was ideal in the Senate, but was unsuited by temperament and background for the stronger duties of the presidency. "He seems to have the good will of everyone," one man noted succinctly, "he comes from the right section; he has an excellent record. He is, however, rather colorless and nobody seems to be particularly enthusiastic about his candidacy." [59] McKinley pursued the wise course, even when Allison challenged him in Illinois, and won in the end. Though he remained Iowa's favorite son, Allison on convention eve had no hope of being struck by lightning.[60]

McKinley's most obvious public opponent was not Harrison or Allison, but Speaker Thomas B. Reed. Like McKinley, Reed was a party regular, rigidly devoted to party principles. A familiar figure on stumps from Maine to Colorado, he too could command the loyalty of men in many states. His caustic wit, which reflected a genuine if cutting ability, also reflected a cynicism that McKinley lacked utterly. A master of legislative maneuvering, he was also a strict disciplinarian, with little regard for public opinion. Nominally a gold-standard man, his views on the currency alienated some, and when he gently tried to change them, he alienated still more. His fame was his weakness, for his rigid beliefs, caustic tongue, and ultraconservatism made him unpopular outside of New England. Unlike McKinley, he had not consciously tried to build a set of nationalistic principles. Told by a friend that he was the man of the hour, the convention's logical choice, Reed answered with a becoming mixture of false modesty and realism: "The convention could do worse, and probably will."

McKinley knew at once that Reed's real strength lay in his contact with the Eastern party leaders and in his national reputation. As early as 1892, the Major had sounded his own strength in Boston, where he was a familiar and respected figure for his tariff stand.[61] Reed supporters, on the other hand, disliked what they called Mc-

Kinley's "trimming" and his equivocal stand on the currency question, which was important to New England. "I like a bold, strong character, a man who has the courage of his convictions and who has convictions, and so I almost intuitively leaned toward Mr. Reed," one of the Speaker's followers wrote.[62]

As 1895 opened, Reed's position seemed potentially good. Powerful Republicans like Lodge, Manley, and Aldrich supported him.[63] Hoping to stem this tide, McKinley went to Hartford in the spring of 1895 to speak discreetly before the nation's first McKinley club, founded by a wealthy dilettante, John Addison Porter. The Major's reception gratified him, and he wrote John Hay that "the sentiment [was] in every way most favorable." [64] He had entered his wedge in New England.

Reed refused to campaign, maintaining that his duties forbade it, but privately he loathed McKinley and unleashed his acid tongue on his former colleague with unequalled ferocity. This hatred lasted until McKinley's death and finally drove Reed from politics. Reed's weaknesses were clearly his sectionalism and his stand on gold; the former gave him no real appeal outside New England, and the latter meant that he could not carry delegates in the crucial West and Midwest.[65] As long as he remained silent, he seemed cold and aloof. Never a charmer, he did nothing to offset his adverse public image, choosing to run instead on his record and position as a party leader. "The reasons which are pulling me are old ones and result from the position I have taken the whole of last year," Reed wrote in January, 1896, in declining to speak for himself. "It [seems] to me more consistent with the position I am in and the duties I have to perform to keep myself always free from the charge of going about seeking something people would not give me if I did not seek it. You know what comments the unjust make in a sinful world. Then, having broken the rule, I should offend all sorts and conditions of men by refusing to repeat the fracture." [66] It was a curious attitude for a politician, but it reflected Reed's long security against defeat in ultra-Republican Maine, a security that McKinley never had in Ohio. This attitude delineated the basic difference between the two men and the wings of their party. Reed could afford rigidity; McKinley could not.

Hanna quickly saw that a break in New England would cripple

Reed's chances, and he carefully nurtured the McKinley clubs in that heavily protected area. The Major's face was as familiar in industrial centers as Reed's, and the organization poured in a steady stream of literature and speakers. As Reed's rage rose, so did the Major's strength. And all of this came without a public challenge to the Speaker, for as McKinley said, it would not do to meddle in another state's politics—except privately.

In New Hampshire, Senator Chandler worked hard for Reed, thinking he was a bimetallist, but failed at the last moment. The McKinley men there secured an endorsement of both Reed and Mc-Kinley in the state convention, and cracks appeared in the Reed wall that widened into a major fault in neighboring Vermont, where Red-field Proctor steered an endorsement of McKinley through the state convention late in April, 1896.[67] The walls of Reed's Jericho were tumbling down.

In Massachusetts, Reed advisors candidly admitted that they could hardly hold their delegates as McKinley sentiment filtered through their ranks.[68] Senator Gallinger of New Hampshire, who lacked "Wild Bill" Chandler's volatile temper and Reed's sarcastic tongue, had a realistic if hard view of the situation in New England:

> . . . you will be disappointed in your view that New England will be solid for the great Speaker. [McKinley] has a thorough organization, which is not true of any other candidate, and in politics organization counts for more than anything else. Mr. Reed made a great mistake when he was nominated for Speaker in not taking a more aggressive attitude on public questions. . . . I know McKinley reasonably well, and am bound to say that I think you do him un-intentional injustice in your well meant criticisms. I know him to be a scrupulously honest man, and if he makes mistakes it will be those of judgment rather than intention.

Noting that Reed was McKinley's only real opponent, Gallinger assumed that McKinley's nomination was "a foregone conclusion" if the Speaker failed.[69]

Though Reed's remaining supporters held together, they clearly would break for McKinley on a second ballot. The Reed men were always the bitterest of McKinley's opponents, making liberal accusations about his alleged weakness and Hanna's use of funds. Reed himself detested both the Ohioans who defeated him. "Now we can make no mistake about this," a bitter manager exclaimed. "McKinley has out-generalled us all to pieces." [70]

While the major candidates sparred back and forth and their organizations worked to catch up with Hanna's commanding lead, the combine strove desperately to organize a bloc against McKinley. One of their key pivots was Matthew Stanley Quay, the Republican boss of Pennsylvania. Matt Quay was no ordinary political boss, and no ordinary man, for that matter. Suave, dignified, cultured, he was a past master at political manipulation. He conferred with men as easily as McKinley and his tastes ran to good conversation, fine wines, and luxurious surroundings. As a chief Harrison lieutenant in 1888 he proved that he could win the most doubtful of elections, given men and money. He was also the equal of many men in literary circles. A close student of Greek and Latin literature, he was fluent in both dead tongues, and carried the ancient authors, as well as political know-how, in his elegant pocket. Unassuming, though a senator from Pennsylvania, he ran his bailiwick as smoothly and deftly as a great business, which it was to him.

Pennsylvania's big delegation figured prominently in Hanna's plans, as his preliminary conversations with Quay showed. Quay must first have wondered if the realtively inexperienced Hanna could actually weld together an organization, but he was a shrewd judge of men and never underestimated an opponent. With time, he saw in Hanna the wave of the future and accorded him the respect of an equal. After his chief vetoed any deals with Quay, Hanna worked assiduously in Pennsylvania, establishing McKinley clubs and feeding a steady stream of literature into the state. If Quay would not deal on the Major's terms, they would challenge him.[71]

Quay professed friendship and was eager to keep a foot on the bandwagon should the McKinley boom get out of control. He publicly praised McKinley while he privately greeted all inroads into Pennsylvania with ruthless retaliation. Through 1895 he was charming and cordial to all ambassadors; his smiles lighted the trips of trusted agents as Hanna sought his support without the customary strings or bargaining. But Quay dealt from both sides of the deck, and late in January, 1896, John Hay warned Hanna that the Pennsylvania boss's promises were worthless; he had conferred with Platt, and insiders bet on Quay's secret support of Governor Morton of New York. Quay and Platt could deal better with each other than with Hanna.[72]

Quay had an iron in every fire; dexterity was his trademark. In mid-February, 1896, he announced his candidacy as a favorite son, and Pennsylvania was his. Angered by what they considered his duplicity, for they had thought him about to break for McKinley, Hanna's agents demanded an end to "coddling" Quay. Congressman Charles Grosvenor wanted a full-scale fight, with clubs and offices in every county of the Keystone state.[73]

But Quay was hardly finished. In April he boarded his private car for a trip to Canossa; he would go to McKinley himself for a talk, Latin grammar in hand. The smiling Major met him at the station, dined him, talked to him for several hours, and then, still smiling, saw him off. What they said was their secret, but tremors ran through both the Reed and McKinley organizations. Was this the break that would kill Reed and insure McKinley's success? Other anti-McKinley men were angry with Quay for seeming to deal with the Major, for it weakened the favorite sons' movement.[74]

But Quay surrendered nothing, for McKinley would not deal on his terms. The Major knew by now, as did Hanna, that he could win without bargaining; his dream of entering office unfettered by demands seemed about to become a reality. Quay kept control of his favorite-son votes, hoping to bargain at convention time, but when that time came, Hanna was past bargaining. Quay remained cordial and outwardly calm toward the McKinley group. As late as mid-May he could write the Major, "There is no antagonism toward you anywhere in Pennsylvania except what arises from the alliances Hanna seems to have made with the municipal thieves of the two great cities of our state." [75] The letter must have brought a smile to McKinley's face and a frown to Hanna's.

While Quay straddled and dickered, a foot on two bandwagons and holding out for more, his neighbor in New York, Tom Platt, grew increasingly spiteful toward Hanna and the McKinley men. He did not like Hanna's organization, nor did he savor defeat in having backed the wrong man. Like Quay, he was no ordinary mortal. Small, wiry, bearded, and bald, he moved with a trace of languor that belied a man given to thought rather than acrobatics. He was the "Easy Boss," for he hated contention. His iron grip on

New York's "Organization," whose capital letter was an icon to him, rested on detailed organization, trusted lieutenants, and an immense boodle fund, little of which lined his own pockets. A man of fairly simple tastes, he lusted after power, not wealth; he gave his whole being to scheming, and politics was his ideal mold. Years in New York's vicious politics put an edge of cynicism on his senses that no amount of charm could dull. He smiled, he promised, but he trusted no one. He rose the hard way, from selling patent medicines to the inner circle of Roscoe Conkling's powerful machine. The passing of "Lord Roscoe" left him momentarily in the shadows, but his talents for the devious gave him absolute control of the New York party by the 1890's. "What Tom wanted, Tom got," the old timers said. So did Mark Hanna. Their meeting on the field of political battle would be an interesting clash.

Platt had no ambitions for himself beyond a Senate seat. He chose another and more willing instrument for his presidential scheme, Levi Parsons Morton, the aging Governor of New York. Any man who commanded New York was a formidable adversary, but the conservative, dull old Morton also had a national reputation. He had been Harrison's vice-president and was a familiar figure in party councils, especially in the East. If Reed was the recognized Eastern leader, Morton was that section's most likely dark horse.

Morton was potentially formidable. His solid pro-gold record endeared him to Eastern financial interests, and Platt's backing provided him with astute managers.[76] If he could force McKinley into the open on the currency question he might rally support for his sound-money stand. Realizing this, Hanna early entertained him, and his charm impressed the aging statesman, though they did not trade promises.[77]

In reality, Morton was merely Platt's stalking-horse. The Governor's position seemed formidable, but he was a member of Platt's machine, which traded on his past record and known integrity. He was old, sectional in outlook, and utterly devoid of popular appeal. Even those around him accepted his candidacy as a front for Platt; apparently only Morton took it seriously. Behind this sheep in wolf's clothing Platt mounted his crusade to stop McKinley, or at least to force him to bargain for the nomination.

Late in 1895, Platt wrote Morton candidly that Hanna was hard at work. "He has already captured much Southern territory (some of which he cannot hold when you get in the field). . . . As I have intimated before, it is the present purpose of certain men of the 'Old Guard' to stand together in the final 'round-up' and secure the nomination of a stalwart Republican who will not forget his promises and *cheat his friends.*" Tom had not forgotten Harrison's refusal to bargain in 1889. Pledging his and Quay's support—Quay seems to have supported everyone—he urged the Governor to set to work. "Missionaries (discreet men) must be sent at once to the South." [78] Waxing optimistic on such flattery, Morton followed Platt's every wish.

The faithful Republicans in New York tendered their Governor a dinner, where Chauncey Depew told his usual inane stories and Morton announced that he would accept the nomination. Feeling it unwise and undignified to campaign or seek support, Morton left such dirty work to his friends, who took the whole project with elaborate mock seriousness.[79]

Morton had toured the South late in 1895, and his reception gratified him, but his "missionaries" were laughed out of the section, securing pledges from only four Southern delegates.[80] The McKinleyites in New York rallied with swift decision, carrying literature into the rural sections and sponsoring speakers and organizations in the cities. "I think this combination of Quay–Platt–Clarkson and others is for Reed and this Morton candidacy is to throw us off our guard," Will Osborne wrote his cousin.[81] He was never more right, though the bosses were more for themselves than for any candidate. Characterizing the Morton boom "a stale little farce," and condemning Platt's "snap conventions" in the rural districts, the McKinley men kept up a steady pressure to avoid endorsement of Morton at the state convention. They failed, for the Governor was New York's favorite son, but they showed their strength and McKinley's popular appeal. So many New Yorkers were pro-McKinley that it seemed doubtful that Platt could hold his lines; in fact he did not, for seventeen New Yorkers voted for McKinley on the first ballot at the national convention. On the eve of the national convention, Morton's agents gave up in disgust and admitted that "there was no use keeping up the appearance of a fight any longer," though they put his name before the convention.[82]

Hanna's lines lay in dozens of places, and his private car heated the rails between conferences and meetings. His drive and energy, as well as the momentum of success, kept his organization in high gear after January, 1896. Sour notes from New York and Philadelphia, plus Reed's growing irascibility, indicated that the bandwagon was running successfully. Bitter at being bested by an amateur, the Eastern bosses stubbornly refused to surrender, and Hanna and McKinley turned to the fertile Midwest, where large blocs of delegates were more friendly.

Illinois was crucial to the McKinley forces. Its large group of delegates would comfortably increase the Major's lead, but more importantly, the state boasted a favorite son whose destruction would show other uncommitted states the power behind McKinley. The state was boss-ridden, and victory there would prove again the truth of McKinley's slogan, "The Bosses Against the People." Illinois' favorite son was her senior senator, Shelby Cullom, distinguished chiefly for his work on interstate commerce regulation, and known for a fancied resemblance to Lincoln. He could be little more than a favorite son, for he had neither strength nor appeal outside Illinois. But if he could beat Hanna in Illinois he could give his mite to the Eastern bosses and perhaps hold the Midwestern line against McKinley.

Hanna had a stroke of good fortune in Illinois in gaining the services of Charles G. Dawes of Chicago. A self-made man, the youthful Dawes had built up an impressive gas business in the Windy City and her suburbs. Quiet and plain, his appearance was highlighted by big ears and a large mouth. "He doesn't *look* much," Hanna exclaimed after first meeting him. But his extraordinary efficiency and his burning desire to introduce business methods into politics caught Hanna's fancy. Dawes asked nothing for his services and paid his own expenses. He was consumed by a deeply felt ambition to help make McKinley president. His father had served in the House with the Major and introduced his son, as a boy, to the great man. The young Dawes never forgot the impression McKinley made on him. He hated the Republican machine in Illinois, and vowed as he began his work that he would "make the machine sick before we get through with them." [83]

Illinois newspapers were not overly enthusiastic about McKinley for they were controlled by the state machine and conservative editors. At first only Kohlsaat's *Times-Herald* lighted the gloom in Chicago, but Hanna forwarded prepared editorials from other newspapers for wide distribution. McKinley clubs sponsored rallies, picnics, parades, and speeches; volunteer workers carried the word from block to block, even in Cullom's home district. Dawes reported in March that the machine verged on surrender, but others urged complete victory. "If we fight to the end there must be but one result, and that is you will carry the state solid; that means more than even the voting of New York solid for McKinley," Osborne wrote Dawes.[84]

Kohlsaat's paper published daily reports of McKinley's growing strength in the Midwest and West which captured the interest of businessmen and farmers.[85] McKinley had declined to campaign in any state, but his casual appearance before the Tippecanoe Club in Chicago at the height of the battle in Illinois, and his "magic name" elsewhere, drew thunderous applause. And all the while the eager and methodical Dawes kept the Major posted by long-distance telephone.[86]

Efforts of Allison men to catch Cullom's votes failed as they fell under the Hanna steamroller. Cullom himself was angry at McKinley's "invasion" of Illinois, but vacillated on what to do; his pride was at stake, but he did not wish a showdown with the Hanna organization. "He wants to withdraw but cannot without deserting his friends and abandoning his hopes," a McKinley advisor wrote.[87] This was sweet music to Dawes' ears, and others around McKinley counselled a final drive to nail Cullom's aspirations as a lesson to others. "He must be crushed if he still continues to resist the friendly overtures that have been so generously extended to him." [88] What those overtures were no man knows, but it is not likely that Hanna promised much, for victory was already his. McKinley had refused to deal with the machine; it must be taught a lesson.

The lesson came home with telling force when an uncontrollable state convention endorsed McKinley on April 28. The victory was complete, and Dawes smiled with satisfaction as an earthquake of cheering greeted his hero's name. Swathed in confetti, streamers, posters, and ribbons, the Major's lieutenants enjoyed the snake dances and demonstrations around the floor as Illinois broke for the

Advance Agent of Prosperity. It was a handsome victory: the Midwest seemed secure; Allison was utterly routed; other state leaders were warned that to hold out would invite defeat and loss of later favor. "The very air is full of McKinley," one man wrote.[89] On hearing that Illinois had abandoned Cullom, William Pitt Kellogg of Maine, a Reed manager, threw up his hands and exclaimed, "That settles it; McKinley will be nominated." [90] Victory never tasted sweeter than in Illinois.

Elsewhere in the Midwest and Northwest the Hanna organization moved forward irresistibly. Illinois merely confirmed the Midwestern sentiment for McKinley. By May, Illinois, Kansas, Indiana, Ohio, Nebraska, and North Dakota were safely in the Major's column. In Michigan, Russell Alger prevented all attempts to make him a favorite son and worked hard for McKinley. In Minnesota, where McKinley drew cheering crowds in 1894, Hanna denounced the Reed forces, and when Senator Cushman K. Davis withdrew, he penned jubilantly: "Nothing can stop us now." [91]

In Wisconsin, just emerging into the dawn of progressivism, young Robert La Follette battled the state machine and allied himself with McKinley as the people's choice. The Major's popularity impressed even such stalwarts as conservative Senator John C. Spooner. The latter refused to be a favorite son and noted that the insurgent La Follette group "will attempt to succeed on the strength of the McKinley enthusiasm. . . ." La Follette, a favorite of McKinley's, drew strength and inspiration from the Major's "warm handshake and . . . understanding look" at one meeting. When the state convention met late in March, "Battle Bob" was "an active and earnest McKinley man," helping to steer Wisconsin's endorsement of McKinley.[92]

Further west, McKinley strength was somewhat hampered by his failure to favor free silver, but friends assumed that he was still a bimetallist, and Dawes reported enthusiasm in Nebraska, North Dakota, and Wyoming. Myron Herrick, vacationing in California, sounded sentiment for McKinley while enjoying the sunshine. The Golden State's endorsement of McKinley was a mixed blessing, however, for it was accompanied by a free-silver declaration.[93]

And so it went in state after state as the commonwealths filled

the McKinley column. The South, most of the Midwest and Northwest, and much of the unpredictable West were firmly with Mc-
Kinley by convention time. Only the eastern seaboard held for Reed,
Morton, and Quay, and McKinley even captured Vermont, Connecticut, Delaware, and Maryland. By June, 1896, everyone with eyes
and ears conceded a first-ballot nomination to McKinley, though
some die-hard opponents hoped for a second ballot to stop the
Major. A Democratic paper summed it up when on May 1 it said
flatly, "He may die before the convention meets, or be incapacitated
by paralysis, but hardly any other event can deprive him of his
present advantage." [94]

How had he done it? There is an air of destiny about any man
who attains a presidential nomination; so much is the result of
chance and fate that some men seem foreordained for the role. Certainly, McKinley's belief in his own destiny was the foundation of
his personal balance and view of life. But both he and Hanna knew
that they had insured that destiny with years of hard work. Without Hanna it would have been more difficult—and McKinley was
the last to deny his friend's genius as a political organizer—but it
seems likely that McKinley could have attained the nomination anyway. His position in the party, the loyalty of other state organizations to him in gratitude for his past help, his personality and record
in Ohio, and above all his position as the leading nationalist of the
day made him the chief contender for the nomination from the
first. Hard times gave him a glamor that no other candidate could
command, so closely was his name identified with protection and
prosperity. In many ways his superb organization only served to
bring his career to this logical climax.

But that organization *was* superb, and carried over into the
presidential campaign it proved an even greater success. It rested
first and foremost on McKinley's standing; then on Hanna's genius
and drive as an organizer. His adaptation of business methods to
politics showed how clearly and how much better he perceived the
currents and needs of the time than did his political opponents.
Hanna grew with experience in his role of party leader. He saw
the force of public opinion, the ways to guide and direct it, and
realized that its power was greater than behind-the-scenes maneuver-

ing alone. The genius for propaganda, office organization, and dispatch that carried him through the campaign of 1896 so successfully was very evident in the McKinley boom.

The evidence of McKinley's standing with the people at large was impressive. To a greater extent than any contemporary he captured the popular fancy. His record as an honest politician, his incessant drumming of the prosperity theme, his personality, his wide travels, the simplicity of his life and views, as well as his refusal to engage in calumny made him the most popular Republican of his day. His organization capitalized on that popularity but they did not manufacture it. Literally hundreds of thousands of people in every state already felt it. Moreover, he appealed to the people as the most liberal Republican candidate and as the one most attuned to their needs and wishes.

Already history called toward St. Louis, where delegates to the national convention prepared to choose their standard-bearer. Further west, the thunder of free silver poised to upset the best laid political plans of both parties. Could the McKinley organization meet this new challenge? Would the destiny that had carried him this far protect him even in the midst of a national political upheaval?

XI

The Front-Porch Campaign

AN AIR OF EXPECTANCY compounded the heat of early June in Canton. Visitors noted the tension and though the town tried to proceed about its business as usual, it seemed braced for a storm. At a certain house on North Market Street, a house surrounded by a neat fence, with flowers pouring over the sides of garden urns and geraniums circling neatly in their beds, the vigil of newspapermen took on fresh importance as the day approached that would decide the occupant's fate. To all intents and purposes, Major McKinley was unruffled by the excitement. He chatted easily over the fence with neighbors, entertained his wife and friends as usual, and had a brisk hello and ready smile for the people who greeted him on the street during his occasional forays into town.

Windows up and down the street were laden with wares boasting Canton's favorite son. Flags and portraits, silver tea sets and spoons, glasses, canes, fans, and handkerchiefs bore his picture. His bust could be bought in tin, marble, terra cotta, or Parian, and bunting was ready for instant use when the great moment came.

The scene was much the same some six hundred miles away in St. Louis, where the eleventh national Republican convention was slated to meet on June 16, 1896. The casual stranger might have thought that the city was named McKinleyville, so lavishly did the Major's followers show their loyalty. Hotels were full of delegates, alternates, party workers, visitors, and curiosity seekers. The elaborate temporary structure that housed the convention drew hordes of the curious and faithful. In their strolls through the flag-decked city they could buy almost anything they wanted with McKinley's name or picture on it. Hotels boasted McKinley bars and a McKinley drink concocted of bourbon, lemon juice, and sugar drew an unusually large following. Arriving guests and delegates passed under McKinley arches on their way to hotels, saw his picture as they mounted the stairs to their rooms, and waved to each other with canes boasting replicas of his features done in tin.[1]

The McKinley machine was ready to carry its chief to a first-ballot victory in a city that McKinley had not selected, for it was too far west—he preferred Chicago. Many of the men who gathered to begin the show were McKinley followers. Charles W. Fairbanks was temporary chairman, Joseph B. Foraker chaired the resolutions committee in charge of the platform, and John M. Thurston of Nebraska was permanent chairman, ready to second McKinley's nomination. Hanna controlled the important credentials committee, which passed on disputed delegations, and his hand was evident everywhere.

The trusted Perry Heath had been in St. Louis for some time, watching McKinley delegates, attending to their wants, and rebuffing all attempts to raid his strength.[2] Before the convention got under way the credentials committee heard the cases of disputing delegations, and Hanna's firm hand never released its grip. When Reed's contesting delegates from Alabama were denied credentials, Joe Manley said that the Speaker's cause was hopeless. Platt dared Hanna to seat any anti-Organization men from New York, and when the committee chose five of the eight anti-machine men, Platt swallowed his words and stayed. The proceedings exasperated one committee member until he turned to Judge Thompson, Hanna's lieutenant, and exclaimed, "Judge, which is your set of rascals? Let us vote 'em in and be done with it!" The discontented were heard to mutter then and later that delegates were seated according to "who they were for and who against," as Senator Allison put it.[3]

Checking disputed delegations was not the crucial business in the week before the convention opened, for McKinley's commanding lead assured his nomination. Hanna's greater worries centered on the party platform plank dealing with the crucial currency question. Ranking Republicans had completely misjudged the swelling sentiment for free silver in their own and the Democratic party. "I do not think we will have any trouble about the money plank, although there will probably be some dissent," Foraker wrote complacently a month before the convention. "The sentiment for free coinage will be so slight comparatively that it will not amount to anything."[4]

Other voices told a different story; those in business and those who took the trouble to listen to sentiment west of the Mississippi knew otherwise. "[I] Have been pretty well over the country since last we met, travelling through twenty-four States, more than ten thousand miles, South and West," a Democrat wrote a friend in 1895. "The people in that section are simply crazy upon the money question; they cannot discuss it rationally." [5] This long groundswell of feeling, child of hard times, farm failures, and Populist agitation, was left on the Republican doorstep in 1896. Business interests were already under pressure and Russell Alger wrote flatly, "This money question is absorbing all others and the commercial world is almost in a state of paralysis." [6]

McKinley at first seemed deaf to discontent and played down all fears. Convinced that the tariff would be the campaign issue, he was still reluctant to commit himself. Hanna was his agent in this as in all matters, and his first utterances in St. Louis did not give the impression that he favored a strong stand for gold. Eastern Republicans were more alive to the problem than their Ohio counterparts; Wall Street knew the mortgage market better than Columbus or Canton. Reed pressured for a strong gold statement. His agent, Henry Cabot Lodge, now Massachusetts' junior senator, went to Hanna during the quarrel on the gold plank and got a drawling, "The hell you say!" when he threatened a floor fight if Hanna did not support gold.[7]

Other voices in the party favored compromise, and gold men feared a bimetallic straddle in the platform. Harrison's friends were divided, but many agreed with the compatriot who exclaimed, "For heaven's sake don't let the 'money plank' bear the suspicion of a straddle." General Harrison was a little more cynical, favoring bimetallism with a proposed international agreement as long as no such compromise was likely.[8]

Mark Hanna himself was not well; Missouri heat did not agree with him, and his tender skin broke out in hives, especially around his ankles, to make his life miserable almost as soon as he entered the convention city. Nonetheless, he spent his time and energy prodigally, interviewing and placating all sides on the currency question. When all else failed, he donned his night shirt for relief from the itching and in that garb soothed the Silver Republicans, who were already talking of a bolt. An endless procession of business-men and politicos passed through his hotel room to ascertain Mc-Kinley's stand on the question.[9]

The Major's silence had been profitable but would have to end. In May, in response to mounting demands that he define his position, he had delegated Charles Grosvenor to say that "No man's friends have a right to call upon him to foreshadow the party's platform. . . . Major McKinley will respond to the platform, but he will not dictate what the platform shall be." [10] Such a statement illustrated McKinley's continuing caution and his apparent oblivion to the silver sentiment. He could quite properly have stated what he would accept or what he would not accept in the platform without seeming to dictate.

McKinley personally still favored the double standard. His bi-metallism increased as the crisis mounted, and in the months prior to the convention he doubtless would have preferred an old-fashioned platform straddle. Only when he realized that silver would be crucial did he abandon his old stand and come out for gold. He knew that whatever side he chose would cost him strength. If he took bimetallism the East would be dissatisfied, and if he took gold the West would leave and might take the Mississippi Valley with it in a bolt that could make his nomination an empty honor.[11]

He had not been entirely idle on the subject that spring, however. His talkative friend, Whitelaw Reid, whose potent *New York Tribune* was a welcome addition to any candidate's bandwagon, was the object of his search for advice. The mails told no secrets, so McKinley sent Reid a draft plank and authorized him to circulate it among his influential friends in Eastern financial circles. The plank seemed the traditional compromise, but, significantly, it favored "sound money" and also "the existing standard," a new departure in McKinley's thought. Reid showed the draft to J. P. Morgan and others without revealing its author, and Morgan's response was somewhat cool. The banking fraternity demanded a stronger stand; they were not prepared to wage the fight on the tariff issue alone, as McKinley hoped.[12]

As the delegates gathered for the convention, McKinley at last sensed the direction of the tide and told Fairbanks, "Tell our friends at St. Louis they can't make the platform too strong for me." [13]

When Hanna left Canton for St. Louis he carried in his pocket a draft plank, penned in the Major's own hand, which marked his advance in the last few weeks. Demanding gold and silver at par, it went on to say that the candidate and party would "welcome bimetallism based upon an international ratio, but until that can be secured it is the plain duty of the United States to maintain our present standard, and we are therefore opposed under existing conditions to the free and unlimited coinage of silver at sixteen to one." [14] McKinley was ready for the gold standard when the convention met. He would fight for it if necessary, utilizing his followers in the East. It was Hanna's task to fit this declaration into the final platform. Clearly the Westerners would not accept it. Senator Teller said later that McKinley's original draft was just as unacceptable as the plank finally adopted.[15]

In after years a whole literature grew up over the disputed authorship of the gold-standard plank in the Republican platform of 1896. Men as diverse as Lodge and Kohlsaat claimed to have written it or to have made it possible. A variety of talent, ranging from Henry Clay Payne of Wisconsin to Myron Herrick and Joseph B. Foraker of Ohio, not to mention dozens of congressmen, senators, governors, editors, and reporters, claimed to have been employed writing the plank. Nearly all those involved favored gold. Nearly all got a hearing from Hanna, who must have patted the draft in his pocket when they threatened catastrophe unless they had their way. Platt seized on the chance to embarrass McKinley, and they all insisted that Hanna "surrender" to their demands. Should the word "gold" be used? Should the party leaders declare for international bimetallism, and if so, how seriously? Would not a straddle catch the most votes after all? Or should they stand on principle and take the risk? Lodge challenged Hanna, whom he considered a boor. "How is the most unreasonable man in St. Louis this morning?" Hanna asked pleasantly one morning. "I am not unreasonable," Lodge replied, "as long as the engine is painted red I do not care what color you paint it." [16]

A self-constituted committee set to work writing a plank that McKinley would accept, and many dreary hours and nights passed before they agreed on the exact wording. Hanna knew the outcome all the while, comforted by his draft from the Major, but let them play their game while he played his. Just who wrote what was the subject of a lively debate in after years. Who wrote the word "gold" is still uncertain, but in 1901, Senator Chandler paid Senator Lodge $100 for having written in the words "which we pledge ourselves to promote" after the sentence dealing with an international agreement.

McKinley had little to do with the actual final authorship except to furnish the core of the plank to Hanna and approve the final draft over the telephone before it went to the convention. The final plank which the convention adopted was as unequivocal as anyone could remember:

> The Republican Party is unreservedly for sound money. It caused the enactment of a law providing for the resumption of specie payments in 1879. Since then every dollar has been as good as gold. We are unalterably opposed to every measure calculated to debase our currency or impair the credit of our country. We are therefore opposed to the free coinage of silver, except by international agreement with the leading commercial nations of the earth, which agreement we pledge ourselves to promote; and until such agreement can be obtained, the existing gold standard must be maintained at parity with gold, and we favor all measures designed to maintain inviolably the obligations of the United States, and all our money, whether coin or paper, at the present standard, the standard of the enlightened nations of the earth.[17]

Though Hanna favored this stand, he recognized the political dynamite involved. Silver Republicans were scattered from New Hampshire, where "Wild Bill" Chandler orated, to the Rocky Mountains, where Henry M. Teller led the movement. Would they all bolt in the face of a gold declaration? No wonder he bided his time and let his Eastern associates show their hand, for he valued their favor more.[18]

Hanna carefully fostered the impression that he favored bimetallism and surrendered only reluctantly to Eastern pressure, for his political acumen showed him that he could unify the party in the East by "surrendering" to what he wanted anyway. He placated the East with a hollow victory, for that section would be more important than the West in the end.

Hanna later denied that the East had won its victory. Midwestern men like Payne, Herrick, Merriam of Minnesota, Kohlsaat, Foraker, Hanna, and McKinley himself really drew the plank; the Easterners had only "secured" its final adoption. They stole something that Hanna wanted them to steal. "I do not desire to detract from the efforts made by these gentlemen for the cause of sound money," he said after the convention, "but I do wish to state most emphatically that the plank defining the party's position was advocated by Western men, drawn up by Western men, and approved by me before any man from the East reached St. Louis." [19]

On the third day of the convention, June 18, 1896, chairman Foraker of the resolutions committee reported the platform to the convention. No one was interested in its strong protection plank, or the stand for the annexation of Hawaii, or sympathy for the Cubans and the call for a large Navy. But storms of applause greeted Foraker's reading of the gold plank. Senator Teller, a member of the resolutions committee, had already filed a minority report and waited for the applause to subside to make his swan song as a Republican.

When Foraker finished, Teller asked permission to speak. The delegates knew what he would say. It was a dramatic moment as the great hall hushed. The sad, deep-set eyes that Teller turned to his audience revealed his mission. His slightly rumpled clothing, gray beard that spilled down over a hard collar, and his weary voice showed the internal pressures and sense of dedication that sustained him in his hopeless fight. Absentmindedly addressing the chairman as "Mr. President" out of habit as a senator, he turned to the rows of delegates whose unfriendliness to his cause was tempered by their respect for a man of character and belief. How bitter that he should come to this, he who had fought to establish the infant Republican party in Colorado and the West, he who held its past and its principles so dear. But how much greater were the beliefs that now forced him to abandon his party. "There are few men in [the Republican party] who have been more attached to the great principle of this party than I have been, and I cannot go out of it without heartburnings and a feeling that no man can appreciate who has not endured it, and yet I cannot, before my country and my God, agree to the provision that shall put upon this country a gold standard, and I will not." His voice was a low monotone, and many delegates cupped their hands to their ears to catch his words; newspapermen poised tensely; there were damp eyes among Western delegates. "And I do not care what may be the result. If it takes me out of political life I will go with a feeling that at least I maintain my consistency and my manhood, and that my conscience is clear and that my country will have no right to find fault with me."

Teller then placed his own substitute free-silver plank before the convention; the roll call defeated the measure 818½ to 105½. The Canton Grand Army Band struck up "Silver Threads Among the Gold" to ease the tension, but Teller again sought recognition. Would the chair permit Senator Frank Cannon of Utah to read a declaration on behalf of the Westerners? As the curly-haired Cannon made his way to the rostrum and began to read, Hanna grunted in his seat, asked who he was, and said acidly, "Perty, ain't he? Looks like a cigar drummer!" When Cannon characterized the Republican party as "once the redeemer of the people, but now about to become their oppressor unless providentially restrained," a massive onrush of hisses and boos drowned him out. He continued, and when he paused after one statement, Hanna's harsh voice rang out over the delegates' heads: "Go! Go!" An electric moment galvanized the whole hall, and cries of "Go! Go!" swept the Westerners from the chamber. Teller paused to shake Foraker's hand and then led his little band from the hall. The schism was a fact; how important it would be time alone could tell.[20]

Reaction to the Western bolt was mixed. "Silver is, we think, the first raw metal that has ever been wept over," *The Nation* sneered.[21] The silverites themselves were not sanguine, and the smallness of their diminishing band was a comfort to Hanna, who hoped it would not increase. But an unknown observer reaped the greatest satisfaction of all. As the Silver Republicans moved for the door and the crush of humanity urged them on, a dark-haired, handsome young man who was sitting in the press section, attentive to every detail, rose suddenly and walked across the desks to get a better view. He stood in rapt attention as though the full import of the event registered on him. His name was William Jennings Bryan.[22]

The afternoon of the third day brought nominations for president, an event for which the delegates and spectators waited anxiously. It was anticlimactic, for McKinley's selection was a foregone conclusion and Teller had provided the only real drama of the convention, but all eyes turned to the rostrum as names were placed before the convention. Behind the scenes the bosses still bargained, but Mark Hanna was not receptive. Platt supposedly told him that he could have New York for the proper promises, but Hanna was not in a promising mood; inside information told him that the Easy Boss could not hold his lines intact. Reed's managers gave up, but the Speaker's loyal followers stood by his name even amid the McKinley avalanche.[23]

The convention awaited its nominees, and speakers' voices scarcely rose above the steady hum of conversation and jostling on the floor. Chauncey Depew placed Morton in nomination; Lodge named Reed; and an Allison cohort put the Iowan to the test. The inevitable demonstrations alleviated the tension, but they were more homage to their candidates than reflections of hope.

In Canton a different scene took place. Reporters flooded over the McKinley porch, sprawling in wicker chairs or straddling the porch railing, joking, smoking, and placing bets on the Major's strength. Inside, friends and Mother McKinley sat with Ida in tense heat. A privileged few talked with the candidate himself, who was as calm as stone. The Major's group sat in the library near the long-distance telephone, and the insistent click of the specially installed telegraph instruments punctuated the conversation. From time to time McKinley crossed the hall to Ida's sitting room to twit the ladies. "Are you young ladies getting anxious about this affair?" he asked with banter in his voice.[24] Even the cynical newsmen remarked on his iron composure.

While Depew nominated Morton and the New Yorker's demonstration wound its way around the hall, the immense bloc of McKinley men sat silent, passing banners and bugles among themselves, preparing for the onslaught of Foraker's oratory. The new senator from Ohio made his way to the rostrum on a tidal wave of applause, while the already defeated Reed and Morton men sat in bitter silence. Foraker opened with a slashing attack on the Cleveland administration as "one stupendous disaster. . . ." He then outlined what the people demanded in a president: "They want something more than a good business man; they want something more than a fearless leader; they want something more than a wise, patriotic statesman; they want a man who embodies in himself not only all these essential qualifications, but who in addition typifies in name, character, record, ambition and purpose"—and here he rose on tiptoe and slashed the air with his arm for emphasis—"the exact opposite of the present free trade, deficit making, bond issuing, labor saving Democratic administration." The crowd loved it; they were all good Republicans, if not good McKinley men. When Foraker continued, the roof caved in. "I stand here to present to this Convention such a man. His name is William McKinley." [25]

The mention of McKinley's name halfway through the speech caused an eruption on the floor. Canes, hats, posters, buttons flew toward the ceiling as cheering delegates rushed into the aisles, placards in hand, to embrace each other and snake dance around the floor. Several bands competed for attention but one triumphed with "Marching Through Georgia." Horns blared as Hanna tapped his foot to the music of a band near his seat and waved a McKinley handkerchief. The demonstration had begun to subside after some twenty minutes when a delegate hoisted aloft a Napoleonic hat, and bedlam broke loose for another ten minutes before the chairman began to impose order.[26]

In Canton the telegraph wires told the city that her favorite son was being nominated, and business halted as citizens met on the street corners in hushed attention to the bulletins. In McKinley's library the telephone operator told him on the long-distance phone that the demonstration was under way. McKinley thanked him and sat back, only to be drawn to the receiver by a curious distant hum, which turned out to be the roar of the demonstration six hundred miles away. The operator had left the receiver off the hook in the booth and McKinley heard himself cheered over the humming wires "like a storm at sea, with wild, fitful shrieks of wind." McKinley chuckled and said that it was hard on Foraker, "like stopping a race horse in full career." When the pandemonium finally settled enough for Foraker to resume, he said: "You seem to have heard the name of my candidate before," and in distant Canton, McKinley smiled through his cigar smoke: "Ah, that is like him. He knows what he is doing, and is all right." [27]

The rest was formality, and when Foraker finished, another demonstration ensued while Hanna, Bushnell, and Grosvenor embraced on their chairs and tap-danced amid the delegates. But the balloting began in tension; nothing is certain in politics until the vote is in. As the clerk called the roll, the states behind McKinley stood firm. In Canton, the Major and his guests were suddenly quiet, and Ida's knitting needles flew faster than ever. The scratch of pens and pencils was audible as McKinley and his friends worked in tense silence over their tally sheets. When Ohio's turn came, McKinley was within 20 votes of the nomination, and the 46 Buckeye votes gave him his victory. Rising quickly, he crossed the hall to Ida's sitting room, embraced her, and kissed his mother. "Ida, Ohio's vote has given me the nomination," he said quietly as she breathed a sigh of relief.

In St. Louis, Hanna burst out: "I love McKinley! He is the best man I ever knew!" When the delegates quieted, Chairman Thurston announced the vote as 661½ for McKinley, 84½ for Reed, 61½ for Quay, 58 forMorton, 35½ for Allison, and a scattering elsewhere. Lodge and Depew rose to make the nomination unanimous. Calls rose over the convention for "Hanna! Hanna!" and he rose reluctantly to face the sea of men amid great applause. He was already known as the new national chairman of the party. Obviously embarrassed, for he was no speechmaker, Hanna pledged himself to a fierce campaign: "What feeble efforts I may have contributed to the result, I am here ready to lay . . . at the feet of my party and upon the altar of my country." [28]

It was a moment of rich victory for Hanna. All his dreams came true on a tally sheet in St. Louis. His hard labors had brought success, and he might well pause in the lull before the real storm to attest his affection for McKinley. It was not so rich a moment to others. Herrick stepped outside the hall at sundown and noted a familiar figure watching the sinking sun. It was Thomas Collier Platt. [29]

The nomination came to McKinley as the climax of hard work and a long political career; there was little magic in it. In after years, with his usual dispassionate view, McKinley himself stated clearly the reason for his success. He told a reporter, "It will occur to the close student of political events that, all things considered, it was desirable to take a man from the Middle West, and that a man who had twice carried Ohio during troublesome times previous to 1896 was entirely available as a candidate. I cannot subscribe to the idea that accident or luck had very much to do with making me President of the United States." [30] It seems curious that he did not attach greater importance to Hanna's organization, which had made his availability a sure thing.

In Canton, the pandemonium matched that of St. Louis. When Ohio put McKinley over the top, the town erupted and all the carefully prearranged plans for a formal parade and bell-ringing jubilee vanished in a mad rush to the Major's house, as thousands of cheering citizens poured down Market Street. "You have my sympathy," General Russell Hastings flung over his shoulder as he fled out the back door. The crowd surged over the fence and around the porch, cheering madly when McKinley appeared to acknowledge their ovation. The ladies of Canton abandoned modesty to dance rings around the candidate.[31] In minutes, 2,000 people arrived from nearby Alliance; 19 carloads of pilgrims flooded in from Massillon about dinner time, riding on cars so packed that many men clung to their sides. Later, 40 cars disgorged 4,000 people from Akron, and trains from Carrollton, Niles, and other hamlets kept McKinley on his front porch greeting guests until midnight. Dawn revealed a litter of handkerchiefs, parasols, and rifled wallets, attesting not only to the excitement, but also to the dexterity of Canton's pickpockets. Between 5 P.M. and midnight, McKinley had spoken to 50,000 people. The pattern of the front-porch campaign was set early.[32]

The following day, the convention finished its business by choosing a vice-presidential candidate. McKinley frankly wanted Reed, but the Speaker would have first place or none; nor would Morton take the second spot. McKinley had long since realized this and wished someone to help carry the eastern seaboard states. Populous New Jersey, therefore, furnished the running mate in the form of Garrett Augustus Hobart, a wealthy lawyer well known for his work within the party. He had already displayed the tact and charm that would make him more than customarily important once in office.[33]

The excitement was not over, for as the Republicans dispersed, the Democrats gathered in Chicago early in July. Their cause seemed hopeless; McKinley's advisors anticipated an easy victory based on the tariff issue, for the Democrats were split into warring factions. The East favored President Cleveland, while the South,

Midwest, and West would accept no one endorsed by the hated President whose financial policies had wrecked their dreams.

Few people paid attention to the dark-haired, handsome young William Jennings Bryan of Nebraska, who did not yet even have a seat on the floor; he was contesting with another Nebraska delegation. When he was finally seated, he wangled a position on the crucial resolutions committee, where he fought for free silver in the platform. He should have been more widely known, for he had been seeking the presidential nomination since his election to Congress in 1890. The Nebraska congressman was a compelling orator and excellent debater. He had a flair for demolishing Republican tariff arguments that made him the best Democratic spokesman on the subject in the House, and many were sad to see him desert the tariff for the silver siren.[34]

Bryan's intuition led him to silver, for he saw that it was the coming issue and that it had greater popular appeal than the tariff would ever boast. Working closely with Midwestern Populists, he drew advice and inspiration from James B. Weaver, the Populist presidential candidate in 1892. Men as distant as North Carolina hailed him as the chief Democratic dark horse for 1896, and a friend of Governor Altgeld of Illinois told an acquaintance, "Keep your eye on William Jennings Bryan." Bryan himself beamed confidence in private as the convention assembled; he declined to nominate Senator Teller because "I am going to be nominated myself at Chicago." [35]

Bryan was right, and in the tumult and shouting of the strife-ridden Democratic gathering he had his hour, an hour such as comes to few men in history. Answering his opponents in both parties, he exclaimed in a phrase of world renown: "You shall not press down upon the brow of labor this crown of thorns, you shall not crucify mankind upon a cross of gold!" In a flash he had called all dissident elements to his side and enunciated clearly in a speech noteworthy for its commonplace ideas all the old American ideals that seemed dormant in the midst of doubt and depression. Silver and the Democracy had found their leader, not only because he spoke eloquently for a new cause, but also because he spoke to all Americans on behalf of their historic idealism and for the wider cause of humanity itself. One young newsman cried "Marat, Marat, Marat has won!" when Bryan was later nominated, and that utterance gives the clue to the opposition that finally defeated him. His war was a class war, a sectional war, the result of the discontent that shook the foundations of the old American way. When he finished speaking, he was the new Democratic leader. "If it be true that destiny shapes our ends then destiny surely reached down into the body of that convention, grasped him firmly in her hands and raised him to an eminence which I think even now he but faintly realizes," wrote one watching silverite.[36]

In the campaign that followed, Bryan was caricatured as an anarchist, socialist, communist, country hick, rabble-rouser, and windbag. In after years, grown old and paunchy, bereft of the aura of vigor and the tinge of youthful rebellion that made so many millions love him, he was painted with the brush of ridicule by men who never understood him. William McKinley did not view him as stupid or a mere rabble-rouser. He knew the forces behind Bryan, and he knew the effectiveness of Bryan's appeal. He was an opponent worthy of his cause, and McKinley's major purpose was to find a remedy for the discontent that produced such a candidate.

The weakness of McKinley's nationalism was its materialism; it promised more goods to more people, but it lacked the essential mystical vision of the American dream. Bryan's platform had precisely that dream. His own weakness as a thinker was beside the point, for he was a crusader, not a theorist. Unlike McKinley, he did not grasp the picture of the nation as a whole, but he cast a magic web of belief over his shortcomings. Essentially uneducated and narrowly read, Bryan seldom moved beyond his limitations and ended his career in the drabness of Chautauqua bonfires and real estate speculation. Rural and middle-class in outlook, he never really understood the forces on whose crest he rode and could not master the means or manner to appeal to all Americans. Ignorant of business and finance, he viewed both from the closet of a conscience that told him they were simply oppressors.

Yet for all his limitations, there was a tone in Bryan's words, an attitude in his figure, a bent in his mind, and a clear call to remedy the distress of his section that cut through the political platitudes of the day like a sharp knife. He gave voice to a great protest move-

222

ment that rested on genuine distress. He revived the American dream of equality and freedom with a deeply American rhetoric that touched the hearts of the people everywhere as no common-sense program of action could. He thought himself radical when in fact he was conservative. The nation was passing from agriculture to industry, and Bryan fastened the blame for his section's distress on an artificial medium which was actually a symptom rather than a disease, The Money Power. America had become a nation of three forces: labor, agriculture, and industry. McKinley already had won the support of industry, and his great accomplishment in 1896 lay in winning labor. The spokesman of the new rising industrial order, of triumphant economic and political nationalism, was not Bryan but McKinley.

The platform on which Bryan ran served notice to the Republicans that their anticipated easy fight had vanished. It flatly favored free silver, anti-trust action, reform in the federal courts, new labor legislation, and a long list of reforms inherited from Populism. The Republicans would have to answer the challenge in ways they did not dream.

With McKinley safely nominated, the Republicans scattered to vacation retreats and countinghouses. They would let the summer wane, as they had in the past, and begin their campaign in September. There was no hurry; McKinley was as good as inaugurated. Bryan's nomination jolted their complacency but did not at once change their plans. However, the Democrats' fusion with the Populists, Bryan's announcement that he would campaign in a national tour, and reports that bordered on hysteria from Republican weathervanes moved Hanna into action in mid-July. On the Sunday after his nomination, McKinley took his mother to church. Ida stayed home listening over a special telephone. The text was never more appropriate: "Wherefore the rather, brethren, give diligence to make your calling and election sure: for if ye do these things, ye shall never fall." [37]

Mark Hanna was not busy in church, but the inevitable political business dogged his steps. "Take care of yourself," McKinley wrote him before the convention. "You will be under great strain." Neither knew then what a great strain and how long it would last. Hanna paid his respects in Canton late in June, and met a wreath of smiles. "I never felt in better health," McKinley said in response to Hanna's inquiry, "and you do not at all look like a sick man." Later, in Cleveland, participating in a victory parade, Hanna spied an acquaintance on the sidewalk and winking broadly, pointed to his own chest, exclaiming: "Big Injun! Me Big Injun!" [38] Still, the sweetness of victory did not blind Mark Hanna to the chances of politics; another turn of the wheel might have made him a small Indian.

Complacency seemed to reign everywhere in party circles as the managers prepared for a repeat of Harrison's campaigns of 1888 and 1892. McKinley himself was not yet fully awake to the dangers of his position. In July, resting briefly on his porch with a circle of friends, he put down his cigar and said, "I am a tariff man standing on a tariff platform. This money matter is unduly prominent. In 30 days you won't hear anything about it." Judge Day looked at him and replied laconically, "In my opinion, in 30 days you won't hear anything else." [39] Whitelaw Reid urged Hanna to come East at once, even before the Democrats nominated Bryan, so that he could contact financiers before they left for summers abroad.[40]

By mid-July, as all concerned realized that their opponents would break precedent by a nationwide campaign pitched to the sentiments of the hour, Hanna woke to the danger. Moving with his old speed, he called his lieutenants together and established headquarters in both New York and Chicago; he would wage the fight in earnest for the crucial Midwest. "I will be in the saddle, so to speak, and be found at both places at different times," he told reporters.[41] Hanna's lieutenants included the trusted members of the McKinley organization, Dawes, businessman Cornelius Bliss as treasurer of the national committee, Henry Clay Payne as head of the Chicago headquarters, and Platt, Quay, and Manley from the executive committee. But publicly and privately, everyone knew who was at the helm. "There is only one man in the National Committee," Clarkson wrote. "That man is Hanna, of course. . . ." [42]

Hanna quickly impressed everyone he met with his vigor and common sense. "He was candid, genial and straightforward," one man remembered. "No pretenses, no intrigue, to gain his ends. He was openly for you or against you. He was a business man in politics, and naturally had a businessman's judgement of the policies best to pursue." [43]

McKinley's hand was also much in evidence, though he wrapped himself in more dignity than ever and studiously tried to avoid factions. Hanna conferred with him by telephone constantly, and few political details escaped the Major's eye. Taking a group of party workers to Canton, Hanna told them candidly: "Now don't you fellows fool yourselves by thinking that we will be able to give McKinley instructions as to how to run the campaign. After you have talked with him you will find that he knows more about politics than all of us." [44]

McKinley's ear was closer to the ground than Hanna's, so close that Uncle Joe Cannon once said it was full of grasshoppers. He recommended Quay's appointment to the national committee to heal old wounds, but questioned the choice of Payne for the Chicago office; he had reports that Payne was unpopular because of his big-business connections.[45] Counselling caution and conciliation, he asked Silver Republicans everywhere to forget their differences and work with the regular organization. How badly he underestimated the silver sentiment, which divided husbands and wives and whole families! No old-fashioned campaign would do in 1896.

The party organization's first need was efficiency. Dawes bent himself to this task with a will. Placed in charge of funds in Chicago, he watched transactions carefully. Contracts for printing and supplies were opened to bidding, office help received strict salaries, callers were carefully screened, and favors were few and far between. He chose his associates from business, not politics, and Hanna endorsed his every move toward efficiency.[46]

Through July and into early August, the Republicans mapped their campaign. McKinley and Hanna agreed that they would have to appeal to labor in the East and to farmers in the Midwest. Conferring in Cleveland with Hanna, the candidate himself endorsed a "blanket campaign," with heavy emphasis on the currency question for sixty days, then a switch to the tariff. The national committee approved the decision and reported in early August that demands for literature and speakers were already overwhelming state and local organizations as they felt the pressure of Bryan's swing around the circle. Bryan was coalescing dissident elements, debtors and the property-less, around the poles of free silver and his own personality. ". . . The people who have got property are all right and can take care of themselves," Osborne wrote McKinley as the organization prepared to flood literature into the disaffected areas.[47]

Alive to the full danger, Hanna hurried East to establish the New York office, make peace with former opponents and, above all, raise money. "The situation is pressing *active* operations and *at once* so we must get our rooms open and at work." His fast moving figure, wrapped in cigar smoke, his swift replies to reporters, and his brusque demands for speed and dispatch became familiar in party circles in the East. Breathing sweetness and light, he hurried to Boston to make peace with Reed's former managers; upon leaving he calmly informed them that they would be responsible for raising $400,000 for the campaign fund. His dispatch impressed the Easterners, who were relieved that the national chairman was awake to the danger.[48]

As he worked for party unity, Hanna took comfort in the encouraging words that came from Canton, and he said later that McKinley's calm assurance saved him many worries. The enthusiasm that greeted Bryan's whirlwind tour jolted many Republicans into action. "I am not so sure as you are about the 'great victory,' " Senator Hale wrote Senator Chandler. "The political situation was entirely changed by the Chicago performance. We could have beaten an old-fashioned democratic nomination and ticket without half trying, but the new movement has stolen our thunder." [49]

Capitalizing on this steadily growing awareness in his ranks, Hanna dealt with Platt. In a long secret conference he recognized Platt's leadership of the New York machine for unqualified support of the national ticket. He would not recognize insurgent New York Republicans at so crucial a juncture. ". . . There was nothing else for Mr. Hanna to do except recognize the regular Organization of the Party in this State or any other State, and particularly in *this* State, at *this* time, when it was evident to the wayfaring man though a free silverite that the Republican party has confidence in its present management and desires them to remain in control," Platt wrote Morton. Asked if he had been redeemed when he emerged from the conference, Platt replied wryly, "Yes, I have been washed in the blood of the lamb." McKinley approved Hanna's agreement, which was not unusual, though he referred to it guardedly; he could clip Platt's wings after the election.[50]

Meanwhile, Dawes hammered out an organization for collecting and disbursing funds in Chicago, while letting immense contracts for printing and office supplies on the best terms he could get. "I am afraid that we are mistaken in assuming that we are going to have more funds than in 1892," Dawes warned McKinley on August 1. "While the interests of businessmen is greater, in our contest, it is more difficult for them to spare the money for subscriptions." Many businessmen were afraid to donate to the campaign fund for fear of losing everything in the expected revolution that would mark Bryan's election. As John Hay so succinctly put it in a dry aside to Henry Adams: "[Bryan] has succeeded in scaring the Goldbugs out of their five wits; if he had scared them a little, they would have come down handsome to Hanna. But he has scared them so blue that they think they had better keep what they have got left in their pockets against the evil day." [51]

Contributions trickled in slowly. Hay, Frick, and other wealthy men sent funds from time to time to McKinley or Hanna, but their donations were more than offset by the frantic calls from state and local offices, which were especially cramped for funds as the national office decided to pour everything into the presidential race and let local candidates worry for themselves.[52]

A worried Hanna left for New York early in August, and after his conference with Platt he made the rounds of the New York corporations seeking funds, but he met evasion and outright fear. "I am having moderate success in getting funds. . . ." he wrote Dawes.[53] He had never had harder sledding, for the Eastern financial world was strange to him, and powerful men there did not know him except by his newspaper reputation. Oddly enough, Hanna's reputation as a businessman did not precede him; the Midwest, where he had made his reputation, was far from the East.

On August 15 a stroke of good luck brought him to James J. Hill, an old acquaintance. He was so evidently depressed that Hill took him by the arm and led him through the great commercial houses, vouching for his integrity and ability. In five days the two collected enough money for immediate expenses and got promises of more.

227

Hanna appointed men to oversee the collection of funds. Banks and insurance companies were levied a percentage of their assets, and commercial houses were billed according to their business volume.[54] Few refused to pay once they saw Hanna and his methods. Still dissatisfied in late August, Hanna wrote Reid, "I am devoting my whole time to this matter here, and on the whole I feel rather discouraged." [55] In the end he had no cause for discouragement, for as the campaign swung into high gear in September, funds were more plentiful. Ultimately the two headquarters spent over $3,500,000, of which $3,000,000 came from New York.[56] As always, Hanna refused any payment for his services or expenses.

The big headache was still the West. "Everything in the East is all right," Hobart wrote McKinley in mid-August. It seemed certain that New England would hold for McKinley, Hobart would carry doubtful New Jersey, and Platt's machine and cooperation would carry New York.[57] Party managers prepared a veritable onslaught in the West, where free-silver sentiment was almost out of control. The Corn Belt and the wheat states like the Dakotas and Nebraska, not to mention the Rocky Mountain silver-producing states, were aflame, though California and Oregon seemed safe.[58]

In two weeks time, Hanna reported that the Chicago office had poured 15,000,000 pamphlets on the silver question into the Western states. Boxcars laden with pamphlets for the hungry masses left Chicago hourly. "Our workshop in Chicago is a great institution," he said proudly. "Fifty or sixty employees are busy all day keeping up with the demand for literature and information and meeting the people who come there from all parts of the West for consultation." [59] Meanwhile, his literary bureau hired ghost writers to prepare speeches for public men too busy to do their own.

Hanna himself had devoted a share of his time to overseeing the Chicago operations. The curious and faithful could see him sitting at his big roll-top desk, fanning himself as he leaned back in a swivel chair to get a better view of the men who talked to him. The national chairman missed none of their earnest conversation as they leaned forward and gestured.

Before the advent of radio and television the printed word was the most effective campaign instrument, and Hanna used it ruthlessly until Theodore Roosevelt exclaimed, "He has advertised McKinley as if he were a patent medicine." [60] By election day the organization had sent out 250,000,000 documents. Five million families got McKinley material weekly. Two hundred and seventy-five different pamphlets went out in 5,000 freight packages and 1,500,000 mail packages from the Chicago office. The New York office sent 20,000,000 pamphlets east and north of the Ohio River, and the remainder avalanched upon the Mississippi Valley. No wonder one Republican could say candidly, "We have carried the Middle West by main strength and by an unprecedented use of money." [61]

Obviously Hanna knew well how public opinion was formed, and adopted new techniques to meet a new situation. Their effectiveness was evident when demand for printed matter exceeded supplies, when printers ran out of paper and ink, and when the assembly lines producing written copy were exhausted.

By late September, when Hanna's vast educational program turned the tide against silver, men around McKinley, though conceding the mountain states to Bryan, confidently predicted that many of the farm states were now safe.[62] The press, then as now, was heavily Republican and drew thanks from McKinley himself for its heroic work.[63]

As the Republican campaign poured forth its torrent, Democratic abuse centered on its manager, and Hanna became the butt of caricatures and libels that time has not erased. Unable to attack McKinley's probity, the Democrats chose to lambast him indirectly through his manager. Homer Davenport's cruel and unjust cartoons of the bloated monster covered with dollar signs went into millions of homes, and it was said that farm wives hid their children when his name was mentioned. Nathan B. Scott remembered that one morning during the campaign Hanna grew suddenly silent over a newspaper and then with tears in his eyes, passed it to him. The familiar bloated Hanna stared up monstrously from the front page. "That hurts," Hanna said. "When I have tried all my life to put myself in the other fellow's place, when I have tried to help those in need and to lighten the burdens of those less fortunate than myself, to be pictured as I am here, to be held up to the gaze of the world as a murderer of women and children, I tell you it hurts." [64]

There is no concrete evidence that Hanna or his agents bribed voters or repeated anything like Quay's performance with "blocks of five" in 1888, despite charges to the contrary. Hanna was in charge of the national offices and did not oversee the local and state organizations where such activities were more likely. McKinley told a meeting of party leaders in September that he would not countenance any bribery or wrong use of funds, and the available record shows that his wishes were respected.[65] Hanna did buy whole newspapers, subsidize whole organizations, draw liberal funds from business interests, but he used these for what he considered legitimate propaganda, not for bribery. So morally squeamish an observer as William Allen White, later in the van of reformers who opposed Hanna, never believed that he bribed voters in 1896.[66] Hanna himself hotly denied all such charges during the campaign. Freely admitting generous use of funds for propaganda, he answered one critic by saying that "he must produce his proof of the charge he makes against me or stand a self-convicted liar before the people. He is a liar if he said that." [67]

While Hanna pushed his organization forward and spread the nets of his vast educational program, McKinley was already speaking to an endless chain of visiting delegations in Canton. In spare moments he sat at his desk writing party leaders and conferring on the telephone. It was imperative that every leading Republican take the stump in a show of unity. Former President Harrison was reluctant to speak. "I cannot go about the country making speeches. I have not the time and I do not think it would be appropriate," he wrote a friend. Though he was reluctant to leave his lucrative law practice in Indianapolis, he was also reluctant to see Bryan win; in the end he spoke after personal appeals from McKinley. By late August, Harrison even thawed enough to address a mammoth rally in New York, where he coined a phrase that became a stock answer to Democratic claims: "The first dirty errand that a dirty dollar does is to cheat the workingman." [68]

McKinley turned next to Reed, whose potent voice was needed in the East. "I am sure we shall hear from him very often during the campaign," he wrote Herrick. Still bitter at his defeat and loathing McKinley, Reed was nevertheless a Republican and loathed Bryan even more. Taking the stump in the East, he hammered his opponents so mercilessly that one paper reported, "He stirs the blood, he stimulates the fancy, he actually flatters men by making them believe they have weak minds." [69]

Among the penitents who now came to Canton to make amends with the Major were Lodge and Roosevelt who, much to John Hay's amusement, went "to offer their heads to the axe and their tummies to the hara-kiri knife." The Major did not eat them after all, and they returned satisfied that he was sound. McKinley himself invited Hay, who thought first that he "would not struggle with the millions on his trampled lawn." In the end he went, and was wiser for the journey. A brief talk with the sociable candidate deeply impressed Hay. "I was more struck than ever with his mask. It was a genuine Italian ecclesiastical face of the fifteenth century. And there are idiots who think Mark Hanna will run him!" [70] McKinley smoothed all paths, even Quay's, with a cordiality and charm that denied any inner tension. "It has been my endeavor to keep free from all factional trouble," he gently admonished a maverick New Yorker. "Upon consideration, you will, I am sure, agree with me that I cannot refuse the aid of anybody. You would not, I am sure, ask me to rebuff whoever might come forward to tender support." [71]

While the two party headquarters spewed forth their speakers and literature, and Hanna collected the funds necessary for the operation, the real campaign unfolded in Canton. It was a changed city, to say the least. A holiday atmosphere greeted the delegations that unloaded at its overtaxed depot. En route to the Major's home they marched past store windows overrun with bunting and pictures, under arches of "protected" tin covered with McKinley's face, and by hot dog stands, cigar drummers, candy sellers, lemonade vendors, and souvenir peddlers. The streets wore down under the tramp of marching feet, and lucky was he who could find a decent meal or a quiet moment between dawn and midnight.

Bryan's rousing campaign from his private train, a break with precedent itself, alarmed McKinley's advisors, and even while the candidate entertained guests and small delegations in Canton in June and July, they gathered in Chicago to confer on techniques. Hanna was worried, and said so. "We have got to get McKinley out on the road to meet this thing and I wish you would go out to him . . . and map out a campaign for him," he told Herrick. When the two later went to Canton and told McKinley of their plans, the candidate surprised them by bluntly refusing. "Don't you remember that I announced that I would not under any circumstances go on a speech-making tour?" he asked. "If I should go now it would be an acknowledgment of weakness. Moreover, I might just as well put up a trapeze on my front lawn and compete with some professional athlete as go out speaking against Bryan. I have to *think* when I speak." [72] He saw that it would be wiser to let Bryan and his enthusiasm wear themselves out. He believed that the more people heard Bryan's appeal, the better off Republicans were. He should stay in Canton as a dignified, responsible statesman, trusting to public opinion and the party organization to do the rest. McKinley refused all invitations to speak and left Canton only three days during the campaign to fill pre-convention promises to speak at the Cleveland Centennial and at Mount Union College. "I have made up my mind to remain in Canton all Summer and Fall . . . ," he wrote in declining an invitation. [73]

What then should he do? Remain safely at home and let his managers run his campaign, risking the charge that he was only a front? Such a role was unthinkable to anyone as attuned to public opinion and as used to politics as he. He knew how successful Harrison's "front-porch campaign" was in 1888, but curiously, he was at first averse to "anything like an effort to bring crowds here" early in the campaign. [74] As he realized the gravity of the situation he changed his mind and planned a campaign that would overshadow Harrison's.

Any delegation was welcome to come to Canton simply by writing McKinley and stating its affiliation. Joe Smith then summarized each group's background and membership in a brief dossier which McKinley rapidly memorized, so that he astonished many by using their first names on being introduced. A felicitous inquiry about a wife's health, a chance remark about a delegation leader's son in college, a careful inquiry about affairs in some rural district all endeared him to the faithful pilgrims who flooded about his porch day after day. He pinned hundreds of carnations in willing lapels and shook tens of thousands of hands with the special grip that spared him lameness.

Before bringing their groups to Canton, delegation leaders talked

232

with McKinley in private. He would ask them what they proposed to say. They would reply, "Oh, anything that comes to mind." Ever mindful of the deadly "Rum, Romanism, and Rebellion" slip that cost Blaine the election of 1884, McKinley would gently remind his guests of the obvious pitfalls of such a course. He would suggest that the delegation chief write out his remarks. The candidate checked the speech, knowing in advance what every delegation leader would say in introducing his group. McKinley prepared dozens of short talks in advance, laboring over them with great care for just the right tone and proper content for varying groups. He dictated them while striding up and down, smoking, his hands clasped behind his back. No one ghost-wrote anything for him, and his own deft touch, ease of explanation, and knowledge of his audience made his front-porch speeches the most effective he ever gave.[75]

When the delegation duly appeared, it waited in respectful attitude on the Major's lawn. A hush ran through the crowd as the door opened, and cheers rent the air as the candidate appeared in smiling dignity. The delegation leader read his remarks, McKinley listening "like a child looking at Santa Claus." The assembled faithful gaped at the famous man and the famous house, some taking pictures with awkward black boxes. When the delegation leader finished, McKinley mounted a chair and read off his speech, punctuated by frequent applause. Often as not he would glance toward the fence of his neighbors, the Harters, and wave to a little girl who clung there in abject adoration, her dress a splash of color against the assembled people. When she was not there the Major chided her. "Where were you today, Mary?" he would ask. "I was looking for your pink dress." [76]

The idea of delegations caught on in Republican circles, and applications flooded in on the managers. It required careful scheduling, in which the railroads cooperated an offered special low fares; careful timing, for one delegation came as another went; and a temporary expansion of Canton's facilities. It was all hard on the homestead, for between June 19 and November 2, McKinley spoke to 750,000 people from 30 states in over 300 delegations. The front lawn looked "as if a herd of buffalo had passed that way, . . ." and the pilgrims took so many souvenir pieces of wood from the porch that it threatened to fall on the candidate's head. As McKinley spoke, those nearest the house pried off splinters of wood; the picket fence had long since disappeared; and for a time blades of grass served as souvenirs, so that the denuded yard became a lake of mud when it rained. On rainy days, meetings were held in the civic auditorium or under a specially constructed tent.

McKinley had only to look out his window to see another delegation, representing farmers, workers, businessmen, college students, or someone, swinging down the street, trumpets blaring and drums banging. Rain or shine, hot or cold, the delegations came. They were handled by a civic organization which attended to their travel schedules, met them at the station, accompanied them to the house, and saw them off. Inside the house an overworked staff handled correspondence and souvenirs, typed speeches, and set up schedules. They did not rest even at night, for electricity lighted the way to the McKinley home. In one day 16 delegations came from 12 states. McKinley wrote a message for a carrier pigeon, which carried it to the distant faithful. Children came in droves chanting:

> Governor McKinley, he's our man;
> If we can't vote for him our papas can.

Five thousand Pennsylvanians representing 65 different factories came to hear McKinley speak on protection, and cheered him to the echo, though some may well have been Democrats simply grateful for a day off.[77]

As the currency question consumed time and energy, McKinley's belief that it would fade did not waver. "We must all realize the necessity of education upon the financial system, but I have no doubt that long before the campaign is ended, the working men of the country will generally concede the correctness of the position taken by the Republican party," he insisted. Late in July he confided privately that he thought the worst was over; he was more prescient than many advisors, for the reaction against Bryan was already setting in.[78]

To the audiences he faced he hammered home three basic themes: free silver would be inflationary and disastrous to labor and the middle class; prosperity rested upon a Republican tariff policy that benefited all sections and all classes; the Democratic platform and candidate were unsound because they spoke for class interests at a time when nationalism was imperative. His gift for simplification matched that of the silverites as he preached that cheap money meant hard times for workers. "Good money never made times hard," he said in a widely quoted epigram. "This money question presents itself to me in this homely fashion," he told one delegation:

> If free coinage of silver means a fifty-three cent dollar, then it is not an honest dollar. If free coinage means a one hundred cent dollar equal to a gold dollar, as some of its advocates assert, we will not, then, have cheap dollars, but dollars just like those we now have, and which will be as hard to get. In which case free coinage will not help the debtor or make it easier for him to pay his debts.

"We do not propose to vote in favor of money, the value of which you have got to ascertain every morning by consulting the market columns in the newspapers," he said, outlining the basic fear of inflation inherent in the great middle class whose support meant so much to him. Insisting that more silver did not mean more money for everyone, and arguing that debts honestly acquired should be paid, he held that since everyone had property of some kind, free silver and depreciation threatened everyone.[79]

Deploring the Democratic arraignment of capital and labor, he asked for unity and patriotism:

> My countrymen, the most un-American of all appeals observable in this campaign is the one which seeks to array labor against capital, employer against employed. It is most unpatriotic and is fraught with the greatest peril to all concerned. We are all political equals here—equal in privilege and opportunity, dependent upon each other, and the prosperity of the one is the prosperity of the other.

This sense of nationalism shrewdly capitalized on the average man's unwillingness to believe in classes in a land that stressed individual opportunity. Hanna also put the shoe on other feet by wisely calming down his rich friends, thus preventing a panic in their ranks that would have hardened the class-struggle theme. "There won't be any revolution," he had snorted at the Union League Club in darker days in 1894. "You're just a lot of damn fools." [80]

The delegations that came and went left behind a litter of gifts. Watermelons, cheeses, canes, flags, cakes, clothing all went to the back rooms, where the staff used them when possible. Tons of flowers went on the trash heap. The more difficult gifts, such as the sixty-foot sheet of tin especially rolled for the Major by foundry workers, and the endless American eagles named "McKinley," "Protection," "Mark Hanna," and "Republican," went to special storage or to the zoo.[81]

Scurrilous stories rose up to greet the candidate. It was rumored that he beat his wife, that he was a drunkard, that he had swindled Ohio out of $3,000,000 in a phony canal scheme, and that he was the front for a gang that made the Tweed Ring look respectable. His managers worried about such lies but were more upset by the vicious stories that Mrs. McKinley was insane, a hopeless cripple, an English spy, a Catholic, a Negro, and heaven knew what else. No one around McKinley ever answered such stories, though many worried letters circulated behind the scenes.[82]

McKinley had little rest from his arduous labors, but he never showed the strain. His stamina was remarkable for so sedentary a nature, and reflected his self-control. He did go for occasional drives and sometimes accompanied Ida to their small farm where she stayed when excitement or heat proved too much. Short walks at night sometimes revived his spirits, but he had few diversions.[83]

Elsewhere the tempo of the campaign was the same, as local politicians worked mightily for the national ticket and also to carry their districts on McKinley's coattails. Ten million tin dinner pails were sold, to be filled when McKinley was elected; the Negro vote received attention in the border states; the ladies got more than their usual due; and every special group got special propaganda. McKinley's virile appearance swayed many women whose force was felt at home, and somewhat offset Bryan's good looks, as one lady revealed when she exclaimed, "I think Major McKinley is just lovely!" [84]

In New York City 150,000 men paraded on Broadway the Saturday before the election, wearing gold bugs in their lapels and carrying miles of banners. Hanna called for an immense national celebration on Flag Day, October 31, to capitalize on McKinley's patriotism. A generation that loved the flag savored the occasion.[85]

Early in September William C. Beer conferred with Bliss in New York and organized a trainload of Civil War veterans to be carried across the country in General Alger's private car. Such colorful figures as Dan Sickles piled their gear into the car and were off for patriotism and the Republican party. Hurrying from pillar to post, Beer cared for the old men, filled bourbon decanters, and kept track of Sickles' wooden leg. He heard the war fought and re-fought countless times, and searched for mineral water and vitamin pills at country stops. Still, the old fighters were a colorful and apparently effective link in the endless chain of ideas that came from the party headquarters.[86]

Garret Hobart, McKinley's running mate, who made speeches and received delegations on his own front lawn, came to Canton with his formal letter of acceptance for the presidential candidate's approval. During a lull in the storm of delegations, he and Kohlsaat accompanied McKinley to the attic, where the latter sat on a table, his legs swinging idly as he squinted through cigar smoke while Hobart read. "McKinley ripped it to pieces . . ." Kohlsaat remembered, but more likely he made only his usual tactful suggestions. Little but phraseology separated Hobart and McKinley.[87]

In August, McKinley greeted a stiffly formal, silk-hatted and frock-coated group and read out his own formal Letter of Acceptance. It was an excellent, concise, clear document. He attacked free silver as a threat to business, investment, and the income of all; stood firmly on the gold-standard plank and promised to work for an international agreement; propounded that the Democrats were sustained by an unholy alliance of Western silver mine owners and Populists; and repudiated the idea that legislation could cure the depression with fiat money. He devoted the last part of the Letter to prosperity and the tariff, deftly avoiding any injury to gold-standard Democrats. Hanna immediately ordered a million copies of the document. McKinley successfully appealed to Silver Republicans, bimetallists, all gold-standard advocates, and protectionists. He had begun uttering the word "gold" with conviction, and many who came doubtful left convinced. "Now that Major McKinley has once said the word 'gold' he feels like the boy who, after long deliberation, finally ducked his head under water," a skeptical Eastern paper reported. "He will keep doing it over and over again just to show that he wasn't afraid."[88]

McKinley faced a vigorous, unorthodox, and effective Democratic campaign. Bryan's youthful idealism, splendid voice, obvious good intentions, and courage in the face of great odds deeply impressed hundreds of thousands of people as he carried his message across the country. He had the tone of destiny that McKinley lacked, for the latter based his appeal on the head rather than the heart. Pressed for funds, with only a skeletal organization, and with time against them, the Democrats nonetheless mounted a formidable crusade against "The Masters of Capital."

Realizing its importance, Bryan hit hardest at the Midwest, attempting to hold silver sentiment at a high pitch until election day and capitalizing on farm discontent and the fruits of Populist agitation. Of his 249 major campaign stops, he made 160 in 8 Midwestern states. Concentrating everywhere on free silver, he let the remainder of his platform die, hoping that the one great issue would carry all before it. That proved an error, for when silver sentiment inevitably waned under Hanna's attack, Bryan had nothing to replace it. The weakness of his crusade was his unwillingness or inability to devise a truly national appeal, a protest movement resting on many issues, not one. Republican newspapers lampooned him ferociously as a windbag and fanatic, pumping his one idea, free silver, day after day. The Chicago Tribune termed his utterances on silver "a fog bank," and even friends said frankly: "His one great weakness is his loquacity, and that I have warned him to be on his guard against." His single-minded attention to silver was not only embarrassing to friends but comforting to enemies. "He's talking Silver all the time, and that's where we've got him," Hanna said, thumping his desk.[89]

In August Bryan journeyed into the lion's den itself, New York, determined to prove that his program appealed to workers as well as farmers. For two hours he spoke to a great crowd in Madison Square Garden. But he was in alien country; hundreds left the hall as he spoke, openly sneering at the country boy in the big city. Bereft of his splendid voice in the huge amphitheater, Bryan also made the mistake of reading a prepared address rather than relying on his eloquence to hold his audience. Republicans and Gold Democrats rejoiced at the failure. William L. Wilson, Cleveland's postmastergeneral, termed the speech "a dreary two hours essay, full of fallacies and the crudest half truths of finance and political economy." Clearly, the Boy Orator's talents lay in speaking not in logic. He

238

could not carry the East for he could not ally labor and agriculture around free silver. He must have sensed in his heart that McKinley had already won. As a correspondent wrote from Berlin, even at that distance "Bryan's 'March to the sea-board' fell quite flat." [90]

Hope sprang eternal in the ranks of the coalition of Populists, Silver Republicans, and Democrats behind Bryan. "I think, on the whole, [Bryan] is doing well, and we are at least reaching the people and creating in their minds a spirit of inquiry that in the end will be valuable, even if this campaign results disastrously," Teller, already sensing defeat,[91] wrote in September.

The coalition which made Bryan's campaign possible was also his biggest worry, for unlike the Republicans, he lacked a unified organization. He ran with two vice-presidential candidates, for the Populists had declined to fuse with the Democrats entirely. If Bryan used his personality and the one argument of silver to unify his followers he risked divisions if silver sentiment waned. The Silver Republicans were more trouble than the Populists, for as Senator Stewart said privately, "Bryan is more of a Populist than Democrat." [92] Teller's prestige made him the leader of the Rocky Mountain silverites, and he fostered their cause while supporting Bryan. "It appears to me very necessary that those of our friends who went out of the St. Louis Convention should not become the subject of the combined attack of the Democrats and Populists and McKinley Republicans," he wrote Bryan, outlining the former Republicans' real dilemma.[93] Acutely conscious of his own Republican past, and knowing that many Democrats distrusted him and his followers, Teller still considered himself a real Republican. "I am not a Democrat because I vote for Bryan," he told one correspondent bluntly.[94] Many Silver Republicans frankly feared full unity with Bryan because his defeat would brand them as party traitors and hamper their future success; after all, they might one day wish to return to "McKinleyism." The failure of the Democratic National Committee to appoint a Silver Republican to the campaign committee rankled in many former GOP breasts and drove a firm wedge between the two groups.[95]

The Democrats' most pressing need was money. Their sources were practically dry as the great depression ground its way through its final year. Industry and finance were closed to them, and they relied instead on small contributions from the party faithful, and subsidies from the silver mine owners. Retreating steadily in the face of the Republican assault, they relied more and more on Bryan's personality, and in the end that was not enough. Local organizations failed for lack of funds. "We could have raised $100,000 four years ago easier than we can raise ten now." [96]

Many Western Silver Republicans, with their eyes on wool and hides, hesitated to vote for Bryan because of his tariff record.[97] Some Democratic leaders also frankly distrusted the Boy Orator while publicly supporting him; Governor Altgeld was not convinced of Bryan's soundness. The Republicans capitalized on all such internal dissensions and heavily attacked the beleaguered local candidates like Altgeld, who were thus forced to devote their time to their own race rather than Bryan's. "It looks to me as if it were impossible for the Chicago ticket to win," Benjamin Harrison noted. "The party is divided and demoralized and the strife between the two nominees for vice-president and other like things has begun to give the appearance of a farce to the whole business." [98]

The greatest crack in the Democratic front was that which separated the Party's Eastern and Western wings. Bryan's nomination on a free-silver platform drove whole state organizations, like the one in crucial New York, from his crusade. Gold-standard men to the end, loyal supporters of Cleveland, and Easterners fearful of a Western triumph, these Gold Democrats found little solace as the campaign unfolded. "I am still a Democrat; very still," New York's David Bennett Hill wrote.[99]

Some Gold Democrats were in a more difficult position than the Silver Republicans, for they could not desert the President, even if they wished to. "It is pretty tough to ask a Democrat to vote for McKinley . . . but it is a choice of two evils, and an Independent Sound Money Democratic ticket at this time will simply give the election to the Populistic element," one Democrat insisted. Others were not so sure. "It is perfectly evident that we cannot be silent during this fierce campaign . . . ," Secretary of the Treasury Carlisle wrote. Many Eastern mugwumps frankly inclined toward McKinley, willing to swallow his protectionism for sound money and his civil service reform record.[100]

The Gold Democrats knew when they went to Chicago that their cause was lost and that they would have to bolt or join McKinley. Early in September, therefore, they formed the National Democratic party at a convention in Indianapolis which excoriated the silverites and promised an independent ticket. Lashing out at the radical Bryan platform as "the Ishmael of platforms . . . ," and calling Bryan "ambitious, unsteady and unsafe . . . An untried man, a demagogue, a word juggler . . . ," the Gold Democrats chose a national ticket. General John Palmer of Illinois and General Simon Bolivar Buckner of Kentucky were nominated for president and vice-president, respectively, on what they took as a serious ticket. Denying that they hoped only to elect McKinley, the Gold Democrats took to the field in a vigorous campaign supported by many banks and fiscal concerns whom Hanna could not touch.[101]

President Cleveland maintained a calm silence during the campaign but privately supported the Gold Democrats. Their hastily erected organization used literature, speakers, and a national campaign tour, though not on Hanna's scale. The Republicans at once made tactful overtures to the Gold Democrats and independents, inviting such figures as Carl Schurz to speak for either McKinley or Palmer. They also quietly extended funds to organizations in Kentucky, Tennessee, and West Virginia, where their support could be crucial to McKinley, though some die-hards counselled fellow Democrats to "spurn the gold of the protectionists." [102]

The Democratic bolt was welcome news to the Republicans, who used it widely to show the diffuse sectional nature of Bryan's protest movement. "General Palmer's nomination was surely very pleasing to us all," Dawes wrote, "and of the fact that he will secure a good many votes which otherwise would have gone to the Bryan ticket, there can be no doubt." Many believed that the Gold Democrats would offset the lost Silver Republicans.[103]

Palmer and Buckner entered upon a campaign as though they expected to win, the one taking on the Midwest, the other the border states. Talking to generous crowds, sprinkled with old soldiers in both blue and gray who came to see their old commanders, they urged Democrats to stand by gold and the Cleveland administration. As election day approached, Palmer told his last audience in Warrensburg, Missouri: "I promise you, my fellow Democrats, I will not consider it any very great fault if you decide next Tuesday to cast your ballot for William McKinley, though you may, if you desire, vote for Palmer and Buckner." [104] By October the Gold Democrats were confident that Bryan was beaten, and when the results were tabulated, were equally sure that their balance of power had carried Michigan, Indiana, Kentucky, and West Virginia for McKinley. "It was your work that made Mr. McKinley President," one Gold Democrat told William D. Bynum. [105]

While the Democrats quarreled among themselves and the Bryan campaign steadily lost its force, McKinley's followers rejoiced. Their candidate's studied attitude of statesmanship, his record, and his personality convinced many doubtful voters that he was the wiser choice. With September, the silver sentiment began to cool as the campaign of education had its effect in the Midwest. "The free silver sentiment in these states began to wane the latter part of July, and is still waning," a Gold Democrat noted. John Hay was more explicit: "I think we have got The Boy on the run," he wrote Whitelaw Reid. [106]

In Canton, as the autumn leaves fell and the Major's homestead slowly disappeared before the souvenir hunters, the Republican candidate deftly switched from silver to a more congenial issue, prosperity. In October he began to push his labor sympathies, publicly praising labor and privately writing: "My sympathies are naturally with the wage-earners, and I can confidently appeal to my record as to my relations with organized labor." [107]

The larger issue of prosperity appealed more to McKinley than that of silver, and as early as August he was sure that the tariff would claim its place as the chief campaign issue. ". . . I am now thoroughly convinced that from this time out, there will be less agitation upon the Silver Question and more talk on the cardinal Republican doctrine of Protection," he wrote on August 2. [108] To the delegations around his front porch he repeated an endless theme: "I do not know what you think about it, but I believe it is a good deal better to open the mills of the United States to the labor of America than to open the mints of the United States to the silver of the world." [109] McKinley argued cogently that the farmers' interest was the same as the workers'. Since he believed that silver did not affect farm prices, which were dependent upon supply and demand, his answer to farm ills was not inflation but an expanded market;

that market would be insured when the factories opened for full production under tariff protection. The most sacred American dream was the sanctity of the farmer; he was the supposed basis of society and prosperity, hence he claimed special attention. The Republicans perceived in 1896, however, that this was no longer true, and that the worker and his industry were the basis of the American economy and society. McKinley's steady appeal for the two groups to recognize their mutual interests, not in free silver or monetary inflation, but in protected prosperity and a closed home market, swung many normally Republican farm voters back to their old allegiance and away from the silver siren that first wooed them.

McKinley realized that as soon as the silver sentiment waned he could fill its place with the tariff, and counselled steady work. "Get your tariff army ready for the battle," he wrote the head of the American Protective Tariff League. "There will be work for them to do and they can get to work with the full assurance of a sweeping victory." [110] By late September his managers agreed, and suspended preparation of printed matter on silver in favor of the tariff question.

Ten days before the election the exhausted Hanna thanked Harrison for his help and added, "The outlook is generally encouraging, and I feel there is no doubt of our success." [111] And Quay, who had never really made peace, penned a charming note to the Major. "You are doubtless glad the agony is nearly over. It is marvellous that you bear up under the tremendous demands upon your physical and intellectual resources." [112]

In Canton the candidate proceeded as usual, anxious not to appear overconfident. In Chicago, Chairman Hanna confidently predicted 311 electoral votes for McKinley, with inroads into the early Democratic lead in the Midwest and border states. On election eve McKinley received his last delegations and chatted amiably with friends. Election day dawned clear, and he and Abner appeared at 8:55 A.M. at their polling place to vote. The Major then returned home, where he talked with visitors and gave out interviews. To all intents and purposes he was confident of election. [113]

Specially installed long-distance telephones and telegraph wires brought the election returns to clerks' desks in the McKinley house. As soon as the figures were prepared in long columns under the proper states they were rushed to McKinley, who sat quietly smoking a cigar in his library as dusk fell and the first returns came in. Periodically he took a paper in his hand and went to the parlor to show Ida some promising figures or check on her comfort. He presented a solemn face to all early celebrants, saying that he would trust only the final tally. Elsewhere the returns released pent-up emotions. "The feeling here beggars description," Hanna wired jubilantly from Cleveland as McKinley took an early lead. "The boys at the Union Club send love and congratulations. I will not attempt bulletins. You are elected to the highest office of the land by a people who always loved and trusted you." [114]

All evening McKinley sat at his desk digesting the returns, watching the sheets pile up, knowing that he had won the highest office in the land. Cigar after cigar went into the ash tray. It seemed almost unbelievable that the long and wearying months and years of toil had resulted in victory. The sound of hurrying feet drew him back from his thoughts, and he smiled at the tired but cheerful clerk who handed him yet another check list. His neighbors passed the house, cheering and calling congratulations that rang crisply through the chill November air. He glanced through windows covered with mist and waved back as if he thought they could see him. Midnight came and still he sat at his desk, watching his lead solidify into sure victory. About 4 A.M. he reached for a piece of his light green stationery, with his name at the top, and wrote down three digits, "241," the number of electoral votes that seemed absolutely safe; others in the border states and Midwest seemed possible, but he would wait to see. All of New England and the eastern seaboard down to Maryland were his; populous Pennsylvania and her tier of sister states north and west as far as the Dakotas were in his column; he seemed likely to carry Kentucky and West Virginia. It was not a landslide, but it was a safe and comfortable majority in both the electoral and popular votes. [115]

In far away Nebraska a different story unfolded as Bryan watched the columns fill with lost votes. Remembering at what cost he had campaigned, he must have winced. All the hurried speeches, the private and unspoken doubts and fears, all the lonely pain and weariness ended in defeat. The miles of campaigning that led him across the darkening prairies, through sleepy hamlets, into the bustling cities added up in the end to only a lost cause. But Bryan was not bitter, even as he watched state after state shift into McKinley's column. He would recall with pride in after years that he had polled over 6,000,000 votes in his first campaign, when he was only thirty-six years old. He had fought his fight well; he would be heard from again.

All that night a watchful nation gathered the returns, for this was by common consent the most crucial election since 1860. In the Midwest farmers muttered that The Money Power had won again. In Wall Street distinguished gentlemen heaved sighs of relief. In Times Square a gigantic crowd milled excitedly, watching a magic lantern screen high up on a building flash the returns and McKinley's picture. Some members of the crowd jostled and cursed, but most were enthusiastic, carrying torches and sporting McKinley paraphernalia. There were sporadic fist fights, but they did not dampen the sense of victory. In the distant West stage drivers and railroad clerks called out the returns from town to town where there were no telegraphs.

Mark Hanna and McKinley were right: the country preferred the head over the heart, safety to speculation. The prosperity theme and the economic nationalism he symbolized carried McKinley to victory. Then and later some said that he bought his victory with money and threats, that he had stayed comfortably at home receiving rigged delegations while the brave Bryan carried his crusade to the people. But William McKinley knew better as he tabulated the returns. His hands ached from handshaking, his eyes were tired, his whole body felt the strain of three months of campaigning. He had worked as few other men ever worked, keeping careful control of his organization, watching every decision with the care of a trained politician who leaves nothing to chance or fate—or even to Mark Hanna. He knew the cost of such an effort; he had only to look in a mirror to see it.

That evening, when McKinley's victory was secure, Kohlsaat picked up his telephone in Chicago and called Canton. He had some trouble locating McKinley but finally got James McKinley, the Major's nephew, on the wire. Kohlsaat asked where the new President was and James left the receiver for a few minutes. He returned

245

to say that he had found Uncle Will and Aunt Ida kneeling beside his grandmother's bed, and the old lady was saying calmly, "Oh, God, keep him humble." [116]

After a brief but refreshing sleep, McKinley rose the following morning to hear Canton's cheers. A slight drizzle obscured the street and washed down across the McKinley posters along the way, causing wet bunting to slap against the store fronts and telephone poles. The President-elect took his mother a bouquet of flowers and returned home to sort through the piles of congratulatory letters and telegrams, one of which had come by pony express from Buffalo Bill. On November 6 a special messenger brought a telegram from Bryan. "Senator Jones has informed me that the returns indicate your election and I hasten to extend my congratulations," it read. "We have submitted the issues to the American people and their will is law." Interviewed at his home, Bryan merely said: "The fight has just commenced." Canton, though worn out, outdid itself with a monster parade and fireworks when the victory was official.[117]

In the flush of victory there was one man McKinley could not forget. Six days after his official triumph he took another sheet of paper and carefully penned one of his most heartfelt and remarkable letters to Mark Hanna:

> We are through with the election, and before turning to the future I want to express to you my great debt of gratitude for your generous life-long and devoted services to me. Was there ever such unselfish devotion before? Your unfaltering and increasing friendship through more than twenty years has been to me an encouragement and a source of strength which I am sure you have never realized, but which I have constantly felt and for which I thank you from the bottom of my heart. The recollection of all those years of uninterrupted loyalty and affection, of mutual confidences and growing regard fill me with emotions too deep for the pen to portray. I want you to know, but I cannot find the right words to tell you, how much I appreciate your friendship and faith. God bless and prosper you and yours is my constant prayer.

Then, asking Hanna to think of joining his cabinet, he signed his name, "Your friend, William McKinley." [118]

A tedious post-mortem followed the election, though McKinley's plurality of 271 to 176 in the electoral college, and 7,100,000 to Bryan's 6,500,000 in the popular vote, gave him the greatest victory of any president since Grant. The half-million votes cast for Palmer had helped a great deal, but he could have lost several doubtful states and still won. Chauncey Depew charged that it was absurd to say that workers had been forced to vote for McKinley, because no one could check on their ballots, but many workers did, in fact, vote for McKinley under threats. Bryan himself believed that the Democratic ranks held firm, but he could not win enough independent Republicans to offset both the regular Republicans and the Gold Democrats.[119]

Charges of purchased votes and corruption were more serious, though impossible to prove. Undoubtedly both parties engaged in such dealings on local and city levels; Altgeld felt that Bryan could have carried Illinois had every legitimate ballot been counted, but this does not seem likely in view of the 140,000 votes that separated Bryan and McKinley there.[120] If men were bought, it seems unlikely and impossible to prove that they were bought with Hanna's consent or knowledge. That the Republicans' money figured prominently in the victory is certain; it alone permitted the vast educational program that flooded the country with literature and speakers. But McKinley himself was undoubtedly the most potent figure in the campaign. His attitude of statesmanship in a time of crisis, his economic nationalism, and his deft handling of the prosperity issue in a national rather than sectional context, as well as his long and distinguished record, won the fight.

Bryan's mistakes were just as responsible for his defeat as was McKinley's organization. The failure to fuse with the Populists hurt his cause in the border states. His emphasis on campaigning in the Corn Belt cost him potential strength in the Northwest and on the border. The defection of the Gold Democrats undoubtedly was important, although McKinley may have won handily without them, for they would probably have stayed at home, enabling him to maintain his normal lead.[121]

It was often said that had the election been held in July, Bryan would have won, so effective was his first appeal, and so compelling was silver sentiment. True or not, the fact remains that McKinley's ultimate victory showed how thoughtful arguments dispelled the silver sentiment and how false a Bryan victory on that issue would have been. Bryan's failure to win all the farmers from their normal

Republican allegiance was a signal defeat. New discoveries of gold doubtless had little to do with the result as they came too late to be of much significance. Bryan's failure to capture the urban vote was a telling blow, and his inability to tie the workers' interests to the farmers' carried his crusade down to defeat through economic and geographic sectionalism.[122]

The deeper meanings remained for historians to ponder; William McKinley knew only the taste of victory. All his life he had sought elusive political power. Phenomenal success had come to him, and with it a host of friends and supporters more important than the riches he spurned. Gratified and exalted by his victory, he was nonetheless sobered by the awesome responsibilities that lay ahead. It would be no easy task to make his vision of nationalism a reality, but it was one to which he would devote his whole being.

XII

Cabinetmaking

PRESIDENT-ELECT William McKinley spent many hours in his study between his election and inauguration, some broken only by the sound of wind beyond the frosted panes and the even ticking of his clock. He watched its hands in occasional fascination through the cigar smoke that accompanied his reverie, marvelling that so small an instrument could record the swift passage of so much time. But few and precious were such hours of contemplation. He spent far more time gazing intently into the faces of fellow politicians and listening to advisors and supplicants who came from the four corners of the country to ask favors and give advice.

Where does a new president find a cabinet? To whom does he turn and from whom does he have the right to expect the loyalty and ability that can withstand the drudgery as well as the power and importance of a cabinet post? Few cabinet members in the late nineteenth century could hope for great political advancement, and businessmen hesitated to accept small salaries, public calumny, and gruelling routine by turning their administrative skills to government.

McKinley turned to his task after a brief rest, though his early decisions were fluid. "I have concluded but a few things and they are likely to be disturbed before the 4th of March," he wrote the inquisitive Whitelaw Reid at Christmas time.[1] Alive to the powers of patronage, he anxiously watched the men in Congress with whom he would have to work and who would expect proper recognition. He did not need Matt Quay's proffered advice not to "distribute your plums before you secure your legislation."[2] One man kept silent; Mark Hanna held that he had nothing to do with cabinetmaking. His action gratified many ranking party men who agreed with John Hay on "the vital necessity for McKinley of asserting himself at the start and letting all and sundry know who is boss."[3]

The new President did not lack advisors. Everyone who came

through Canton was likely to cast a word his way, and the editors, reporters, and local politicians of the nation wholeheartedly devoted themselves to affairs in which they had as little practical influence as the emperor of China. Nor was there any dearth of candidates for patronage. A multitude of good Republicans, some of recent conversion, came forward. "In October an Irish Raypublican's so rare people pint him out on th' street, an' women carry their babies to see him," Mr. Dooley said presciently. "But th' day afther iliction, glory be, ye run into thim ivrywhere. . . ." [4]

One place to look for cabinet material was in the Senate. There a group of veteran Republicans, seasoned by long tenure, inured to the ways of politics, wise in administration and legislation, had held power for decades. McKinley knew the ability, soundness, and congeniality of views of men like Allison, Aldrich, Orville H. Platt, and others. They knew him, agreed with his program, understood what his administration would have to do. But he moved cautiously, for he could not weaken the Senate to strengthen his cabinet. If he took Western or Midwestern Republicans, silverites would fill their seats; if he took only Easterners he would split the party. Every outstanding senator presumably had presidential ambitions, and McKinley had not survived political life to raise up an opponent by giving him prominence in the cabinet. What if a strong man in his cabinet, with a national following, disagreed? It was unlikely, but the unforeseen was his specialty. He preferred no Blaines in his cabinet who, though they added luster, also added dissension.

There were other places to look. Many prominent Republicans in private life were "available." The new administration would need a cabinet composed of sound, respected men, representing the geographic and economic interests of the country. Brilliance was not necessarily required, for solid, businesslike administration was the major Republican campaign promise. To find men who could thus represent local interests in a national framework was no small task, even for a judge of men of McKinley's ability.

McKinley's most pressing problem was Mark Hanna. After his election victory, the national chairman took a well-earned rest, but he was followed everywhere by the nagging question: would he join the cabinet? McKinley had already asked him to join his official family as postmaster-general, from which post he could direct both his department and the party. Though Hanna denied any part in the cabinetmaking that went on in Canton, his name was prominent in all such discussions.[5]

Rumor said that Hanna wished the Treasury portfolio, feeling that his managerial feats during the campaign qualified him for the post. This was doubtful, for Hanna knew his own limitations. McKinley himself honestly said: "I don't think Mark knows enough about governmental finance to fill the position." [6] It is unlikely that either Hanna or McKinley thought seriously of him for that position.

McKinley fully understood the problem involved. If Hanna were appointed would it not look like payment for services rendered in 1896? "The people would consider him as your owner and the administration his not yours," wrote a trusted friend.[7] McKinley himself certainly had such thoughts, but his loyalty to and belief in Hanna would not have prevented his giving him a cabinet post had the latter been willing. Hanna had his own doubts and did not wish to be taken out of Ohio politics or away from his business connections by a cabinet post.[8]

But Hanna also had his ambitions. When told that he had said he desired no political office, he snapped back, "I don't know that I ever said that." His heart was set on a prize that had occupied his dreams since he first dabbled in politics, a seat in the United States Senate. "I would rather be a Senator in Congress than have any other office on earth," he told a friend in 1892. Shortly after the election he told Will Osborne frankly that he wanted to go to the Senate, where he thought he could help McKinley more than in the cabinet, but he didn't know how to do it.[9]

An avenue opened to McKinley and Hanna as they pondered the problem late in 1896. McKinley's eye turned to Senator Sherman for the State Department; if Governor Bushnell would then appoint Hanna to Sherman's vacant seat their problem would be solved. As soon as McKinley resolved on this plan of action and Sherman agreed, the wheels were set in motion. Sherman informed Governor Bushnell that he would resign, effective March 4, and asked that Hanna be appointed to succeed him. Hanna meanwhile rallied influential friends to pressure Bushnell, for the Governor was a major backer of Foraker and felt scant affection for either Hanna or McKinley. Unity had its merits, but the election was over. While Bushnell procrastinated both in silence and in manuever, Hanna and Sherman pressured the Foraker people in the name of party unity.[10] The President-elect remained aloof, though in the end his voice too was required.

Early in January, in the weeks after Sherman accepted the cabinet post, Hanna's tension mounted as he became ever more fearful that the coveted prize would slip from his grasp. It seemed for a time that Bushnell would temporarily appoint a figurehead and seek the seat himself, or that he would call a special session of the legislature to choose a new senator. National attention focused on Ohio, for it rapidly became a testing ground of Hanna's strength and McKinley's influence. "There will be a deadly fight for the senatorship," John Hay wrote. "We shall do all in our power to avoid trouble," Hanna said privately, "but if it *must come* better now." [11]

The key to the puzzle was not Bushnell, a rather pompous, handlebar-mustached, and conveniently wealthy manufacturer of farm implements, but Foraker. If he could challenge Hanna's power he might increase his following; on the other hand, if he failed, he might lose it. Hearing of Sherman's appointment, Foraker, suddenly overcome by pious patriotism, went to Canton to protest that Sherman was too old, the State Department too important, and so on. He found McKinley immovable; his Scottish stubbornness was very evident. From there he went to Columbus for closed-door talks with Bushnell. Declining to say what he recommended, Foraker went his way, impressed by the popular force behind Hanna.[12]

McKinley remained publicly aloof and discreetly silent, while steadily supporting Hanna, relying on public opinion and his own private emissaries to do the real work. "McKinley is having his share of worry now," Hanna wrote, "but is trying his best to meet the situation bravely." In the last week of February Bushnell capitulated and told Judge Day, whom the President-elect had sent to Columbus with an ultimatum, that he would appoint Hanna. "I know that this information will be agreeable to you inasmuch as it is in accordance with your request conveyed to me by Hon. William R. Day," Bushnell wrote McKinley curtly.[13]

The story had a strange and tense ending, for Bushnell added insult to injury by refusing to deliver Hanna's formal commission until after the inauguration, thus permitting Foraker to act as Ohio's senior senator. On the morning of March 5, 1897, Hanna received his commission in the lobby of the Arlington Hotel in Washington.[14]

The story ended on a different note for McKinley. Though he was happy at the outcome, he had sincerely wanted Hanna in his official family. In mid-February, with Hanna's final refusal to enter the cabinet, and with his senatorial future apparently assured, McKinley wrote another warm letter to his old friend:

It has been my dearest wish since I was elected to the Presidency, to have you accept a place in my Cabinet. This you have known for months and are already in receipt of a letter from me, urging you to accept a position in the administration, written a few days after the election. You stated to me that you could under no circumstances accept a Cabinet place, and have many times declined both publicly and to me personally to have your name considered in that connection. As from time to time I have determined upon various distinguished gentlemen for the several Departments, I have always hoped and so stated to you at every convenient opportunity that you would yet conclude to accept the Postmaster-Generalship. You have so often declined and since our conversation on Tuesday last, I have reluctantly concluded that I cannot induce you to take this or any other Cabinet position. You know how deeply I regret this determination and how highly I appreciate your life-long devotion to me. You have said that if you could not enter the Senate, you would not enter public life at all. No one, I am sure, is more desirous of your success than myself, and no one appreciates more deeply how helpful and influential you could be in that position. It seems to me that you will be successful, and I predict for you a most distinguished and satisfactory career in that greatest of parliamentary bodies.[15]

If McKinley promoted Sherman to the State Department only to create a place for Hanna in the Senate, as has often been charged, it is singularly odd that as late as mid-February he was still trying to get Hanna to join the cabinet.

The Hanna problem ran concurrently with the larger problem of choosing a secretary of State. Contrary to popular opinion then and later, McKinley was especially aware of the post's importance. Not only was it the premier position of the cabinet, but he sensed already the growing importance which it would acquire under his administration. Senator Lodge stopped at Canton to discuss Hawaii and Cuba with the President-elect. Surprised by McKinley's grasp of the subject, he wrote Theodore Roosevelt, "He is entirely prepared to face the responsibilities [of foreign relations] at the earliest possible moment and deal with them. Indeed his whole attitude of mind struck me as serious, broad in view, and just what we all ought to desire. I brought from it many good hopes." [16]

McKinley's first choice for the post apparently had been Senator William B. Allison. Drawn to his tact and great experience as well as his proverbial caution, the new President had felt him suited for the job. No matter that the Iowan knew little of foreign relations; he could learn, and his natural talents would offset his factual deficiencies in the meantime. To travelling Iowans who stopped to see him in December, McKinley had let it be known that he would welcome Allison to his cabinet in the premier post.[17] Those close to Allison doubted that he would leave the Senate for either the State or Treasury Departments; his Senate term had time to run, re-election was sure, and he liked his work. "My situation is such that I could not afford to accept either the State or Treasury Department," Allison himself wrote after declining.[18] It was just as well, for Allison proved invaluable in the Senate. But the Iowan, who had twice sought the presidential nomination, must have reflected in after years on how he had inadvertently lost the White House, for in 1900 he was to refuse the President's request that he be vice-president in McKinley's second term.

By January, 1897, however, McKinley had made up his mind to ask Sherman to enter the cabinet as secretary of State. He did so after much reflection and not, as his enemies charged, only to create a place in the Senate for Hanna. Sherman was one of the most famous and respected men in the United States. His great national prestige and administrative ability lent themselves well to the State portfolio. He had been a member of the sacrosanct Senate Committee on Foreign Relations since 1883, and its chairman since 1886. It would be a signal honor for the elder statesman to end his public life as chief of the cabinet.

But rumors reached McKinley that Sherman's health was poor, that his age told, and that he was in fact unable to carry out such duties as the State Department bade to impose on its new incumbent. Ever cautious, McKinley sent private emissaries to check the stories. Will Osborne reported after a cordial dinner with the usually frosty

Senator that he seemed as alert and strong as ever despite his seventy-four years.[19] Similar reports reached McKinley from other sources. After appointing Sherman he felt acutely conscious of the gossip that he had misused the aged statesman and shown scant respect for the State Department in order to make room for Hanna. He testily wrote Joseph Medill that "the stories regarding Senator Sherman's 'mental decay' are without foundation and the cheap inventions of sensational writers or other evil-disposed people. When I saw him last I was convinced both of his perfect health, physically and mentally, and that his prospects of life were remarkably good." [20]

As early as mid-December, Sherman himself let it be known that he would accept the secretaryship. McKinley's formal offer, on January 3, 1897, came as no surprise, for Sherman knew that he was the leading contender. "After a day's reflection I have concluded to accept your tender of the portfolio of Secretary of State, and will heartily do all I can to make your administration a success," he wrote his former lieutenant.[21]

Sherman had his own reasons for accepting the post with alacrity. He would face a costly and uncertain battle for re-election in 1898; he wished to end his public career in a useful and distinguished capacity. He felt duty bound to the new President. "Still I feel a sense of duty to McKinley and am strongly inclined to accept his offer," he wrote on January 10. "The chief impediment in the way is the fear that Governor Bushnell will not appoint Hanna to fill my unexpired term." [22] Though he apparently had some second thoughts after his appointment aroused criticism, he was never disposed to decline the offer. "I could see by Mr. Sherman's letters that he was not adverse to a Cabinet appointment," an aide noted. ". . . and did accept the Premiership without any pressure on Mr. Hanna's part." [23] If it was all a plot to kick the old man upstairs, Sherman kicked first.

The newspapers greeted Sherman's appointment with a mixture of resentment and regret. Most felt he was too old and infirm to undertake the new duties. Many felt that it was a stop-gap appointment and that he would not last a year. The Foraker group rallied to the elder statesman with a devotion they had never shown in his younger days. In the meantime, McKinley opened cordial relations with Sherman by asking him for suggestions on the Cuban problem for use in his inaugural address. A long, confused memorandum came from the new Secretary, arguing that intervention was inevitable. McKinley digested it, softened it, and finally discarded it in favor of his own tone. It was a bad beginning.[24]

Sherman's position became intolerable with the outbreak of war. His hearing and memory all but failed, and subordinates conducted the department's business. McKinley and Assistant Secretary Day were in fact secretary of State. Day attended cabinet meetings and was close to the President, facts that never escaped the touchy Sherman.[25] It is difficult to believe that McKinley ever wished the appointment to end sadly, or that a man of his responsibility and tact used Sherman merely to create a place for Hanna. It is also curious that Sherman's associates thought so little of the office he held, regarding it as one unbecoming his age and dignity.

McKinley had selected his good friend William R. Day to be assistant secretary of State despite the latter's surprised insistence that he did not want the job. The quiet, legalistic judge became a familiar and well-loved figure in the State Department, and his country-lawyer's bearing hid a sharp acumen and common sense. The second assistant secretary was equally able; Alvee A. Adee seemed to have been there forever, and served under a long series of presidents with unusual modesty, efficiency, and ability. His deafness helped, for he heard little dissension. The position was really a clerkship, but Adee made it a policy-making post. Handling all routine business in the department, he knew more details of foreign affairs than any man in Washington, and McKinley found his chits of advice, written on scraps of paper and signed with a familiar triple A, indispensable. The whole arrangement worked, but it had disadvantages. As one foreign diplomat said in 1897, "the head of the department knew nothing, the first assistant said nothing, and the second assistant heard nothing." [26]

The secretaryship of the Treasury was the second most important cabinet position. The very issue of the campaign raised the office to fresh importance, and its occupant would show how seriously the new administration took its mandate on the currency issue. Many expected the post to go to a Gold Democrat as a reward for that group's indirect support of McKinley. But the fiery "Marse

Henry" Watterson said bluntly after the election that the Gold
Democrats and Republicans would not work together because of the
tariff. However tempting the post might be, leading Gold Democrats
refused it, for it might look like treason; like the Silver Republicans,
they might one day wish to return to the fold.[27]

The "Gold Democracy" had less immediate appeal to McKinley
than did his fellow Republicans. His first choice for the Treasury
post was his old friend Nelson Dingley, the slight, unassuming
wizard of tariff figures. A perpetual congressman from Maine,
Dingley had such an eye for figures and was so cold-bloodedly
analytical that his robust confrere, Tom Reed, said he would rather
hold a tariff schedule on his knee than a pretty girl. Already he was
writing a tariff bill that would bear his name when the new administration passed it.

Dingley's appointment would have satisfied New England and
would have been wise, for he knew governmental finance. But he
was not well and not inclined to leave his tenure in the House for the
pressures of a cabinet post. While newspapers peddled rumors that
Hanna wanted the job, Dingley weighed the pros and cons of acceptance. By late December he reluctantly declined, while pledging
his best work in Congress.[28]

With Dingley's refusal the newspapers resumed their speculation and rumor manufacturing. The post, they said, would go to
Nelson Aldrich, an even more formidable financial wizard, but that
hard-driving New Englander was far too cold blooded to sit next to
McKinley; nor would he have left the safety and power of his
Senate seat for a cabinet post.[29] McKinley apparently thought of his
friend Myron Herrick, but the Ohio banker would not leave his
growing business and felt himself too closely identified personally
with McKinley, as well as too inexperienced in national finance to
consider the post.[30]

From Illinois the winds of opinion brought the name of Shelby
Cullom, strongly endorsed by his own and by Senator Allison's
friends. Cullom himself remained discreetly silent; after being run
over by the McKinley steamroller in his own state, it would add insult to injury to ask for a cabinet post. Such an appointment, if
McKinley ever considered it seriously, had only politics to recommend it, for Cullom knew little of finance. He may have wanted the

honor of declining more than that of a cabinet post itself. But it was not likely that the Major, who also remembered the salt of Illinois' wounds, would make such overtures, though Cullom called at Canton and basked in McKinley's friendliness.[31]

A certain nervousness haunted McKinley's dealings with Illinois' demands for patronage, for the figure of Charles Dawes shadowed him there. The youthful Dawes took McKinley aback earlier in the fall by calmly saying that he wanted to be secretary of the Treasury. He felt adequate to the task and his work in the campaign proved his ability. McKinley, who looked upon Dawes almost as a son, was torn between his awareness of Dawes's limitations and his desire. The aspirant's youth and national obscurity overbalanced his proven ability. Yet McKinley hesitated to offend Dawes or seem ungrateful; he was relieved when Dawes accepted the comptrollership of the currency instead.[32]

But Illinois could still lay claim to a cabinet post, for her electoral votes had helped McKinley's cause mightily. Mr. Kohlsaat had an inspiration, and calling McKinley on the telephone, asked him if he had considered the Chicago banker, Lyman J. Gage, for the Treasury. "Have I ever met him?" McKinley asked after a moment's hesitation. "Oh, I remember him," he said suddenly, vividly recalling Gage's splendid white chin whiskers on the occasion of a formal dinner they had both attended. "That is an inspiration," McKinley said. "Let me think." He quickly dispatched Dawes to talk with Gage, whose banking affairs made him a power in Midwestern finance. The newspapers speculated rampantly, and reported great pressure on Gage's behalf. "Where in hell is the great pressure?" Hanna grunted publicly. "I never heard him mentioned for the place." [33]

Talk of Gage surprised Eastern Republicans who had confidently expected the post for themselves; moreover, Gage's politics were not clear and he had no stature in national affairs. He had been on the fringe of radicalism, having publicly supported the pardon of the Haymarket rioters, and had participated in several "reform" movements in Illinois. The Cullom organization hated him. McKinley was drawn to Gage by the fact that his affiliations would satisfy both sound-money Republicans and Gold Democrats, by his apparent lack of deep interest in politics, which marked him as a man of finance, and by his lack of connection with any factional group in Illinois. His appointment would show that the Midwest as well as the East favored the gold standard.

Dawes talked several hours with Gage in the latter's Chicago office, informing him frankly that McKinley would like him to accept the Treasury portfolio if his tariff views were not extreme. Gage, always honest, said that he opposed any tariff "which might foster trusts and monopolies," but did not oppose the protective principle as such. He said frankly that he had voted against Blaine, and feared that Sherman's financial record might overshadow him in the cabinet. Bowing Dawes out with a smile, he promised an answer in forty-eight hours.[34]

On January 23, Gage announced publicly that he would not refuse the Treasury post if offered it. Making the pilgrimage to Canton, he impressed McKinley with his forthright and honestly expressed views. In a long private interview, Gage bluntly said that he would press for monetary reforms and oppose any further purchase of silver. The gold standard would be his signpost, to which McKinley replied easily: "As to the gold standard, you cannot be more firmly convinced of our interest as a nation in maintaining it than I am." This did not forbid negotiations for an international agreement, toward which McKinley was already working.[35]

Gage accepted the post and pleased by the prospects before him, left Canton. Like many independent Republicans, he had thought McKinley weak and found him strong. "I expected a cross examination, but there was nothing of the kind. . . ." he told reporters after the meeting. "Major McKinley is a man with a mind of his own. Instead of asking me what *I* thought, he told me what *he* thought. We agreed on everything we talked about." [36]

The courtly, charming, and kindly Gage was among McKinley's happiest selections. Looking for all the world like Santa Claus behind his beautiful chin whiskers and twinkling eyes, the modest, gentle banker became a social favorite and close confidant in the administration. While not a genius, he gave his department a sound financial administration, and the fiscal problems of the Spanish-American War did not interrupt his smooth progress. His selection offended no one except the silverites and satisfied many who feared that the crucial Treasury post would go to a political hack or bimetallist. Eastern bankers, Gold Democrats, and most Republicans applauded the choice.[37]

Only one man was in the lead for the War Department, Russell Alger, the genial McKinleyite from Michigan. Slight and of delicate build and frail health, his narrow face offset by a fine white goatee and mustache, the cordial Alger was popular and respected in many Republican circles. He had risen to brevet general in the Civil War, entered the lucrative lumber and railroad boom in postwar Michigan, and became the state's governor and a power in the Republican party's inner councils. A favorite son in 1888 and 1892, he had had a taste of national politics, which he abandoned for McKinley in 1896. He was rich, addicted to ease, often indolent because of his bad heart as well as his nature. Alger's appointment had little to recommend it except politics, and hope was voiced that there would be no war during his incumbency, for he showed no ability to meet the pressures of a real emergency. Why McKinley was so drawn to him is a mystery, except to repay the Northwest for its support.

A circle of loyal friends set to work as soon as the polls closed in November to make Alger secretary of War. "I shall be utterly confounded if we do not succeed," the trusted Senator Julius Caesar Burrows of Michigan wrote Alger by January. "I believe we will." [38] The newspapers steadily reported that Alger was "first, last and all the time Mr. McKinley's choice." Sherman stated flatly early in January that he felt Alger would join the cabinet, and few other names vied with the Michigander's for the War Department.[39]

McKinley would not be hurried. Rumors reached him that Alger's war record was not clean. He had been absent from duty in the Shenandoah Valley campaigns of 1864, and though subsequently honorably discharged and given brevet promotions, a cloud of doubt hung over his past. McKinley said nothing, as was his wont, but sent the trusted Joe Smith to Washington for a thorough search of the War Department records and a report on the case. His friend Burrows undertook a similar mission, and both reported that the charges were untrue.[40]

Satisfied of Alger's past, McKinley asked him for a conference late in January and the eager candidate hastened to Canton.[41] Upon being offered the appointment, he emerged from the conference beaming a self-confidence that never vanished even in the disasters of his wartime bungling: "The policy of the administration will be the policy of the department . . . ," he said. "I am a man of peace. The country wants and needs peace for a number of years. With these and a moderate tariff this country will reach a prosperity not equalled for some years." [42] This strangely garbled statement must have given McKinley pause for thought if he heard or read it.

Alger's appointment was worse than Sherman's, for there was no Day or Adee in the War Department to restrain or advise the touchy Secretary. He knew little if anything about the War Department, and unlike his colleague Long in the Navy Department, he did little in the year given him before the war to prepare for the conflict. If McKinley ever regretted an appointment, he must have regretted this one most, though he treated Alger with great deference and stood by him loyally during his darkest hours. It is significant, however, that when the time came to dismiss the luckless Secretary, the President asked someone else to carry the bad news.

The Navy Department offered fewer problems. There was only one real candidate, John Davis Long, former governor of Massachusetts and an old friend of McKinley's. The stooped, kindly Long was a popular and respected figure in all the circles he graced, but nowhere was this more true than in his native New England. "Mr. Long is probably the most popular man in public life in Massachusetts," a supporter wrote McKinley. "He is a lovable man, a loyal friend, and has every qualification for a Cabinet post of this kind, *and there would be no mistake in making such an appointment*." [43] On January 30, McKinley formally tendered Long the post.[44] Long's surprising energy, quickness of mind, and willingness to experiment made his department one of the best in the new administration. His courtly manners, easy conversation, and scholarly mien also gave him entry into Washington society.

The most vexing problem in the Navy Department was the assistant secretaryship. Pressure came from everywhere for Roosevelt. Lodge rushed to Canton early in December to put an iron in the fire for "Teddy," and his embarrassment at having opposed the Major before the convention dissolved in McKinley's genial smiles. "I have no feeling about what went before the nomination," he said. "You have a perfect right to ask a favor and I understand what you want." He admitted that he was considering Roosevelt, among others. "I hope he had no preconceived plans which he would wish to drive through the moment he got in," McKinley said bluntly, betraying an understanding of Roosevelt. "The truth is, Will, Roosevelt is always in such a state of mind," he said to William Howard Taft at another interview.[45]

McKinley was first inclined to let the Secretary choose his assistant; his second inclination was to pass over Roosevelt, both because Platt hated the pushy "dude," and because the Bellamy Storers supported him. They had contributed to the Walker fund of 1893 and it might look like repayment of debts. "[Platt] hates Roosevelt like poison and moreover, I don't like the idea of making an appointment solicited by the Bellamy Storers on account of the fact that they sent a subscription to that Fund," McKinley said frankly. He was even more frank to Mrs. Storer, who called on him in Canton. "I am afraid he is too pugnacious. . . . I want peace and I am told that your friend Theodore is always getting into rows with everybody." He listened in silence to Mrs. Storer's admonition to "Give him a chance to prove that he can be peaceful," and promised nothing.[46]

Hay, Taft, Hanna, even Reed, as well as the Lodges and Storers, recommended Roosevelt, but Senator Chandler of New Hampshire showed remarkable foresight in opposing the New Yorker. "It is a curious situation," he wrote his own candidate for the post. "Here is a man in every way fitted to be a member of the cabinet, and yet who is not adapted to be an Assistant Secretary. If he were a Secretary and responsible to the world, he would be cautious as well as energetic; as an Assistant Secretary he might be uneasy and troublesome." [47] Roosevelt was not inclined to go to Canton to plead his own cause. "He saw me when I went there during the campaign, and if he thinks I am hot-headed and harum-scarum I don't think he will change his mind now. . . . Moreover, I don't wish to appear as a supplicant." Roosevelt's friends did his work, Platt finally capitulated, and McKinley appointed him in April.[48]

Hanna's definite refusal to be postmaster-general left Henry Clay Payne of Wisconsin the front runner for that post. Payne's charm and dispatch recommended him to fellow politicians, and his smooth management of the Chicago headquarters in 1896 brought Hanna to his side when the time came for cabinet appointments. "You may wipe out every obligation that you feel toward me, and I'll ask no further favors of you, if you'll only put Henry Payne in the Cabinet," Hanna asked McKinley in person.[49] Isaac Stephenson and Philetus Sawyer, Wisconsin's senior Republicans, went to Canton on Payne's behalf and came away feeling that they had moved the mountain, though McKinley said little.[50]

Actually he was having second thoughts, for Payne was popular only with professional politicians. Robert La Follette counteracted Payne's conservative support by coming to Canton for a drive with McKinley and his mother, "a beautiful old lady." La Follette bluntly told McKinley that Payne was a railroad lobbyist and lumber dealer, and was anathema to Wisconsin's progressive element and young Republicans. McKinley thought a long time and then said frankly: "Bob, I may not be able to appoint Hoard [La Follette's candidate], but I will say to you that Henry Payne shall not be a member of my cabinet." [51] McKinley remembered Payne as a lobbyist from his own congressional days and would not risk branding his administration in the eyes of the younger Republican element who had helped so much in 1896.

Finally he turned south for his postmaster-general, and in doing so clearly left Hanna in charge of the party organization; he could be a senator as well as the national chairman. In replying to Hanna's final decision in February, McKinley noted that he had offered the cabinet post to James A. Gary of Baltimore, "a prominent Republican of the South. . . ." [52] To an Ohioan the South began on the Chesapeake. Gary, whose appointment was only temporary, served without distinction or luster.

McKinley originally intended to make the attorney-general his Southern appointment, and first inclined toward Judge Nathan B. Goff of West Virginia, who talked with him about the post. But Goff declined late in January for personal reasons. The President-elect had already weighed the possibility of John J. McCook of New York, who was urged by Platt. He had also moved west in search of a secretary of the Interior to give geographic balance to the cabinet and to repay California for her electoral votes. His first choice as secretary of the Interior was Judge Joseph McKenna, a prominent lawyer and jurist whom he knew from his days in Congress.

McKenna was reluctant to join the cabinet for financial reasons; it would involve a cut in salary, and a recent "unfortunate loan" compelled him to rebuff McKinley's first offer late in December. Harrison Gray Otis, prominent Republican publisher, called on McKenna and talked long and earnestly about his duty and the willingness of friends to help him out, so the Judge went to Canton to confer with McKinley.[53]

Greeting McKenna with smiles, McKinley proffered a seat and cigar as the two talked pleasantries before beginning earnest political conversation. McKenna said that he was honored and happy to be considered for so important a post, but seeming a trifle embarrassed, he said suddenly that he was a Catholic and many people might oppose his control over Indian education as Secretary of the Interior. McKinley was surprised but smiled as he said blandly that he didn't want McKenna for Interior, but as attorney-general. The flustered McKenna could do nothing but accept. McKinley later laughed over the interview. "I don't believe the Judge suspected that I switched him," he said. "We were in Congress together several years and it never occurred to me that he was a Catholic." [54]

McKinley had hoped that his cabinetmaking troubles would end when he talked with McKenna, but his unexpected switch reopened the Interior Department and threw out his tentative choice of John J. McCook of New York for attorney-general. The situation in New York was thus further complicated, for McCook would not think of the Interior Department.

The Agriculture Department posed fewest problems of all. Inevitably it would go to a Midwesterner, and James H. "Tama Jim" Wilson of Iowa commanded McKinley's attention.[55] No one foresaw the close relations that developed between McKinley and Wilson, or that Wilson would hold his post until 1913, serving under three presidents. Looking like the farmer he had been, the lanky, dark-bearded and shrewd-eyed Wilson had his ear to the ground alongside McKinley and served as a leading administration weathervane for Western and Midwestern affairs. McKinley entrusted him with delicate political trips that he gave no one else, and Tama Jim's long reports from "the folks back home" constituted a prime source of information on trends and events west of the Mississippi.[56]

Wilson's administration of his department was wise if not colorful, and prudent if not spectacular.

Of all those who offered the President-elect advice on his cabinet, none came forward more frequently, more volubly, or to be greeted with greater respect than Whitelaw Reid. The distinguished-looking publisher of the *New York Tribune* had been prominent in Republican circles since the disputed election of 1876, in which he played a leading role. His steadfast loyalty to his party and to McKinley made him a friend worth having. Always elegantly attired, charming and courtly behind a white beard, wealthy and at ease in luxurious surroundings, the voluble Reid had one great failing; he could not keep a secret. His lengthy letters poured advice on the Major, concerned largely with the New York scene, where his very name was anathema to Tom Platt, who thought him a mush-headed reformer.

A man who could not keep a secret and who talked as freely as Reid got respect but limited confidence from McKinley. A foreseeing fate had temporarily isolated Reid in Phoenix, Arizona, a frontier environment singularly incongruous for the elegant New Yorker but where he basked in the sunshine, writing long letters and trying to cure the painful asthma that made him wretched in the East. The election was no sooner over than he bombarded the patient McKinley with long and tedious letters warning against any compromise with Platt. "They have talked so long and so much about Major McKinley's yielding character, that they have come to believe themselves, and think they can bully him into taking the advice of the men who said he was unfit to be President, as to those who are fit to be in his cabinet," he complained as the papers reported Platt emissaries in Canton. Talk that Cornelius Bliss was anti-machine and a suitable compromise irritated Reid, who warned that Platt had planned to foist Bliss on McKinley even before the election. Arguing that Platt had proven to be a double dealer and was circulating the story that he had written the gold plank and won the election for McKinley, he advised that New York receive no cabinet post as a punishment.[57]

No cabinet post, that is, except for himself, for he was willing, as he put it, to be secretary of State. That failing, he enlisted his friend John Hay to pressure the Major to make him secretary of the Navy. And that failing, he would like to be ambassador to England. While Hay reported privately to Reid that Platt threatened "hell with the lid off" if Reid got anything at all, the disgusted Colonel informed McKinley that "I have ceased thinking about Reid; he thinks enough about himself for two." [58]

McKinley solved the problem in a masterful way. In mid-February, unable to defer the decision on New York any longer, and unwilling to alienate Reid, McKinley wrote him a lengthy letter, a masterpiece of tact, stating that while he would like to have Reid in his cabinet or as the ambassador, he would not risk the publisher's health in either spot. When his asthma was better, would he please stop by Canton for a chat? And he could be sure that McKinley would always value his counsel above that of all others.[59] Reid could only accept in silence.

McKinley was not nearly so impressed by Reid, whose song was an old one, as he was by Hay, who had donated liberally to the campaign fund of 1896, and had proffered sound advice only when asked. McKinley decided to make him ambassador to England, the first step in making him the most influential secretary of State since Seward. Hay, who came to fame as Lincoln's youthful secretary and later biographer, married wealth and enjoyed an ease that often gnawed at his conscience, which demanded more of him than idleness. A famous poet and novelist, he knew most of the literary and artistic illuminati of the day. Well-educated and widely read, urbane and sophisticated, slightly irritable due to chronic ill health which his hypochondria magnified into fatal diseases, aristocratic in his tastes, and possessed by a loathing for the United States Senate that curiously did not destroy his diplomacy, Hay was a wise choice for the Court of St. James. Deeply Anglophile, he believed mystically in the emerging union between the two great English-speaking peoples. He bent all his energies to welding that alliance into a historic reality, a policy which McKinley himself fostered assiduously. The more eloquently and faithfully Hay spoke for Reid, the more McKinley admired him. Of all his appointments, only that of Elihu Root spoke as well as this one did of his ability to judge men.

The last and most vexing cabinet appointment remaining was the Interior Department. McKenna's selection as attorney-general reopened that question and sharpened the problem by throwing it back to New York. Victory had not simplified the situation there. Three groups appealed to the new President for support: the McKinley clubs that had first organized his victory, the Platt machine that had made that victory a fact, and the Union League Club, which contained many prominent Republican reformers in the state.

McKinley was not anxious to placate Platt, so lately an enemy. He knew that the Republicans controlled the Senate by one vote, and that Platt could be that vote, but he gambled that the Easy Boss would not risk defying the other bosses and alienating himself from the party by playing that card. He recognized that most of Platt's talk was idle threat, and while he did not object to dealing with him on patronage matters, he would not allow him a free hand in a cabinet appointment from his state. "Of course you will know how to talk to him," Hanna wrote early in January, reporting that Platt's lieutenant, Edward Lauterbach, was on his way to Canton. "They must not *dictate*." [60] He need hardly have reminded McKinley.

McKinley would have liked to mollify New York by making former Vice-President Morton ambassador to England, but the aging statesman hurriedly declined. Abner McKinley and Will Osborne then went to New York to chart the lay of the land. Talks with Platt were fruitless; he was backing Stewart Woodford or McCook for attorney-general, assuming that McKinley would have to compromise with him. McCook, a wealthy and haughty corporation lawyer, was not overly receptive, and when told that only the Interior Department remained, positively refused the appointment. He would not even make the journey to Canton, "that now doubly famous Chinese city." [61]

Finding everyone but these two unacceptable to Platt, and feeling that neither Woodford nor McCook would really do, McKinley found a way out in Cornelius Bliss, a famous dry goods merchant and recent treasurer of the Republican National Committee. Bliss was acceptable to many around Platt, for he had tried always to appear the businessman and efficiency expert. Well-known friends finally appealed in his behalf to Reid, who changed his mind and thought he might not be so bad. [62]

Early in January, McKinley asked Bliss to join the cabinet, presumably then as attorney-general, but he declined because of his business and his wife's health. He was also averse to the heavy entertainment schedule which Washington society would impose.[63] But Bliss' refusal was edged with conciliation, and McKinley bided his time until inauguration eve, not mixing in local politics and allowing Platt's invective to wear itself out before appealing to Bliss' party loyalty a second time. Only on the eve of inauguration did Bliss capitulate and accept the Interior Department in a show of harmony. Though the appointment was something of a surprise, since it had been conceded to the West, Bliss fulfilled his duties well until succeeded by Ethan Allen Hitchcock.[64]

While worrying over cabinet appointments, McKinley thought also of diplomatic posts and of his own staff. Diplomatic posts were often more open to politics than cabinet posts, for local state leaders demanded such patronage in return for campaign funds and support. Hay's assignment to Great Britain was McKinley's only coup, and the remainder of the appointees were much as could be expected, local men recommended by local politicians. New York took Paris, with General Horace Porter, U. S. Grant's former aide, as ambassador. Andrew D. White, president of Cornell University, went to Berlin, while Charlemagne Tower, a friend of the Pennsylvania Senator and Republican boss, Boies Penrose, went to Vienna and then to St. Petersburg. The faithful Powell Clayton went to Mexico City; John K. Gowdy, who had helped swing Indiana into line, went to Paris as consul-general; and Will Osborne filled the same post in London.[65] In two crucial posts McKinley left Democratic appointees for the time being, Hannis Taylor at Madrid, and Fitzhugh Lee at Havana.

For his personal secretary McKinley chose John Addison Porter, whose original McKinley club in Hartford had entered the wedge in New England and set the pattern elsewhere across the country. It was an unhappy selection, for the wealthy, dandified Porter was not the Major's kind of man. Preoccupied with his own dignity and items of petty protocol, he grated against the homespun President. Only when Porter died mid-way during the first term and the businesslike George B. Cortelyou replaced him, did efficiency come to the White House.

The end result of the Major's cabinetmaking was not spectacular, but he had produced an average assembly. He played politics in rewarding the faithful and in representing the sections, but that was only normal. Later he appointed men of a different caliber, like Root and Hay. The outstanding thing about his first cabinet was its age; the members ranged from the elderly Sherman, seventy-four, to McKenna, fifty-four. "The Major is very nice, and we all wish him well," Henry Adams remarked acidly, "but he has collected a fine old hospital around him, and I think he will find the bottom drop out of his bathtub within a twelve-month." [66] Adams' feeling reflected much public opinion, but the public was not as interested in the cabinet as in the new President. It expected a sound, no-nonsense, businesslike administration, and the finished cabinet stood ready to give it. The business world and the people who voted for McKinley in 1896 expected performance rather than pyrotechnics.

As December passed and January brought fresh snow and cold winds to Canton, while the bright days brought an unending procession of visiting statesmen to talk with the Major, the Ohio city settled to its normal tasks. But with February and the advent of March, fresh preparations marked the city's farewell tribute to the new President as he prepared to leave for Washington. Ida had twice visited in New York to buy new clothes. Her absence added to McKinley's worries, for her health was poorer, but he could not accompany her. She returned laden with fine clothes and the best wishes of friends for the new role she was about to assume in the nation's capital.

On the morning of March 1, the presidential entourage of some fifty relatives and friends boarded the luxurious train furnished by the Pennsylvania Railroad and began their trip to Washington. Canton provided an enthusiastic citizenry, the usual bunting and flags, and brass bands to send off her leading citizen. [67]

A stiff formal reception committee greeted him the following morning in Washington. A large crowd of both curious and well-wishers saw the President-elect alight from his car and walk to the engine, where he shook hands with the grimy crew and gave each a carnation. Mrs. McKinley leaned on her husband's arm, but Mother McKinley, a spry eighty-seven, alighted gingerly from her car, carrying an armload of deep red roses she had thriftily gathered in the train, and faced the cameramen with a smile and light wave. Not even her widely beloved son would receive as much praise and press adoration as did Mother McKinley. She filled many places in the nation's heart that her ailing daughter-in-law could not reach. But the photographers, the smiling crowds to whom she waved, never turned her head. The spectacle and pageantry of power meant little to her. William was her dearest, but she cherished another dream for him that died hard. On inauguration eve, the President's brother Abner was overheard pleading with her: "But, Mother, this is better than a bishopric." [68]

Smiling and doffing his hat as he walked quickly through the crowd, McKinley entered his victoria to a round of cheers and drove rapidly past waving onlookers to the Ebbitt House, whose lobby overflowed with flowers. Governor Bushnell was his formal host there, and tried to break the ice as deftly as possible in public view. The Major shook more hands and conferred with more advisors all day.[69]

Before inauguration he had one final formal call that filled him with pleasure, his visit to President Grover Cleveland. The formality of the traditional call did not make it less inviting. Cleveland had sat stolidly for the last few hours signing bills and documents from the dying Congress, and he extended ink-stained fingers to his successor, explaining apologetically that he did not stand because his painful gout hurt his feet.[70] As a congressman, McKinley had said cutting things about the corpulent man he now faced, the only Democratic president since Buchanan. But in the last four stormy years he had grown to admire and deeply respect the stubborn President's integrity, if not always his methods. Mrs. McKinley did not accompany her husband because of last-minute illness, and the gracious and beautiful young Mrs. Cleveland did not note the omission as she retired so that her husband and his guest might talk privately.

The moment was laden with drama for both men. In it the one prepared to relinquish his burdens and his power; soon he would be simply another citizen. The other understood with a suddenly oppressive sense the responsibilities and labor that awaited him. Now he was but a private citizen; soon he would be chief magistrate.

Cleveland talked of many problems, but returned time and again to Cuba. "I was struck by the sadness which characterized this interview on both sides," he remembered. The one question on McKinley's mind was the threatened war with Spain. McKinley surprised Cleveland with his knowledge of the details of the latter's Cuban policy and expressed his firm desire to continue it. "He adverted to the horrors of war, and was intensely saddened by the prospect incident to the loss of life, the destruction of property, the blows dealt at the higher morality, and the terrible responsibility thrust upon him." McKinley rose to go, reluctant to leave. Extending his hand he said firmly: "Mr. President, if I can go out of office at the end of my term, with the knowledge that I have done what lay in my power to avert this terrible calamity, with the success that has crowned your patience . . . I shall be the happiest man in the world." Cleveland too was moved by his quiet determination. ". . . No man ever gave me a stronger idea of his unyielding determination to do his duty when thus confronted by a great crisis," he recalled.[71]

So saying, McKinley turned to go, walking through the White House that would be his own home, out between the portals through which greatness and pettiness alike passed. He paused on the steps. Adjusting his hat, he squared his shoulders and stepped into the waiting carriage. The night swallowed him as he made his way back to his last hours of privacy and peace. Tomorrow he would be president.

XIII

The New Administration

MARCH is often Washington's most fickle month. Cold skies and chill winds alternate with high humidity and snow as the month that bridges winter and spring comes to the nation's capital. But clear skies greeted the morning of March 4, 1897, and a relatively mild wind blew across the Potomac; "McKinley weather," the newspapers called it, auguring well for the new administration. The President-elect rose early in his suite, dressed carefully in a dark suit of American-made goods, ate heartily and attended to the final details of the first of many elaborate ceremonies that would occupy him as president of the United States.

A crack honor guard of Ohio cavalrymen escorted McKinley from the Ebbitt House to the Executive Mansion, where he joined President Cleveland and an official escort for the ride up Pennsylvania Avenue. People lined the famous thoroughfare and blue-coated policemen and uniformed soldiers stood out against the background of darker masses wrapped against the chill. Flags waved and steady cheers greeted the procession, while photographers worked with their heavy black boxes as the party passed. The Treasury building was aflame with flowers and bunting, and sported large pictures of McKinley. "Mr. President, you are a happier man today than I am," McKinley told his host. "I am sure of that, Major," his burly companion replied drily.[1] The two men chatted between waves to the crowds, each occupied by his own thoughts. "What an impresive thing it is to assume tremendous responsibilities," McKinley said as they neared the Capitol. He had already surprised Cleveland by remarking that he hoped he could do the people's will; Cleveland had always done his own and no one else's will. Cleveland, in turn, had saddened his successor by remarking that he regretted leaving him a war with Spain.[2]

Arriving at the Capitol, the official party proceeded to the Senate chamber past kinetoscopes designed to produce a moving record of the occasion for posterity. There Vice-President Hobart took his own oath of office. Cleveland and McKinley, surrounded by their senatorial escort, entered the chamber. Glancing at the galleries, they saw their wives in a profusion of distinguished guests. Cleveland, still nursing his gout, wore a soft shoe and leaned on an umbrella.

The ceremonies in the Senate chamber finished, the party moved slowly to the Capitol's east front, where hearty cheers greeted McKinley's appearance. When order returned he stepped before Chief Justice Melville Fuller and repeated the oath of office. Facing the expectant crowd, he unrolled a sheaf of manuscript and read his address. Behind him, his mother sat placidly holding a large spread of roses, while his wife's ashen profile touched many in the crowd who would not have been surprised had she collapsed.[3]

McKinley's address was relatively long but contained no surprises. His chief concern was government revenue, for which he advocated tariff revision; until revenue was secured he would make no specific recommendations for currency legislation. He supported the move for international bimetallism. His foreign policy would be cautious and conservative. "We want no wars of conquest," he said significantly. "We must avoid the temptation of territorial aggression." He favored arbitration, tariff reciprocity, and work toward domestic prosperity. Financial reform would be postponed, the tariff raised, and the Cubans would get but moderate comfort from the new administration.[4]

Lavish receptions consumed the remainder of the day; the most gala event was held that night in the huge Pension Building, with a crush so great that dancing was impossible. Mrs. McKinley became ill and had to leave. Dawn greeted a mass of trampled flowers and paper litter from which the presidential couple had long since escaped to the solitude of the White House.

But the new President's solitude did not extend beyond the morning, when he was up early and hard at work even before crowds of well-wishers and curiosity-seekers crowded around the White House. The afternoon of his first day in office brought a thousand people to shake his hand. A steady stream of official callers filtered past the secretaries and into the sanctity of the presidential office. Public interest reflected McKinley's popularity with the people, surprising in comparison with the bitterness of the recent campaign.

"It is clearly apparent that Mr. McKinley assumes the office of President with the good will of the country," a Chicago paper noted.[5] This was among the first reflections of a popularity that eventually reached a level approached by no presidents in the nineteenth century except Andrew Jackson and perhaps Lincoln.

McKinley quickly assumed his duties. His rapid step, clear greeting, and demands for dispatch and order became familiar to the White House staff. "With the manly strut so characteristic of him, he acted as if he were true master of the situation," steward Ike Hoover recalled.[6] McKinley looked first to the new Congress, for his fate lay in its hands. At first glance he saw little comfort, for the Democrats and Silver Republicans in the Senate could easily block any legislation. The House, however, was safe with 204 Republicans to 153 Democrats and allies. Himself a former legislator, McKinley never forgot the thinness of congressional skins, nor did his tact languish in his dealings with the "Hill," especially in view of this close division.

He had an invaluable ally in Vice-President Hobart. Kindly, with an open face and eager hand, easy in conversation, and rich enough to entertain lavishly with his equally charming and witty wife, Hobart smoothed many paths in the upper house over which he presided. Seldom at a loss for words, he strolled easily through cloakrooms and committee sessions, lunching with doubtful brethren, staging dinner parties, and displaying all the talents for charm and compromise that made him well liked and respected in the capital. More than once his informal dinners and afternoon smokers, which the President attended freely, won doubtful votes.[7]

The President himself conciliated Congress, especially the Senate. His door was always open to legislators, though he tired of their incessant demands for patronage and their often rude and bellicose language when refused favors. Democrats as well as Republicans came, and even "Pitchfork Ben" Tillman left his favorite implement at home to call at the White House. Those around the President admired his equanimity, but he himself had a simple answer. "I have too often seen the results of losing patience," he told Dawes, and only once did the latter see an exhibition of McKinley's Scottish temper. A politician who he knew hated him and his administration, and who told malicious stories behind his back, beamed cordially at him during an interview. When he left, McKinley pounded the desk in rage and blurted out that he knew the man to be a scoundrel. The demonstration was so sudden and unexpected that Dawes jumped from his chair.[8]

But such temper fits were rare. The President preferred to sit quietly through a tirade and then say placidly, "Now you feel lots better, don't you," as he told one spouting congressman. "In view of the language you used you are not entitled to know why I made that appointment, but I'm going to tell you. Any man has a right to get mad when he doesn't know the facts." Thus shamed, the legislator sat silently while the President outlined his reasons for refusing the favor. Never one for letters, he much preferred face-to-face contacts, where his powers of persuasion and kindly firmness usually moved even the most recalcitrant politicians. Told that the peppery Senator Chandler would introduce a Senate resolution opposing his use of senators for diplomatic jobs, the President said idly to a visiting senator, "Bring Chandler down some time." Chandler came, and after a few words, McKinley suggested a walk in the garden, or "yard" as he was likely to call it. Chandler's opposition left with him. McKinley vetoed a mere fourteen bills in his entire administration; he vetoed the rest in his office and garden before they were introduced.[9]

The result was a surprising and long standing spirit of equanimity between executive and Congress. Shelby Cullom admitted that "We have never had a President who had more influence with Congress than Mr. McKinley." And stubborn old Senator George Hoar of Massachusetts, who opposed many of his policies, admitted equally that "President McKinley, with his great wisdom and tact and his delightful individual quality, succeeded in establishing an influence over the members of the Senate not, I think, equalled from the beginning of the Government. . . ." As Elihu Root remembered: "He had vast influence with Congress. He led them by the power of affectionate esteem, not by fear. He never bullied Congress. He never threatened compulsion." Many in Congress would have agreed with Senator Chandler's warm note as he left his own seat: "Your kind treatment of me has drawn my affection to you as to no other President, . . ."[10]

The same spirit of temperance, conciliation, and affectionate regard warmed the President's approach in his own official family. Declining to interfere with departmental details, McKinley accorded his cabinet administrators a free hand in their duties. He did not pose as an expert on their various affairs, and did not go over their heads without prior consultation. His gifts as an administrator consisted of his ability to delegate, his willingness to take advice, and his frequent consultation with his lieutenants so that he knew fully the details of the various departments. The cabinet worked harmoniously, and as Elihu Root remembered: "He understood the art of administration with a minimum of interference." [11] His chief weakness as an administrator was procrastination and delay in making crucial decisions, and his softheartedness that often made him refuse to face facts.

The President met with his cabinet on Tuesday and Friday mornings, when they crowded into the dark, somewhat cluttered room whose big desk served as McKinley's work table when his own office and reception rooms became crowded or noisy. An "admirable raconteur," in Long's opinion, McKinley opened the proceedings with a story to put the men at ease. In time the cabinet worked so smoothly that it resembled a club; there was no pomposity in McKinley's dignity. Discussion was informal and the agenda was always loose. Someone would suggest a problem, unless the meeting had been called for a specific purpose, and each member responded in turn to the President's nod. When they had all spoken, McKinley would state his decision and then say: "You agree? You all agree?" and the matter was closed. Everyone thus knew the details of each policy adopted and was identified with it. Root noted a deeper force at work in this light bantering and courtesy to the cabinet members; McKinley had often already made up his mind on a problem and drew the cabinet to his support by making them think the idea and decision were theirs. "He was a man of great power because he was absolutely indifferent to credit," Root remembered, complimenting the President's lack of ego. "His desire was to 'get it done!' He cared nothing about the credit, *but McKinley always had his way*." [12]

McKinley needed all the good will and cooperation he could muster, for he turned at once to the tariff problem, summoning Congress into special session on March 15.[13] A bill drafted by his friend Nelson Dingley had languished in the dying Democratic Congress, and was now rushed to the House for quick passage. Between November, 1896, and March, 1897, McKinley kept in close contact with Dingley and the tariff-framers, sending them information and suggestions, and making it clear that he considered tariff legislation a party responsibility. Nor did he hesitate to extract promises of support in return for patronage, ever aware of the power of grease in the legislative machinery. "In my judgement, formed after a personal conversation with Major McKinley, there will be no appointments made until after the passage of the Tariff Bill or at least very few. . . ." one politico wrote.[14]

Politicians greeted tariff revision with clenched teeth, for as one wrote: "You and I know that whenever tariff revision begins the end is not in sight." [15] But for once the Republicans had solid popular support for upward revision, as the ground swell of hard times deposited on most legislators' desks a mass of petitions and correspondence demanding the protected prosperity the Republicans had promised in 1896. The situation was complicated, however, by the usual endless demands for protection from every interest. The President himself clearly wanted a modest revision without a riot of protection. He let it be known that he would not favor any radical increase over the Wilson-Gorman rates. The press warned legislators that debate would have to be cut short; the public demanded action, and the state of business would not tolerate windy discussion. Importers would also bring in excess quantities of goods if the debates lengthened, depriving the government of needed revenue. The evenly balanced Senate was unsafe, and Chandler warned that only speedy work would bring satisfactory results.[16]

The House posed no problem, for its obedient majority had returned the acid tongue and iron hand of Tom Reed to the chair. The Dingley bill sailed through the lower house on March 31, after a minimum of debate, by a party vote of 205 to 122.[17] The House bill, drafted with McKinley's blessing and assistance, was moderate in tone, raising few rates and accepting many of those in the act of 1894. Hopes for its speedy adoption in the Senate faded quickly as a recalcitrant minority trumpeted for higher rates and full debate.

Senatorial dignity would not countenance a Reed in the chair, and when Hobart opposed cloture, the Capitol settled for a typical tariff battle.[18]

Many chambers of commerce, factories, and individual business-men deluged the Senate with petitions demanding reasonable rates and fast action, often even suggesting that some House rates be lowered. Like McKinley, the great majority of the business community seemed to realize that the days of exclusion were past and that America must find overseas markets to prosper; tariff barriers would only hinder this expansion. The bill passed into the hands of the Senate Finance Committee and under the direction of Nelson Aldrich, who startled many of his colleagues and gained unexpected applause by his own moderation. The mad rush for tariff favors repelled Senator Hanna. "Mr. McKinley stands for protection, not exclusion," he reminded the more rabid protectionists who gathered around the Chinese wall of exclusion. In more colorful moments he later blurted out that manufacturers were "squatting behind the tariff like a lot of God damn rabbitts. . . ."[19]

Two factors worked for higher rates and complicated the situation: the stubborn silverites, who used their balance of power for higher rates on wool, hides, and ores; and the general momentum for raising rates as the scramble developed. The debates rose and so did the rates, and tariff-fixers and rate-jugglers haunted hotel lobbies and committee rooms. T. C. Platt argued for higher levies on this and that; Hoar wanted granite protected; Foraker spoke for wool; Maine and Wisconsin joined hands to save lumber; and so it went as the inevitable log rolled through Republican ranks.[20]

The Western silverites were in an anomalous position; on the surface they should have desired lower rates, for their colleagues were in Europe working for an international bimetallism agreement in return for which the French and others expected lower American tariff duties. But the silverites were divided; the real free-coinage men did not favor an international agreement and demanded protection if they could not have free silver; higher rates were their price for any tariff at all; and their Eastern colleagues not only bowed to the bandwagon spirit but gave it a push. Some Westerners, like Teller, were merely bitter, vowing that they would oppose protection if it did not include free silver. As in the past, the troublesome and shortsighted silverites were the key to the problem.[21] McKinley was publicly silent, but he favored postponing any comprehensive currency legislation in the hope of winning the Westerners in the meantime with some tariff favors, a little patronage, and a lot of charm.[22]

Senator Aldrich fell ill, probably of disgust, in the midst of the Senate debate, and the leadership passed to Allison, who was more prone to high rates. Many charged him with bad faith and weakness, though Chandler denied to his colleagues abroad that Allison or the administration had scuttled bimetallism for higher rates. McKinley himself called Allison "one of our strongest and ablest Republicans and an acknowledged leader in the Senate. . . ." It was unfortunate that McKinley did not publicly denounce the tariff-raisers, but such an act would have been utterly uncharacteristic of him. It would also have cost him support among moderates, and might have angered the protectionists to push the rates even higher in spite.[23]

The Senate labored over the bill schedule by schedule. The Republicans chose not to speak in order to expedite passage, but the Democrats and silverites and pro-Cuban jingoes more than made up for any such sacrifices; further compromise was in order as the long debates weakened the lines.[24] "I wish however that the tariff could be [gotten] out of the way," Hoar wrote his junior colleague, "a new disturbance seems to arise every day." Others shared this sentiment, and Foraker, weary of the midnight conferences and endless talk, belabored "this awful tariff question" that swept all before it.[25]

Outraged cries from foreign consuls and diplomats greeted every rate increase. The French were enraged by duties on wine, art works, and agricultural products, and their consul even said that relations would be strained if it did not stop. Chinese and South American representatives volubly protested increases on their exports. But all such cries merely added to the protectionists' momentum, as they pointed out how unpopular the bill was with America's competitors. Early in June, as the bill finally took form, McKinley counselled caution and restraint until the final results were in, but seemed helpless to stem the tide.[26]

On July 7 the Senate passed and sent the bill to a House conference committee, which accepted most of the increases. On July 24 the President signed the bill after some private demur.[27] The resulting tariff, undisturbed for twelve years, was the highest to date, and marked the protectionists' victory. Foraker was right when he said flatly: "Tariffs are guesswork modified by compromise." The newspapers commended the new administration's comparatively rapid action, but frankly expressed disappointment at the apparent return to ultraprotectionism.[28]

McKinley was more interested than ever in reciprocity, and looked upon that section of the new act as a loophole through which he might lower some duties. In his inaugural address he had said flatly: "In the revision of the tariff especial attention should be given to the re-enactment and extension of the reciprocity principle of the law of 1890, under which so great a stimulus was given to our foreign trade in new and advantageous markets for our surplus agricultural and manufactured products." He also asked for executive discretion in negotiating reciprocal trade agreements, and made it clear that the power would not rust in his hands.[29]

It is surprising that he did not exert more pressure upon Congress for greater latitude in the reciprocity clause, for the final provision was inadequate. The Dingley Act provided for three kinds of reciprocity: (1) the president could negotiate executive agreements with European nations on art works, wines, liquors, and minor items; (2) he could negotiate agreements with Latin American countries on tea, tonka, and vanilla beans; (3) he could negotiate treaties with any country relative to an enumerated list of goods, reducing the Dingley rates as much as 20 per cent in return for similar reductions on American goods. These last agreements had to be negotiated within two years of passage of the Dingley Act, were operative for only five years at a time, and were subject to Senate approval. Had McKinley pressured for more, he would likely have ended with less, for the majority of Congress were far behind him on reciprocity, and still viewed the whole plan as "commerce on paper," as Reed had said in 1890.

With all its limitations, the plan was a hopeful beginning, and McKinley fell to his task with a will. Many of the Dingley rates were so high that they would serve as levers against foreign governments, and the President expected great progress. Using his persuasive charm on the talented but somewhat aged career diplomat, John A. Kasson of Iowa, McKinley made him head of a special reciprocity division of the State Department and began negotiating agreements with the major world powers.[30]

McKinley's interest in reciprocity was not an overnight conversion; the years between 1890 and 1897 had taught him much, and he began to see that America's prosperity depended upon world prosperity. As this vision broadened, showing his search for the greatest possible context for his own and his country's actions, and as events projected America onto the world stage as an international power, he saw that tariff barriers would have to fall. The protective system that had made America a great industrial power must give way to a system of reciprocal internationalism that would keep America great. His vision of nationalism steadily enlarged into an internationalism that made him the first truly modern American president. His speeches after 1898 took on a new tone, and those who talked with him were much impressed by his sincerity in desiring reciprocity and world trade. "Good trade insures good will," he told the Cincinnati Commercial Club late in the summer of 1897. "It should be our settled purpose to open trade wherever we can, making our ships and our commerce messengers of peace and amity." A few months later he carried this message to the commercial centers of New York. "The government, however, is restricted in its power to promote industry," he said in warning tones. "It can aid commerce, but not create it." [31]

The tariff symbolized prosperity, and McKinley closely questioned visitors during the hot months when Congress wrangled over the schedules. Were the people happy with the beginning? Had the first signals of returning prosperity of early 1897 matured? Certainly the nation's condition in mid-1897 was not equal to that of 1890, but the triumph of the gold standard, reviving international trade, tariff legislation, and restored confidence in the government all combined to turn expectations and business indexes up by the fall of 1897.[32]

The tariff question lay embroiled in the bonds of an equally devious and even more frustrating problem, international bimetallism. The fires of victory had not died in 1896 before the voluble silverites hammered at the Major's door for a favorable statement on the platform pledge to work for an international silver convention. Late in 1896 and early in 1897, he wrote Senators Hoar, Chandler, Wolcott, Gear, and Carter that he was "anxious to bring about an international agreement and carry out if possible the pledge of our platform in that behalf." Before his inauguration he assured a correspondent that "I am exceedingly anxious that we should carry out the pledge of our platform to promote international bimetallism; and everything I can do in that direction will be done." [33]

The outgoing Congress authorized such a commission, and Senator Wolcott proceeded quickly to Europe, even before March, to lay the groundwork, confident that McKinley would later make him the commission's chairman. Voluble, charming, somewhat stout, and with impressive mustaches, the junior senator from Colorado was considered the greatest senatorial orator of his day. Though he differed from Teller and Stewart in shunning free coinage, he was always hopeful that the dream of bimetallism would come true. Chandler, always ready to be deceived for silver, joined his enthusiasm, as did many other prominent Republicans and Democrats. But even before the commission began its labors a warning voice told the silverites that the Republican party would not solidly support them. "We have got trouble enough ahead of us, don't let's add to it by committing ourselves to anything that we may be sorry for," wrote Connecticut's cold-blooded, straight-laced Senator Orville Platt.[34] On April 12, 1897, McKinley appointed a special commission consisting of Wolcott as chairman, former Vice-President Adlai Stevenson of Illinois, and Charles J. Paine of Massachusetts, all avowed bimetallists. The administration's promise of support seemed ready to mature.

The formal instructions issued to the new commission should have caused some tremors in the silver ranks. The commission was charged with working for an international conference if the continental powers agreed. Such a conference would set the proper mint ratio and would be the first step toward general world bimetallism. But success hinged on tariff concessions, especially for the French, and the instructions stated flatly that: "You will state that this government will deal with the question of its customs revenues and its tariffs as entirely separable and distinct from that looking to a settlement of the money question by international agreement." In short, an agreement was doubtful if tariff concessions were the *sine qua non*.[35]

There was, however, some hope for an agreement. The Bi-Metallic League in England enlisted the aid and sympathy of such men as Arthur Balfour. The Liberal party was also tinged with silver sentiment. The French and even the Germans seemed more than willing to adopt bimetallism if an agreement could be reached. But England's powerful private financial community was utterly opposed, and the Chancellor of the Exchequer, Sir Michael Hicks-Beach, was a gold-standard advocate. Furthermore, three attempts at international conferences in the last ten years had failed.

McKinley felt that France was the weakest link in the golden chain and instructed Wolcott to sound out Paris before London.[36] This irritated the shifty French, who intended to agree only if England did so first. From France the exuberant Wolcott sent back glowing reports in February, as French statesmen wined and dined the mission with all the courtesies of Gallic hospitality. They could well afford it, for the tariff was not yet under discussion in America. "*Nothing* can prevent our reaching an International Agreement, restoring silver to its old place, . . ." Wolcott wrote. "Friction over the tariff may bring trouble, but I think this can be avoided," he added innocently.[37]

As the negotiations developed it became increasingly evident that the French wanted tariff favors first and a silver agreement second, that they were waiting on the English, and that the French government itself was divided on the question.[38] While the French moved with maddening slowness, Wolcott and Ambassador Porter worked to soothe them. Porter assured them that his government was not discriminating against French goods. The Dingley Act's final form outraged the French, and the likelihood of a cabinet crisis also slowed negotiations on silver. Chandler urged McKinley to make a reciprocity treaty with the French at once, but the damage was done. At home, the French consulates and embassy worked for concessions, but found Sherman immovable and confused; the Secretary could not remember the details of business from day to day, and the French gave up in disgust.[39]

Next on the commission's itinerary was London, where they appeared with due pomp early in July. A court presentation, at which

Stevenson's knobby knees, encased in the black knee breeches prescribed by protocol, amused Hay, was followed by an endless round
of receptions and social events. The English were cool toward silver,
though Wolcott's enthusiasm was not entirely dampened. He had
earlier stopped in London en route to Paris, and his reception
flattered him.[40]

Acutely aware of the potent residue of anti-English feeling in
the United States, Hay took his post as ambassador in London with
considerable caution. Like McKinley, he preferred face-to-face
diplomacy to the spotlight, and the quiet of the private conference
room to the glare of the public council table. "I have determined to
appear in public as little as possible," he wrote the President, "and
resolutely avoid slobbering over the British." Though not a bimetallist himself, Hay worked to help Wolcott and followed McKinley's
instructions to the letter. Talking privately with Lord Salisbury, the
prime minister, Hay reported that the English were not enthusiastic
and that they would not open their own mints to silver, but that they
would participate in an international conference and would discuss
later whether or not to open the crucial Indian mints to silver.
Privately, financial powers assured Hay that gold would soon be
the world standard. English financiers were amazed that the Americans did not protect their gold reserve, much of which had flowed
to England in the preceding years.[41]

Wolcott's enthusiasm and hope carried him through the initial
conferences with the English, though he began to doubt his mission's
outcome. Lord Salisbury touched a sore point when he bluntly told
the commission that tomorrow's newspapers might announce a new
French government. By late July, Wolcott saw the drift of events;
the French would not act without the English, and the English would
not act without the French. Only the commission was on the merry-
go-round. Though some members of the English government were
willing to "experiment with silver," they were a minority, and the
powerful private financiers were unalterably opposed. The negotiations dragged on, even as the commission prepared to sail for home
with defeat on its banners, and mid-October brought the final English refusal: the Indian government would not open its mints to
free coinage. France was still enraged by the Dingley Act, and England was definitely committed to the gold standard. "You thought

England would be afraid to have it said that she blocks the way," Wolcott wrote Chandler bitterly, "she doesn't care a straw about it." [42] As the last strains of the silver siren's song died in November, Hay wrote home that he had talked on the subject with Sir George Trevelyan, who left him with a Biblical quotation: "Reprobate silver shall never call them; because the Lord hath rejected them." [43]

McKinley had called bimetallism one "of the administration's greatest efforts," and he followed the commission's work with close interest. [44] Charges that he had scuttled the bimetallism commission flew as silver's chances waned, but there was no evidence that the President ever worked against the commission; in fact, he suppressed one unfavorable report that Sherman wished to give to the press. [45] Chandler persistently urged the President to take a stronger public stand and especially to silence the pro-gold remarks of Sherman, Gage, and others in the administration. But the President declined to do so because he felt that they were entitled to their opinion and that the administration's chief aim was to assure business that no radical agreement would be negotiated. Grudgingly admitting that McKinley had done everything he could "except to stop the profuse mouths of some of his subordinates," Chandler argued that the administration's failure to keep the tariff rates down ruined silver's chances. Though grateful for the President's special instructions to Porter and Hay to cooperate, Chandler nonetheless felt that McKinley could have spoken out. [46]

Wolcott himself thanked McKinley, saying that he had been "uniformly kind and frank in your relations with me. . . ." [47] But, like Chandler, he felt that the administration had not really put its full weight behind the movement. The hopes for a real silver agreement died with the autumn leaves of 1897. As the trees turned to gold, so did sentiment among leading financiers and politicians, and by November even the staunchest silverites admitted defeat. [48]

In addition to diplomatic and political complications of the problem, finance took a hand, for the price of silver steadily declined on the world market through the summer and autumn, as if to mock the bimetallist claims that an international agreement would stabilize the white metal. Explanations that the decline was due to the commission's apparent failure and to speculation did not move the financial and political world, as more and more men refused to risk anything on the silver question.[49] The silverites were dead; all they lacked was a public funeral.

That was not long in coming, for though he mentioned the problem in his annual message of December, 1897, McKinley abandoned hope for an agreement.[50] His attitude, if not his action, was that of a gold adherent. In October, 1897, Japan adopted the gold standard; in December, Russia followed suit; in 1900, Germany began calling in her outstanding silver notes. The commission's failure convinced McKinley more than ever that the currency issue was settled in favor of gold, and that commercial and industrial expansion depended on adherence to the gold standard. Henceforth he planned legislation and government policy on that assumption, culminating in the Gold Standard Act of 1900.

The bimetallism commission was not the only fiscal problem demanding McKinley's attention in 1897. It was really part of the larger problem of national legislation on the currency. The new administration faced a formidable problem in the Treasury. Cleveland's bond sales to sustain the gold standard had cost over $260,-000,000, while Treasury deficits in the four depression years of his second term totalled over $155,000,000. No one doubted the soundness of the Treasury or the government's ability to meet its obligations or to borrow, but McKinley was loathe to rely on deficit financing. He warned in his inaugural address that new revenue must be found. Gold Democrats as well as Republicans supported this attempt to apply balm to the business and financial world.[51]

But silver again intruded, for the gold-standard adherents lacked a majority in the Senate, and the slightest attempt at gold legislation would provoke a storm of stale oratory and obstructionist tactics from the upper house's silver bloc. McKinley wished Congress to create a monetary commission to study the problem and make recommendations, much as he had sponsored a tax commission while governor of Ohio. The plan was strongly endorsed in the business community.[52] But Allison, with whom the President talked, warned that the Democrats and Silver Republicans would talk the tariff to death if currency legislation were introduced at the special session. And no such legislation would have a chance after the tariff was passed, "because you cannot keep a quorum of the Senate here twenty minutes after the tariff is cleared away." [53] Any such legislation would have to wait until the gold-standard men had a congressional majority, not likely until the regular session of December, 1899.

McKinley had one avenue of expression: public statements. Secretary Gage, never an ardent speaker, nonetheless told a Cincinnati businessmen's dinner late in May that the government would seek comprehensive currency legislation in the near future. "That is exactly what I want you to say," the President told him after reading a draft of the speech.[54] Both wanted a comprehensive series of laws to create a more flexible currency resting on more national banks, to reform the currency itself, and to redeem greenbacks only in gold and pay them out only for gold.

But they knew the obstacles. "The prejudices and pre-conceptions which surround the subject in the minds of political leaders is an obstacle very difficult to overcome," Gage noted later.[55] In December, 1897, McKinley urged the re-issue of greenbacks only for gold as "an obvious duty." Gage himself hoped for legislation to retire the greenbacks and thus solidify the gold standard. "The desire is strong; the hope is weak," he candidly admitted as late as September, 1898. There was no hurry for financial legislation. Not only was there little hope for it; there was little real practical need for it. As long as the administration pursued a gold policy the country was on the gold standard, and many Republicans opposed retirement of the greenbacks for fear that contraction would deflate the growing prosperity bubble; as long as they were backed by gold, Lodge argued, why tamper with them? The stubborn Teller, never one to say die, introduced a resolution in January, 1898, stating that United States bonds were payable in silver. The ease with which it passed the Senate, though the House killed it, was a slap at the administration and a clear indication that any real currency legislation would have to wait for another session.[56]

Neither the tariff nor the currency was the chief grist in the political mill in the first months of the administration; the humdrum routine of politics was not nearly so elevated. The honor belonged to patronage, as in time-honored fashion it dominated the minds of politicos who talked hourly with the patient President. Long before inauguration, McKinley had warded off droves of office seekers; the train that brought him to Washington also carried six steamer trunks

of job applications. The crush for office was incredible; 2,500 applications poured in on Senator Foraker, and Senator Spooner swept
1,400 off his desk in 20 days. "It is one of those disagreeable things
which makes one wish he had remained in private life," Senator
Fairbanks lamented. Crowds of job hunters followed Hanna in his
daily rounds. One morning a young lady was busily trying to photograph the White House when the Senator's bulky, fast moving figure
swept past her, cane tapping the ground. "I'm Eliza crossing the
ice, and there come the bloodhounds," he remarked, pointing to the
unwanted retinue behind him.[57]

Cleveland had compounded the problem for the Republicans by
increasing the civil service coverage from 42,000 to 87,000 places.
No sooner had the patronage mill moved into high gear than Congress demanded reclassification. Only Long in the cabinet really
favored the present state of things, and most Republican members
of Congress were frankly bitter about it. "[Cleveland] waited until
he saw the offices of the country well filled with democrats, and then
extended the civil service blanket over them," Spooner said bluntly.[58]
Charles Grosvenor, chief "spoilsman" in the House, warned that
office seekers "are not to be excluded by a bureau from participating
in the government." Tom Reed, whose lip curled at the sight of a
reformer, snapped that the reformers "seem to have walled up"
every office. And Senator Gallinger fairly shook with rage when he
thought about it. "The average American citizen will never be able
to understand why Theodore Roosevelt, a rabid and unreasoning
advocate of civil service reform, should keep them out of a chance
of securing public employment while *he* clings to office with the
tenacity of grim death." [59]

Like most presidents, McKinley doubtless wished that every
office were under civil service to spare him the deadly monotony of
choosing candidates. He had also been a staunch advocate of the
merit system as a congressman. But he knew the power of patronage
in politics; like money, it talked. His formal messages to Congress
did not interest the lawmakers nearly as much as did the private
talks on patronage with him. Asked what Congress did on receipt
of a presidential message, Mr. Dooley smiled. "Congress didn't say
anything. Congress yawned. But Congress'll get th' rale message
whin it goes over to th' White House wan at a time to see about

th' foorth class post-masters." The President was not averse to rewarding the faithful, but he would move slowly in changing the laws. As he told Sherman, ". . . my rule is to 'make haste slowly.' " [60]

Some kind of system was necessary simply to process the great number of applications. The White House staff digested each letter, typed up a summary of its contents with identification of the sender and his references, attached it to the letter, and forwarded it to the proper agency. Most letters were simply sent on to the required department, but McKinley himself read much of this mail. Post-office appointments went through congressmen, larger offices through senators. Recommendations were necessary but not always crucial, for the President appointed on merit, experience, and ability as well as on party loyalty. [61]

The South, where there was no real party organization to dispense patronage, posed a special problem. Hanna, who knew the Southerners best, handled a great deal of this patronage, and the administration relied on recommendations from defeated Republican candidates in the South. Larger Southern offices were filled by recommendations from a Republican board composed of the candidate for governor, the state chairman, and the national committeeman from the state. Often there was no Republican in a Southern district to accept the postmastership, and the state chairman chose a Republican to move to the job. The great majority of offices, of course, lay outside the South, but both McKinley and Hanna were anxious to reward that section's pre-convention support and to try to build a Republican party there. [62]

McKinley at once informed congressmen that he would not remove Cleveland appointees without cause, and himself appointed men who were former Democrats. Disappointment was inevitable, for the President simply could not please everyone. "The President is not to blame," John Hay wrote. "The pressure is so cruel that he must use these offices to save his life." One congressman angrily demanded to know McKinley's reasons for refusing an appointment, and the President replied calmly: "Did it ever occur to you that in matters of this kind the President does not have to give his reasons?" Disappointed applicants wrote poison-pen letters addressed to "an Ingrate Politician"; old soldiers were especially out-

raged at not picking the first plums; and one man wrote that Mc-
Kinley had packed the civil service with the pope's agents in return
for Catholic support.[63]

One group got no favors; the Republican silver-bolters of 1896
were not consulted on appointments. Senator Teller said sadly in
1901 that nobody had asked his advice on a patronage matter since
1893.[64] Senator Stewart offered to help an office seeker, but added
honestly that "my influence with the administration is nil." [65]

But McKinley was not a man of vengeance; grudges died easily
with him. Foraker quickly suggested burying the hatchet, and Mc-
Kinley smiled through his cigar smoke as he read the capitulation;
he carefully divided Ohio between its two senators thereafter. But
it was at first a different story with Shelby Cullom, for McKinley
saw a copy of a letter in which his erstwhile Illinois opponent charged
him with distributing the offices before the election. The charge
rankled, and a slight chill greeted Cullom on his frequent visits to
the White House. The tension mounted one day until Cullom raised
his voice, whereupon McKinley calmly drew the letter from his desk
and showed it to the Senator. Cullom swallowed his gorge; it was,
to say the least, an embarrassing moment, followed by "a general
overhauling." In the end McKinley asked what Cullom wanted and
gave it to him; the whole affair ended in a love feast. But the President used all his arts to sidetrack the persistent Cullom. Insisting
on appointing an old Civil War friend whom he had seen "shot
through," instead of one of Cullom's men, McKinley made a show
of tears; the Senator threw up his hands and left. "I never have
any trouble to get the President to do what he wants to do," Cullom
said with the voice of experience, "but to get him to do something
that he does not want to do is a different proposition." [66]

The story was much the same with Tom Platt, for McKinley
wished to be conciliatory and firm at the same time; Platt must be
kept in the fold but taught a lesson, a lesson borne in upon him in
a series of adverse appointments. Roosevelt went to the Navy,
Andrew White to Berlin, Stewart Woodford to Madrid, and all were
anti-Organization Republicans. Platt swallowed his pride, admitting
even before the inauguration that "I have no assurance, however,
that I shall have any influence with the new administration." He
agreed to Bliss's appointment for party harmony, but his temper

rose in August, 1898, when the newspapers said that Whitelaw Reid would replace Hay as ambassador to England. Pleading that the appointment would disrupt the New York party and promising future help, Platt asked the President not to name the hated publisher; McKinley, who did not think seriously of Reid for the post, complied. Platt knew when he was bested, and he was grateful for McKinley's kindness and frequent consultation. In the end he cooperated well, for he remembered favors as well as faults.[67] McKinley's technique of reconciliation furthered the cause of party harmony and illustrated his understanding of the political powers he applied.

The civil service reformers watched the developing patronage show with alarm. Though McKinley favored civil service coverage in his inaugural address, he agreed that changes were in order. Any change of administration threatened the civil service system, and hard times sharpened the pressure in 1897. "I am very much afraid . . . that there is trouble ahead," a member of the Civil Service Commission wrote a month after the inauguration; but by midsummer he sighed with relief that "for a while, at least, we have little to fear." While stating frankly that he found many regulations irksome and petty, McKinley told the reformers that he had no plans for quick or drastic change and promised to study the question fully.[68]

Even mugwumps and reformers realized the stringency of the orders that kept cabinet secretaries from choosing their own staffs and that placed many technical positions at the mercy of examinations. McKinley argued that technical posts ought to be open to experience as well as education, and circulated a memorandum among the bureau chiefs asking for recommendations. Gage informed correspondents that changes in the laws were inevitable, but that they would not be "in the nature of a pandering to the aspirants for political patronage." Senator Hanna found the whole business irksome, for he had less patience than most with distribution of the plums. Departing for a European vacation in 1899, he bade the President goodbye, and added: "But if you don't get that civil service order out soon, so I can fix things up here, I am never coming back."[69]

McKinley's executive order reclassifying posts in the federal civil service appeared on May 29, 1899. Though the reformers greeted it sourly as a backward step, it did not greatly lessen the coverage. It merely placed some posts on the classified rather than the restricted list, making them open to appointment on the basis of merit as well as education; removals could not be made without written cause, subject to hearings, and the Civil Service Commission was untouched. The professional politicians were not especially happy for few jobs were opened, and even Theodore Roosevelt grumbled that it was not bad, but seemed to play into the hands of Grosvenor and "similar cattle." [70] McKinley showed admirable restraint and wisdom in dealing with the patronage. Freely using the offices at his disposal for his own political benefit, he did not remove or appoint solely for partisan purposes; nor did he give subordinate politicians a free rein with patronage.

Domestic problems were irksome and exhausting, but foreign affairs intruded on McKinley's thoughts even before his inauguration, an omen of the increasing role they would play during his administration. Aside from his personal tact and diplomacy, McKinley seemed ill-equipped to control the nation's foreign affairs. His speeches of 1896 were concerned exclusively with domestic problems, and he had never manifested much interest in world affairs. He knew little if anything of the actual workings of diplomacy. Yet he quickly displayed an amazing ability to choose men who had the talents and information he lacked. He took advice easily, and his endless industry permitted him to digest and master the mass of detailed information involved in foreign relations. Almost every foreign diplomat with whom he worked commented on his natural talents for diplomacy.

The first problem in foreign affairs was a holdover from the Cleveland administration, the annexation of Hawaii. The islands, whose very name was magic to many Americans, lay over two thousand miles off California like a string of rich jewels. American seamen, traders, and explorers frequented the Sandwich Islands, as the nineteenth century knew them, bringing back tales of great wealth and tropical splendor. Sugar, molasses, fruits, jute, and other products found a ready market in the United States, which gave the islands tariff favors. Hawaii also bore souls, and to save these, missionaries invaded the islands after 1850. Coming to do good, they stayed to do well; quickly controlling the great sugar plantations, they were the economic, political, and social arbiters of the islands by 1890.

Capitalizing on the supposedly corrupt rule of Queen Liliuokalani and the popular demand for annexation to the United States under Blaine and Harrison, the white element staged a revolution in 1893. The dying Harrison administration forwarded a treaty of annexation to the Senate early in 1893. But hopes of annexation faded when the stubborn Cleveland, opposed to all overseas expansion, sent a special mission to investigate the revolution. He summarily withdrew the treaty, arguing that the whole movement was directed from the United States and did not represent the will of the Hawaiian people.

Cleveland's opposition to expansion reflected the Democratic foreign policy of the late nineteenth century. Like so many other features of that policy, it passed with him when he left office, for the future rested with the Republican vision of overseas expansion pursued by Blaine, McKinley, and Roosevelt. Already the Democrats were divided over expansion toward Cuba, and in the end would join the Republicans to free that island. The days of those who looked upon Hawaiian annexation merely as a plot "of sugar, by sugar and for sugar" were numbered. The annexation of Hawaii was but the first step in a conscious policy of national assertion that culminated in the acquisition of the Philippines after the war with Spain.

Though McKinley's election had not involved foreign policy, the Republican triumph inevitably meant a different attitude. The Republican platform of 1896 was expansionist in tone and purpose, favoring Hawaiian annexation, purchase of the Danish West Indies, an isthmian canal, and strong sympathy toward Cuba. Already a potent group of intellectuals, legislators, and administrators in the national government, like Lodge, Roosevelt, Captain A. T. Mahan, and others, thought of overseas possessions that would give America command of the seas, a leading role in the world's commerce, and above all, would fulfill America's destiny. This "large policy" appealed to many Democrats as well as Republicans, for with the settlement of the silver question in 1896, their eyes turned increasingly toward Cuba and other foreign trouble spots. In July, 1897, a Trans-Mississippi Congress, meeting in Salt Lake City under the chairmanship of William Jennings Bryan, favored the annexation of Hawaii, an isthmian canal, and a free Cuba.[71]

McKinley's early views on foreign affairs were hard to gauge, so silently did he wend his way through diplomacy. As early as 1891, however, before leaving Congress, he had helped retain American naval rights at Pearl Harbor, and knew of American interest in Hawaii. He also favored naval expansion and subsidies for the merchant marine as early as 1890, and did not slow construction of the new Navy begun under Harrison. His steadily enlarging ideal of an America dominant in world commerce inevitably brought him to internationalism and overseas expansion. He lent a ready ear to the expansionist theme. True, he told Carl Schurz early in his administration: "Ah, you may be sure that there will be no jingo nonsense under my administration," and early in 1897 he supposedly opposed expansion.[72] But he doubtless referred to Cuba, where he hoped to crown his diplomacy with peace; and he still trusted Spain. He also hoped that a pending Hawaiian treaty would lessen jingo pressure on the Cuban problem.

An early visit to Canton convinced Lodge that McKinley was sound on foreign affairs. The inaugural cheers had hardly died when he, Roosevelt, and others poured their troubles into the patient President's ear. The problem was how to annex Hawaii. The party lacked a two-thirds majority in the Senate and McKinley was inclined to caution. John W. Foster, an experienced diplomat who had been Secretary of State in 1892–93, and William Pierce Frye of Maine, president pro tem of the Senate, conferred with him on March 15, and all agreed that a joint resolution was best, since it required simple majorities in each house. Hawaiian representatives in Washington hopefully cabled home that the new administration was as favorable as the old one had been unfavorable.[73]

McKinley was the guiding spirit behind the annexation of Hawaii, showing an unexpected interest in the subject and a firmness in pursuing it. Early in June, 1897, the President decided rather suddenly after a cabinet meeting to frame a new annexation treaty. Assistant Secretary of State Day assigned the task to Foster, and Secretary Sherman knew little if anything of the transaction. Caught en route to Europe, Foster hastily drafted a new treaty and took it, rolled up in a rubber band, to Day. The Judge looked solemnly at the little tube. "And that little roll can change the destiny of a nation," he noted drily. On June 16, 1897, McKinley forwarded the treaty to the Senate with the injunction: "Annexation is not a change, it is a consummation." [74] He had now abandoned the joint resolution scheme because it smacked of weakness, and he wished to gauge opinion while the treaty was debated. If he realized that this was the first step in his full and final adoption of the "large policy" he did not say so, but he knew that the expansionists would not be satisfied with Hawaii.

Embroiled in the tariff and lacking a clear majority, much less a two-thirds vote of the membership, the Republican senatorial leadership delayed action. In the meantime, the jingoes welcomed Japanese agitation against annexation as a godsend, for it stiffened American pro-annexation sentiment. Fearful that annexation by the United States would upset the status quo in Hawaii and the Pacific, and anxious to protect their nationals in the islands' labor force, the Japanese government entered sharp protests and even sent warships to the islands. Roosevelt and Lodge led the van of pressure on the Senate to act. Roosevelt spoke heatedly against the Japanese in a public address, and McKinley took him for a drive one afternoon to congratulate him. "Of course the President is a bit of a jollier," Roosevelt wrote Lodge, "but I think his words represent a substratum of satisfaction." [75]

Indeed they did, for McKinley sensed the demand for annexation in many Republicans to whom he talked, despite the Senate's recalcitrance. He was alive to the Japanese menace. The aged Senator Hoar, whom he respected while disagreeing sharply with him, reported a frank conversation with the President. "We cannot let those islands go to Japan," he said. "Japan has her eye on them. Her people are crowding in there. I am satisfied they do not go there voluntarily, as ordinary immigrants, but that Japan is pressing them in there, in order to get possession before anybody can interfere." [76] McKinley from the first acted in his new policy with a consciousness of American defense, an appreciation of the desirability of Pacific possessions, and an awareness of the designs of other powers. That consciousness would settle into a hardened conviction that America must assume her destiny in the Philippines as well as Hawaii.

The Japanese scare, however true or false, generated heat, but not enough to accomplish annexation. The new Congress of December, 1897, heard McKinley advise annexation in his message, but the Senate turned its attention to Cuba. The expansionists were quick to point out that suffering Cuba tied in with Hawaii; it was America's destiny to redeem them both. As war with Spain loomed, Hawaii took on new strategic importance for the war in the Pacific. The Hawaiian government spared no effort to impress this on visiting soldiers and sailors, and increased pressure in Washington for annexation. As the expansionist fever caught on, constituents pressed senators with demands for Hawaiian annexation. "The Hawaiian Islands are necessary to the protection of the United States," one New Englander wrote Senator Morrill. "If we do not take them some other nation will. We cannot play the dog in the manger forever." Whitelaw Reid had long since advocated that McKinley finish Harrison's start, and at a later date even the cautious Judge Day told Senator Lodge flatly that we could not escape our destiny in the Pacific. The project appealed to the initiated expansionists for its inflation of America's role, and destiny accompanied in many minds the spectacle of greater profits and wider trade in the Orient.[77]

The chief congressional opposition came from Speaker Reed, who set up a large terrestrial globe in his office, where he showed with a piece of string that the Orient was closer via the American-owned Aleutian Islands than Hawaii. But his sharp tongue and obvious hatred of McKinley soured many, and his efforts were vain. The issues of overseas expansion were never those of the head but rather those of the heart; no piece of string could prove them wrong. War provided the heat that generated annexation, though the opposition held bitterly, and some feared that the United States would simply have to occupy the islands. By the first week in June, 1898, Reed "caved in" and agreed to let a joint resolution pass. Leaving the chamber to avoid humiliation, the Speaker raged at the cheers that greeted annexation. He might well have surrendered, for as Lodge said, "the President has been very firm about it and means to annex the Islands anyway. . . . The whole policy of annexation is growing under the pressure of events." Privately McKinley was more explicit, telling George Cortelyou: "We need Hawaii just as much and a good deal more than we did California. It is manifest destiny." The annexation of Hawaii placed him in the expansionists' camp.

Lodge hopefully wrote Roosevelt: "He did everything to secure the annexation of Hawaii, and speaks of it as a step in a policy." At 7:00 in the evening of July 7, 1898, with Ida and staff members watching, the President signed the joint resolution annexing Hawaii.[78]

His mind then already filled with the Philippine problem, McKinley saw the connection between the two groups of islands. He had thought of Hawaii for a year while the treaty languished in the Senate, and finally adopted the medium of a joint resolution for speed's sake, though he still disliked its quality of evasion. He later urged the retention of the Philippines not for the sake of public opinion, but after reflection on and work with the similar Hawaiian problem.

Though tariff schedules and demanding congressmen occupied most of the President's time, and the mounting Cuban crisis claimed ever more attention during 1897, the new administration spent much time and thought on other aspects of foreign relations. The outgoing Cleveland administration left behind a general arbitration treaty with Great Britain, which McKinley heartily endorsed in his inaugural address. "The importance and moral influence of the ratification of such a treaty can hardly be overestimated in the cause of advancing civilization." Time wrought many changes in American attitudes as the nation slowly emerged into world power. Chief among these was the transformation of England from a historic enemy to a historic ally, a long and carefully planned rapprochement nurtured by McKinley and Hay. The arbitration treaty was not ratified, but McKinley lived to see diplomatic ties binding the two English-speaking peoples together.

Relations with Canada endangered the broader problem of American-British relations, for the two powers pursued a tangled foreign policy. The disputed Alaska boundary, the Bering Sea fisheries, and tariff reciprocity headed the list of issues between the North American neighbors. McKinley showed a friendly disposition to arbitration with Canada before his inauguration, and worked throughout his administration toward settling these long outstanding issues.

McKinley's general public silence on foreign affairs did not indicate the lack of either interest or effort on his part. Sherman's physical condition and the President's own sense of responsibility made him follow foreign affairs closely. Constant consultation with

Day at home and with embassies abroad gave unity to the administration's foreign policy. From the first it rested on two general bases that were to be the foundation of American foreign policy in the twentieth century: an awareness that the age of isolation was drawing to a close for America and that she would have to assume her rightful place as an international power; and a belief in arbitration of differences with foreign powers whenever possible, which led to American participation in the general movement for world cooperation.

The figure of Mark Hanna stood on the edge of the administration circle throughout its first year in office. Newspapermen and the public speculated on his real power in the government. Both Hanna and McKinley understood that neither could afford the spectacle of a national boss, and both showed their independence. Ever watchful of his reputation, McKinley would never have permitted his affection for Hanna to raise him into a dominating power. "Hanna was a strong and vigorous man, but McKinley was the controlling spirit of the two," Elihu Root insisted emphatically.[79]

Special groups from Negroes to Gold Democrats looked to Hanna to reward their work of 1896, and he often brushed his way through milling crowds of favor seekers as he left his hotel suite in the Arlington. Hanna was close to fellow politicians; his corned beef breakfasts and jolly evening smokers were famous in senatorial circles, and his suite was not far from those occupied by other powerful Republicans who lived in and near the Arlington. He was often a welcome guest at the White House, offering advice and receiving instructions from McKinley. But his power with the administration was only a shadow of what the press often attributed to him. His share of the patronage was limited to Ohio, advice on Southern appointments, and choice of men who ran the party organization. He wrote candidly that he had nothing to do with overseas appointments, and often had little success with those at home. Much of this was evasion; his voice carried great weight with McKinley. But he was wise enough not to overstay his welcome at the White House, and told one friend that he never went unless called for.[80]

Hanna had his own troubles as the administration settled to its early tasks. His appointment to the Senate ran only until January,

1898, when Sherman normally would have been re-elected. The turbulence of Ohio politics had not subsided for a moment in the great contest of 1896, and Bushnell was still wary of Hanna's ambitions. The state elections in the fall of 1897 found Hanna in the thick of a fight for his political life. Would he be a senator for only a year? Was this the reward for all his work? And would his defeat serve notice that the Republicans were not unified and that McKinley would not or could not help him?

Electing a safe Republican majority of the legislature that would choose a new senator was a formidable task, even for Hanna, for it required an exhausting and expensive campaign in every legislative district in the state. Hanna plunged into the fall elections with McKinley's blessing. "I hope you will stand it through," the President wrote. "I sympathize with you in the hard work you have before you. Be of good courage, I am sure you must win." [81] McKinley was frankly loath to intervene in the state contest, for it seemed undignified and he did not wish to jeopardize his national standing by seeming to pressure state leaders. Yet he realized that a combination of dissident Republicans and Democrats would strive mightily to defeat Hanna as the public symbol of "McKinleyism." He could hardly afford such a defeat in the first months of his administration. Much to the President's relief, the Republicans carried the election. "Under all the circumstances it is a most significant triumph," he wrote Hanna. "You made a great campaign. You measured up. . . . I hope there will be nothing to change the results. . . ." [82]

But the victory at the polls was close; disgruntled Republican legislators might yet defeat Hanna. In December it was apparent that Hanna lacked a majority, that some Republicans elected on his pledge might defect, and that every pressure would be necessary to assure his victory. Grosvenor and others managing Hanna's contest looked to McKinley for support, and he quietly dispatched Dawes to Columbus with a private letter stating his views to doubtful Republicans. To White House visitors he said that Hanna's fight was his own, yet he responded to calls from Ohio to send speakers and to pressure individual legislators. [83]

Early in January the legislature gathered and elected Hanna by a bare majority for the full term ending in 1904. Though charges of bribery emanating from his opponents provoked a close investigation by the Senate, Hanna was cleared. His friend's re-election relieved McKinley. In the first week of January, as the battle became tense, the President wrote Hanna a remarkably intimate letter:

> I cannot tell you how much I feel for you under the great strain you are subjected to. I hope you will not lose your courage. I have every confidence that you will be elected and the integrity of the Republican party and its conventions fully vindicated. You have the deepest sympathy of everybody here. Senators and Representatives are surprised and shocked at the situation in Columbus, and all of the many who come here daily have only words of confidence and good wishes for you.
>
> I need not tell you how deeply I feel about the result, and how anxious I am that you shall be returned to the Senate. If any man ever won his election, you did, and if ever a man deserved the support of a united party in his State you are that man. I feel more than I can write. I will not trust myself further.

Hanna's final triumph filled the President with relief and gratitude. "We have a common sentiment and feeling about the Ohio election," he wrote Alger. "Of course you knew how profoundly interested I was and how comforting the result is to me." [84]

Hanna's election was the spice of personal satisfaction in a year that ended well for the new administration. A weary president in search of rest fled Washington for Lake Champlain when Congress finished the Dingley bill; it was his only vacation in 1897. The session had enacted a tariff law; the Cuban crisis seemed dormant through most of the year; the bimetallism commission had at least redeemed the party's pledge and also sounded the death knell of the silver question. Hanna's election revealed party unity under pressures of necessity. McKinley's foreign policy augured well from an expansionist viewpoint, while his steady efforts to solve the Cuban question peacefully gained the support of most Americans. Even Theodore Roosevelt admitted that "it certainly seems to me as though this administration was opening, unlike every other administration for the last twenty years, with prospects steadily brightening for its continuance during a second term." [85]

Business confidence returned, and while prosperity and full production were some distance off in the summer of 1897, the long curve of depression definitely turned upward. "The 'dawn of prosperity' has come, and come in time to save the party which is responsible for it, even a temporary set-back," Dawes wrote the President. McKinley himself, though admitting some dissatisfaction with the "difficult as well as very important session of Congress," was pleased with the record of his first months in office.[86]

Less tangible matters were important too. McKinley had begun the long and hidden restoration of presidential leadership that he passed on to Theodore Roosevelt. He strengthened the spirit of cooperation between president and Congress that had lapsed under Cleveland. He had set the basic outlines of his nationalism in motion. He had won cooperation in many areas of action from every major figure in his party by using charm, pressure, and patronage. Grover Cleveland held that the people sustained the government, not it the people. William McKinley disagreed. More democratic in his outlook, he felt that the government existed to serve the people. Cleveland left office bankrupt of party support, devoid of public following. McKinley had already attained a great measure of both these and now prepared to use them and his close relationship with Congress to complete his program.

But while the office seekers, tariff-makers, and bimetallists went steadily about their work, and as the President himself worked to solidify his hold on the people and Congress, a greater menace arose. In the long night hours after full days of work, and in earnest reflection and conversation among friends, McKinley thought of it. He spoke often and earnestly about the fortunes of the palm-fringed island to the south whose agony was now a part of America's destiny. *Cuba libre!* the newsboys shouted beyond his window, and daily the pressure from politicians and plain citizens alike mounted. As domestic affairs settled into expected grooves, he often reflected on what he had told his listeners in his inaugural address. "It will be our aim to pursue a firm and dignified foreign policy, which shall be just, impartial, ever watchful of our national honor, and always insisting upon the enforcement of the lawful rights of American citizens everywhere. Our diplomacy should seek nothing more and nothing less than is due us. We want no wars of conquest; we must avoid the temptation of territorial aggression. Wars should never be entered upon until every agency of peace has failed; peace is preferable to war in almost every contingency."

Heads shook in the crowd. Most of his listeners expected more, and in 1897 some worked avidly to ruin his peace policy. Could he withstand the pressures for intervention in Cuba? And could he triumph in the end over those who believed that Cuba's fate was America's destiny, and that peace was not always preferable to war?

XIV

Presidential Profile

LATE APRIL, 1897, brought leaden skies and icy winds to New
York, but did not prevent the lavish spectacle of the nation's
last tribute to a great warrior. In that month thousands
braved the cold gusts that blew off the Hudson to stand in silence as
the solemn catafalque of Ulysses S. Grant moved through glittering
horsemen and splashes of uniforms to its final resting place in the ornate mausoleum that the nation's largest city provided for a hero who
had never claimed her as a home. On the platform among the speech-
makers and dignitaries the President of the United States chatted
with his Vice-President, and listened to the oratorical flourishes of
others, then rose to present his own. It was the first large ceremony
in which the new President participated after his inauguration, and
New York, no stranger to him, took him to heart, welcoming his
pleasant and patriotic remarks. As he spoke, McKinley shifted im-
perceptibly in a hidden armor of newspapers, for both he and Hobart
wore them under their coats to keep out the freezing blasts.[1]

That homely gesture said much of the new President; the for-
malities of public office did not prevent his adopting a time-tested
method of keeping out the cold. At heart he was still a man of simple
and unostentatious tastes, though he never forgot his dignity or
denied that he relished the powers and prestige of office. His election had brought a notable thaw to Washington society and to public opinion in general. The unpopular Cleveland claimed little affection from the people as he left office, and his gruff manners had
alienated most of social Washington. He stood for the East, which
was cold; McKinley stood for the West, which spelled warmth and
homely tastes, which the public could understand and appreciate.[2]

Though Cleveland gained popularity in the years that followed,
his countrymen ignored him as he left office, giving their best wishes
to his more genial and seemingly more human successor. Democratic congressmen who had shied from Cleveland found a warmer

welcome in a Republican White House, and reporters noted the more relaxed atmosphere. The public could stroll through the White House gardens again; the mansion was more accessible to everyone; and the new President himself moved with greater freedom than his predecessor. "No other administration has been so like the period of James Monroe from 1817 to 1825 as McKinley's—an era of good feelings," one reporter remembered.[3]

McKinley's love of people hardly dictated otherwise. A life in politics had given him the common touch which, combined with his dignity, made him the ideal representative of the decorum the age prized so highly. His wife, though ailing, bespoke a tender affection and an obstinate will that endeared her to many. The President's homespun family, headed by his aged and beloved mother, duplicated thousands of households in America, and gave him an appeal that Cleveland never had.

The Washington which the McKinleys left in 1891 greatly differed from that they faced in 1897. Six years had made it a larger city. More buildings, more people, reflecting a growing government, greeted the new President. The lavish and impractical Congressional Library, newly finished atop Capitol Hill, spoke volumes of the era's taste. The city's fundamentally beautiful plan was enhanced by cables that ran underground to avoid unsightly poles and wires. Even an automobile huffed and puffed occasionally along its streets.

Fashion had not changed radically, nor had the people, though they hurried more now. Ladies were still venerated, and encased in wrappings fit for mummies. Gentlemen in politics and society moved with an ease that bespoke assurance and habit, sporting an elegance that in a few years would fall before the scissors of mass production. The city's air was quieter than a later generation would know. It was a different world, provincial, given to confident insularity.

It was the last generation of Americans to face every tomorrow with confidence. McKinley was ideally suited to preside over such a country in such a time. He breathed the spirit of the age and radiated the confident destiny that had made him famous. As late as 1899 he could voice his countrymen's assurance: "In this age of keen rivalry among nations for mastery in commerce, the doctrine of evolution and the rule of the survival of the fittest must be as inexorable in their operation as they are positive in the results they bring about." [4] There was nothing cruel in this law of life either to him or his people; it had always been the American way. Though it had begun to quicken amid the signs of disturbing change, the pace of daily life was still slower than in the mid-twentieth century.

The home which the McKinleys claimed, the nation's most famous, was an anachronism, boasting little more than a historic dignity, an eighteenth-century mansion utterly unsuited to the nation's chief executive as the twentieth century dawned. Its paint was cracked, and closets and basements were discolored with age and neglect. The wallpaper in the state dining rooms and reception parlors peeled irresistibly and showed patches that even a modest house-. wife would have scorned. Behind President Arthur's ornate glass screen, age took its toll in sagging furniture, threadbare carpets, and faded drapes. Attics bulged with an excess of sheer junk and cast-off mementoes of bygone administrations. The floors creaked to the step, and staircase bannisters often leaned crazily under the arms of distinguished guests. The immense receptions incumbent on the first family called forth the best efforts of all the staff, who rushed to the cellars to bolster the floors with beams and bricks. They sighed with relief when each event was over, grateful that no elegant leg had pushed through the flooring, or that no nation's visiting embassy had died in a general collapse of the rickety structure.

Congress had loosened its purse strings enough to wire the house for electricity and install modern plumbing, but the legislators preferred to patch rather than rebuild. The staff telegrapher, B. F. Montgomery, noted for his elevator shoes and diminutive size, knew all the dangers of the house wiring.

People poured through the mansion daily, and its grounds were a city park where tourists could picnic, take snapshots, and gawk at visitors. The main entrance opened into a vestibule from whose left, stairs led up to the staff's work space. The President's office lay between the cabinet room and his secretary's rooms. Visitors waited to be received singly or in groups. Secretary Porter's pomposity lent itself to exact scheduling, and he was more conscious of the President's time than was McKinley himself. He kept careful appointment schedules, and often reminded his chief when a visitor exceeded his time limit.

The staff consisted at first of six clerks and typists, one of whom handled Mrs. McKinley's mail and callers. The younger men played baseball on the White House lawn after hastily gobbled lunches, and the President often smiled out the window at their antics, for he loved young people. Their spontaneous and carefree actions gave him vicarious compensation for his own cramped and confined personal life. The staff quickly grew to love the genial and kindly McKinley, who always stepped in their door to say: "Gentlemen, I am glad to see you all again," after returning from a trip.[5]

To the west lay the McKinley's private quarters. Five bedrooms and two dressing rooms must suffice for them and their guests. An endless array of junk and overused furniture, a tangle of gas lights and electric lamps, whatnots, and bric-a-brac greeted Mrs. McKinley, who did not mind in the least. The simplicities of Canton and the Ebbitt House had long since inured her to modest surroundings, and since she lived an interior life it did not matter. Only her husband, his career, and her life with him mattered. Mementoes dotted the dressing tables and little Katie smiled down from the wall, where her ailing mother saw her every morning upon awaking. A maid was nearby, ready for instant call, and the approach to the room was easy so that the President could reach it in haste if an emergency arose.

The service staff was inadequate to the tasks imposed upon them, for the budget dated from the Grant administration. They often voluntarily worked late into the night and on holidays. Nearby conservatories produced the flowers that Ida loved so much and carnations for the Major's buttonhole. Gardeners tended the lawns as best they could amid the tourists, and preparations for formal affairs found them carrying in and out droves of potted palms and flowering plants. A chief steward presided over the household staff. For his own family, McKinley hired a plain cook at forty dollars a month, but formal dinners brought a fancy French chef from New York. The President paid the head coachman and the stable expenses. McKinley replaced the housekeeper after Cleveland complained that she was "too frivolous and flirty." [6]

McKinley was always inclined to attend to many details himself, but he doubtless overburdened himself from sheer necessity. The pompous Porter was no match for the hordes who pressed for audience with the President. Even the chilly Cortelyou, who succeeded

Porter, had his troubles, though he maintained close schedules with icy efficiency. In palmy days, the staff handled 50 to 100 letters. But patronage, the war with Spain, and problems of empire increased this load enormously, and Porter begged for more help from Congress early in the administration. "As you already know the clerical force at the White House is very limited and the utmost dispatch is required to keep up with each day's work," he wrote to Senator Fairbanks in a bid for help. He played on congressmen's sympathies by reporting that he and his staff often worked until midnight, and hinted strongly that more help would mean faster service. The complaints brought some results. By the end of the first administration the total White House staff had increased to more than 80, with 13 clerical assistants to help with the flood of mail and paper work.[7]

The miscellaneous household staff boasted a barber who shaved the President at irregular intervals, for McKinley liked to do that himself on first arising. When discharged for unknown reasons, the man pleaded for reinstatement, and as usual, the softhearted McKinley relented.[8] He also interceded for an aged Negro retainer, Jerry Smith, known generally as "Worthless Jerry," whose slipshod methods were the mansion's scandal. A crisis arose when he threw a bucket of sudsy water from an upstairs window and drenched a policeman. But a misspelled and ungrammatical plea to the President on a scrap of purloined formal stationery brought his reinstatement.[9]

Some of the staff took advantage of the President's kindness and busy schedule. Porter detailed his aid, Colonel Bingham, to make a surreptitious investigation of the household staff, and the latter replied that most staff members did their duties but that the janitors were remiss. "I took a look at the radiators at once and found waste paper, remains of lunches, cigars, cigarettes, and other trash at least a foot deep between the radiators and the window sills."[10]

The staff's chief worry was the President's personal security, for the mansion was literally a public thoroughfare, the police force inadequate, and McKinley himself averse to security measures. More soldiers were detailed to the White House, to McKinley's displeasure, for he disliked uniforms. Threats against the President went to the superintendent of the Washington police, and though

Secret Service agents were assigned on his trips, their attention was sporadic. Theodore Roosevelt was the first American president to be guarded adequately. Cortelyou was more alive to the security problem and investigated the police force on his own and through deputies. A deputy made the rounds one evening and found the staff working except for the Secret Service man, "whom I discovered asleep on a lounge in one of the bedrooms on the second floor. After watching him in that condition for twenty minutes, I awakened him in the presence of one of the officers." [11] Cortelyou's icy stare kept many of the staff on their toes, but McKinley's light dismissal of danger to his person did not help his secretaries.

McKinley followed his staff's schedules as closely as possible, realizing their efforts to spare him embarrassment and overwork, but he often detained guests longer than Porter and Cortelyou wished. A steady worker, he spent hours each day almost immobile at his desk, reading reports and signing papers. Callers were often a relief and delight for him, for he liked company, and a steady flow of conversation and banter highlighted the visits of many to his office. He was anxious to see everyone quickly, but senators and representatives had first claim on his time. He was, after all, a politician.[12]

His sedentary nature and long tenure in politics inured him to the daily grind of paper work and visitors. He appreciated the chatty letters that John Hay, Horace Porter, and others at home and abroad wrote him, though he could not repay them in kind. He genuinely disliked few of his daily tasks, but he hated signing the endless flood of military commissions that could better have been left to a subordinate. "Let's get busy," he would say after greeting a secretary, as he downheartedly eyed a fresh stack of commissions. The commissions had to be spread out to dry because their sheepskin would not blot. While one drying batch covered the floor and tables, the President would wring his hands and say impatiently: "Something ought to be done about this. Somebody else ought to be able to sign these." [13]

McKinley enjoyed the glitter and flurry of official entertaining, often checking on seating arrangements himself, with a tactful eye on who rubbed elbows. Some informal receptions were necessary, in addition to the inevitable New Year's ball, annual military ball, affairs for Congress, and the ornate dinner for the Supreme Court. There were normally three noon receptions a week for the public, at which McKinley, resplendent in a frock coat and genial smile, stationed himself near the door to greet the visitors. Staff members figured that he could shake hands with 30 people a minute, or 1,800 an hour, and could increase his pace to as many as 50 a minute if necessary. If she felt well, Ida would sit beside her husband, nodding to the guests as they passed by; if not, she stayed in her room. The President obviously enjoyed the task far more than she did, though she seldom missed a formal function.[14]

The larger dinners and receptions brought heroic efforts to save the White House floors, to provide extra hat and cloak stands, and to take care of the refreshments. A crowd of 1,000 taxed every facility of the mansion, but crowds three times that large were not uncommon. Officers had their sabers broken, expensive dresses were trampled, what remained of furniture and draperies disappeared or was crushed, women fainted and could not be helped because of the mass of humanity, and no one could find sitting space, much less room to dance, at many of the larger affairs. Gate crashers compounded the problem, for the doors were open to anyone off the street, and congressmen unloaded visiting constituents on McKinley with a will. Secretary Porter and Colonel Bingham tried mightily to limit the number of receptions and to make attendance at each one dependent on an invitation. The President absently agreed to their plan, with little thought of its consequences. When Bingham stuffily wrote that "the greater part of these people [the gate crashers] have been such as butchers, cabmen, market and grocery clerks, and the scum of the city," McKinley called a halt.[15] The pompous secretaries got on his nerves anyway, and he saw at once that it would never do to omit the common people from his social affairs.

The President preferred the convivial dinners with the cabinet and a few friends to the larger affairs. He was more genial around a smaller board, and after dinner, when the ladies had gone, he could retire to the smoking room to talk horses, family affairs, or personal problems with the men he knew best. He scattered many such relaxed evenings through his appointment book, and often invited people like the William P. Fryes over for a small "family dinner."[16]

The state dining room was inadequate for the larger dinners, and tables set up in the halls accommodated an overflow of elegant guests, though protocol was always strictly followed in seating and serving. Such stiffness did not accompany the smaller dinners, when the state dining room sufficed, and the informal atmosphere reflected the ease of living and lack of pomposity of the McKinley inner circle. There were, however, numerous special problems, such as the lady soprano who sang for Mrs. McKinley's party in the Blue Room, and the painter who politely nagged the President to sit still for his formal likeness done in oil for posterity.[17]

The President's chief personal concern was his wife, for the promise of improvement in her health, which he had noted while governor of Ohio, was not fulfilled. She was to all intents and purposes a sickly invalid who tended to her official duties and stood beside her husband only through sheer determination. She spent most of her time in her chair, seldom going for drives and walking little except from bed to chair, downstairs, or across a room. The President sometimes took her for an afternoon drive, and she accompanied him on most of his trips around the country. The ladies of the cabinet assisted her. Mrs. Hobart was Ida's closest friend and greatest helper, just as her husband so often helped the President.

It was not that Ida disliked the formal affairs; she was simply not equal to the strain. On the contrary, her pride at being with her husband and her love of the limelight were often evident. She had a keener eye for the details of social intercourse than she admitted, and was acutely conscious of her position. Unlike her mother-in-law, she was fascinated by the glitter of pomp and power. No adverse words about her husband ever passed in her presence. If they did, the speaker was instantly reprimanded with a display of the short temper and irascibility that her illness sharpened, and which her husband mollified by his constant attention.

McKinley's hope for her recovery or betterment died hard. He seldom spoke of her illness now except to answer polite questions, though he admitted privately to his sister Helen late in 1899 that Ida was "very miserable," and spent all day in her room.[18] "Mrs. McKinley is not at all well," he wrote Hanna in the same year, "[and] has not been for four or five months." Doctor P. M. Rixey, a Navy physician, was later at her constant call, but there was little his science or experience could offer but barbiturates for sleep and various sedatives to see her through her worst days. Her headaches, which came and went with maddening severity, baffled treatment, and her fainting seizures became more and more frequent during the latter part of the presidential term. Special medicines and doctors came from New York and other centers of medical knowledge, but availed little. Nor did the home remedies and fantastic suggestions that came in daily from quacks, frauds, and misguided well-wishers help her distress.[19]

Her illness was distressing and her determination not to sacrifice her position added to its painful and embarrassing aspects. More than one luncheon, dinner, or reception was interrupted by one of her seizures.[20] In such circumstances the President displayed all the firm tact and patience that a life of attention to her wants had given him. Apparently oblivious to her spasm, he was apt to continue the conversation as though nothing had happened, as much to ease her feelings when she momentarily recovered as to spare his guests fright or embarrassment. William Howard Taft remembered talking with the presidential couple one day and asking McKinley for a pencil to make a note. As the President reached in his pocket for it, "a peculiar hissing sound" came from Ida and McKinley quickly dropped his handkerchief over her face and proceeded as if nothing had happened. When Mrs. McKinley recovered in a few moments, she continued her part of the conversation where she had left off.[21]

She thought that she comforted her husband by remaining at his side, and doubtless his life would have been harder had she entered an institution or remained entirely at home. She made every effort, as she had in Canton, to fulfill her obligations and to carry out her role as first lady of the land. McKinley lavished on her jewels and clothing such as she had never had before, fulfilling her old taste for fancy things. Partial to blue, she had several embroidered and jewelled costumes available in that color at all times; she dressed very well every day and was never seen informally. The vestiges of her beauty remained, and her sharp profile was accented by the Greek bob in which she wore her hair. Though the marks of pain and suffering were all too evident on her face and in her eyes, McKinley might well remind visitors that Ida was the prettiest girl he had ever seen. His devotion to her had long since endeared him to a large segment of the public. "President McKinley has made it pretty hard for the rest of us husbands here in Washington," Mark Hanna once said. But the nation also admired Ida's determination, perhaps realizing, as a military aide told her husband: "I believe her determination to be with you is the determining factor in her strength." [22]

Ida's valiant efforts to meet the public that crowded around her husband were not always successful. She often sat in the receiving line beside him, sometimes "looking rather blankly at the procession passing in front of her." The formal dinners were most trying, for protocol decreed that she sit opposite her husband so that she could entertain the guests on one side of the table. This placed her beyond his reach in emergencies and worried him until he finally asked Mrs. Hobart if she thought it would be proper for Ida to sit beside him. "Could it possibly offend anyone for me to have my wife sit beside me?" he asked naively. "Mr. President, you are our Chief Executive," Mrs. Hobart answered. "This is your home. It is your privilege to do as you choose." Ida thereafter sat beside him.[23]

Despite his work, he dropped in to see her several times each morning and evening, and usually managed to have lunch with her, though often they had guests. The President seldom spoke of business at the table, for mealtime was a vacation for him.[24] Ida spent most of her time, as always, crocheting slippers and wearing apparel for friends and relatives, steadily adding to the formidable list in her pocket. Her husband, as in the past, often wrote for her little notes asking Mrs. Herrick and other friends about thread and styles of stitching.[25]

The formal crushes at the White House sometimes irritated and tired her, but she liked the informal evening talks and dinners as much as her husband did. She also delighted in the sprawling glass-enclosed conservatories on the White House grounds. From them, as she sometimes toured them with her nieces and friends, she plucked the red roses that were her favorite flowers, or took a carnation back for the Major's lapel.

In the evenings, when time permitted, McKinley sat with her

and talked of the day's events or of family affairs. He might read a newspaper or glance through a book, rising periodically to stir the fire in winter or open a window in summer. Her needles continued at their murderous pace through it all unless she played cards, a delight of which she never tired. She and the Major often played euchre, he contriving to have her win through one artifice or another, by dropping his cards or exposing his hand inadvertently, for she did not like to lose. If she felt bad, her victor might savor her temper. "I had the misfortune to beat Mrs. McKinley in one game," Whitelaw Reid noted drily, "but recovered myself soon and presently said goodbye to the ladies and rejoined the party downstairs." [26] Frequent guests and friends quickly learned her habits and displayed silence if not patience. She was thoughtful and sweet when well, and her love for children and for her husband endeared her to many. Her faults were those of her illness, not her nature, and an age accustomed to sickly matrons forgave her everything.

McKinley's own health continued to be good despite his lack of physical conditioning and his confined life. The newspapers often reported him ill with "la grippe," the age's elegant name for virus colds. While he was prey to colds, he hastily informed his worried sister in 1900, he had not been sick at all except in the newspapers. "But as I have said a good many times, it is less painful physically to be sick in the newspapers than in the body, but the former always gives pain to my friends, which I regret." [27]

The President resolved to keep as fit as possible by frequent walks, horseback rides, and drives, the methods he had pursued with mixed results to date. Evenings during his first weeks in office often found him riding the Washington street-cars, walking the city's streets while reading a newspaper, or looking in store windows in a most "un-Cleveland-like" manner. Guards would have hampered his progress had he paid them any mind; he generally simply left without telling them. Though he had to abandon his walks on the street because of business and appointments, he became familiar to many who lived near the White House in the first week of his administration. Children lay in wait around corners for him, pestering him with congratulations and delighted exclamations, and he was his avuncular best with them or their mothers. Only the office seekers who occasionally shadowed him got a chilly greeting.[28]

Physically, he had not changed much in the last few years except for added weight. His face was unlined and the deep-set eyes under the large brow did not look older. Conservative clothes and an air of great dignity heightened his physical appearance. When he spoke he used few gestures, though his right hand might cut through the air "as though driving a nail into the atmosphere." [29] His face bespoke an inner attention to what the visitor said, for his brow often knitted in concentration as he listened closely. He listened a great deal more than he talked, though his language was rather slow and deliberate, and his voice was flavored with a slight Midwestern drawl.[30] He impressed most visitors with his personal dignity; he seemed never off guard with visitors, catching their every word and nuance to match in his reply. Some, like William Allen White, disliked and distrusted this formality, feeling that it hid some essential aspect of the man and that he used it to cover an ignorance on the subjects he discussed.[31] His reticence and caution were ingrained into habit now. His consciousness of his position did not lend him to frivolity or even to informality except among friends and family.

The President boasted a larger wardrobe than ever before. His handsome salary, despite its encumbering housekeeping bills, enabled him to indulge his and Ida's taste for good clothing. "McKinley was rather dressy," Ike Hoover remembered. "Particular always to have on a clean white vest." He sometimes changed his vests three or four times a day as they became wrinkled.[32] Most of his clothing came from New York, tailored to measurements which he carefully provided. Brother Abner, who lived in New York, often shopped for him, especially for shirts. On formal occasions he dressed in the white tie and tails prescribed by protocol. He received his daily visitors in his customary black Prince Albert and striped pants, usually with a white waistcoat, boiled shirt, and high collar. His ties were dark and might sport a stickpin, though he wore little jewelry and his watch chain and cuff links were usually the only visible ornaments. Unlike Ida, fancy things did not appeal to him. His glasses hung on the end of a black silk ribbon when not pinched on his nose. He seldom wore them in public, betraying a touch of vanity. The total effect was one of unending dignity, for his greatest concession to the weather was the short black alpaca coat he sometimes wore in place of the Prince Albert when Washington broiled beneath the summer sun. Andrew D. White mopped his brow on the way to a White House appointment in the summer of 1900, but the President, as he greeted him, appeared cool and uncannily dry in the stifling room. White remarked of this to Secretary Hay, who replied: "Yes, he is a source of perpetual amazement to us all. He allows no question, no matter how complicated or vexatious, to distract him." [33] It all reflected his inner control and the habits of a lifetime in politics.

McKinley's chief diversion was smoking. Friends and admirers sent him gift boxes daily, so his supply of cigars never ran out. He might smoke ten or even fifteen a day. "McKinley had a passion for cigars and was perhaps the most intense smoker of all the presidents during my time," Ike Hoover recalled.[34] Like Ulysses Grant, he felt more at ease with a cigar in hand. Though he still did not smoke in Mrs. McKinley's presence for fear of upsetting her, he smoked in conferences and private talks with friends and politicians. Evening usually found him sitting placidly in a rocker on the back piazza of the White House, looking out toward the Washington Monument, smoking idly or interspersing his puffs with comments to friends. He and Mark Hanna relaxed in this manner while talking politics. Friends detained after dinner in summer would talk a few moments with him here in the cool of the evening, and listen to the city's traffic work its way toward another busy evening.[35]

In an age of decorum and morality, the President of the United States did not think it proper to set a poor example, so he always put his cigar aside before the camera's eye. "We must not let the young men of this country see their President smoking," he told William Allen White.[36] Touchy about the camera anyway, McKinley carefully supervised all formal photographs, and tried to look his best for those in the crowds where he appeared. One reporter remembered that only once did he forget himself and pose for a photograph with the back of his hair sticking up.[37]

Other pleasures were rare, though Andrew Carnegie's secretary carefully forwarded a barrel of Scotch whiskey for the President's use, saying that if he did not drink it himself he was free to give it away.[38] History does not record its disposition, though he liked good Scotch. He was never anything but a moderate social drinker, but full courses of wine greeted guests at the White House. He was not bothered by temperance scruples as much as by lack of a taste for liquor. He drank moderate amounts of wine with dinner, though the White House cellar was never famous, and friends often sent him special bottles of wine and liquors. "The President says he likes the taste of the wine very much," Porter wrote Herrick in thanking him for a special shipment.[39]

His days were mostly work, with few interruptions in his routine. Trips out of Washington to make speeches or dedicate monuments were actually vacations for him despite the tedious preparations involved. Travel was not difficult on a special train, and he always had company. He loved the music of the brass bands that accompanied him, which must have brought back nostalgic recollections of his youth. Or perhaps he had simply heard so many that he had to like them.[40]

As president, he was naturally at the mercy of publicity seekers. He consistently refused to use his name for any commercial advantage. Scores of babies were christened with his name, and proud parents usually expected a presidential accolade. He even had a race horse named after him, "Kinley Mac." [41] His innate kindness and patience led him to tolerate quacks and favor seekers, and the War and Navy Departments complained frequently during the war with Spain that he unloaded more than their share of inventors on them. He would scribble a note and "W. McK." on a small card which gained the inventor admission to the proper department. He knew absolutely nothing of mechanical gadgetry, though it fascinated him. The most intriguing quackery came from spiritualists. Mother McKinley died in the winter of 1897, and the following spring a Washington medium reported contact with her; would her son please get in touch with her via the medium? The first letter to the White House went unanswered, filed carefully in a space the staff reserved for crackpots. Nothing daunted, the lady wrote again to say that if references were required she could summon the shades of Washington, Lincoln, Grant, and Garfield, as well as Mother McKinley, to her aid.[42]

McKinley's patience was evident in all his personal dealings, though the inventors and mediums must have taxed it. "He has a patience that is almost sublime. . . ." wrote crusty old Harrison

Gray Otis, who had none himself. But those around him knew that this patience was a means as well as an end in itself, and quickly understood, as John Hay wrote, that he had "a very strong will, as you know, and . . . likes to have things his own way. . . ." Mc-Kinley could not please everyone, the politician's ideal goal, but in declining requests he knew that the right words lessen the blow. His temper often rose but he seldom showed it. One congressman noted that Harrison used to freeze people out, Cleveland kicked them out, and McKinley kissed them out.[43] The President's charm often soothed ruffled feelings. Told that a senator was behaving badly, he followed Hanna's advice to "send for him and apply that *never failing remedy* of yours to his wounds." [44]

The President's natural tact and kindness, so successful in gaining friends, also delighted visitors whom he could not help. If he declined to do a favor he often as not removed the flower from his button-hole and pinned it to the caller's lapel, with the injunction to give it to his wife with the President's best wishes. How could anyone hate such a man, one congressman asked? Nor did this talent for the thoughtful gesture extend only to public men. George Cortelyou's young sons called at the White House one afternoon for a breathless and boyishly exciting meeting with the President. McKinley carefully shook their hands, inquired after their mother and their chief wants in life and, as they turned to go, gave the carnation in his lapel to the older brother, Bruce, while the younger, Win, looked on jealously. The President then took a fresh carnation from a vase, put it in his buttonhole for a moment, and gave it to Win, whose older brother thus could not lord it over him.[45]

The President showed some irritation at the endless stream of favor seekers. The White House elevator was an antique, among the first of its kind in the country, and ran from the water pressure of a tank on the roof. Its groaning ascent was precarious, but it was a blessing to stout congressmen who disliked the stairs. When it broke down, which was often, they had to walk and complained to the staff. "Let them complain," McKinley said one day. "It's too easy for them to get up here the way it is." [46] The politicians imposed on him, and many callers found themselves in Joe Choate's position, with their own appointment time taken up by unwanted visitors and favor-seeking congressmen.[47]

McKinley loved the people who simply came to shake hands. He had never found this an arduous or unrewarding task, though it was a burden to his less congenial predecessors who, like Harrison, had simply not seen people, or who, like Cleveland, had been so formidable that people did not come. The new atmosphere in the White House and McKinley's reputation for kindness and approachability brought hundreds of tourists and visitors to the mansion weekly, and they crowded in to shake his hand at the noon receptions. His handshake was a thing thousands remembered. "He had a way of shaking hands with you all his own—close up as if he were really interested in you," cartoonist Art Young remembered.[48]

McKinley got more from his friendly callers than they got from him, as he often said. They brought him greetings from afar and individual contact, personal touches that he prized highly and feared losing in his busy days and august position. "Everyone in the line has a smile and a cheery word," he said. "They bring no problems with them; only good will. I feel better after that contact. It is the visitor to the Cabinet room, pressing some policy or seeking some office who tires. . . . There's where the wear and tear is." The staff and friends were less cordial and more suspicious. As Hanna snorted: "What would happen, do you think, if some crank got in there with a revolver in his pants?" [49]

But as long as McKinley lived in the White House it was open to all. A variety of visitors came to see him. A departing oriental potentate on tour might brush past a housewife waiting her turn, or Samuel Gompers, who came often and talked long, always feeling that he had impressed the President. The door swung inward even for rivals, and a month after the inauguration, William Jennings Bryan called to pay his respects, accidentally meeting Hanna, who was leaving. Cordial talk ensued and Bryan left after a brief chat with the President.[50]

McKinley's memory for names and faces was an asset to him as a politician. His unflinching, often disturbing stare was one method of fixing a caller's face in his memory. "Once known, ever so slight[ly] to McKinley, you were rarely forgotten," a reporter noted.[51] He watched his guests so closely and with such obvious interest that Archbishop Ireland once exclaimed: "What a priest he might have made," perhaps not knowing of his mother's dream.[52]

He surprised many with this gift. While waiting for the ceremonies to begin at the dedication of a monument at Antietam battlefield, he walked to the edge of the platform and called down to an aged veteran in blue: "Hello, Comrade. I saw you in the crowd at Gettysburg, last month when I spoke there, didn't I?" The astonished spectator said, "Yes, but how did you recognize me?" The President only waved and smiled; his photographic memory for faces had done the trick. Asked later how he did it, he replied cheerfully, "Oh, I don't know, it just comes naturally." [53]

The round of activities and unceasing pressure of responsibility would have tired a man even in prime physical condition, but McKinley had a knack for throwing off the day's cares. Once decisions were made, he seldom reflected on them; he did not rehash what might have been. His basic problem was making up his mind, and he often moved with maddening slowness, his ingrained caution impeding his way. Once his course was clear, however, he was inflexible. Like many famous men in responsible positions, he could shift thoughts of state from his mind in a moment and change easily from the statesman to the husband or uncle or friend. He could relax when he wished to, an indispensable thing for men in his position.

He did not like outings or rugged relaxation; the strenuous life was not for him. From childhood he had never cared for hunting or fishing, but to please a staff member he once tried his line in a stream while on vacation. Miraculously hooking a fish, he hauled away but unbalanced the boat in which he was standing, causing it to sink and ruin his shoes and pants. Seemingly oblivious to his danger, he did not lose his composure while the frantic staff worked to save his dignity, and if need be, his person. Needless to say, he had not removed either his frock coat or silk hat while fishing. The unfortunate result doubtless persuaded him that he was wise in pursuing other recreations. [54]

The two outdoor sports he loved were horseback riding and driving. His dignity, not to mention his expanded girth, forbade further riding, but he often took the White House carriage for a turn around the town. A favorite form of relaxation, it gave him time to think, and such diverse people as Ida, Theodore Roosevelt, Hobart, or some visiting constituent might be seen at his side as the carriage rattled out of the gates and down the street. He was an expert driver and the horses soon knew him; the stable master kept them in fine condition at all hours, never knowing when the President would call on him. His dexterity with horses came in handy, for he averted a bad accident while driving with his niece Mabel, when he calmed a horse that had slipped and almost run away.[55]

The automobile, coming into vogue as a rich man's toy, held few charms for him; it was too impersonal as well as too erratic. The chances of a broken chain or exploded boiler were never far from his mind and, like most of his countrymen, he preferred reading about autos to riding in them. But once again his associates, who were accustomed to a certain amount of teasing and chaffing from him, prevailed on his good nature. They persuaded him one lazy afternoon to ride in a new steamer. Gripping the seat front, the President endured the agony until the machine reached eighteen miles an hour and his hat threatened to fly off. At that the party ended, and by common consent was not repeated.

The evenings he spent smoking and rocking with Mark Hanna were not altogether humorless.[56] Both he and Ida enjoyed occasional evenings of group hymn singing, much as they had when visiting Rutherford and Lucy Hayes twenty years before. McKinley, sweetly insisting that Hanna had a lovely voice, always begged the Senator to join in. Hanna, wisely realizing that his talents lay elsewhere, persistently declined, firmly holding his hymn book in one hand and just as firmly keeping his mouth closed.[57]

Sunday found McKinley in a pew at the First Methodist Church. He preferred to come and go as an ordinary parishioner, but the congregation paid him the courtesy of standing when he left after services. He kept his membership in many advisory Methodist organizations. Sunday he still set aside for rest, though his best intentions often failed under the onslaught of events.

His family ties were close, and the affection he showed his sisters as a young man did not diminish with age. The unobtrusive Helen taught school in Canton as if her brother were not president. Several charming young nieces and a nephew somewhat compensated for the President's lack of children. The death of his nephew, young James McKinley, while serving as a soldier in the Philippines brought home America's troubles on the world stage with peculiar force. Abner's daughter Mabel was married in the White House in 1900, and the festivities and bright young people cheered Ida. Mrs. McKinley's nieces were a special consolation to her, for they devoted time and energy to her wants when they visited, and were always on call to help care for her when she was ill.[58]

In the late nineteenth century, the presidency was taxing but not nearly as time-consuming as it is today. The adjournment of Congress in the early summer usually marked the end of the executive's greatest headaches, and summer and early fall, except in election years, passed more comfortably than did the winter and spring. The entertaining schedule was also cut drastically as politicians and businessmen left for world tours or long summer vacations. For McKinley it was time to go to Canton, which he regularly visited in summer and where he voted in national and state elections. He stayed in the old house while there, seeing family and friends. Charles Dawes remembered one such evening when Mother McKinley sat up later than usual, talking and knitting. She finally retired with a good-night kiss for William and the injunction, "You will find some pie on the dining room table under a cloth which I have put there for you." The men later sampled the pie and found it good. Mother McKinley's death on December 12, 1897, made her son break down and cry, the only time Dawes ever remembered seeing him so much affected.[59]

In July, 1899, the McKinleys bought back their old home and looked forward to refurnishing and remodeling it for their retirement years. To McKinley, who had spent his adult life in other people's homes and in hotel rooms, it was indeed a happy prospect. When visiting in Canton, he liked to sit in a chair on the porch, fanning himself gently with his hat or a palm leaf fan, watching the people go by, often waving to passers-by or stopping them for a chat.

The pressures of business and his natural aversion to figures and deals kept McKinley from attending to his financial affairs. His salary was more than ample, allowing savings which his friends Myron Herrick and Garret Hobart took each month to make careful investments for his future. He often sent money to members of the family or shared in a family project.[60] Of course, he got his share of requests for money and was not above tinging his replies, at least those made verbally, with sarcasm. Presented with a dunning letter beseeching funds for a worthy cause, he handed it back to Cortelyou with the wry instruction, "Call that to my attention when I feel richer than now." [61]

The McKinley Block in Canton still brought in rents, and the President delegated the worries there to a manager who was often hard put to collect from tenants. "It does seem to me that they take advantage of me on account of you being President of the United States," he wrote plaintively. "It is much harder to get money from your tenants than it is to get money from other people." [62]

McKinley's chief concern was for his wife in her widowhood should he die, and his will bequeathed everything to her. His life insurance was substantial, and Hobart's careful investments and Herrick's equally careful management left Mrs. McKinley a tidy sum at his death. They would have been able to live free from financial worry had he survived to be an ex-president.[63]

The President had little free time for reading anything but governmental reports and official correspondence, but he always had a talent for rapid assimilation and digestion of facts and information. His reading was scattered and eclectic, though he liked history, biography, and non-fiction in general. In the past he had digested great quantities of dusty tables and labyrinthine figures on the tariff, but that was no longer possible or necessary. He did manage occasionally to read some of the gift volumes sent to him, including James Ford Rhodes' *History*. ". . . It has been so engaging that I have gone well into the night in perusing it," he wrote the author.[64]

One thing he did read was newspapers, for his eye was always ready to judge public thinking. There was an unwritten law that the newsmen who hung around the White House might not approach the President unless he spoke first, but he read their wares. White House facilities for them were meager, though tables, chairs, and sofas were set aside for their use in the corridors. News releases generally came through Cortelyou and were given to the representatives of the big press associations first so that the administration could count on quick and impartial coverage. Both pro- and anti-administration papers got equal treatment. Though he held no press conferences and afforded no special treatment, McKinley at least fostered the idea that the presidency was a news source. When he travelled, Cortelyou arranged for a car of reporters to be attached to the presidential train.

The President read his home town newspaper to keep in touch with local affairs and personalities. The White House staff kept careful clippings from daily newspapers of all political leanings for his rapid digestion, and subscribed to papers from all parts of the country.[65] Public opinion counted for much with McKinley, and the newspapers as well as his visitors brought him most of his information on that attitude. In the back of his mind McKinley regretted his inability to read much, feeling perhaps that gathering information largely from men was really not as good or as rewarding as gathering it from books. "You make me envious," he told Theodore Roosevelt somewhat wistfully in 1901. "You've been able to get so much out of books. . . ."[66]

There was no systematic ghost writing in the White House until Warren Harding employed that leisurely method, and McKinley's extreme caution forbade his using anyone else's text, though he relied heavily on others for information and ideas. Writing speeches and reports and messages to Congress consumed a great deal of his time, and he often sat thoughtfully at his desk, a searching expression on his face as he strove to remember a fact or to find the right word.[67] He wrote on small slips of paper, with soft pencil and in his usual crabbed hand, then often read his speeches aloud to friends and advisors, making corrections as he went so that in the end only he could read the jumble of words that assaulted the eye. He might then make out a legible copy, or merely call in a secretary and dictate the text, which was typed for further correction and emendation.

His formal state papers required great quantities of information, and his annual message to Congress and special reports required the help of the cabinet officers and bureau heads. When McKinley went on tour the Bureau of Statistics felt the brunt of the assault as the White House staff demanded facts and figures on the locality to be visited. The resulting presidential style was not great literature, but like his speeches it was simple and comprehensible. "It is a hopeless task trying to correct your English," John Hay wrote his chief in a burst of enthusiasm that passed criticism. "I have read this over a dozen times and can find no fault in it. Either I am no critic or you know what to say. Perhaps both." [68]

McKinley's greatest asset in this line was his ear for anything that might offend or lead to misunderstanding. Cabinet officers read their reports and suggestions at cabinet meetings, and often the President sat silent for a moment after the reading was finished and then tactfully suggested rephrasing a passage to clarify its meaning.

McKinley's public speechmaking was accompanied by a fanfare that to many seemed almost royal, so dignified was the guest of honor and so deferentially did his prosperous fellow countrymen receive him. "Th' proceedin's was opened with a prayer that Providence might r-remain undher th' protection iv th' administration," Mr. Dooley gouged in a famous sally.[69]

McKinley and his staff carefully chose his appearances, and many institutions and groups were inevitably disappointed. In arranging visits outside Washington, the staff allowed local authorities to plan a schedule within the time limits they imposed, provided that they avoided conflicts by informing the staff of their arrangements well in advance of the trip. McKinley himself was always nervous lest someone talk with feet in mouth, and warned friends and associates who asked his presence to caution their own associates. "Do not have anybody who will be sensational or say foolish things," he wrote Webb Hayes in accepting an invitation, "as we are always beset, you know, with dangers of that sort." [70] He capitalized on his popularity with the people by appearing frequently and in widely scattered places. His tours of the Midwest in 1898, through the South in 1899, and to the Far West in 1901 made him the most widely known president of the nineteenth century, and were valuable to him, giving him a sense of the country and its people. And after the speeches were over, he always met interesting and kindly people.

Those who knew them did not doubt that Ida and William McKinley enjoyed life in the White House during most of their occupancy. The glamor and excitement, the presence of famous and powerful men, and the relative ease of living had their psychological rewards for the first family. McKinley had not pursued the phantom of political power all his life not to enjoy it on the pinnacle of success. But he also knew the deep responsibilities of his post, and the grim labor and unrewarding tedium of much of his duty. No place in life offers rewards without effort, not even the presidency, and success calls forth ever greater efforts to retain that success.

But as the administration moved into its second year, clouds gathered. The President worked longer and rested less. His callers were more and more short tempered, and his popularity with the people seemed to decline somewhat. His health was poorer and the circles around his worried eyes grew darker. The cause of the trouble was not imaginary, nor could it be assuaged with a message to Congress or a plea for calmness. A hundred miles off the shores of Florida, ragged and bearded revolutionaries nightly toasted the health of the President of the United States, sure in their belief that sooner or later he would come to their rescue.

⌘ XV ⌘

Cuba Libre!

CUBA lies in the Caribbean, a scant hundred miles from the shores of Florida. "The Pearl of the Antilles," once the treasure house and seat of government of much of Spain's vast empire in the New World, held many allures for her neighbors to the north. Boasting a rich Spanish culture and agricultural wealth, the island was important to the United States not for economics alone. History, some said destiny, joined the fortunes of these two lands; the affairs of one inevitably affected the other.

The post-Civil War generation in America took special pleasure in Cuba's sporadic struggles for independence. An oppressive political system run by Spaniards, economic domination by the mother country, repression of attempts to elevate the populace, and sharp awareness of their lot among Cubans led to violence that flared into open revolt between 1868 and 1878, and again in 1895. Each uprising sent tremors northward to stimulate ambitious, sympathetic, or mercenary men. To most Americans the struggles were birth pangs of freedom. To others, like William Randolph Hearst, they were the chance for fame, enshrinement in history books, and a kind of power. To several presidents they were a source of chronic and time-consuming worry and doubt. While the demands for intervention were often loud and persuasive, no president except Grant lent them a willing ear. The severe and protracted economic problems of the 1880's and 1890's drew American attention inward. McKinley's election ended those issues and inevitably turned American attention outward.[1]

The "Ever Faithful Isle," whose loyalty the mother country did not forget even as the other colonies declared independence, was the richest of Spain's jewels. Her emotional ties with Cuba were strong, just as emotion evoked most of America's sympathy. This depth of feeling fed the tenacity with which the Spanish suppressed the two Cuban rebellions of the late nineteenth century. In Spain

326

itself the people were poor, sullen under the weight of political oppression, sharply divided into classes, but also alive to the echoes of an imperial past that found its focus in the very name Cuba, to give the nation a kind of unity in foreign affairs. The government was reactionary and the dynasty weak. Queen Regent Maria Christina ruled for her young posthumous son, Alfonso XIII. Her ministers were slow, steeped in punctilio, given to delay and inaction, but always stubborn with the pride of past grandeur.

Cuban rebels gained little from their mother country. The conservative ministry of Canovas del Castillo that ruled between March, 1895, and August, 1897, cared only to suppress the costly rebellion that disrupted trade, cost men and money, and above all, revived the old American threat to drive Spain from the New World. A famous epigram governed his policies: "Politics is the art of applying in every epoch of history that part of the ideal that circumstances render possible." [2]

By the end of 1896, some 160,000 Spanish soldiers had tasted life in the lazy towns and tangled countryside of Cuba. But the insurrection dragged on dismally, with no conclusion in sight, its course written vividly in declining trade and a ravaged countryside. Exports from Cuba to the United States were cut in half between 1894 and 1896, and by 1897 were a fourth of what they had been three years before. By 1896 half the taxes collected in the island supported the Spanish military establishment, and public works and governmental services declined even as their need rose. [3]

In January, 1896, the government relieved Marshal Campos, whose "lenient" policies had not proved effective, and installed a new captain general, Valeriano Weyler. A veteran of colonial wars elsewhere, he had no patience with rebellion. To the United States, his name symbolized Spanish cruelty. His reconcentration policy became a hiss and byword. In a year New York newspapers would say succinctly: "Weyler has turned the island into a prison." [4]

The rebels, spurred on by their leaders Jose Marti, Estrada Palma, and General Maximo Gomez, struck for freedom. Moved by desperation, heedless of false promises from Spain, they would hear nothing of autonomy or compromise. They commanded respect and much support in America, for Spain's inability to reform the island after the end of the Ten Years' War in 1878 predisposed

American public opinion against her.[5] Surveying his motley legions, ill clad, often unarmed, desperately poor and illiterate, Gomez could only say, "With these oxen we must plow." [6] Such sentiments found a ready hearing in America.

While emotion pulled American sympathies toward Cuba, there were also practical reasons. Mistreatment by the Spanish of American citizens, whose rights were defined by old and sacred treaties, was greatly resented. The fact that many of these "citizens" were Cubans who used their naturalization papers as shields made no difference to Americans. Naturally there were incidents between American ships accused of filibustering and Spanish authorities, and more than one of these set coastal cities ablaze with ardor to "Beat the Spanish Dons." [7]

To those with financial and commercial interests in Cuba, the insurrection was devastating. Cane fields were put to the torch systematically, both to break the rebellion and for mere vengeance. The rebels hoped to embarrass the Spanish by such lawlessness, and the Spanish hoped to bring the rebels to terms. Systematic destruction of property, regardless of ownership, appealed to Gomez, who used it frankly to keep the issues of Cuban freedom alive in the press and in the hope of American intervention. Clouds of smoke by day and flickering tongues of flame by night lighted the rebellion's progress. Many plantation owners paid large bribes to both sides to escape destruction.[8]

Political repercussions in the United States were inevitable and, like other issues, they crossed party lines. Southern Democrats joined Republicans to embarrass Grover Cleveland's policy of strict neutrality, and every congressional session after 1895 found many pro-Cuban resolutions in both houses. Like a contagion, the desire to aid Cuba spread through American politics, and even so staid a man as John Sherman said that "no earthly power" would keep America out of Cuba.[9]

Cleveland pursued neutrality regardless of Congress, and yet even he, in all his stubborn disregard for public opinion, clearly perceived the crisis. In April, 1896, Secretary of State Richard Olney forwarded a famous note to Spain, making it clear that the American government could not remain aloof indefinitely. The Spanish answered in phrases that outlined the policy they carried to Cleveland's successor: the problem was internal, Spain was crushing the rebellion, and no aid could come to Cuba except through Spanish auspices. "In brief, there is no effectual way to pacify Cuba apart from the actual submission of the armed rebels to the mother country." [10] Cleveland's notes disclosed a basic difference of opinion that also passed to his successor: Spain held that her colonial system was not at fault and that she was free to suppress the rebellion with her own methods, while the United States insisted that the system itself was wrong and must change unless Spain wished American intervention. Such differing attitudes boded ill for the future, and even Cleveland noted in his last annual message to Congress, "The United States is not a nation to which peace is a necessity." [11]

The most vexing immediate problem which both Cleveland and McKinley faced was filibustering. Endless inlets, coves, and small islands along the American shoreline from New York to the Florida keys afforded hiding places for arms and debarkation points for Cuban sympathizers. The material aid sent from the United States helped the rebellion, but each successful dash bolstered Cuban hopes and vitalized the yellow press. Filibustering hurt Spanish pride, taxed resources, and was a constant irritant. Spanish authorities vigorously denounced what they felt was lax enforcement of the American neutrality laws, holding fast to the convenient thought that the United States prolonged the rebellion with actual aid and, more importantly, with the hope of ultimate intervention. [12]

Though Spanish spies checked suspicious ships, some filibusters made the run to Cuba. But the vigilance of the American Navy made such a journey a gamble at best. Of seventy-one such reported expeditions, only a third reached Cuba. Stephen Crane cursed the Navy for its efficiency in bottling up a crew of reporters in Florida, and the Cuban junta in New York candidly admitted that both Cleveland and McKinley kept vigilant navies. [13]

The influence that kept many politicians awake at night was far more dangerous, the yellow press. Politically, the influence of the press was often alarming in the 1890's, especially in foreign affairs. "Every congressman has two or three newspapers in his district, most of them printed in red ink, shouting for blood," one congressman complained. [14] The Cuban revolution was a godsend for the American newspapers and they kept it alive year after year.

As the conservative New York *Times* said acidly of its upstart brethren: "The most alarming Cuban revolutions have occurred in New York for many years—in speeches." [15]

By 1895, coincidental with the fresh outbreak in Cuba, two men appeared on the New York newspaper scene, each determined to outdo the other. The scholarly appearing but ruthless and canny Joseph Pulitzer poured all his energy and talents for exaggeration into the potent New York *World*. Not to be outdone, William Randolph Hearst did the same for the *Journal*. Neither professed fixed policies or steady ideals; both were concerned with their empires' growth. Of these the most public was Hearst. Consumed by some terrible ambition for fame, love, and power, young Hearst, backed by fabulous family wealth, carved out a newspaper empire almost as a plaything. Aloof, imbued with a kind of amoral arrogance based on a lust for power, his deceptively guileless blue eyes and slit mouth hid an iron determination.

Cost was no object and, as the war fever mounted early in 1898, the yellow dailies lost money to run extravagant extras. Atrocity stories flowed north steadily in 1897 and 1898. Vivid language, striking sketches made by men who had never seen Cuba, lurid details composed in the back rooms of taverns and press rooms mingled with the truth about Cuba and Spain's policies until the whole fabric dazzled millions into a kind of stunned belief. Dispatching Frederic Remington to Cuba for battle sketches, Hearst demanded only the best. Told that there was no war after all, he allegedly wired the artist in reply: "You furnish the pictures; I'll furnish the war." For every horror that the *Journal* printed, the *World* countered admirably, and their reporting served more than New York. Damsels in distress were rescued by reporters; private navies ferried supplies and newshawks to Cuba; an elaborate system of spies and rumormongers created what they did not know for sure, until one man suggested acidly that Hearst's reporters simply free Cuba.[16]

True or false, it had its effects. "This reporting was fragrant with circulation results, while we commoner folk began to boil and seethe with ardor to kill a Spaniard," remembered one who later became a soldier.[17] The McKinley administration itself took note of the press. "As to the objectionable newspapers, their sensational and unfounded reports are the cause of as much embarrassment at home as they can be abroad," Judge Day remarked. "The only real remedy seems to be the sober sense and judgement of the people." [18]

In Washington and New York, the Cuban junta, composed of exiles and sympathizers, furnished endless rumor and information to their friends in the press. Every day the newsmen came to the "Peanut Club," as the afternoon gathering in New York was called, to eat peanuts, drink beer, and hear the latest word from Cuba. The junta itself, established in 1895, was a clearing house for information, propaganda among congressmen and the public, and filibustering. Aided by funds and sympathy from many Americans, it exercised considerable influence through the press. It consistently opposed McKinley's efforts for peace, and functioned as a kind of government-in-exile, awaiting the day when it could announce American intervention to its friends in Cuba.[19]

Just how potent the press actually was in fomenting the war with Spain is unanswerable, for its power is indefinable. The Cubans themselves held that however valuable it was to them, it did not create public opinion, but merely fed the public appetite already there.[20] Newspaper distortions helped cause the war by maintaining diplomatic tension, and yet McKinley never entirely lacked newspaper support for his own policies. Nor did he himself pay special attention to the yellow press, despite his interest in public opinion. He had many friends in the fraternity, and such major papers as the New York *Times* and the *Tribune* generally stood by him.

The yellow press directed unrelenting scorn toward the business interests. If the very words "Wall Street" had spelled greed, crass materialism, and arrogance to many in the campaign of 1896, that symbolism was now transformed by the interventionists into the caution and timidity that would deny freedom to suffering Cuba while coveting her dollars. That the conservative business elements sustained McKinley is undeniable, and they had potent representatives in Congress. Fearful that war would disrupt returning prosperity, afraid of its cost and undetermined consequences, they bartered for peace at almost any price.[21] To many, business was "the soulless sordidness which dignifies itself with the title 'business interests' . . ."; Wall Street stood against Cuban freedom as "the colossal and aggregate Benedict Arnold of the Union, and the syndicated Judas Iscariot of humanity." [22] McKinley welcomed business support for his policy. He had promised prosperity and deemed it his first duty; he wished to buy time, and the conservatives in and out of Congress could help him greatly. But in this as in so many other things, he stood between two fires: if he acted to end the war in Cuba he risked alienating business; if he did not, he alienated public opinion. In the end he helped maneuver business into favoring intervention.

A small but potent group of intellectuals preached a new doctrine of "expansion," artfully linking it with the slogans of "Manifest Destiny" that had captured the allegiance of prior generations of Americans. Captain A. T. Mahan, doctrinaire in person as well as in his writing, stood aloof but powerful in the Navy. Whitelaw Reid spoke for the "large policy" through the potent New York *Tribune,* and often found it hard to curb criticism of his friend in the White House. John Hay had visions of an alliance of English-speaking peoples which it fell his rare lot to consummate later, and he had ready access to the President's ear. And always the pushy, aggressive, enthusiastic, irritating, but impressive Theodore Roosevelt, toward whom McKinley maintained a fatherly air of indulgence, grimaced his way through tiresome conferences, making his points with vigor and confidence. Any day might see him hurrying across the lawn from the awful marble pile of the State, War, Navy building to enter the White House on the run, where he "educated" the tolerant and often amused President in foreign affairs. It was America's destiny, these men said, to command continents and seas with actual as well as moral force. McKinley did not read their works, but he knew their tone.

Congress had long been pro-Cuban. In the spring of 1896, both houses passed resolutions favoring Cuban belligerency but these languished under Cleveland's icy gaze. The extensive debates in that session of Congress may well have made much of McKinley's policy inevitable, for they polarized beliefs and aroused the country.[23] Endless resolutions were introduced, great quantities of mail showered on congressmen, and impressive petitions from folks at home bade the new administration treat Cuba kindly. After all, the Republican platform of 1896 had favored a free Cuba.[24]

The House posed less of a problem than the Senate, for there the determined Speaker Reed held fanatics in check with both rules and sarcasm. As late as the eve of war one member could complain that ". . . Mr. Reed has the members of that body bottled up so tight they cannot breathe without his consent." [25] The most superficial poll showed, however, that the administration lacked a clear majority in either house, especially in the Senate, on the Cuban question. There the Foreign Relations Committee was staffed by Democratic and Republican expansionists, willing to differ from the President on Cuba. His influence with powerful committee chairmen somewhat offset this, but his hope for a free hand in making foreign policy was soon dashed. He could count only on such men as Aldrich, Hanna, and O. H. Platt in the Senate—the Old Guard.

When Congress assembled in special session in March, 1897, to deal with the tariff, Democrats in the Senate flooded the upper chamber with resolutions and oratory on suffering Cuba. In the House, belligerent members of both parties favored such resolutions.[26] Hanna was frank when asked if he thought action on Cuba was possible during the short session. "I don't know," he told reporters, screwing up his face and tapping the ground with his cane. "You can't tell about that. A spark might drop in there at any time and precipitate action." As he waddled quickly away, he threw over his shoulder the thought that action might not be possible after all; the administration opposed it, and the new President had public opinion, prestige, patronage, and endless persuasive abilities at his disposal.[27]

But the jingo senators, whether Republican or Democratic, followed their own course. McKinley thought it wisest to deal with them informally, and they met quietly at Sherman's home to receive official information on Cuba. They hinted that there would be no tariff unless there was also a Cuban resolution. Administration opposition took a familiar line: conduct of foreign affairs was an executive problem, and Congress could not interfere; any resolutions it passed would only be expressions of opinion, not binding on the President. It sounded suspiciously like Cleveland, and many Republicans who had expected McKinley to take a different tone began to wonder. The Senate passed its resolution favoring recognition of Cuban belligerency, but the House killed it.[28] Congress always thought less of Spanish power and sensibilities than did the executive. Wild Bill Chandler was heard to remark many times that a war with Spain would last from fifteen minutes to ninety days.[29]

These were the opposing conditions that confronted the new President as he began to outline his Cuban policy. His first responsibility was to restore prosperity and party harmony, but in his heart he know even as he spoke the oath of office that foreign affairs, centered in the bright and compelling name of Cuba, would consume his time and energy. His nomination in June, 1896, had brought choruses of approval from the Republican press. It assumed that he would be more "liberal" on Cuba than Cleveland and that he would not abandon the party platform that clearly favored Cuban independence. He was a party regular, and Republican policy in the past had always favored overseas expansion. A pro-Cuban stand would endear him to the public and McKinley had never spurned the people. So, at least, the newspaper talk ran during the campaign and after his election.[30]

Though partisans of a vigorous foreign policy had faith in the new administration, they sobered when they looked at the diplomats around McKinley. True, he chose politicians, presumably open to pressure, but by and large they were not excitable politicians. It was quickly apparent that the President himself would conduct foreign relations and that Judge Day would be the actual secretary of State rather than the assistant secretary. "I see that the newspapers talk about the diplomacy of this administration as 'amateurish,' " Day said with a slight smile, "and I must confess that it is." [31]

What did a regular Republican know of the details of foreign policy? McKinley had never taken a stand on foreign affairs before, nor had they touched to any degree upon his public life. Exactly what his attitude might be on Cuba no one really knew, for in all his speeches in 1896 he had said nothing on the subject. Privately he worried to friends that Cleveland might leave him a hot potato by precipitating action on the subject, and he was relieved when the Democratic administration passed on the whole issue intact.[32]

But appearances were deceptive in this as in so many things about McKinley, for though he lacked formal experience in diplomacy, he had natural talents that enabled him to learn the facts of diplomacy quickly. Basic to all his actions was a deep sense of humanitarianism that made him look with horror upon the savage events in Cuba; that they transpired elsewhere than in his own country did not lessen his shock or their importance to his policy. His concern for his country's welfare caused him to continue Cleveland's basic policy of watchful care for American interests. His conservatism and caution led him to explore every avenue. His adaptability gave him a flexibility which Cleveland lacked utterly, allowing close contacts with the elements that both supported and opposed his policy. His habit of taking advice spread responsibility for actions and laid careful groundwork for any policy chosen. His extraordinary patience, coupled with regard for Spanish sensibilities, and a certain clearness of mind made him see workable solutions to many problems.[33] Though he delegated much authority, he accepted ultimate responsibility for all foreign relations. He read his mail assiduously to ascertain public opinion and kept a firm grasp on the details of policy, a fact which surprised even the Spanish. Nothing emanated from the State Department which he did not know or approve.[34] Even the critical expansionists in his party grew to respect his methods. ". . . I think he could be depended upon to deal thoroughly and well with any difficulty that arises," Roosevelt remarked rather condescendingly.[35]

McKinley's chief concern seemed to be his Secretary of State, for Sherman's public utterances indicated a certain confusion that age compounded. Late in the summer of 1897, when finally the Dingley Act was on the books, the McKinleys departed for Lake Champlain and a brief summer outing. The peace of blue skies, calm lake waters, and hazy days was rudely interrupted by newspaper reports of an interview with Secretary Sherman. Jealous at his isolation, Sherman spoke out to a canny and straight-faced reporter who played his subject to the limit. Yes, said the Secretary of State, Cuba should be freed; no, Spain could not hold her. In the Orient, he thought, Japan bore watching, and elsewhere one could never trust England. Alarmed, McKinley sent Day to Washington to calm newspaper fears and to mollify the Secretary until he himself could return and explain away Sherman's words and tone.[36]

335

Sherman had already said privately that he felt American intervention in Cuba was inevitable, but he had said little in public.[37] Now he recanted to the President but not before tongues wagged, in and out of the administration. John W. Foster privately hoped that something would be done about Sherman's failing memory. "Even the lowest servant in the State Department knows and talks about it." [38] To his chief Sherman was candid, but he edged his frankness with an appeal to the President's notoriously soft heart. "As to my getting old I will not deny it. Whenever you think I am too old I will retire with thanks to the Ruler of the Universe for extending my life beyond the allotted three score and ten years." [39] The bitterness with which Sherman later treated McKinley was not yet obvious, and naturally the President could not dismiss so honored and famous a name. But thereafter, McKinley and Day tightened their hold on the department.

McKinley had need of both caution and judgment as he confronted the Cuban problem, for the men with whom he dealt were past masters at manipulation and intrigue in the classic European mold. Chief of them was the Spanish minister in Washington, Enrique Dupuy de Lome. Cynical, worldly-wise, and deeply experienced in all the turns of Spanish diplomacy, de Lome in his chilling person was a reminder of Spain's grand past. A vision of empire and faded glories seemed to follow him at the ornate diplomatic receptions. Though he was not McKinley's kind of man, the President went out of his way to please the Minister. Too late did the proud and narrow Spaniard understand that the President, his apparent foe, could have been a valuable friend. The arrogance and vanity that tinged his dealings merely reflected the strong beliefs held among his people and their government in Spain. There were those in Madrid, just as in Washington, who had no taste for compromise and peace. "We may perhaps introduce an epic into history," one said.[40]

McKinley relied chiefly on two men for his direct information on Cuba, the American consul-general in Havana, who was closest to the scene, and the Minister in Madrid. In Havana, McKinley inherited a Cleveland appointee, the jingoistic Fitzhugh Lee. Stout in body, addicted to Panama hats, white suits, and colorful language, Lee, while working assiduously for his country's interests, made no secret of his hopes for Cuban freedom. Related to the great Lee and himself a "Confederate brigadier," he had influence in his party. He carefully chose the information and recommendations that went north to the State Department. His hurrying fat figure was a familiar irritant to Spanish officialdom; his potential for harm was great. Cleveland had his doubts about Lee, and said so, but left him for the new administration.[41]

With all his temper and occasional bluntness, Lee was not irresponsible. He understood McKinley's special reliance on his reporting and, while it would have been easy to exploit the advantage, it would also have offended his sense of responsibility. He was honest; he never denied his feelings. But he was not any more anxious for unnecessary intervention than was the President. If diplomacy would work, so be it; if not, so be that too.

McKinley thought briefly of replacing Lee—it might be dangerous to rely on his reports—but he feared this dismissal would seem weak to the Spanish. As early as March he assured Lee that the latter would remain at his post, though like Mr. Dooley the President might have thought, "He's ca'm, an' he waits part iv th' time. That's whin he's asleep." But Lee had experience, knew Cuba and the Spanish, and his views could always be discounted.[42]

The embassy in Madrid was a touchier matter. McKinley again inherited a Cleveland appointee, Hannis Taylor, who remained at his post through almost six months of the new administration. He too was a jingo—how curious that the pacific Cleveland retained jingoes at two such crucial posts as Havana and Madrid— but McKinley again did not wish to lose an experienced man until he was ready to choose the right successor.

Many thought it curious that McKinley should delay so long in selecting a new minister. Delay did not trouble the President, since it brooked no change of policy and gave him more time to consider his new departure, if there was to be any. In March he talked candidly with Henry White and John Hay. "What am I going to do about the Spanish mission?" he asked, spreading his hands in a little gesture of frustration. "I must have a trained diplomatist there." He turned to White and asked him to take Madrid, but the latter declined for personal reasons. He next asked Foster, who also declined for personal reasons, and bluntly said he thought it impossible to avert intervention.

Politics entered into the selection. New York demanded the post, and McKinley inclined toward the Empire State, but he would not appoint Tom Platt's man. He thought briefly and publicly about Reid, which panicked Platt, but turned instead on June 16 to a compromise candidate, Stewart Woodford. Woodford was acceptable to most New York Republicans and was a straightforward and honest man who accepted the post though he doubted that he could keep the peace. The choice surprised some, who thought a more colorful appointment wiser, but McKinley wanted soundness and common sense at the embassy.[43]

Newspapers predicted a sound and sane policy toward Cuba, coupled with firmness. Many still remembered, not always with gratitude, the inaugural address with its calm phrases that had glided over the problem. Few could as yet see any emerging design in the President's policy; perhaps he himself had not made up his mind, or perhaps he preferred to veil his plans while he worked. Lodge dined at the White House and noted with pleasure that McKinley would continue naval expansion. But the Spanish Minister reported home that he expected no immediate danger; the new administration seemed well disposed toward Spain's halting promises to reform Cuba.[44]

Yet filibustering, voices in Congress and the press, mistreatment of American citizens in Cuba, and other irritants kept the problem in the forefront of American news even while the President worked slowly and methodically for peace. Every day's headlines told of new atrocities and magnified the all too apparent horrors of war in general and the reconcentration policy in particular. McKinley obviously could not sit idle; his inaction would only invite further irritation and opposition. Still he was loath to define a hard and fast policy until Woodford arrived in Madrid and made his basic intentions clear to the Spanish.

Could he trust Lee's reports and the volatile Southerner's automatic presentation of the case against Spain? Was relief as desperately needed as he said? McKinley temporized, thinking that he would send Day on a special mission. But that would indicate apparent divisions in American policy. In the end he chose a characteristic method: a private emissary who would cooperate with Lee and secretly report on general conditions in the island. William J. Calhoun, prominent Illinois attorney and the President's friend, embarked early in May for a Cuban fact-finding tour.[45]

Meanwhile, Congress wrestled with the tariff in special session, employing every chance to thrust at Cuba and to record its opinions. Resolutions placed by many members of the Senate called for recognition of Cuban independence, belligerency, or extension of aid in some form by the United States. Of these resolutions, John Tyler Morgan's was most popular, and despite administration pressure, it was reported out for action early in May. Over protests from conservative Republicans it passed the upper house and brought a hasty conference between McKinley and his supporters in the Senate.[46]

One good thing came from all the talk. On May 17, a presidential message asked Congress for $50,000 in relief funds for American citizens in Cuba, to be spent through Lee's office. Congress did not delay, spurred by reports of widespread hunger.[47] Grateful that his words and Cuba's cause had at last been recognized officially, Lee assured the State Department that the money was needed and would be well spent. His staff began to work among the needy at once, though reports of extensive starvation and destitution among American citizens were, admittedly, exaggerated. Intervention in Cuba, he hinted broadly, was the only answer to the problem, for famine and poverty were widespread among the reconcentrados in Cuba's cities and towns.[48]

The most remarkable aspect of McKinley's diplomacy was its lack of public focus. In the first weeks and months of his administration, harried bureaucrats faced other problems, but those who talked with the President knew that Cuba lay always in his thoughts. Yet defining his policy was almost impossible. Fearing to add impetus to the problem by discussing it, he followed his customary silence. All who talked with him noted that as usual he listened rather than talked. In all of his personal correspondence no position is outlined; the word "Spain" is never mentioned.

"Where to turn?" he must have asked himself as he shook hands with visitors and sat quietly through long hours of unwanted advice.

339

He desired peace, but he knew also that he must obtain certain concrete modifications of policy from Spain or he would have war. He did not wish to annex Cuba, though there were those who did. Would it not be politically wise, some said, to buy the island and either keep it as a protectorate or prepare it for independence under American auspices? [49]

It was an intriguing prospect. Perhaps the whole question could be settled painlessly and finally by American purchase. Through the summer he developed the idea briefly as he formulated his plans, the crisis conveniently held in abeyance by the rainy season in Cuba. He toyed with the idea, dropping hints here and there, sounding out visitors and diplomats.[50] But Spain was not interested. Confident that they could crush the rebellion once and for all in the fall before the United States could act, Spanish authorities did not incline to selling the island to anyone. A newspaper report had already brought blunt words from Canovas himself: "Spain is not a nation of merchants capable of selling its honor." [51] The plan died a-borning; the President knew in his heart that a solution could not be that simple, anyway.

As the summer wore away, McKinley looked hopefully toward the adjournment of Congress for removal of a major irritant, thus permitting him to conduct his first diplomacy without public interference or strict definition of his means. The secrecy which McKinley employed in his dealings was remarkable. In private, he spoke freely, although in generalities, of his aims and hopes to those who questioned him. He said nothing in public, however, and made no appreciable effort to placate any opinion arrayed against him. By maintaining this statesmanlike pose above the battle he hoped to rally all as yet undecided sentiment to his side and to hold his own ranks firm, while at the same time denying information to the press and public that might be distorted. The danger was that he seemed inactive. He hoped also to accomplish much before Congress reassembled in December; if he could present that body with concrete executive accomplishments, the public would not countenance interference from partisan politicians.

From Havana, Lee directed a steady stream of information and opinion which he hoped would guide the State Department in formulating policy. On March 17 he forwarded a response to Day's inquiry about conditions, outlining the position to which he clung persistently until war came, and which was accurate: the insurgents could not defeat the Spanish, nor could the Spanish defeat the insurgents, who had the support of the people; the war would continue until Spain was financially exhausted or until another power intervened; in the meantime, Cuban agriculture would be destroyed, with attendant loss of life and property. He flatly denied that the Spanish intended reform or that anything approximating autonomy could be instituted.[52] A month later he was even more specific in his indictment of Spanish policy, stating that Spanish claims of reforming the island were simply false. "No one can fully appreciate the situation without being here in person," he said in a careful thrust that outlined his own key position.[53]

The news from Spain that summer was equally disheartening. In June, a cabinet crisis by which Liberals hoped to oust the Conservatives and the increasingly unpopular Canovas, failed, and the Queen Regent's support of the cabinet caused Taylor to lose heart. "All who were hopeful of amicable settlement on the basis of conciliation profoundly discouraged," he cabled home.[54] Yet he held out a glimmer of hope to the anxious President: the summer's abeyance in the rebellion had sharpened distaste for its resumption in the fall; Spanish public opinion grew restive; there might be some softening if proper pressure were applied.[55]

Matters differed, however, in Cuba, at least according to Lee. Autonomy within a newly constituted Spanish empire, in which Cubans would rule Cuba, had often been suggested as a way of settling the problem to everyone's benefit. Canada was suggested as the proper model. But as Lee and others often pointed out, Spain was not England. She had held Cuba far too long to release her even partially now. "No one who is well acquainted with existing conditions now has any hope that Spain can grant reforms *approximating,* even, to Canadian autonomy, such as is so often mentioned," Lee wrote home bluntly.[56] Furthermore, talk that the insurrection would not be resumed in the fall, that the rebels were exhausted or ready to deal with Spain, were false. The failure of Spanish officials to take the promised reforms seriously only heightened the rebel desire to succeed.[57]

Though McKinley preferred to present his first formal policy through Woodford, who was scheduled to arrive in Madrid in September, a statement of policy was necessary lest the Spanish feel free to act on their own. On June 26 Sherman forwarded to de Lome the first of the long series of notes that outlined McKinley's Cuban policy. The note took high ground, arguing in traditional American fashion that the rights of humanity exceeded the rights of men and states. The note also stated the basic terms on which the United States expected the conflict to be settled: revocation of reconcentration, rapid pacification of the island to end its devastation, proper measures to care for the populace, better treatment of American citizens, and reform of the system to better the Cuban lot and prevent a future rebellion. McKinley did not deny Spain's right to suppress the rebellion, but pointed out that for better or worse the United States was involved, due to American interests in the island and for the cause of humanity. To him as to other Americans the method of warfare was most repugnant, and the reconcentration policy of crowding the cities with helpless and untended victims of warfare from the rural areas must cease: ". . . against the cruel employment of fire and famine to accomplish by uncertain indirection what the military arm seems powerless to directly accomplish, the President is constrained to protest, in the name of the American people and in the name of common humanity."

To the Spanish it had a familiar ring; it sounded all too much like Cleveland. But if anything, its tone was firmer:

> He [the president] is bound by the higher obligations of his representative office to protest against the uncivilized and inhumane conduct of the campaign in the island of Cuba. He conceives that he has a right to demand that a war, conducted almost within sight of our shores and grievously affecting American citizens and their interests throughout the length and breadth of the land, shall at least be conducted according to the military codes of civilization.[58]

McKinley's Cuban policy always contained this firm threat of ultimate intervention unless Spain bowed to American demands. Conceding that such reforms as he demanded could not be instituted overnight, he made it clear that the Spanish must end the long and tedious delays by which they had staved off America's wrath while failing to end the conflict. Having taken this position, he could not recede. It may well have determined all that followed, for the United

342

States permitted itself the right to judge Spanish conduct and to set the due speed with which reform progress was to be made. It insisted on the methods to be employed in Cuba but accepted no responsibility for them. While assuring the Spanish and Cubans of American neutrality, it held the threat of intervention over the heads of all. McKinley's diplomacy was simply a logical extension of Cleveland's, consisting at heart of steadily tightening the screws of diplomatic pressure in the hope of speedy Spanish reform in Cuba. The implicit danger was that Spain would choose in the end to fight her way out of the corner into which she backed.

Madrid's reply was not at once forthcoming. The marble halls of Spain's foreign ministry seldom echoed to hurrying footsteps, nor did harried diplomats often pass within its portals intent on speed and dispatch. Late in August, de Lome transmitted to the State Department his government's reply. It breathed the tone of truculence which characterized all of Spain's dealings over Cuba. Its substance was simple: the Cuban problem was Spain's alone, the United States was not enforcing neutrality legislation, the rebels had started the conflict and could end it whenever they wished by approaching the mother country. It held out no hope that Spain would transform her methods of warfare or fail to prosecute the rebellion in the fall.[59]

As Woodford travelled toward Madrid, the cables brought the news that Canovas had been assassinated on August 8, 1897. The flinty Premier was the chief hope of the conservative elements in Spain that fought reform, and his passing was not altogether regretted. A successor might be more conciliatory, especially in view of mounting American pressure.[60]

Woodford had worked his way toward Madrid with genial slowness, obliging the Spanish request that he not appear until the new government, an interim army ministry, was settled in power. Conferring with Hay in London, Horace Porter in Paris, and American diplomats from Berlin and other countries, he sounded opinion and concluded that the continental powers posed no real threat. While they were pro-Spanish because of economics, politics, and monarchical sympathies, they would not risk a war to rescue Spain's chestnuts.[61]

What tone should Woodford take, and what specific proposals

would he lay before the Spanish? The administration made it clear that it wished neither annexation of Cuba nor war. McKinley wanted merely to mediate the conflict, insuring a peaceful settlement amenable to all sides. He would not recognize the Cubans as belligerents, for that would be tantamount to intervention.[62]

In the first week of September the Woodford party rolled into Madrid, lazy in the sunshine, her white walls and tiled roofs sparkling in contrast to the ancient monuments that dotted her hills and lined her streets in a profusion of Old World splendor. The new Minister settled in his embassy, took afternoon drives, watched bullfights, and was tactful and courteous to all. He delayed offering the President's good offices, feeling that the time was not quite right.[63] Though de Lome felt that the new Minister was pacific, in retrospect the Madrid government held that his coming ended an era. "His first official actions made it clear that the new representative of North America had instructions to approach the Cuban problem with the idea of overshadowing or limiting the sovereignty of Spain." [64]

The foreign minister, the Duc de Tetuan, received Woodford informally late in September. He hid any tensions he felt with a legendary Latin charm, talking sincerely and with some animation for three hours as Woodford repeated what McKinley had told him: the United States could not permit an indefinite war in Cuba and would not hesitate to intervene unless concrete reforms were enacted in not only the method of warfare but also the status of the island. Woodford's tact did not conceal his frankness, and he felt sure that the dignified Spaniard understood both the unspoken and spoken words. But despite all the Spanish courtesy, he left with an uneasy feeling. "I have little hope of peaceful solution, but am doing the best I can to get peaceful results." [65]

Two days later he wired home in an even franker tone that thus far he felt little reason to trust Spanish promises. Like Mr. Micawber, they were waiting for something to turn up. Delay was their chief implement, and de Lome fed their hopes from Washington, apparently taking McKinley's public silence and official slowness for weakness. "It is a hand to mouth policy." [66]

From Washington, McKinley still refused to conduct open diplomacy and resisted pressures to release Woodford's dispatches. He preferred silence to further complications, wisely insisting on a free hand. If he was quiet publicly he was firm privately, feeding a steady stream of instructions to Woodford which, though they appeared over Sherman's or Day's signatures, expressed the President's views. Late in September, Woodford presented the President's formal tender of good offices to mediate the Cuban conflict. If Spain refused, she should understand that McKinley would feel free to pursue a different course. Such an offer was not, however, pro-Cuban.[67]

The passing of the interim ministry brought the Spanish Liberals to power on October 4, 1897, in the form of Praxedes Sagasta, whose party had often openly criticized Canovas' harsh policies. The McKinley administration believed that the Liberals would be friendly toward American good offices, but recognized the dangers of seeming to force the issue.[68]

The oppressive silence from the foreign ministry and the incredible slowness of Spanish diplomacy made Woodford uneasy. Like his chief, he was eager to show some progress to the new Congress that would assemble in December; unlike McKinley, he was not at all sanguine. The autonomy scheme was fine, he reported, except that the Spanish did not seem to understand it; when they did, likely as not they smiled and shrugged. "I doubt whether the Spanish official mind comprehends real autonomy as Englishmen and Americans would understand autonomy. I doubt whether Spain could give in theory or enforce in fact such autonomy as Canada has." [69] It was the first of much similar cold water that washed away the President's hopes for Cuban autonomy.

On October 26, the new ministry delivered a comprehensive reply to past American notes. While they declined to permit presidential mediation, they promised to step up the fall campaign, employ humane methods, and grant ultimate autonomy of some kind to Cuba, which, however, would remain carefully in Spanish hands. Suggesting inevitably that the United States might enforce her neutrality laws more strictly, the note ended with vague assurances that at least a change was in the offing.[70] On October 9, the Spanish had assured Washington that the hated Weyler would be recalled, a major breakthrough for McKinley. Pressing the advantage, Day applied another turn of the screw, pointing out to de Lome that atrocities continued in Cuba. There was little evidence that the Spanish there understood the change of policy in Madrid. Measures of relief must be accomplished at once, if only as a sign of good faith.[71] De Lome must have sniffed irritably, for he had grown to hate McKinley, this rural politician who had wrung large concessions from the new regime. The regal Minister had no taste for reform and, as he would shortly prove, cared less for McKinley and his talents. From Madrid, however, Woodford congratulated his chief on having achieved the first steps of his program. While the new policies were only promises, they were at least new, and McKinley in a matter of weeks had forced an apparent redefinition of Spanish aims and methods.[72]

De Lome replied to the new American protest by saying that miracles of speed were impossible, but if McKinley noted the icy aloofness he said nothing. It did not prevent his giving the Spanish Minister an unusually warm greeting in mid-November. His hand outstretched, face wreathed in smiles, the President congratulated de Lome on what he felt was a joint success, expressing confidence in Sagasta's new trend.[73]

The Spanish ministry did not fail Woodford's and McKinley's best hopes. Later in November it assured Woodford that the Queen Regent would proclaim the long rumored reforms shortly. The concentration camps would be broken up, Weyler would return home for a more moderate successor, and autonomy would be outlined. The most significant point to Woodford was simply that such a policy could be announced. "The Ministry have now entered upon their path of promised humanity, reform and autonomy. . . . If they should ever attempt to turn back or evade the logical results of what they now do, they will practically break their pledges to Cuba and to the United States. This would not only justify but might compel intervention." [74] The Ambassador was dealing in prophecy.

For the moment he was hopeful, eagerly grasping at every Spanish smile and promise. On November 25, the Queen Regent formally proclaimed the long awaited Cuban policy, repudiating Weyler's methods and outlining a formidable and complex system of autonomy. To those who looked closely, however, it was not autonomy at all. The proposed Cuban legislature was dominated by a council of Spanish appointees and was at the mercy of a Spanish governor, while all ultimate authority remained with the mother country. The New York newspapers dismissed it as a hodge-podge scheme thought up for publicity purposes, and the administration was not publicly impressed.[75] McKinley's lack of public statement at this logical point indicated his own disappointment.

Woodford's cordial and rather informal interviews with the Queen Regent impressed on him her earnest desire for peace. She feared the dynasty's fall if she lost her empire, but she feared war with the United States even more.[76] However charming and sincere she was, as Woodford left her presence he must have thought of the news reports of the wild receptions accorded Weyler on his landing at Barcelona. He who supposedly returned in disgrace found himself the hero of the hour for Spaniards, who shouted slogans about empire and glory, waving flags that had been hated symbols in another hemisphere.[77] In Havana, General Lee smoked his endless cigars, made his rounds on behalf of beleagured American citizens, and filed his dispatches to Washington, reiterating a single theme: intervention was the only ultimate answer; the rebels would not accept reform, and the Spanish could not enforce it. Almost incidentally he repeated an old request that warships be placed at his disposal at Key West.[78] Privately de Lome penned similar and even more sinister thoughts. Early in December he cabled home: "My opinion has not changed in any respect. So long as a government is not formed in Cuba, and until the decrees are put into effect, the situation must remain expectative." [79] Delay, the ancient Spanish weapon, would serve them again. But time was running out, for Congress was now on the President's doorstep, filling his ear with complaints and ready to hamper his policy at every turn.

The first snows of December brought congressmen straggling into the capital eager to resume their labors. They longed to turn now to Cuba, a far more dazzling and compelling prospect than tariffs or currency legislation. Though the administration's congressional lines seemed firm around such men as Reed, Hanna, and Aldrich, the jingoes and moderates in both parties were irritated by McKinley's silence and his insistence on executive formation of policy. His apparent victory in winning concessions from the new Spanish ministry that would presumably be the first step in reform without war called militants in Congress and the press to battle.

De Lome had written his superiors that they might expect a pacific annual message from the President.[80] Congress agreed as it sat restively listening to clerks read McKinley's words, reciting the history of the first few months of the administration, asking for legislation on such dull things as the banking system and tarriff reform. The section dealing with Cuba was general, rather vague in its recommendations, and counselled caution and watchful waiting. Reciting the history of the insurrection and the horrors of its warfare, the President listed three alternatives: neutral intervention, recognition of Cuban belligerency, and annexation. Of the latter he spoke bluntly. "I speak not of forcible annexation, for that can not be thought of. That, by our code of morality would be criminal aggression." He dismissed Spain's contention that the United States did not enforce its neutrality laws with a somewhat curt aside. On the whole, he would wait and see. "It is honestly due to Spain and to our friendly relations with Spain that she should be given a reasonable chance to realize her expectations and to prove the asserted efficacy of things to which she stands irrevocably committed." But he included a warning that rang familiar in Spanish ears and which gave some comfort to many who listened:

> Throughout all these horrors and dangers to our own peace this Government has never in any way abrogated its sovereign prerogative of reserving to itself the determination of its policy and course according to its own high sense of right and in consonance with the dearest interests and convictions of our own people should the prolongation of the strife so demand.

The screw was tightened another turn; Spain must make her promises real or the old threat of American intervention would become real.[81]

Reaction to the message was swift from those who heard it. In the Senate the Democrats opposed it almost to a man. The pacific ring of the message alienated many Republicans, and Foraker, Chandler, and the ultra-jingo "Billy" Mason of Illinois frankly rejected it. Ex-Ambassador Taylor thought it weak and pro-Spanish, and constituents showered congressmen with protests. ". . . His Cuban policy is cowardly, heartless and idiotic," a friend wrote Alger. "McKinley is a Chinese statesman." [82] From Spain, Woodford reported that the government appreciated the patient tone and the

President's whole attitude. Later more personal reports from others indicated that the tone behind the ladies' fans at court and on the streets among the people was different. Proud Spaniards of every class resented American pressures and implicit threats.[83]

In Havana, General Lee fumed and pounded his desk, caught between the fires of Spanish official delay and what he considered a heartless policy in Washington, reiterating his old stand in cables home. As if to supplement the President's message with deeds, Day arranged to have warships on call at Key West; in the event of revolution or troubles, Lee might cable the code letter "A" and the Navy would respond.[84]

In Madrid, Woodford hastened to explain that the President's patience was not lenience and that Spain must mollify public opinion in the United States with actions in Cuba. McKinley himself would not outline a plan of autonomy, but he expected Spain to implement one at once, "the scope and effects of which must remain to be judged by their realization." [85]

As the old year died, ushering in a new one to be filled with tensions of which the already weary President could only be faintly aware, the need for relief mounted in destitute and ravaged Cuba. Once more the appeal went out to distribute private charity through the Red Cross. And silently, anonymously, the President himself sent a check for $5,000.

With almost a year of diplomacy behind him, McKinley faced 1898 with misgivings. He might take some pride in the concessions he had wrung from Spain, but they were after all only promises. The new session of Congress would demand much more from both him and his foreign adversaries. The days of free diplomacy were already gone. His chief danger was that the middle-of-the-road sentiment in Congress and among the public would shift to intervention unless Spain acted. Speed was of the essence and yet daily dispatches from Havana and Madrid revealed no sense of urgency among the Spanish. McKinley would have appreciated what Senator Lodge wrote a critical friend, Lodge who was still willing to wait and see:

> I do not feel that you are just to the President in regard to Cuba. By the firm attitude which he has assumed he forced the withdrawal of Weyler, the release of all the American prisoners, the revocation

349

of the concentration edict and of the tobacco order. Spain having made all these concessions, he would hardly say that they should not have the opportunity to try to pacify the island by autonomy, and I think he has acted wisely in so doing.[86]

Comforting words, and yet dangerous, for they showed how much the critical and undecided demanded. If the President's plans failed, there was nothing to do but intervene. He had built no bridges behind him. His policy, like Cleveland's, was one of unrelenting pressure, requiring speed and results to offset rising public opinion at home. The problem really rested now with Spain. Could she break the log jam of promises in 1898, or was she fated to lose Cuba?

From Peace to War

HAVANA in 1898 bore the marks of its divided character. To the casual visitor and tourist it was a charming, if inconvenient, city. From this seat of imperial power expeditions had set out under banners of glory and God to conquer an empire. From this same regal city, arrogant viceroys and captains-general had held sway over that empire. In 1898 the city still boasted this air of grandeur, but now it was uneasy, sitting in the midst of a crumbling world, prey to terrors and fear from all sides as the conflict ate at Cuba's vitals. Now within its confines stood not a conquering army but a mere garrison, surrounded by the rabble and misery bred by war, prey to disease, fearful of tomorrow. It shared the dubious honor of Spanish power with only one other major Cuban city, Santiago de Cuba.

Havana was not Madrid, nor were the attitudes of its people the same. Conditioned by events and interests in Cuba, both its civil and military officials saw things in a different light from that which filtered through the instructions and correspondence from Spain. The military commander who undertook a Cuban responsibility soon lost heart when he faced his command and surveyed the scene of battle. The civil administrator who determined to reform the island to save it for his country soon fell into laxness and defeatism on facing the ingrained delay and lack of insight in the inland's bureaucracy. From the somewhat seedy but still ornate government palaces in Havana there issued a stream of edicts and pronouncements intended to change Cuba to American satisfaction, but they seldom impressed anyone but the printers.

Much of the problem was inherent. Spaniards born in the island ran the Cuban economy and political system. Their interests and passions dictated greater stubbornness than that in Madrid. Loss of the island would mean loss of office to them; their control over the fiscal system, the debt, and the economy in general would vanish. The Cuban Spaniards clung largely in the past, urging the Captain-General, Marshal Blanco, to subdue the rebellion at once. Their opposition to insular reform, together with the rebels' manifest refusal to accept anything but independence, was the basis of Lee's skepticism about autonomy, no matter what intentions motivated Madrid.

American pressure had only sharpened that sullen opposition during 1897, for the Spanish elements in Cuba were far more conscious of the "Yankees" than was the government at home. On January 8, Lee reported that reconcentration seemed as bad as ever despite the new edicts against it, and on that same day in Madrid, Woodford warned the Spanish bluntly that "the result must be wrought out in Cuba and by facts, rather than at Washington or Madrid and by negotiations." [1]

As New Year's Day and the flurry of receptions which inaugurated 1898 passed, McKinley looked hopefully toward the warm shores of Cuba for speedy results in instituting autonomy that would relieve the pressures upon him. He had assured many visitors to the White House during the holidays that he expected the first royal proclamations setting the autonomy scheme in motion to be issued on January 1. Lee was skeptical and his usual pessimistic cables flowed into the State Department and then into the President's office. The sense of calm which presaged the storm broke on January 12 with reports from Lee and distorted stories in the yellow press describing anti-American riots in Havana, led by elements opposed to autonomy. First reports caused alarm for loss of life and property, but the President remained calm, expressing mock surprise to callers "that the war should be beginning outside the White House, and [I] know nothing about it." [2]

But the trace of humor did not conceal his uneasiness, nor did subsequent reports that the riots had been exaggerated remove the gnawing doubt that had now entered his mind, to remain there until intervention. Spanish and anti-rebel elements in Havana had revolted against the very proclamations of reform; Lee quickly pointed out that such an attitude forbade constructive diplomacy.

In the days that followed McKinley remained silent, but the riots shook his faith in Spanish ability to reform Cuba more than anything had in 1897. This was the first of the series of events in early 1898 that swept his diplomacy from under him. To callers he seemed more grave, and de Lome, calling out of courtesy and to allay administration fears, found him more reserved than usual. ". . . The change of sentiment has been so abrupt, and our enemies, influenced by it, so numerous," he cabled to Madrid, "that any sensational occurrence might produce a change and disturb the situation. . . ." Even he was alive to the President's firm purpose, adding in another dispatch, "For public opinion to be completely tranquil here, it is essential that action shall be taken which will prevent a repetition of the events just past." [3] All the Minister's charm, which could be persuasive, was of no apparent avail, for while McKinley listened and talked of peace, de Lome sensed that he was growing impatient and perhaps thought of war. As rumblings of discontent continued to come from Havana he cabled home on February 16 in alarm:

> The news from Havana is not improved; if it continues it will cause the situation here to change. The sensational press is just as bad as it was in the worst period, and the government and Cabinet, although they have said nothing to me, seem to have lost all faith in Spain's success, and, to some extent, to have lost tranquility.

Private sources whispered that McKinley himself had lost faith in Spain's ability to institute autonomy.[4]

In Madrid, Woodford hastened to an audience with the Queen Regent, determined to use bluntness where tact and charm had failed. With Hapsburg regality Maria Christina insisted that the American government cease its indirect assistance to the rebels and abandon its pro-Cuban policy. For the moment, Woodford lost his surface charm and replied with equal vigor: "Let there be no misunderstanding in your mind or in the mind of any Spaniard. General Weyler will never be allowed to land in Cuba again. The old conditions of barbarity can never be restored. Any attempt to return to the old methods will be met by instant, effective, and final intervention." [5] Faced with such frankness the Queen's tone softened and she assured Woodford that no such return was considered, but demanded more time for Spain's policy. As he walked from the royal presence through echoing corridors and past the statuary and tapestries of Spain's past, the Minister's neck stiffened and his heart sank. Never optimistic about the prospects of peace, he felt heavier of heart now than before, for he realized that however fine Spain's intentions might be—and he did not think they were that elevated —she was powerless to fulfill her promises.

McKinley might well have paused to reassess his year's labor and to look coldly at the chances for successful autonomy in Cuba. Though he did not know it, de Lome himself had privately sneered at the autonomy scheme, saying flippantly that it existed "for the purpose of printing it in the newspapers." [6] Whatever the Spanish intended, they had really ceased to be the major factor, for the Cuban rebels now publicly spurned the Spanish solution. In Cuba's jungles and on the ragged edges of her plantations, Maximo Gomez' tattered army took new hope; only independence would suffice.

The Cubans had good reason to distrust their fickle mother country. Promises of self-rule had come to nothing in the past; interests in the island worked against it; the scheme itself was inadequate to the Cubans for it did not obviate Spanish control; it left the economy at the mercy of the mother country. As winter drifted toward spring the insurgents hoped for American intervention. Their newspaper friends assured them that McKinley would not defy Congress and rising public clamor; he would surrender in a matter of weeks. Why should they compromise with Spain when they could thus attain full independence? This sentiment, together with the real obstacles to successful autonomy, gave McKinley pause. That pause lengthened as he pondered the Havana riots and an apparent stiffening in Madrid, which seemed less inclined to yield. "There is no longer any doubt that the President of the Republic is very much impressed with Lee's statements regarding the failure of autonomy," de Lome cabled home on January 20.[7]

McKinley still shrank from any open declaration of his stand or redefinition of his hopes lest this drive the Spanish further toward a break and solidify his opposition. Congress began debating resolutions; the administration moved quickly, realizing acutely how disastrous an anti-administration declaration from Congress might be now. The House responded to Reed's gavel and squelched budding plans. For a moment the President sighed with relief and late in January went out of his way to assure de Lome of his hopes for peace. At the annual diplomatic reception, filled with the color of foreign uniforms and decorations, alive with soft music and the

354

clink of glasses, McKinley sought out de Lome and greeted him warmly. His hand outstretched and his face wreathed with a benign smile, the President made way for de Lome through other ranking foreign diplomats. "I see that we have only good news; I am well satisfied with what has occurred in the House, and with the discipline of the Republicans," McKinley said genially. "You, who comprehend this, will understand how strong our position is and how much it has changed and bettered in the past year; you have no occasion to be other than satisfied and confident." As the President smiled his way beyond the Spanish Minister, de Lome looked at his retreating form with a mixture of puzzlement and gratitude. Of the man's sincerity there could be no doubt. He might be a rural politician, eager to please and to succeed with his homemade diplomacy, but he was sincere. And yet there was an edge of iron in his voice; he clearly meant to say that while the situation was good it could easily worsen. Spain must see that it did not.[8]

If de Lome had a conscience, it must have twinged that night as he talked with the President and as he rode back to his embassy through Washington's dark streets, echoing to the comforting clop of the horses' hooves. Perhaps even then he thought a moment of the storm that might soon break over him, for he remembered writing a letter. In the first week of February, sources he could not impeach were to say that the letter was about to be printed.

The history of his letter revealed much of the whole Cuban problem. Irritated by what he considered the hypocritical quality of McKinley's annual message in December, 1897, de Lome answered a query from a friend in Havana. In the middle of that month he wrote a frank opinion of the American President to Don Jose Canalejas, a Spanish editor touring the United States and Cuba gathering information on autonomy. But Canalejas was a busy man, moving through Havana in a welter of teas, receptions, and siestas. Secretaries handled his correspondence and Cuban spies were carefully planted on his staff.

Noting the Spanish embassy's return address on one letter, with a careful injunction to personal privacy on the envelope, a secretary opened it, removed de Lome's letter, and inserted a blank sheet of paper, hoping the theft would not be discovered until he sent the letter to New York. In New York, Horatio Rubens, a loyal juntist with connections in the newspaper fraternity and among friendly politicians, realized the letter's importance. A facsimile went to the New York *Journal,* which could always be counted on, and the letter's text went to the other principal dailies.

The bomb exploded on the *Journal*'s front page on February 9. Readers unfolded their sheets with a morning yawn to sit up in surprise at the headline above the facsimile and its translation: "Worst Insult to the United States in Its History." As he scanned the text the average reader might have thought that it contained less vitriol than the rest of the paper, but it was, after all, from the Spanish Minister himself. To the casual reader and to a subsequent generation, the letter's importance lay in de Lome's aspersions on the President. In reviewing the annual message he lashed out at McKinley in words that found their way into all the history books:

> Besides the ingrained and inevitable bluntness with which is repeated all that the press and public opinion in Spain have said about Weyler, it [the message] once more shows what McKinley is, weak and a bidder for the admiration of the crowd, besides being a would-be politician who tries to leave a door open behind himself while keeping on good terms with the jingoes of his party.

However accurate or inaccurate this description of McKinley's policy was, its tone revealed all the hypocrisy, arrogance, and stubborn pride with which Spain ran her Cuban affairs. For most who read the letter, de Lome must go.

In the State Department and the White House eyes lighted on the last paragraphs. They were profound in their implications and far-reaching in their results, though the man on the street might have overlooked them. In the supposed privacy of the mails, de Lome stated his own opinion of autonomy and the peace policy in general:

> It would be very advantageous to take up, even if only for effect, the question of commercial relations, and to have a man of some prominence sent hither in order that I may make use of him here to carry on a propaganda among the Senators and others in opposition to the junta and to try to win over the refugees.

In an earlier passage he clearly stated his opposition to negotiating with the Cubans or to any idea of success for autonomy not preceded by Spanish victory in the field. To the man on the street the letter was an insult to his President; though he himself might oppose McKinley's policy, he now rallied to his Chief Executive. To the diplomats in the administration and the moderates in Congress the letter revealed that their fears were correct: Spain was deeply insincere in her policy.[9]

This juicy morsel effectively unseated de Lome, who cabled home his resignation the evening before the letter's release. Popular outcry echoed across the land and a little ditty jangled through the yellow press:

Dupuy de Lome, Dupuy de Lome, what's this I hear of you?
Have you been throwing mud again, is what they're saying true?
Get out, I say, get out before I start to fight.
Just pack your few possessions and take a boat for home.
I would not like my boot to use but—oh—get out, de Lome.[10]

For the Cuban junta the letter was a godsend. "The de Lome letter is a great thing for us," a member candidly admitted.[11]

Rubens took the original letter to the State Department the day after its release, where he talked with Day, who examined it without comment. Alvee Adee first thought it was a forgery but then changed his mind. Rising with his customary languor, the Judge asked to keep the document for a day or two, promising to return it to Rubens, and bowed him out. Hurrying across the lawn to the White House he showed the paper to McKinley, who looked at it without comment. Why hadn't it been brought to him first, he asked? Rubens had already said that he suspected the President would have forbidden its release, fearing its effect on his policy.[12]

While the newspaper war raged during the week, McKinley remained silent. To comment in any way seemed beneath his dignity. In the administration itself, many were sorry to lose de Lome. He may have been supercilious and arrogant but he knew Spanish diplomacy. A successor would be hard to find.[13] Whatever his private thoughts, McKinley remained dignified. A lifetime in politics had inured him to even the harshest epithets. Administration papers approved his course, and they were more sympathetic than ever, for the moderate sheets began to drift toward intervention. "His attitude in the de Lome affair commands the approval of all but the extreme radicals at home and is unstintedly praised by the civilized foreign governments through their official presses," a Chicago paper noted.[14]

Privately, however, McKinley fully understood the letter's importance. No such slur could go unanswered, and de Lome's mere resignation would not allay American public opinion. A formal apology was necessary, and he outlined on a scrap of paper what he thought it should contain: "Expression of pained surprise and regret at the Minister's reprehensible allusions to the President and the American people, which it is needless to say the Govt of His Majesty does not share, and promptly disavows." [15]

In Madrid, Woodford was not idle. The first cable reports had alarmed him, for like McKinley he saw that unless the affair was closed at once it would jeopardize the administration's whole policy. Delay in Spain worked against her own best interests, for in failing to disavow de Lome at once she seemed to approve his words.[16] But speed was still difficult to impress upon the Spanish, and Woodford's sense of urgency did not extend into the marble corridors of the foreign ministry, which echoed to the rapid step with which he approached the Foreign Minister. De Lome's resignation had already been accepted, that worthy said blandly, and a new minister was on his way. Woodford pointed out bluntly that an apology was expected and that it must come quickly to quiet the American press. The Foreign Minister was noncommittal, saying that Spanish public opinion might be excited by a hasty apology. Woodford left, depressed as usual, but cabled home that negotiations on the new reciprocity treaty with Spain, provided for under the Dingley Act, should be rushed; victory there would strengthen his hands on the Cuban matter.[17]

On February 14, Woodford called again at the ministry and said frankly that unless an official apology were forthcoming he would resign, for he could not remain accredited to a government that slandered his chief. The Spanish assured him that an apology was ready. In the quiet of his office he wondered if he had been right. Would McKinley approve? "With your generous and forgiving nature, you may think that I was possibly too positive and probably too severe," he cabled the President, "but I know that my decision is right. It is due alike to the affection I bear you and to my duty to our country." [18]

On February 16, Woodford at last received the Spanish apology, which Washington accepted despite its insolent tone and allusions to thefts from the mails. McKinley was anxious to conclude the whole matter. "If a rupture between the two countries must come, it should not be upon any such personal and comparatively unimportant matter," Day wired early in March as the last problems of the affair were settled.[19] As the incident faded into history, the administration hardened its lines. Only days before the letter's release Woodford had cabled home that the Spanish seemed genuinely interested in commercial reciprocity; success here would bolster the Cuban diplomacy.[20] And now the Spanish Minister himself had ended all such negotiations as irrelevant, implying either Spanish insincerity or divided policy, either of which was fatal.

McKinley might well have wished to end the vexing affair, for a week after the letter's release a far greater tragedy, which ended his peace policy, swept all before it in the newspapers and in administrative circles. The return of cooler weather in the fall of 1897 heightened tensions in the Cuban capital, and though anti-American feeling seemed to subside, Lee still insisted that warships be kept available on his call at Key West. The consul's repeated dispatches had fed a gnawing doubt in the President's mind: how sure could he be that American citizens in Havana were safe? The anti-autonomy riots of January 12 solidified his belief that perhaps Lee was right: closer protection was necessary. After the newspaper and diplomatic flurry over the riots subsided, Day told de Lome that the President wished to resume formal naval visits by sending the battleship *Maine* to Havana early in February for a courtesy call. It was, he said, an effort to alleviate tension between the two countries and to show that neither feared the other. A Spanish battleship would be welcome in New York or some other eastern port. De Lome was not overly happy, for he read easily between the lines; to him it was another turn of the diplomatic screw. McKinley seemed animated only by his usual friendliness.[21]

Lee at first was not anxious to have the ship call, feeling that it might increase tension. But when she sailed into the harbor, "a beautiful sight and one long to be remembered," the consul-general reported that the *Maine* "has greatly relieved by her presence the Americans here." Lee opposed any move to withdraw the ship unless it were replaced by another, lest this cause America to look weak.[22] The American press was franker on the matter: the ship was there in case of emergency. And reports from Spain indicated that already ruffled official pride was not smoothed by the ship's dispatch.[23]

In Havana itself the *Maine* arrived with dignity, greeted by Spanish and American flags. Sailors from the two fleets fraternized, and many townspeople came down to the docks to see the gleaming vessel, which was among the Navy's best second-class battleships. The air was clear and warm; the sailors' expeditions into Havana resulted in the usual hauls of souvenirs. All were gratified at the apparent hospitality.

The *Maine's* commander, however, noted an undercurrent of tension; boos mingled sometimes with the cheers, and the populace at the bull ring seemed set for trouble.[24] But the days drifted past, punctuated by nothing more exciting than ship's drills. On the evening of February 14, he sat in his cabin writing letters and filing the day's last dispatches. As the clock moved through the evening hours of February 15, he picked up his pen to write to his wife. As it scratched across the paper the ship shuddered with a massive explosion and sank slowly. Dawn revealed that nearly all the crew had perished; some 260 men lay dead in the twisted wreckage.

Tired from a day's work, the President had gone to bed early that night. About three A.M. a watchman who had Secretary Long on the telephone aroused him. McKinley hurried to his office and listened incredulously as the Secretary repeated the cables he had received from Havana. Half-dressed, his mind fogged with sleep, McKinley sat silent as Long spoke and then hung up. He shook his head, repeating slowly as if to himself: "The *Maine* blown up! The *Maine* blown up!" Hurrying back to his room he calmed Ida, dressed, and prepared for a busy day.[25]

The Spanish chargé d'affaires had also been aroused from his sleep, and he clattered through the early morning hours behind a frantic team to deliver his personal condolences at the State Department and to offer his government's assistance. The officials he

360

met were wary, silent, not yet having absorbed the full import of the tragedy, but as he descended the steps half an hour later he thought to himself that the Americans seemed to feel that it was an accident. He hoped so, for if they did not, his country would have much to explain.[26]

As dawn broke and the American people awoke, ill-prepared for the frantic headlines that seemed to rush at them from their front porches and newsstands, McKinley hastily contacted the cabinet members and congressional leaders. Hurrying toward the White House for the appointed discussions, they sensed that at last the long delay over Cuba would end. To his old friend Nelson Dingley, McKinley extended a hand of friendship and warmth, though Dingley had never seen the President so worried. Lack of sleep, the tragedy itself, and fear for the future had already put dark circles around his eyes and a slight tremor in his voice.[27] There must be no war, McKinley repeated, because "the country was not ready for war." [28]

All that day McKinley conferred and waited for fresh news from Havana. The cables brought distressing tidings: the ship was utterly lost, few bodies had been recovered, the cause of the explosion could not be determined, the city was tense, but everywhere the Spanish were helping. As he read the cables McKinley's feeling of hope, which he had impressed on de Lome a scant month before, vanished. The de Lome letter and now the *Maine* shattered his following and coalesced his enemies. In his heart he knew that intervention was but a matter of time. To Secretary of the Navy Long, with whom he conferred on the seventeenth, he seemed aged. "Am sorry to find him more oppressed and careworn than at any time since I have been in the Cabinet. Am afraid he is in danger of overdoing," he recorded in his diary.[29]

As the public devoured every fresh report from Havana, congressional tempers flared. Lodge would only say that "it is too serious to talk about at present," but Cullom expressed a more blunt and widespread feeling. "I am too mad to talk about it," he snapped at an insistent reporter. "I can't see how the explosion could have been the result of an accident and I think the time is rapidly approaching when this country should do something." In the House, both Reed and Dingley fought their way past angry members. Joe Bailey, of Texas, insisted that war be declared then and there, and not all of Reed's sarcasm could calm him.[30] The Spanish chargé noted the rising congressional temper and something even more alarming. "But aside from the belligerent feeling, I observe in the Administration a certain apprehension." [31]

The cabinet and administration were divided on the cause of the disaster. Lee and Captain Sigsbee of the *Maine* both held that it was an accident and urged a suspension of popular feeling, and McKinley himself felt that an investigation would prove the consul right.[32] He tried to smile at the increasing lines of congressmen and reporters outside his door and went quietly about his usual routine to prevent panic. To friends the President stated bluntly that he would never ask for war until all else failed. "I have been through one war," he told a friend. "I have seen the dead piled up, and I do not want to see another." [33]

Now was the time to break his long silence, to rally public opinion to his side by a firm declaration of his intentions, to repudiate the jingoes in public. But he remained inexplicably silent, the captive of caution, fearing that any statement would feed the jingo fire. Late in the month he entrained for Philadelphia, smiling somewhat hesitantly at his well-wishers, but moving with his customary speed and assurance. At the University of Pennsylvania he spoke to an enormous crowd, and counselled caution and patience on the whole Cuban problem. "Such judgement, my fellow citizens, is the best safeguard in the calm of tranquil events, and rises superior and triumphant above the storm of woe and peril." [34] The applause was not enthusiastic. Should he have been more forthright, or would anything he said matter now?

As February wore into early March, administration newspapers were less and less firm. "We all owe a debt of gratitude to the President, and we shall be under obligation to him whatever may be the outcome of the *Maine* disaster," noted a Boston paper, "for should worse come to worse his devotion to the duty of silence will have gained us time from the enemy." [35] But the number of people willing to wait was dwindling under the pressure of events.

McKinley realized at once that an official investigation was necessary lest inaction anger the public. Two days after the disaster the Navy appointed an official commission consisting of Captain W. T.

Sampson as chairman, Captain F. E. Chadwick, and Lt. Commander William Potter to report on the explosion. With a presidential injunction to withhold nothing from their report, they hastened to Havana with divers and experts on naval armor to examine the ship's wreckage.[36] Spain's request for a joint investigating commission was rejected. McKinley knew that the American public would never accept a Spanish report, and a mixed commission would only invite conflicts of opinion.

From Washington, as the March days turned warmer and spring began to spread blossoms along the capital's thoroughfares, tempers waxed even hotter in congressional quarters, though most Americans waited tensely for the official report. The Spanish chargé warned his government. "All await with feverish anxiety the American official report. If it declares that the catastrophe was due to an accident, I believe I can assure your excellency that the present danger will be over; but if, on the contrary, it alleges that it was the work of a criminal hand, then we shall have to face the gravest situation." [37]

Madrid had hardly digested this warning before Day cabled, on March 3, a lengthy note to Woodford. Seizing the opportunity to leave no mistake in Spanish minds about American purposes and to capitalize on fears of American public opinion, McKinley turned the screw again:

> The de Lome incident, the destruction of the Maine, have added much to the popular feeling upon this subject [Cuba], although the better sentiment seems to be awaiting the report of the facts, and to follow the action of the President after the naval board has made its report. Whatever that report may be, it by no means relieves the situation of its difficulties. The policy of starvation, the failure of Spain to take effective measures to suppress the insurrection, the loss of our commerce, the great expense of patrolling our coast— these things, intensified by the insulting and insincere character of the de Lome letter, all combine to create a condition that is very grave, and which will require the highest wisdom and greatest prudence on both sides to avoid a crisis.[38]

To underscore this warning, McKinley called Joe Cannon to the White House for a very special conference. When "Uncle Joe" visited "Mack," as he had once called his fellow congressman, he left his colorful language at home, for McKinley disliked it. But

363

the President knew Cannon's importance in the House and he trusted him. He spoke briefly and sincerely with Cannon, outlining a plan for national defense while walking about the room. He wanted a quick appropriation for national defense, he said, without congressional debate, for he did not wish the jingoes to use the issue for oratory, or the Spanish to feel that peace was now impossible. He suggested that Cannon in the House, and Allison or Aldrich in the Senate, pilot the bill through. He wanted $50,000,000 to be spent at his discretion, without congressional strings. Taking a blank sheet of telegraph paper from his desk, he wrote a single sentence on it which became the bill's title: "For national defense, fifty million dollars." [39]

Cannon hurried home, worked into the night on the bill draft, and introduced it in the House the following day. At the other end of the Capitol, administration senators worked with efficient calm; on March 9 the bill was law. It granted the President complete control of the money. It passed without dissenting vote, though there were absentees, for news that Spain was bargaining for new ships spurred on the solons.[40]

The Spanish were shocked. "It has not excited the Spaniards, it has simply stunned them," Woodford cabled home on March 9. "To appropriate fifty millions out of money in the treasury, without borrowing a cent, demonstrates wealth and power. Even Spain can see this. To put this money without restrictions at your disposal demonstrates entire confidence in you by all parties. The Ministry and press are simply stunned." [41] And yet there was an air of unreality about all of Woodford's dealings in Madrid, as if not even the Spanish understood the Cuban problem. If the President's purpose was peace, it seemed odd that he should ask for arms. If he had gone over to intervention, on the other hand, diplomacy was pointless. As usual it was hard to say just where McKinley stood. Woodford assumed that the President still stood for peace, and that Congress now sustained him, not realizing that all parties could vote for "national defense" with no abatement of ideology. From this time forward the administration had no alternative to intervention except a complete revolution in Spanish policy. This was now McKinley's goal.

In the midst of these confused March days the new Spanish

Minister arrived, somewhat innocently, to present his credentials, an event almost overlooked by the press. His remarks to the effect that autonomy was successful in Cuba sounded incredible, and even the aged Sherman shook his head in disbelief.[42] If he was at first innocent of the real situation, he learned quickly. McKinley received him with rather stiff dignity, reading off a little speech which contained no surprises. "I have just been received by the President of the Republic, who made a most gracious address," Polo y Bernabe cabled home. "I fear, nevertheless, that the acts will not bear out the words." [43]

He was right, and had reason to fear from many quarters. While McKinley made his last efforts for peace, Senator Redfield Proctor, of Vermont, reported to the Senate on a recent tour of Cuba in toneless words and dull phrases that nevertheless set both houses aflame. On March 17, he spoke for several hours, giving a dispassionate review of what he had recently seen in Cuba, concluding that Spanish promises were fruitless, that the rebels would not accept autonomy, and that American intervention was inevitable for peace and justice.[44]

The Senate was stunned. Accustomed to intemperate speeches on Cuba, it had awaited Proctor's speech without enthusiasm. Instead, he had spoken normally, almost coldly, of the horrors he saw. The moderates and conservatives were badly shaken. "It is just as if Proctor had held up his right hand and sworn to it," said William P. Frye. Speaker Reed's caustic remark that "a war will make a large market for gravestones," an allusion to Proctor's marble interests, passed unnoticed. His recent visit to the White House convinced many that Proctor reflected McKinley's views, for surely he had told the President of his speech. Commercial papers reported that business groups everywhere were deeply impressed, and that last stronghold of support for the President's policies seemed now to be slipping into the interventionist camp. Spain's new Minister cabled home that all was not well. "Senator Proctor yesterday made a speech which has produced great effect because of its temperate stand. . . . My impression is that the President will try to withstand the powerful public sentiment in favor of the insurrection, but any incident might hinder his purposes." [45]

Public eyes now turned to the elaborate report which the *Maine* investigation commission had finished. On the quiet Sunday after-noon of March 20, Long hurried to McKinley with a confidential dispatch from Havana that the report was finished and should be in his hands by Friday, March 26. The Spanish commission which also investigated the wreck reported that accident had destroyed the *Maine* and offered to discuss the problem with an American commission. But the American court of inquiry would report that an external explosion of undetermined origin and nature had sunk the ship. McKinley was upset, for he knew that whatever the facts might really be, the American people would immediately assume that Spanish agents had destroyed the *Maine*.[46]

In distant Madrid, Woodford sat through edgy hours by the telegraph and spent long afternoons vainly arguing for more speed from the Spanish. His mood darkened as he talked. "They want peace, if they can keep peace and save the dynasty," he cabled on February 26. "They prefer the chance of war, with the certain loss of Cuba, to the overthrow of the dynasty." [47] On February 28 he reported incredulously that the Cortes had adjourned until April 25, intensifying the vacuum of Spanish diplomacy. It was too trans-parent: by April the rainy season would be upon Cuba again and the Spanish could invoke the old seasonal argument to explain their delay in pacifying the island.[48]

On March 1, Day forwarded another note which showed that American patience was ended. Spain must reform or face war. The following day McKinley assured Woodford that Lee would not be removed from Havana in response to an old Spanish demand.

As the tension mounted in the two capitals, with Madrid still not seeming to understand the pressures at work against McKinley, American official and public patience was exhausted. By mid-March Woodford conceded frankly that autonomy would never work be-fore the rainy season, and was a lost cause. He suggested that Wash-ington insist bluntly on Spanish dispatch to show that "the United States means business and means it *now*. The Spanish mind is so ingrained with 'mañanaism' that few Spaniards ever act until they have to act." Washington obliged in the last week of March, stating bluntly that the *Maine* disaster could be arbitrated, but that "the general condition" of Cuba could not be tolerated longer. McKinley set April 15 as "none too early for accomplishment of these purposes," and added an appendix that must have given Woodford pause. "It is proper that you should know that unless events otherwise indicate, the President having exhausted diplomatic agencies to secure peace in Cuba will lay the whole matter before Congress." That could only mean war.[49]

Between March 20 and March 26, McKinley entertained a series of congressmen, hurrying from conference to conference, as he sought support from every agency and person he could command. The three weeks after the *Maine's* destruction were a nightmare for him and his advisors, when public opinion seemed to abandon them utterly. The pressure was such that he reluctantly promised to surrender necessary diplomatic papers to Congress if the problem were not settled by late April. He shrank from dealing with Congress, for he knew, as a friend said, that "Congress is never a good diplomat." [50]

Even the most optimistic of the President's friends and followers lost heart. "It was manifest that the loss of the *Maine* would inevitably lead to war, even if it were shown that Spain was innocent of her destruction," Long remembered.[51] "If it is found that the *Maine* was blown up from the outside, it will be difficult to restrain the American people," Lodge wrote.[52]

To the newspapers the discussion was academic as they impatiently awaited the *Maine* commission's report which they were sure would implicate Spain. "Nine out of ten American citizens doubtless believe firmly that the explosion which destroyed the *Maine* was the result of the cowardly Spanish conspiracy, and the Report of the Court of Inquiry will not tend to destroy that belief," the Cleveland *Leader* trumpeted on March 27. The Hearst press was rabid, especially proud of having coined the potent phrase: "Remember the *Maine* and to hell with Spain!" [53]

In Virginia a raging mob burned twin effigies of McKinley and Hanna. McKinley's picture was hissed in theaters and torn from walls in some cities.[54] This personal indignation climaxed late in March when Theodore Roosevelt shook his fist under Hanna's nose at the annual Gridiron Dinner and exclaimed: "We will have this war for the freedom of Cuba in spite of the timidity of the commercial interests!" [55]

On Friday, March 25, the President received the commission's report and closeted himself for six hours with the cabinet and Army and Navy officers, poring painfully over the tedious finely printed pages, examining charts and diagrams. They ate lunch working. For the rest of the weekend McKinley thought about the report, listened to advice, and then on Sunday afternoon began dictating the message that would accompany the report to Congress the following day.

When the impatient congressmen received the report and the President's message the following morning, on March 28, they were for the most part incredulous. It was the same story they had heard from McKinley for a year. His request for "deliberate consideration" and his whole tone infuriated Congress.[56] The Chicago *Tribune* had spoken for most of the public:

> The people want no disgraceful negotiations with Spain. Should the president plunge his administration into that morass, he and his party would be swept out of power in 1900 by a fine burst of popular indignation. An administration which stains the national honor never will be forgiven.[57]

A closer reading showed that the President's message breathed a sense of inevitability. He held Spain responsible for the conditions which presumably destroyed the *Maine,* though he did not insist that her agents had set the blast.

That tone now flavored the dispatches that went to Spain, and on March 27, with the *Maine* report ready for Congress, Day cabled Woodford the administration's last plan. "A feeling of deliberation prevails in both houses of Congress," he said, stretching the truth for diplomacy's sake, and then outlined the President's plan: [58]

> 1. An immediate armistice, freely granted by Spain, to last until October 1, both sides to accept McKinley's good offices.
> 2. A final end to reconcentration and Spanish relief for Cuba.
> 3. If peace terms were not reached by October 1, McKinley as arbitrator would settle the Cuban problem.
> 4. McKinley would approach the Cuban rebels directly for their participation in this plan if Spain *first* agreed.

The whole plan depended on speed. Three days later Day cabled bluntly that the President could hold out only a few days unless Spain capitulated.[59]

Why McKinley felt that Spain would accept this ultimatum is

a mystery. Since 1895 she had spurned all efforts to make the President of the United States a mediator in the Cuban problem. She had always held that overtures for peace must come first from the rebels. She could manifestly not reform the island to anyone's satisfaction by October 1 or by any reasonable date. There was no assurance that the Cuban rebels would accept such a plan even if approached by the President. Indeed, there was every reason why they should not. Who among them would take half the loaf now that it all seemed within reach, for the American people would have their war, they thought, regardless of what the timid President wished.

Isolated in Madrid, Woodford still had only a general idea of the pressures at work against McKinley's policies. Late in March he had reiterated his view that while autonomy might ultimately succeed, it could now only force continuation of the Cuban war, but he held out hope for further Spanish concessions. The Spanish Premier, seemingly oblivious to the need for dispatch, was kind but bland.[60] Time was running out, as McKinley knew, and one afternoon he sketched out a tentative ultimatum, expressing "the gravest apprehension" that Congress might declare war on its own.[61]

Congress was angry and uneasiness spread through the ranks of the men who had sustained McKinley. As congressmen of both parties looked at the virtues of Cuban intervention, their clamors grew. To the Democrats it was a chance to end the frustration of their defeats of the last few years and to exercise an ancient right to free suffering Cuba. To the wavering Republicans it was a chance to end the issue and to draw attention from domestic problems. "I trust we shall escape without a war," Lodge wrote with tongue somewhat in cheek, "but if we should have war we will not hear much of the currency question in the elections." [62]

McKinley was certainly alive to the politics of the problem. He had already stretched the painfully built Republican coalition to the breaking point. If he resisted public pressure further he might destroy his party and any hope of a constructive national and international program in the future. Congress was the major problem, for its pressure was immediate and dangerous, and grew daily. "He shivers a little but he will go," Chandler wrote confidently of the President, saying bluntly that if he did not, Congress would go alone, and what president could resist such a demand? [63] Ugly scenes occurred at the White House as angry politicians converged on McKinley during the last of March and first of April. The State Department got its share too, and one day an angry, cane-waving senator stormed into Day's office and pounded on the table. "By ———!" he thundered, "Don't your president know where the war-declaring power is lodged? Well tell him, by ———! that if he doesn't do something Congress will exercise the power and declare war in spite of him! He'll get run over and the party with him!" [64]

Whether Congress alone could have declared war is not clear. The administration ranks were not yet quite broken, though Hanna, Aldrich, and Orville Platt canvassed the upper house every day, armed with assurances that McKinley would veto a war resolution. But the President had bought only limited time with assurances that he would do something. One sunny afternoon, Hobart took him for a relaxing drive, where the wind had no ears, and said flatly that he could not restrain the Senate much longer. McKinley looked startled. "Say no more," he exclaimed, and lapsed into silence. [65]

These were the hardest days the President ever knew, compounded by the terrible worries that assaulted him every night, and which even sleeping potions would not ease. Would history remember him, the gentlest of men, as a war president? How bitter that he should face the agony of affixing his name, two lines of ink, to a paper that meant death and destruction. How could he forget the sincere and hopeful words with which he had left Grover Cleveland that pre-inauguration night that now seemed so distant? And perhaps General Woodford's almost pathetic reminder rang through his mind in the hours of strain: ". . . you as a soldier know what war is, even when waged for the holiest of causes." [66]

He often mused out of the window in his few free moments, watching the traffic hurry by his fenced mansion, whose very walls reminded him of the trust he owed the people. The round of entertainments went on with glacial inevitability, and at one he took visiting Mr. Kohlsaat aside and poured out his troubles, with tears in his eyes. His lack of sleep affected his nerves, and he was tired and unsure much of the time. Perhaps it affected his policy too. [67]

Whatever his personal phantoms, the processes of diplomacy carried him now to the inevitable end. The last week of March produced a Spanish response: yes, they would reform Cuba; yes, they would increase autonomy; yes, they would undertake relief; but they would not suspend hostilities unless the rebels asked first. It was not enough, and McKinley renewed his old demand for presidential mediation. Woodford was frankly confused, but the Spanish seemed more so; he wondered if they understood the problem at all, for the ministers did not seem to know what each other did. On the twenty-ninth, the Spanish Minister came to the White House and left with the usual presidential demands: relief, reform, and presidential mediation.[68]

On that same day Woodford cabled frantically that he had conferred with the cabinet, which had adjourned until March 31, when they would make a final offer. Could McKinley hold his lines until then? Day, fearful that he could not, managed to secure promises from congressional leaders, and the President continued the handshaking and personal charm that had bought so much time already. Yes, they would wait.[69]

On the evening of March 31, McKinley and the cabinet members sat expectantly awaiting the message from Spain that would be fed to decoding clerks over a special wire. By eleven it was apparent that no text would be given out, and Day dismissed the waiting reporters with the promise that they would have it for their morning editions.[70]

The message which McKinley read in the small hours of April 1 was not heartwarming. Spain offered to arbitrate the *Maine* incident; she would abolish reconcentration in the western provinces; she would undertake relief; she would accept American aid or relief; and she would turn over the Cuban problem to the insular parliament to meet in Havana on May 4; but she would not suspend hostilities or accept American mediation.[71] This was "the ultimate limit to which [Spain] can go in the way of concessions," but it was not enough. It did not end reconcentration, promised only further delay under an uncertain autonomy government, and above all was couched in such an insulting tone that Long felt it ended McKinley's diplomacy.[72]

In the two days that followed, Woodford continued to work for peace, but without confidence. "They know that Cuba is lost," he insisted, admitting that the concessions were "a sorrow for me," because of their stale and inconclusive nature, and because he now feared that the ministry would prefer war for honor rather than peace by concession.[73]

On April 4, Day returned the expected formal answer which indicated clearly that intervention was inevitable:

> We have received today from the Spanish Ministry a copy of the Manifesto of the Autonomy Government. It is not armistice. It proves to be an appeal by the Autonomy Government of Cuba urging the insurgents to lay down their arms and to join with the autonomy party in building up the new scheme of home rule. It is simply an invitation to the insurgents to submit, in which event the autonomy government, likewise suspending hostilities, is prepared to consider what expansion, if any, of the decreed home-rule scheme is necessary or practicable. It need scarcely be pointed out that this is a very different thing from an offered armistice.[74]

Woodford's reply was familiar: if he could have time it could all be worked out.[75]

But McKinley had no more time. After reading the Spanish note he turned reluctantly to composing the war message he must now send to Congress, aware that the opinion beyond his windows made Woodford's hopes seem absurd. On April 4, Joe Bailey spoke for the Democrats. "But if the President of the United States wants two days, or if he wants two hours, to continue negotiations with the butchers of Spain, we are not ready to give him one moment longer for that purpose." [76]

Capitulating, McKinley set April 6 as the date for his war message, but the expectant crowds that gathered at the Capitol that day were disappointed, for a last-minute cable from Lee stayed his hand; he would wait until American citizens had been evacuated from Cuba, and send the message on April 11.[77] The congressmen who angrily crowded into his office demanding war met a rare show of presidential wrath. Summoning Cortelyou, McKinley ordered the message locked in the safe until he called for it.[78] For once the clamor angered the President. His old faith in the people had wavered and then turned sour as he read his mail and saw his visitors. "The country should understand that we are striving to make our course consistent not alone for today, but for all time," he had told Cortelyou. "The people must not be unreasonable." [79]

On April 6, Woodford grasped at the hope of papal intervention, which the Spanish might accept, and hurried a fresh note to Washington. A leak caused considerable embarrassment and irritation at home, for to many it seemed that the President had sought the Pope's help. But McKinley's hands were now tied, and he answered Woodford with the weak assurance that he would transmit to Congress any further Spanish offers.[80]

One small act in the drama remained. On April 6, representatives of Europe's major chancellories filed into the Blue Room where the weary President heard Sir Julian Pauncefote, dean of the diplomatic corps, read a joint note urging the United States to maintain peace. The very expression "the Powers" was distasteful to most Americans, conjuring up images of continental meddling in American affairs, all edged with monarchical despotism. Nor was it a secret that Germany, France, Italy, and Austria-Hungary all favored Spain. McKinley saw but one friendly face in the group, Pauncefote's. When the august delegation finished its little speech, McKinley read one of his own, to which all listened attentively and then withdrew. The New York *World* paraphrased it neatly the following day. "We hope for humanity's sake you will not go to war," said the diplomats. "We hope if we do go to war you will understand that it is for humanity's sake," McKinley replied.

On April 8, crowds of sullen Spaniards surged past the American embassy in Madrid, looking up questioningly at the flag that fluttered there. On the following day Woodford cabled home frantically that the holy days had induced the Queen Regent to submit to a papal request to avoid war; tomorrow she would proclaim unconditional suspension of hostilities and take steps to implement autonomy.

On April 10, the cable brought the news to Washington. Day hurriedly took it from the operator's hand and almost ran across the grass to the White House, where he found McKinley and cabinet members in conference. It was a fact; hostilities were suspended. McKinley turned the message over in his hand. Did it change anything? "I hope that nothing will now be done to humiliate Spain," Woodford wrote in the accompanying dispatch, "as I am satisfied that the present Government is going and is loyally going to go as fast and as far as it can. With your power of action sufficiently free you will win the fight on your own lines." [81]

A quick talk with Lodge, Aldrich, and the cabinet convinced

the President that the stroke came too late. Events had rushed past the Spanish; it seemed doubtful now that such an armistice could be enforced in Cuba. "It comes late," said Senator Elkins, long Spain's friend. "Had it come a few days ago I think we could have averted war." [82] Fulfilling his promise to congressional leaders, the President appended it to his war message and prepared to transmit the whole document to Congress the following day.

And so it ended. History would say that he should have accepted the final Spanish program, thus avoiding conflict, but history affords hindsight that McKinley did not have. He had lost freedom of action. He had no reason to believe that Spain was either sincere in her promises or capable of fulfilling them. Officials in Cuba were corrupt, and money voted for relief was often spent for arms; arbitration had been denied; autonomy seemed an impossible dream; the insurgents would accept nothing now but full independence. As he would say in his annual message the following December, the whole scheme depended on factors that were no longer present. [83]

Delay beyond April was impossible. The summer would suspend hostilities, giving the Spanish a convenient excuse for inaction. McKinley's diplomacy by that time would transpire in a vacuum, devoid of support in press or Congress, or among the people. If by some miracle he could wait until fall, the elections might turn his party out. Above all loomed the simple conviction that in any event he could not trust Spanish promises.

Surely it was the bitterest time of the President's life, and if he read the letter he received a few years later from an elderly man who knew Lincoln, he must have paused for agreement and reflection. "Yours is a strange fate indeed. No man in all the land exists more averse to war than yourself. When you were elected president you did not dream of war as a possibility. When the possibility presented itself, no man strove harder to avert it." [84] And all for nothing, he must have thought as he surveyed the end results of a year's diplomacy. More than a year later, in a reflective mood, he pencilled some notes for his own use on a scrap of paper, and the efficient Cortelyou filed them away. From the smudges emerges a final sentence. "Nor would I shirk the responsibility of a single step in the progress of our relations with Spain, from the beginning of my administration to the close of the war. I did what I believed was right in the sight of God and my own conscience, and accept all responsibility." [85]

What had gone wrong? What had ruined his hope of peace? The real flaw in McKinley's diplomacy was not a lack of consistency or of courage, but a lack of imagination. Desiring peace more than anything else, he sought it by threatening war and chose to continue Cleveland's policy of ever increasing pressure against Spain, gambling that in the end she would give way rather than face war. Fearful of preceding public opinion—and in this he was doubtless wise—he stood against the current until the fateful point where his last alternative to war disappeared, and was then swept forward with the tide. The real flaw in his diplomacy was its lack of alternatives to ultimate intervention. He would attain reform in Cuba by neutrality if possible, but by force if necessary.

How easy it is to say with all the textbooks that an addition to the President's spine would have averted war, or that had Cleveland been president there would have been no war. True, the diplomacy of the two presidents was similar in maintaining neutrality while pressuring Spain, in upholding American interests in Cuba, and in restraining public opinion at home. But the conditions that worked against McKinley differed from those which Cleveland confronted. Cleveland did not face the de Lome letter of the *Maine* incident; nor was the issue ablaze in the press and Congress as much as under McKinley.

The methods McKinley employed also differed from Cleveland's. The Democratic President was notoriously rigid and unheeding of public opinion, while McKinley was more flexible, conducting his diplomacy in consultation and with the nation's various interests in mind. Only when he saw his coalition of followers threatened did he give way. But he did not surrender to public opinion. He only accepted in the end the implicit aim of his policy; intervention when peaceful pressure failed. He was aware of the public feeling that eddied outside his doors, and in retrospect he felt that this pressure more than anything else defeated him.[86] This attitude seems ironic, for the chief personal weakness in his diplomacy was his failure to rally public opinion. Fearful of being misunderstood or of adding impetus to the movement for Cuban relief, he remained silent in public, thus *seeming* to drift. Had he defined his position

375

firmly in 1897, and certainly in the great crises of 1898, he might have rallied public opinion and congressional support with which to buy more time. He could not have prevented the war, but such a declaration would have improved his standing. The pose of statesmanship above the battle had won him many laurels in domestic politics. He failed to see that it did the opposite in foreign affairs, where conditions were different, and where it gave his enemies ammunition by making him seem vacillating.

A bolder and more vigorous mind might have cut through the tedium of diplomacy with a striking idea to move ahead of both the Spanish and the Cuban rebels. McKinley might have called for an international meeting, a kind of nineteenth century summit conference, between his government and that of Spain, at which a settlement could have been made or at least proposed. But American public opinion would probably not have tolerated a scheme so fraught with the perils of compromise that might weaken America's diplomatic independence. Such a meeting, though intriguing in retrospect, had little to recommend it at the time. It would have created more problems than it might have solved. What, for instance, would have been the rebels' status at such a meeting? Would not both Spain and the United States have insisted on an agenda for the conference, and would not agreement upon such a program itself have consumed endless debate, thus feeding Spain's policy of inaction? In any event, McKinley was not the man to set such a precedent. He might have served Spain with an ultimatum to reform or free Cuba by a certain date, but that would have amounted to a war declaration. He might have called for an investigation of conditions in Cuba by impartial powers, whose recommendations could become the basis of a settlement. But would Spain ever have permitted such interference in her affairs? And would American public opinion have accepted such arbitration? All such suggestions have about them an air of unreality when set in their late nineteenth century context.

What policy might have saved the peace? Inaction was impossible, and whatever course McKinley chose would offend some major group. Any alternative policy to the one actually pursued depended upon events and conditions impossible to attain. It is a question of "ifs." If McKinley could have conducted his diplomacy alone; if

376

the press had allayed public opinion; if Spain had acted on her promises; if there had been no de Lome letter and *Maine* incident, perhaps the story would be much different. But there were none of these "ifs." Conditions rather than the quality of presidential leadership determined the outcome. The problem was old, complex, fraught with unseen difficulties. Blame for the intervention falls fairly among the Cubans, the Americans, McKinley's policies, and especially the Spanish.

The rest was anti-climax, as the whooping Congress received the war message it had awaited so long. On April 4, McKinley had read it to the cabinet and Long recorded his disappointment in his diary. It was long, inconclusive, without any ringing declarations of intent or definition of policy. It seemed vague, especially weak in thrusting the whole matter at Congress. Only lack of sleep, worries, and nervousness, Long felt, could account for this failure.[87] A stronger hand would have been more forthright, seized the moment, and proclaimed a ringing manifesto to unite the country on a common course.

The Congress that heard the message found it astonishing. Its elevated tone and recital of history irked many. McKinley's refusal even now to recognize Cuban independence angered the more rabid element of both parties. The President recommended neutral intervention in Cuba on four grounds: for humanity's sake and to stop the bloodshed in Cuba; to protect American citizens in Cuba; to end the danger to our commerce; and to end the strategic danger to the hemisphere. Of these the first was doubtless deepest in McKinley's mind. If there was a single purpose to his intervention it was to end the destruction of the island, with its attendant horrors. He could have softened all the other issues at stake, but this one finally determined his action. The last Spanish offer was appended as if by afterthought, illustrating how little the President thought of it, and it went unnoticed.[88]

Little genuine applause greeted the message and the Senate, especially, found it weak. "It is the weakest and most inconclusive speech sent out by any President," Bailey snapped. "President's message on Cuba—disappointing," Chandler noted in his little red pocket diary. "I have no patience with the message and you may say so," Foraker told a reporter. "I have heard nothing but condemnation of the message on all hands," said Senator Rawlins of Utah. "The message is weak, impotent, imbecile, and disgraceful." [89]

Failure to extend even a hint of recognition to the Cubans angered the Senate and seemed to indicate that McKinley thought his hands would remain untied.[90] As if to underscore the administration's collapse in the upper house, the Turpie resolution favoring Cuban independence passed by a vote of 67 to 21; some 24 Republicans joined the Democrats to humiliate the President, and only Reed squelched it in the House.

McKinley asked for intervention under his direction rather than an outright war declaration, and Congress granted the ultimatum on April 20, adding Senator Teller's famous amendment forbidding the annexation of Cuba. On that same day McKinley signed the resolution and forwarded the text to Spain. Once more he was President of all the people, for public sentiment closed ranks behind him and the dissident congressional Republicans followed his lead. Spain's rejection of the ultimatum brought the nation expectantly to April 25, when Congress considered a war declaration.

On that afternoon McKinley lay down, feeling the utter exhaustion that comes with relief from strain. He expected the joint resolution from Congress and left instructions to be awakened. But he could not sleep. Ida was gone and he worried about her. He asked visiting Webb Hayes, his old friend's son, to stay in his room with him and then tried to nap. But sleep would not come and he walked softly down the hall toward the sound of voices, where a group of acquaintances talked animatedly. He waved aside their apologies and lay down on a sofa, comforted by their sounds. About four o'clock the doorkeeper brought the resolution, and the President arose, dressed, and prepared to sign it. He wrote "William" and "McKinley" separately with a set of pens which Hobart had sent, giving them to Webb Hayes as souvenirs.[91]

As the tension drained from his body and at last he could sleep, the President might have recalled a clipping from the New York *Sun,* dated April 20. "We are all jingoes now; and the head jingo is the Hon. William McKinley, the trusted and honored Chief Executive of the nation's will." He must have felt slightly sad if he did recall it, for in view of his past labors for peace, this was the unkindest cut of all.

ᏬᏯᎧ XVII ᏬᏯᎧ

Commander-in-Chief

To THE MAN ON THE STREET April, 1898, was a very special
month. If he was of military age he might pause at the
sight of long lines of grinning, joking young men, impatiently waiting to volunteer for service in Cuba in search of warfare's rumored thrills. He might be impressed by the rather jaunty
air with which most Americans welcomed the war. His heart was not
especially heavy, if he was an average man, for the war with Spain
promised to be a spirited adventure, not a war at all. When it was
all over no less a person than John Hay would say that it had been
a splendid little war; and Theodore Roosevelt would sigh wistfully
that while it wasn't much of a war, it was the only one we had.[1]

The conflict was not little or splendid to the administration in
Washington. Natural American suspicions of foreign powers in this
hemisphere or anywhere else sharpened under world events. Mc-
Kinley had already canvassed his ambassadors abroad on the possibilities of foreign intervention. The ambassadors reported that
while the governments to which they were accredited seemed pro-
Spanish, there was no thought of actual intervention.[2]

One capital conspicuously favored American designs, London.
There the Stars and Stripes flew from the same pole with the Union
Jack, and British politicians scored oratorical triumphs at Spanish
expense. Even in Parliament and in discreet murmurs from the government the pro-American stand was obvious. The Anglo-Saxonists
saw in the conflict a chance to cement the mystical alliance of
which they talked. Andrew Carnegie reported to McKinley that the
British government "would be swept from power in 24 hours if it
failed to show leanings towards its kin beyond the seas."[3]

John Hay worked assiduously for an Anglo-American understanding, reporting his success to McKinley, who heartily approved.
When the conflict was over, Ambassador Pauncefote could congratu-

late the Americans in private, and Judge Day said that the new feeling for England was the war's greatest legacy. In September, the conflict safely settled, McKinley read with pleasure a letter from his new Secretary of State. "I consider it not the least weighty of the results of your Administration to have changed the condition of dull hostility between us and England which existed a year ago into a friendship firm enough to bear any test you might choose to put upon it." [4]

At home, McKinley faced a small but long expected diplomatic crisis of his own. Secretary Sherman must now depart. His dead weight could not be tolerated in the crisis. His relations with the President had declined embarrassingly during the last year, and he had grown to dislike McKinley with the spite that often comes tragically with age. He was part of an anti-administration cabal, though publicly he maintained his cool demeanor.

Happily for the embarrassed President, Sherman resigned on April 25, and McKinley quickly named Day his successor. Day did not desire the office, knowing its burdens, and looked forward to the federal judgeship which was his for the asking. The country might have wanted a more spectacular successor but they could not have asked for a more experienced one at the moment. The nation's eyes and ears had turned elsewhere anyway, for diplomacy now took second place to the problems of raising and outfitting an army to redeem the claims of American greatness.

A friend of Lodge had boasted that if the Spanish ever landed at New York they would be selling oranges before they got to Fourteenth Street, but others did not share this confidence. Visions of Spanish men-of-war hovered in many fevered imaginations, and state governors wired Washington for naval protection against the Spanish armadas which were rumored near at hand. Admiral Cervera's squadron was somewhere out of the Azores, and those given to pessimism placed it within gunshot of New York, Boston, and Providence, despite patient assurances from the Navy that it was impossible. Of course there were inconveniences to those who summered at Newport. Society editors warned their readers not to open their summer cottages "until they shall know something more definite as to the probable movements of the Spanish fleet." [5]

Strong support materialized for the war cause. Helen Gould gave the government $100,000 and her yacht. A regiment was especially organized among Wall Street brokers, as if to redeem that street's reluctance to start the war, and William Astor Chandler gave the government a regiment. From the West came a familiar voice: William Jennings Bryan offered his services to his erstwhile opponent and got a rather formal reply from the President asking which branch he preferred. McKinley was not one to make an enemy a hero. The Boy Orator got his colonelship in a Nebraska regiment, but he never got out of Florida where, as Mr. Dooley said, he could preach his hellish doctrines to the alligators.⁶

The Army which McKinley commanded was, in time-honored American fashion, pathetically small and ill-prepared for war. Congressional penury, the long absence of conflict, and traditional dislike of standing armies kept it at a level that any European nation would have scorned. The Civil War had demonstrated what the nation could do under pressure, and a generation later minds still labored under the cherished belief in a citizen soldiery. There had not been a brigade formation in the army since Reconstruction, most officers had never seen more than a regiment of men even on maneuvers, and staff work, supply, and procurement were all set on this monumentally inadequate scale.

When the war came, despite a year's warning, there were 57 men in the quartermaster corps which must now be stretched to supply 250,000 soldiers. Most of the $50,000,000 appropriated in March went to the Navy, the country's traditional first line of defense. Equipment was antiquated and irregular; uniforms issued varied so much in color, due to age, that a formation took on a rainbow effect. There were never enough rifles raised for the army. One bewildered quartermaster summed it all up when he said weakly: "There were so many changes." ⁷

But American citizens did not think their country weak, which explains their jingoism. On April 22, the President blockaded Cuba; on the following day he called for 125,000 volunteers, and before the war ended some 270,000 men had been mustered into the Army and Navy, half of whom never left training camps. The administration wanted 104,000 men in a new regular army, but the national guard lobbies pared the figure to 60,000 regulars for two-year enlistments.

Those who saw the first regulars, hastily called from their scattered Western posts, march briskly into Washington and the new training camps where they would be the nucleus of a new army, felt a little thrill. The regulars were few but efficient, for the most part young, healthy men, versed in discipline and hardship. They could not be retained as an invasion force because they were simply too few. Instead, they were partly scattered among the volunteers as a cadre, while some whole units were kept for invasion purposes.

How to make an army of regulars out of the volunteers? Speed was of the essence, for backed by fervent jingoism, the country demanded action. "The United States must make thorough work while it is about it," a Boston paper said in May, and this would require large forces. In the cities and towns, flags fluttered above makeshift recruitment booths. No young man could pay for his own drinks, buy a meal, or avoid being kissed by girls once he had enlisted. An air of festive enthusiasm, incongruous to the task at hand, filled the air. "Patriotism was not merely aroused; it was in conflagration," one soldier remembered.[8]

Fittingly, Ohio was the first to respond, sending her favorite son a regiment raised in eight days.[9] Confronted with this mass of enthusiastic but raw volunteers, champing for overseas action, McKinley moved slowly. His unwillingness to send raw troops into battle won praise from more sober judgments. He might well hesitate, for as the volunteer army grew mushroom-like, crowding into state capitals and preparing to converge on debarkation points and training camps, the administration had not yet devised its strategy. Army and Navy officers counselled caution and delay. All could agree with the President's simple dictum: "We must not scatter our forces." [10]

McKinley's first worry was not the troops but the rush of applicants for office, now fully as ferocious as they had been a year ago. Every train into the city brought commission-hunters and contractors, all eager for personal gain and public position. McKinley wished to avoid the political generals he had seen in the Civil War, and all in all he did well. Of the 26 major generals he appointed, 19 came came from the Regular Army; of the 102 brigadiers, 66 were regulars. In the administrative posts so crucial to a modern army he placed experienced men. Yet even in June, with victory almost in sight, Cortelyou could write drily: "All hands are still interested in the Army appointments." [11]

McKinley did not forget his geography in making appointments. It was not mere politics, but an effort to make the war national, for he wanted to erase the last vestiges of sectionalism. He could not overlook the South, which was so vociferous in its desire to free Cuba, and whose "Confederate brigadiers" were anxious to wear Federal uniforms again. The first logical choice was Georgia's aging "Fighting Joe" Wheeler, a jingo Democrat in Congress, who wanted to serve the old flag. The President greeted him with outstretched hand early in May. "There must be a high ranking officer from the South. There must be a symbol that the old days are gone— you are needed," he said. He did not have to argue, and Wheeler subsequently fought bravely, though not always wisely.[12]

As May passed and the Army began to take some form, the larger and more vexing problems of equipping and supplying it grew in McKinley's mind as he sat through the laborious conferences necessary to make policy. An army must be taken to Cuba and the Navy was not equipped for the task. The government began buying private transport, converting lake steamers, yachts, steamboats, and pleasure craft into troop transports, often at excessive cost and with unhappy results. Supply posed special problems, for no one in Washington knew anything about amphibious operations that required transporting huge quantities of supplies to a foreign country. Food was a special problem, since there were few prepared rations; refrigerator ships for fresh beef were expensive and impossible to find, though the Armour Company promised to procure one.[13]

As the country gradually saw the War Department ensnarled in its own red tape, inadequate staff, and poor planning, it grew angry. Eager for war, the public found it hard to excuse or understand the confusion and delay, conveniently forgetting that the country had never had an adequate military establishment. The very Congress that had helped provoke the war had done little to prepare for it. To those in the planning, the confusion was doubly clear, though it perhaps was what "no more than naturally follows the transition from a state of peace to a state of war in a country situated as ours is," as John J. McCook noted.[14]

If matters were confused in Washington, they were frightful in Tampa, chosen for dubious reasons as the army's debarkation point for Cuba. Located in a fairly mild climate, on Florida's west coast, with what was thought to be an adequate harbor and port facilities that could be expanded, the city seemed logical as a jump-off point. It might have been in theory, but in practice it became a nightmare, for only one railroad led over the sandy wastes to its few inadequate piers. The jumble of boxcars backed up for miles was incredible, and since bills of lading and invoices were lost or forgotten, no one really knew where anything was. Food, water, and medicines were short; fodder for animals was rare; more than one regiment was assigned the same transport, and many commanders like Theodore Roosevelt, simply took what they wanted.[15]

To Senator Lodge, waiting impatiently at the war's other end, all the blame rested upon Alger and his encrusted bureau chiefs. If he would only use a broom, or if McKinley would use one on him, matters would be vastly improved. McKinley began to share this suspicion of Alger before the war began, though he retained his usual cordiality with the Secretary, whose alternate boasting and complaining got on his nerves. "I do remember that you had your war days and your anti-war days," the President would say a year later of Alger's inconsistency.[16] Perhaps he took it out elsewhere, or perhaps he was simply strained; at any rate, McKinley grew testy, sharply reprimanding Adjutant General Corbin once on the theory, as he told his brother, that it made sense to call people down sometimes. But even the strain of war did not kill his sense of humor, and he knew of many things that he did not discuss. When the war was over, he asked a major, well known for having boldly stolen another regiment's supplies, to do a job. When the man protested, McKinley smiled knowingly. "Charlie, any man who can steal the rations of a whole regiment can do anything." [17]

McKinley's problems were now compounded by the men to whom war planning fell. There was no chief of staff or central planning agency. In the Army he encountered the impressive figure of Major General Commanding Nelson A. Miles. One of the last "boy generals" of the Civil War, Miles had earned a fabulous reputation as an Indian fighter and climbed the ladder of Army success until there was nowhere to go but to his present ornate but empty office. Married to John Sherman's niece, he had long criticized the administration and disliked McKinley personally. Even Theodore Roosevelt found this "brave peacock" insufferable, for the General did not hide his ambitions.[18] It was no secret that the presidential bee had stung him deeply.

Miles could not command the field army, for theoretically he supervised all actions. Command fell by lot of seniority to an embarrassingly comic figure, General William R. Shafter, for he weighed over 250 pounds. Slow of movement and cautious in thought, he did not inspire vigor in his troops. Steeped in the routines of paper work and addicted to form, he seemed a wholly illogical choice for command. But he was a brave and responsible officer, with considerable good sense, whose caution saved lives that others might have wasted. His corpulent, half-comical, half-pathetic form, swathed in a tight-fitting uniform and topped by a pith helmet, became a familiar figure to the front lines in Cuba. He rode down the lines in his celebrated sagging buckboard or perched atop his "stout hearted mule," the subject of soldier songs and poetry.

In the Navy the command situation was somewhat better, for that branch of the service had been more prosperous than the Army since the Civil War. A decent navy was a matter of national pride, and conversion to modern steam vessels began under Arthur, to be carried forward by every subsequent president. In the Atlantic, command lay between the chilly but efficient Admiral William T. Sampson and the more colorful and erratic Commodore Winfield Scott Schley. In the Pacific there was but one hero, the victor of Manila Bay, George Dewey.

If McKinley had his private doubts about the Army and Navy command, he kept silent. He had no alternative, for they were inevitably the best names which the system produced. He relied on them fairly heavily, though he often superseded them by virtue of a broader view of the conflict. Happily for all concerned, McKinley did not fancy himself a warlord; he developed no tactics, but devised the basic strategy.

While the warlords convened in Washington and army officers tried to create a new force, the chief drama of the war transpired half a world away in the waters of Manila Bay. In the fall of 1897, partly persuaded by Senator Proctor and Roosevelt, McKinley promoted George Dewey to command of the Asiatic squadron. Though he did not know Dewey, he trusted Long's judgment. "Are you satisfied that Dewey is a good man for the place and that his head is level?" he had asked Long.[19]

The taciturn Navy veteran was set on the road to glory. Not given to the politicking that brought other officers favors, he had counted on an orderly retirement from the service. But Roosevelt and others had sensed in him a steadiness and hidden ability for the dramatic that would make him an excellent commander and, as it turned out, an ideal hero. On April 21, Long urged McKinley to authorize the departure of Dewey's fleet from Hong Kong to Manila, but McKinley demurred, thinking it was not yet time. On April 24, however, he agreed, and the signal went to Hong Kong.[20]

The night of April 30 found Dewey's squadron hesitating at the entrance to Manila Bay. The Channel was mined, the guns of Corregidor, the rock fortress which sat in the bay, were formidable, and the Spanish navy was larger than the American. But as Dewey discovered later, the mines had no fuses, Corregidor was silent, and the Spanish navy was a collection of hulks. Admiral Montojo, determined on saving face prepared for battle by anchoring out of the city's range in shallow water, so that his men could swim ashore after the fight.

In Washington, May 1 developed into a lazy, placid day, but it was tropical and hot off Manila, whose buildings glared whitely in the piercing morning heat. As Dewey's ships moved to battle, a crew member exclaimed: "We people don't have to worry, for Hell ain't no hotter than this!" [21] The day was far hotter for the Spanish, for Dewey's fleet destroyed the enemy force without loss. To insure the safety of isolation, Dewey cut the cable to Hong Kong. On May 2, rumor via Madrid told of a great naval battle in the Philippines, but the United States got no official word until May 7, when one of Dewey's cutters reported from Hong Kong.

When America heard the news she went wild, for at last action had emerged from the welter of confusion surrounding the efforts to free Cuba. That it had occurred in another hemisphere, in islands of which most people had never heard, was irrelevant. A member of the Coast and Geodetic Survey, thinking that the President might need some maps, carried a load to the White House, where Secretary Porter showed him into McKinley's office. The President looked up from a small map of the Philippines torn from a schoolbook, and gratefully took the larger map his visitor offered. The two men talked for half an hour and then McKinley signalled that he must go. As he bowed his visitor out, he said with a sigh: "It is evident that I must learn a great deal of geography in this war. . . ." [22]

The very name Philippines drew a blank with most Americans; later Mr. Dooley said he did not know if they were a place or canned goods. But it did not matter; the Stars and Stripes had won somewhere. The name was familiar to the administration. At a conference on May 2, the President authorized an expedition to the islands, setting in motion the chain of events that caused him much grief in the years ahead. General Merritt was charged with conquering the islands with a force of some fourteen thousand regulars and volunteers.

The battle was no sooner reported than countless Americans rushed to their maps. Then in a second breath they demanded retention of the islands as a steppingstone to empire, beginning the chorus of approval for McKinley's final decision to keep them. Almost all the consular officials in the Orient had already urged Washington to prepare to take the islands in the event of war. Though cautious administration organs held their fire, jingo and expansionist newspapers demanded retention. "Common sense tells us to keep what has cost so much to wrest from an unworthy foe." Said a Baltimore sheet, "Back of that is the solid, irresistible sentiment of the people." [23]

Suspicions of foreign powers sharpened this demand. Were not Germany and France and England and heaven knew who else ready to take the islands if we did not? And would this not give them more than a toe hold in the oriental sphere of influence? Such questions ripened into dogmas under the impact of events. Congressmen pressured the administration to state a policy and to send a land force to seize Manila itself. Militant Senator Frye was forthright. "The fear I have about this war is that peace will be declared before we can get full occupation of the Philippines and Porto Rico." Expansionist appetites sharpened everywhere, and in the Navy, Captain Alfred Thayer Mahan raised a potent voice in favor of expansion in the Orient. In the confusion that followed, one paper asked a plaintive question. Why was Uncle Sam like a lady throwing a stone? Because he had aimed at Cuba and hit the Philippines.[24]

Within the administration, opinion was divided. The influential and usually reliable Washington *Post* said in mid-July that the administration would not retain the islands because it was un-American. Judge Day was heard to remark laconically that "Unfortunately there is nothing we can do but give those islands back to Spain." [25]

McKinley neither confirmed nor denied the rumors. It was a momentous problem, and one on which he may not have counted. Mr. Kohlsaat remembered the President's saying in after years that he could not have located the islands within two thousand miles before Dewey's victory. Since he had already authorized an expedition to the islands, however, this story, like so much of Mr. Kohlsaat's memory, seems apocryphal. But he could repeat with greater certainty another saying of McKinley's: "If Old Dewey had just sailed away when he smashed that Spanish fleet, what a lot of trouble he would have saved us!" [26]

As July closed and the President had not yet said anything publicly, those around him felt that he was "conservative," but awaited events in the island. To one visitor, however, he clearly showed the drift of his thinking, saying that while he favored retaining as little as possible, he did not know how much that little might be. He favored "the general principle of holding on to what we get." If events dictated, he would not hesitate to retain all the archipelago. Impressed by his sincerity and calmness, the visitor hurriedly assured Senator Lodge that McKinley was at heart already in the expansionist camp.[27] From the first, McKinley was inclined to retention of the islands, and now began the long search for support for that position.

The situation in the Philippines was terribly complex, as the President quickly learned. The Filipinos welcomed the Americans as liberators from Spanish oppression, but they already had a full-fledged independence movement of their own, complete with a George Washington in the person of Emilio Aguinaldo. They had revolted against Spain in 1895 and were not now disposed to welcome another conqueror. Dewey's ships sat grimly in the harbor, their guns upon the city, awaiting land forces to consummate the victory. The Admiral warily watched the insurgents in the meantime, fearful that they would dislodge the Spaniards before Merritt arrived.

Alive to the danger, the State Department quickly forbade Dewey's cooperation with the insurgents. Washington made it clear that the islands were under American authority alone until the peace settlement, and acknowledged no insurgent rights. Though he worried over the "insurgent complication," as he called it, the politically inept Dewey did not fully understand the problem's explosive nature. He conferred with Aguinaldo but apparently did not promise independence, though American consular officials in the past had certainly led the Filipinos to expect the Americans to come as liberators, not as conquerors.[28] In June, Aguinaldo proclaimed a republic, with himself as president.

To counter this situation and relieve Dewey, the first part of Merritt's hastily gathered force left San Francisco on May 25. The General had McKinley's first instructions on treatment of the Philippine problem; these breathed his legendary caution and underscored his ignorance of the full situation. McKinley radiated good intentions, promising friendly relations with Aguinaldo as long as the later understood American sovereignty in the islands. Enjoining strict accountability on the American army, the President assured the Filipinos that the Americans came as liberators, not as conquerors, and that a firm policy would be announced in the near future. He would not share authority with the insurgents but he held out the slender, unspoken hope of some kind of joint rule later. In the meantime, "Our occupation should be as free from severity as possible." [29]

The uncertainty and doubt about the future of the islands was hidden from public view, however, for attention turned in late May and early June toward the army in Florida, which now prepared to debark helter-skelter on its crusade in Cuba. The same conference of May 2 which decided to send an expedition to the Philippines also formulated plans for the assault on Cuba. As the raw troops poured southward, the President's desire for invasion grew firmer. "If you have too many troops," he told an officer, "that is my fault—if you have too few, that will be your fault." [30] He must have known of the ill-prepared army, and doubtless had his misgivings about sending it into conflict. But he had great faith in the navy and in the regular troops who would compose the initial landing force. Despite Alger's vacuous bluster and his already proved incompetence, McKinley mysteriously counted on him to devise an army in the thirty days the voluble Secretary allotted to the task. The confusion attendant on training the army should have shown how vain was this dream, but McKinley hoped that a strong threat would bring a negotiated peace.

Miles wished to delay the assault until cooler weather in the fall, spending the summer in training the army, but political pressures dictated otherwise.[31] Under the pressures of organization which this decision created, Alger was left to wrestle daily with men and problems others criticized but could not alleviate. He grew touchy, and he had some light on his side. "It is one thing to be a National Guardsman with all the convenience of a few days in camp once a year, and another to buckle down to the duties and hardships of real soldiering," he told one correspondent. He added a postscript that rumors of his resignation were "a silly fiction." [32] He was oblivious to McKinley's rapidly wilting belief in him.

In Tampa itself Shafter surveyed his army with dismay. The chief problem was equipment and supply, and he did not frankly know how the army was to get to Cuba. Plaintive letters and telegrams went north to Washington but produced little except executive irritation. By the first week in June, McKinley's patience was at an end. Sampson's fleet blockaded Santiago on June 6, and the Admiral called for land forces. On the evening of June 7, angered by excuses and delay, McKinley ordered Shafter to debark for Cuba the following day. The result was a melee in which conflicting regiments simply seized their supplies and ships and drifted defiantly into the harbor to await sailing. Shafter retired for the night with resignation, but was awakened by a message saying that debarkation would be delayed while the navy hunted a rumored Spanish squadron. The men roasted in their ships' holds for a miserable week before finally sailing on June 14.

On June 20 the force arrived off Santiago de Cuba, and between June 22 and June 26 landed amid confusion at Daiquiri and Siboney. Many ships would not come close to shore because the government had not insured them and they feared damage. The soldiers rowed ashore against nominal or nonexistent resistance, and horses and mules swam. The supplies landed in jumbled heaps as the first waves of men pushed into the unknown terrain. The presence of news reporters hampered operations, and Shafter gained the "bad press" that followed him thereafter. By the twenty-ninth, Shafter's men had come within a mile and a half of the city, and the corpulent general began devising ways to avoid storming the city, for he feared a pitched battle.

On the morning of July 1, newsmen in Washington and Florida perked up their ears, for news of a major engagement filtered north. When it was all over, San Juan Hill had been engraved in history and the city's formidable ring of outer defenses had fallen, allowing Shafter's army to lay siege to the city. In the triumph of the moment memory overcame reality and Joe Wheeler yelled: "We've got the damn yankees on the run!" [33]

The momentary flush of victory turned to apprehension at home as word came on July 3 that the enemy fleet, bottled up in Santiago's harbor since May 29, had emerged for a running fight. Already worried about Shafter's gloomy reports that he could neither storm Santiago nor hold his present position indefinitely, McKinley spent a tense July 3 as no report of the naval engagement came. Schley's first message was ambiguous, seeming to say that the American fleet had been destroyed, and the President's face fell visibly as Long handed him the cable. McKinley waited hours by the cable, smoking with "Tama Jim" Wilson and friends. At one A.M. a message went to Shafter: "We are awaiting with tense anxiety tidings of yesterday." Early that morning Sampson cabled: "The fleet under my command offers the Nation as a Fourth of July present the destruction of the whole of Cervera's fleet, not one escaped." The capital and the country awoke to delirium like that which greeted Dewey's victory. [34]

Shafter now began his role of negotiator rather than conqueror. Aware of his command's difficulties, the threat of yellow fever, and criticisms at home, he was anxious to avoid an assault on Santiago. He feared that the Spanish garrison had been reinforced before the siege, and wished to avoid casualties among the city's undefended people. Many at home shared the view, disturbed by Shafter's blunt warning that McKinley "should be prepared for heavy losses among our troops." [35]

McKinley did not object to peace by the pen rather than the sword, and authorized the General's negotiations on the basis of unconditional surrender. The Spanish offered to leave the city if given the advantage of a day's march on the Americans, to fight somewhere else to save their honor. McKinley sternly vetoed such an absurd scheme. "What you went to Santiago for was the Spanish army. If you allow it to evacuate with its arms you must meet it somewhere else. This is not war. If the Spanish commander desires to leave the city and its people, let him surrender and we will then discuss the question as to what shall be done with them." In true Spanish fashion, General Toral than demanded that his troops keep their arms and that the Americans pay their fare home. This, too, raised tempers in Washington. "It is not possible that you are entertaining the proposition of permitting the Spanish to carry away their arms," Alger cabled angrily. "Such a suggestion should be rejected instantly. You have been instructed on the terms of surrender acceptable to the President, and they must be concluded on those lines." [36]

McKinley had begun to wonder about Shafter's fitness and thought of removing him on the grounds of ill health. His slowness and indecision were proving dangerous. When Miles, in Cuba on an inspection tour, cabled his assent to the proposed armistice, McKinley relented and the Spanish won some concessions. Shafter saved many lives and much time by negotiation, though his slowness irritated the administration and angered the public.

The surrender of Santiago on July 17 practically ended the war, and the nation basked in the warmth of foreign praise and a new self-confidence. McKinley welcomed the momentary relief. As the first war president since Lincoln, he was beset with new and baffling problems. While government officials and private citizens fled steaming Washington that summer, he stayed dutifully behind, assisted by the loyal office seekers and favor-mongers who stuck to their posts with him.[37]

He did not relish the role of war lord, for aside from the interminable conferences and the necessity for decisions, he remembered the days when he had been closer to war. In this situation, as in diplomacy and politics, he relied on conference to form policy, not only to spread responsibility but also to gather information and to provide coherence to war plans. He was often at his desk until after midnight, and watched closely the colored pins on the maps in his war room that denoted military positions. His callers and mail increased heavily, taking more time and energy. Nevertheless, he often surprised callers by his grasp of the problems involved.[38]

The physical strain proved hard to bear, and circles appeared under his eyes. He was even more silent than usual, saving his strength, but in mid-July, as the victories in Cuba were announced, he seemed to improve.[39] He did not direct the conflict first-hand, but felt it was his duty to give coherence to the total effort, while accepting responsibility for the grand strategy involved. He was in this, as in other things, a kind of mediator and final authority rather than an actively planning leader.

Party politics and favoritism did not diminish in the emergency. Senators rushed to the White House to speak for their states' interests; state politicians wanted martial glory for the coming elections; inventors with political friends sought special favors. They got few from McKinley, for charges of corruption and official favoritism angered him. He often dispatched curt notes to various departments, demanding reports on this or that alleged wrong. Alger, who was getting on his nerves, felt the President's temper when he asked if it would not be politically wise to send the men in the training camps to Porto Rico, that they might taste foreign service before the war ended. McKinley eyed him stiffly and spoke with an alarming chill. "Mr. Secretary, what do you think the people will say if they believe we unnecessarily and at great expense send these boys out of the country? Is it either necessary or expedient?" Alger's answer was silence.[40]

One Spanish colony remained, Porto Rico. In mid-June, McKinley had anxiously inquired about outfitting a Porto Rican expedition. His thinking had already turned to overseas expansion; as he had said in the case of the Philippines, common sense or destiny dictated that the United States acquire all the territory it could and dispose of it later. Alger feared that Porto Rico might require more troops than expected. "Too many is just enough," McKinley replied curtly, and Miles left Cuba with an army that landed in Porto Rico on July 25.[41]

Alarming news now came from Santiago, where heat and the threat of yellow fever descended on the nervous, exhausted, and frightened army. As early as July, Miles had spoken of yellow fever, and by the first week of August medical officers warned that all supplies, especially drugs, were low.[42] On August 2, Shafter cabled urgently that the army must be moved or it would perish. The War Department ordered the army to the mountains outside Havana, where cooler temperatures would banish the fever, but lack of rail transport made the transfer impossible. At this juncture, Roosevelt and a group of fellow officers sent their famous "round robin" to the newspapers at home, protesting the delay in evacuating the army, saying that it must move or die, and charging the government with inefficiency and corruption.

McKinley first read the letter in the morning paper on August 4 and was enraged. Alger shared his view and reprimanded both Shafter and Roosevelt. The administration had already ordered the debarkation to the United States of all troops but those necessary to hold the city, and the letter only revealed the army's weakness to the Spanish. Anyone else, Alger said, would be court-martialled, but the Secretary confined himself to a monumental understatement on Roosevelt: "He evidently has little idea of army discipline."[43]

As August opened, the army began moving as many troops as possible to demobilization centers in the United States. The sandy wastes of Point Montauk, Long Island, christened Camp Wikoff, were set aside for recuperation and mustering out, and a tent city mushroomed across its dunes overnight. Naturally it was inadequate; food was short; doctors were scarce; materials were hard to find and expensive. Behind the hurried work at the camp loomed public fear of yellow fever and contamination from the contagion which the emaciated army brought home from Cuba as its war legacy.

Late in August, Alger visited the camp and agreed that the men ought to be mustered out soon. He felt that while conditions were admittedly bad, they were greatly exaggerated in the press, and he still seemed oblivious to his own precarious position. While some in the administration admitted the bungling, they discounted it as inevitable. Alger curtly informed the governor of Massachusetts that the returning army was not made up of invalids, and assured him that the government would spare neither effort nor expense to care for it.[44]

In September, the President himself went to Camp Wikoff in company with Alger and other officials; it was his only holiday in 1898. There in the seasonal heat and dust he passed down the rows of beds in the temporary hospitals, questioning the sick and greeting the well. His coat became dusty and his face showed the marks of what he saw during the long and tiring day.[45]

The criticism around Alger now rose as public fury vented itself against the man whose name had been slurred into an ugly word denoting incompetence, "Algerism." The Secretary continued to excuse his mistakes. In public he grew self-righteous, snapping at an inquisitive reporter that he would not "get down in the gutter with these people" who were criticizing him. To himself he repeated a bitter rhyme from Lord Byron:

> A man must serve his time to every trade
> Save censure—critics all are ready made.[46]

In keeping silent on the question, McKinley seemed to sustain Alger. He would not throw the hapless Secretary to the wolves of public opinion, but he was increasingly conscious of the chorus of criticism. He told Cortelyou that it was inevitable, but he seemed defensive on the subject. An old friend, worried over the political repercussions of Algerism, was blunt. "If he is not corrupt, as many believe, his incompetence has reached the magnitude of a crime." Others around McKinley had long since given Alger up for lost. "He maintains that his prerogatives are being encroached upon," Dawes noted icily late in May. "Fortunately for our cause at war, he tells the truth." Even the faithful Cortelyou thought that Alger's record might be "one of the few blots" on McKinley's record unless he were removed. McKinley could not very well fire the Secretary under such pressure, but perhaps he also had a deeper reason. If he removed him, would it not appear that he accepted as valid the criticisms of the whole administration? [47]

The chief business of late July and August was not resettlement of the army or Algerism, but the peace negotiations, for the fall of Santiago and the destruction of Cervera's fleet ended Spain's hope for victory. She quickly sought peace to avoid the capture of Porto Rico and the Philippines.

McKinley had already refused to state his peace terms until the Spanish asked, and the first overtures came from Madrid on July 18, when the Spanish asked France to state her case to the United States. Due to delays and confusion, the French did not appoint their ambassador in Washington, Jules Cambon, to conduct the negotiations until July 22, after American occupation of Porto Rico.[48] On that day Cambon hurried to the White House, where he talked with McKinley and Day.

Cambon had no sooner left than McKinley called the cabinet together. A crucial problem now must be met: how to dispose of the Philippines. Any decision taken now might affect all that followed. The cabinet was about equally divided. The President did not force his views, but heard out his advisors.

To escape the city's heat and to provide a more relaxed atmosphere, the President suggested a short cruise down the Potomac on a lighthouse tender, and one hot July day the stiffly-attired cabinet debarked from a pier that swarmed with reporters. As the little boat chugged into mid-channel, where there were no prying eyes and listening ears, the fate of the Philippines was discussed.

The President was genial and pacific as he listened to the conflicting views. Day was frankly reluctant to take anything but a naval base; Gage joined him, but Bliss and Griggs saw commercial possibilities in the islands; Wilson wanted them all to evangelize, which later brought a humorous reply from McKinley: "Yes, you Scotch favor keeping everything including the Sabbath."

Cabinet sessions followed as the members worried over fine shadings in proposed wordings for the peace protocol. Day's first draft would have kept only a naval base; the President tactfully buried it. On July 29 the cabinet worked most of the day. As they continued on Saturday, July 30, personal attitudes among the President's advisors emerged clearly. When a vote was taken, expansion won, though by a narrow margin. After one session, Day said: "Mr. President, you didn't put my motion for a naval base." McKinley, who had already said that Day wanted only "a hitching post," smiled. "No, Judge, I was afraid it would be carried!" He had played his usual waiting game and won support for a predetermined stand.

On July 30, as the cabinet and President worked over a final draft, Cambon appeared and waited discreetly in an anteroom while the finishing touches were applied. McKinley presented the document to Cambon, who was startled by its demands, and they talked until about half-past five, when the Frenchman left to cable the text to Madrid and Paris.[49]

The proposed protocol to end hostilities held some unpleasant surprises for Spain, and the friendly French tried to soften the American demands. McKinley, with his usual skill, had guided the cabinet and negotiators to produce a firm document. Spain must leave Cuba and the hemisphere; Porto Rico would go to the United States as an indemnity; the Americans would hold the bay, harbor, and city of Manila pending the disposition of the islands at the subsequent peace conference. The protocol only suspended hostilities, and a joint peace conference would settle all matters later.[50]

Madrid's answer was pained surprise, outlined in a note of August 7. They would not quarrel with leaving Cuba or ceding Porto Rico, but the United States could not claim any part of the Philippines by right of conquest or by any other right. When he received the long-winded Spanish complaint, Day looked at McKinley and said wearily: "Let us get it down in black and white." It was the old Ohio lawyer talking, and it made sense. Despite Cambon's gentle persuasions, McKinley was not inclined to compromise, saying to the Spanish, through Cambon, that the peace conference would have to settle the question of the Philippines. "The Madrid government may be assured that up to this time there is nothing determined a priori in my mind against Spain; likewise, I consider there is nothing decided against the United States."[51] Further Spanish delay was futile, for McKinley would not back down despite the questionable ability of the American army to enforce his demands. The exasperated but impressed Cambon burst out at one meeting that McKinley was "as firm as a rock." [52] The Spanish capitulated on August 10, and in the following two days the final act took place. The war was over.

A few days later a Philadelphia newspaper ran a disturbing editorial: "With peace will come new responsibilities, which must be met. We have colonies to look after and develop." [53] The average American who looked at the protocol had reason to be gratified, for his country had swept away the Spanish empire and seemed now ready to take it as the spoils of war. The Philippine problem remained, potentially more dangerous than the issues that caused the war, for even now party lines were re-emerging.

McKinley had momentarily solved the complex and vexing Philippine problem in characteristic fashion; he had left it open to be settled by a later conference. He later quietly revealed that this was his purpose all along, and he had followed the cabinet's discussions only to sound out opinion and maneuver for support. When the final decision was taken to retain Manila and leave the problem to negotiation, the President showed Cortelyou a scrap of paper, which he had in his pocket and on which he had written that plan some days before. "If the American forces have remained until now in their positions it is in obedience to a duty which respect to residents and strangers and the progress of affairs imposes upon me," McKinley told the Spanish.[54] That last phrase, or a subtle variation concerning destiny and duty, became the basis for subsequent negotiation over the islands.

In leaving the Philippine question open to later discussion McKinley in effect committed himself to their ultimate retention. Whatever he might say to the contrary, he knew that this device merely bought time to develop and sound out public opinion on the issue of territorial expansion. His whole tone indicates that his own mind was already made up. In July he signed the Hawaiian annexation with a reference to manifest destiny; in July he also authorized the conquest of Porto Rico for frankly expansionist motives; and even before knowing fully of Dewey's victory at Manila, he authorized a land force to conquer the islands. The whole direction of his policy after May was toward retention of the Philippines. Now that peace had come he would bide his time, employ the same discreet pressure, and use the same tactics of silence and public generalities to avoid alienating foes and overly enthusiastic friends. He had decided upon his position; the public must now come to it.

Though he felt relieved at the war's end, the President knew that endless troubles lay ahead in making the peace. As he looked upon the war's results he saw that it had created more problems than it solved. As he looked from his window upon a capital now at peace, he might have reflected on how much his country and his own office had changed in the last two short years. In his youth and middle years a man might enter public life championing one issue and retire forty years later with that issue still in the public eye. The tariff, silver, internal improvements—they seemed dead and alien now. He would be the first American president to face an ever mounting array of bewildering challenges at home and abroad as his country moved into an era marked not only by a new chronology but by a new spirit.

The war with Spain was a small affair, brief, relatively cheap, seemingly glamorous, but its consequences were far-reaching and important for the whole world. Placid, insular, isolated America was forever gone, and in her place there was a different nation. "No war in history has accomplished so much in so short a time with so little loss," Horace Porter wrote Hanna. "The nation has at a bound gone forward in the estimation of the world more than we would have done in fifty years of peace," said Senator Proctor. "It is almost a creation or new birth." Such was official opinion, but as usual Mr. Dooley perhaps summed up the new tenor best. "We're a gr-reat people," said his friend Mr. Hennessey. "We ar-re that," replied Mr. Dooley. "We ar-re that. An th' best iv it is, we know we ar-re." [55]

ᕙ᎒ᕗ XVIII ᕙ᎒ᕗ

Making Peace

 O NE HOT DAY in mid-August, Judge Day came to the White House on a pleasant mission; he was to resign as secretary of State. He could not resist joking with McKinley, for while they were somewhat formal together even as friends, both remembered calmer days at the Canton bar. Day laughed and told the President that he was sorry to leave him in mid-administration, depriving him of priceless counsel. McKinley smiled and quipped: "Well, Judge Day, every change so far in the office of Secretary of State has been an improvement!" [1]

McKinley's humor bespoke the truth, for he turned to John Hay as Day's successor. He was pleased with the Ambassador's work in England before and during the war, and had long since decided to have him in the cabinet's premier post. On August 15 he formally tendered the post, expecting a ready acceptance. But in England, Hay was not so eager. A curious mixture of indolence and ambition, he was not anxious to return to Washington. He enjoyed the English capital. Furthermore, he hated the United States Senate, with which he inevitably would have to work as secretary of State. Henry White found him restive as he debated, but in the end he "shouldered his pack" and accepted. [2] McKinley promptly frightened him by saying that he himself would not worry any longer about diplomatic details.

The choice bespoke McKinley's growing awareness of foreign affairs. No mere front, or domestic politician, would do in the State Department. Hay's world travel, urbanity, intelligence, and diplomatic experience recommended him to the President. Hay's acceptance relieved him, though the Ambassador did not take his post until September 30.

Selection of Hay's successor posed a knotty problem and a fascinating possibility. Could he not send Senator Hoar to London as ambassador, removing the old man from the scene at a time when he had already betrayed disquieting symptoms of revolt against the President's policies? He sounded out the Senator, whose innocent face hid one of the sharpest tongues in public life, and tendered him the appointment. But the canny old man brushed it aside. His temper was roused; he had no intention of going abroad at his time of life, or just when the choicest fight since Reconstruction loomed.[3] McKinley's offer then went to a more logical choice, the rich, witty Joseph Choate.

His mind filled with the problems of demobilization, affairs in the distant Philippines, and countless other burdens, McKinley faced a formidable problem in choosing the peace commission to make the Treaty of Paris. The thought of going personally did not enter his mind. No president had ever done so before and he was not one to set such a precedent. It was a wise decision, for it gave him closeness to events at home and freedom from foreign pressures in making his decisions.

With a shrewdness that belied his past experience and his understanding of the controversy around the peace, the President sought a balanced commission. He had already decided to send Day as chairman. Whitelaw Reid, ever anxious for office, would also go. the Senate must be represented, and President wanted Allison, whose careful glove would have been of great use, but the Iowan declined. He chose instead Minnesota's Cushman K. Davis, chairman of the Foreign Relations Committee and an expansionist. To accompany him, McKinley selected Maine's fiery jingo, William P. Frye, and Delaware's anti-expansionist Democrat, George Gray. John Bassett Moore, distinguished international lawyer from Columbia University, went as secretary to give advice and counsel. As he surveyed his handiwork, McKinley was satisfied. Day would speak for the administration and was a moderate on the Philippines but open to persuasion. Reid would speak for the expansionist public. Davis and Frye were expansionists with powerful Senate posts. Gray would act as ballast, representing the Democrats and, presumably, anti-expansionist sentiment in general. The President might have temporized a moment over choosing senators, but in the end he politely ignored Chandler's protest that he ought not to use men who would ratify their own work. He was not blind; that was exactly what he had in mind.[4]

As August progressed to September, domestic problems confronted him with sharp reality. It was inevitably an election year, and a bad one at that, as Senator Hanna reminded him. Though the peace treaty would not be finished by election day, it would be the real issue; the whole administration would be on trial, with the voters' minds focused on the Philippines. Few things would be more disastrous than a Republican defeat, and to Hanna and stark realists this possibility seemed all too predictable, considering the Democrats' eagerness to talk of Algerism and a new and uglier word, "imperialism." The President, said Hanna, must show himself, must enter the elections if he wished his party returned, and must explain his stand on the Philippines.

That was all very well, some might have said, but just what was the President's stand on the Philippines? The peace protocol seemed to outline all he had to say on the subject for the moment; the question would be settled somehow later. To all intents and purposes he had not made up his mind yet.

He did not lack advisors and advice that hot summer; nearly everyone who came to see him or wrote him a letter offered a solution to the problem. The missionary element wanted to keep the islands to Christianize and Americanize them, conveniently forgetting that the natives were supposedly Catholic. Rumor said that Ida was interested in saving the Igorrotes, though her political feelings rarely influenced her husband.[5]

Some callers from the business world were frankly worried; would it not be best not to risk anything, but rather to hand the islands back to Spain or leave them to self-government?[6] This sentiment was not very strong, however; far more callers and correspondents, dazzled by the prospects of commercial empire in the Orient, urged retention of the islands and their development as a stepping-stone to the China trade. Reluctant to engage in the war originally, by October the business element championed expansion.[7]

A far more touchy problem confronted the peacemakers in the United States as they pondered their course toward the islands. Foreign ships still lingered in Manila Bay, and McKinley knew that American success there had aroused European chancelleries. The Germans were a great irritant. Their activities during the battle of Manila Bay had aroused most Americans to fever pitch.[8] Whatever their real motives, they seemed ready to take the islands if the United States did not; if the bellicose Kaiser Wilhelm failed in this, diplomats reported, the islands would be divided among the powers. At home, the jingo press did not lessen these fears. "Hoar is crazy," Hanna said surprisingly, for he had never been an expansionist. "He thinks Germany is just fooling." [9]

Consular agents, newsmen, businessmen, and tourists in the Orient reported to the government all suspicious foreign activity. The French were impressed, someone wired. The Japanese must be watched, for had not Sherman himself said only a year ago that they were a major power? Of all the powers, only England forthrightly desired American acquisition of the islands, Hay reported to his chief with the tacit assumption that England would sustain American action.[10] The President did not really think another power would forcibly take the islands, but the threat was there and entered into his thinking. As he said of the Philippines in his annual message of 1899, in a felicitous allusion, the United States could not "fling them, a golden apple of discord, among the rival powers."

If news from abroad fortified the President's inclination to take all of the islands, that from home solidified it. While the war raged McKinley wrote on a scrap of paper: "While we are conducting war and until its conclusion we must keep all we get; when the war is over we must keep what we want." [11] He quietly studied intelligence reports on the islands and digested all the information he could find. A ready chorus from the newspapers swelled the volume of expansionist sentiment. As early as July, 43 per cent of some 65 newspapers polled favored retention of the islands, and 33 per cent were undecided; a mere quarter were opposed. There was no doubt that the press, which presumably reflected public opinion, favored retention.[12]

The politicians had their say, and while the President made up his mind, they found an open door at the White House. In July, Western congressmen urged Hanna to speak to McKinley about retaining the islands, apparently feeling that they afforded a rich agricultural market. Others reminded the President that "George Washington has been dead 100 years, and a great many things have happened since his day. . . ." The logical Orville Platt spoke for many in the party when he pointed out the position which Mc-

Kinley's conscience had already reached: duty presented no alternative but to retain the islands. "Shall we reach out beyond ourselves, shall we go forward or stand still? If we would maintain ourselves in the front rank we must go forward." [13]

By September all media available to the President indicated that the people favored retaining the islands.[14] Anti-expansionists in the party admitted that they were unpopular. "You and I don't want the Philippines," Secretary Long wrote a friend, "but it's no use disguising the fact that an overwhelming majority of the people do. . . ." Dawes perhaps reflected McKinley's thinking when he wrote flatly: "Whatever the result to our Nation, the retention of the Philippines was inevitable from the first. No man, or no party, could have prevented it." [15]

And what did the President think? As he sat smoking and listening to his endless callers, what thoughts passed through his mind? Did he smile at their earnest emphasis, thinking that they only fortified a conclusion he had already reached, or did he wait to be convinced of a policy from which he shrank? As early as May, Lodge reported to Roosevelt with satisfaction that the President was "sound." "Unless I am utterly and profoundly mistaken the Administration is now fully committed to the large policy that we both desire." Late in June he and Mahan worked on Day with thoughts of destiny, and the quiet Judge finally agreed. Early in July, Lodge thought that McKinley was "a little timid," but by the last of that month felt that he was convinced. "I think his imagination is touched by the situation, and I think he grasps it fully." [16] As the final preparations for the departing peace commission ended in September, the usually sedate Washington *Post* could report that the administration would keep the islands.[17]

The really crucial problem did not develop in the United States or in Paris, but in Manila, where the situation resembled a powder keg. McKinley knew that he was ignorant of the full situation there; yet he hoped that his pacific intentions would prevent trouble. Consular reports strengthened this hope for a pacific policy. The military commanders who had relieved Dewey in August were divided, but General Otis reported at first that he expected no trouble. The conservative Filipino citizenry, it was said, wanted American rule and order.[18] The correspondents failed to say how few in number such citizens were.

The "little brown brothers" who sat encamped near Manila watched their American liberators with experienced eyes; how much they looked and acted like the Spanish. Blissfully ignorant of their real situation, the American soldiers were often uncouth and overbearing toward the "niggers," as they called the Filipinos. Tragically, the Americans never realized or never admitted until it was too late that Aguinaldo headed a full-scale independence movement, and would be satisfied with nothing else.

In the year between December, 1897, and December, 1898, a score of private emissaries had passed between the two camps, Filipino and American. The Filipino junta in Hong Kong had been cheered by American officials there, who without authorization spoke in veiled terms of independence and American aid. After Dewey's victory, as the American ships swung slowly at anchor in the blazing harbor day after day, other officials assured the natives that some kind of deal would be worked out later. As time ran out late in 1898, the Filipinos still clung to the hope that the Americans would grant some kind of self-rule. Dewey's later categorical denial, "I never dreamed that they wanted independence," smacks of naiveté remarkable even in the Admiral.[19]

Aguinaldo often seemed comical. His childish preoccupation with fancy clothes and court etiquette obscured for many his talents for leadership and the respect he commanded in the islands. "They are big children whom one must treat as little ones," one correspondent to the President noted in words he must have rued a year later. The military, naturally suspicious of any potential enemy, tended to brusqueness in dealing with the natives. General Thomas Anderson warned the administration in mid-July to expect trouble.[20] Manila fell after a joint effort with the insurgents on August 13, one embarrassing day after the signing of the peace protocol, due to delays in communication. But while the Filipinos might fight the Spanish with the Americans, Washington still forbade any official joint occupation of the city, or any recognition of their rule.[21]

Disturbed and puzzled by the protracted silence from Washington, Aguinaldo ordered his trusted advisor, Felipe Agoncillo, then in the United States, to speak to McKinley himself to dispel the growing suspicion that liberty had not yet come. On October 1, Agoncillo met the President in his office. McKinley listened to a long account of Spanish misrule and the Filipino struggle for freedom, delivered tediously through an interpreter. The afternoon was pleasant and drowsy; time passed idly through the hands of a clock at which the President looked from time to time. He noted Agoncillo's allusions to promises of independence and shifted uneasily in his chair. When he had finished, McKinley asked politely if that was all. Agoncillo asked if he could speak to the peace commission, but the President declined. He suggested tactfully that the Filipino commit his remarks to paper so that he might study them at his leisure. Ten prosy points resulted, and Adee took the paper from the little brown men with a chilly injunction that this did not imply recognition.[22]

Mid-September brought the President an opportunity to define his position. On September 16 the peace commissioners gathered at the White House for dinner and a last conference before going abroad. McKinley talked informally and ascertained their own views. Day still opposed taking the islands. Reid and Frye wanted them all. Davis wanted only part, but was clearly open to persuasion. Gray still adamantly opposed taking any part of them. The President said with surprising frankness that he felt the people demanded full retention, but did not go further.[23]

The formal instructions which he read held no surprises. The United States did not wish to annex Cuba, he reaffirmed, but would acquire Porto Rico and end Spanish rule in the hemisphere. The Philippines were a different matter; the tone of his remarks indicated that they too would be taken. The old tone of destiny was there. "The march of events rules and over-rules human action." The least the United States could demand was Luzon, and clearly this would not be enough.[24] The dignified group left early in the evening, almost fearful of the coming negotiations to begin in two weeks.

How rapidly the scene shifted. The cables ran from Manila to Hawaii, to the United States, and on to places he had never heard of a year or two before. The problems all loomed up, growing like weeds if left untended. In the days that followed he remembered Hanna's insistent voice: the party's salvation depended on a presidential tour; the people must see their victorious chief. In the silence of his own thoughts, McKinley knew that Hanna was right. It was also an excellent chance to see if opinion had come around to his position.

In late September the national committee forwarded to him data on all Republican candidates in the Midwest, and McKinley announced that he would tour the area. The response was quick; he must come into every district. Of course, it was said, he would not come as a Republican, but as president of all the people. But naturally he would help the Republican candidates, defend his own record, and define his stand on the Philippine issue.

The President's entry into the off-year elections was little short of historic. Wary of partisanship, McKinley chose to stand on general principles, assuming rightly that all voters would connect him with the Republican candidates. He moved west in a special train, and for two weeks in October spoke several times daily in most of the states between Ohio and the Dakotas. The chief event of the tour was an appearance at the Trans-Mississippi Exposition at Omaha on October 12.[25]

The President did not disappoint his party or his people. Wherever he went he evoked storms of approval. At the crossroads and smaller stops the people turned out in droves to hear the man whom many of them had hissed a year ago. Speaking in generalities he offended no one with his brief, careful remarks, tailored to each stop. He said little of note, for characteristically he was listening "with at least one ear to the ground," as an Iowa politician recalled. He sounded opinion among politicians and shook hundreds of hands. He was in his milieu. He loved contact with the people, and the reporters who tagged along noted the tonic effect his appearance had on local campaigns. The Democrats admitted privately that he insured a Republican victory. Peace, prosperity, the strength of a revitalized America were his texts. But his subtle references to expansion, duty, and destiny roused the greatest cheers. "We have good money, we have ample revenues, we have unquestioned national credit," he told a people basking in unprecedented prosperity and ignorant of foreign complications, "but we want new markets, and as trade follows the flag, it looks very much as if we were going to have new markets." [26]

Late in October he and Ida returned to Washington, aglow from their experience. It was all "most delightful," he wrote Reid in

Paris. "Everywhere there were the most enthusiastic demonstrations and the Government seemed to have the hearty support and encouragement of the people." [27] His private callers noted a change in him. "None of us have been able to move him since he returned from the west," Secretary Bliss told Andrew Carnegie. The stubborn Scotsman found his old friend committed to keeping the islands; the people would permit nothing else, he said. The November elections pleased the President; the new Congress in 1899 would not be overwhelmingly Republican, but there were safe margins in both houses. Enough safe senators had apparently been endorsed to insure the treaty's ratification later should it fail at the present session. He would have disagreed with Lodge, who called it "a sweep," but it would do. Hanna saw that the President's coalition had weathered a crucial mid-term election in good form. Free silver had failed to catch votes. "That means continued prosperity and Republican success." [28]

In distant Paris the cheers surrounding the President's tour came only vaguely through the cables to the American commission that gathered in the French capital late in September to negotiate the peace treaty. The French hosts spread before the two delegations a traditional Gallic hospitality that combined conviviality and dignity. The diplomats of Spain and the United States met in a high-ceilinged, well-aired room in the French foreign ministry at the historic Quai d'Orsay. Though the Americans faced with dread the prospect of tedious discussions with the Spanish, their counterparts seemed to be "men of ability and dignity." [29]

The Spanish hoped to dispose of the Philippine problem first. At the initial meeting on October 1, they assumed the tone of "rather proud supplication" which they retained throughout the conferences. Their demand that the United States evacuate the islands met the quick answer that the Americans would discuss the other problem first; they must wait upon formal instructions from McKinley on the Philippines.[30]

The disposition of Cuba consumed the remainder of the month, and the tedium with which the Spanish pursued the vain hope of giving the island and its debts to the United States cost Senator Davis many cigars as he sat somnolently through the long-winded talk. The American refusal to take the island exploded the Spanish belief that the war had been for conquest after all. The Americans would take the island in trust, following McKinley's directions, and the Spanish argued that this involved taking the Cuban debt. The debt, estimated at as much as $400,000,000, did not entice the Americans, who held that none of it had been spent on pacific internal improvements, but their sour looks and persistent refusals did not stop the Spanish argument. "The Spanish mind is infinite in its resources . . . ," Day wired home mournfully as he perused the complex and endless papers with which his counterparts flooded him.[31]

Courtesy required that dinners and receptions occupy most of the evenings. At one such affair late in October, Senor Montero Rios cornered Reid with a proposition on the Cuban debt. It was, the Spanish chairman said, a small price to pay for Cuba. Reid replied that he did not want Cuba at any price and would not accept responsibility for the debt. The Spaniard hinted darkly that this might disrupt the conference, but Reid spurned any suggestion that a mixed commission discuss the debt.[32]

When all else failed, the Spanish asked the Americans at least to use their good offices with a future Cuban government to settle the debts, but all talk was futile. The more the Spanish talked the more rigid the Americans became. Angered by the slowness, McKinley abruptly wired on October 25 that the United States would not deal over the debt, and the Spanish accepted the position two days later.[33]

Both parties now turned to the more fascinating question of the Philippines. Gray still refused to be converted to empire, and Day still hoped that the United States would take only Luzon. But in the weeks following their arrival in Paris the persuasive Reid and Frye wrangled with their unconverted fellows amid much cigar smoke and arm-waving. As the commission met for the first time, Reid reported a definite weakening in Day, though Gray seemed as stubborn as ever.[34]

Feeling acutely their isolation from events, the commission took the President's advice and heard expert testimony when they were not negotiating. A parade of witnesses, distinguished and unknown alike, filed past them, answering their questions, reading statements, and leaving quantities of information behind. General Merritt, returning home from the Philippines, answered their questions with first-hand knowledge and favored retention of all the islands. Visiting "authorities" bent forward eagerly to describe the beauties and wealth of the islands. Army and Navy officers confirmed the feeling that it would be impossible to take only one island.[35]

Admiral Dewey's opinion weighed heavily, and the commission earnestly asked the President to forward his views to Paris. But Dewey was hard to pin down; now he would and now he wouldn't take the islands, and his evasiveness baffled the commission until they concluded that the Admiral wanted all the islands.[36] As the placid Sundays passed in this interrogation, the positions fell into place. The military opposed taking only one island or base; it would be impossible to hold or develop and it would divide the Filipinos themselves. The expansionists like Reid and Frye had but one choice. To the hesitant, like Day, the argument of duty appealed strongly; the natives were incapable of self-rule and we could not, as the President had once wished, simply sail away. On October 13, Dewey warned that a policy should be settled to alleviate the tension, adding as an afterthought the clinching argument to the moralists: "The natives appear unable to govern." [37]

Spanish long-windedness on Cuba foreboded a tedious discussion once the Philippines were reached, and Davis shuddered at the thought. "But I am getting tired of this ——— toil of dropping buckets into empty wells, and growing old in drawing nothing up, and so also are my associates." [38]

The problem of McKinley's silence remained. The peace commission followed his route across the country in October, assuming like everyone else that he was gauging opinion, but his lack of statement on expansion disturbed Reid and Frye. October 25, McKinley broke his long silence with a personal cable to Day, asking for the commission's opinions, saying in passing that "a very general feeling" dictated that the country "cannot let go." [39]

The presidential communication impelled Day to activity, and that same evening the cable wires carried the commission's views to Washington. Davis, Frye and Reid wanted all the islands, feeling that the fall of Manila delivered them all, since it was their focus. Opinion forbade retaining only part of the islands, and it was impossible to return them to Spain or to another power. Day still

favored the "hitching post" which the President had already ridiculed, fearing the consequences of total retention. Only the doughty
Senator Gray was still inflexible, pointing out with much cogency
that events there were unpredictable. Defense fixtures would cost
money, trade was uncertain, and it would be years before the islands
would repay the cost of taking them. For himself he stated the position which opponents to the treaty later assumed: empire was alien
and unconstitutional, since it involved government over people
without their consent.[40]

McKinley read the commission's views with interest, but he had
already made up his mind. While the commission had wrangled
over the Cuban debt in mid-October, the last act of the President's
little drama took place. He had heard on his tour the voice of the
people emphasizing the stand he had long since accepted with his
usual fatalism as inevitable. His visitors and heavy mail told the
same story. Of course there would be opposition; it would be a
party issue to the Democrats.

The alternatives available were not happy ones. It was manifestly impossible to release the islands to Spain; the people would
never agree. Simply to abandon them to another power would not
only be reprehensible, but dangerous as well. Taking just one island
would only deepen the problem, leaving it for later settlement. Proclaiming them autonomous under American auspices came to be the
least favorable course to the President, for it implied responsibility
without power. The only possible choice for him was acquisition of
all the islands.

On paper it was a prosaic decision, but it was not without its
drama, as he revealed in after years. The pressures on him were
great. With uncharacteristic self-revelation, he later told a group
of ministers how he had reached his final decision. "I have been criticized a good deal about the Philippines, but don't deserve it," he
said. Holding that he had never wanted the islands and did not
know what to do with them when they came "as a gift from the
gods," he explained that his only thought had been military victory
over the Spanish in Manila. He thought at first of retaining only
Manila, then only Luzon. He sought help from all parties but got
no comfort. After much prayer it came to him late one evening that
he had four choices: he could not return them to Spain, "that would

be cowardly and dishonorable"; he could not turn them over to another power, "that would be bad business and discreditable"; he could not leave them to themselves, for they were unfit for self-rule; "there was nothing left for us to do but to take them all, and to educate the Filipinos, and uplift and civilize and Christianize them, and by God's grace do the very best we could by them, as our fellow-men for whom Christ also died." Sleep followed, buttressed by belief in the soundness of his decision.[41]

What the ministers thought of this remarkable statement as they filed out into the night was unrecorded. A later generation, not knowing of McKinley's sincere if simple Christanity, finds it easy to scoff; God, they say, was unusually clear that night. The temptation is to credit McKinley rather than the Deity with the idea, which is doubtless true, for few of the President's statements more exactly describe his thought processes.

The statement is a classic outline of the alternatives available to the President, but he prefaced them with a somewhat ingenuous explanation of how the islands came to the United States. It is true that he later told many people that he had never wanted the islands and took them only after passing through the stages he mentioned. And yet the suspicion lingers that he must surely have known what unforeseen dangers he invited in ordering Dewey to Manila. No man in politics as long as he had been could think otherwise. In a sense, acquisition of the islands was not new, but was merely the logical conclusion of his administration's drift toward world power. Nor did he simply yield to public opinion, slavishly assuming that whatever a majority of the people wanted was right. In the end his sense of duty and responsibility, as well as a strong feeling of destiny, forced him to demand all the islands.[42]

He was conscious of the visions of empire that dazzled less sober men. In the summer of 1899 he told a group of visitors at Canton that "one of the best things we ever did was to insist upon taking the Philippines and not a coaling station or an island, for if we had done the latter we would have been the laughing-stock of the world." [43]

Thus McKinley at last declared publicly his allegiance to the expansionist dream. Did the expansionists envision the tragedies that lay in store for their policy? Some may have, but to most it did not matter. The fascinating question remains: did McKinley foresee the coming struggle in the Philippines? It is unlikely that he would have shrunk from it even if he had, for events made any other course untenable. He doubtless felt as he had so often in the past, that he was a prisoner of events. He had to gamble that the natives, faced with American power and intentions, would not start a revolution.

In Paris the crucial negotiations had almost come to an impasse when the President's final instructions came on October 26. The Spanish were tense and threatened to break off the conference unless they could return home with some kind of concessions. They must satisfy public opinion too, they reiterated, and the American commissioners saw some truth in their demands. The Spanish feared that their being saddled with the Cuban debt would bring down the monarchy.[44]

Realizing this, Senator Frye had an idea which might soften the coming blow for Spain. On October 30, he cabled home a solution. To sweeten the pill and strengthen the American stand, would it not be wise and fair to offer a money settlement for the Philippines? It could be justified at home as payment for internal improvements, it would somewhat mitigate the questionable American claims to the islands by right of conquest, and it would insure further negotiations by giving the Spanish something to take home. On November 1, McKinley agreed to paying the sum Frye had mentioned, between ten and twenty million dollars.[45]

Now united in the President's demand, the American commissioners awaited the session of November 1 with mixed emotions. The air was strained, and they knew the burden under which the Spanish already labored. The demand for the islands might cause either a rupture in the talks or a fatal delay. The Spanish listened with an air of "resigned attention" as Day read the American demands. When the translation was finished, Montero Rios jumped up and asked for time to consult his government.[46]

The wires to Madrid burned with indignation as the Spanish delegation expressed their "amazement" and outrage at the American demands, which the home government called "the greatest extreme imaginable. . . ."[47] On November 2, the Spanish leaped at the loophole in the American claim: the islands were not theirs by right of conquest since Manila had fallen after the armistice. The American delegation felt a certain embarrassment in defending its own position, recognizing all too painfully that "we are dealing with people marvellously expert in argumentation. They are resourceful in obscuring that which seems plain." [48]

On November 13, McKinley curtly said that he expected the negotiations to close soon. Hay reinforced this warning three days later, saying that the Spanish would be responsible for any break.[49]

The Spanish dilemma was a cruel one. They valued the islands at ten times what the Americans would pay, but economics was not the problem. As always, Spanish pride hurt more than the Spanish pocketbook. But it was hopeless to prolong the negotiations, as the Queen Regent saw, for though the two commissions had worked courteously together "in a cloud of tobacco smoke diligently maintained by Senators Davis and Frye . . . ," the Americans would not weaken.[50]

In mid-November, Day determined to conclude the negotiations. "We are now disposed to force this matter to an issue, realizing that we have been here a long time, and that argument is exhausted on the subject," he wrote the President. Reid continued his personal diplomacy and on November 22, frankly told Leon y Castillo that it was all over.[51]

The end came quickly. On November 28, Reid watched the Spanish as the dignified old Montero Rios capitulated. The day was cloudy, and just as the conference adjourned in "mournful dignity," the sun broke through and threw a shaft of light onto the green-topped table. Reid remarked that it was a bright omen, smiling pleasantly at his opponents. "No, everything is gloom around us," a Spaniard replied, and the group filed slowly out of the room and down separate corridors.[52] On December 10, Day wired home that the treaty had been formally signed.

To the Spanish it was all tragedy. "The treaty is the pure expression of the immoderate demands of a conqueror, who, in order to appear great in history, ought to have made moderate use of its victory," Montero Rios wired home.[53] But to the Americans it was different. The usually laconic and restrained Day, touched perhaps by visions of the empire his country gained from the treaty, was unusually ebullient. Their work had brought the country "a goodly estate indeed!" [54]

December had brought cold weather but a warm inspiration to the nation's capital. Would it not be fitting and wise, McKinley suggested, for him and an official party to journey to Atlanta to take part in a mammoth celebration of the country's victory over Spain, and just as importantly, to show that the last vestiges of sectionalism were gone? The idea appealed to McKinley, who realized fully just how much his name had come to symbolize not only to his party but to the whole country: victory over foreign foes, peace, prosperity, and now empire.

The President's tour to the South in mid-December was an unqualified success and a demonstration of the effect his personality had had upon the country. Every crossroad between Washington and Atlanta boasted a group of cheering citizens, and every city and town vied for his presence. In the crowds that came to see him gray mingled with blue and an occasional khaki uniform on a younger man.

In Atlanta the state legislature assembled in joint session amid a crush of flowers and visitors to greet McKinley, whose appearance in company with Joe Wheeler and dignitaries of both parties set off an eruption of applause. The gray badge on his coat indicated that he had made his peace. His speech breathed the sense of well-being, amity, and prosperity which he had detected across the country. The great capitol dome rocked with cheers in response to his suggestion that Northern groups "share with you the care of the graves of Confederate dead." His reception elsewhere in the South was equally invigorating, and he returned home resolved to conclude his long-sought domestic program, confident that all sections supported him.[55]

He had need of all the support he could gain, for he returned to find party leaders fraught with worry over the treaty just returned from Paris. "Whatever treaty we get here, I suppose, will meet with considerable opposition in the Senate," Day had wired from Paris almost offhandedly, "but no doubt you are much more familiar with that situation than we can be." [56] As the President looked over the Senate that would pass on the treaty he saw four groups: the administration Republicans, committed to its ratification; the anti-administration Republicans like Hoar and Hale, opposed to it; the Democrats under Gorman opposed to it; and the Democrats under Bryan who, for differing motives, favored its ratification.

The opposition was worrisome; not only would it delay the treaty and make it a partisan issue, it had formidable arguments against ratification, defined first and best in the resolution introduced by Senator Vest of Missouri on December 6, even before the treaty was finished. Empire, it read, was alien to the American spirit and unconstitutional; the Philippines could not be acquired. The treaty's opponents could easily wrap themselves in historic American rhetoric, as Hoar did, about freedom and self-government.

Of all the groups that opposed the treaty, the Democrats irritated McKinley most. Had they not helped start the war over his objections? And now, having helped so much to provoke the conflict, they refused to accept the responsibilities for their actions. He could forgive Senator Hoar, not merely because he was a Republican, but because he felt he was sincere in his opposition, but he could not forgive the short-sighted and unpredictable Democrats. It promised to be a bitter fight, with many unexpected turns. Lodge's injunction to Roosevelt early in December that "we are going to have trouble over the treaty" was an understatement.[57]

The President's most baffling problem was Senator Hoar. Long a party regular and powerful with much of the public, his defection could be serious. McKinley's tact and charm were vain. Asked how he felt, the Senator responded with a glitter in his eyes, "Pretty pugnacious, I confess, Mr. President." McKinley took his hand. "I shall always love you, whatever you do." Hoar was not moved to change his mind.[58] His grounds were the highest, and he argued consistently that the constitution forbade acquisition of lands not intended to be organized into states.

Though he continued to entertain a high opinion of McKinley, Hoar thought him his chief enemy. He knew that the administration would spare neither ruthlessness nor the subtler charms of patronage to have its way. He did his share to fill the *Record* with finely printed pages of rhetoric, and he made enemies. "It is difficult for me to speak with moderation of such men as Hoar," Roosevelt said. "They are little better than traitors." [59] That Eugene Hale could actually join Hoar in the teeth of expansionist sentiment in his own state was salt in Republican wounds.

It was one thing to face opposition in Congress, but quite another to find a formidable body of influential men in private life willing to fight the treaty by arousing public opinion. Chief among these was an old beneficiary of Republican programs, Andrew Carnegie. The doughty steelmaster, who was a familiar figure to McKinley, and whose purse had been open in many campaigns, now called on his old friend with different matters in mind. He found McKinley exasperatingly determined to retain the Philippines.[60]

Carnegie was not above accusing McKinley of desiring to be a dictator and of seeking to use the new expanded army to enforce his hellish will after he had dazzled the mob with visions of empire. In this he made an ironic judgment, common to many of McKinley's opponents. They called him weak, and a pleaser of the crowd, even as they accused him of harboring dictatorial ambitions. Carnegie's shrill voice rose even in October. "Our young men volunteered to fight the oppressor; I shall be surprised if they relish the work of shooting down the oppressed." [61]

To the men around the President, Carnegie seemed almost mad. "Andrew Carnegie really seems to be off his head," Hay wrote Reid. "He writes me frantic letters signing them 'Your Bitterest Opponent.' He threatens the President, not only with the vengeance of the voters, but with practical punishment at the hands of the mob." [62] Carnegie's real danger was not his voice, but the impetus he could give to an anti-treaty coalition, for money was his magic wand. "You have brains and I have dollars," he told the aged but active anti-expansionist Carl Schurz. "I can devote some of my dollars to spreading your brains." [63]

Carnegie was not alone, and as winter deepened over the nation a curious group of men took up the anti-expansionist cause. Carnegie, Hoar, Hale, Schurz were joined by the prominent businessman, Edward Atkinson; representatives of labor who feared Filipino competition; Thomas B. Reed; ex-president Grover Cleveland, and assorted figures. "What a singular collection the so-called anti-imperialists are getting together," Lodge wrote in exasperation.[64]

The most curiously ironic was the man who came to Washington in mid-December to help ratify the treaty, William Jennings Bryan.[65] His contention that the Democrats must ratify the treaty took many, especially Republicans, off guard, for he was the natural leader of McKinley's opposition. During the war, "military lockjaw" had mercifully kept his mouth closed, but when peace came he was voluble in opposing expansion. As early as June he charged that the war had turned from one for humanity to one for conquest. Throughout the fall and early winter he kept up his attack on the expansionists. "Shall we keep the Philippines and amend our flag?" he asked on Christmas eve. "Shall we add a new star—the blood star, Mars—to indicate that we have entered upon a career of conquest?" In the tense days of early January, he swept aside expansionist clichés about duty and destiny. The commandment to "preach the gospel to every creature," he would say, did not include a "Gatling gun attachment." [66]

To those around him, Bryan's motives seemed confused, despite his insistence that they were simple. He wished at first simply to ratify the treaty in order to kill the imperialism issue before the election of 1900, which could then be fought on silver. Andrew Carnegie's angry protests that silver was dead and that expansion was now the paramount issue in American politics met a short rejoinder from the Great Commoner: ". . . you need not delude yourself with the idea that silver is dead." [67] Tom Reed's remark that Bryan had rather be wrong than president seemed true after all.

Bryan's motives were more complex. He perceived that it would be suicide for the Democrats to defeat the treaty and take the responsibility for technically continuing the war, as he told Senator Pettigrew in unsuccessfully asking him to vote for ratification. He had a rather curious view of the treaty as a whole. "By ratifying the treaty we settled the question with Spain and gave to ourselves the entire control of the Philippine situation," he remembered.[68] He never seemed to have understood that ratification would be a blank check for the administration to do with the islands as it pleased.

Carnegie was beside himself with rage at Bryan, feeling that he and his helpers had brought the treaty to defeat, only to have Bryan throw the question into doubt again. Hoar felt that Bryan swung doubtful Populists toward the treaty and was a deciding factor. But Bryan persisted in his demands through January. "To reject [the treaty] would throw the subject back into the hands of the administration and those who prevented its ratification would be held responsible for anything that might happen," he wrote Carnegie. In the end he was willing to have the people vote on the whole issue in 1900.[69]

The debates in the Senate themselves were historic, since they were concerned with the nature of the constitution itself. Debate began on the treaty in mid-December, with Orville Platt's strong speech in its support. "Providence has put it upon us. We propose to execute it." In the arguments that followed he stated the administration point of view succinctly: the constitution implicitly permitted all acts of sovereignty, and the acquisition of land was among these.[70]

Hoar's labored speeches contained sardonic wit. The President's cry, "Who will haul down the flag," should read, "Who will haul down the president," the old man said acidly to a mixture of applause and laughter. The men now avid for acquiring the islands were remarkable for their ignorance, a Democrat rejoined. "Why, six months ago men who talk that way did not know where the Philippines are!"[71]

The tedious arguments over constitutionality passed most Americans by, but they were susceptible to both logic and emotion. Lodge made a telling argument when he said bluntly:

> The President cannot be sent back across the Atlantic, in the person of his commissioners, hat in hand, to say to Spain with bated breath: "I am here in obedience to the mandate of a minority of one third of the Senate to tell you that we have been too victorious, and that you have yielded too much, and that I am very sorry that I took the Philippines from you." I do not think that any American President would do that, or that any American would wish him to.[72]

Leadership for the administration fell to Lodge, Aldrich, and Hanna, who spoke little on the issue but who did the necessary work in the cloakrooms. In the Democratic party, Bryan's entry split the opposition. Maryland's Arthur P. Gorman seized the opportunity to lead dissident Democrats; if he could defeat the treaty and Bryan, perhaps he could wrest party leadership from the Boy Orator for the nomination in 1900. He knew that the lame duck vote of senators defeated at the last elections could defeat the treaty, and he was not above cooperation with Hoar and Hale.

As the debates developed in executive sessions, ugly charges of bribery and coercion mounted: The administration was dangling patronage plums before wavering Republicans and bribing sympathetic Populists and Democrats with promises of jobs; Aldrich was willing to juggle committee assignments for the faithful. Hoar charged George Gray later with taking a federal judgeship as a reward for his work.[73]

McKinley himself remained unobtrusive, refusing to entertain any idea of amending the treaty. He was not averse, however, to using all his charm and persuasive powers, as well as the more solid offerings of patronage, in return for votes. The genial Hobart, almost the President's alter ego, turned every screw with his legendary politeness. Hanna presumably spoke for the President and interceded several times, promising his listeners that McKinley would not forget them. As January passed and the date for the vote, set for Monday, February 6, approached, Lodge took some heart, feeling that at the last moment the crucial wavering Republicans would return safely to the fold.[74]

As tension mounted in Washington the focus of events shifted quietly to Manila, where insurgents under Aguinaldo, feeling betrayed and seeing the administration's designs at last, prepared to take up arms. By late November some officers warned the administration to expect trouble if all the islands were retained. And yet this tension was but vaguely reflected in Washington, for while General Otis in one breath gloomily predicted trouble, in the next he thought otherwise, and to this were added conflicting reports from other quarters. On January 30, Admiral Dewey, in whom McKinley placed a great deal of faith, wrote Long: "I do not think the insurgents will fight." [75]

McKinley's persistent silence angered the Filipinos almost more than the American army. What could they expect? Had he only given Agoncillo some hope in October, things might have been less tense now. If only he would say that he favored ultimate independence for the islands, perhaps a clash could be averted. The President's position remained that of the silent watcher, but this time was more complicated than usual. He did not wish a struggle in the islands, but he felt sincerely that he could not properly speak on future policy until Spanish sovereignty was relinquished with ratification of the treaty. Visitors to the White House said he favored ultimate independence, but there was no confirmation.[76]

It was a touchy problem. Alive to public demands and political pressures, he could not risk a conflict and yet could not take steps to prevent one. "We are in an anomalous position," he complained to Cortelyou. "The people want us to hold everything but the soldiers, forgetting that without them we could not hold anything." [77] In retrospect his strict construction of his rights during the treaty discussion seems a singular error; he could at least have allowed a "leak" through reliable sources to define his proposed attitude toward the islands. It may not have prevented conflict but it would have clarified his own position, focused his policy, and improved his standing with all parties.

Initiative now passed to Manila, where Aguinaldo and his advisors, upon learning that the treaty gave the islands to the United States, began the events that led to the insurrection. On January 5, he proclaimed an independent Philippine Republic, and warning cables crossed the Pacific. The conclusion came on the night of February 4, when an American sentry challenged a Filipino who failed to respond properly, and in a matter of hours the whole perimeter of the two forces was engaged.

In Washington, McKinley received the first cables with dismay and then with a kind of resigned sadness. "It is always the unexpected that happens, at least in my case. How foolish these people are. This means the ratification of the treaty; the people will insist on ratification." [78] He was right, for as the country digested the news over the weekend, recalcitrant senators made up their minds; the doubtful Republicans came back.

The President did not say what the news meant to him, though he later remarked that he "never dreamed" the Filipinos would return "our mercy with a Mauser." [79] As had been the case so often in the last two years, unpredictable events swept his hopes from under him. But he retained good intentions toward the Filipinos. They were a sacred trust, and it was not too much to say that for the rest of his life their welfare was second in his mind only to that of America.

On Saturday, Lodge counted 58 sure votes and 4 doubtful ones. On Sunday one of these went over to the opposition, and Monday came with only 58 votes certain; he needed 60 if all the senators voted. As the Senate balloted, 3 of these 4 came over, 1 after the roll call, giving the treaty the necessary two-thirds plus 1, with a vote of 57 to 27. When the result was clear, Lodge felt a great weight pass from his shoulders, as if he had been climbing a mountain. He, Hanna, Aldrich, Chandler, and Elkins got little credit because they seldom spoke. "We were down in the engine room and do not get flowers, but we did make the ship move." [80]

As Hobart announced the vote, Hanna rushed through the chamber doors into the packed corridors, hands over his head in a victory gesture. Moments after the Senate's action McKinley had the treaty, surrounded by friends and well-wishers. He could have agreed with Lodge: "We ratified the treaty yesterday, after the closest, most bitter, and most exciting struggle I have ever known, or ever expect to see in the Senate." [81]

As McKinley accepted the congratulations, controversy eddied around the Capitol as to who "saved" the treaty. "The war at Manila helped us," Chandler noted in his diary, but Lodge disagreed, noting to his surprise that opposition ranks did not break after February 4. He laid success "partly to the Senate, partly to Providence, and partly to the Filipinos." [82]

Andrew Carnegie brooded darkly over the result, blaming his new nemesis, Bryan, saying once in retrospect that "one word from Mr. Bryan would have saved the country from disaster." But when he thought about it more deeply, he was wiser in laying the credit, or blame, for the treaty's ratification at McKinley's doorstep. He had all the advantages and used them well. "This is the President's own Pandora's box—this New Year's gift to the country, for which he is responsible," he wrote Schurz. [83]

One more test remained when a few days after ratification, Senator Bacon's resolution favoring ultimate independence for the Philippines was defeated by Hobart's deciding vote, showing how closely the Senate was still divided. To McKinley fell the task of healing the party's breaches, and Hay and Lodge were surprised and a little angry to see Hoar's placid countenance in the President's office a few days later, smiling under McKinley's kindness. They felt more than a twinge of bitterness, but Hoar left feeling that McKinley would do his best to uplift the islands. [84]

Thus the wearisome congressional session ended, and the President was not sorry. He would have some nine months to define and implement a new Philippine policy before Congress reassembled. By that time perhaps he could solve the basic problems and retain in the process his ever growing stature as a national president. He must define his policy now that the treaty was safe, must give some hint of the things to come. He entrained for Boston, despite a blizzard that swept down out of New England, to speak on February 16 to his old friends at the Home Market Club.

Almost two thousand guests flooded out over the great ballroom, served by a corps of waiters directed by a flag system. The room lay swathed in flowers and bunting, and portraits of Washington and Lincoln flanked McKinley's. When he rose to speak applause engulfed him, and he gathered uncommon fire for his words. His resonant tone rolled out over the great audience. He justified acquiring the Philippines as the only alternative available, given the political and humanitarian forces at work. Invoking a higher law to justify the pacification of the islands, he turned scornfully against his late opponents who talked of self-determination in the islands. "It is not a good time for the liberator to submit important questions concerning liberty and government to the liberated while they are engaged in shooting down their rescuers." He emphasized that he alone would direct policy in the islands, and that he accepted full responsibility for past and future decisions. "That the inhabitants of the Philippines will be benefited by this republic is my unshaken belief. . . . No imperial designs lurk in the American mind. . . . Our priceless principles undergo no change under a tropical sun." In closing he outlined his own vision of the future Philippines:

> . . . a land of plenty and of increasing possibilities; a people redeemed from savage indolence and habits, devoted to the arts of peace, in touch with the commerce and trade of all nations, enjoying the blessings of freedom, of civil and religious liberty, of education, and of homes, and whose children and children's children shall for ages hence bless the American republic because it emancipated their fatherland, and set them in the pathway of the world's best civilization.

It was a noble dream and a forceful speech, a major utterance in McKinley's presidency, and many who had derided him as weak and without character took fresh note.[85] The problem now, as winter skies cleared for spring, was to make the dream come true.

✺ XIX ✺

Problems of Empire

O N SEPTEMBER 24, 1898, a group of distinguished men met at the White House for a talk with President McKinley. They were entrusted with a task that demanded both speed and diplomacy. Officially constituted as the Commission Appointed by the President to Investigate the Conduct of the War Department in the War with Spain, it was their official task to see if the rumors, charges, and countercharges that swirled around Secretary Alger were true. The Secretary himself had asked the President to form the commission in a formal letter on September 8. He was confident that a board of the "most distinguished soldiers and civilians that can be selected" would absolve him and his department.

The commission chairman, Iowa's old General Grenville Dodge, about whom still hung not only the glamor of war but the faint flavor of conquests on the western frontier on behalf of the Union Pacific Railroad which he had helped build, greeted the President cordially. McKinley wasted no time, and left no doubt about the commission's task. He emphasized the formal statement, which he read with flourishes of his hand, looking now and then at his attentive listeners. He was disturbed, he said, both officially and as a citizen, by the charges levelled against Alger and his department. The public was entitled to know who, if anyone, was to blame, and if criminal acts were committed the guilty parties would be punished; "I put upon you no limit to the scope of your investigation," he said earnestly. With his instructions in mind, the commission shook hands and left the mansion, hurrying through the afternoon heat to begin their unenviable task.[1]

Their problem had not lessened in the weeks since the war's end. The cessation of hostilities did not end criticism, and though the President remained persistently silent on the subject and retained cordial public relations with Alger, there could be no doubt that he

424

was disturbed. He was not blind to the political implications of such charges in this election year, but his concern and distress ran far deeper than party feelings. Of all the charges put forth during the war, none so angered him as those dealing with corruption and favoritism. If Alger had been criminally negligent, he wished it known.

Public feeling had reached such a pitch at the war's close that the Secretary was not always at ease in his tours of the demobilization camps that housed returning soldiers. Their facilities were crude, their food poor, medical attention sporadic, especially at Point Montauk. When it was announced that Alger would visit the camp in September, the soldiers chose a spokesman to present their case. As Alger came abreast of the grumbling men he asked rather gently if anything was wrong. The spokesman hesitated, but behind him a chorus called insistently, "Go on, get going!" and the soldiers unloaded their woes on the Secretary.[2]

Personal confrontation was one thing; it could be dismissed as the result of ignorance or personal spite. But the swelling chorus of opinion in the newspapers that Alger must go was more alarming. Tama Jim Wilson was frankly worried, hoping privately to Senator Allison that Alger could take a hint and have a commission appointed to air the charges. An even better solution would be the Secretary's resignation.[3]

Alger reacted with predictable irritability and intransigence. Ambition and pride of place had long since combined to give him the political skin of an elephant. It was all, he insisted, the work of political malcontents. On October 2, as the Dodge Commission began its labors, he said crankily to a reporter: "I am not on trial. Nobody is more anxious than I am to have everything righted. . . . If all the Departments had a year or two to get ready it would have been different." [4] To the end he posed as the victim of public opinion, and as time turned his wounded pride to the canker of personal spite, he blamed the President for "abandoning" him.[5]

General Dodge could devise no such simple explanation. He was an old friend of Senator Allison's, an arch-conservative, with connections in the business world as well as the Republican party, but he was fair-minded and honest. He was so closely connected with Alger and the party that he rejected the President's first offers of the task, though finally surrendering to McKinley's usual appeal to patriotism.[6]

The opposition Democrats smelled a whitewash, pointing to Dodge and his colleagues as ample proof that the President intended to smother the charges of neglect and incompetence with the cloak of discreet inquiry. Dodge never hid his own views, saying later privately that the Democrats had no grounds for their charges. "This attack is not on beef," he bluntly told a friend, "it is on the administration," and added in an unconscious pun that the opposition press had "cowed" the Republicans into an investigation.[7]

Whatever others may have thought, the President was in no mood for a whitewash. He did not doubt that much had been mismanaged in the War Department under the pressure of events, but that was not criminal negligence or corruption. He was anxious to air the whole problem in the hope that Congress would use the commission's recommendations to reform the Army, a subject to which he had already turned.

The commission's star witnesses came from the Army and Navy, and as they passed in a monotonous procession to fill many fine columns of type with their reports and opinions, the hearings lost public interest. And then General Miles appeared in December with sensational charges that rated headlines in the press and alarmed the administration. Stung by his fancied ill-treatment during the war, and angered by the administration's policies, Miles lashed out with surprising venom and dark connotations of evil designs at the men and agencies which had supplied the army.

He objected chiefly to the beef supplied his men. "I do not think that beef such as was sent to Cuba or Porto Rico would be good in any country in the stomach of any man," the "Brave Peacock" said forcefully. As he proceeded his tone grew more sinister. "I do not know what may have been injected into it," hinting that the beef had been preserved with poisons. As he talked, the ugly epithet "embalmed beef" dropped from his lips. Shades of a sinister plot on the part of the Beef Trust rose in the press. "The understanding is that this is a secret process of preserving beef," he reaffirmed. Not once did he substantiate his charges with anything but personal recollection and opinion, which was always aimed at the press gallery, but he created a public sensation.[8]

426

The President was at first shocked and then outraged at Miles's testimony. Dignity forbade any direct reply, but the General was never again welcome except on formal business. Alger related in after years that McKinley determined to break Miles, though he would not agree to the court martial which Alger recommended. As usual, the Secretary ridiculed the President's lenience as weakness, not recognizing the same balm when applied to his wounds.[9]

Through the winter and into the spring, after the commission made its formal report, the charges of "embalmed beef" continued. One bystander could not keep silent when his name was mentioned. When newspapers hinted that Senator Hanna had been allied with the Beef Trust that fleeced the Treasury and poisoned the troops, he exploded to the President. Heads should roll, he affirmed in a hasty, torrid scrawl. "I bring this to you for I am in serious earnest, for I won't stand for this sort of thing any longer!"[10]

The President wisely counselled prudence and caution, for it was not his place to reply. Interference would look like dictation; they would do better to wait. The formal responsibility for reply lay with the commissary general, Charles P. Eagen. Eagen was shocked into a loss of judgment by Miles's charges, and spent the days before his own testimony in a mounting fever of rage and nervous irritation. When he appeared he covered the Major General Commanding with verbal offal, calling him a liar and a traitor, spicing his written statement with language that the commission ruled out of order. Breaking down during his testimony, Eagen was relieved of his command and court-martialled for conduct unbecoming an officer. He was sentenced to dismissal from the service, but the lenient President softened it. There was no victor in the sally, only a blotch of tarnished reputations, questionable rhetoric, and unfounded charges.

The yellow press revelled in the display of dirty laundry and rioted again in disclosures, red ink, and extras. Nothing seemed to satisfy its craving for the lurid. And it was not only the questionable press at that, for such staid and hitherto reliable organs as the *Tribune* joined the catcalls for a time. The latter's defection shook the President, for he had tolerated a great deal from Reid. It all proved one thing anyway, he told Cortelyou, "and that was that you could get at a man's true character" in such a crisis.[11]

427

Through January the commission took testimony, and returned a report on February 9, 1899. Its nine packed volumes held not only a kind of history of the war, but a wealth of conflicting testimony. Miles was not alone in his charges, but other responsible officers in the Army like the fast-rising Leonard Wood noted honestly that yellow fever struck the best as well as the worst camps. The real problems arose from inexperience rather than dishonesty.[12]

The commission's report bore reading in Congress, for it was testimony to the Army's needs. There must be a central staff system for future conflicts, a logical and rapidly expanded method of supply, new equipment, new methods of training, and centralized authority. The commission found no evidence to support the spectacular charges of "embalmed beef." The tinned roast beef had often been tasteless and revolting in appearance, but chemical tests revealed no poisons.[13]

Dodge left no doubt in the President's mind that while there had been mismanagement and incompetence, there had been very little criminal negligence.[14] But he was not overly sanguine about military reforms in Congress. "It seems a foregone conclusion that this country will never do anything for the Army until we are placed in some position some time that will compel action to be taken," he wrote a friend.[15]

The commission disbanded in February with the President's thanks. The yellow press swept aside its findings as irrelevant, and unfortunately many good recommendations smothered in its report. Alger's successor used much of its findings in the brilliant annual reports that outlined America's modern army after 1899.

The commission said in effect that Alger's sins were those of omission rather than commission, and the Secretary blithely assumed that he was cleared. The President still showed no inclination to fire him. McKinley went out of his way to ease the tension around him, for everyone in the administration except Alger seemed to know that his end was at hand. Jokes were current within the cabinet itself, but not within the President's earshot. Returning from an official engagement in Boston in February, he soothed Alger's ruffled feelings when the Secretary took umbrage at another cabinet member's remarks.[16]

Alger always shuffled the blame for wartime mistakes, pointing

428

like the boy in the circle to the next man when guilt was mentioned.[17] But the public thought otherwise and did not hide its feelings. In mid-February, after the commission's report, Alger met cries of "Yah! Yah! Beef!" at a Grand Army encampment.[18]

The men around McKinley had assumed that he would ask Alger to resign after the commission reported. There was no reason to cater to him any longer; he could now depart gracefully, having been officially vindicated. But McKinley maintained a baffling silence for five more months. "Much pressure is being brought upon the President to ask for his resignation," Dawes noted, "but he pays no attention to it." [19] McKinley may well have felt that Alger need not now resign, having been cleared. But the real reason was more personal; he was simply too squeamish to face a showdown with Alger, whose temper fits were notorious and who could be vindictive. He counted on his own increasing formality toward the Secretary and the continuing pressure of events to bring a graceful departure.

Others were not so patient. True, the party had not apparently suffered at the November elections because of Alger, but he was still politically dangerous. "I do wish that President McKinley would get rid of Alger," Roosevelt fumed in April. And then a month later: "When McKinley's foreign policy is so good it is misery to see him keep Alger." Of course, idle tongues said that the new governor of New York was not entirely disinterested, since he supposedly craved Alger's post so that he could reform the Army.[20]

A political event solved the problem for McKinley. Late in June, Alger announced that he would seek the Michigan Senate seat to be filled in 1900, and would run with the assistance of Hazen S. Pingree, Michigan's chief maverick Republican, a deadly enemy of Hanna, and a man whose curious and questionable reform tendencies smacked of demagoguery to the President. Either Alger simply did not understand his position or he wished to humiliate the President.

Early in July, Alger sat down one afternoon in McKinley's presence and wrote out his resignation, effective January 2, 1900. The President demurred, and Alger could not see that this was not enough either to placate public feeling or to relieve McKinley's embarrassment. And yet McKinley, incredibly squeamish after all that Alger had done, would not demand his resignation. Instead, he unburdened himself silently, writing in soft pencil on a scrap of paper his attitude toward the whole affair. The document reflected his misery, and underlined his softhearted weakness when it came to such things. "I was unwilling to have you offer your resignation while you were under fire, and being attacked for official delinquency and if it had been tendered because of the attack I should not have accepted [it]," he wrote in logical explanation of his stand. "You well know my unwavering devotion to you while the assault upon your official integrity and administration was being made," he continued in a tone of supplication that ended lamely. "I was willing to bear all rather than the slightest injustice should fall upon you. It is not for me to ask you to resign—our relations should require you to spare me that painful course as well as save you from any humiliation which such action would cause. You must determine without any suggestion from me whether the time has not come for you to place your resignation in my hands. It will be for me to judge of the propriety and wisdom of its acceptance." [21] But there is no evidence that he sent the letter. His desire to avoid hurting Alger dictated another and more characteristic course.

On July 12, Alger publicly denied news reports that he would resign before the Philippine insurrection was over. He wished to finish his task, he said, and cynical reporters wondered if his task was to wreck the administration. The following day, Secretary Hay sent the clipping to the President with a small injunction: "This is deplorable—after all the trouble we have taken to save his dignity." Cortelyou showed McKinley all the adverse press reaction, but the President was silent, though admittedly Alger continued to be "the topic of the hour." [22]

McKinley had another plan, dependent on a long-trusted advisor, now enduring a painful and fatal illness, Vice-President Hobart. He appealed to Hobart, a friend of Alger's, to ask the Secretary to resign at once and end the administration's embarrassment. The witty and urbane Mrs. Hobart shared the burden with her husband. Alger called with smiles in answer to the Hobarts' summons and left wreathed in frowns, surrounded by an air of spite and bitterness. He hurried to Washington to see the waiting President, where a tense conference took place. Alger remonstrated briefly against McKinley's squeamishness, deploring his roundabout methods. The President said bluntly that the proposed alliance with

Pingree irritated him. He needed a man with wider training for the tasks now at hand. Alger wrote out his resignation and left.[23]

It was a hot July 19, and McKinley hastened to Cortelyou's office when the interview was over. He had come to like and trust the efficient secretary who managed his affairs far better than he could himself. "Get your hat and we will take a walk on the grounds," he said rather brusquely. When they were out of any earshot, he sighed and patted his pocket. "Well, he was over and left it with me," meaning that Alger had left his resignation. "The interview was brief and devoid of any embarrassing features. It is to take effect at my pleasure." Cortelyou was relieved, for he knew what the news would mean to the party and the Republican press. "The President seemed much relieved but was, as always, gentle and charitable in his talk," Cortelyou noted.[24]

The two pieces of paper that passed between Alger and McKinley ending the long, tortured affair, were formal and devoid of the pleasantries with which the President released other subordinates.[25] One other scene remained in the little drama, for the Hobarts had watched the end of the affair from New Jersey. The President was grateful to them both and wired his thanks, saying that the Vice-President was "a man of crystal insight and velvet tact." To an inquiry about Hobart's health, McKinley received a cryptic but illuminating reply: "My crystal insight is as clear as ever, but the nap on my velvet tact is somewhat worn." [26]

The resignation was effective August 1, which gave McKinley two weeks to find a successor. It did not require much deliberation, for he had already made his choice, but the object, Elihu Root, might have to be persuaded. Root's selection had a curious history. He knew McKinley only through a fellow New Yorker, Secretary Bliss, and no man thought himself less suited to government service than Root. A successful corporation lawyer with a truly brilliant legal mind, Root was not politically active, though he had high-ranking friends in the Republican party. He called men like Reid and Roosevelt by their first names, and he was not unfamiliar with Tom Platt. The President did not forget the homely, large-nosed Root, his face topped by a curious bang of hair, his mouth not given to smiles, his eyes clear, almost cold, in their appraisal of men. He detected in this rather stiff and formal figure a talent for administration. He saw in Root a deep demand for efficiency and speed, two things that he always needed and prized in the men around him. Root was silent but strong; he could make policy and would carry it out. He was McKinley's kind of man.

With his usual skill, McKinley maneuvered to make Root's appointment acceptable to New York Republicans. In effect Root would be nonpartisan, for his Republicanism would not overshadow his sense of duty. New York's member of the cabinet, Bliss, was leaving, and Tom Platt eyed his successor anxiously. In September, 1898, when Hay was appointed secretary of State, the President idly mentioned appointing Whitelaw Reid to some future post, perhaps as ambassador to London, when his work on the peace commission was done. Platt exploded to the President. He hated Reid, and hurried to suggest almost anyone else. The President let the Easy Boss stew through the winter, though he did not appoint Reid to London, and Platt did not object to the latter suggestion that Root enter the cabinet, despite his lack of connection with the Organization.

Root, knowing nothing of the long prelude to his choice, was astonished to be called to the telephone in late July, 1899, to hear Lemuel Quigg, one of Platt's associates, say: "The President directs me to say to you that he wishes you to take the position of Secretary of War." Dumbfounded, Root could only reply: "Thank the President for me, but say that it is quite absurd, I know nothing about war, I know nothing about the army." The line was silent a long moment before Quigg returned. "President McKinley directs me to say that he is not looking for anyone who knows anything about the army; he has got to have a lawyer to direct the government of these Spanish islands, and you are the lawyer he wants." [27]

Root asked for time to think, which the President granted. It was no small decision; he risked an income in six figures for a government salary in four. But his law practice had ceased to challenge him, and Root was a man who loved challenge and work. The news leaked out, and many pressed him to accept. Alger himself urged him to take the post. "With your great knowledge of law and your excellent health you can serve the country in a way given to few men." [28] McKinley was always effective in appealing to men's sense of duty, and on July 24, Root was in Washington.[29]

Root's acceptance relieved the President of the same kind of problem that had preceded Hay's appointment the year before. McKinley was replacing a strictly political appointee with a man well-fitted for the post. He said honestly that he did not know what to do if Root declined, and prepared at once to give the new Secretary full powers to implement a colonial policy.[30]

McKinley's desire to have an experienced lawyer in the War Department to govern the colonies showed his understanding of the problems involved, but it did not find favor everywhere. The politicians, disappointed and otherwise, thought Root was too chilly. The easy days of Algerism were obviously gone. With a slight tone of pique, Roosevelt noted his own reaction. "Personally, the desire to have a lawyer in the War Department seems to me simply foolish —so foolish indeed that I can only regard it as an excuse." [31] The answer said much of the immature Roosevelt's concepts of the President's problems. Did he himself wish to be Alger's successor? Probably not, and in any event McKinley would not have appointed him.

To those concerned with efficiency and erasing the blots that Alger left on the administration, it was a happy choice. Even Platt was pleased. "He will be cautious and conservative, but what he does, you may be sure, will be right," he assured Allison.[32] "I like the 'hang' of your new Secretary of War," Senator Proctor told McKinley after a conference with Root.[33]

Root was not blind to the chances of jealousy and suspicion within the cabinet itself; might not Attorney-General Griggs, himself a formidable lawyer, resent the intrusion of other counsel? Griggs was not envious, but Root allayed any such qualms with a rather shy note. "I think the main feature of the change I am making is the formation of a new law firm of 'Griggs and Root, legal advisors to the President, colonial business a specialty,' " he wrote.[34] Griggs, already deeply embroiled in the tangled Insular Cases, cooperated admirably with him.

Root fell to his task with a will, clearing out mounds of papers, replacing old staff, adopting strenuous hours, and hastily absorbing huge quantities of unfamiliar information. He had what the reporters called X-ray eyes; he could see the favor seekers through the closed door and gave them short notice. The President promised to take care of the patronage hunters, and lines of them moved across

433

the lawn to the White House, where they got more charm if not more satisfaction. But McKinley softened some of Root's first orders. "I think one duty of a President is to act as a check upon a hard-hearted Secretary," he told Cortelyou with a smile.[35]

McKinley needed Root and all the strong counsel he could obtain as 1899 wore on. The ratification of the treaty and the insurrection were only the beginning of the Philippine problem. As month wore drearily into month in that other distant world, with no end of the conflict in sight, the people at home grew progressively apathetic toward the contest. Each day's newspaper catalogued the events in the islands, but the mass of Americans preferred simply not to think of the endless conflict that swallowed men and money as desert sands drink water. The Splendid Little War that had brought America the Philippines begot the Forgotten Little War, and young volunteers and regular soldiers disappeared in the conflict to "pacify" the islands and "uplift" the natives.

Criticism of the administration and of the whole imbroglio deepened at home and then turned to sourness in the press and among the public. The trumpet blasts of imperialism sounded false, and a people who a scant year before had burned with eagerness to save Cubans and Filipinos now felt otherwise, as one cynical poem denoted: [36]

> We've taken up the white man's burden
> of ebony and brown;
> Now will you tell us, Rudyard,
> how we may put it down?

The soldiers who swung through the steaming jungles with heavy packs, grimy beards, and at the mercy of silent death in myriad forms had another and more bitter song: [37]

> Damn, damn, damn the Filipino
> Pock marked Khakiac ladrone;
> Underneath the starry flag,
> Civilize him with a Krag
> And return us to our own beloved home!

"Do ye think Hivin sint us th' Philippeens?" Mr. Hennessey asked his friend Mr. Dooley. "I don't know," came the answer of many Americans, "but th' divvle take thim." [38]

The anti-expansionists in and out of public life revealed an astonishing bitterness. Tom Reed, whose gall was such that he retired from public life after the war to practice law, could not contain the acid sarcasm that had stung a generation of political opponents. "I have got to hunt all over your figures even to find out how much every yellow man costs us in the bush," he wrote a correspondent. "As I make it out he has cost us $30 per Malay and is still in the bush. Why didn't you purchase him of Spain F.O.B. with definite freight rates and insurance paid?" [39] None was more bitter than Andrew Carnegie. "It is a matter of congratulation that you have about finished your work of civilizing the Filipinos," he wrote Whitelaw Reid. "It is thought that about 8,000 of them have been completely civilized and sent to Heaven. I hope you like it." [40]

The President faced such criticism with his usual stoicism. He was sustained by belief in his programs and ideals. He too was bitter at the cost of the war, saddened by the casualty lists, and by the damage done to the Filipinos. And he could not read his mail without twinges, despite twenty-five years in politics. Calling the insurrection "the greatest international crime of the century," Senator Pettigrew of South Dakota did not shrink from calling McKinley "among the most dishonored rulers of all time." [41]

But the expansionists did not fade under the assaults. Of the imperialists who revelled in the name, none talked more or to greater effect than Indiana's young Republican senator, Albert Beveridge, a sport in that state's politics, a maverick elected by a fluke of fate. Fair-haired, young, vigorous, and handsome, with a spellbinding voice, Beveridge elected to make his maiden speech on imperialism in the early days of 1900. He spoke with some authority, for he had toured the Philippines before taking his seat.

Beveridge's speech was a vivid exposition of the mystical belief in Anglo Saxon institutions which such steady men as Lodge and Roosevelt professed to share with English counterparts around Joseph Chamberlain and a host of more or less profound thinkers. The war in the Philippines was but part of a grand design, wrought under God's law. Jealous tongues whispered that Beveridge spoke for McKinley, and willing hands carried the news to the White House. McKinley was upset; he did not like Beveridge's pushy ways, and he did not really believe in the rhetoric of the Anglo-Saxonists. He saw pacification of the Philippines first as a sober duty and then as a civilizing mission, to be sure. To believe in destiny was one thing, but talk of racial superiority nettled him.

McKinley had already spelled out his own answer to the anti-imperialists. It appealed to many because it was practical. Late in August, 1899, he went to Pittsburgh to welcome returning volunteers from the islands. He was blunt, for the anti-expansionists had angered him. The insurgents had struck the first blow, he said; they represented a small minority of the people. He freely accepted all responsibility for the government's policies and intended to see them through. "They assailed our sovereignty; and there will be no useless parley, no pause, until the insurrection is suppressed, and American authority acknowledged and established." He called the roll of state regiments that had fought in the islands, and after each name a chorus of cheers arose from the ranks. In that moment of drama all the horrors of jungle warfare blended easily into the already growing nostalgia of veterans' memories.[42]

In October, he toured the Midwest again, speaking in the states holding elections, taking the opportunity to define his policies and to quell the murmur of criticism and sense of apathy that both seemed somehow to spread among the people. He was candid. "It is no longer a question of expansion with us; we have expanded. If there is any question at all it is a question of contraction; and who is going to contract?"[43]

But this common-sense approach of dealing with facts was not enough. He had his theory too. "There can be no imperialism," he told a banquet of the Ohio Society of New York in March, 1900. "Nations do not grow in strength, and the cause of liberty and law is not advanced by the doing of easy things. . . . It is not possible that seventy-five millions of American freemen are unable to establish liberty and justice and good government in our new possessions."[44] In his second inaugural he reaffirmed this belief. "Our institutions will not deteriorate by extension, and our sense of justice will not abate under tropic suns in distant seas."[45]

But the theory of Philippine freedom was implemented by war, a

436

cruel fact to the President, for he never conceded sovereignty to the Filipinos. They must first accept American control and then freedom would be worked out. He did not doubt the policy's wisdom, and left Root to implement it. He must also clothe the administration's promises with the reality of constitutional government, a task made more formidable by lack of American precedents.

The President's first statement of intention came in his annual message of December, 1899, which held some surprises for the Congress that heard it. His moral justification for his policy remained the same. Promises of independence to the Filipinos had "no foundation in fact . . ." and the rebellion was caused by "the sinister ambitions of a few leaders of the Filipinos. . . ." The President thought that most Filipinos wanted American rule. Beyond that he would not go, except to enunciate a policy of executive leadership that he pursued the rest of his administration. "It does not seem desirable that I should recommend at this time a specific and final form of government for these islands. . . . As long as the insurrection continues the military arm must necessarily be supreme." He would favor and foster local self-government in the dependencies under American rule, but he clearly would not turn the problem over to Congress, however eager that body might be to take the responsibility. This insistence on presidential control of colonial policy was remarkable in a supposedly weak president, the more so for its lack of precedent.[46]

The distance between Manila and Washington was vast, and good intentions did not add luster to the jungle war in the Philippines. The most caustic comments on the administration's policies came from the news correspondents who plagued General Otis in Manila, and that rather stuffy martinet had a bad press. The general unwritten rule at Otis' headquarters was to release only information favorable to the American cause, a policy bred by military narrowness. The correspondents, desperate for news, were not above manufacturing and inflating it for themselves, but many honestly felt that the full horror and mismanagement of the campaign were being kept from the United States. Otis had no tact and did not desire to please the newsmen. Interviews with him produced only ill will and a hardening of his policies. In desperation and partly out of spite the correspondents pooled their resources and cabled home their own "round robin," exposing what they felt were the injustices and misconduct of the army in the islands.

The President was not impressed by their exposure, and most Americans seemed content to discount it at the rate generally applied to yellow journalism. But the news was disturbing, for it showed that all was not well within the army command. It was easy to say, as did some of the soldiers in the islands, that "some of our newspaper correspondents can give the Filipino pointers in lying—and that is saying a good deal," but they reflected something.[47]

General Elwell S. Otis, the focus of this newspaper war, was a curious man, seeming in his stiff attitude and unbending manner a figure from another era. The seniority system placed him in command of the Philippine expedition, but McKinley trusted his judgment for some ill-defined reason, and sustained the General before all detractors. His bald head fringed by an astonishing set of white sideburns, his eyes chilly in their glance, his hands nervous and busy, Otis was an extraordinary officer. Swathed in red tape and unable to delegate even a minimal amount of authority, he delighted in studying and mastering the minutest and most irrelevant details of his command. His desk lay hidden in papers, which his successor literally shovelled out the door. A Confederate bullet robbed him of the ability to sleep easily, and he craved work as a palliative from insomnia. It was not unusual for him to be at his desk eighteen hours a day. Yet he did not venture beyond Manila; all his information came at second hand. To the end he persisted in the disastrous belief that the insurrection was a formal conflict, little realizing that guerrilla tactics could not be matched or mastered by the knowledge in military manuals.

Yet with all his faults he was an honest and courageous soldier. He did not lie, nor did he really bungle, for he kept sharp eyes on all his operations. He was simply the wrong commander for the task. Otis' opinion that the Filipinos ought to surrender and "be good Indians" revealed his ignorance of the larger political problems involved in the insurrection.[48] McKinley's good opinion of him came largely from the General's written reports, models of clarity, breathing a confidence that in Washington did not seem misplaced. At the mercy of distant advice, McKinley always trusted the senior officer in command, assuming that he spoke for his entire group. But Otis' refusal to delegate authority and lack of taste for conference robbed his reports of that broadened vision. He left in May, 1900, relieved at his own request, confident that the insurrection was over, when in fact it had another year to run under his more imaginative but not especially more successful successor, General Arthur MacArthur.

The insurrection was no less real in Washington, though men there did not face the daily threat of disease, the jungle, and death at the hands of a crazed native. The President resigned himself to a long struggle, but for political reasons he was not anxious to do more than was necessary.[49] Just how many men Otis needed remained speculative, for the General's predictions varied during 1899. He envisioned a vast encircling movement, sweeping through Luzon and some of the southern islands with trains of infantry, safely garrisoned behind forts, which tactic would, of course, end the rebellion and pacify the islands. That required men. By April, he was beginning to realize the complexity of his problem; it was one thing to beat the rebels in a battle and another to hold the position they evacuated.[50] The natives fled before their opponents, firing their villages and telling tall tales about American atrocities to keep wavering districts in line. An unhappy incident hampered the program. Otis had changed the wording of the President's first proclamation, but a subordinate elsewhere issued the original text. Natives who could read compared the two, and never again trusted the Americans.

By August, Otis was asking for 60,000 men, and the War Department called for ten more volunteer regiments.[51] But this expansion could not go on indefinitely, for the law required that the army revert to its 1898 size of some 25,000 men in July, 1901. By February, 1900, Otis had more than the 60,000 men he asked for.[52] The President also had his own observers in the islands. Among them was Joe Wheeler, who wrote home in August, and made a similar statement later in the fall when he returned to go to Congress, that only vigor would end the rebellion.[53] McKinley wanted just that, but he got instead another campaign season of struggle and half-success. The Filipino garrisons vanished at the touch, clad in uniforms of rags, adept at using native weapons, using a rice sack as a supply base, united by an often vague but emotionally potent loyalty to independence.

439

The insurrection itself was bad enough, but far more complex problems had to be solved as it drew sluggishly to its inevitable conclusion. Root's appointment as secretary of War signalled interest in establishing government in the colonies, and late 1899 brought controversy over their status. The President believed that the Philippines and Porto Rico were dependencies to which the constitution did not extend. John William Griggs, the attorney-general, had already begun the formidable arguments on the Insular Cases, decided in May, 1901, that would sustain this view. The President's insistence on executive rule in the islands was recognized by the Spooner bill, debated in the session of 1899–1900, though later dropped. McKinley was loath to extend the full rights of citizenship to the Filipinos in particular. If they were citizens and the constitution followed the flag, as popular parlance put it, their products automatically entered the United States duty free. The whole elaborate idea of the Open Door in China, then under negotiation, depended partly on the administration's ability to control the Philippine trade and offer concessions there to other powers in return for concessions in China.

Root, a novice at politics, suggested a special session of Congress to solve the problem in the form of legislation. The President demurred. It would be bad enough to have Congress back in December, with the insurrection still ablaze, but it would be impossible to cast the whole problem into that body's lap. Root then saw the President's position clearly. "Without a clear conception for thought and legislation to crystallize around we should inevitably drift into a hopeless entanglement of contradictions," he wrote Lyman Abbott in December.[54] McKinley, an older and wiser hand at the game, wished to present a plan for Congress simply to ratify.

He had already chosen a characteristic method of dealing with the islands. Before the treaty was ratified, Dewey had suggested a civilian commission "composed of men skilled in diplomacy and statesmanship . . . to adjust differences" and to report to the President. General Otis was less agreeable, not wishing to face civilian conflict, but would not disagree with Dewey. The President appointed the commission on January 20.[55]

Men with sound knowledge of the islands were scarce, and unbiased men scarcer still. He turned to a man in private life, Jacob

Gould Schurman, the president of Cornell University. Schurman faced the offer of the commission chairmanship with dismay. He said frankly that he disagreed with the administration's policy: he did not want the islands. "Oh, that need not trouble you," McKinley explained with a winning gesture, "I did not want the Philippine Islands either; and in the protocol to the treaty I left myself free not to take them; but—in the end there was no alternative." [56] His familiar appeal to duty swayed Schurman, who duly departed with his colleagues, Charles Denby and Professor Dean C. Worcester of the University of Michigan, a noted zoologist with firsthand knowledge of the islands. Dewey and Otis would also be members of the commission.

Its duty was to gather information and recommend a policy for the administration. It was not empowered to deal with the natives or to infringe upon the military suppression of the insurrection. The commission sat listening in ample rooms within the old city of Manila, as a parade of witnesses from every field spoke their recommendations, voiced their criticisms, and suggested plans for the future. The lazy afternoons and soft accents belied the war's existence in the back country, but the commission did not lose its sense of purpose. Its initial proclamation of April 4, 1899, was well received in the areas already pacified, but did not visibly affect the insurrection. Clearly, the natives would not surrender without military defeat.[57]

McKinley authorized Schurman to outline the future plan of Philippine government to the responsible elements of the population. It was neither new nor surprising, providing for a governor-general appointed by the president, a legislature chosen by selective native electors, a cabinet and general civil system presided over by the governor-general, whose authority and Washington's clearly overrode that of the natives.[58] McKinley sincerely wished to establish self-rule in the islands, but he did not trust the natives' ability to govern without American supervision.

Schurman visited most of the pacified areas, and Worcester packed into the back country, combining his politics with his interest in natural science.[59] Late in June, Schurman left for home, anxious to return in time for the fall semester at Cornell, presenting a four-volume report. The commission's findings did not surprise McKinley. It sustained the past stand against independence, repeated that the natives could not yet rule themselves, favored presidential control until Congress enacted legislation, and urged the latter body to make haste.[60] Schurman left behind a sanguine Otis; the General began his massive encircling movement on Luzon when the rains lifted, and fall weather shone with tropical beauty through the jungles that stirred to the crack of rifle fire. By November he cabled home the end of organized resistance.[61] He neglected to add that far more vicious unorganized resistance was about to begin.

McKinley's views were less hopeful as 1899 closed, and the double problem of the insurrection abroad and Congress at home remained. Schurman had not been quite adequate to his task. Early in 1900, McKinley cast about for a more definite solution; his eye fell upon the ample figure of William Howard Taft, then a federal judge in Ohio. As in choosing Root, he wanted a lawyer to draw up a blueprint for government in the islands, and possibly to be groomed as the first governor-general. Day knew Taft, and McKinley urged the Judge to pressure him to take the post.[62]

Taft was not inclined to go. Like Schurman, he had opposed taking the islands. He asked for time to consider the offer, and Day quietly urged his fellow jurists not to dissuade Taft. His friend Root, immersed in his great and satisfying work, bluntly demanded that Taft accept. "You have had an easy time of it holding office since you were twenty-one. Now your country needs you." McKinley promised that if he were able to later, he would appoint Taft to the Supreme Court, the office he really coveted, as a reward for his service. Taft capitulated, beginning a long and eventful career.[63]

One group did not welcome the commission, despite its presidential support and powers. General MacArthur, later to be Otis' successor, wanted no part of civilian meddling, and when Taft's ship docked at Manila, the air was frigid. "The populace that we expected to welcome us was not there, and I cannot describe the coldness of the army officers and army men who received us any better than by saying that it somewhat exceeded the coldness of the populace," Taft remembered. The absence of military men on the commission belied the President's purposes. MacArthur was blunt, fearing that the civilians would lessen his own power. To him they were "an injection into an otherwise normal situation." [64]

Like many seemingly easy-going men, Taft had a temper that

induced determination rather than tantrums. He measured his opposition and bided his time. His chief support was in Washington, and he never forgot the consistency with which McKinley sustained him. "I have always cherished the recollection that he gave me this promise and kept it to the letter," Taft remembered.[65] Through the summer of 1900, beset with the worries of diplomacy and re-election, the President still managed to retain close contact with the commission, and even read the lengthy chatty letters which Taft sent home.[66] This interest reflected his deep concern over the islands and their peoples. "From the beginning up to the end the real good of the several peoples of the archipelago came first with him, and no one who had the privilege of knowing him well doubts it," Worcester recalled.[67]

Taft's friction with the military, especially with MacArthur, whom he called "a martinet," did not prevent exhaustive sessions on all topics relevant to the islands. The tariff, "about as interesting as the multiplication table" to Taft, got special interest, for the island's economy was unsound. Like Schurman, he did not argue that the Filipinos were ready for self-government; for their own good, they must remain under American paternalism. The people, he reported, had great potential for self-rule and full development, were bright, engaging, and quick to learn, but it would be years before they could successfully grapple with the problems of government.[68] For seventy-five searing summer days Taft and his entourage toured the islands, gathering information and meeting the native peoples. Taft on tour was an impressive sight, and the natives came in time to view him with an almost superstitious awe for his inflexible honesty and sincere good intentions.[69]

Late summer brought conferences with the rebels, which proved to the army that the insurrectos were holding out only in the hope that Bryan would be elected president and would reverse McKinley's policies.[70] Whether the inference was true or false—and the rebels did doubtless gain morale from the anti-expansionist feeling in the United States—McKinley rushed the expansion of civil government through the election months. Safely re-elected, the President informed Taft early in 1901 that military government would shortly end and assured him and the other commission members that they would remain as civil administrators.[71]

In the spring of 1901, the Supreme Court declared that the

islands were dependencies subject to congressional authority, thereby endowing the inhabitants with a curious mixture of civil rights and non-citizenship that caused Root to drawl: "Ye-es, as near as I can make out the Constitution follows the flag—but doesn't quite catch up with it." [72] In April plans were set to establish civil government on July 4, 1901, with Taft as governor-general, marking the end of military rule. The capture of Aguinaldo in April, and his acceptance of American sovereignty, ended the insurrection.[73]

McKinley did not live to consummate his colonial policy, and the public did not credit him with the final results. Had he lived, he would have sustained a more popular kind of self-rule in the islands. The leadership he exercised in making colonial policy was deceptive. As in his diplomacy, he saw himself as the arbiter of differences within the administration. His willingness to delegate authority to men he trusted, like Root and Taft, removed him from the public eye in the complex diplomatic negotiations of his last years in office. But no policy was devised without his consent, and he was surprisingly well informed on the events and problems of each area.

The President viewed with satisfaction the progress of his and Root's efforts to define the status of the Philippines, but the islands were not his only such problem. Cuba, lying as close to America as ever, must be dealt with. The island had hardly been occupied before he made it clear that while the United States would not acquire it, Cuba would not be released unconditionally until after the peace settlement. It would be held in trust under the army's control until stable democratic government was established. Executive rule through the army would continue.[74]

Cuba posed fewer problems than did the Philippines, for there was no insurrection to deal with, but the situation was far from satisfactory. A devastated countryside greeted the new liberators in many areas; mere relief for the population was in itself a huge task. Inevitably there were political frictions. The Cuban army was anxious to be paid for its efforts. Cuban leaders viewed with alarm American reluctance to leave Cuba to their rule. Suspicion grew in many quarters that the efficient men in khaki, so obsessed with cleanliness and an un-Latin emphasis on speed, would not leave the people they had freed.

Official friction was embarrassing and potentially dangerous enough, but private quarrels between American soldiers and the populace were more irritating. Though the Americans did a great work in cleaning up the island and preparing it for independence, there was inevitable hostility to any foreign rule. The American soldiers considered the Cubans inferior "niggers" and "dirty dagoes," and were often arrogant, hostile, and insulting. Government imposed by uniformed officers smacked of tyranny to the touchy Cubans; change was rapid, in the American tradition, and often bewildering. The Americans, both at home and abroad, compounded the problem by expecting gratitude, that rarest of repayments.

Army rule, preoccupied with the basic problems of sanitation and transportation, continued until Root replaced Alger, but mid-1899 brought changes. The problems facing any civil government were formidable. Three-fourths of the population lived in the country under substandard economies. Only a third of the population could read and write rudimentary Spanish. The system of schools, roads, and public works was utterly inadequate. The proposed republican government, therefore, could hardly be entirely popular in practice. It would not do to leave the island at the mercy of demagoguery and dictatorship, inevitable in such conditions. While he desired a real republic in Cuba, McKinley would not simply abandon the island. Root explained to critics early in 1900 that the administration desired "conservative and thoughtful control of Cuba by Cubans during the formative period, [to] avoid the kind of control which leads to the perpetual revolutions of Central America and the other West Indian islands." [75] At the same time he stated clearly that American military rule must end quickly, and McKinley could report at the end of 1899 that there were only some 11,000 American soldiers in Cuba.[76]

The first American overseer of Cuba was General John R. Brooke, a rather stiff Army officer with more seniority than political skill to recommend him. The President could not leave him permanently in charge. His usual good judgment of men, when not hampered by restrictions of military seniority, brought the President to Leonard Wood's name. With a long career in army garrisons, a strong sense of duty, common sense combined with a lust for work, and a demand for dispatch, Wood was McKinley's kind of administrator. In talking to him in 1900, the President outlined his own ideas. "I want you to go down there to get the people ready for a republican form of government. I leave the details to you. Give them a good school system, try to straighten out their courts, and put them on their feet as best you can. We want to do all we can for them and to get out of the island as soon as we safely can." [77] As usual, he would delegate much authority to a man he trusted.

Wood had been in Cuba after the war, sending information to the President and political friends. He fortified the belief that paternalism was necessary for the moment, since the masses of people were ignorant and indifferent.[78] Both as a deputy to the military governor, Brooke, with whom he disagreed, and then as commander himself, Wood toured the island to gather accurate information and to allay Cuban fears. Bluff but honest in his dealings with local Cuban leaders, he affirmed the goodness of American intentions. "The government of the islands shall be delivered to the Cubans," he promised.[79] He was not a martinet, refusing, for instance, to gag the press, but he brooked no opposition from the Cuban rebel leaders, who were jealous of his power and purposes. General Garcia demanded payment for his troops and other rights, and when Wood refused, threatened war. ". . . I told him the sooner he began the better, because as we had taken a mean job on our hands, that might be the best way out of it." [80] The Cuban soldiers were finally paid for their services to the Americans during the war, largely as a way to put money into circulation, and Wood's firmness impressed them.

The General did not spare himself, often working eighteen hours a day, dashing into the interior, without warning, to check on subordinates, daily driving his men to greater feats. He ordered a subordinate to check on the island's insane asylums, and when the man protested his ignorance, the General said calmly: "Find out how much it will cost, how long it will take, what machinery you will need, what you will have to do for discipline, and report." [81] Wood's driving energy inspired a poem that made the rounds among his staff: [82]

> Don't stop to drink or spit,
> to smoke or scratch your ear.

Go work while yet the stars are lit!
Come home when night is near.
There is no time for food.
Write till the ink runs dry.
The man who works for Wood
is one who wants to die.

McKinley's satisfaction with progress in the island was rudely shaken in May, 1900, by a major scandal in the Cuban post-office system. Estes G. Rathbone and a group of friends in the politically corrupt postal system were suddenly charged with misappropriating funds. The Democrats howled with glee as the only major scandal of McKinley's administration broke. Moreover, it was an election year, and Rathbone was Hanna's friend.[83] Orville Platt, Chairman of the Senate's special committee on Cuba, was openly worried. "The Cuban scandal is really sad and mortifying," he admitted. "The Democrats and Populists are making all they can of it and the worst is they have too much ground to go on." [84]

The scandal was not only mortifying and politically dangerous, but personally shocking to McKinley. He quickly sent Fourth Assistant Postmaster General Joseph L. Bristow, long familiar with political patronage, to investigate. The President feared that the scandal might set back plans for evacuating the island; it seemed to many Cubans to give the lie to American rhetoric. "In making this investigation, be thorough," the President told Bristow, "do no one an injustice, but shield nobody who has committed a wrong. I want every offender properly punished." Bristow knew that Hanna's friends would appeal to the Senator for protection. But the President was adamant. "As for the complaints against you, do your duty and leave that to me." [85]

Root, entrusted with overseeing McKinley's instructions, was equally adamant. "I want you to scrape to the bone, no matter whose nerves are hurt by it," he ordered Wood. "The first essential of administration in the island is that we shall be perfectly honest with ourselves." [86] The postal system was put under Wood's control, and Rathbone and others, caught in flight in the United States, were duly convicted, only to be pardoned under a general amnesty by the new Cuban government in 1902. Fears that the scandal would hurt

447

the Republicans in the campaign of 1900 proved groundless as the country accepted the evidence of McKinley's sincerity in prosecuting the guilty.[87]

Preparations for a Cuban constituent assembly moved forward in the fall of 1900. In September, the Cuban electors chose delegates who met in November under Wood's direction to begin the tedious process of drafting a constitution and establishing a republican government.

These events in Cuba sharpened a fresh problem. What attitude should the United States take toward the new Republic of Cuba? Could the United States simply leave the island, in view of the population's inexperience with self-rule? Would it not be wise to protect the great American investment, both public and private, in the island? But could this be done effectively without curtailing the authority of the new Cuban government?

As early as January, 1901, Root had formulated an outline of what became the Platt Amendment. He had instructed Wood to insist upon real republicanism in the new Cuban constitution, but republicanism run by the conservative elements in the island.[88] The United States would assure this type of government in Cuba. The administration felt it only just that the new Cuban government accept the American viewpoint by agreeing to five things: the United States would retain the right to intervene in Cuba to assure a republican government; Cuba would enter into no treaty with a foreign power that might threaten her independence; Cuba would contract no debts beyond her ability to pay; land would be leased to the United States for a naval base; and all acts of the American military administration were legalized.[89] In February, these demands were officially forwarded to Wood, whose duty it became to secure their adoption by the Cuban assembly.[90] The demands did not seem onerous or threatening to the President, and he urged their passage by Congress as a rider to the annual army appropriation bill. Given Senator Platt's name, the bill became law on March 2, 1901.

In Cuba a different attitude prevailed. The Cuban assembly balked at accepting what seemed to be American dictation. There the amendment was defeated on April 6, and a special delegation was sent to Washington to confer with McKinley. They had some sympathy from Wood. "The Cubans have been so dishonestly dealt with, always and in all things, that it is next to impossible to make them believe that we have only their own interests at heart," he wrote Roosevelt.[91] The Cuban committee found McKinley charming, sympathetic, understanding, and adamant. He promised to use his influence with Congress to grant them special tariff favors if they accepted the amendment, a promise which his successor fulfilled. He assured the Cubans that the Platt Amendment defined an American responsibility, not a privilege.[92]

Sullen but somewhat reassured by McKinley's sincerity and the promises of commercial favors, the Cuban assembly surrendered, and by the narrowest margin accepted the Platt Amendment on June 12, after Wood and the President again refused to compromise on the issue.[93] Elections followed in December, 1901, and again in February, 1902, resulting in the final establishment of an independent Cuba.

In retrospect the Platt Amendment seemed questionable to many, but few Americans felt at the time that it was unjustified. Within McKinley's strict definition, it implied no threat to Cuban sovereignty. Its real danger lay in the interpretations which other presidents would give it. Its fault was not in its content but in its potentialities. McKinley's successors used it in ways he never dreamed of, and would surely not have used himself.

As 1900 closed and the President came to the end of his first eventful administration, he could look with considerable pride upon his work in the dependencies. The tragic Philippine insurrection lay like a pall on his conscience as it dragged to a close, but he was proud of the civil government that would shortly arise there. In Cuba he had even greater cause for congratulation, for he lived to see the island run by responsible and efficient men.

Both he and Root questioned many aspects of the new Cuban constitution, and clearly would continue their policy of paternalism toward the island. But Cuba was free, fulfilling the American promise that had been made so forcefully in 1898.[94] Travellers in Cuba reported to the President their gratification with work done under the American regime.[95] McKinley found foreign affairs increasingly absorbing, but less bewildering than when he first entered office. He might have hoped for an end to them, but no such prospect was in sight.

ᐁᐁ XX ᐁᐁ

The Diplomacy of Power

ECRETARY OF STATE John Hay hated nothing quite so much as
the Senate of the United States. He was never noted for his
liberal views; service as Lincoln's secretary had not apparently included a course in tolerance. Even with his aristocratic
temperament, his dislike of senators amounted to a disease. The
tolerant McKinley did not share this view, not at least publicly, for
he had sat in a legislative body and had spent all his adult life in
the give-and-take of American politics. Hay hated the Senate for its
power to block treaties. "A treaty entering the Senate is like a bull
going into the arena," he noted later. "No one can say just how or
when the final blow will fall—but one thing is certain—it will never
leave the arena alive." [1]

There was some justice on his side. He had long harbored the
dream of consummating an alliance with England. He understood
that it would have to be unwritten to avoid objections from the
public and Congress, but he knew that it must be implemented by
certain formal arrangements. He did not hide his feelings. "As long
as I stay here in Washington no action shall be taken contrary to
my conviction that the one indispensable feature of our foreign
policy should be a friendly understanding with England," he wrote
in 1899.[2] The President, with whom Hay was closer than most associates, shared these views, though with less volubility. He was more
likely to laugh when the Senate was mentioned. Exasperating, yes,
he might say, but there it was. A way would have to be found to
placate or implicate the Senate in the administration's foreign policy.

The President's friendliness was invaluable to Hay, for he could
influence public opinion while the Secretary carried on the details of
diplomacy. The President was more than willing to do this. He
understood the changed role of America in world affairs and had
begun assiduously and unobtrusively to lead the people into a better

understanding of foreign relations. He justified it, as usual, in terms of duty and reality. "In this age of frequent interchange and mutual dependence, we cannot shirk our international responsibilities if we would," he told his audience at Omaha in 1898. "This must be met with courage and high wisdom, and we must follow duty even if desire opposes." [3]

He needed public support, for in the last years of his administration he faced a formidable array of complex negotiations. The first and most irritating of these was the dispute over the Alaska boundary. The discovery of gold in Alaska in 1896 revived an old quarrel over the boundary in the "Alaska panhandle" that lay adjacent to Canada. The Anglo-Russian treaty of 1825 was vague, for the area was a tangle of indentations and bays which the discovery of gold and the settlement of Alaska made important. Did the boundary line run inland, as the Americans claimed, giving them control of the bays, or across the heads of the inlets, as the British and Canadians claimed, giving them control of the potential harbors?

Hay was loath to enter the negotiations, but conflicts between Americans and Canadians made a settlement imperative. McKinley was also reluctant to have the explosive issue aired in public for political reasons. Though he was a convinced Anglophile, Hay had no illusions about British diplomacy, which could be "tricky and tortuous." [4] The Canadians further complicated the problem. They could not well surrender to either the United States or England, since in either case it would lose votes at home. Canada was fiercely proud of her independent status in the Empire. ". . . Our Lady of the Snows is disposed to be a daughter in her mother's house, but mistress in her own, with a wanion," Adee noted crisply early in the administration.[5] As if this was not enough, the English insisted that the boundary affair was part of a larger problem; they might favor the American boundary scheme if the Americans gave in on building an isthmian canal.

A Joint High Commission, established in 1898, was to arbitrate the twelve outstanding differences between the United States and Canada. The commission met in Quebec and in Washington with much dignity and amid great talk, but accomplished little. McKinley was not disposed to arbitrate the differences because of politics; the Irish vote might be offended. Hay had a better reason for his dislike of arbitrating tribunals, "the besetting sin of which is to split the difference." [6]

The President of necessity remained aloof during the negotiations. Over all there hung the question of what the Senate would say, and Hay was apt to be bitter over this and other treaties he was then negotiating. ". . . The real duties of the Secretary of State seem to be three," he wrote Henry Adams: "to fight claims upon us by other states; to press more or less fraudulent claims of our citizens upon other countries; to find offices for friends of Senators when there are none." [7] The President's calmness both amazed and gratified Hay. McKinley told Hay frankly to make his treaty and then they would fight it through. "I have been greatly struck since I came here with his coolness and courage in regard to such matters," Hay, who had never made a tariff, said in wonder. "Having passed the greater part of his life in Congress he is, of course, a thorough parliamentarian, with the greatest respect for the Legislative department, and a loyal regard for its legitimate authority." [8] Of course, the President did not want any treaties to fail, so Hay hesitated and then refused to run the risk of humiliating him.

The negotiations with Canada hung fire through the summer and winter of 1899, producing only a temporary *modus vivendi* that brought some law and order to the territory in dispute. Delay, however, was dangerous, for it might undermine other more important dealings, throwing the country back into "our old relations of simmering hostility with England, with all this implies in Canada, Nicaragua, China and elsewhere." [9]

The administration's chief concern was not really the Alaska boundary, exasperating as it was, but a plot of land at the continent's other end. McKinley, in common with most Americans, wanted a canal across the narrow waist of the two Americas to unite the Pacific and Atlantic. His imagination, like that of the average American, was aroused by the project and was sharpened by a specific event during the war. The U.S.S. *Oregon,* isolated in Puget Sound, had made the long journey to Cuban waters amid a welter of newspaper headlines and had arrived too late to affect the war. If only there had been a canal, the downhearted noted, she could have saved two-thirds of the distance. Why, the public asked, was there no canal? The answer was simple: the Clayton-Bulwer

Treaty of 1850 between the United States and Great Britain forbade unilateral construction of a canal. Treaty or no treaty, after 1898 the people wanted a canal, an American canal. McKinley and Hay must somehow arrange it.

McKinley had not been in office long before Alabama's insistent senator, John Tyler Morgan, pressed for a canal agreement, as he had so often in the past. It was the dream of the old Senator's life; he would sacrifice all else if he could die knowing that the canal would be built. The Senator's fearful handwriting and delightful drawl were familiar to McKinley. In fact, he had easier access to the White House than did many Republicans. McKinley was not averse to Morgan's views. The Republican platform of 1896 called for a canal, and early in his administration he supported a commission of experts which investigated various proposed routes and methods of construction in Nicaragua and Panama.[10]
whom Morgan talked incessantly and not always tactfully. McKin-

Beset with other worries, he delegated the task to Hay, with
ley once again urged Hay to make his treaty and they would fight it through. The President apparently favored the Nicaraguan route, but in 1899 he talked with William Nelson Cromwell, agent for the French interests that had started a canal in Panama under the great Ferdinand de Lesseps, architect of the Suez Canal. Morgan took note; he wanted Nicaragua and did not wish to quarrel or waste time over routes.

The basic problem of the Clayton-Bulwer Treaty remained. Many familiar with the problem felt that England did not really care who built the canal, so long as it was built. The only question was whether it would be unfortified and neutral, or fortified and under exclusive American control. The English were naturally reluctant to surrender to unilateral construction, devoid as they would then be of insurance for future transit of English goods and ships. They preferred an open canal, modelled after the Suez.[11]

In early December, 1898, after an early morning breakfast, Henry White formally approached Lord Salisbury upon the subject and found the English Prime Minister cordially disposed to the American suggestions. He frankly felt that the canal could be built only by a government and that the United States was the logical choice. Of course, he reminded White, some new arrangement must

453

replace the Clayton-Bulwer Treaty, and England assumed that any canal would be unfortified. White felt that the English stand was just and cabled jubilantly: "I do not believe if it is to be open to all nations on equal terms that there will be any serious difficulty in effecting such an agreement satisfactory to both nations." [12]

Through 1899 and into early 1900 this mood continued, though the negotiations proceeded slowly because of tangential problems like the Alaska boundary. American Ambassador Choate reported home in January, 1900, that the English assumed that the United States would build the canal. The problem was simply how to avoid friction in negotiating a new treaty. Choate's talks with Salisbury grew more firm and more productive. The Ambassador did not hesitate to sweep aside English protests that Canada's problems must be settled first; Canada had nothing to do with it, Choate responded.[13]

The negotiations proceeded through January, 1900, to the satisfaction of Hay and McKinley. They discussed their work with few people; the Senate was not consulted and only professional diplomats had a hand in drafting the first Hay-Pauncefote Treaty. A peculiar gleam of satisfaction shown in Hay's eyes, therefore, as he received the dignified figure of the English Ambassador on the morning of February 5, 1900. Sir Julian's bald head shone as he bent to sign the necessary papers, and Hay's face was wreathed in smiles at the thought of his coup. The shiny red drops of red sealing wax formed around the necessary seals, and the treaty was to be rolled up with impressive ribbons before being dispatched to the White House. It was a "great achievement" as the President said in forwarding the document to the Senate that very day, together with a special message recommending ratification.[14]

McKinley expected rapid confirmation of the treaty, permitting the United States to choose a route, acquire the property, and begin construction. He saw nothing startling in the proposals. The agreement superseded the Clayton-Bulwer Treaty and permitted the United States to build a canal alone. The canal would be open to all vessels in peace and war, and would not be fortified. It was simple; it was what the country wanted. The President and Hay shook hands on a job well done.

They faced a rude surprise, for the treaty was no sooner at the Senate than cries of outraged protest echoed through the press and across the land. The degree and kind of protest surprised McKinley. The focus, of course, was in the Senate. Perhaps out of spite at not being consulted, but largely out of sincere opposition to the scheme, a majority of the senators opposed Hay's treaty.[15] Hay, on tenterhooks, was plagued at night and in his frequent fits of depression with visions of the treaty's defeat. His spleen rallied him. "I have never seen such an exhibition of craven cowardice, ignorance, and prejudice," he wrote Henry White. "I am old enough to have foreseen it, but I confess it never entered into my mind that anyone out of a madhouse could have objected to the Canal Convention. It gained all we have longed for and worked for for twenty years, and without an atom of compensation." [16]

As the criticism mounted, Hay grew depressed. He had failed McKinley, for whom he had developed great devotion as well as respect. The President was worried and preoccupied with other things. When the Foreign Relations Committee reported the treaty out with amendments for debate, McKinley felt sorry and angry. Hay took it closer to heart. On March 13, he took McKinley aside after a cabinet meeting and handed him a sealed envelope. The President absently put it in his pocket, and saw the Secretary leave. Later that evening he opened the envelope to find Hay's resignation. The attacks in the Senate, Hay felt, had ruined his "power to serve you in business requiring the concurrence of that body as an end."

The President was amazed. He had said nothing which the Secretary might construe as lack of confidence. He had supported Hay at every turn, trusting his judgment and ability. He did not consider the Senate's action a catastrophe, and he could not afford to lose Hay now in the midst of so many complex negotiations. No one knew of the letter except Cortelyou as McKinley took up his pen to answer it. "I return your resignation," he began. "Had I known the contents of the letter which you handed me this morning, I would have declined to receive or consider it." He paused. Perhaps some advice was in order. He knew how Hay chaffed at the slowness of political dealing, and how much he hated the Senate. He continued: "Nothing could be more unfortunate than to have you retire from the Cabinet. The personal loss would be great, but the public loss even greater. Your administration of the State Department has had my warm approval. As in all matters you have taken my counsel, I

455

will cheerfully bear whatever criticism or condemnation may come. Your record constitutes one of the most important and interesting pages of our diplomatic history. We must bear the atmosphere of the hour. It will pass away. We must continue working on the lines of duty and honor. Conscious of high purposes and honorable effort, we cannot yield our posts however the storm may rage." The most effective thing about the letter was the signature: "Yours devotedly, William McKinley." [17] Hay did not need to be pressured; he was moved by a sense of necessity rather than desire. The letter deeply touched him, and he smothered his old feelings. If he had had McKinley's experience in politics he would have turned the other cheek. With the President's confidence, he would stay.

As he faced his vocal opponents with a fresh grimness and determination, Hay saw no virtue in their ranks. Spite and politics motivated them to opposition. But this hardly accounted for such notable defections from Republican ranks as Lodge and Davis, or Governor Roosevelt. They had a point, which Hay came in time to see. Few Americans would accept the task of building a canal without controlling it. "I do not see why we should dig a canal if we are not to fortify it so as to insure its being used for ourselves and against our foes in time of war," Roosevelt wrote Mahan.[18]

Hay carried on a voluminous correspondence with politicians. Others spoke publicly for the administration. John Bassett Moore argued that an unfortified canal was the historic American position. Some military officers felt that a neutral canal was a blessing, since it would be controlled by sea approaches anyway. Any other arrangement would upset Latin American nations, who might see in the fortifications further evidence of American imperialism.[19]

As the Senate amended the treaty, the attacks on Hay increased. The usual charges mounted that it was all a surrender to the British; Hay was their tool and McKinley a willing or unwilling dupe. The Irish, the Democrats, the discontented everywhere seized upon this chance to twist the English lion's tail. The talk nettled McKinley. The charge that Hay had been "educated in the English school" provoked an acid rejoinder: "I wish someone had replied to that by saying, 'Yes, he was trained under Abraham Lincoln.'" [20]

Troublesome, shortsighted, exasperating, and frustrating as the senatorial objections might be, they were nonetheless real. Through the spring they were increasingly fortified by the anti-imperialist press, joined occasionally and ironically by the jingo press, which felt that lack of fortifications would slow overseas expansion.[21] While Lodge was reluctant to alienate his friend Hay, with whom he generally agreed, he could not accept the original treaty. "The plain facts of the case are these," he wrote Henry White. "The American people will never consent to building a canal at their own expense, which they shall guard and protect for the benefit of the world's commerce unless they have virtually complete control. There is no use arguing about the wisdom of this attitude."[22] Lodge dealt with reality, and those around him increasingly saw that he was right.

As the treaty lay fallow during the summer months, controversy over the canal continued. The tiresome discussion of routes revived. The President was inclined toward Nicaragua because it involved fewer political problems, and the canal commission would recommend that route. Senator Morgan always agreed. Morgan did not believe, correctly as it turned out, that Colombia would part with a canal zone in the isthmus without a struggle; nor did he feel that the French assets in the uncompleted canal in that area would be usable. But that was not the worst of it to Hay; the problem of political attacks at home remained, and the campaign of 1900 induced Bryan to oppose the treaty. It was the last straw to Hay, then sick from nervous exhaustion and worry. "He struck at it in mere ignorance and malice, as an idiot might strike at a statue because he happened to have a hammer in his hand; but he has thus made it a political question and lined up his party strength against it."[23]

Rising resentment in the House compounded the President's worries over the canal. There seemed an excellent chance that the House would simply pass a resolution abrogating the Clayton-Bulwer Treaty and authorizing a unilateral canal. Senatorial opposition took form when on December 20 the upper house ratified the treaty with amendments giving the United States control of the canal, with the right to fortify it.

Hay was mortified, as he hastily informed Ambassador Choate, whose task it would be to present the amended treaty to the English. The administration looked upon the Senate's amendments as a violation of American honor and an insult to England. "*We* have suffered a rebuff at the hands of the Senate," Hay wrote Choate.

"It is *our* dignity that has suffered and not that of England." The blame rested with the Senate, he said, and the chief culprits were the maverick Republicans like Lodge who "panicked" and started "tacking on" amendments until England could not accept the treaty.[24]

Hay felt that the President had done all he could. Resentful of the Senate's encroachments on executive authority, and convinced that the treaty was proper and that England could not be expected to go further, McKinley had met opposing senators with a marked chill. Lodge, Aldrich, and Foraker came to a White House conference to state their views. The President was not happy, and looked it. The treaty was right, he said, as it stood, and ought to be ratified. Foraker and Lodge disagreed. Amendments abrogating the Clayton-Bulwer Treaty and removing the necessity of the consent of other powers were necessary for the treaty to pass at all. McKinley said that this would mean rejection in England. "That puts the onus of rejecting the treaty on England!" Lodge said. The President frowned. All agreed that unless some treaty were ratified, the Senate would do violence to the Clayton-Bulwer Treaty. A Hay-Pauncefote Treaty with amendments would at the very least buy time to negotiate a further convention, Lodge argued. The awful thing was, as everyone knew, that it must all be done over again.[25]

The President's attitude was clear to everyone who talked with him. Hanna found him "much exercised" over the whole affair during a friendly call, and McKinley spoke his mind freely about the Senate's action. To senators who called he was unusually frank, saying simply that he did not "see it" their way. He told Hoar bluntly that England "is as kind as she can be and desires to do exactly as we want." The Senate's recalcitrance might yet cost the United States the canal.[26]

In March, 1901, the English rejected the treaty as amended by the senate and assumed that the Clayton-Bulwer Treaty was still in force. They would view with alarm any construction not preceded by adequate treaty arrangements; thus Hay could not retire from the field. Nor did he wish to. He devoted most of the remaining months of 1901 to a second Hay-Pauncefote Treaty, signed on November 18, 1901, and duly ratified by the Senate on December 16. Hay's only sorrow lay in McKinley's absence, for his late chief's patience had done much to achieve the final agreement. In this

458

second treaty the English abandoned all their claims and left the canal to the Americans. "We must bear the atmosphere of the hour," McKinley had said. "It will pass away."

The story of the isthmian canal was not finished. It would be years before actual construction began, but McKinley had done much to make it possible; his patience, support of Hay, and calmness had avoided any hostility with England. McKinley may well have been converted to the shorter and more convenient Panama route, but he would not have acquired a canal zone in the manner employed by his successor. The bluster and violence in Theodore Roosevelt's whole Latin American policy never found any welcome in the McKinley administration. It was a major tragedy in American diplomacy that McKinley did not live to consummate the policies he set in motion in Latin America.

The President was rewarded elsewhere by minor encouraging successes, such as the American adherence to the Hague Conference, called by the czar of Russia to attempt to establish machinery for international arbitration. McKinley and the cabinet received the initial invitation to attend as a tribute to America's growing power in world affairs. The President did not doubt the czar's sincerity, though like most Americans, he did not expect much of the conference.[27]

The American delegation which sat at the Hague during the summer of 1899 was impartial and distinguished. Andrew White, of Cornell University, and Seth Low, of Columbia, returned chatty and interesting reports which the President read. The nations were unwilling to surrender any sovereignty, Low reported, but the conference had already eased some tensions. White gauged the rather good-natured skepticism at home well, but saw hopeful signs. "Of course it will come short of what the enthusiasts and dreamers expect, but I believe that the more thoughtful men and women in the world will see in it not only a plan good in itself but one which will prove to be a germ out of which better and better things will be developed in the future," he wrote Chauncey Depew.[28] The President saw the conference as another step in the long road to world peace, for which he was anxious to use America's growing stature.

When the problems of isthmian canals, Alaska boundaries, open doors, and Boxer Rebellions did not plague Hay, he devoted some

459

attention to routine duties and such minor matters as the flurry of interest in the Danish West Indies that struck certain parts of the Senate after 1899. A deal for the latter was finally consummated under Woodrow Wilson, and formed the last step in guaranteeing American control of the Caribbean area. The Danes were willing to sell the islands for a stiff price provided it could be arranged quickly. But a cabinet crisis in Copenhagen ended the immediate chance of selling the islands. The President's interest, however, was aroused, and he read several long reports from Henry White, who handled matters in Denmark, and Hay, who conducted negotiations from Washington.[29]

One event called for more than ordinary tact, the Boer War that erupted in South Africa in the fall of 1899. Confident claims that it would be settled in a matter of weeks turned to ashes as the resources of the British Empire seemed necessary to quell the rebellion of Dutch farmers. Much American sympathy naturally went to the Boers, on the assumption that they were fighting for freedom. The administration was between two fires; an inevitable election loomed next year in which the anti-English vote might count, but the administration could not upset pending negotiations with England by a pro-Boer announcement.

The eve of conflict in South Africa brought appeals for McKinley's mediation from American consular officials there and from elements among the Boers themselves. The first response from the White House was a calm assurance that the President would do what he could by offering his good offices to the parties involved. Beyond that he could not go. Despite political pressures, he stated, in his annual message of December 5, 1899, only that the United States would of course be neutral in "the unfortunate contest between Great Britain and the Boer states of Africa." [30]

The presence of Hay's son Adelbert in the consular service in South Africa fortified the Secretary's already rampant Anglophile attitude. Hay viewed with disdain any suggestion that the Boers merited anything but suppression, and his formal comments on the war exuded a noticeable chill. In the spring of 1900, McKinley renewed his offer of mediation, but the English returned the expected polite refusal. The President was only extending the gesture required of him.[31]

But he was not to escape without a public display of his pro-

English attitude. Boer envoys, in search of funds and diplomatic support, arrived amid some celebration and much publicity to attend a rally in Washington late in May. Their partisans thoughtfully forwarded two tickets to the proceedings to the White House. The disapproving Cortelyou promptly returned them for all too obvious reasons.[32] The following day the Boers called on Hay, who met them with frank impatience, and his coldness ended any hopes they may have had of American aid. He listened to their formal statement requesting American good offices and hinting that more concrete assistance would be welcome, then fixed his eyeglasses and read the prepared paper which he had held all along. "It was a bit discouraging to see our answer lying on the table as we entered and before we had had opportunity to open our mouths," one of the Boers said.

Daunted but not defeated, the group crossed the lawn to the White House, where they were sure a warmer reception awaited them. Once safely in the presidential presence, however, their hopes faded. McKinley was calm and as cordial as ever. But when they broached the subject of their visit, innocently as a child he drew their attention to the splendid view from his window. As he talked, their time vanished in this pleasant subterfuge. They left, after the President graciously excused himself, richer in nothing but antiquarian lore on the Washington view. Like Hay, McKinley proposed to be passive in the affair, election year or not. Later in August he revealed a deeper suspicion of Boer designs. Rejecting the idea of American asylum for defeated Boer leaders, he noted stiffly that "it looks to me very much as though there might be some purpose in it which is not altogether manifest now. . . ."[33] It would never do to have vocal Boer exiles in America.

Of necessity the President had not taken a prominent role in the long and tedious negotiations with England over the canal treaty and other issues. He tried only to watch the total picture. He had promised Hay a full and responsible hand in running foreign affairs and was only too glad to abide by his agreement. He trusted Hay's discretion and judgment, and agreed with his ideas, while Hay looked upon McKinley as a source of political strength and as the arbiter of differences that arose within the government. It was an ideal arrangement for both men.

One aspect of foreign affairs did not escape the President's close attention, however. As the promised prosperity returned after the war, he turned with greater force to the reciprocity treaties negotiated under the Dingley Act. He accepted commercial reciprocity after much thought. Since the tariff of 1890 he had been interested in it, and urged Congress to include it in the Dingley Act. He believed that the age of commercial exclusion was past. He saw in reciprocity an excellent chance to attain much of his goal of world harmony and peace under American direction by economic means, avoiding the harsher realities of direct political action. He believed that the country's unparalleled prosperity proved that protection was no longer the necessity it had once been. The tariff must now be lowered gradually if the nation was to capture the world's markets in the future. Political isolation was obviously ending, and economic isolation must inevitably pass.[34]

The President made the influential and experienced Iowan, John Kasson, head of a special reciprocity division in the State Department, giving him confidence and a free hand. Though harrassed by troubles with Spain during 1897, the war in 1898, and other entanglements in 1899, the President and Kasson negotiated a series of treaties with European powers and their colonies before the time limit expired.[35] Kasson's success won McKinley's gratitude, but both knew that making and ratifying treaties were two different things. Like Hay, Kasson often wished out loud that the Senate would disappear.

Once committed to the Senate Finance Committee, the treaties were heard of no more. Senator Cullom, to whose nominal charge they fell, worked in vain. Conservative Republicans paled at the thought of the President's proposed system of international reciprocity. Who knew where it would lead? The Senate proposed to kill the treaties with neglect.[36]

Much of the conservative opposition was sincere. Men like Connecticut's Orville Platt feared the precedents implied in reciprocity. They were old, reluctant to change; they had never been in the liberal wing of the party, as McKinley had. Reciprocity seemed a logical extension of protection to him; it seemed a new and radical innovation to them. The Democrats, theoretically committed to free trade, opposed reciprocity as being a means of saving protection.

The focus of opposition lay in the Finance Committee, where

462

Aldrich and Allison reigned supreme. But the situation was not without some hope. Neither of these was an ironclad protectionist; it all depended on how well they could control those who were. McKinley realized his error in not consulting the Senate while the treaties were being drawn up, and now liberally applied his personal charm. Allison, always a weathervane, began to waver, after hearing rumbles of discontent from the Midwest. The tariff, some said, was the mother of the trusts. His ear to the ground, the aging Senator did not like what he heard, but he hesitated to speak out.[37]

The logs began to roll as soon as change was mentioned. The usual interests, potent as ever and liberally supplied with funds, issued arguments that had long since been hackneyed. Kasson sighed with weariness at his opposition. "The chief difficulty is that each interest speaks for itself," he wrote Allison in 1898, "and none for the general interests of the country." The American Protective Tariff League came forward with its well-phrased talk about home markets and domestic prosperity, pressuring congressmen to oppose the President's plans. The whole thing had a trace of humor; few had expected the author of the McKinley Tariff ever to favor downward revision. That, of course, was a moot point; the President was no free trader. The system of reciprocity he envisaged was both gradual and moderate, but it was a beginning. "These treaty arrangements are not to be confused with any proposals for tariff revision," Kasson assured a businessmen's banquet in 1901. "They simply execute the provisions of the Dingley Tariff as it now stands." [38]

McKinley had barely registered any success with the complex program when the war brought further complications. What was the status of the new dependencies? Did they have ready access to the American market, duty-free? Of these, Porto Rico was the most complicated and politically dangerous. The island's situation appealed to most Americans; it was presumably a war indemnity, but it had no insurrection such as there was in the Philippines. Its main crops were sugar and coffee, both used amply in the United States. Its people were poverty stricken and desperately in need of relief. It seemed only right that the United States should help. The President accepted that view. "Our plain duty is to abolish all customs tariffs between the United States and Puerto Rico and give her products

463

free access to our markets," he said in his annual message of December, 1899, in a phrase that would boomerang on him.

In December, McKinley and Root began to replace military government in the island with a system of civil government. The necessary legislation would be prepared under the auspices of Foraker's special Senate committee on dependencies. The committee drafted its bills under great pressure from American military authorities in the island and interested groups there who warned that relief was doubly necessary due to the disastrous hurricane that ravaged the island in August, 1899. A special relief measure, an outline of civil government, and an act recognizing free trade were therefore drawn up and introduced early in January.[39]

As the bills slumbered in committee, awaiting debate, no one doubted where McKinley stood. He was apparently willing to face the protectionists at long last. In late January, however, the bees began to swarm from the hive which the President had kicked, as the "protectionist fraternity" awoke to the full danger involved.[40] Through February and into March they pressured Foraker and others not to set the precedent of free trade with Porto Rico, lest this also imply free trade with the Philippines and give a boost to the President's reciprocity program. By February, New York's Sereno Payne had drafted a substitute House measure that levied 25 per cent of the Dingley rates on Porto Rican products. On March 1, Foraker yielded to the call for compromise with a plan of his own: why not levy 15 per cent of the Dingley rates for a two-year period, the money to be spent in Porto Rico itself? Was it not fair to repay some of the American investment in the island by this means of self-help? Republican and Democratic newspapers for once joined in condemning the protectionist lobby, and saw in all the compromise schemes merely other ways of defeating any reform. Recalcitrant conservatives were reminded of what their own President had said of free trade.

It all made McKinley somewhat nervous. He had not counted on this sort of controversy. He had wanted a quick settlement of the matter. Burdened with other concerns, the last thing he wanted was a quarrel with Congress, especially in view of the pending election of 1900. He looked at the problem again from every angle and wavered. He knew that he faced formidable opposition within the party. Hanna was agitated over tariff reform; Orville Platt was "much distressed" by the move for free trade with Porto Rico; prominent members of Congress feared a party split in an election year.[41] Would it not be wise, he asked himself, to delay on the issue until after the election; then, re-elected with popular support, he could assault the whole protectionist fraternity through reciprocity. To quarrel now would court disaster. He weakened.

Foraker debated the relief bill and amendments grant civil government in the first week of March. He was reluctant to call a vote, not knowing how his lines would hold or just what the President would do. He favored the compromise 15 per cent rate to avoid an election year struggle; what did it matter, he reiterated, for the money would be spent in the island and the tariff would last only until 1902, or perhaps not that long if the Porto Rican economy revived. Many Republicans wavered with the President, but were pressured by angry constituents. A prominent Republican said that "a few weeks ago we were united and invincible; now we are divided and in danger of defeat!" [42]

It all came back to the President, and the more criticism he heard from the party the more cautious he became. He favored the compromise rate. He called recalcitrants to the White House, where he explained his stand. Party harmony dictated this partial surrender, he said; protection was too ingrained on the pattern of Republicanism to be endangered just now. It was an election year. He was perfectly willing to take the blame for it. Those who had wavered left his presence committed to the compromise, though some, like Senator Davis, were frankly bitter at his surrender.[43]

On April 3, after much heated debate, the 15 per cent rate bill passed the Senate; on April 11 the House concurred, and McKinley signed it the following day. McKinley always justified his action in terms of party unity. "We need party harmony on the greater and more important question of the Philippines. I know I shall be charged with weakness, but I prefer to endure such charges rather than face the future with a disunited party." It seemed weak, especially to Kasson, who had fought so hard and to such little avail for a lower tariff. "I could not allow the Republican party in the House to be defeated by the votes of the Democratic minority," the President explained to Kasson.[44] He would not risk a nonpartisan appeal to Democrats and Republicans alike, for that might alienate a large wing of his party in the election year.

The President had his way; the money was raised and spent in the island, and he was able before his death to proclaim free trade with Porto Rico. As usual, his plan worked out. But at the time it smelled of petty politics. Much of the public never saw him in quite the same light again. The newspapers had a field day, and though the words were harsh, there was some justice in the assertion that "it is not a question of brains but a question of backbone." [45]

McKinley had basked in unprecedented popularity since the war. His course resembled true statesmanship, and his deep personal sincerity impressed the people. He had become a truly national president, and the people not only admired him, they loved him. The tariff controversy momentarily broke the spell. Ugly memories of the vicious charges of 1896 rose in some minds again. He was Hanna's tool, the front for "The Interests," a weakling given to compromise and inaction, noble sentiments and shady dealings. He was, after all, a politician, many said. Had he been a different man, McKinley would have seized this opportunity to challenge the protectionists in an election year, gaining support from both parties, redeeming his promise to the new colonials, and cutting the ground from under any Democratic talk of reform. But he was not that other man; the party was his life, and his habits of conciliation did not permit such drama.

As the warm spring turned to a warmer summer in Washington, he faced the prospect of another election with resignation. It was bad enough, though he would not campaign again, but the year brought no relaxation in the procession of foreign crises that had occupied him since 1897. The last great question remaining between the United States and Great Britain concerned China, a complex problem with which Hay had been wrestling since 1898. To most Americans China was a dim and mysterious continent of its own, presided over by yellow orientals of fabled cunning and devious designs. Its culture, art, peoples, and history were closed books, but its mystery and a sense of enchantment with its ways always remained. It was not very real; Americans could not discuss it very intelligently. The war changed this somewhat; acquisition of the Philippines inevitably sharpened interest in the whole Orient.

It fell to Hay and McKinley to devise a China policy, and its results were peculiarly American, centering around a famous phrase, "the Open Door." Hay knew how anxious the English were to ally the United States with their own policy of keeping China neutral while not disturbing existing treaty-port arrangements whereby nearly every major European power controlled a portion of the China trade and maintained an armed watch over the tottering empire. In March, 1898, Ambassador Hay journeyed south to the warmth of Egypt, where he talked of China with interested Englishmen. Perhaps an understanding could be worked out between the United States and England. The Ambassador remembered the arguments when he became secretary of State in the fall. At about the same time, in the United States, Ambassador Pauncefote informally suggested to McKinley that discussions on the subject might be fruitful. Immersed in other worries with Spain, wary of all propositions implying an alliance, and ignorant of the Chinese situation, McKinley politely demurred with the suggestion that the United States would informally agree with England in favoring Chinese territorial integrity.[46]

The war threw the problem into sharper relief. "The outcome of our struggle with Spain may develop the need of extending and strengthening our interests in the Asiatic Continent," Day wrote Hay as the war continued.[47] The President, still ignorant of the problem, did not persuade so easily; he thought for a moment that it might be well not to stand for an open door. "May we not want a slice, if it is to be divided?" he asked when China was mentioned, an opinion supported sometimes by the minister to China, Edward Conger.[48] But McKinley quickly saw the advantage to the United States of sustaining Chinese territorial integrity. It would stabilize a dangerous situation and help prevent quarrels among the great powers if China survived. Devoid of the power to enforce her will in China, the United States must devise a policy dependent upon other powers. The President saw that the Open Door would at least suffice for the moment to assure double security, to prevent tension that would follow division of China by the powers, and to assure American participation in the China trade. He was the first to use the phrase, later garlanded with so much approval, in his instructions to the Paris Peace Commission: "Asking only the open door for ourselves, we are ready to accord the open door to others." [49]

Hay pointed out, however, that the administration would not

467

shrink from bargaining. "Open door does not mean free trade but admission of other nations to the Philippine trade on equal footing with ourselves," he cabled Henry White late in 1898.[50] Whatever doubts the President may have had faded during 1899 as the necessity of a China policy became clearer. Schurman, returning from the Philippines, assured him of the commercial advantages in China.[51] Besides, there was always the chance of an impressive victory in the growing understanding with England, for the China policies of the two countries now coincided.

Hay did not take too seriously the President's rather absent dismissal of the idea of an understanding with England over China, and in 1899 began to formulate his policy. A famous and competent Asian expert, W. W. Rockhill, called to head the innocuous Bureau of the American Republics in Washington, helped him and also advised the President. Hay had read Charles Beresford's popular book, *The Breakup of China,* and was aware of the explosive situation within the empire. He feared the growing power of the Germans, but the Russians and Japanese also posed a menace. A travelling Englishman in the consular service in China, Alfred Hippisley, joined Hay and Rockhill in making a policy. McKinley talked privately with Hippisley and was much impressed by the Englishman's striking recitation of his Chinese adventures. Long memoranda flowed from Rockhill to Hay to the President.[52]

It was said in after years that the Open Door was all a British subterfuge, like so much of Hay's policy, accepted by the United States as part of the Anglo-American accord. The English had much to do with its formulation and adoption by the United States, but the English furnished only the general idea. Hippisley's draft memoranda, shown to McKinley during August, confirmed his policy and ideas. McKinley would doubtless have come to the same policy without promptings from the English. It was the most feasible one for the United States at the moment because of its commercial promises and diplomatic protection without the invocation of force.

As it developed through the spring of 1899, Hay firmly opposed the partition of China, insisting at the same time that the United States would not "take part in the great game of spoliation now going on [in China]." The pressures continued from diplomats and business interests. As rumors flew of a departure in American policy, more and more newspapers favored participation in the China policy. The result was popular support for the formal announcement on September 6, 1899, that Hay had dispatched a circular note to the major European powers dealing with the Open Door.[53] The terms were as expected; Hay asked that the powers in China agree to three things: noninterference in the leases and vested rights within each power's treaty port; application of the Chinese tariff collected by the Chinese within each sphere of interest; and nondiscrimination by each power in favor of its own nationals on railroad rates and harbor dues within its sphere of influence.

To the English, Choate was frank; commercial reasons dictated the notes, for the United States wished to expand its China trade. To the Chinese, Hay extended assurances of the policy's altruism, spiced by commercial realities, and insisted that the United States wanted no Chinese territory.[54] The response from the powers was unenthusiastic. All accepted in principle if all the others would accept. This did not deter Hay from consummating his bold stroke. On March 20, 1900, he blandly informed the world that all of the powers had accepted the policy. The United States considered the Open Door's acceptance "final and definitive."

American public reaction to Hay's deceptive success was instant and rewarding. Coming as it did on the verge of the frustrating dealings over the canal, and in the midst of the Philippine entanglement, the Open Door negotiations seemed a relief from tedious diplomatic defeat. There seemed to be no diplomacy involved; Hay seemed simply to have impressed his will upon the powers, saved China, and enlarged America's role in the Orient. Here was diplomacy that the ordinary American could understand, devoid of treaties and bickering, bright with promise for the future, gilded over with the wonderful combination of moral altruism and commercial success so peculiarly appealing to Americans.

The challenge to the whole policy which the Open Door notes sought to alleviate came not from the Europeans but from the Chinese themselves. As spring drifted into summer in the pleasant last year of the century, Americans thought little of China except to congratulate Hay for having solved the problem. Facing re-election, McKinley was not disposed to raise the issue further. But it raised itself. As the nation and the world watched in horror in early summer, the seemingly dormant and helpless Manchu empire erupted in revolution and international tragedy.

Smarting under foreign domination, the younger element in China turned hated eyes upon the arrogant and wealthy foreigners. Forming a group called by various names, but nicknamed the Boxers because of their gymnastics, the younger Chinese boasted the secret support of the aged and much-feared Empress Dowager. Publicly aloof, the old Empress secretly sympathized with her restless subjects, and her imperial troops were not to be trusted to sustain the foreigners should there be a general insurrection.

As the tension rose, the Western Powers seemed oblivious to their danger. Conger appealed vainly for American participation in a naval demonstration in north China waters. Diplomats and missionaries reported that the revolt which flared in the northern provinces in the spring of 1900 was merely local. Rockhill discounted the possibility of a general uprising.[55]

The silence of cable wires from Conger late in May and early in June at last alarmed Washington, and on June 3 the world learned of a general uprising. The foreign navies at Tientsin were landing marines and available troops to relieve the impounded foreign legations in Peking. Early June brought a statement of American policy as the public imagination ran riot over first fragmentary reports of the murder of missionaries and destruction of the area around the imperial capital. "We have no policy in China except to protect with energy American interests, and especially American citizens and the legation," Hay wired Conger. "There must be nothing done which would commit us to future action inconsistent with your standing instructions. There must be no alliances." [56]

The siege of the foreign legations must now be lifted by an international expedition, for the first relief columns perished as they crossed the inflamed countryside. Admiral Kempff, in command of the American China squadron, could do little. A raid on the army in the Philippines proved necessary, though McKinley was reluctant to deprive MacArthur of much-needed troops. The President was wary of the undertaking, which might seem to the public to involve an alliance, but public opinion sustained his course.[57]

The President went to Canton after his nomination, refusing to campaign. He conducted business over a special long-distance telephone to Washington, and matters there fell to the senior cabinet officer present, generally Root, who bore these added duties gracefully, though he was immersed in his own work.

Laid low by overwork, heat prostration, and a bad case of nerves, Hay fled in August to his summer home in New Hampshire, but his conscience gnawed at him, compounding his physical illnesses. He regretted his isolation from events in Washington, and feared that his absence would spark rumors that the President distrusted him. "It is a great affliction to sit apparently helpless at such a vast distance, knowing that scenes of tragic horror are taking place so far away and not being able to prevent them," he wrote the President.[58]

In Washington, "the faithful remnant of the cabinet," generally Root, Gage, and Smith, tried to keep McKinley posted. The deaf Adee knew most, but he had trouble communicating with Root, who in turn had trouble making the long distance telephone to Canton work. Root wrote his wife that he had first to "yell at Adee" and then "yell at the president." "I feel as if China had me by the throat," he said ruefully.[59] McKinley returned to Washington for special cabinet meetings and found the capital steaming and deserted. He dispelled rumors that he would summon Congress into special session; that, as usual, was the last thing he wanted. He spent most of his time in Canton, not only directing the China policy, while anxiously awaiting news of the legations, but also trying to keep calm and statesmanlike during the campaign. He never liked the telephone, and often kept a secretary at hand to take down what was said if necessary; such was the caution bred by Ohio politics. He disliked it chiefly because of its impersonality and inhuman qualities, and often had trouble making it work. One afternoon as he talked to Washington, his gardener ran water into a bucket beneath his window. It was hot, the window was open, and the sound carried. The President leaned out the window, hand over the mouth piece, and called down, "Mike, won't you please stop that noise till I get through?" The gardener obliged with a wave—he was an old friend—sat down and smoked, knocking the ashes out of his pipe when the President finished. "Major," he asked, with Canton's usual familiarity toward its illustrious citizen, "what are ye goin' to do with thim haythen?"[60]

McKinley might well have pondered the question, for the necessity of answering it loomed nearer in August. On the fourteenth the legations were freed by the international army, and Hay restored communication with Conger, whom many had given up for dead. The ingenious Secretary confirmed Conger's presence by asking him to name his sister, a homely stroke that pleased the public. The public was avid for news from China, which easily rivalled the rather dull presidential election. "The drama of the legations interested the public much as though it were a novel by Alexandre Dumas," the cynical Henry Adams remembered.[61]

The public drama may have ended, but the necessity of careful diplomacy sharpened, for a settlement must now be devised to save China from the rapacious designs of the Germans, Japanese, and Russians. On July 3, Hay had circulated another note saying that the United States would oppose any efforts to use the rebellion as an excuse to end the Open Door policy or to partition China. "What I want is the friendship of China when the trouble is over," Mc-Kinley told a Canton visitor.[62] Hay agreed, but did not quite know how to keep the other powers from seizing Chinese territory. "Of course we are not the policeman of the world and cannot take by the collar every nation which commits a crime," he wrote the President. "But certainly we cannot hold our tongues completely in such a case." [63]

McKinley presided at the White House on August 28 when the cabinet considered a Russian proposition to withdraw from Peking pending a settlement. The resulting American answer was an unhappy marriage of McKinley's prose and Root's ideas, that smacked of uncertainty and divisions. The President frankly wanted to get out of Peking because of the issue of "McKinley imperialism" in the campaign, because of the ever-present danger of quarrels among the powers, and because the American soldiers were needed in the Philippines. At the same time he could not think of partitioning China, and agreed with Adee that holding Peking as a kind of hostage would expedite the settlement.[64] He wanted to withdraw, but only with all the powers.

August lengthened into September and still the powers wrangled over the proposed indemnity and treaties to be wrung from China. In the middle of the month the President unburdened himself to Hay. He wanted to get out of China, but was not sure just how to do it except to get out, plain and simple. "We want to avoid being in Peking for a long time and it must be a long time if we stay there for the diplomatic negotiations, and without our intending it, we may be drawn into currents that would be unfortunate." [65] Hay was more realistic: unilateral withdrawal, or one in concert with the Russians, would be an admission of defeat. He advised awaiting events.[66] It was admittedly exasperating, as he wrote Adee. "It all sums up to this: we shall get no credit whatever we do; our friends will take it as a matter of course, and our critics will kick us all around the lot." The United States could not leave lest it look like surrender, yet could not enforce any decision. "The talk of the papers about 'our pre-eminent moral position giving us the authority to dictate to the world' is mere flap-doodle," the Secretary said with sharp candor.[67] The President dropped the subject, though the American force was later reduced to a legation guard.

While McKinley wished proper punishment for the Chinese offenders, he did not wish a heavy indemnity. He refused the German demand that the powers punish the Chinese ringleaders. And above all he and Hay wished to preserve the Open Door. Beyond this they could not go; talk of an alliance with England irritated both, who had had more than enough of these temporary alliances. The negotiations dragged through the winter of 1900 and spring of 1901, but the President could report with some satisfaction in his annual message of December 3, 1900, that the outcome would be satisfactory. "I am disposed to think that due compensation may be made in part by increased guarantees of security for foreign rights and immunities, and, most important of all, by the opening of China to the equal commerce of all the world," he said confidently. England's support of the American demand for leniency was not entirely successful, but the final indemnity settlement was not exorbitant. The story eventually had a happy ending, for the United States disavowed its monetary settlement in 1924, and China used the money to educate students in the United States.

McKinley's growth in ability after the war with Spain is striking. He seemed ever more sober and thoughtful to the men who talked with him. He had a large and surprising grasp of the problems at hand, and greater perspective from which to make judgments. He seemed to grow more firm, more confident of his own powers, as the central design of his foreign policy slowly emerged from the welter of diplomatic detail that surrounded its construction. He needed patience, calmness, and dignity as he faced a second mandate from the people that hot summer of 1900. It was the last election of the century, and there seemed little doubt about its outcome. But he had long since learned that in politics, nothing is ever certain.

XXI

President of All the People

THE SUMMER OF 1899 brought McKinley a brief rest from the ceaseless complexities of foreign and domestic problems, and added a great personal pleasure—he was at last to have a real home. He often reflected to friends that he and Ida had not really had a home of their own since he entered politics; they had lived most of their married life in hotels, executive mansions, and other people's houses. That summer he returned to Canton after purchasing his old house. He proudly conducted visitors and dignitaries around the yard, pointing to the flower beds, the neat fence, then standing back at the front gate to get a full view of the house and its setting. It sat on an ample, quiet lot, not far from the center of town but not in the traffic. It was not pretentious, but it was comfortable. "We began our married life in that house; our children were born there; one was buried from there," he told friends. "Some of the tenderest memories of my life are centered there, and some of the saddest. I am as happy as a child to have it back. It's a fine old place."

He saw it as a kind of summer White House. He showed Cortelyou on a scrap of paper the improvements and additions he wished to make so that he could entertain when necessary. "Now I shall have a home, what I have wanted so long; a home I can go to. If I have a place like that, I can get away any time, and could take you with all the help we need, and we could transact all the Executive business there."

Not everyone who came was impressed. Mrs. Hanna, not given to snobbery though she was socially conscious, got a presidential tour and was not excited by the house or by McKinley's almost boyish exclamation, "And the best thing about it is that it's all paid for." [1] Theodore Roosevelt thought that the house resembled that of a railroad superintendent, hardly the home of the nation's chief executive. His simple pleasure in the house hid any defects of architecture or elegance from McKinley. He told Long and others that he and Ida would redecorate it themselves to live in after he left the White House.[2]

The President's sense of well-being only reflected the larger attitude of the America over which he presided. Whatever the prosperous and hazy years after the war with Spain were to others—self-righteous, smug, provincial, or happy, gay, contented, and blissful—they were the golden age of the Grand Old Party. Most Americans breathed the air of confident equanimity that radiated from commercial prosperity and pride of national accomplishment. All of this national and international glory reflected in turn upon a Republican party not unwilling to take perhaps undue credit for the nation's situation. Never again would Republicans bask so happily in the reflected glow of prosperous contentment and peace. Seldom again would America seem so much the land of opportunity where, as Mr. McKinley proved, any man could hope to be president. If it was a false dawn, or a twilight, few admitted it. Those occupied with power strengthened their positions; those concerned with money relished and expanded their situation; the vast mass of people, concerned with neither, would look back with nostalgia upon this last generation of the nineteenth century. No facade is a house; success is bought at a price. Republican security rested upon successful bargaining with the powers that were, with only limited attention to the powers that would be. The temper in politics and elsewhere was conservative, and many ignored the forewarnings of coming upheavals. But the years merited their title: the Age of Confidence.

The President was given to confidence but not to complacency. He had been in politics too long to make that mistake. He read with pleasure such letters as the one Tama Jim Wilson sent to Canton. "Nobody is thought of for your successor but yourself." [3] McKinley knew the power his name commanded among the people; it was not only his party that looked upon his successes among the people with a kind of superstitious awe. He was often compared to Lincoln for his management of men, but he let no comparisons blind him to the temporary quality of any public success. His chief personal satisfaction lay in having come to the threshold of his ancient dream of nationalism. He had lived to see sectionalism blur and almost disappear. "The present war has certainly served one very useful purpose in completely obliterating the sectional lines drawn in the last one," he told John B. Gordon, former Confederate from Georgia.[4]

Supporting this feeling of national unity was the high level of prosperity, based on full production, a gold dollar, and an excess of exports over imports. Factories turned away orders for lack of time and trained workers; railroads reported that they had no spare cars; wages were good, prices stable, and dividends handsome.[5]

Covering its commercial prosperity like a bright garment was the nation's increased pride in its status as a power. There was the unpleasant war in the Philippines, there would be a Boxer catastrophe, there were tense moments in Mr. Hay's dealings with other powers, but few Americans doubted their country's right to claim equality with the great powers of the world. Confidence was the war's chief emotional legacy. Ambassador Horace Porter noted it in a letter to his chief:

> I have frequently heard a number of public men in Europe express the opinion that we did in three months what the great powers of Europe had sought in vain to do for over a hundred years, in having secured a chain of island posts in the Pacific, secured the Philippines, captured their trade, paved the way for a Pacific cable of our own, virtually taken possession of that ocean and occupied a position at Manila easily defended, only a couple of days in time from the Chinese coast with no fear of Chinese or Russian armies at our back and yet near enough to protect our interests in the Orient. So that while some of our citizens of "mental malformation" are bemoaning our unlucky fate, the most experienced statesmen here envy our transcendent achievements and see clearly the future benefits.[6]

Such was the talk of politics, made real to the people in addresses and editorials. The burdens that came with those possessions were not yet apparent to the generation that first acquired them.

The sense of contentment and prosperity brought McKinley's political thinking full circle. His satisfaction with his national program was common knowledge, yet his reluctance to articulate his philosophy publicly, and his aversion to the glare of personal publicity obscured the deeper meanings of the quiet changes over which he presided. As always, politics was the center of his life, and even his opponents now recognized and admitted the deftness with which he had transformed potential political disaster into popular approval.

477

His understanding of the people and of the divergent forces of the American system was his greatest asset. He was not the people's slave, but their servant. He had done much of which they disapproved, and they had failed to sustain him and his policies too often for him to think that they were infallible, but he understood public opinion with a keenness not seen in the White House since Lincoln. To him the art of politics was the reconciliation of divergent interests. Government, he thought, functioned for the people, to further the total good. He had few qualms about federal power; he would be alien to subsequent generations of Republicans if they properly understood him. If the programs of subsidy or government action were national in scope, he saw no evil in them.

By some curious rapport with the people, through the indefinable but real intuition which had saved him so many times, he understood both the people and the system. The more rational, if less popular, Henry Adams grudgingly admitted that the Major was "a marvellous manager of men." In his intellectual way he perceived clearly what McKinley felt to be true:

> Mr. McKinley brought to the problem of American government a solution which lay very far outside of Henry Adams's education, but which seemed to be at least practical and American. He undertook to pool interests in a general trust into which every interest should be taken, more or less at its own evaluation, and whose mass should, under his management, create efficiency. He achieved very remarkable results. How much they cost is another matter; if the public is ever driven to its last resources and the usual remedies of chaos, the result will probably cost more.[7]

McKinley took this vision to the people in a more rustic and compelling form. His understanding of the power of public opinion and the virtues of its use is reflected in the mere fact of his travels. More than any previous president since Lincoln or perhaps since Jackson, he toured every section of the country, allowing himself to be seen, and, in turn, seeing men and women from all walks of life.

He believed that government functioned to reflect the people's best wishes; he could discover these wishes and gauge his popular strength only by travel and personal contact, at which he was masterly. Like any sucessful leader he strove to become a symbol rather than a mere man; death prevented the completion of the process, but he had accomplished much by 1901. His tour of the South in 1898 had helped everyone in that section, Booker T. Washington wrote him.[8] The East and Midwest knew him, and the Far West would see him in the summer before his death.

He was not above combining discreet politicking with his tours, but he always appeared as an American rather than as merely a Republican president. In the summer of 1899 he categorically refused to campaign if he were renominated the following year.[9] He could conveniently tour the Midwest that fall, therefore, as his last national campaign tour, testing the public support for his diplomatic policies as he went. Immense crowds greeted him, eager to shake his hand, to hear his voice, or to see him in procession. Lest this detract from his growing strength, he spoke of no specific policies or candidates as he passed among the people, despite Senator Hanna's hope that he might join him in some old fashioned "bushwhacking." [10] The elections were not crucial, but they were another Republican victory in which McKinley took pride and renewed confidence. They were, as Hanna said, "certainly a magnificent endorsement of this administration. . . ." [11]

If the President radiated confidence and a sense of well-being which he found in the country as a whole, he was not blind to other forces. He recognized a growing threat in the trust issue. Though he seldom mentioned the trust problem in public, it was much on his mind during 1899 and 1900. He sensed that it was the coming political issue; the settlement of the issues of expansion inevitably meant a turning inward, just as the settlement of the currency question in 1896 had meant a turning outward. The President listened more than he talked on the subject, but it was common knowledge that he was disturbed for more than political reasons; he felt personally that the trust magnates had gone too far for everyone's good. Perhaps they did threaten the American dream of individualism. He was heard to hint that maybe the Sherman Act ought to be dusted off.[12]

The opinion was not universal among his associates. "I cannot, however, excite myself with much alarm at the direction which the industrial movement has taken," Lyman Gage wrote a correspondent. "In a free country the corporations cannot rise superior to their creators—the people. The repressive hand of legislation can be laid upon them when occasion calls." [13] Senator Hanna was naturally more blunt. He thought of the whole issue as a Democratic delusion with no support among the people. It was to him a question of business, not a matter of social conscience. He thought the party might better keep silent on the issue. "I have as yet been unable to see any way to stop the combination of industrial interests in this country," he wrote Senator Chandler, who had begun to feel the ground rumble under him with distant protest that might ripen into political revolution. "In the numerous discussions that I heard upon the Constitution and the Declaration of Independence during the last session I got a sort of an idea that a man had a right to do what he pleased with his own, and I see no way to prevent it, if distinguished Senators like yourself and Senator Hoar are reliable in defining the Constitution." [14] It was a narrow and belligerent view, reflecting the self-made capitalist. Roosevelt, still a conservative Republican, felt that most of the talk against the trusts was "aimless and baseless," though they doubtless had their bad side.[15]

Worried Republicans like Chandler felt that McKinley would do all he could against the trusts.[16] McKinley was in an anomalous position. He knew little of business; it did not interest him, and his past experience in financial matters was not so pleasant as to prompt further personal study. But he did try to view the anti-trust agitation out of its mere political framework. He genuinely feared the growing trusts. When his friend George Perkins went to work for the Morgans in 1901, McKinley asked quizzically if he knew what he was getting into in joining such a large impersonal organization; might not such work "squeeze the humanities out of him"? [17] He shrewdly understood the emotional aspect of the problem that gave it force as a political issue.

With his usual penchant for the concrete, he did not indulge in arguments as to whether or not trusts were an inevitable outgrowth of capitalism; he only knew that they were there and would have to be faced. Dawes once raised the issue, suggesting that combinations must inevitably rule the economic system in the future. The President shifted uneasily and looked aside. He "guessed" that was so. The people as well as the companies must, however, be protected in any governmental action, he said before changing the subject.[18]

McKinley apparently first favored state legislation against the trusts to avoid making the question a national issue.[19] But he soon saw that this would not be enough to arrest the trusts or allay public fears. Early in 1899 he told Dawes that he would ask Congress for anti-trust legislation in the near future and began gathering material for a personal study of the problem.[20] His annual message of December, 1899, contained a statement on the subject: "Combinations of capital organized into trusts to control the conditions of trade among our citizens, to stifle competition, limit production, and determine the prices of products used and consumed by the people are justly provoking public discussion, and should early claim the attention of the Congress." [21] But no suggested legislation, no clear-cut call followed. As in the case of reciprocity, he would bide his time until re-elected; then his hand would be strengthened.

What McKinley would have done about the trusts had he lived to formulate a program cannot be known, but he would surely have recommended at least a minimal program. Roosevelt's subsequent discrimination between good and bad trusts is so McKinleyesque in its solution to the explosive problem that it may well have been McKinley's answer. In any case, his awareness of the issue would have led to action.

The President faced other vexing domestic problems during the summer of 1899. Labor violence erupted in the mines of Coeur d'Alene, Idaho, and inevitably the mine owners called for state militia and federal troops to quell the outbreak. The rugged wilds of the then-isolated state flared into open warfare between the partisans of labor and capital, and ugly charges flew that the administration permitted itself to be used to break the strike. The President was anxious that the federal troops sent to restore order do just that, not merely break the strike. Stories of violence on the part of state militia filtered eastward, but the federal troops were under strict orders not to go beyond their avowed purpose of restoring order.[22]

The lazy summer drifted past, its heat alleviated for McKinley by frequent stays at Canton, where he permitted himself his first real vacation in almost two years. He placed more confidence in the first session of the Congress to assemble in December than in any of its recent predecessors. For the first time since the dark days of the silver crusade this session would boast gold-standard majorities in both houses. Inevitably there would be legislation on the currency question. Republican majorities were such that the seating had to be rearranged to accommodate the surplus members in both houses.

There was a new speaker in the House, for Tom Reed had packed his bags after the war and left. In his place sat David B. Henderson, a one-legged Civil War veteran from Iowa, who could be counted on to sustain proper Republican votes. At the Capitol's other end, the powerful committees still worked under the direction of such men as Aldrich, Allison, and Orville Platt. The beloved Hobart was gone, and in his place the gavel fell under the humorless eye of William P. Frye. The President was wise enough not to interfere with the organization of the new Congress.[23] But though he knew most of the men well and had worked with them in the past, he grew increasingly restive about their attitude toward many of his wishes, such as reciprocity, the Porto Rican tariff, and the trust issue.

The one thing on which all Republicans could agree was the necessity of final legislation on the gold standard. The President had made his stand clear as early as the winter of 1897, when the last hopes of an international agreement on silver faded. In October of that year he called upon Congress to "strengthen the weak places in our financial system, and remove it forever from ambiguity and doubt." [24] It was a hopeless task so long as the rump of silver Republicans cooperated with the Democrats to howl down any hint of gold legislation, but McKinley assured a convention of the National Association of Manufacturers early in 1898 that he would press for legislation as soon as the composition of Congress changed. He had long since ended his dalliance with silver, perceiving that only gold could be a final national solution to the problem. "It will not suffice for citizens nowadays to say simply that they are in favor of sound money. That is not enough. The people's purpose must be given the vitality of public law. Better an honest effort with failure than the avoiding of so plain and commanding a duty." [25]

As if to mock the President in his own house, Senator Teller introduced a resolution to pay holders of government bonds in silver, and to Republican mortification it passed the upper chamber in January, 1898; again the House defeated it. The vote shocked the Republicans into an awareness of their continuing weakness on the issue. "The fact that the Senate can pass such a resolution will give

482

you some idea of the difficulty of getting desirable currency legislation through it," Lodge told an insistent correspondent.[26]

The fall elections of 1898 changed all of that, and McKinley fairly gloated in confidence that the silver issue would finally be buried. "Both branches of Congress on the 4th of March next will have an unquestioned majority opposed to any demoralization of our currency, and committed to uphold the world's standard," he told his audience at Boston's Commercial Club on February 17, 1899. "Certainly for two years every branch of the government will be united for good currency and the inviolability of our national obligations and credit." [27]

Through 1899 he laid his lines carefully, for even with a congressional majority he could not afford the luxury of an expanded public debate that might revive the ghost of free silver. Speed was essential. The administration recognized the genuine shortage of currency. Gage assured correspondents that the Treasury replaced large notes with smaller issue in an effort to inflate.[28] This was a half-measure at best, that the expanding state of business could not endure much longer.

For all his charm and affectionate demeanor, Secretary Gage was no politician and did not try to be one. He was available to all who wished his views, but he conducted his diplomacy and lobbying quietly among friends in Congress and elsewhere; the President would, as usual, handle whatever public relations the issue required. Gage spoke for McKinley when he outlined to Henderson what the administration wanted: a clear-cut statement in law on the gold standard, an expanded system of national banks, and parity of gold and silver by legislation if possible.[29]

Congress hesitated to go that far. The banks were, after all, inviolate to the Republicans like Aldrich and Platt. Conferences with Gage and the President did not produce a complete overhauling of the banking system, but clearly the congressional leaders would act. Early in May, the House Republicans caucused and agreed to pass a gold declaration with McKinley's support. They were all still cautious. "To have attempted more or less than this plan at this time would have been unwise, both from a commercial and political standpoint," Dawes wrote.[30]

Aldrich and Allison, who would manage the bill, were attuned to caution. They admitted the President's correctness in believing that the public would now sustain the gold standard, yet they were reluctant to touch the issue. McKinley demanded that something be done to redeem the greenbacks. A special fund ought to be set aside to redeem them in gold. They need not be recalled, but they should be equal to gold.[31]

As the new session approached, Gage felt that it was time to face the issue and to run political risk if necessary with a "bold, straight-forward, unequivocal declaration for the single standard." By November, the President's views took form for his annual message, but he still dallied. He wanted the substance, not merely the form, of a gold declaration, he told Dawes. His annual message of 1899 called for a revision of the banking system and for gold-standard legislation. Gage swept away as an illusion the old cry that there was still hope for an international agreement on silver.[32]

McKinley's caution seemed excessive to men like Lodge, who felt that there were no serious obstacles to gold legislation. But there was some danger that legislation might cause deflation, which the Republicans feared. New Year's Day brought predictions that Aldrich would bring up the bill for vote without delay, avoiding debate and cautioning the Republicans to silence lest they feed any fires the silverites lit.[33] Discussion of the complex measure faded in the public imagination before such things as Senator Beveridge's great speech and the reports on diplomacy abroad. World events stole the scene from the once potent money question. It was dull. "Speeches on the financial resolution seem like hammering nails in a coffin," one newspaper reported as the discussion wore on.[34] The silverites could clearly play only a delaying hand; they simply did not have the votes to prevent passage. On March 14, 1900, the Gold Standard Act became law. The President was jovial as he signed it that same day with a special gold pen brought for the ceremonies by a group of elder statesmen. The Act set the content of the gold dollar, and declared it the standard of American currency. A gold reserve, to be maintained by the sale of bonds if necessary, was established to redeem the greenbacks. The number of national banks of small capital was increased for the rural areas.

The President was not fully satisfied, but it was the first major piece of gold legislation in many years. "I think myself it is a great step forward to the interests of all the American people, high and low, rich and poor," Gage assured a correspondent. "Legislation always makes haste slowly, but with this advance gained the issue is narrowed, and we may look hopefully forward to the time when the consideration of a truly scientific currency may find its place in the proceedings of Congress," he added.[35]

The Act's passage centered public attention on the fact that it was a presidential election year, something that McKinley had never forgotten. Persistent rumors said that he faced dissension within his own party and from other quarters. It seemed impossible, in view of his public standing. Most such talk combined seriousness and humor to focus on the resplendent figure of Admiral George Dewey. It was said that he, like many military heroes, would like to be president, and that many men, even good Republicans, would like to see him unseat the President.

The Admiral came home in October, 1899, to an immense reception at New York and Washington. His tour through the nation's largest city exhausted even cynical reporters, and from the moment his ships anchored, saluted by the delirious whistles of a host of tugs and other craft, to the hour when he received the city's freedom in a tumultuous greeting, his progress was an unending triumph. Some who watched from the curb or who looked down from the tall buildings along his route, and who saw the Admiral's face wreathed in smiles of almost childish gratitude for the honors paid to him, wondered if he might not be groomed for public office. Many politicians would benefit from such a figure's manifest inability to understand either his public position or his political potential. The word went to the President that New York's fickle political rulers were cultivating the Admiral for obvious reasons.[36]

But the Admiral was silent, soaking up the admiration of the crowds with pleasure. The preparations for his reception at Washington, where the President was to present him with the ornate ceremonial sword voted by Congress as a token of the nation's thanks, were elaborate. McKinley thought for a moment that he would go to New York to greet the republic's greatest hero in a generation. But John Hay threw cold water on the plan. It would not do, he noted stiffly, for the President to lower his office by calling on Dewey first; the Admiral could come to him.[37]

At the elaborate ceremonies McKinley tactfully refused to invade Dewey's popularity. As he mounted the steps of the temporary flag-draped structure near the Capitol, the President thought nothing amiss either, on seeing the splendid figure of Cardinal Gibbons, who gave the benediction. As the Admiral brushed forward to accept his sword, rustling in his uniform, the emblems of the republic's honors flashing from his figure, McKinley discreetly stepped back that the people might see their hero. Then the President quickly returned to the White House to receive with him at a public reception, instructing the hand-sore Dewey in his own method of grabbing the callers before they grabbed him.

Voted the country's highest naval rank for his lifetime, Dewey duly departed, with presidential good wishes, for a tour of other cities that vied for his presence. But he proceeded to make a series of political blunders that tarnished his public image. His subsequent marriage to a woman of Catholic persuasion nettled some. "No fool like an old fool," the wits were heard to say. When he signed over to her the deed to the home which the nation had given him, many more among the common folk began to wonder.

But inevitably, as 1900 loomed on the political horizon, there was talk of Dewey for president. In the spring of the year multitudes still hailed him in the major cities. In April, Dewey replied to reporters with disarming candor that he might be a candidate for president if the people insisted. He hadn't thought too much about it, he said absently, but if they really wanted him he couldn't very well refuse. After all, he would say, it wasn't much of a job anyway, consisting of doing what Congress said. "What party did he belong to?" the straightfaced reporters asked as they mercilessly pumped their unsuspecting quarry. "I do not know on what ticket I will be nominated," the Admiral said blandly. "I have no politics. I am the people's candidate." [38]

A chorus of good-natured laughter greeted Dewey's remarks. The Bryan followers in the Democratic party took momentary fright, and some Republicans felt a chill for a different reason. "Mark Hanna and those who share with him the responsibilities of Republican management would never forgive the Democrats if they nominated anybody but Bryan," said the staid New York *Times*.[39]

Criticisms of the Admiral's remarks blended with pity in many mouths. "Of course among right thinking people there can be but one verdict upon it," Roosevelt said of Dewey's remarks, "and I cannot help but believe that he will be laughed out of court." But willing hands were ready to help him. "Say nothing, nor write anything that can turn away support and your campaign will be irresistible," a confidant remarked with becoming candor. By early summer, however, with the conventions at hand, the Admiral's serious chances were gone. The public had loved him as a hero, not as a politician.[40]

The President had never worried about the Dewey boom. Dewey was not spiteful like Miles, and McKinley sincerely respected his military feats. Senator Hanna was apt, as always, to be more blunt and curtly fended off all questions about Dewey's threat. "I have no time to discuss the matter," he snapped at an insistent reporter. "I am too busy arranging for the Philadelphia convention, where William McKinley will be renominated by acclamation." The President was more tactful, saying only that the Admiral knew he was safest in Republican hands. The whole thing would blow over; he had seen it before in politics.[41]

As 1900 approached, McKinley's friends expected an announcement of his candidacy, but McKinley always felt slightly uncomfortable about seeming to seek an office. His old-school attitude dictated that he must somehow be asked. In September, 1899, he listened to a group of friends sing his praises at Canton and then rather abruptly talked about the coming election. He said, with gestures of sincerity amid silent attention, that he would like to step down. He motioned to the yard outside and the freedom it would mean. "I have had enough of it, Heaven knows! I have had all the honor there is in the place, and have had responsibilities enough to kill any man." He paused and shifted. He would welcome any strong Republican of similar views as a successor, knowing as he spoke that his position had eliminated any such rivals. He would not seek renomination, knowing that he would not have to, saying that when the time to decide came he would be guided "absolutely upon whether the call of duty appears to me clear and well defined." It was an elegant and typical way of saying yes; he did not intend to step down with his work half done. He would not welcome a change of administration that might threaten his programs. "If I were to announce that I would not stand for re-election my party would be torn to pieces in a contest over my successor, and the only course open to me is to go ahead and bear the burdens as best I can," he told Joe Bristow.[42] He was only reassuring the necessary leaders, for no one, least of all he, contemplated his retirement.

The new year opened on a small personal crisis. Senator Hanna had not been well, and doubts about his standing with the President and his future control of the party sharpened his temper, already made painfully public by his searing rheumatism. McKinley was displeased with some of the Senator's recent remarks. Hanna's obvious enjoyment of his vicarious power often nettled the President, who was somewhat touchy about revived charges of his subservience to Hanna. This alarmed Hanna, for his own power depended on the President; without McKinley he would have been only another Ohio senator. Once asked if her husband had power over the President, Mrs. Hanna replied that he had power "of a kind." [43] She meant that it was personal. That power's unwritten and ephemeral quality, dependent upon presidential patronage and party direction, was in turn McKinley's power over Hanna.

Hanna put out feelers in 1899 to test his situation. He would be happy, he said, to resign as national chairman. Let someone else manage next year's campaign; he was getting old and tired, his senatorial duties were heavier, perhaps the President needed someone else. He cocked his ear for the expected reply, and when nothing followed but silence he grew worried and nervous. His physical appearance deteriorated as the new year brought no answer from McKinley.[44]

The President was using his usual indirect pressure and the power of silence. He needed and wanted Hanna, but on his own terms. Perhaps it was time to tone down the Senator's public remarks and remove the slight tarnish that still lingered on their relationship. "Anticipation is sometimes a good regulator," the President once said. By May he had done enough; the louder Hanna protested his unwillingness to run another gruelling campaign, the more surely he became aware of McKinley's purpose. The President asked Hanna to return with his old vigor for the campaign.[45]

Hanna's chief concern soon also came home to McKinley. That the President would be renominated without a contest was as sure as sunrise. The only problem lay in the running mate, and there the brash, colorful, and politically uncertain figure of Theodore Roosevelt once again intruded. Covered with glory, Teddy came home from Cuba to enter politics in the Empire State, snagging a victory as governor in 1898. As governor he was a double danger to Tom Platt: he was both an incipient reformer and a popular leader who conceivably could run the state without the Organization. He would have to be checked. The most convenient spot was the vice-presidency, a limbo from which few politicians emerged alive.

Teddy was certainly vexing. It was no secret that Hanna disliked and distrusted him. The President said nothing, but the tolerant amusement with which he had faced Roosevelt before faded now that a serious threat emerged from the new occupant of the statehouse at Albany. Rumor quickly placed Roosevelt in the vice-presidential sweepstakes. "Mr. Roosevelt, I hear you are being groomed by the Republicans as my husband's successor in the coming election," Mrs. Hobart asked point blank. Teddy grinned nearsightedly, his mustache quivering. "No, by George! I've had a good time as governor and I want to be governor again." [46]

Like McKinley, Roosevelt took the grand tour for the party, travelling through the Midwest to help state candidates in the fall of 1899. He met an immense reception, western jamborees, corps of Rough Riders, and general public acclaim. Eyebrows were raised in the councils of elders. Hanna was mad and the President was doubtful. Friends of Roosevelt like John Hay hastened to vouch for the Governor's views. "If the Governor ever had any leanings in the direction of mugwumpery, he seems to have lost them," the Secretary of State assured McKinley.[47] He spoke well, for in those days Roosevelt was more conservative than McKinley. Yet Roosevelt thought it necessary to allay fears by announcing during the summer of that year that he favored McKinley's renomination.[48] The very statement seemed impertinent. As Roosevelt's popularity grew, local politicians wanted to know where McKinley stood. "The question of the next Vice President is being considered here," a New Yorker wrote McKinley. "A little confidential tip from you would settle it." He obviously did not know McKinley, who never gave confidential tips. Hanna fumed that winter and as the new year broke, frankly admitted that while McKinley's nomination was secure, "when it comes to choosing his running mate and deciding on the platform, there is likely to be an abundance of excitement." [49]

Roosevelt was only too aware of his predicament. He wanted the limelight, but not at the expense of alienating the party elders; he might need them some day. His friend Lodge pointed out the dangers. "There are plenty of men who would like to get up a fight with McKinley and use you for that purpose, but I do not at present see any advantage to you in such a course." Roosevelt knew how double-edged Tom Platt's smiles could be. The Easy Boss would like nothing better than to check Hanna and McKinley with the ironic tool of Teddy Roosevelt. Roosevelt wrestled with his conscience, feeling that the chance of his being considered presidential timber in 1904 was slight; the public would have forgotten San Juan Hill by then.[50] There could be only one course. "It is proper for me to state definitely that under no circumstances would I accept the nomination for the Vice-Presidency," he intoned in February.[51]

He was not so firmly decided in his own mind. Friends like Hay watched his vacillation with amusement. Now he would and now he wouldn't listen to the call of duty. "I think you are unduly alarmed," Hay would say. "There is no instance of an election of a Vice-President by violence." Such cynicism was well and good; it lightened the load of deliberation, but Roosevelt worried about the future. In January, Lodge asked McKinley "point blank" if he had any plans for Teddy. The President thought a moment and said he would not send Roosevelt to the Philippines; no, he had no plans. Lodge was silent, looking wise and noncommittal. The President matched his mien and smoked.[52]

March brought Nicholas Murray Butler to Washington. The distinguished educator talked earnestly about his young friend's chances. The President smiled and laughed over some of Roosevelt's past antics. He was still noncommittal, and suggested a talk with Hanna, who as national chairman would of course have to be consulted. The Senator was blunt, and the objects on his desk rattled under his fists; he did not want and would not take Roosevelt on the ticket. Butler told his story to Roosevelt, who was somewhat angry. Many said later that Hanna's opposition and McKinley's coolness caused Roosevelt to seek the office.[53]

Yet in April he said again that he was not a candidate, but he was saying the same thing with alarming frequency. He stopped to see the President late in the spring. Any visit from Roosevelt was an event, Hay reported, which left indelible impressions for a wide radius. "He came down with a somber resolution thrown on his stupendous brow to let McKinley and Hanna know once for all that he would not be Vice-President, and found to his stupefaction that nobody in Washington except Platt had ever dreamed of such a thing," Hay recorded with glee. "He did not even have a chance to launch his *nolo episcopari* at the Major. That statesman said he did not want him on the ticket—that he would be far more valuable in New York—and Root said, with his frank and murderous smile, 'Of course not—you're not fit for it.' And so he went back quite eased in his mind, but considerably bruised in his *amour propre.*" [54]

The administration faced a dual problem; how to stop Roosevelt and how to find an adequate popular replacement. As in 1896, the party bosses were perfectly willing to relieve the President of the problem. "If you have none [recommendation for the vice-presidency] the middle states will proceed to effect a nomination before the Convention meets," Quay wrote McKinley blithely.[55] Pennsylvania's boss agreed with Platt that the rambunctious Roosevelt must be kicked upstairs lest he ruin the party organization. Platt awaited his opportunity to see Roosevelt "take the veil," as he said with his slit smile.

McKinley did not intend to permit the bosses to name Roosevelt. He did not oppose Roosevelt for partisan reasons; he simply felt that there were better men, and in terms of experience and party regularity he was right. But if Roosevelt was to be chosen by popular demand, the administration would have to find a way to identify itself with the boom. The President was sincere in saying that he would not dictate the choice; he left that to the convention, but he also had his private choices. One of these was John D. Long. The Secretary of the Navy had few recommendations for the post beyond his party regularity, identification with the administration, and a certain ill-defined appeal to those delegates opposed to the bosses' dictation. But at the same time, he had no illusions; Hanna's favoritism could not offset the disabilities of geography and his questionable popularity. "I tell my friends I am like the boy at school who gets honorable mention if no prize," he wrote Alger. "I have

491

never counted on the Vice-Presidency going as far east as Massachusetts." [56]

Months before the convention met, McKinley tapped Elihu Root as his running mate, but the Secretary of War adamantly declined. The President's next choice was Senator Allison, whose twenty-eight years in the upper house and legendary caution made him "the father of the Senate." The Iowan declined the offer; he would not risk the certain power incumbent in his Senate seat for the potential power in the vice-presidency. McKinley's insistence that he had expanded the office under Hobart and would continue to do so did not move Allison, who thus declined a major post under McKinley for the third time.[57]

Hanna turned to Secretary Bliss in an effort to compromise with Platt, but "Corny" was unwilling. As a delicate ruse he suggested to Hanna that if he could get Mrs. Bliss to agree, he would run. Hanna fled, having tangled with that formidable lady before. When Allison declined, the President also turned to Bliss, but the wealthy merchant was adamant. He had taken his post only as a favor to McKinley and would not continue in politics.[58]

When that failed, the administration managers looked to the West, for that section might properly be recognized in the ticket. The leading young contender there was Allison's protégé, the great orator Jonathan P. Dolliver, then a faithful servant of arch-Republicanism, betraying no hint of the progressive temper that later made him famous. He was willing, but saw clearly that Hanna wished to use a number of state candidates to divide Roosevelt's strength, the same tactic which the bosses had unsuccessfully tried on McKinley in 1896.[59]

The President persisted in his usual public silence, though those around him knew that he did not especially relish the idea of having Roosevelt on the ticket. He chastened Foraker somewhat by not asking him to make the nominating speech until the last minute. Calling in a huff, Ohio's senior senator met the familiar presidential charm and assurances that his stock had not fallen at the White House. As he turned to go, Foraker remembered, the President said suddenly. "I hope you will not allow the convention to be stampeded to Roosevelt for Vice-President." [60] It seems doubtful that McKinley made the remark; perhaps it was Foraker's interpretation of what he did say. The President was not close enough to Foraker to make such a bald request and he would not have revealed his opposition to Roosevelt so bluntly to an erstwhile opponent.

And so the confused situation developed as the convention prepared to meet in Philadelphia in mid-June. The City of Brotherly Love outdid itself to play host to the Republicans, building special accommodations, lining hotels and streets with miles of bunting, staging torchlight parades, and organizing corps of celebrants who flooded into the city in the wake of the arriving delegations. The convention would open formally on Tuesday, June 19, but the week prior to the gavel's fall was devoted to hectic conferences. The situation must be settled before the delegates arrived, Hanna felt, or they would stampede. The President's renomination was but a matter of form. "If it were not for the uncertainty over the Vice Presidency, there would be absolutely nothing to relieve the monotony of the Republican gathering in Philadelphia," the papers noted.[61]

Hanna was not feeling well. His rheumatism had returned with such distressing severity that he often had to be helped up and down his hotel steps. His disposition deteriorated accordingly, for mental worries added to the physical strain. The President had not yet said just where he stood on the vice-presidency, and though Hanna assumed full powers to deal for the administration, McKinley's hesitation of the earlier spring had impressed upon him the ephemeral nature of his authority. That he opposed Roosevelt, none doubted. In a fit of temper he snapped, "It must always be remembered that there is only one life between the Vice-President and the Chief Magistracy of the Nation. . . ." Followed by growing clouds of discontent at his rough dictation, the Senator would only say as the battle began: "May the best man win." [62] Roosevelt was not that man.

On Saturday, June 16, Roosevelt breezed into town with Platt and the New York delegation as a delegate-at-large. He told Lodge that he must come, or seem a coward; Lodge in turn warned that to go was to be nominated. Roosevelt was silent. His teeth and eye-glasses flashed as he talked to reporters who dogged his footsteps. He was not above acknowledging the ragged cheers that often arose as he passed little knots of onlookers, much to Platt's covert amusement. He made sure that he would be noticed by abandoning the fashionable straw boaters which most delegates wore in deference to the muggy heat, for a large Rough Rider hat. "Gentlemen, that's an acceptance hat," a wily politician noted. "The Governor was in a state of rare excitement, even for him," Platt remembered, though his reluctant candidate still persistently denied that he was available.[63]

Hanna had left town to stay with friends at Haverford; Roosevelt had said that he would not run, and apparently Hanna took him at his word. News on Sunday, June 17, brought him back to Philadelphia in a rage. Late that evening Charles Dick telephoned the White House on the special long-distance connection and talked with Cortelyou, who had the President at his elbow. "The Roosevelt boom is let loose and it has swept everything," Dick said frankly, remembering the flood of badges and banners which had miraculously appeared to disrupt Philadelphia's Sabbath calm. "The feeling is that the thing is going pell mell like a tidal wave." Other candidates were simply vanishing. "I think up to this moment Roosevelt was against it, but they have turned his head." Hanna was frankly sour, but the problem remained of how to check the apparently spontaneous demonstration; would presidential interference not look like dictation? Dick asked that McKinley talk with Hanna. "We cannot afford to have it said that something was done in spite of ourselves." [64]

The President was loath to act at all, but toward midnight he dictated a formal statement that Cortelyou then read to Dick and the managers at Philadelphia: "The President has no choice for Vice-President. Any of the distinguished names suggested would be satisfactory to him. The choice of the convention will be his choice; he has no advice to give. The Convention is the lawfully constituted body to make nominations, and instead of giving advice he awaits its advice, confident now as always that it will act wisely and for the highest interest of the country and of the party." [65] Hanna's reaction to this pompous statement may be imagined. McKinley had, in effect, conceded the fight; he would not oppose the popular demand for the Rough Rider.

Hanna was not by any means finished. That same afternoon the Senator hobbled to Roosevelt's hotel rooms, and put the question to him squarely: was he a candidate? Roosevelt hung back; could he risk his political future by refusing such a call, he asked. Hanna persisted grimly; he had only honestly to withdraw. The talk was free and full, seasoned with some of Hanna's profanity. The Senator bluntly told Roosevelt that Platt was using him as a tool. Roosevelt persistently said that he could not refuse a popular call. That was simple, Hanna said, withdraw. Roosevelt hesitated and then agreed. He would withdraw.[66]

The following day, Monday, June 18, the Governor put out his statement, but it was still ambiguous; clearly, he would accept a "draft." Just as clearly, he could get one, for as one paper noted: "There is more genuine spontaneous, hearty enthusiasm for Roosevelt than for all the other Vice-Presidential candidates combined." [67] Desperately striving to harmonize the situation and to break the Roosevelt boom, Hanna spent convention eve in a frenzy of work, whipping obedient Southern delegates into line, promising everything he could think of to the wavering. He was still not committed to the President's passive course. McKinley's attitude angered and perplexed him. "I am not in control!" he shouted at harassed deputies who demanded a rout of the Platt–Roosevelt combination. "McKinley won't let me use the power of the administration to defeat Roosevelt. He is blind, or afraid, or something." [68] It was the closest the angry Senator had ever come to lese majesty.

On Tuesday, June 19, according to schedule, Hanna's gavel fell to open the convention shortly after noon. As the echoes of his hammer died away into the hall's vastness, a commotion announced Roosevelt's carefully timed entrance and signalled a demonstration which Hanna could not quell.[69] Hanna was terribly bitter now, feeling that Roosevelt had played him false. He ruthlessly collared every delegate he could find, angrily using any and all means at his command. He was still the President's agent, he said; the administration must not be defied by Roosevelt or the men behind him, Platt and Quay. McKinley had not trimmed the feathers of these two only to see them identified in a gullible public's mind with the glamor around Theodore Roosevelt.

He seemed to have lost his head. Dawes saw that it would not do to have the President's official spokesman as the only man seriously bucking the tide. He had a violent quarrel with Hanna, whose red face and strident voice betrayed his tension and bitterness. Dawes

495

then returned to his hotel, called the White House, and talked to Cortelyou, with the President listening on an extension. The danger of a split in the party was real, he warned; every minute made the contest seem more like a fight between the Old Guard and the Young Lions, and Hanna was identifying the President with the Old Guard.

Once again McKinley decided that a formal statement was in order, and Cortelyou read Dawes his answer: "The President's friends must not undertake to commit the Administration to any candidate. It has no candidate. The convention must make the nomination; the Administration would not if it could. The President's close friends should be satisfied with his unanimous renomination and not interfere with the vice-presidential nomination. The Administration wants the candidate of the convention, and the President's friends must not dictate to the convention." The tone irritated even McKinley's cohorts at Philadelphia, but at least it clarified his stand.

Dawes hurried to Hanna with the message, read it slowly, and watched the Senator, calmer now, digest its import. At about 1 A.M. he called the White House again to say that while Hanna was "a little perplexed" by the message, he would, of course, abide by it. A subsequent conference of administration leaders decided emptily to support Long, but Hanna kept silent; he was out of it, he said. "Well, that settles it, it will be Roosevelt," someone said.[70]

Wednesday, June 20, was a dull day, set aside for routine business and the platform. It ran true to form in endorsing everything McKinley had done and promising more of the same for the next four years, and no one was especially interested in it anyway. It was dull, that is, until Senator Quay arose to move that the power of the Southerners be curbed in the national conventions. The Southern delegates, who delivered no electoral votes, were Hanna's hard core. Pandemonium reigned on the floor until Quay blandly suggested that the motion be carried over to the next day. The gesture was enough. Hanna could come over to Roosevelt gracefully or face a floor fight. Hanna gave in, and George W. Perkins returned from Washington with assurances that the President would welcome Roosevelt.

On Thursday, the convention came to life, for nominations were in order. A sense of vitality flowed through the crowded aisles and across the rows of expectant faces in the galleries. Ladies' hats mingled with bowlers and boaters in excited conversation, and fans waggled as celebrities strolled into view for identification. Senator Hanna's figure, still stiff and limping, excited enthusiasm, but Roosevelt brought the greatest cheers. Tickets quadrupled in price, and soon there was standing room only. "Bim the Button Man" did a booming business in McKinley–Roosevelt banners and buttons, and state delegations unlimbered their paraphernalia and their lungs. For Bim, a familiar figure at conventions, it was an act of faith. "If it isn't Roosevelt there will be a dent in the Delaware River caused by Bim committing suicide," he said.[71]

When Foraker rose to nominate McKinley, waves of applause greeted him. His speech repeated the party's achievements and the glories of her greatest statesman, William McKinley. The whole story was paraded before the impatient crowd that murmured in approval of the record and in the expectation of the tumult that would greet the mention of the sacred name. At last it came, and tidal waves of delegates poured into the aisles. The lethargy vanished, as all paid homage to William McKinley, the party's most popular president since Lincoln. Hanna revived, abandoned his rheumatism, and ran from delegate to delegate "yelling like an Apache" as the contagious enthusiasm swept up to, and over the stand of dignitaries. The Senator waved a huge plume and passed it on to a friend with the injunction: "Isn't this glorious? Take a plume and whoop 'er up." [72] Announcement of the President's unanimous nomination provoked another storm.

It had hardly subsided when Lafayette Young, a former Dolliver man from Iowa, rose to nominate Roosevelt. Hanna had already surrendered, telling Young to "put in San Juan Hill and the proper coloring." The din of enthusiastic cheers that greeted Roosevelt's name and the three seconding speeches attested to the Rough Rider's popularity. He received all the votes except his own, which he held out to perpetuate the fiction of his unwillingness.[73]

And so the convention faded into history. The party's cheers foretold its unity as all ranks closed automatically behind the ticket. Hanna feared the result. He had some terrible premonition of Roosevelt's succession, a faint, undefinable feeling that Teddy had not been shelved. But a different air prevailed in the party councils. "Everyone feels very happy this morning over the situation," Perkins telephoned the White House. No bitterness was discernible. In his hotel room, Tom Platt smiled at reporters as he nursed a broken rib that had kept him swathed in plaster of paris and isolated from public view, but not from the devious dealings he so enjoyed. "I am glad we had our way. The people, I mean, had their way." [74]

Roosevelt left Philadelphia resigned to his fate. He felt that he had defeated Platt in some indefinable way, and friends assured him that he was young enough to survive the vice-presidency. Senator Lodge warned the voluble Teddy to play the silent game during the campaign, and to follow the caution that had brought McKinley such success:

> We must not permit the President, or any of his friends, who are, of course, in control of the campaign, to imagine that we want to absorb the leadership and the glory. I want you to appear everywhere as the champion of the President. That is, on every occasion I want you to appear, as you did at the convention, simply as a leading advocate for McKinley and to make this clear in everything you say. Fortunately his policies on the great questions are our policies. He is doing admirably so far as I can see in all directions, and especially in the difficulties in China, and I am anxious that your advocacy of him should appear in everything you say. My purpose in this is to secure by every righteous means the confidence and support for you of the President and of all his large following. This is going to be of immense importance to us four years hence, and that is why I desire that you should appear, not only during the campaign but after the election, as the President's next friend, just as Hobart was.[75]

Such is hard political advice in every age. Roosevelt took it.

The President sent his usual felicitous greetings, and Roosevelt replied that he was "proud to be associated with you on the ticket." [76] To friends, McKinley expressed himself less formally. "It is going to be hard for Roosevelt to sit still long enough to preside in the Senate," he told Joe Butler.[77] As usual, Hanna had the last word, flavored by a curious foreboding: "Well, it was a nice little scrap at Phila., not exactly to my liking with my hands tied behind me," he wrote the President with disarming candor. "However, we got through in good shape and the ticket is all right. Your *duty* to the country is to *live* for *four* years from next March." [78]

McKinley was perfectly content to mollify Hanna by permitting him to control the campaign that followed.[79] Affairs in China and the Philippines took most of his time, and it would have been awkward to arrange even a front porch campaign. This did not preclude appearances. On July 12, a formidable committee appeared on the Major's front lawn to inform him of his nomination in time-honored fashion. The President was the essence of dignity as he smiled at the onlookers. The heat seemed oppressive, though an occasional breeze lifted the corners of the bunting on the porch and straightened the flags that stood like sentinels on their poles. Mrs. McKinley sat in view, anxious not to miss another historic occasion. The President's speech of acceptance was later amplified and printed as his formal Letter of Acceptance, the chief Republican campaign document.[80]

The opposition was familiar. The Democrats, not to be impressed by history or experience, clung to free silver at Bryan's insistence, and combined this with the "paramount issue" of imperialism for a potentially powerful assault on the administration. The Boy Orator was older, but spoke in tones that appealed to historic Americanism in pointing out the weaknesses in McKinley's Philippine policy. Bryan wished an immediate assurance of Philippine self-rule, which he felt would end the insurrection and also uplift the natives. The rest of the Democratic platform, like its Republican counterpart, was all too familiar, garnishing accepted party platitudes with the rhetoric of politics. Except for the manifest absence of strife and tension, it might have been 1896 again, and of course that absence made all the difference in the world.

The President elected to answer his adversaries in his only real campaign speech by touching on the usual high grounds. His speech was long and intricate, not among his best prose efforts, but it breathed the spirit of sincerity and honesty which the people had grown to associate with him, and that in the end was more impressive than rhetoric. He reviewed the foreign affairs of his administration, justifying his stand on the Philippines. It would not do, he said, to promise self-rule now in the midst of the insurrection, lest this seem weak. The natives must still accept American sovereignty. He would press on and finish the work of pacification, pointing to the Taft Commission's labors as proof of his and the country's good intentions. He dismissed as absurd the hoary charges of imperialism now revived for the campaign.[81]

He retired from view to greet the delegates and to preside at an informal luncheon arranged in special tents in the back yard. The remainder of his speech had dealt with such mundane matters as the pending diplomatic negotiations, the gold standard, and growing references to the prosperity that flooded across the country.

The weeks between the speech and the formal printing of the Letter brought the ugly charges of imperialism emanating from Bryan's camp into sharp relief. "We dare not educate the Filipinos lest they learn to read the Constitution," the "Commoner" affirmed. Might it not be wise to promise the natives independence? Senator Hoar wrote earnestly that such a statement would insure Bryan's defeat and clarify once and for all the whole Philippine problem. The President thought and wondered. On September 5, he dictated to Cortelyou a paragraph for inclusion in the Letter stating that the United States would grant self-government to the Filipinos "when they are ready for it and as rapidly as they are ready for it." [82] Still he hesitated. Would it not look like a weak election year promise? At last he demurred; the statement was not included in the Letter.

The President was too wise in the ways of politics to take anything for granted. Most Republicans smiled when the campaign was mentioned. It was their year, they assured themselves; it was as good as in the bag. McKinley contrived to look that way, but he had a pang of doubt early in the campaign. If defeated, he told Dawes and Cortelyou, he would retain the Army at expanded strength so that Bryan could not say he had failed in his duty.[83]

But these fleeting phantoms faded quickly as the campaign unfolded. It was Hanna's show, and he had long since mastered the details. The President seemed more imperturbable as the ballyhoo progressed. He would not even speak from his home, he told a friend; it was not 1896. "Now I am president of the whole people, and while I am a candidate again, I feel that the proprieties demand that the President should refrain from making a political canvass in his own behalf, and I shall not engage in speech-making this year, save on one or two occasions when I shall speak upon national questions rather than partisan politics." [84] It made for dignity, but it was also dull. "They ain't been so much as a black eye give or took in th' ward and it's less thin two months to th' big day," Mr. Hennessey said. " 'Twill liven up," Mr. Dooley answered. "I begin to see signs iv th' good times comin' again. 'Twas on'y th' other day me frind Tiddy Rosenfelt opened the battle be insinuatin' that all dimmycrats was liars, horse thieves an' arnychists." [85]

Hanna might have disagreed with Mr. Dooley; the President's nonchalance worried him, as did the public's apathy. Nothing is so easily lost, he reminded friends, as sure-fire elections. In addition, a host of nagging problems absorbed his time, energy, and campaign money. Doubtful Indiana, as always, swung from one camp to the other. "There has been more money spent in Indiana to carry that Infernal State than almost any other in the Union," Senator Cullom exploded. John Hay suffered in silence as the Democrats distorted his foreign policy. Old soldiers bombarded the President with complaints against his Pension Bureau chief, H. Clay Evans, whose tight fist protected the Bureau's funds but alienated many veterans.[86] McKinley ignored the complaints; Evans stayed on until Roosevelt removed him.

But for the managers, indifference was a problem. "I cannot arouse any fears in myself that McKinley will not be elected," Senator Chandler frankly wrote. Other prominent Republicans embarked on their usual European vacations, and it was hard to get speakers in some areas. The burden fell on Hanna, and the Senator was growing more and more irascible about it all. It was no snap, he would thunder, to elect a president; they would all see how easy it was when the chips were down. "I think I am entitled to the support of all departments for this is no boys' play this year," he wrote Dawes testily, "and I find my disposition is not as sweet as it used to be." [87]

Everyone had too much of a good thing, Hanna grumbled, waving his cane and nursing an aching joint. The country was too prosperous; McKinley had succeeded too well; people easily forgot the dark days of 1896, and now they would risk it all with stark indifference. He seemed right. "The workingmen in other parts of the country are receiving fine wages and are not inclined to overturn matters," Taft's brother wrote him. "Everybody is making money, silver men, gold men and farmers," he added later in the summer. Hanna advised standing pat, as the newspapers garbled his phrase: it was the full dinner pail versus the specter of Democratic misery, he told his listeners time and again. But he still feared the apathy of contentment and prosperity. "We are filling the doubtful states with spellbinders and ploughing the fence corners," he assured McKinley.[88]

The problem of campaign finance remained, though not with the urgency of 1896. Some familiar pocketbooks snapped shut. Andrew Carnegie gave "not a cent to imperialism—not a cent to renegade Americanism," and even adopted a new love, the Boers. The President gave up on Carnegie, but Hanna's agents did not need the steelmaster's money. Perry Heath, an old hand at fund raising, reported that they could pay the party bills and have cash left over. Hanna and Bliss, seeking funds, toured Boston and came away happy. Things were so rosy that when the election was safely over, officials of the Standard Oil Company were stunned to receive a $50,000 refund from Hanna, who had not needed all their contribution.[89]

Bryan's magnetic voice and old appeal stirred many hearts that profited from McKinley prosperity. The Boy Orator still inspired also some of the hate of 1896, for he was a symbol of recklessness to many. "Mr. Bryan starts out on his second race for the Presidency still the head of a rabble half fanatical, half demagogic," Reid's *Tribune* said. "His mouth has been a mint," J. Sterling Morton snapped. "His voice, his lungs and his brain have been continually emitting coinage to the profit of their proprietor. The returns have been more than $16 annually to every one invested. No other trust or monopoly has declared dividends of such magnitude on so small a capital." [90] And John Hay harbored his grudge against Bryan, sharpened now by the latter's assaults on his diplomacy. "He is his own best opponent. That slack jaw will give him away every time he sets it going." [91] But Bryan's followers had their old confidence, which shone through a funny story some thoughtful soul sent to the President. At a whistle stop someone said that Mrs. Bryan would be sleeping in the White House next spring. A hardy Republican at the edge of the crowd yelled that if so she would be sleeping with McKinley.[92]

As the campaign progressed, however, all signs pointed to a lack of interest in silver, even in the Rocky Mountain states. "Silver is but little discussed," Senator Wolcott assured McKinley. It seemed the year "to make an end of Bryanism this time for good and all." A few bolters like Senator William M. Stewart returned humbly to the fold of party unity. Nevada's silver-haired silverite had never really been comfortable with Bryan, and now condemned him. "When the remedy came from the output of gold he should have claimed a vindication of his theory," Stewart remembered. "One of two things must be said of him—he either did not understand the money question or he was willing to deceive the people." [93]

Bryan's talk of imperialism was far more disturbing than the hollow echoes of free silver. The forgotten war in the Philippines was revived for the public, and its horrors sparked a repetitious account of its origins. Talk of destiny, Bryan said, was "the subterfuge of the invertebrate," a telling phrase which cast implications on the President's backbone. The Republican reply that "the so-called issue of 'imperialism' is a fiction" did not set the party managers' minds at ease. In mid-September, McKinley released the Taft Commission's instructions, together with other documents that showed the gradual fulfillment of American promises to the Filipinos. [94]

The President, ensconced in a rather informal state at Canton, receiving visitors, posing for pictures, talking with Root on the telephone, and following Hanna's election efforts, tried to weather this last major storm of his career. "I deeply sympathize with you in 'some of your trials,' but all will end well," he assured Root. "We are moving on safe lines and can disregard the petty consequences of the hour," and added in his dark scrawl an affectionate and unusual signature: "Your friend, William McKinley." [95] It was difficult to say just how potent the issue of imperialism was to the voter; it never outshone Republican prosperity. [96] Much bitterness salted Republican words as they reflected that only the hope of a Bryan victory, with an attendant change of policy kept Aguinaldo's rebels active in the distant jungles of the Philippines. For many, Democracy bore the stamp of treason, stained with the blood of American soldiers. [97]

The campaign was not without its hidden drama, for Hanna and the President almost clashed, and their old friendship, already strained that spring, was further stretched. Hanna wrote McKinley early in August that he understood that work in some navy yards was being held up; this meant lost votes, he said bluntly, and asked that McKinley investigate the matter. The President answered in a formal tone, chiding Hanna for suggesting that work be made for the election year. "This is a time when every effort will be made to have the administration do questionable things," McKinley wrote. "It is a period of great temptation, just the sort that will require the highest courage to meet and resist. If elected I have to live with the administration for four years. I do not want to feel that improper or questionable methods have been employed to reach the place, and you must continue, as you have always done, to stand against unreasonable exactions which are so common at a time like the present." Somehow the President could seldom unbend in writing Hanna; the letter was signed: "Very Sincerely yours, William McKinley."

As he read, a flush crept over Hanna's face. The President presumed to give him advice; the hurt was compounded by a realization that he should have known better than to write McKinley such a proposition. He crumpled the letter and threw it on the floor. His stiffness did not prevent some stamping. As far as he could see, McKinley was writing pious letters for his biographer.[98] Hanna's anger subsided; he swallowed his gorge and faced the task resolutely. But he did not give up his rather huffy tone. He complained volubly that Secretary Long was talking openly about building a government armor-plate plant unless private industry met his price. It was maddening, he said, to think that administration spokesmen could say such things in the midst of a presidential campaign, alienating the very men who were financing the Republican effort. "I will not trouble you about all the grievances that come to me," Hanna wrote the President in a wounded tone. "But I do think that when I have such responsibilities that my advice should be taken. Under *other* circumstances I would quit the job in just one *minute*." [99]

McKinley ignored the letter. He knew Hanna and his touchiness too well to be worried. He still felt that the Senator should be toned down. Hanna's frank comment that the election was "a business proposition purely," and his rank materialism repelled McKinley; he saw the same vision of plenty in a different form. The Senator's easy dismissal of the trust question as so much rabble-rousing disturbed McKinley, who had already taken a public stand in favor of regulation in some form. In September, Hanna came to lunch and when he left he issued a more complete statement, talking of good and bad trusts in the best McKinley tradition.[100]

Hanna now discovered that he had more than managerial talents. He decided to undertake his first speaking tour. As a senator he had not been vocal, preferring the cloakroom and manipulation to the more vocal talents his colleagues so liberally displayed. But he had spoken occasionally with an impressive directness and cogency. His earthy, common-sense approach to life and his frankness impressed many who would have found another attitude in him mere cant or humbug. He liked the plaudits of the crowd. The President once tried to help him write a speech, but it was no use; he preferred informal speaking on the stump, attuned to the crowd, to McKinley's elaborate statesmanlike approach. The Senator decided to tour the farm country of the Northwest and Middlewest.

The party managers greeted the announcement and Hanna's determination with some misgivings. Who could tell what he might say, or what reaction the people might have toward him? After all, he was to many the bloated monster of 1896, covered with dollar signs, cloaked in evil designs, the mouthpiece of Wall Street. Could he shake off that stereotype with even the best intentions? The President himself was somewhat uneasy. Postmaster-General Charles Emory Smith arrived in Chicago one day to talk with Hanna about the proposed tour. He was not enthusiastic. One by one he tactfully listed the impediments to such a tour. Hanna watched his visitor shrewdly and then blurted out: "The President sent you, didn't he?" Smith nodded slowly, with obvious embarrassment, and Hanna snapped: "Return to Washington and tell the President that God hates a coward!"[101] In all justice, it was an act unworthy of McKinley.

Hanna turned to the rails and invaded enemy territory in the Midwest. In a special train, amply stocked with all the necessities of the campaign trail and shadowed by the inevitable reporters, some anxious to report Hanna's defeat, the Senator set out to convince the farmers face-to-face that they must favor Republicanism. In many areas he drew larger crowds than did Bryan. People who came to see the monster, prepared to touch the dollar signs on his coat, saw instead a kindly gentleman in conservative clothes who gesticulated vigorously as he talked in a rather flat and nasal, but not unpleasant, voice.[102]

Hanna's party was astonished by the large turnouts in Illinois and Indiana. "I have never seen the laboring men so eager to get up close where every word could be heard. . . ." a member of the party wrote McKinley. The more he spoke, the better Hanna liked it. Warmed by his receptions, he grew positively eloquent, revelling in the role of public figure which he had hitherto shunned. The politician had become a kind of rustic statesman. "Quietly and in strict confidence, I think that our good friend is rather enamored with the flattery and high praise which he is receiving for his very effective work," Charles Grosvenor wrote the President.[103]

The Senator's tour combined humor and earnestness, for he was well aware of the stereotype affixed to him. At a Nebraska town he was met by a typical placard that shrieked a mock warning to the faithful:

POPULIST FARMERS,

BEWARE!!!

Chain Your Children to Yourselves

or

Put Them Under the Bed

MARK HANNA IS IN TOWN

Laughing jovially over similar incidents, he smiled at another crowd, pointed to his head, and cried: "I do not wear horns." [104] But he was deadly serious; the tour was not a matter of comic relief. He lambasted Bryan with a fervor that showed his experience in politics. "Bryan will stand on any platform they make for him, ride any hobby horse, endorse any issue: yes, he will even abuse me for the sole purpose of being President. That is all he wants," Hanna cried, and got a cheering echo of, "You are all right!" Amid the excitement he did not lose his good humor. When a wooden speakers' stand at a meeting collapsed under the weight of dignitaries, he emerged unscathed with a wry smile: "This was a Democratic platform, I think." [105]

But Hanna's tour was only one highlight of the campaign. If the effort was in fact more noisy than earnest, most of the noise reverberated around the vice-presidential candidate, who undertook a gruelling tour, speaking at countless crossroads and in most major cities. Wrapped in all the glamor of his war heroics, his zeal fed by his own ebullience, Roosevelt swept along the campaign hustings with dazzling success. The real exhibition of the whole campaign seemed to be his teeth, which he bared prominently and to good effect to thousands all over the country. His schedule was monstrous. "They do not give me time to eat or sleep," he complained to Henry C. Payne.[106]

There was no lack of showmanship, either, for Roosevelt was thinking of 1904 all the while. He thought it well to be accompanied by a troop of Rough Rider veterans in South Dakota, and no audience was likely to forget his heroics as he described the glories of Republicanism. His endless energy and high spirits amazed thousands. "Has he been drinking?" asked an astonished Iowan as he watched Roosevelt grimace his way through hundreds of hand-shakes, telling stories and cracking jokes. "Oh, no," came the answer, "he needs no whiskey to make him feel that way—he intoxicates himself by his own enthusiasm." The President's absence from the campaign highlighted Roosevelt's importance to the ticket. The people doubtless loved him for himself, whatever he said, but he was probably right in feeling that his tour, next to McKinley's name and Hanna's organization, did most to win the victory.[107]

The campaign ground to its inexorable close. On election eve, Canton paid homage to her favorite son in grand style. A brass band, blaring the President's favorite marches and popular tunes, escorted several thousand townspeople to the famous front porch, where repeated calls and cheering brought him out to say a few words before introducing the visiting Judge Day, who spoke briefly.[108]

The election fulfilled the President's expectations. His popular vote exceeded that of 1896 by 100,000, and in the electoral college Bryan was swamped by a total of 292 to 155, or 21 more than in 1896. McKinley lost Kentucky but gained Kansas, Nebraska, South Dakota, Utah, and Wyoming, which seemed to prove that free silver was forever dead, and that the West and Midwest endorsed "imperialism." "God bless and keep you for the patriotic purposes to which you have dedicated your life's work," Hanna wired shortly after midnight on election day. "I am deeply sensible of your untiring efforts since the very beginning of the campaign and I am sure I voice the sentiments of all Republicans when I say that the service you have rendered the party and the country is incalculable," McKinley later responded. A more perfunctory message came on November 8: "At the close of another Presidential campaign it is my lot to congratulate you on a second victory. W. J. Bryan." [109]

Victory elated Vice-President-elect Theodore Roosevelt. But from time to time he reflected on his new job, telling friends that he "now expected to be a dignified nonentity for four years." He heaped praise on the man he had once called as weak as a chocolate eclair. "I do not think I am wrong in my historic judgement of contemporary matters when I say that President McKinley's administration will rank next to Lincoln's during the whole 19th century in point of great work worthily done," he wrote Hay. "Other presidents such as Jefferson, Madison, and Polk met great crises, but they did not do the great work as well." [110]

To McKinley the victory was doubly rewarding. Not only did it seem to endorse his past actions and promise support for his future work, but the majority also seemed to indicate in the form of cold figures the realization of his old dream of nationalism. Still, it was sobering. "The President seems more impressed with his responsibilities than his triumph," Dawes noted. Two weeks after the election, McKinley told an attentive crowd at a Union League banquet in Philadelphia that it was a sobering victory. "It has to me no personal phase. It is not the triumph of an individual, nor altogether of a party. . . ." The new issues which they would all face were "too exalted for partisanship," and meeting them was the task of "the whole American people." In private he was more explicit, outlining in a simple utterance to a friend all that the victory portended for him: "I can no longer be called the President of a party; I am now the President of the whole people." [111]

XXII

Journey to Buffalo

FTER CHATTING with cabinet members and friends, the President retired toward midnight on the last day of the old year, to wake to a new century. Tomorrow would bring floods of callers for the customary New Year's reception, and McKinley would not permit any curtailment of the numbers of people to be greeted. "I come away better for meeting them," he would say. "I get more out of them than they get out of me." [1] On the morrow the people stood four abreast in cold lines outside the mansion, waiting for the somewhat pompous retainers to open the doors and allow them to shake the smiling President's hand. Most came out of kindness and curiosity. Ida reported in her little pocket diary that over 5,300 people greeted him that day.[2]

McKinley had been so seldom ill that the people around him assumed him immune to sickness. Everyone was surprised, therefore, when he came down with a case of the flu. Confined to bed, he was a cooperative patient, for there were dangers of pneumonia, a serious disease in 1901. Two years before, Cortelyou had dismissed rumors about McKinley's supposedly failing health as "foolish stories . . . ," and the private secretary worried about his chief, so unusual was the attack.[3]

His illness was kept discreetly quiet, for fear the press would inflate it. Ida relished for a moment the role of nurse which her husband had himself fulfilled for her for so many years. Friends like John Hay dropped by to commiserate with the patient, who chafed at inaction more than illness. The finicky Hay could not help alluding to his own still delicate condition. "I feel like 30 per cent— with a discount for cash," he wrote McKinley.[4] Worried inquiries came from Canton as friends and relatives read the scanty news reports. Told that a friend had the flu, the President, from the benefit of experience, recommended bed. "When you get the grippe, that is just the best place to be." [5]

The dying Congress refused to die as quietly as the President could have wished. There were rumors that an outrageous rivers and harbors bill would be rushed through to take advantage of the favorable Treasury balance to which Secretary Gage had recently pointed with pride, and McKinley firmly told Cortelyou that he would veto it. Senator Hanna was lobbying for a federal subsidy to merchant marine operators, which he said would give the United States an independent fleet. The newspapers fell on the morsel with glee, pointing to Hanna's ship operations, and McKinley was tactfully silent on the subject, though he favored a subsidy of some kind.[6] The President and administration leaders had no illusions about congressional speed. ". . . You might as well ask a football team in full play for their autographs as expect to get legislation on any important new subject from Congress at present. . . ." Root wrote Leonard Wood.[7]

March 4 approached, and the sound of hammers and the flash of colored bunting across Washington's major thoroughfares heralded the coming pageantry of another presidential inauguration. The country did not forget that this was not only the last inauguration of the century, but was also the centenary anniversary of the first inauguration in Washington. The city had changed vastly since then, and took pride in the face it presented; then it had been mud, now it was marble.

The formal services were to be held, as usual, at the east front of the Capitol, in the center of the plaza, in a specially built pavilion resembling a Greek temple. By the day before the ceremonies, hotel rooms were at a historic premium. Prosperity added a certain glamor to the event, and brought more people to the capital for the spectacle. The White House had been somewhat refurbished; a glass-enclosed booth for reviewing the inaugural parade would protect the presidential party from any inclemency. Dazzling honor guards and spanking teams of well-fed and festooned horses stood ready to transport and accompany the official party to and from the Capitol in specially varnished and gleaming carriages, thoughtfully provided with covers just in case it rained.

When inaugural day dawned, the sound of conflicting music rolled down Pennsylvania Avenue as the various bands competed for the attention of the crowds which grew with the approach of the mid-morning hours that would take McKinley to Capitol Hill. General Corbin and Doctor Rixey—to accompany Mrs. McKinley —Senator Hanna, the cabinet, and other high-ranking dignitaries arrived by ten o'clock. At ten-thirty the President emerged to doff his hat to the cheering crowd beyond the iron fence, before he climbed into his carriage for a swift ride up the Avenue.

Congress seemed to have been in session ever since anyone could remember, and to the bewilderment of foreigners Senator Carter of Montana was busy talking the rivers and harbors bill to death; he had to be interrupted so that Roosevelt could be inaugurated. Nonetheless, a stack of last-minute legislation awaited McKinley, who sat in the ornate President's Room signing the measures. From time to time men walked in to watch, chat with others, or return the President's cordial nod. There was no sense of tension in the air. All except the most die-hard Democrats agreed that the sweeping mandate of November ended the fierce strife that had marred the first part of the decade.[8]

Roosevelt was duly inaugurated. At about noon the President's party emerged from the Senate wing of the Capitol and walked briskly toward the little white temple where the oath was to be administered. McKinley seemed spirited and vigorous as he walked to his position, ignoring the sudden rain with bared head and turned-up collar. To others in the crowd the rain and leaden skies seemed an ill omen. "This is not McKinley weather," one congressman said as he returned from the ceremonies.[9]

But the rain did not dampen either the President's brief address or the crowd's responses. Some shuffled under heavy umbrellas and squinted through fogged spectacles as they strained to watch his figure, but his ringing tones carried well into the huge crowd.[10] His short speech held no surprises. He alluded to America's fulfilling destiny, to the need for patience in foreign affairs, to the promises he had made and would fulfill for the dependencies.

The President acknowledged the cheers, shook hands with the members of the Supreme Court and other statesmen, bowed to the cheering well-wishers, and hastened to his closed carriage. Rivers of water poured off the coachmen's rubber capes, and Pennsylvania Avenue wound from the Capitol to the White House like a dark mirror as the party returned for the parades and receptions. But the weather did not dampen the cheers. McKinley came to his second term on roars of popular approval.

Popular approval of the Chief Executive, and the country's sense of well-being and prosperity did not mean, of course, an end to partisan politics, but no really sharp issue faced the President in the following weeks. There were minor personal problems with public overtones, like the departure of Attorney-General Griggs, anxious to return to private practice, who was replaced by the aloof but efficient Ohioan, Philander C. Knox.[11]

Congressional adjournment brought some relief, but the petty irritants of patronage, to which men like Hay never seemed to become inured, remained always. The Secretary of State raged at senatorial demands for offices. "I wonder if we can *ever* make an appointment on its merits," he wrote the President after enduring a harangue from a windy senator.[12] McKinley was also warned of another impending coal strike, and union officials asked him to mediate it, pointing to his record as governor of Ohio as proof of his pro-labor sympathies.[13] Despite visits from Senator Hanna on the subject later in the year, presidential mediation died aborning; the big strike was reserved for McKinley's successor.[14]

Though publicly silent on the subject, McKinley was thinking more of the trusts. With his recent mandate from the people, the experience of four years in office, and the sobering reality of having met many varied crises with general success, McKinley now grew more inclined to use new authority on the Congress that would meet in December. He could have agreed with Roosevelt that the common man was unfair in pointing to the trust while forgetting his own prosperity, but there was no singing the trust issue away. It would have to be met.[15]

The President was, as usual, excessively cautious about the problem, but he warned Hanna and the party leaders that anti-trust action was inevitable. In 1902, when Roosevelt moved against the Northern Securities Company, Hanna grunted: "I warned Hill that McKinley might have to act against his damn company last year. Mr. Roosevelt's done it. I'm sorry for Hill, but just what do you gentlemen think I can do?"[16]

But public affairs did not absorb the President as much after the inauguration as did the details of the transcontinental tour he planned to make between April and June. It seemed both fitting and felicitous to inaugurate the second term with such a tour. He had not seen the Far West, and the six weeks tour would take him south, across the desert Southwest, and then up the coast to San Francisco, where he would launch the recently finished battleship *Ohio*. The return would be climaxed on June 13 at the newly inaugurated Pan-American Exposition at Buffalo, where he would make a major address in celebration of President's Day.

He originally hoped to take a large official party, including the cabinet, with him, but at departure time on April 29, this proved impossible. The cabinet officers had too much work to do. Hay and Smith accompanied him, to be joined at San Francisco by Secretaries Long, Hitchcock, and Wilson. Root and Knox simply could not leave their offices. The President, Mrs. McKinley, and a party of forty-three braved the tremendous welcome staged for them through the sympathetic South, which already loved McKinley, and the Western states that revelled in the presidential tour as evidence of their growing importance.

The trip was not altogether a pleasure jaunt. McKinley was mindful of his standing with the people; he wished to see them, to have them see him, and above all to discuss some controversial topics in public as a warning to Congress that it might expect not only a new kind of presidential leadership, but the necessary public opinion to implement it. Nor was Congress unmindful of this aspect of the tour.

The tour was all that could be expected and more. In the South his every appearance signalled cheers and flowers. Jovial and radiating confidence, McKinley was ideal in the role of travelling statesman, choosing always the right word, the proper tone, the expected reference at every stop and for every delegation. At one stop a welcoming party told him that his appearance had drawn the crowd away from a visiting circus. "Why, of course," he laughed, "you can't expect a fifty cent show to draw any people when there's a free show in town." [17] In Arizona and New Mexico, still in a semi-frontier state that added to the spirit in the crowds that welcomed the party, there were occasional calls for "Teddy!" which may have irked the President.[18]

The train paused briefly in the rugged beauty of the desert, now springing into life and dotted with sweeps of blooms and greenness, so that Doctor Rixey could lance a felon on Mrs. McKinley's finger which was causing her considerable pain. Still confident that Ida would withstand the trip without difficulty, the President alighted from the train while the minor operation was performed to admire the desert beauty.

Fiesta celebrations covered Los Angeles with flowers during the second week of May, and McKinley's appearance in the City of the Angels was an unqualified demonstration of popular affection. Rose petals poured down on his reviewing stand until they covered his shoe tops, and he stood smiling and waving his hat for what seemed like hours. With typical California zeal, the citizenry could not do him enough honor. Pickpockets circulated freely in the crowds, however, and the flustered Secretary Wilson lost his wallet.[19] One watcher refused to leave the line of march when told that his house was burning; the house was doomed anyway and he might never again get to see the President of the United States.[20] Even with partisanship considered, there was much truth in a reporter's assertion: "No President—certainly no president since the days of Lincoln—has been so close to the hearts of the people as Mr. McKinley." [21]

The route of conquest lay north along the fabled trail of the Spanish friars who had first civilized the Golden State. San Francisco waited impatiently to outdo all others in homage to the official party. On Friday, May 10, the entourage left Los Angeles for Del Monte and a quiet weekend before beginning the visit to San Francisco which was scheduled for Tuesday. But Mrs. McKinley showed signs of failing health. Her seizures threatened, and weakness and a general fever caused by a blood infection in her finger brought her to the edge of collapse. On Sunday the President rushed her to San Francisco. Trained nurses watched over the invalid, put to bed in the home of H. T. Scott, whose firm had built the *Ohio*.

In the days that followed, the city and nation rallied silently to the President's side as Ida sank inexorably toward death. It seemed impossible that she could survive such a general assault on her frail being. On Wednesday, after she had lapsed into semi-consciousness, her saddened husband made arrangements for her funeral train's departure to Washington, and cancelled the rest of his tour. Silence prevailed around the house where she lay, and the crowds that came to see the celebrities come and go merely raised their hats in silent greeting.

Then suddenly Ida showed her famous stubbornness, called on hidden reserves of strength, and to everyone's amazement, rallied. By Thursday she could sit up and talk weakly, and the doctors pronounced her out of immediate danger. The President hurried to the docks, crossed the bay to the shipyards, and dedicated the ship named after his native state. At the same time he gave public thanks. "I am inexpressibly thankful to the Ruler of us all for His goodness and His mercy, which have made it possible for me to be with you here today," he told the rather sober crowd of workers and dignitaries. Fidgeting on the ferryboat that took him back across the bay, and almost panic-stricken by his absence from the sick bed, he fairly ran to the waiting carriage that returned him to the Scott house.[22]

For almost another week he remained in the city, though Mrs. McKinley was still in bed, trying to make amends for the misfortunes that had kept him from public view. If there were no cheers around the Scott house, the same could not be said for other areas of the city where the citizenry gave vent to their joy at seeing their first president with wild shouts and showers of roses. The party then bade a reluctant farewell to the city, and entrained for Washington, where further medical consultations were in order for Mrs. McKinley.

Ida remained dangerously ill due to the weakness which the fever and blood condition brought, and McKinley could not go to Buffalo for the Exposition. He dispatched Hay and Root to make some amends, carrying the promise that he himself would appear later in the fall to speak at the Exposition and to view the many marvels that were already a topic of national interest.

He was scheduled to depart for a summer's rest at Canton, whose quiet and familiar surroundings would help Ida's recovery. He was eager to escape public duties before going on to the Exposition, attendance at which required writing a major speech. But one small matter intruded. There had been persistent rumors, repeated eagerly by such powerful men as Hay, that he would seek a third term. His popularity was already such that he could easily win in 1904, the pollsters said. The President had no such inclinations. After a cabinet meeting, he dictated and, surprisingly enough, signed a press release to end such talk. "I will say now, once for all, expressing a long settled conviction, that I not only am not and will not be a candidate for a third term, but would not accept a nomination for it if it were tendered me." There could be no mistaking either the tone or content, all the more remarkable in view of his usual cloudiness on such controversial matters.[23]

On July 5, he and Ida left for Canton, planning to spend some months in their home there. This would be his longest absence from the White House. He could afford it, for now there was no crisis in China or elsewhere to claim his attention. He enjoyed the little town again, moving as freely as ever, entertaining a few friends, talking more of horses and houses than of politics, and watching Ida improve in the cool air that flowed down from the lakes. "It is really so comfortable here that unless I am needed I shall be in no hurry," he wrote Hay. "I would like very much to talk with you about three or four things, but dislike to suggest your running out here rather than Washington. Washington is such a hot place, and you know Canton being so near the Lake, is perpetually cool." [24]

There was the speech to think about, and the routine correspondence and business that Cortelyou handled efficiently, and the days were not idle. One note of tragedy had intruded on McKinley before he left. Hay's son Adelbert, who had worked in the consular service, and to whom McKinley had taken an instant liking, was killed in an accidental fall from a window, and the Secretary's grief was limitless. Having lost two children himself, McKinley felt a strong sympathy for the tortured father, whose tendency to morbidity the tragedy heightened. The President could only suggest resignation. "Time, I know, is the great healer—but have I time to heal?" Hay answered despondently.[25]

The President had not forgotten his promise to the Exposition managers at Buffalo. It would be an ideal setting from which to discuss reciprocity, since it displayed inventions and manufactures from the whole hemisphere. Late in August a distinguished committee called at Canton to discuss the arrangements, and the President agreed that September 5 would be a good day for his speech. He was to address a Grand Army of the Republic meeting in Cleveland in mid-September, and it would be well to have the Exposition speech out of the way.

One evening after dinner in Canton, with Mrs. McKinley safely resting, the President and Cortelyou repaired to the library, where cigar smoke soon wound above McKinley's head. Suddenly he turned to his secretary and said: "Expositions are the timekeepers of progress." Cortelyou hastily wrote the sentence down, and McKinley continued: "We'll build the speech around that." [26] It illustrated his methods: the germ sprouted only after long and careful thought.

McKinley had already decided that the speech would take a forceful stand in favor of reciprocity and international commercial dealings. He wished to ally this with the total idea of America's new role in world affairs. "Our trusteeship is a large and sacred one," he wrote in notes for his private use. "We must not be faithless to our high mission, or falter before its high responsibilities, nor permit pride or might to taint our motives, or lead us from the plain teaching of duty or divert us from the sacred principles of liberty." [27]

His vision of commercial reciprocity not only as a tool of commercial expansion but as an implement of world peace fitted neatly into this larger design. He had already chuckled to Cortelyou that it would be "amusing" if the tariff issue revived; but he said also that the Republicans must handle it, since the Democrats had never been sound on the issue. [28] Before his recent western tour, McKinley promised Kasson and others to fight for the pending treaties during the coming session even if it meant party disharmony. [29] During the summer, visitors to Canton like Dolliver noted an increasing vigor in the President's insistence that reciprocity could not be delayed. [30] "I never saw him more determined on anything than this," Cortelyou remembered. [31]

The knowledge that he faced party opposition did not deter him. He had had enough of senatorial dalliance. "I suppose you realize that that policy is going to be pressed upon us next winter . . . ," Lodge wrote Aldrich candidly, pointing out that while they could accept reciprocity with Latin America, it would not do on a large scale with Europe. [32] The President was quite willing to contradict this attitude. "We must awake out of the long dream that we can sell everything and buy nothing," he wrote in other private notes. "A one-sided arrangement cannot last forever. We should take from our customers such of their products as we can consume without harm to our own industries. Reciprocity is the logical outcome of our enormous industrial development. The home demand is more than supplied by our present productive capacity. Our surplus products must seek a market abroad." [33]

As the September date for departure to Buffalo approached, a small specter worried some of the President's staff and friends. Crank letters during the campaign of 1900 had sharpened Cortelyou's fears of assassination, which he considered doubly likely in view of McKinley's nonchalant attitude that no one would want to hurt him. Hanna was especially alarmed at the lax security measures around the President, and cautioned his friend in vain. Joe Butler, visiting Canton shortly before the departure to Buffalo, raised the subject and was waved aside.[34] With his usual fatalism, McKinley left all such matters to destiny. He would not risk the isolation and curtailment of freedom that full security imposed. "If it were not for Ida," he was once reported saying, "I would prefer to go as Lincoln went." [35] Cortelyou tried to screen visitors and supervise public arrangements to thwart assassins. A special detective was assigned, a barrel-shaped, walrus-mustached man named George Foster, to accompany the President at Buffalo. Special plain clothes detectives from the Buffalo police force and Pinkerton men would stand guard over the Milburn home, where the President would stay, but there remained the problem of the crowds at the Exposition.

Time rushed past, and though reluctant to leave Canton, McKinley nonetheless made the necessary arrangements and left for the Exposition on September 4. The Exposition to which his special train drew him was a historic event, celebrating the progress of the Americas. Its electric marvels and water fiestas vied with its architecture for public attention. Prosperity and a lazy summer brought thousands to the fair; on President's Day, 116,000 paid admission, and 50,000 heard McKinley's speech in the main plaza.

On the appointed day, September 5, the boom of cannon and clatter of horses' hooves raised cheers in the massed thousands as the presidential party swept down the Triumphal Causeway toward the specially constructed platform from which McKinley was to speak. A field of domes and towers, glistening whitely in the sun

518

above the huge crowd, claimed attention and bespoke the marvels of the age. Colorful costumes dotted the crowd as foreign visitors and dignitaries strained to see the presidential party. Accompanied by his wife and the president of the exposition, John Milburn, his host, McKinley acknowledged the cheers and stepped up to the flag-draped platform for perhaps the most important speech of his career. With his right hand thrust into his pocket, his left holding a sheaf of papers, in a characteristic pose, the President's figure was impressive.

The speech captured the crowd's attention, and the muttering and cheering died as he raised a practiced voice in his last public utterance. His words were frank but felicitous. He wanted reciprocity to foster world peace, and prayed that all Americans would face the facts which recent world events had proved true. "Isolation is no longer possible or desirable," he said candidly. He sang the praises of the country's wealth and industrial system. "No narrow, sordid policy will subserve it. . . . Only a broad and enlightened policy will keep what we have. No other policy will get more." He was not advocating free trade, but "sensible trade arrangements which will not interrupt our home production. . . ." And then the ultimate truth: "The period of exclusiveness is past. The expansion of our trade and commerce is the pressing problem. Commercial wars are unprofitable." [36]

The speech captured the fresh spirit in the crowd, which underlined each telling phrase with growing applause. The sense of victory lingered in the cheers as the President left the rostrum, greeted the waiting foreign diplomats, and escorted Ida to her carriage. She was to return to the Milburn home while he toured the Exposition.

His progress was an uninterrupted ovation. Mechanical gadgetry, none of which he ever understood, always fascinated him, and he toured each building like any tourist, pausing here and there to let his picture be taken, to shake a hand, or to wave to people. He saw in all the instruments symbols of national progress and the implements of welfare that would make his dream of world harmony true.

Friday, September 6, was a special day. He rose, dressed in his usual dark frock coat, striped pants, boiled shirt, and hard collar, for a visit to Niagara Falls, after which he was to have a formal luncheon and then greet the public in the Temple of Music. Special cars carried the dignified party to the Falls, and the President ventured half-way across the suspension bridge that connected the United States and Canada. Protocol forbade stepping on foreign soil. A visit to Goat Island and its steep inclines did not damage his dignity. The party duly witnessed the spectacle of the Falls and then went on to the International Hotel for luncheon. Mrs. McKinley, who had abandoned the tour, met him there. Luncheon was a jovial affair, after which he smoked on the veranda and then freshened up on the train that took him back to the Exposition grounds. The reception at the Temple of Music was to be held at four, and while he would be there only some ten minutes, he wished to look his best. Ida was now too tired to accompany him, and the President saw her off to the Milburn home, and then turned for the trip back to the Exposition grounds. He paused some time later near the Temple of Music for refreshments before beginning his favorite chore, greeting the people.

The large Temple was especially decorated for the President's brief stop. Potted palms, flowers, and screens gave it a comfortable atmosphere, and the huge pipe organ provided soft background music to the rustle of skirts and tap of shoes as the people filed past McKinley. Thousands who could not possibly enter waited in front of the Temple. The lucky ones who would actually shake the President's hand had waited in the heat for hours. Among them was a rather nondescript young man with wide-set eyes. Dressed in plain dark clothes, and wearing a childish and vapid expression on his face, there was no air of sinister intent about him. No one, certainly not McKinley, would have taken him for what he was, a professional anarchist. His name was Leon Czolgosz. He had come to kill the president of the United States. He did not know Mr. McKinley, nor had the President wronged him. It was a matter of principle. Government was evil and must be stamped out. The place to start was at the top.

Cortelyou posted special guards as best he could, and lined up the ropes that guided the visitors so that the detectives could watch each person approach. Some ceremonial soldiers and officers did double duty as detectives, scrutinizing each person as he came up to the President. Cortelyou had talked in vain against the public reception. "Why should I?" McKinley had asked blandly when cancellation was mentioned. "No one would wish to hurt me." It was bad enough to circulate among the crowds, Cortelyou told the President, but to greet people would be dangerous. Besides, he couldn't greet more than a few, so why run the risk? "Well, they'll know I tried," McKinley answered blandly, and would not be dissuaded.[37]

The President arrived promptly at four o'clock, stepped lightly from his victoria, and walked briskly toward his assigned spot. He nodded toward the doors and said, "Let them come in." The doors opened and people pushed or were pushed into the room, passing quickly before him, saying a few words, nodding shyly to his warm greeting before hurrying along to where attendants showed the route of exit. Cortelyou watched the door sourly, watch in hand, anxious to cut off the flow of people. He would raise his hand as a signal to close the doors at about ten minutes after four. He was too late.

About seven or eight minutes after the doors opened, as the big organ softly exuded a Bach sonata, the pleasant rustling of clothing and shuffle of feet, the murmured greetings and directions, were interrupted by two pistol shots. For a moment nothing stirred. The President raised on his tiptoes and looked in astonishment at the blank eyes in front of him. Smoke curled from a hole in the bandaged right hand of the young man he had obligingly reached out to greet with his left hand. It seemed incredible. The President had been shot.

In a moment the full import of the sound registered on the crowd, and screams rent the air as women rushed for the exits. The assassin stood rooted, making no effort to escape or destroy himself, until he was pinned down and disarmed. The President was led to a chair. The hand he held to his vest came away sticky with blood. He stared at his fingers in disbelief and turned to Cortelyou. "My wife—be careful, Cortelyou, how you tell her—oh, be careful!" He had already looked at the assassin. "Don't let them hurt him," he said.[38]

The crowd's stupefaction gave way to panic that threatened to block all entrances and exits with seething humanity, but miraculously the ambulance arrived from the Exposition's small emergency hospital. At eighteen minutes after four, the President was being undressed for an examination, in shock but conscious. One bullet rolled from his clothing, apparently deflected by a button, but the other had cut a path through his stomach, perhaps a kidney, losing itself somewhere in the muscles of the back. It was not found. The Exposition's medical director was away, but attending physicians counselled an immediate operation to probe and clean the wound, lest gangrene interfere, and to survey the damage. As ether was administered, the President spoke the Lord's Prayer.

The operation was only a partial success; the bullet remained hidden and X-ray was never used, though one of the new machines was on display at the Exposition. In the failing afternoon light, Doctor Rixey focused the sun's rays on the surgeon's work with a mirror. The incision was closed without drainage, and antiseptic bandage applied. Still under sedation, McKinley was transferred to the Milburn home, where Ida waited.

Friends and relatives feared that the shock of the news would simply kill Ida McKinley outright, but as so often happens with invalids, she received it well. She wished to see her husband, but the doctors refused, since he needed rest and quiet. She reposed in the fancied belief, shared by the doctors, that the wound was not fatal; he would live. In the week that followed she clung persistently to that vain hope, relinquishing it only at the last moment. It did not seem possible that fate would take the one thing for which she lived, the man who had made her life bearable.

The news was telegraphed across the Associated Press wires within minutes, in time for the late afternoon editions, and the nation heard it in stunned horror. Anarchism was a strange and vague word to most Americans, but its intent was clear. The last decades had seen the assassination of many European princes and rulers at anarchist hands. The empress of Austria, king of Italy, president of France, shah of Persia, czar of Russia, and lesser notables had fallen before the doctrine.

When the news reached Vice-President Roosevelt, vacationing on an island in Lake Champlain, he emitted a thundering "My God!" A later amplification was more explicit, speaking in tones that the people shared. "I am so inexpressibly grieved, shocked and horrified that I can say nothing." [39] Senator Hanna was thunderstruck. "McKinley never had any fear of danger from that source," he told reporters as he flagged down a mail train in Cleveland. [40] Editorials on every front page reflected the nation's shock at this act against the republic, for Czolgosz had said that he had nothing against Mc-Kinley. To assault so obviously kind, sincere, and able a man as William McKinley seemed to most Americans the ultimate act of madness.[41]

On Saturday, Roosevelt and the cabinet members except Hay and Long were in Buffalo, anxiously watching the doctors and eagerly devouring the news bulletins. The Milburn house became a hospital, its halls and vacant rooms jammed with equipment. Adjacent streets were roped off so that traffic noise would not bother the patient. Soldiers posted at intervals served notice that no similar attempt could be repeated.

For the week after the assassination a current of hope ran through public expectations. The President recovered consciousness with no apparent complications, and could talk, move, and even smile at the doctors. His hearty constitution, everyone said, would see him through. The doctors seemed hopeful, even confident. On September 7, Cortelyou's medical bulletin relieved the country: "The President passed a fairly comfortable night and no serious symptoms have developed." [42] In the days that followed the public read with consuming interest every morsel of news released, and the doctors retained their rosy view.

It is difficult to understand the cheer with which they viewed their patient. He was nearly sixty years old, overweight, and the wound itself had not been thoroughly cleaned or traced. Precautions against infection, admittedly difficult in 1901, were negligently handled. Informed that the President would undoubtedly recover, Roosevelt left for his summer camp in the Adirondacks, twelve miles from any communication. The cabinet dispersed and once again Cortelyou shouldered the burden of managing affairs.

McKinley himself lent credence to the cheerful view. He complained of being lonely in his sick room, so Ida was allowed to see him briefly each day. He was concerned about the reaction to his speech, and smiled when told that the public approved.[43] As usual, he worried about his wife. The day after being shot, he had taken her hand and said, "We must bear up. It will be better for both." [44] Hanna shared the public's confidence, and on September 9 said he might go home if the President's improvement continued.[45]

As the week closed, disquieting symptoms appeared in the patient. He was unable to take nourishment except by enema; the light foods taken by mouth did not digest. His fever rose, and the doctors realized by Friday, September 13, that their worst fears were true: general infection resulting from gangrene along the bullet's track had set in. The President rallied briefly, then collapsed. Bulletins went to the press, and Cortelyou called the officials and friends back to the dying President's side. In the Adirondacks, a messenger rattled over the rough mountain roads to the Vice-President's retreat. Theodore Roosevelt returned over the same route, behind wild horses, to learn at the train station that he would shortly be president.

At the bedside that dark Friday, the friends and associates of a lifetime gathered in response to the official bulletin: "The President is sinking." Some clung to hope. "I cannot bring myself to believe that he is not to recover—sad and disheartening as this morning's news appears," Hay wrote Senator Morgan in despair. The Secretary was convinced that he had the touch of death about him. He had been a friend of Lincoln, Garfield, and now McKinley.[46]

Late in the afternoon McKinley rallied from his comatose state and talked to his doctors. Life was prolonged by the use of oxygen and heart stimulants, but the President felt that it was hopeless. "It is useless, gentlemen. I think we ought to have prayer." As the day ended he asked for his wife, and Cortelyou led her in. A small knot of relatives and friends stood and sat around the bedside as she wanly bade him farewell. "Good-bye, good-bye all," he said weakly. "It is God's way. His will, not ours, be done." He murmured as best he could his favorite hymn, "Nearer my God to Thee." They were his last words.[47]

Sometime that terrible evening, Mark Hanna had approached the bedside, tears standing in his eyes, his hands and head shaking in disbelief that thirty years of friendship could end thus. Near collapse, he composed himself with the aid of Myron Herrick and James Wilson, and paid his final respects. The President was weak and moaning incoherently as his friend approached. "Mr. President, Mr. President, can't you hear me?" Hanna asked plaintively. "Don't you know me?" There was an ineffectual response from the dying McKinley and Hanna, abandoning formality, cried out over the years of friendship, "William, William, don't you know me?"[48]

Downstairs, members of the cabinet and officials milled restlessly, stepping outside now and then for air, resigned to the inevitable end. Upstairs, Mrs. McKinley's pleading, in sobs, "I want to go too, I want to go too" was of no avail. The death rattle continued fitfully, and then toward a quarter after two Saturday morning, it ceased. Doctor Rixey put his stethoscope to the President's heart. "The President is dead." [49]

A state funeral was not to be avoided, for the nation must pay its last homage to the man it had so lately loved and honored. He had come to them and now they would come to him. There was a new president, and the nation endured. Roosevelt arrived, ashen and shaken, to take the oath of office and to promise to carry out McKinley's policies. There was a panic on the stock exchange, but the public had no time for it. The black-bordered extras and carloads of flowers in Buffalo, Canton, and Washington were all eloquent testimony to the nation's grief. Tolling bells heralded the progress of the special train that brought the body to Washington for solemn services.

The coffin rested a time in the flower-smothered East Room of the White House. At the Capitol the humble and the mighty alike passed in review. The immense funeral parade escorting the body to the train that would carry it to Canton for interment crossed streets slick with falling rain. Even the heavens seemed to weep. For Ida McKinley, it was the cruelest journey of her life as she sat carefully attended amid the evidence of her grief. In every town the train passed flag-draped poles and houses clad in mourning. Silent and bareheaded crowds lined the route and stood in homage at every crossroad.

In Canton, the nation's dignitaries gathered for the final rites. President Roosevelt strictly forbade any undue attention to himself, but he sat in the front row of the Methodist church for the funeral services, backed by congressmen and members of the administration.[50] Five minutes of silence enveloped the land as the people paid an extraordinary act of final homage; vehicles, factory wheels, and conversation stopped.

At the cemetery, amid the floral pomp and the black emblems of grief, the bier was laid to rest in a temporary vault. Already there was talk of a fitting monument. The soldiers snapped to attention. The vault doors closed. Slowly, sadly, the crowd dispersed. The long journey that had carried William McKinley from Canton to Washington and the seats of power had led him to Canton again.

Epilogue

I
DA McKINLEY lived until 1907, spending six years in the isolation of her private world, pouring out her grief and loneliness
to friends on heavy black-bordered paper. Few hours of any day
passed not spent in reverie over her husband and his accomplishments. All around her, objects evoked his presence in her solitary
rooms. Often she rallied from her illness to be kindly, thoughtful,
and interesting. But despite attending nieces and friends, time
weighed heavily on her hands. "I realize more and more that I am
not company for anyone but I do not wish to forget my friends," she
wrote plaintively to Webb Hayes. "I am more lonely every day I
live." [1]

When she died in Canton in 1907, Ohio and the nation that had
perhaps passed her by mourned her sincerely, remembering with
a touch of sad nostalgia her pride in sharing her husband's public
life. She lived to see many honors accorded him. On a green hill in
Canton's cemetery there arose a stately tomb that would house her
remains along with his and the two small coffins of their children. In
Niles, a many-pillared memorial combined utility with majesty to
remind travellers and residents that a president came from those
humble surroundings.

Ida McKinley did not question her husband's greatness or the
magnitude of his accomplishments. To her they went without saying. She only knew, as did millions, that his passing seemed to close
a whole era. The men, movements, and ideas she lived to witness
seemed to bear little relation in their urgency and threats to the
placid America she thought she had known. At his death, McKinley
was the subject of sincere eulogies, for he died the most widely
beloved president in memory. "There have undoubtedly been greater
and stronger Presidents than he was," George McClellan, Jr., would
say, "but none was a more kindly nor a more courteous gentleman,

and none has died more regretted by his countrymen, nor more beloved. . . ." It was no small epitaph.[2]

An inexorable personal sadness filtered into the ranks of the people who watched William McKinley's funeral cortege pass slowly by. Somehow he had mirrored in his life a calm assurance, a personal and public stability that they would not find in the new century and new order that followed him. The new era would bring alien forces to flood tide, expansion abroad in wars, political and social unrest at home. The imposing edifice of prosperity, peace, and public trust that William McKinley represented would be severely tested. His generation grew to await tomorrow with a kind of foreboding. In a few short years many would look back on his administration with nostalgia.

The years of his presidency were transitional. He stood not as the last old-fashioned chief executive nor as the first modern one, but as something in between, trying through his policies of conservative conciliation to ease his country and his people into the new position their responsibilities demanded. His successors awakened and used the latent powers of his office. They could not have done so had McKinley not paved the way by ameliorating the diverse forces that disturbed the country in the tumultuous nineties. "Your administration will go down in history next to that of Lincoln as one having more difficult problems to solve than any that preceded it," James Gary once wrote McKinley.[3]

Men would say, however, in his lifetime and long afterward, that he had expressed only that which was desired by a majority of the people at the moment. But any review of his career dispels that facile judgment. Many harsh critics apologized while he was alive, seeing at last the outlines of the system he tried to build. "I was brought up in a Reed-Allison atmosphere, and I accepted the 'no backbone' yarn only too readily," Raymond Chandler admitted to Dawes in reviewing a study of McKinley's administration. "This review, therefore, is my recantation, and the tribute is the more honest because it involves a confession of my own previous injustice." [4]

McKinley had few qualms about popular government; nor did he deny that he was a leader of the people, but he did not simply reflect their views. He did not hesitate to oppose their will when he thought it wrong and when events permitted. But he radiated the historic American confidence in democracy. To him what others called the American myth was real; had his own career not proved it? "We have the broadest opportunity for advancement, with every door open. The humblest citizen among you may aspire to the highest place in public favor and confidence," he once said. "As a result of our free institutions the great body of men who control public affairs in State and Nation, who control the great business enterprises of the country, the railroads and other industries, come from the humble home and from the ranks of the plain people of the United States." [5]

This trust in the people was the source of his strength, for through the alchemy of political technique he transformed it into support for practical policies. "Your voice, when constitutionally expressed, is commanding and conclusive," he told the people. "It is the law to Congress and to the Executive." [6] But he also knew how to interpret, to develop, and to create that voice for his own ends.

The weakness of his thinking was its contemporaneity, yet by his tenure's end he had devised a striking set of long-term goals and ideas in both domestic and foreign aflairs. He lacked the articulate manner that would have explained his philosophy of government and life and made it more compelling. Distrusting emotion, he always appealed to reason and logic. His reliance on manipulation and conciliation required unwritten understandings and personal agreements that kept him from history's limelight, for he could not advertise his methods without destroying them. His power over men lay in persuasion rather than in force, and persuasion is seldom dramatic. He cared little for the showmanship and personal publicity in which his immediate successor reveled. It did not fit his nature, and he wished dignity rather than display to restore executive leadership and the national stature of his office which had declined under Cleveland. McKinley often lacked creative vigor, but he had great ability to synthesize diverse views into policies acceptable to a majority of his people and his party. He did not move more rapidly in many fields simply because he detected no support for such motion. He was not a "great" president, but he fulfilled an exacting and critical role with success and ability displayed by no other contemporary.

It may seem strange that a man so experienced in the political system, so skilled in the nuances of public feeling that he seemed to hear things before they happened, lacked the vigor and imagination to perform bold new feats. But as a traditionalist, McKinley was sometimes the captive of his thinking and the political system which he would not or could not challenge. Nor did merciless events permit him the freedom or power that he or any president wishes. He came to the presidency when old ideas and institutions felt the first signs of discontent and change. Who could tell if this were merely a warning tremor or a deeper challenge? He faced issues with old ideas sometimes simply because no precedent guided him, and it was difficult to tell how far he could go and still retain the authority of public support. But he could and did make his own precedents in foreign affairs where his hand, like that of most presidents, was more free than in domestic matters. It was natural that a man of his temperament, attuned to caution and patience, built slowly, establishing first a spirit of conciliation and slow progress to prepare public and party for later bolder measures.

He helped heal the breaches in the GOP caused by the divisive issues of the 1890's, and restored the party harmony so necessary to carry out his long-term policies adopted after the war with Spain. To this task he brought many skills, born of patience, experience, and calmness of temper, fortified by his belief in the national system that party unity and public trust could construct. He did not always have his way, but even when he failed, as in tariff reform, he lighted a path for his successors. He was deft in telling the people things they did not know or did not wish to hear. He proclaimed the end of diplomatic isolation, called for international cooperation, and insisted that America accept the burdens of greatness in world affairs whether she wished them or not.

With his deep faith and sense of fatalism, McKinley did not question history's judgments. He understood his limitations as well as his strengths. He once summed up his own historical thinking in a sentence whose confidence and simplicity says much of both the man and his era: "That's all a man can hope for during his lifetime —to set an example, and when he is dead, to be an inspiration for history." [7]

He is not forgotten. His name is familiar nearly everywhere in his beloved Ohio. The McKinley carnation is the Buckeye State's flower, and his statue stands in many of her cities and towns. His birthday is the occasion for commemoration and celebration. Canton especially remembers her favorite of all sons, and in many ways it is still the same Canton. Tourists visit the impressive monument. They walk a graceful promenade to the hillside, pausing before a bronze statue of the twenty-fifth President, struck in a characteristic pose, then mount the steps that lead to the dome. From the top the view of the Ohio he loved is often beautiful. The color, the homes, the hills are there, as well as the fields and factories. The seasons come and go. Autumn touches every hillside with its brush and winter is the prelude to a varied spring. As though it were eternal, the great building looks out over Canton's environs. As they go about their business, the people often glance toward the monument and its green hillside that runs down to the edge of town.

Notes to Chapters

KEY TO ABBREVIATIONS

AHR	American Historical Review
DUL	Duke University Library, Durham, North Carolina
HAHR	Hispanic American Historical Review
HML	Hayes Memorial Library, Fremont, Ohio
HPSO	Historical and Philosophical Society of Ohio, Cincinnati
HSP	Historical Society of Pennsylvania, Philadelphia
ISDHA	Iowa State Department of History and Archives, Des Moines
JMH	Journal of Modern History
LC	Library of Congress, Manuscripts Division, Washington, D.C.
MHS	Massachusetts Historical Society, Boston
MVHR	Mississippi Valley Historical Review
NA	National Archives, Washington, D.C.
NHHS	New Hampshire Historical Society, Concord
NHS	Nevada Historical Society, Reno
NU	Northwestern University Library, Evanston, Illinois
NYPL	New York Public Library
OAHQ	Ohio Archaeological and Historical Quarterly
OAHS	Ohio Archaeological and Historical Society (now OHS), Columbus
OHQ	Ohio Historical Quarterly
OHS	Ohio Historical Society, Columbus
PHR	Pacific Historical Review
SCHS	Stark County Historical Society, Canton, Ohio
SHSC	State Historical Society of Colorado, Denver
SHSI	State Historical Society of Iowa, Iowa City
SHSW	State Historical Society of Wisconsin, Madison
UNC	University of North Carolina Library, Chapel Hill
WLCL	William L. Clements Library, Ann Arbor, Michigan
WRHS	Western Reserve Historical Society, Cleveland, Ohio
WVU	West Virginia University Library, Morgantown

WILLIAM MCKINLEY AND HIS AMERICA

I: *ORIGINS AND ANCESTORS*

1. The best sources on McKinley genealogy are Reverend A. Stapleton, "Genealogy of William McKinley," OAHS, *Publications,* 10 (1902), 236–242; Charles S. Olcott, *The Life of William McKinley,* 2 vols. (Boston: Houghton-Mifflin Co., 1916), I, 1–12; Edward A. Claypool, *The Scotch Ancestors of William McKinley, President of the United States* (Chicago: Schulkins and Co., 1897).

2. Olcott, *William McKinley,* I, 3ff.

3. See Duncan papers, WRHS.

4. Robert P. Porter, *Life of William McKinley, Soldier, Lawyer, Statesman* (Cleveland: N. G. Hamilton Pub. Co., 1896), 29ff.

5. Eugene Smalley, "William McKinley: A Study of His Character and Career," *Review of Reviews,* 14 (July, 1896), 33–45.

6. Olcott, *William McKinley,* I, 4–5.

7. W. H. Hunter, "The Pathfinders of Jefferson County," OAHS, *Publications,* 8 (1900), 133–262.

8. *Canton Repository,* January 7, 1892.

9. Porter, *William McKinley,* 36ff.

10. Joseph G. Butler, Jr., *Recollection of Men and Events* (Youngstown: N.P., 1925), 26.

11. Porter, *William McKinley,* 46–47.

12. Olcott, *William McKinley,* I, 5–6.

13. Murat Halstead, *The Illustrious Life of William McKinley, Our Martyred President* (Chicago: n.p., 1901), 114.

14. Andrew J. Duncan, "A Sketch of the Life of William McKinley," Duncan papers, WRHS.

15. *Canton Repository,* September 4, 1890.

16. See Porter, *William McKinley,* opposite page 42.

17. *Speeches and Addresses of William McKinley* (New York: Doubleday and McClure, 1900), 340. Hereafter cited as McKinley, *Speeches* (1900).

18. *Speeches and Addresses of William McKinley* (New York: D. Appleton and Co., 1893), 220–224. Hereafter cited as McKinley, *Speeches* (1893).

19. Henry B. Russell, *The Lives of William McKinley and Garrett A. Hobart . . .* (Hartford, Conn.: A. D. Worthington Co., 1896), 49.

20. Halstead, *William McKinley,* 109.

21. *Ibid.*

22. *Ibid.*

23. Butler, *Recollections,* 346.

24. *Ibid.,* 12.

25. Olcott, *William McKinley,* I, 8–9.

26. *Canton Repository,* October 26, 1896.

27. Smalley, "William McKinley," 33–45.

28. *Canton Repository,* November 1, 1896.

29. Olcott, *William McKinley,* I, 14; Joseph G. Butler, Jr., *Presidents I have Seen and Known* (Cleveland: The Penton Press, 1910), 39.

30. Halstead, *William McKinley,* 110.

31. San Francisco *Chronicle,* September 14, 1901.

32. Emil P. Herbruck, *Early Years and Late Reflections* (Cleveland: Central Pub. House, 1923), 218.

33. Julia B. Foraker, *I Would Live It Again* (New York: Harper Bros., 1932), 264–265.

34. Olcott, *William McKinley*, I, 15–16.

35. Porter, *William McKinley*, 54.

36. Russell, *William McKinley*, 57.

37. Olcott, *William McKinley*, I, 20.

38. Halstead, *William McKinley*, 110–111.

39. McKinley, *Speeches* (1893), 218.

40. Olcott, *William McKinley*, I, 18–19; Porter, *William McKinley*, 53ff; *Canton Repository*, October 25, 1896.

41. Halstead, *William McKinley*, 114.

42. The original program is preserved in Case C, in the museum of the McKinley National Birthplace Memorial, Niles, Ohio.

43. Ernest Ashton Smith, *Allegheny: A Century of Education* (Meadeville, Pa.: Allegheny College, 1910), 424; Don Marshall Larrabee, "William McKinley's College Days at Allegheny," *The Alleghenian*, 5 (March, 1940), 2–3.

44. *Canton Repository*, September 26, 1896.

45. John Johnson to McKinley, September 5, 1900, William McKinley papers, LC.

46. *Canton Repository*, June 21, 1896.

47. Charles B. Galbreath, *History of Ohio*, 5 vols. (New York: American Historical Society, 1925), II, 778.

48. Porter, *William McKinley*, 52ff; OAHS, *Publications*, 10 (1902), 232–235.

49. Cleveland *Leader*, August 25, 1895.

II: *THE VOLUNTEER SOLDIER*

1. Butler, *Recollections*, 47–48.

2. *Mahoning Register*, June 16, 1861.

3. Russell, *William McKinley*, 62.

4. OAHS, *Publications*, 10 (1902), 233.

5. *Ibid.*

6. Cleveland *Leader*, August 25, 1895. McKinley was eighteen on January 29, 1861.

7. McKinley, *Speeches* (1893), 362.

8. *Mahoning Register*, June 27, 1861.

9. *Ibid.*, June 20, July 6, 1861.

10. *Ibid.*, June 27, 1861.

11. *Ibid.*, July 6, 1861.

12. McKinley, *Speeches* (1893), 642–643.

13. *Mahoning Register*, July 18, 1861.

14. *Ibid.*, August 1, 1861.

15. H. Wayne Morgan (ed.), "A Civil War Diary of William McKinley," *OHQ*, 69 (July, 1960), 277; hereafter cited as Diary by date.

16. Diary, June 27, 1861.

17. Whitelaw Reid, *Ohio in the War: Her Statesmen, Her Generals, and Her Soldiers,* 2 vols. (Cincinnati: Moore, Wiltstach and Baldwin, 1868), II, 160.

18. Diary, August 16, 1861.

19. *Ibid.,* August 16, 1861.

20. *Canton Repository,* August 13, 1896.

21. McKinley to W. K. Miller, August 11, 1861; reprinted in Olcott, *William McKinley,* I, 29–30.

22. Diary, September 10, 1861.

23. *Ibid.,* September 11, 1861.

24. *Ibid.,* November 3, 1861.

25. McKinley, *Speeches* (1893), 643.

26. McKinley, *Speeches* (1893), 643–644; Olcott, *William McKinley,* I, 34ff; *Canton Repository,* March 6, 1896.

27. See the mass of material in the Quartermaster Papers of First Lieutenant William McKinley, Duncan papers, WRHS.

28. Cleveland *Leader,* July 31, 1891.

29. See Porter, *William McKinley,* 61ff.

30. Cleveland *Leader,* June 17, 1894.

31. McKinley to James McKinley, April 13, November 1, 1899, McKinley papers, LC.

32. Reid, *Ohio in the War,* II, 161.

33. McKinley, *Speeches* (1893), 643ff.

34. Porter, *William McKinley,* 62ff.

35. *Ibid.,* 103–104.

36. William T. Crump to The President [Grover Cleveland?], January 15, 1897; copy in Webb C. Hayes papers, HML.

37. Comly to Hayes, October 15, 1862; copy in William McKinley papers, HML.

38. Cyrus B. Lower to Hayes, January 13, 1891, Hayes papers, HML.

39. Surgeon Joseph T. Webb to Hayes, October 5, 1862; copy in McKinley papers, HML; Charles Richard Williams (ed.), *Diary and Letters of Rutherford Birchard Hayes,* 5 vols. (Columbus: OAHS, 1922), II, 3620.

40. *Ohio State Journal,* August 14, 1891, Webb C. Hayes to William Henry Smith, November 11, 1895, William Henry Smith papers, OHS.

41. McKinley to Hayes, July 2, 1888, Hayes papers, HML.

42. Olcott, *William McKinley,* I, 38.

43. Hayes to Mrs. Hayes, December 14, 1862, Hayes, *Diary,* II, 373.

44. Russell, *William McKinley,* 63.

45. Reid, *Ohio in the War,* II, 162.

46. McKinley to Sarah Duncan, March 18, 1863, William McKinley papers, in possession of author.

47. Tippecanoe Club of Cleveland, *McKinley Memorial Addresses* (Cleveland, 1913), 56.

48. Hayes, *Diary,* II, 398, 548.

49. McKinley, *Speeches* (1893), 644–645.

50. Olcott, *William McKinley,* I, 40.

51. Halstead, *William McKinley,* 118.

52. Reid, *Ohio in the War,* II, 164.

53. Porter, *William McKinley,* Chapter VI.

54. See *ibid.*, 104ff; Olcott, *William McKinley*, I, 49.

55. McKinley to Murat Halstead, February 16, 1895, reprinted in *Canton Repository*, October 15, 1896; Philip H. Sheridan, *Personal Memoirs of P. H. Sheridan,* 2 vols. (New York: C. L. Webster Co., 1888), II, 81–82.

56. Hayes, *Diary,* II, 486, 502, 534.

57. Statement of the Military Service of Brevet Major William McKinley, Jr., July 15, 1897, McKinley papers, LC.

58. Olcott, *William McKinley*, I, 53.

59. Margaret Leech, *In the Days of McKinley* (New York: Harper Bros., 1959), 8.

60. Porter, *William McKinley*, 106ff; *Canton Repository*, February 22, 1896; John Wise, *Recollections of Thirteen Presidents* (New York: Doubleday, Page and Co., 1906), 215–216.

61. Helen McKinley to McKinley, January 1, 1865, Duncan papers, WRHS.

62. Anne McKinley to McKinley, March 14, 1865, *ibid.*

63. J. M. Comly to Hayes, January 28, 1865, Hayes papers, HML.

64. Reid, *Ohio in the War*, II, 168; Honorable Discharge of William McKinley, Jr., July 26, 1865, McKinley papers, LC; Joseph P. Smith, *History of the Republican Party of Ohio,* 2 vols. (Chicago: Lewis Pub. Co., 1898), I, 697.

65. McKinley, *Speeches* (1900), 42–43.

66. Diary, September 5, 1861.

67. Cleveland *Leader*, August 25, 1895.

68. McKinley, *Speeches* (1893), 518.

III: *OHIO LAWYER*

1. Cleveland *Leader*, August 25, 1895; *Canton Repository*, October 2, 1890.

2. Hayes to McKinley, November 6, 1866; Hayes, *Diary,* V, 149–150.

3. McKinley to Russell Hastings, August 28, 1865, Hayes papers, HML.

4. Smalley, "William McKinley," 33–45; Smith, *History of the Republican Party of Ohio,* I, 697.

5. Olcott, *William McKinley*, I, 57–58.

6. Leech, *In the Days of McKinley*, 10.

7. See McKinley to Lewis O'Conner, June 6, 1900, and to Charles J. Buchanan, June 14, 1901, McKinley papers, LC.

8. *Stark County Democrat,* August 24, 1876.

9. Edward Thornton Heald, *The Stark County Story: The McKinley Era* (Canton: SCHS, 1955), 335.

10. *Canton Repository,* March 22, 1896.

11. Olcott, *William McKinley*, I, 59–60; McKinley to H. S. Belden, December 18, 1897, McKinley papers, LC; Cleveland *Leader*, August 25, 1895.

12. McKinley to Sarah Duncan, December 18, 1867, Duncan papers, WRHS.

13. William McKinley, Sr., to William and Abner McKinley, March 12, 1871, *ibid.*

14. Olcott, *William McKinley*, I, 61–62.

15. Anne McKinley to Sarah Duncan, December 8, 1867, in possession of author.

16. Anne McKinley to Sarah Duncan, May 19, 1868, *ibid.*

17. *Canton Repository,* May 5, 1876.

18. *Canton Repository,* June 24, 1869, March 17, 1876; Charles Miller to J. A. Porter, February 6, 1900, McKinley papers, LC.

19. Edward Thornton Heald, *The Stark County Story: Industry Comes of Age* (Canton: SCHS, 1958), 325; *Canton Repository,* July 24, 31, 1874, June 11, 1875.

20. Olcott, *William McKinley,* I, 73–74.

21. *Canton Repository,* October 16, 1896; Chicago *Tribune,* October 28, 1900; Cleveland *Leader,* August 25, 1895.

22. Olcott, *William McKinley,* I, 74–76.

23. *Ohio Repository,* August 5, 19, September 9, 1868.

24. *Ibid.,* September 9, 1868.

25. *Ibid.,* October 14, 28, November 4, 1868.

26. *Canton Repository,* January 7, 1869.

27. *Ibid.,* March 11, 1869.

28. McKinley to Hayes, November 28, 1869, Hayes papers, HML.

29. *Canton Repository,* October 7, July 1, 1869, January 6, 1870.

30. *Ibid.,* July 1, 1870, August 4, September 8, 15, October 20, 1871; Heald, *The McKinley Era,* 635.

31. Porter, *William McKinley,* 122; Olcott, *William McKinley,* I, 65–67.

32. Leech, *In the Days of McKinley,* 14.

33. Porter, *William McKinley,* 123ff.

34. Leech, *In the Days of McKinley,* 16–17.

35. Foraker, *I Would Live It Again,* 257–258. Jennie Hobart, *Memories* (Paterson, N.J.: p.p., 1930), 28.

36. Smith, *History of the Republican Party,* II, 541; Olcott, *William McKinley,* I, 69.

37. McKinley to Rutherford and Lucy Hayes, December 12, 1870, Hayes papers, HML.

38. *Canton Repository,* January 27, 1871.

39. Olcott, *William McKinley,* I, 69.

40. Heald, *The McKinley Era,* 484.

41. McKinley papers, in possession of author.

42. Leech, *In the Days of McKinley,* 13.

43. Heald, *The McKinley Era,* 483; *Canton Repository,* July 10, 1874; W. Kennedy Brown to Hayes, April 3, 1877, Hayes papers, HML.

44. Thomas Beer, *Hanna* (New York: Alfred Knopf, Inc., 1929), 102–103.

45. Foraker, *I Would Live It Again,* 246–247.

46. McKinley to Thomas W. Bradley, January 13, 1900, McKinley papers, LC.

47. See McKinley to Hayes, June 8, 1875, Hayes papers, HML.

48. *Canton Repository,* June 11, 18, August 27, 1875; Hayes, *Diary,* III, 292.

49. *Canton Repository,* September 17, 24, October 1, 8, 1875; McKinley to Hayes, October 21, November 17, 1875, January 18, March 6, 1876, Hayes papers, HML.

50. See Herbert Croly, *Marcus Alonzo Hanna: His Life and Work* (New York: Macmillan and Co., 1912), 92ff; *Stark County Democrat,* May 4–12, June 2, 1876.

51. Beer, *Hanna,* 78–79, states that Hanna believed the strike could have been settled peaceably, and exploded: "God damn militia, anyhow!" on seeing

uniforms in the streets. On the other hand, Hanna to Hayes, June 16, 1876, Hayes papers, HML, strongly endorses Hayes' action.

52. McKinley to Hayes, July 11, 1876, Hayes papers, HML.

53. Beer, *Hanna*, 79.

54. Joe Mitchell Chapple, *Mark Hanna: His Book* (Boston: Chapple Pub. Co., 1904), 46; McKinley to Hanna, November 12, 1896, McKinley papers, LC. See Francis P. Weisenburger, "The Time of Mark Hanna's First Acquaintance with McKinley," *MVHR,* 21 (June, 1934), 78–80.

55. Hanna to R. W. Taylor, January 29, 1903, Rice papers, OHS.

56. *Stark County Democrat,* March 23, 1876; D. R. Hunter to Hayes, June 18, 1876, Hayes papers, HML.

57. McKinley to Andrew Duncan, August 5, 1876, Duncan papers, WRHS; Heald, *The McKinley Era,* 22.

58. *Canton Repository,* August 4, 18, 25, 1876.

59. McKinley to Hayes, July 1, 1876, Hayes papers, HML.

60. *Canton Repository,* November 10, 1876; William Ganson Rose, *Cleveland: The Making of a City* (Cleveland: World Pub. Co., 1950), 486; Hayes, *Diary,* III, 346.

61. *Canton Repository,* September 22, 29, 1876.

62. *Ibid.,* October 6, 1876; *Stark County Democrat,* September 7, 21, 1876.

63. *Canton Repository,* February 2, 1877.

IV: *RAISING THE STANDARD OF PROTECTION*

1. *Congressional Record,* 45th Congress, 1st Session, 198; 2nd Session, 706.

2. Philip D. Jordan, *Ohio Comes of Age 1870–1900* (Columbus: OAHS, 1943), 150–151. Cf. *Canton Repository,* December 7, 1877, January 4, 1878; *Congressional Record,* 45th Congress, 2nd Session, 1285; Leland Sage, *William Boyd Allison* (Iowa City: SHSI, 1956), 151–155.

3. Jacob H. Gallinger to Charles Marseilles, November 19, 1898, Gallinger papers, NHHS.

4. McKinley, *Speeches* (1893), 544; *Canton Repository,* November 16, 1877.

5. Garfield Diary, February 17, February 28–March 1, 1878, Garfield papers, LC.

6. McKinley to Abner McKinley, March 5, 1878, Duncan papers, WRHS

7. *Mark Hanna: His Book,* 62; Smith, *History of the Republican Party in Ohio,* I, 697; Edward Nelson Dingley, *The Life and Times of Nelson Dingley, Jr.* (Kalamazoo, Mich.: Ihling Bros. and Everard, 1902), 155.

8. McKinley, *Speeches* (1893), 27.

9. See Frank Taussig, *The Tariff History of the United States,* 5th edition (New York: G. P. Putnam's Sons, 1910), 173–174.

10. William McKinley, *The Tariff in the Days of Henry Clay and Since* (New York: Henry Clay Pub. Co., 1896), 50.

11. Cleveland *Leader,* August 25, 1895; Butler, *Presidents I Have Seen and Known,* 40–41.

12. Robert M. La Follette, *La Follette's Autobiography* (Madison: Robert M. La Follette Co., 1918), 114.

13. McKinley, *Speeches* (1893), 190.
14. *Congressional Record*, 47th Congress, 2nd Session, 2743.
15. McKinley, *Speeches* (1893), 17, 97, 105, 215–219.
16. *Ibid.*, 350.
17. *Ibid.*, 376.
18. *Ibid.*, 187.
19. *Ibid.*, 295.
20. *Ibid.*, 71.
21. *Ibid.*, 327.
22. *Ibid.*, 71.
23. See Ida Tarbell, *The Tariff in Our Times* (New York: Macmillan and Co., 1911), 87–88.
24. Henry Littlefield West, "William McKinley," *The Forum*, 32 (October, 1901), 131–137; cf. J. E. Watson, *As I Knew Them* (New York: Bobbs-Merrill Co., 1936), 53.
25. McKinley, *Speeches* (1893), 1–22.
26. Tarbell, *The Tariff in Our Times*, 185; McKinley, *Speeches* (1893), 447ff.
27. *Canton Repository*, April 26, 1878.
28. *Congressional Record*, 45th Congress, 2nd Session, 4515.
29. Foraker, *I Would Live It Again*, 140.
30. Sherman to William Henry Smith, June 2, 1879, William Henry Smith papers, OHS.
31. McKinley, *Speeches* (1893), 171.
32. See Harry Barnard, *Rutherford B. Hayes and His America* (New York: Bobbs-Merrill Co., 1954), 401ff.
33. *Congressional Record*, 46th Congress, 1st Session, 548ff.
34. *Ibid.*, 553.
35. *Canton Repository*, May 17, 1878. Olcott, *William McKinley*, I, 82ff has an excellent map showing the gerrymandering of McKinley's district.
36. McKinley, *Speeches* (1893), 23–32.
37. *Canton Repository*, August 9, 1878; Garfield Diary, LC, August 24, 25, 28, September 14, 1878; Patrick Flaherty to Hayes, October 30, 1878, Hayes papers, HML; McKinley to Hayes, August 13, September 26, 1878, *ibid.*
38. Hayes to J. M. Comly, October 29, 1878, *ibid.*
39. McKinley to Hayes, October 10, 1878, *ibid.*
40. Edward Noyes, "The Ohio G.A.R. and Politics from 1866 to 1900," *OAHQ*, 55 (April–June, 1946), 79–105.
41. McKinley to R. W. Taylor, November 14, 1878, Duncan papers, WRHS.
42. McKinley to Hayes, June 16, November 18, 1880, Hayes papers, HML.
43. McKinley to James M. Tyner, First Assistant Postmaster General, May 2, 1880, Hayes papers, HML.
44. *Congressional Record*, 46th Congress, 1st Session, 621, 1091, 1890, 2289.
45. McKinley to W. M. Crapo, August 23, to Walter Allen, August 24, 1880, William McKinley letterbook, OHS.
46. McKinley to General Robinson, September 9, 1880, *ibid.*
47. McKinley, *Speeches* (1893), 60; John Danner, *My Memories* (Canton: p.p., 1937), 53; McKinley to Garfield, June 8, August 30, 1880, Garfield papers, LC; Garfield Diary, LC, August 31, 1880.
48. McKinley to Garfield, October 16, 1880, Garfield papers, LC.

49. McKinley to George Marsh [?], November 12, 1880, McKinley letter-book, OHS.

50. McKinley to Garfield, November 13, 1880, Garfield papers, LC.

51. Smith, *Life and Letters of James Abram Garfield*, II, 1061.

52. McKinley to Garfield, March 8, 16, 28, 1881, Garfield papers, LC.

53. McKinley to Anson G. McCook, July 5, 1881, *ibid.*

54. *Speech of Hon. William McKinley, Jr., at Mount Vernon, Ohio, Saturday Afternoon, August 18, 1883* (n.p., n.d.); *Congressional Record*, 47th Congress, 2nd Session, 867.

55. *Congressional Record*, 47th Congress, 1st Session, 2227.

56. J. L. Botsford to Hayes, January 9, 1882, Hayes papers, HML.

57. McKinley to Abner McKinley, January 13, February 20, 1882, Duncan papers, WRHS; *Canton Repository*, March 1, 1882.

58. McKinley to Abner McKinley, March 8, 1882, Duncan papers, WRHS.

59. McKinley to Abner McKinley, March 12, 1882, *ibid.*

60. McKinley to W. K. Miller, March 18, 1882, *ibid.;* McKinley to Hayes, May 18, 1882, Hayes papers, HML.

61. *Canton Repository*, October 6, 1882.

62. *Ohio State Journal*, October 19, 1882; *Canton Repository*, October 20, 1882, January 10, 1884.

63. *Canton Repository*, February 15, 1883; Washington *Post*, March 6, 1883, April 20, 1884.

64. McKinley to Unknown Addressee, October 12, 1883, McKinley letter-book, OHS; McKinley to R. W. Taylor, July 23, 1883, Simon Gratz papers, HSP.

65. McKinley to J. B. Foraker, October 31, 1883, Joseph Benson Foraker papers, HPSO.

66. J. B. Foraker to McKinley, March 28, 1884, *ibid.*

67. McKinley, *Speeches* (1893), 70–105.

68. McKinley to Abner McKinley, April 8, 1882, Duncan papers, WRHS.

69. McKinley, *Speeches* (1893), 106–123.

70. Porter, *William McKinley*, 120.

71. McKinley to A. L. Conger, February 18, 1884, Duncan papers, WRHS.

72. McKinley, *Speeches* (1893), 131–159; James A. Barnes, *John G. Carlisle* (New York: Dodd, Mead Co., 1934), 81–82.

73. *Congressional Record*, 48th Congress, 1st Session, 4525.

74. J. H. Wallace to McKinley, December 28, 1882, McKinley to W. K. Miller, February 25, 1884, Duncan papers, WRHS; Hayes, *Diary*, IV, 152; Wise, *Recollections of Thirteen Presidents*, 217–218; *Congressional Record*, 48th Congress, 1st Session, 415–416, 4158, 4595.

75. Olcott, *William McKinley*, I, 244.

76. *Canton Repository*, May 29, 1884. McKinley missed only a few weeks of the regular session, in addition to the short session of December, 1884–March, 1885.

77. McKinley to W. K. Miller, February 25, 1884, Duncan papers, WRHS.

78. Washington *Post*, February 28, 1884; *Canton Repository*, March 6, 1884.

79. McKinley to Foraker, March 15, 1884, Foraker papers, HPSO; *Canton Repository*, June 22, 1884.

80. McKinley to A. L. Conger, April 11, 1884, McKinley papers, HML.

81. Olcott, *William McKinley,* I, 254–255; Ryan, *Masters of Men,* 35–36.

82. *Proceedings of the Eighth Republican National Convention, June 3, 4, 5, and 6, 1884* (Chicago, 1884), 91–94.

83. *Ibid.,* 152.

84. William Henry Smith to Hayes, June 9, 1884, Hayes papers, HML.

85. *Canton Repository,* September 11, 1884.

86. Shelby Cullom, *50 Years of Public Service* (Chicago: A. C. McClurg Co., 1911), 118; *Canton Repository,* October 9, 1884; Ryan, *Masters of Men,* 61–64.

V: *CONGRESSMAN WILLIAM McKINLEY*

1. *Canton Repository,* January 16, 1890; Smith, *History of the Republican Party in Ohio,* II, 541.

2. Hugh Baillie, *High Tension* (New York: Harper Bros., 1959), 29.

3. McKinley to Abner McKinley, January 13, 1882, Duncan papers, WRHS.

4. Belle Case La Follette and Fola La Follette, *Robert M. La Follette,* 2 vols. (New York: Macmillan and Co., 1953), I, 63; William McKinley to Ida McKinley, March 17, 1888, McKinley papers, SCHS.

5. McKinley to Ida McKinley, n.d., 1888, *ibid.*

6. McKinley to Ida McKinley, April 4, 10, 1888, *ibid.*

7. Beer, *Hanna,* 107.

8. La Follette and La Follette, *Robert M. La Follette,* I, 63.

9. La Follette, *Autobiography,* 132.

10. Henry L. Stoddard, *As I Knew Them* (New York: Harper Bros., 1927), 229.

11. To W. K. Miller, February 25, 1884, Duncan papers, WRHS.

12. To Abner McKinley, April 7, 1882, Duncan papers, WRHS.

13. *Mark Hanna: His Book,* 50.

14. Wise, *Recollections of Thirteen Presidents,* 215.

15. Beer, *Hanna,* 110.

16. Wise, *Recollections of Thirteen Presidents,* 216.

17. Adlai E. Stevenson, *Something of Men I Have Known* (Chicago: A. C. McClurg Co., 1909), 55–56.

18. *Mark Hanna: His Book,* 64; William A. Robinson, *Thomas B. Reed* (New York: Dodd, Mead Co., 1930), 135.

19. Cleveland *Leader,* July 15, 1886.

20. Joseph Benson Foraker, *Notes of a Busy Life,* 2 vols. (Cincinnati: Stewart, Kidd Co., 1917, 3rd ed.), I, 119.

21. Cleveland *Leader,* August 25, 1895.

22. La Follette, *Autobiography,* 92.

23. Stoddard, *As I Knew Them,* 231; McKinley to A. W. Whelpley, December 16, 1888, Whelpley collection, HPSO.

24. *Canton Repository,* May 2, 1896.

25. Barnard, *Rutherford B. Hayes,* 219; Webb C. Hayes to W. D. Allen, December 10, 1896, Webb C. Hayes papers, HML; Hayes, *Diary,* III, 463.

26. McKinley to Hayes, October 10, 1878, May 8, 1883, February 27, 1882,

Hayes papers, HML; Mary L. Hinsdale, *Garfield-Hinsdale Letters* (Ann Arbor: Univ. of Michigan Press, 1949), 496.

27. *Canton Repository,* October 22, 1896; Smith, *Life and Letters of James Abram Garfield,* II, 658.

28. Garfield Diary, LC, December 26, 1879.

29. *Mark Hanna: His Book,* 70.

30. *Canton Repository,* June 29, August 15, 1879; John Danner, *Old Land-marks of Canton and Stark County* (Logansport, Ind.: B. F. Bowen, 1904), 55; Rose, *Cleveland,* 518–519.

31. Heald, *The McKinley Era,* 412.

32. Chicago *Inter-Ocean,* June 20, 1888.

33. Heald, *The McKinley Era,* 361.

34. Busbey, *Uncle Joe Cannon,* 301–302.

35. David S. Barry, *Forty Years in Washington* (Boston: Little, Brown Co., 1924), 237; *Canton Repository,* May 2, 1896.

36. Washington *Post,* December 9, 1900.

VI: *SERPENTS, SHARKS, AND COOING DOVES: OHIO POLITICS, 1880–1890*

1. William Allen White, *Autobiography* (New York: MacMillan and Co., 1946), 251.

2. John Sherman, Republican, was a U.S. senator from Ohio from 1861 to 1897, with the exception of 1877–1881, when he was secretary of the Treasury. His Democratic colleagues were: Allen G. Thurman, 1869–1881; George H. Pendleton, 1875–1885; Henry B. Payne, 1885–1891; Calvin S. Brice, 1891–1897.

3. See Jeannette P. Nichols and James G. Randall, *Democracy in the Middle-west 1840–1940* (New York: D. Appleton-Century Co., 1941), 73–96.

4. Cleveland *Plain Dealer,* May 5, 1887.

5. The standard biography of Hanna is Herbert Croly, *Marcus Alonzo Hanna: His Life and Work* (New York, 1912).

6. The standard biography of Foraker is Everett Walters, *Joseph Benson Foraker: An Uncompromising Republican* (Columbus: OAHS, 1948).

7. *Canton Repository,* September 26, 1879.

8. *Ibid.,* October 3, 1879; Garfield Diary, LC, October 10, 1879; Foraker, *Notes,* I, 119.

9. McKinley, *Speeches* (1893), 61.

10. Walters, *Joseph Benson Foraker,* 21–25.

11. Foraker, *Notes,* I, 110; *Ohio State Journal,* June 7, 1883.

12. *Canton Repository,* August 2, 1883.

13. McKinley to Foraker, October 12, 1883, Foraker, *Notes,* I, 126.

14. Ryan, *Masters of Men,* 21; Smith, *History of the Republican Party in Ohio,* I, 481; Harvey S. Ford (ed.), "The Diary of John Beatty, January–June, 1884: Part III," *OAHQ,* 59 (January, 1950), 78–79.

15. *Canton Repository,* May 1, 1884; Foraker, *Notes,* I, 149; Foraker to McKinley, May 10, 1884, McKinley to Foraker, May 24, 1884, Foraker papers, HPSO.

16. *Mark Hanna: His Book*, 47.

17. Foraker, *Notes*, I, 169; Sherman to Foraker, June 9, 1884, Foraker papers, HPSO.

18. Hanna to Foraker, October 29, December 8, 1884, Foraker papers, HPSO.

19. *Canton Repository*, May 21, 1885; McKinley to General Robert P. Kennedy, February 14, 1885, McKinley letterbook, OHS; Hanna to Foraker, April 10, 1885, Foraker papers, HPSO.

20. Hayes, *Diary*, IV, 247.

21. Hanna to Foraker, November 28, 1885, Foraker papers, HPSO.

22. Hanna to Foraker, January 14, 1885, *ibid.*

23. See Walters, *Joseph Benson Foraker*, 81–82.

24. McKinley to Foraker, November 14, 27, 1885, September 2, 1886; Hanna to Foraker, November 28, 1887, February 20, 1888; all in Foraker papers, HPSO.

25. Foraker to R. McMurdy, December 3, 1887, *ibid.*

26. Walters, *Joseph Benson Foraker*, 50–51.

27. McKinley to Sherman, June 12, 1887, Sherman papers, LC; Hanna to Foraker, June 22, July 19, 1887, Foraker papers, HPSO; Foraker to Hanna, July 20, 1887, *ibid.*

28. Walters, *Joseph Benson Foraker*, 56–57.

29. Foraker to Hanna, November 14, 1887, Foraker papers, HPSO.

30. McKinley to A. L. Conger, February 25, 1888, McKinley papers, HML.

31. Sherman to Foraker, May 21, 1888, Foraker papers, HPSO; Foraker to Hanna, May 10, 1888, *ibid.*

32. *Canton Repository*, April 26, 1888.

33. See Walters, *Joseph Benson Foraker*, 62–80.

34. Foraker to R. McMurdy, August 27, 1888, Foraker papers, HPSO.

35. One seat, ultimately filled by a Democrat, was due in 1890; Sherman's seat would be vacant in 1892.

36. Foraker to R. McMurdy, August 27, 1888, Foraker papers, HPSO.

37. Croly, *Hanna*, 153; Foraker, *I Would Live It Again*, 143–144.

38. McKinley, *Speeches* (1893), 378.

39. Butterworth to Daniel J. Ryan, July 6, 1889, Daniel J. Ryan papers, OHS.

40. See Walters, *Joseph Benson Foraker*, 91–97, for an excellent summary of the entire affair.

41. John Sherman, *Recollections of Forty Years in House, Senate and Cabinet*, 2 vols. (New York: The Werner Co., 1895), II, 1053–1054.

42. House of Representatives, *Miscellaneous Document 27*, 51st Congress, 1st Session; Washington *Post*, January 17, 1890.

43. Foraker to Murat Halstead, December 28, 1889, Murat Halstead papers, HPSO; *Canton Repository*, January 2, 1890.

VII: *A NATIONAL FIGURE*

1. See Allan Nevins, *Grover Cleveland, A Study in Courage* (New York: Dodd, Mead Co., 1932), 206–207; Washington *Post*, March 1–7, 1885.

2. *Canton Repository*, February 4, 1886.

3. McKinley to A. L. Conger, February 2, 8, April 5, 1886, McKinley papers, HML; Items 22–29, draft petitions, McKinley papers, LC.

4. Stanwood, *American Tariff Controversies*, II, 225–226.

5. McKinley, *Speeches* (1893), 197–198; *Congressional Record*, 49th Congress, 2nd Session, 811.

6. Olcott, *William McKinley*, I, 234.

7. Cf. *Congressional Record*, 50th Congress, 1st Session, 2303, 1771, 1735, 1988, 2590, 179, 432, 1002, 1575, 4298.

8. See Olcott, *William McKinley*, I, 85.

9. McKinley to A. L. Conger, May 24, 1886, McKinley papers, HML.

10. *Canton Repository*, June 3, September 9, November 3, 1886; Cleveland *Leader*, June 27, 1886.

11. See Nevins, *Grover Cleveland*, 367–382.

12. Stanwood, *American Tariff Controversies*, II, 229–230; McKinley, *Speeches* (1893), 259–260.

13. Tarbell, *The Tariff in Our Times*, 139, 156–160; Nevins, *Grover Cleveland*, 283; Stanwood, *American Tariff Controversies*, II, 231.

14. There are two kinds of tariff taxation, the *ad valorem* system, based on the valuation of imported goods, and the specific system, based on each unit of imported goods.

15. McKinley, *Speeches* (1893), 277–289.

16. Barry, *Forty Years in Washington*, 227ff.

17. See McKinley, *Speeches* (1893), 290–335.

18. New York *Herald*, May 21, 1888.

19. Tarbell, *The Tariff in Our Times*, 162; *Congressional Record*, 50th Congress, 1st Session, 6658.

20. B. F. Jones to S. B. Elkins, April 30, 1888, Stephen B. Elkins papers, WVU.

21. S. B. Elkins to L. T. Michener, March 26, 1888, Louis T. Michener papers, LC; Sherman to Richard Smith, May 23, 1888, Sherman papers, LC; Hanna to Sherman, May 30, 1888, Sherman to Henry C. Hedges, June 12, 1888, Sherman papers, LC.

22. *Canton Repository*, April 26, 1888; Washington *Post*, June 10–12, 22, 1888.

23. Foraker to Murat Halstead, June 11, 1888; Halstead papers, HPSO.

24. Foraker to Thomas Graydon, June 30, 1888, Foraker papers, HPSO; Foraker, *Notes*, I, 342.

25. Grosvenor to Sherman, June 17, 1888, Sherman papers, LC; Washington *Post*, June 15, 1888.

26. W. M. Bateman to Sherman, March 31, 1888, Sherman papers, LC.

27. Foraker was known to be friendly to Russell Alger, to whom he promised his support if Sherman failed; Foraker to Alger, April 3, 1888, Foraker papers, HPSO.

28. Washington *Post*, June 17, 1888; Chicago *Tribune*, June 18, 1888.

29. *Ibid.*, June 19, 1888.

30. Chicago *Inter-Ocean*, June 20, 1888; *Canton Repository*, November 1, 1888.

31. *Ohio State Journal*, June 22, 1888.

32. New York *Times*, June 22, 1888.

33. See *Official Proceedings of the Republican National Convention Held at Chicago, June 19, 20, 21, 22, 23 and 25, 1888* (Minneapolis, 1903), 108–112; Washington *Post*, June 22, 1888.

34. Hanna to Sherman, June 22, 23, 1888, Sherman papers, LC

35. Butterworth to Sherman, June 22, 1888, *ibid.*

36. *Mark Hanna: His Book*, 48–50.

37. McKinley, *Speeches* (1893), 336.

38. Murat Halstead to Sherman, June 23, 1888, Sherman papers, LC.

39. *Mark Hanna: His Book*, 47.

40. Walters, *Joseph Benson Foraker*, 72–74

41. Foraker to C. N. Browning, June 30, 1888, Foraker papers, HPSO: Foraker, *I Would Live It Again*, 105.

42. *Ohio State Journal*, June 23, 1888.

43. Beer, *Hanna*, 110n; Webb C. Hayes to William Henry Smith, June 23, 1888, Webb C. Hayes papers, HML.

44. *Canton Repository*, July 12, 1888.

45. Cleveland *Plain Dealer*, June 24, 1888; Robert Harlan to Sherman, June 23, 1888, George F. Hoar to Sherman, June 23, 1888, Hanna to Sherman, Item 29429, Halstead to Sherman, June 23, 1888, all in Sherman papers, LC.

46. McKinley to Sherman, June 24, 1888; Green B. Raum to Sherman, June 23, 1888; E. E. Wood to Sherman, June 23, 1888; all *ibid.*

47. Sherman to George F. Hoar, June 23, 1888, *ibid.*

48. Sherman to Hanna, June 24, 1888, *ibid.;* Muzzey, *James G. Blaine*, 378.

49. Rhodes, *History*, VIII, 317.

50. "The National Convention of 1888," typescript in Michener papers, LC.

51. Sherman to Richard Smith, June 26, 1888, Sherman papers, LC.

52. Chicago *Inter-Ocean*, June 26, 1888; Foraker to Halstead, July 2, 1888, Halstead papers, HPSO.

53. Hanna to Sherman, June 25, 1888, Sherman papers, LC.

54. Sherman to Hanna, June 26, 1888, *ibid.*

55. W. H. Smith to Sherman, June 25, 1888, Smith papers. OHS.

56. *Canton Repository*, July 5, 1888.

57. See Harry Bernardo, "The Presidential Election of 1888," Unpublished Ph.D. Thesis, Georgetown University, 1949.

58. William Henry Smith to Whitelaw Reid, June 24, 1888, Smith papers, OHS.

59. Hayes to McKinley, June 27, 1888, Hayes papers, HML.

60. *Canton Repository*, July 12, 1888; Allison to Harrison, July 3, 1888, Harrison papers, LC; Sherman to David Harpsteur, July 25, 1888, Sherman papers, LC.

61. William Whitman to Allison, July 26, 1888, Nelson Aldrich papers, LC; Joseph Medill to Harrison, August 2, 1888, Harrison papers, LC.

62. McKinley to Harrison, July 2, 1888, Harrison papers, LC; McKinley to Reid, August 18, 1888, Reid papers, LC.

63. The term was W. W. Dudley's, and originated in his recommendation that doubtful voters be divided into groups of five and escorted to the polls by a financially sound party manager who could watch them vote before paying them.

64. *Canton Repository,* November 22, 1888.

65. Charles Foster to Murat Halstead, April 15, 1889, Halstead papers, HPSO.

VIII: *THE McKINLEY TARIFF: VICTORY AND DEFEAT*

1. McKinley to Hayes, December 31, 1888; Hayes papers, HML.

2. Charles Bawsel to Lydia Lindsay, October 4, 1889, Bawsel papers, SCHS.

3. Robinson, *Thomas B. Reed,* 271.

4. Dunn, *From Harrison to Harding,* I, 300, 302.

5. John Garraty, *Henry Cabot Lodge* (New York: Alfred Knopf, Inc., 1953), 109.

6. Dunn, *From Harrison to Harding,* I, 22; Henry Cabot Lodge (ed.), *Selections from the Correspondence of Theodore Roosevelt and Henry Cabot Lodge,* 2 vols. (New York: Charles Scribner's Sons, 1925), I, 88.

7. Croly, *Marcus Alonzo Hanna,* 150; Robinson, *Thomas B. Reed,* 19.

8. La Follette, *Autobiography,* 92; Busbey, *Uncle Joe Cannon,* 166–167; Washington *Post,* November 24, 30, 1889.

9. Washington *Post,* December 3, 1889.

10. La Follette, *Autobiography,* 92–93.

11. Washington *Post,* February 9, 1890; Ida McKinley to Hayes, January 18, 1890, Hayes papers, HML.

12. Dunn, *From Harrison to Harding,* I, 7; Busbey, *Uncle Joe Cannon,* 243–244.

13. See Robinson, *Thomas B. Reed,* 192–216.

14. Rhodes, *History,* VIII, 343.

15. McKinley, *Speeches* (1893), 387, 393–394.

16. 51st Congress, 1st Session, *Revision of the Tariff,* Misc. Doc., 176.

17. La Follette, *Autobiography,* 110–111; Washington *Post,* July 26, 1890; Gail Hamilton, *Biography of James G. Blaine* (Norwich, Conn.: Henry Bill Pub. Co., 1895), 700.

18. David S. Muzzey, *James G. Blaine* (New York: Dodd, Mead Co., 1934), 444; McKinley to Blaine, December 9, 1891, Blaine papers, LC.

19. Stanwood, *American Tariff Controversies,* II, 260–261.

20. McKinley, *Speeches* (1893), 397–430.

21. See W. C. Cronemeyer, "The Development of the Tin Plate Industry," *Western Pennsylvania History Magazine,* 13 (January, 1930), 34–35.

22. *Congressional Record,* 51st Congress, 1st Session, 5015.

23. *Ibid.,* 4259, 4991, 157 appendix, 931 appendix, 438 appendix; Washington *Post,* April 19, 1890; *The Nation,* 50 (January 16, 1890), 47.

24. *Congressional Record,* 51st Congress, 1st Session, 4341.

25. *Ibid.,* 4028, 4711–4712, 10581.

26. *Ibid.,* 193 appendix, 204 appendix; Allan Nevins (ed.), *Letters of Grover Cleveland* (New York: Houghton-Mifflin Co., 1933), 221–222.

27. *The Reminiscences of Senator William M. Stewart of Nevada* (New York: Neale Pub. Co., 1906), 310.

28. McKinley to Hayes, March 28, 1889, Hayes papers, HML.

29. *Congressional Record,* 51st Congress, 1st Session, 3803.

30. McKinley, *Speeches* (1893), 456–458.

31. Thomas Collier Platt, *Autobiography* (New York: B. W. Dodge and Co. 1910), 215; McKinley to Hanna, July 8, 1890, Hanna Transcripts, Felt.

32. Olcott, *William McKinley*, II, 343–344.

33. Allison to Morrill, June 23, 1890, Morrill papers, LC.

34. *Washington Post*, May 25, 1890.

35. Stewart, *Reminiscences*, 293; Rhodes, *History*, VIII, 353–354; Stewart to John Thompson and to T. B. Baker, January 4, 1890, William M. Stewart papers, NHS.

36. Stewart to H. B. Kelly, March 11, 1890, *ibid.*

37. Edward O. Wolcott to Reed, March 15, 1894, copy in H. M. Teller papers, SHSC; Reed to Wolcott, March 16, 1894, copy *ibid;* McKinley to Teller, March 17, 1894, *ibid.*

38. McKinley, *Speeches* (1893), 454–455.

39. *Washington Post*, July 8, 1890.

40. Fred Wellborn, "The Influence of the Silver Republican Senators, 1889–1891," *MVHR*, 14 (March, 1928), 462–480; Sherman, *Recollections*, II, 1084–1085.

41. Stewart to Q. R. Cooley, February 17, 1890, to Thomas Nelson, E. C. Hardy, Walter Schmidt, April 15, 1890, Stewart papers, NHS.

42. Elmer Ellis, *Henry Moore Teller* (Caldwell, Idaho; Caxton Printers, 1941), 190–192.

43. The final plan called for monthly purchase of 4,500,000 ounces of silver at market price, covered by the issue of Treasury Notes redeemable in gold or silver. The "endless chain" of which Cleveland later complained was thus set in operation as silver flowed into the Treasury and gold flowed out to redeem the Notes.

44. *Congressional Record,* 51st Congress, 1st Session, 6933, 6941; *Washington Post,* July 8, 1890; Stewart, *Reminiscences,* 297.

45. Ainsworth Spofford to Aldrich, July 11, 1890, Aldrich papers, LC; *Washington Post*, July 12, 15, 1890; Robert McElroy, *Levi Parsons Morton* (New York: G. P. Putnam's Sons, 1930), 189–190.

46. *Washington Post*, June 22, 1890; Dunn, *From Harrison to Harding*, I, 44; Muzzey, *James G. Blaine*, 445.

47. Leland Sage, *William Boyd Allison* (Iowa City: SHSI, 1956), 242–243; Louis A. Coolidge, *An Old Fashioned Senator: Orville H. Platt* (New York: G. P. Putnam's Sons, 1910), 238.

48. Butterworth to Hanna, May 26, 1890, Hanna Transcripts, Felt; John W. Foster, *Diplomatic Memoirs*, 2 vols. (New York: Houghton-Mifflin Co., 1909), II, 4.

49. Muzzey, *James G. Blaine*, 437–447.

50. Warner Bateman to Sherman, August 25, 1890, Sherman papers, LC; H. V. Boynton to Halstead, July 30, 1890, Halstead papers, HPSO.

51. H. M. Ashbrook to Sherman, July 14, 1890, Sherman papers, LC.

52. Hanna to Sherman, September 24, 1890, *ibid.*

53. *Harper's Weekly*, 34 (July 12, 1890), 535; *Washington Post*, July 20, 1890.

54. Sherman to W. H. Smith, September 26, 1890, Smith papers, OHS.

55. Morrill to Aldrich, October 7, 1890, Aldrich papers, LC.

56. New York *Herald,* July 11, 1890.
57. Lyman J. Gage, *Memoirs* (Chicago: Field, Inc., 1937), 90.
58. Olcott, *William McKinley,* I, 127.
59. McKinley, *Speeches* (1893), 472.
60. *Canton Repository,* August 21, 28, 1890.
61. Croly, *Marcus Alonzo Hanna,* 157–158, which omits the last phrase found in McKinley to Hanna, October 6, 1890, Hanna Transcripts, Felt.
62. Charles Bawsel to Lydia Lindsay, October 4, 1890, Bawsel papers, SCHS.
63. Olcott, *William McKinley,* I, 186.
64. Reed to Lodge, November 5, 1890, Lodge papers, MHS.
65. Cleveland *Leader,* November 6, 1890.
66. *Mark Hanna: His Book,* 61; Croly, *Marcus Alonzo Hanna,* 158.
67. Hayes, *Diary,* IV, 615.
68. Dunn, *From Harrison to Harding,* I, 72.
69. Chicago *Inter-Ocean,* November 6, 1890; New York *Tribune,* November 7, 1890; *Ohio State Journal,* November 7, 1890.
70. McKinley, *Speeches* (1893), 503–506; McKinley to Hanna, December 11, 1890, Hanna Transcripts, Felt.

IX: *GOVERNOR OF OHIO*

1. Olcott, *William McKinley,* I, 270.
2. Sherman to James A. Hall, January 2, 1891, Sherman papers, LC.
3. *Ohio State Journal,* March 30, 1891.
4. McKinley to Daniel Ryan, May 8, 1891, Ryan papers, OHS.
5. Charles Foster to Ryan, April 12, 1890, Ryan to Foster, April 23, 1890, all *ibid.*
6. Cincinnati *Inquirer,* June 18, 1891; Foraker, *Notes,* I, 444; Foraker to Foster, March 11, 1891, Foraker papers, HPSO.
7. *Ohio State Journal,* June 17, 1891.
8. McKinley, *Speeches* (1893), 523ff.
9. Hahn to Ryan, August 13, 1891, Ryan papers, OHS.
10. Roger Henry Van Bolt, "The Gubernatorial Campaign of 1891 in Ohio," unpublished master's thesis, Ohio State University, 1946, p. 42; Toledo *Blade,* February 13, 1891; *Ohio State Journal,* August 23, 1891.
11. Croly, *Marcus Alonzo Hanna,* 160.
12. McKinley to Foraker, June 21, September 7, 1891, Foraker papers, HPSO; William Dana Orcutt, *Burrows of Michigan,* 2 vols. (New York: Longmans, Green Co., 1917), II, 16; Blaine to A. L. Conger, September 23, 1891, Dent papers, UNC.
13. *Ohio State Journal,* August 23, 1891; Charles Bawsel to Lydia Lindsay, August 31, 1891, Bawsel papers, SCHS.
14. *Ohio State Journal,* August 25, September 11, 1891; Rose, *Cleveland,* 531.
15. Cleveland *Leader,* July 31, 1891.
16. Charles Bawsel to Lydia Lindsay, October 2, 1891, Bawsel papers, SCHS.
17. *Ohio State Journal,* November 27, 1891; Charles Bawsel to Lydia Lindsay, November 8, 1891, Bawsel papers, SCHS.

18. McKinley to Alger, November 5, 1891, Alger papers, WLCL; Blaine to Alger, November 5, 1891, *ibid.*

19. McKinley to Hanna, November 4, 1891, Hanna Transcripts, Felt; *Ohio State Journal,* November 8, 1891, December 16, 1891.

20. Cleveland *Plain Dealer,* January 11, 1892.

21. *Ibid.,* January 11, 12, 1892; *Ohio State Journal,* January 12, 1892.

22. See Mary Aldora Deibel, "William McKinley as Governor of Ohio," unpublished master's thesis, Ohio State University, 1939.

23. *Ohio Executive Documents* (Columbus, 1892), I, 13.

24. *Ohio State Journal,* March 15, 1893; *Ohio Executive Documents 1895* (Columbus, 1895), I, 18–19.

25. Olcott, *William McKinley,* I, 276.

26. McKinley to J. R. White, October 23, 1893, McKinley National Birthplace Memorial, Niles, Ohio.

27. McKinley to Robert P. Skinner, September 22, 1894, McKinley papers, LC.

28. Ernest L. Bogart, *The Financial History of Ohio* (Urbana, Ill.: Univ. of Illinois Press, 1912), 242–246; *Report of the Tax Commission of Ohio of 1893* (Columbus, 1893), 1–70.

29. Hanna to Foraker, April 3, 1893, Foraker to Hanna, April 4, 1893, Foraker papers, HPSO.

30. *Ohio Executive Documents 1895* (Columbus, 1895), I, 3–27.

31. *Ibid.,* II, 123–160.

32. McKinley to Charles Foster, April 18, 1893, McKinley Governor's papers, OHS; McKinley to Peter Murphy, July 5, 1893, *ibid.*

33. *Ohio State Journal,* April 26, 1894.

34. *Ibid.,* January 4, 1893; McKinley to G. W. Collier, May 17, 1894, Webb C. Hayes papers, HML.

35. Leech, *In the Days of McKinley,* 24–25.

36. *Tippecanoe Club Memorial Addresses,* 26–27; Heald, *The McKinley Era,* 466; Charles Bawsel to Lydia Lindsay, January 25, 1893, Bawsel papers, SCHS; *Mark Hanna: His Book,* 66–67.

37. Charles Bawsel to Almina Downes, March 13, 1892, Bawsel papers, SCHS; *Ohio State Journal,* January 3, 1893.

38. Cleveland *Leader,* August 25, 1895; James Boyle to R. G. Haight, August 13, 1895, McKinley Governor's papers, OHS.

39. Cleveland *Leader,* June 17, 1894; Charles Bawsel, "A Day in a Governor's Life," manuscript in Bawsel papers, SCHS.

40. *Tippecanoe Memorial Address,* 25; Smith, *History of the Republican Party in Ohio,* II, 541.

41. *Ibid.,* II, 543; McKinley to Herrick, April 30, 1893, Herrick papers, WRHS.

42. Charles Bawsel to Lydia Lindsay, January 13, 1892, Bawsel papers, SCHS.

43. *Ohio State Journal,* February 8, 1892; Sherman to Hanna, May [?], 1892, Sherman papers, LC.

44. Ross, *Jonathan Prentiss Dolliver,* 101; Beer, *Hanna,* 123.

45. George Harmon Knoles, *The Presidential Campaign and Election of 1892* (Palo Alto, Calif.: Stanford Univ. Press, 1942), 40, 58–60; "The Minneapolis Convention of 1892," Michener papers, LC.

46. *Ohio State Journal,* April 29, 1892; Hanna to Sherman, June 9, 1892, Sherman papers, LC; Charles Boynton to Harrison, June 9, 1892, Harrison papers, LC.

47. Foraker, *Notes,* I, 448–451; Foraker to Hanna, June 20, 1892, Hanna to Foraker, June 24, 1892, Foraker papers, HPSO.

48. See the lengthy letter of Hanna to Sherman, June 14, 1892, Sherman papers, LC.

49. Art Young, *The Life and Times of Art Young* (New York: Sheridan House, 1939), 146ff.

50. New York *Herald,* June 9, 1892; E. S. Powers to Hugh McRae, June 14, 1892, Hugh McRae papers, DUL.

51. Kohlsaat, *From McKinley to Harding,* 7.

52. *Proceedings of the Tenth Republican National Convention . . . 1892* (Minneapolis, 1892), 137–138.

53. Nicholas Murray Butler, *Across the Busy Years* (New York: Charles Scribner's Sons, 1939), 221–222; Kohlsaat, *From McKinley to Harding,* 8–9.

54. Platt, *Autobiography,* 246–247; New York *Herald,* June 12, 1892; Harrison to McKinley, June 13, 1892, McKinley papers, LC.

55. Alger to Foraker, June 22, 1892, Foraker to John Hopley, June 20, 1892, Foraker papers, HPSO; *Mark Hanna: His Book,* 51.

56. Hanna to Sherman, June 14, 1892, Sherman papers, LC.

57. See Croly, *Marcus Alonzo Hanna,* 165–166; Muzzey, *James G. Blaine,* 377–378; Donald M. Dozer, "Benjamin Harrison and the Presidential Campaign of 1892," *AHR,* 54 (October, 1948), 49–77.

58. Knoles, *Presidential Campaign and Election of 1892,* 73; McKinley to R. B. Hayes, June 15, 1892, Hayes papers, HML.

59. *New York Herald,* June 22, 1892; James Boyle to J. H. Bothwell, September 17, 1892, McKinley Governor's papers, OHS.

60. Charles Bawsel to Almina Downes, November 17, 1892, *ibid.*

61. Foraker, *I Would Live It Again,* 236–237.

62. T. Bentley Mott, *Myron T. Herrick, Friend of France* (New York: Doubleday, Doran Co., 1929), 49; Butler, *Presidents I Have Seen and Known,* 44–45.

63. *Ohio State Journal,* February 19, 1893.

64. Olcott, *William McKinley,* I, 289; Kohlsaat, *From McKinley to Harding,* 12, 13.

65. *Ohio State Journal,* February 18, 1893.

66. Olcott, *William McKinley,* I, 290, 291.

67. Myron Herrick to [Unknown Addressee], February 21, 1893, Duncan papers, WRHS.

68. J. L. Botsford to Herrick, February 27, 1893, *ibid.*

69. "You know that Mrs. McKinley *insisted* on giving up her property. But that is in my hands to use at my discretion. We propose to raise [an amount] equal to her fortune from the [governor's] personal *non-political* friends and apply it to pay (we hope) the whole of these endorsements. Then I hand back the deed to her." Hanna to Hopley, Hopley papers, OHS. Mrs. McKinley's fortune was about $70,000 at the time.

70. McKinley to Herrick, February 25, 1893, Duncan papers, WRHS.

71. Mott, *Myron T. Herrick,* 51; Kohlsaat, *From McKinley to Harding,* 13.

72. Charles Bawsel to Lydia Lindsay, February 28, 1893, Bawsel papers, SCHS.

73. McKinley to Herrick, February 24, 1893, Duncan papers, WRHS.

74. Mott, *Myron T. Herrick*, 51–54.

75. Herrick to [Unknown Addressee], February 21, 1893, Duncan papers, WRHS.

76. Hanna to Charles Dick, February 23, 1893, Dick papers, OHS.

77. See Albert Clarke to McKinley, February 23, 1893, W. J. Magee to McKinley, February 22, 1893, Duncan papers, WRHS.

78. Hastings to McKinley, February 19, 1893, McKinley to Herrick, March 7, 1893, *ibid.* George W. Hazlett to McKinley, February 23, 1893, McKinley papers, LC.

79. Kohlsaat to Herrick, March 14, 1893, Duncan papers, WRHS.

80. Hanna to Hopley, February 25, 1893, Hopley papers, OHS.

81. Mott, *Myron T. Herrick*, 73.

82. Kohlsaat, *From McKinley to Harding*, 15–16; Croly, *Marcus Alonso Hanna*, 170.

83. Sherman to Herrick, February 20, 1893, Duncan papers, WRHS.

84. Hanna to Herrick, March 7, 18, 1893, *ibid.*

85. Kohlsaat to Herrick, February 25, March 8, 14, 1893, *ibid.;* Kohlsaat, *From McKinley to Harding*, 16; Herrick to Samuel Q. Marsh, June 8, 1893, Duncan papers, WRHS.

86. *Ohio State Journal*, April 11, 1893.

87. *Ibid.*, June 9, 1893.

88. McKinley to Herrick, August 24, 1893, Herrick papers, WRHS; Henderson to Charles Dick, September 16, 1893, Dick papers, OHS; Cleveland *Leader*, October 15, 1893.

89. Olcott, *William McKinley*, I, 291; Kohlsaat, *From McKinley to Harding*, 16; Mott, *Myron T. Herrick*, 54.

90. Joseph W. Allen to McKinley, February 22, 1893, Duncan papers, WRHS.

91. McKinley to J. C. Howe, December 26, 1893, McKinley Governor's papers, OHS; *Ohio State Journal*, January 7, 8, 1894.

92. *Ohio State Journal*, June 22, 1894; Leech, *In the Days of McKinley*, 54.

93. Cleveland *Leader*, April 21, 1894.

94. *Ohio State Journal*, May 30, 1894; Cleveland *Leader*, May 31, June 2–10, 1894.

95. *Ibid.*, June 12–15, 1894; McKinley to J. C. Howe, June 13, 1894, McKinley papers, LC.

96. Thomas Beer, *The Mauve Decade* (New York: Alfred Knopf, 1926), 78.

97. *Ohio State Journal*, July 13, 1894; *Canton Repository*, June 18, 1894.

98. Cleveland *Leader*, March 28, 1894; *Ohio State Journal*, April 29, 1894; *Ohio Executive Documents 1894*, II, 545.

99. McKinley to W. H. Parham, January 14, 1894, McKinley Governor's papers, OHS; *Ohio State Journal*, February 2, 1896; *Ohio Executive Documents 1895*, III, 14, 20.

100. Olcott, *William McKinley*, I, 281–282; Randall and Ryan, *History of the Republican Party in Ohio*, IV, 407–408; *Ohio Executive Documents 1895*, I, 25.

101. Cleveland *Leader*, September 9, October 2, 3, 1894.

102. Joseph L. Bristow, *Fraud and Politics at the Turn of the Century* (New York: Exposition Press, 1952), 23–25.

103. See McKinley, *The Tariff*, 231–232; Cleveland *Leader,* November 7, 8, 1894; McKinley to J. R. Thomas, December 5, 1894, Thomas papers, LC.

104. Cleveland *Leader,* September 11, October 6, 1895.

105. *Ohio Executive Documents 1895,* I, 27; *Canton Repository,* January 15, 1896.

X: *THE McKINLEY BOOM*

1. McKinley to Reid, January 22, 1896, Reid papers, LC.

2. *Canton Repository,* January 25, 1896.

3. Samuel Leland Powers, *Portraits of Half a Century* (Boston: Little Brown Co., 1925), 163–164.

4. Hay to Reid, May 2, 1895, Reid papers, LC.

5. Hanna to H. A. Humphrey, February 22, 1896, William B. Allison papers, ISDHA.

6. Royal Cortissoz, *The Life of Whitelaw Reid,* 2 vols. (New York: Charles Scribner's Sons, 1921), II, 199.

7. White, *Autobiography,* 295; Dawes, *Journal,* 368; Kohlsaat, *From McKinley to Harding,* 96.

8. Hanna to John Hopley, June 29, 1892, Hopley Family papers, OHS.

9. Olcott, *William McKinley,* 303.

10. Mott, *Myron T. Herrick,* 59–61; Kohlsaat, *From McKinley to Harding,* 30–31.

11. Reid to Hanna, May 4, 1896, Reid papers, LC; Smith to A. B. White, February 15, 1896, White papers, WVU; Smith to Dawes, April 9, 1896, Dawes papers, NWU; Clarkson to Allison, March 10, 1896, Allison papers, ISDHA.

12. Chandler to R. A. Moseley, June 3, 1896, Chandler papers, LC.

13. McKinley to J. R. Thomas, March 21, 1896, Thomas papers, LC; *Canton Repository,* March 22, 1896.

14. Charles Bawsel to Lydia Lindsay, October 25, 1895, Bawsel papers, SCHS.

15. Cleveland *Leader,* February 16, 1894.

16. *Canton Repository,* May 4, 1896.

17. White, *Autobiography,* 249.

18. McKinley to J. M. Cullers, April 1, 1896, to John Grant, April 2, 1896, to Robert Alexander, December 18, 1895, to John Mason, April 25, 1896, in McKinley papers, LC.

19. *Ohio State Journal,* February 23, 1895.

20. Cleveland *Leader,* November 18, 1893. Olcott, *William McKinley,* I, 298, attributes the title to Jonathan Dolliver.

21. Clarkson to Allison, April 4, 1896, Allison papers, ISDHA.

22. Hamilton Disston to Quay, April 1, 1896, Quay papers, LC.

23. Reid to Stephen B. Elkins, February 20, 1896, McKinley papers, LC.

24. McKinley to E. R. Holman, April 6, 1896, *ibid.*

25. Platt, *Autobiography,* 311; Stewart to McKinley, April 28, 1896, McKinley papers, LC; *The Nation,* 62 (May 21, 1896), 389; J. B. Corey to Morton, June 13, 1896, Morton papers, NYPL.

26. Hanna to Foraker, April 2, 1896, Foraker papers, HPSO; *Ohio State Journal,* March 28, 1896; McKinley to Kohlsaat, May 23, 1896, McKinley papers, LC.

27. *New York Journal,* May 4, 1896.

28. McKinley to Alger, April 23, 1896, Alger papers, WLCL.

29. McKinley to Thomas McDougall, December 18, 1894, to W. I. Squire, December 26, 1894, to Edwin Blank, February 18, 1895, McKinley papers, LC; Hanna to Foraker, January 17, 1896, Foraker papers, HPSO.

30. F. N. Wicker to C. S. Kelsey, May 20, 1896, McKinley papers, LC.

31. McKinley to A. E. Buck, February 1, 1895, to Thomas McDougall, December 19, 1894, *ibid.*

32. *Atlanta Constitution,* March 21, 1895.

33. *Ibid.,* April 2, 1895.

34. McKinley to I. Dawson, April 15, 1895, to C. C. Stewart, June 12, 1895, to Samuel Pugh, March 25, 1896, John Grant to J. W. Sansom, January 8, 1896, A. B. Hart to McKinley, January 12, 1896, James Boyle to McKinley, February 6, 1896, all in McKinley papers, LC; H. C. Warmoth to Chandler, February 4, 1896, Chandler papers, LC.

35. *Canton Repository,* March 19, 1896; New York *Tribune,* March 21, 1896.

36. Croly, *Marcus Alonso Hanna,* 184–185.

37. Knox to McKinley, February (?), 1896, McKinley papers, LC; Alger to Clarkson, March 28, 1896, Clarkson papers, LC; Hanna to Hay, October 7, 1895, Hay papers, LC.

38. James M. Swank to Hanna, February 28, 1896, McKinley papers, LC.

39. Albert Boardman to B. F. Tracy, June 20, 1895, Tracy papers, LC; E. G. Hay to Mrs. Hay, December 10, 1895, Eugene Gano Hay papers, LC; Hanna to John Hay, October 7, 1895, Hay papers, LC.

40. Harrison to John Wanamaker, November 7, 1895, Harrison papers, LC.

41. Harrison to Elkins, February 3, 1896, Elkins papers, WVU.

42. Olcott, *William McKinley,* I, 307–308.

43. D. M. Ransdell to E. F. Tibbott, February 27, 1896, Harrison papers, LC.

44. *Canton Repository,* April 7, 1896; J. S. Runnells to Allison, February 23, 1896, Allison papers, ISDHA.

45. Hanna to W. R. Holloway, April 24, 1896, reprinted in *Indiana Magazine of History,* 36 (December, 1940), 374–375, 386.

46. Hay to Reid, February 15, 1896, Reid papers, LC.

47. Depew to Morton, March 4, 1896, Morton papers, NYPL.

48. Morton to Edward Lauterbach, February 21, 1896, *ibid.*

49. Olcott, *William McKinley,* I, 307.

50. McKinley to Reid, February 19, 1896, Reid papers, LC.

51. Reid to McKinley, April 2, 1896, *ibid.*

52. Levi Ferguson to Harrison, August 10, 1895, Harrison papers, LC; J. S. Runnells to Allison, February 23, 1896, Allison papers, ISDHA; Clarkson to Michener, February 24, 1896, Michener papers, LC.

53. Cleveland *Leader,* June 23, 1895.

54. See boxes 59–61, 296–307, and T. W. Harvey to Allison, April 20, 1895, all in Allison papers, ISDHA.

55. Elkins to Reid, March 10, 1896, Reid papers, LC; Louis Gottschalk to Allison, May 21, 1896, Allison papers, ISDHA.

56. New York *Tribune,* March 26, 1896; Dawes to I. M. Raymond, January 10, 1896, Dawes papers, NWU.

57. McKinley to J. W. Brown, February 3, 1896, McKinley papers, LC.

58. E. Rosewater to Chandler, March 12, 1896, Chandler papers, LC.

59. Albert Boardman to Tracy, June 20, 1895, Tracy papers, LC; M. E. Estee to Clarkson, January 11, 1896, Clarkson papers, LC.

60. Allison to James Wilson, May 4 [1896], Wilson papers, LC.

61. Powers, *Portraits of Half a Century,* 163.

62. M. M. Estee to Clarkson, January 11, 1896, Clarkson papers, LC.

63. Robinson, *Thomas B. Reed,* 329–330.

64. McKinley to Hay, April 13, 1895, McKinley papers, LC.

65. F. W. Clancy to Chandler, March 11, 1896, W. J. Fowler to Chandler, April 4, 1896, Chandler papers, LC.

66. Reed to Russell Alger, January 8, 1896, Alger papers, WLCL.

67. Richardson, *William E. Chandler,* 515–517; *Canton Repository,* April 29, 1896.

68. George Lyman to Lodge, March 10, 1896, Lodge papers, MHS.

69. Gallinger to Charles Marseilles, May 30, 1896, Gallinger papers, NHHS.

70. George Lyman to Lodge, April 30, 1896, Lodge papers, MHS.

71. Hanna to McKinley, January 20, 1896, McKinley papers, LC.

72. Hay to Hanna, January 27, 1896, *ibid.*

73. Grosvenor to McKinley, February 19, 1896, *ibid.*

74. New York *Tribune,* February 13, April 9, 1896; Michener to E. G. Hay, May 23, 1896, Eugene Gano Hay papers, LC.

75. Quay to McKinley, May 15, 1896, McKinley papers, LC.

76. McElroy, *Levi Parsons Morton,* 284, 287–288; William Morton Grinnell to Morton, March 16, 1896, Morton to Edward Leach, April 20, 1896, Morton papers, NYPL.

77. Hay to Reid, September 5, 1895, Reid papers, LC.

78. Platt to Morton, December 11, 1895, McElroy, *Levi Parsons Morton,* 291–293.

79. Depew to Reid, December 27, 1895, January 25, 1896, Reid papers, LC; Morton to Depew, December 31, 1895, Depew papers, LC; Elkins to Reid, February 18, 1896, Reid papers, LC.

80. McElroy, *Levi Parsons Morton,* 281–284.

81. Osborne to McKinley, January 16, 1896, McKinley papers, LC.

82. Reid to Depew, March 13, Depew to Reid, June 11, 1896, Reid papers, LC; New York *Tribune,* March 25, June 2, 1896.

83. John E. Pixton, Jr., "Charles G. Dawes and the McKinley Campaign," *Journal of the Illinois Historical Society,* 48 (Autumn, 1955), 283–306.

84. Osborne to Dawes, March 23, 1896, Dawes papers, NWU; Dawes to McKinley, March 13, 16, 1896, McKinley papers, LC.

85. J. W. Gates to Allison, February 17, 1896, Allison papers, ISDHA.

86. Dawes, *Journal,* 63–74.

87. John McNulta to McKinley, April 9, 1896, Cullom to [Unknown Addressee], April 4, 1896, McKinley papers, LC.

88. Joseph P. Smith to Dawes, April 16, 1896, Dawes papers, NWU.

89. S. P. Peabody to McKinley, May 1, 1896, McKinley papers, LC.

90. *Canton Repository,* May 1, 1896.

91. McKinley to Alger, March 10, April 20, 1896, McKinley papers, LC; Cleveland *Leader,* March 29, 1896; Hanna to J. R. Holloway, March 25, 1896, in *Indiana Magazine of History,* 36 (December, 1940), 383.

92. Spooner to Henry C. Payne, December 25, 1895, to W. H. Brimson, February 3, 1896, to Philetus Sawyer, March 12, 1896, in Spooner papers, LC; La Follette and La Follette, *Robert M. La Follette,* I, 103.

93. Dawes, *Journal,* 51; George Peck to McKinley, January 16, 1896, McKinley papers, LC; Mott, *Myron T. Herrick,* 57; *Canton Repository,* May 6, 1896.

94. *Review of Reviews,* 13 (June, 1896), 643–644; *Brooklyn Eagle,* May 1, 1896.

XI: *THE FRONT-PORCH CAMPAIGN*

1. Walters, *Joseph Benson Foraker,* 129–130.
2. New York *Tribune,* June 6, 1896.
3. *Ibid.,* June 13, 1896; Joseph Shafer, "The Presidential Election of 1896," unpublished doctoral thesis, University of Wisconsin, 1941, p. 106.
4. Foraker to James H. Wilson, May 12, 1896, *ibid.*
5. A. B. Farquar to Henry Thurber, May 2, 1895, Cleveland papers, LC; Kenesaw Landis to Daniel Lamont, May 23, 1896, Lamont papers, LC; Beer, *Hanna,* 157n.
6. Alger to McKinley, June 4, 1896, McKinley papers, LC.
7. Reed to Lodge, June 12, 1896, Lodge papers, MHS; Dunn, *From Harrison to Harding,* I, 178.
8. C. A. Griscom to Clarkson, June 12, 1896, Clarkson papers, LC; Harrison to C. S. Smith, April 15, 1896, Harrison papers, LC.
9. Beer, *Hanna,* 145; Cleveland *Leader,* June 13, 14, 1896.
10. New York *Times,* May 18, 1896.
11. McKinley to Sherman, March 22, 1896, McKinley papers, LC.
12. Reid to McKinley, June 11, 13, 1896, Reid papers, LC.
13. Olcott, *William McKinley,* I, 312.
14. *Ibid.,* 312–313; *Mark Hanna: His Book,* 62–63.
15. Leech, *In the Days of McKinley,* 79.
16. Lodge to Eben S. Draper, January 12, 1900, Lodge papers, MHS.
17. See Olcott, *William McKinley,* I, 313–315.
18. The literature on the subject is endless. See Shafer, "The Presidential Campaign of 1896," 106ff; Lodge to W. R. Merriam, March 19, 1923, Lodge papers, MHS; H. C. Hansbrough to Gallinger, August 4, 1896, Redfield Proctor to Gallinger, July 16, 1896, Gallinger papers, NHHS; William W. Wight, *Henry Clay Payne: A Life* (Milwaukee: Burdick and Allen, 1907), 93ff; Beer, *Hanna,* 144n; "History of the Financial Plank of the Republican Party 1896," Typescript in Foraker papers, HPSO.
19. Harry Thurston Peck, *Twenty Years of the Republic* (New York, 1905), 486–487.
20. White, *Autobiography,* 276–278; *ibid.; Official Proceedings of the Eleventh National Convention . . . 1896* (St. Louis, 1896), 75–100.
21. Quoted in Leech, *In the Days of McKinley,* 80.

22. Dunn, *From Harrison to Harding,* I, 181.

23. McElroy, *Levi Parsons Morton,* 303; *Roosevelt-Lodge Correspondence,* I, 216.

24. Leech, *In the Days of McKinley,* 81.

25. *Proceedings of the Eleventh Republican National Convention . . . 1896,* 117–120.

26. Peck, *Twenty Years of the Republic,* 490; *Canton Repository,* June 18, 1896.

27. *Canton Repository,* June 17–20, 1896.

28. New York *Tribune,* June 21, 1896; *Proceedings of the Eleventh Republican National Convention . . . 1896,* 129–131.

29. Mott, *Myron T. Herrick,* 61–62.

30. Dunn, *From Harrison to Harding,* I, 228.

31. *Canton Repository,* June 19, 1896.

32. Olcott, *William McKinley,* I, 317–319.

33. Stephen B. Elkins to A. B. White, December 15, 26, 1894, White papers, WVU; Reed to Lodge, June 10, 11, 1896, Lodge papers, MHS; Telephone Transcript Report, June 17, 1896, Morton papers, NYPL; Reid to McKinley, April 7, 1896, Reid papers, LC; *Proceedings of the Eleventh Republican National Convention . . . 1896,* 143.

34. Thomas Kilpatrick to Bryan, July 13, 1891, Bryan papers, LC.

35. Bryan to Josephus Daniels, June 1, 1895, Weaver to Bryan, May 29, 1896, *ibid.;* Thompson, *Presidents I've Known,* 46; Dunn, *From Harrison to Harding,* I, 184.

36. White, *Autobiography,* 278; C. S. Thomas to Teller, July 14, 1896, Teller papers, SHSC.

37. II Peter 1:10; *Canton Repository,* June 22, 1896.

38. McKinley to Hanna, June 13, 1896, McKinley papers, LC; *Canton Repository,* June 22, 1896; Croly, *Marcus Alonzo Hanna,* 207.

39. Olcott, *William McKinley,* I, 321.

40. Reid to Hanna, July 4, 1896, Reid papers, LC.

41. Cleveland *Leader,* July 17, 1896.

42. Clarkson to H. G. McMillan, October 5, 1896, Clarkson papers, LC.

43. Stoddard, *As I Knew Them,* 262; Beer, *Hanna,* 156; White, *Autobiography,* 291–292.

44. Bristow, *Fraud and Politics,* 61.

45. McKinley to Hanna, July 7, 1896, and n.d., p. 38, letterbook 88, McKinley papers, LC.

46. Dawes, *Journal,* 90–93.

47. New York *Tribune,* July 17, 27, 1896; Osborne to McKinley, August 11, 1896, McKinley papers, LC.

48. Hanna to Reid, July 24, 1896, Reid papers, LC; George Lyman to Lodge, July 31, 1896, Lodge papers, MHS.

49. *Mark Hanna: His Book,* 54; Hale to Chandler, July 16, 1896, Chandler papers, LC.

50. Platt to Morton, August 4, 1896, Morton papers, NYPL; New York *Tribune,* August 2, 1896; McKinley to Morton, August 17, 1896, Morton papers, NYPL.

51. Dawes to McKinley, August 1, 1896, McKinley papers, LC; William

Roscoe Thayer, *Life and Letters of John Hay,* 2 vols. (New York: Houghton-Mifflin, 1929), II, 151.

52. Hay to McKinley, August 3, 1896, McKinley papers, LC; Frick to Quay, October 26, 1896, Quay papers, LC; S. D. Slemmons to Quay, September 30, 1896, *ibid.*

53. Hanna to Dawes, n.d., Dawes papers, NWU.

54. Croly, *Marcus Alonso Hanna,* 219.

55. Hanna to Reid, August 22, 1896, Reid papers, LC.

56. Croly, *Marcus Alonzo Hanna,* 220–221; Dawes, *Journal,* 106.

57. Hobart to McKinley, August 20, 1896, Nelson Dingley to McKinley, July 26, 1896, William P. Frye to McKinley, July 27, 1896, McKinley papers, LC.

58. James Boyle to Perry Heath, August 1, 1896, Dawes papers, NWU.

59. Cleveland *Leader,* August 17, 18, 1896.

60. Hanna to Carl Schurz, September 16, 1896, Schurz papers, LC; Beer, *Hanna,* 165.

61. Shafer, "The Presidential Campaign of 1896," 302ff; John W. Stewart to Justin S. Morrill, November 11, 1896, Morrill papers, LC.

62. W. M. Hahn to Clarkson, September 30, 1896, Clarkson papers, LC.

63. J. G. Carlisle to Stewart, August 25, 1896, Stewart papers, NHS; Osborne to McKinley, August 11, 1896, N. B. Scott to McKinley, September 7, 1896, McKinley papers, LC; White, *Autobiography,* 291–292; McKinley to Reid, June 24, 1896, Reid papers, LC.

64. Nathan B. Scott, in *Marcus A. Hanna: Memorial Addresses,* 39–40.

65. Dawes, *Journal,* 98.

66. White, *Autobiography,* 285.

67. *Canton Repository,* October 24, 1896.

68. Harrison to E. G. Hay, September 8, 1896, Eugene Gano Hay papers, LC, to Powell Clayton, August 10, 1896, Harrison papers, LC; McKinley to Harrison, October 7, 1896, Hanna to Harrison, October 10, 1896, *ibid.;* New York *Times,* August 28, 1896.

69. McKinley to Herrick, August 10, 1896, Herrick papers, WRHS; Washington *Post,* October 27, 1896.

70. Thayer, *Life and Letters of John Hay,* II, 152–153.

71. McKinley to E. L. Osborne, August 26, 1896, McKinley papers, LC.

72. Mott, *Myron T. Herrick,* 64.

73. McKinley to Webb C. Hayes, July 18, 1896, Webb C. Hayes papers, HML.

74. McKinley to [Unknown Addressee], n.d., letterbook 88, McKinley papers, LC.

75. Croly, *Marcus Alonzo Hanna,* 215–216.

76. Leech, *In the Days of McKinley,* 88, 93.

77. *Ohio State Journal,* June 20, 1896; *Canton Repository,* October 25, 1896; *ibid.,* July 18, 1896; Cleveland *Leader,* October 4, 18, 1896; San Francisco *Call,* September 6, 1896.

78. McKinley to George Miller, July 15, 1896, McKinley papers, LC; McKinley to S. W. Fordyce, July 31, 1896, *ibid.*

79. *Canton Repository,* August 18, September 18, 30, 1896.

80. *Ibid.,* August 18, 1896; Beer, *Hanna,* 134.

81. *Canton Repository,* July 20, 1896.

82. Beer, *Hanna,* 156–157.

83. *Canton Repository,* August 11, 1896.

84. Leech, *In the Days of McKinley,* 89.

85. Beer, *Hanna,* 163; Cleveland *Plain Dealer,* October 18, 1896.

86. Beer, *Hanna,* 161–162; Cleveland *Plain Dealer,* October 2, 1896; Alger to McKinley, October 14, 1896, McKinley papers, LC.

87. Kohlsaat, *From McKinley to Harding,* 55.

88. Springfield *Republican,* August 28, 1896.

89. C. S. Thomas to Teller, July 14, 1896, Teller papers, SHSC; Beer, *Hanna,* 153.

90. Festus P. Summers (ed.), *The Cabinet Diary of William L. Wilson* (Chapel Hill: Univ. of North Carolina Press, 1959), 134; Edwin F. Uhl to Lamont, August 17, 1896, Lamont papers, LC.

91. Teller to Brooks Adams, September 3, 1896, Teller papers, SHSC.

92. Stewart to Marion Butler, July 14, 1896, Stewart papers, NHS.

93. Teller to Bryan, July 20, 1896, Teller papers, SHSC.

94. Teller to William Van Nostrand, September 3, 1896, to Bryan, July 22, 1896, *ibid.;* see also Elmer Ellis, "The Silver Republicans in the Election of 1896," *MVHR,* 18 (March, 1932), 519–534.

95. Fred Dubois to H. E. Taubeneck, July 13, 1896, Teller papers, SHSC; James K. Jones to Teller, August 24, 1896, *ibid.*

96. Teller to R. F. Pettigrew, September 3, 1896, Teller papers, SHSC.

97. Pettigrew to Teller, June 26, 1896, *ibid.*

98. Fred Dubois to Teller, June 26, 1896, *ibid.;* Clem and P. E. Studebaker to Harrison, October 12, 1896, Harrison papers, LC; Harrison to W. J. Steele, September 18, 1896, *ibid.*

99. Hill to Lamont, September 14, 1896, Lamont papers, LC.

100. Barnes, *John G. Carlisle,* 465.

101. James A. Barnes, "The Gold Standard Democrats and the Party Conflict," *MVHR,* 17 (December, 1930), 422–450; *Proceedings of the National Convention of the National Democratic Party . . . 1896* (Indianapolis, 1896), 12, 32, 45.

102. Calvin Tompkins to Bynum, September 28, 1896, Bynum papers, LC; C. S. Wood to Bynum, September 11, 1896, Z. T. Vinson to Bynum, October 7, 1896, *ibid.;* Powell Clayton to Schurz, August 6, 1896, Schurz papers, LC.

103. Dawes to A. J. Lester, September 9, 1896, Dawes papers, NWU; Dawes to D. A. Campbell, October 12, 1896, *ibid.*

104. *The Nation,* 63 (November 5, 1896), 337.

105. D. L. Griffin to Lamont, October 15, 1896, James J. Hill to Lamont, October 1, 1896, Lamont papers, LC; Bynum to M. L. Crawford, November 18, 1896, C. H. J. Taylor to Bynum, November 12, 1896, in Bynum papers, LC; Barnes, *John G. Carlisle,* 479.

106. Roswell Miller to Lamont, September 21, 1896, Lamont papers, LC; Hay to Reid, September 23, 1896, Reid papers, LC.

107. McKinley to W. M. Hawkins, September 2, 1896, McKinley papers, LC; McKinley to H. G. Otis, September 2, 1896, *ibid.*

108. McKinley to L. D. Ashley, August 6, 1896, *ibid.*

109. *Canton Repository,* August 14, 1896.

110. McKinley to Wilbur F. Wakeman, August 7, 1896, McKinley papers, LC.

111. Hanna to Harrison, October 23, 1896, Harrison papers, LC.

112. Quay to McKinley, October 23, 1896, McKinley papers, LC.

113. *Canton Repository*, October 31, November 3, 1896.

114. *Ibid.*, November 4, 1896.

115. Fragment in McKinley's handwriting, dated 4 A.M., November 4, 1896, in McKinley papers, LC.

116. *Kohlsaat, From McKinley to Harding*, 53.

117. *Canton Repository*, November 5, 8, 1896; Senator James K. Jones of Arkansas was Bryan's campaign manager.

118. McKinley to Hanna, November 12, 1896, McKinley papers, LC.

119. New York *Tribune*, October 10, 1896; *The Nation*, 63 (October 22, 1896), 300. Bryan believed that he drew 4,500,000 votes from regular Democrats, 1,500,000 from Populists, and 500,000 from Silver Republicans; see Bryan to Teller, March 22, 1897, Teller papers, SHSC.

120. Altgeld to James K. Jones, December 5, 1896, Altgeld papers, Illinois Historical Society, Springfield, photostat furnished by Mr. Thomas E. Felt.

121. Shafer, "The Presidential Campaign of 1896," 436ff.

122. James A. Barnes, "Myths of the Bryan Campaign," *MVHR*, 34 (December, 1947), 367–404; Gilbert C. Fite, "Republican Farm Strategy and the Farm Vote in the Presidential Campaign of 1896," *AHR*, 65 (July, 1960), 787–806; William Diamond, "Urban and Rural Voting in 1896," *ibid.*, 46 (January, 1941), 281–305.

XII: *CABINETMAKING*

1. McKinley to Reid, December 26, 1896, Reid papers, LC.

2. Quay to McKinley, December 15, 1896, Quay papers, LC.

3. Hay to Reid, November 8, 1896, Reid papers, LC.

4. *Mr. Dooley in the Hearts of His Countrymen* (Boston: Small, Maynard Co., 1899), 143ff.

5. Cleveland *Leader*, November 30, 1896.

6. Dawes, *Journal*, 105, 108; Kohlsaat, *From McKinley to Harding*, 56.

7. Thomas McDougall to McKinley, January 9, 1897, McKinley papers, LC.

8. Algert to Foraker, February 1, 1897, *ibid.*

9. Cleveland *Leader*, November 16, 1896; Croly, *Marcus Alonzo Hanna*, 232; Osborne to McKinley, December 11, 1896, McKinley papers, LC.

10. Hanna to McKinley, January 13, 1897, Sherman to McKinley, January 16, 1897, Alger to Foraker, February 1, 1897, *ibid.;* Sherman to McKinley, February 10, 1897, *ibid.*

11. Hay to Reid, January 17, 1897, Reid papers, LC; Hanna to Reid, February 11, 1897, *ibid.*

12. Foraker, *Notes*, I, 500–501; Cleveland *Leader*, February 19, 1897; Alger to Foraker, February 1, 1897, Foraker papers, HPSO.

13. Hanna to Reid, February 11, 1897, Reid papers, LC; Bushnell to McKinley, February 21, 1897, McKinley papers, LC.

14. Croly, *Marcus Alonzo Hanna*, 240–241.

15. McKinley to Hanna, February 18, 1897, McKinley papers, LC.

16. *Roosevelt–Lodge Correspondence,* I, 240–242.

17. J. A. T. Hull to Allison, December 18, 1896, Allison papers, ISDHA.

18. Allison to James H. Wilson, January 18, 1897, Wilson papers, LC.

19. Osborne to McKinley, December 11, 1896, McKinley papers, LC.

20. McKinley to Joseph Medill, February 8, 1896, *ibid.*

21. Sherman to Hanna, December 15, 1896, *ibid.;* McKinley to Sherman, January 4, 1897, Sherman to McKinley, January 7, 1897, *ibid.*

22. Croly, *Marcus Alonzo Hanna,* 235–236.

23. *Ibid.,* 233ff; Wilson, *Cabinet Diary,* 233ff.

24. Sherman to McKinley, February 15, 1896, McKinley papers, LC.

25. Foraker, *I Would Live It Again,* 229, 234–235.

26. Dunn, *From Harrison to Harding,* I, 204.

27. Cleveland *Leader,* November 19, 1896; Reid to McKinley, December 5, 1896, McKinley papers, LC; Schurz to Hanna, November 12, 1896, Schurz papers, LC.

28. Cleveland *Leader,* December 11, 1896; Dingley to McKinley, December 22, 1896, McKinley papers, LC.

29. Cleveland *Leader,* January 16, 1896.

30. Mott, *Myron T. Herrick,* 72.

31. W. P. Nixon to J. R. Thomas, November 17, 1896, Thomas papers, LC; Cleveland *Leader,* January 4, 1897.

32. Dawes, *Journal,* 112–113.

33. Kohlsaat, *From McKinley to Harding,* 58–59. Kohlsaat's memoirs are not always reliable; there is some evidence in this case to show that Dawes had suggested Gage and that McKinley himself had already been thinking of the name. Gage was definitely the choice of the anti-Cullom people. See Dawes, *Journal,* 112.

34. Dawes, *Journal,* 112–114; Dawes to McKinley, January 21, 1897, McKinley papers, LC.

35. McKinley to Gage, January 25, 1897, McKinley papers, LC; Gage, *Memoirs,* 87–91; Cleveland *Leader,* January 29, 1897.

36. Moses P. Handy, "Lyman J. Gage: A Character Sketch," *Review of Reviews,* 15 (March, 1897), 289–300.

37. Cleveland *Leader,* January 22, 1897; Wilson, *Cabinet Diary,* 211; Hay to McKinley, February 2, 1897, McKinley papers, LC.

38. Burrows to Alger, January 27, 1897, Alger papers, WLCL.

39. Cleveland *Leader,* January 14, 1897; Alger to McKinley, January 11, 1897, McKinley papers, LC.

40. Samuel Thomas to McKinley, January 18, 1897, *ibid.;* H. V. Boynton to McKinley, January 18, 1897, J. C. Burrows to McKinley, January 25, 1897, *ibid.;* Orcutt, *Burrows of Michigan,* II, 97–103.

41. McKinley to Alger, January 27, 1897, McKinley papers, LC.

42. Cleveland *Leader,* January 30, 1897.

43. W. Whitman to McKinley, January 25, 1897, McKinley papers, LC.

44. McKinley to Long, January 30, 1897, *ibid.*

45. *Roosevelt–Lodge Correspondence,* I, 240–242; Archie Butt, *Taft and Roosevelt: The Intimate Letters of Archie Butt,* 2 vols. (New York: Doubleday, Page Co., 1930), II, 440–441.

46. Mott, *Myron T. Herrick,* 73; Maria L. Storer, "How Theodore Roosevelt

Was Appointed Assistant Secretary of the Navy: A Hitherto Unrelated Chapter of History," *Harper's Weekly,* 56 (June 1, 1912), 9.

47. Chandler to W. H. Jaques, January 8, 1897, Chandler papers, LC.

48. *Roosevelt–Lodge Correspondence,* I, 253; see Pringle, *Theodore Roosevelt,* 165–169.

49. La Follette, *Autobiography,* 129–131; George F. Stitch to Hanna, November 28, 1896, McKinley papers, LC; Cleveland *Leader,* January 16, 1897.

50. Isaac Stephenson, *Recollections of a Long Life* (Chicago: R. R. Donnelley and Sons, 1915), 198–199.

51. La Follette, *Autobiography,* 129–131.

52. McKinley to Hanna, February 18, 1897, McKinley papers, LC.

53. Goff to McKinley, January 23, 1897, *ibid.;* McKenna to McKinley, December 28, 1896, *ibid.;* Otis to McKinley, December 29, 1896, *ibid.*

54. Kohlsaat, *From McKinley to Harding,* 59–60. McKinley did receive protests that McKenna was "a member of the Roman Hierarchy." See American Protective Association of Taunton, Mass., to McKinley, February 15, 1897, McKinley papers, LC.

55. William D. Bynum to H. E. Fries, January 5, 1897, Bynum papers, LC.

56. Earley Vernon Wilcox, *Tama Jim* (Boston: The Stratford Co., 1930), 157–158.

57. Reid to Hay, November 17, 1896, Reid to McKinley, December 5, 1896, Reid to McKinley, January 2, 1897, all in Reid papers, LC.

58. Hay to Reid, December 10, 1896, Reid to Stephen B. Elkins, February 3, 1897, *ibid.;* Hay to Hanna, January 15, 1897, to McKinley, February 16, 1897, McKinley papers, LC.

59. McKinley to Reid, February 19, 1896, *ibid.*

60. Hanna to McKinley, January 18, 1897, *ibid.*

61. See Hay to Reid, December 10, 1896, Reid papers, LC; Platt to Alger, January 31, 1897, Alger to McKinley, February 9, 1897, McCook to McKinley, February 27, 1897, McKinley papers, LC; McCook to James Wilson, February 17, 26, 1897, Wilson papers, LC.

62. Reid to McKinley, December 5, 1896, Reid papers, LC.

63. Bliss to McKinley, January 8, 1897, *ibid.*

64. Cleveland *Leader,* March 4, 1897; Washington *Post,* March 4, 1897.

65. New York *Tribune,* March 19, 1897.

66. H. D. Cater (ed.), *Henry Adams and His Friends* (New York: Houghton-Mifflin Co., 1947), 399.

67. *Canton Repository,* March 1–4, 1897.

68. Leech, *In the Days of McKinley,* 113.

69. New York *Tribune,* March 3, 1897.

70. Peck, *Twenty Years of the Republic,* 519.

71. George F. Parker, *Recollections of Grover Cleveland* (New York: The Century Co., 1909), 248–250.

XIII: *THE NEW ADMINISTRATION*

1. Wilson, *Cabinet Diary,* 248

2. Olcott, *William McKinley,* I, 367–368; George B. McClellan, Jr., *The*

Gentleman and the Tiger (New York: J. B. Lippincott Co., 1956), 118; Kohlsaat, *From McKinley to Harding*, 64.

3. Cleveland *Leader*, March 5, 1897; Foraker, *I Would Live It Again*, 256–257; Dunn, *From Harrison to Harding*, I, 208.

4. McKinley, *Speeches* (1900), 2–15.

5. New York *Tribune*, March 6, 9, 1897; Washington *Post*, March 6, 9, 1897; Chicago *Evening Post*, March 5, 1897.

6. Irwin Hoover, *Forty-Two Years in the White House* (New York: Houghton-Mifflin Co., 1934), 245.

7. New York *Tribune*, July 4, 1897; Diary of William E. Chandler, June 4, 1897, Chandler papers, NHHS; Hobart to John T. Morgan, June 26, 1897, Morgan papers, LC; Hobart, *Memories*, 17.

8. Washington *Post*, March 27, 1897; Olcott, *William McKinley*, II, 343.

9. *Ibid.*, 338–343; Alexander, *History and Procedure of the House of Representatives*, 359.

10. Cullom, *Fifty Years of Public Service*, 275–276; Hoar, *Autobiography*, II, 46–47; Olcott *William McKinley*, II, 346; Richardson, *Chandler*, 542.

11. Olcott, *William McKinley*, II, 346.

12. *Ibid.;* John D. Long, "Some Personal Characteristics of President McKinley," *The Century Magazine*, 63 (November, 1901), 144–146; John D. Long *The New American Navy*, 2 vols. (New York: The Outlook Co., 1903), II, 142ff.

13. New York *Journal*, March 8, 1897.

14. N. B. Scott to A. B. White, March 1, 1897, White papers, WVU.

15. W. Stewart to J. S. Morrill, December 3, 1896, Morrill papers, LC.

16. The mass of such petitions is staggering, but can best be sampled in the Records of the House Ways and Means Committee, and Senate Finance Committee, 55th Congress, NA; and boxes 308–319, Allison papers, ISDHA; Washington *Post*, March 12, 1897; Chandler to Hobart, January 31, 1897, Chandler papers, LC.

17. Washington *Post*, April 1, 1897.

18. *Ibid.*, May 11, 1897.

19. Stephenson, *Nelson W. Aldrich*, 142; Beer, *Hanna*, 181, 236.

20. Chandler to E. O. Wolcott, June 21, 1897, Chandler papers, LC.

21. Wolcott to Chandler, November 13, 1897, Teller to Chandler, April 21, 1897, *ibid.*; Ellis, *Henry Moore Teller*, 244.

22. Washington *Post*, April 26, 1897.

23. Chandler to Wolcott, June 14, July 20, 1897, Chandler papers, LC; McKinley to Kohlsaat, December 18, 1897, McKinley papers, LC.

24. Spooner to Charles Ray, June 22, 1897, to B. Leiderdorf, June 12, 1897, Spooner papers, LC.

25. Hoar to Lodge, June 15, 1897, Lodge papers, MHS; Foraker to James Wilson, June 22, 1897, Wilson papers, LC.

26. Washington *Post*, April 17, 1897; Wu Ting-Fang to Sherman, June 29, 1897, Sherman to Aldrich, June 29, 1897, Aldrich papers, LC; Oscar Straus to Carl Schurz, June 4, 1897, Schurz papers, LC; New York *Tribune*, June 3, 1897.

27. Washington *Post*, July 8, 1897.

28. Walters, *Joseph Benson Foraker*, 144; Washington *Post*, July 24, 1897.

29. James D. Richardson (comp.), *The Messages and Papers of the Presidents 1789–1905*, 11 vols. (Washington, 1905), X, 14.

30. Laughlin and Willis, *Reciprocity,* 302, 315; La Follette, *Autobiography,* 115; Younger, *John A. Kasson,* 364–366.

31. McKinley, *Speeches and Addresses* (1900), 54–55, 62.

32. New York *Journal,* July 4, 1897.

33. Wolcott to Chandler, November 13, 1896, Chandler to McKinley, December 17, 1896, Chandler papers, LC; Olcott, *William McKinley,* I, 354; McKinley to C. W. Stone, February 13, 1897, McKinley papers, LC.

34. Thomas F. Dawson, *The Life and Character of Edward Oliver Wolcott,* 2 vols. (New York: Knickerbocker Press, 1911), I, 648; Chandler to Frank Challis, December 23, 1896, Chandler papers, NHHS; O. H. Platt to Chandler, November 9, 1896, Chandler papers, LC.

35. General Records of the State Department, Instructions to Special Missions, May 1, 1897, Vol. 4, Record Group 59, NA. All papers in this collection hereafter cited as RG 59, NA.

36. Sherman to Wolcott, Paine and Stevenson, May 1, 1897, *ibid.*

37. Wolcott to Chandler, February 8, 1897, *ibid.*

38. Wolcott to Chandler, June 1, 11, 1897, *ibid.*

39. Porter to McKinley, July 13, 1897, McKinley papers, LC; Porter to Bliss, August 10, 1897, Porter papers, LC; Chandler to E. Bruwaert, August 2, 1897, Chandler papers, LC.

40. Wolcott to McKinley, January 25, 1897, McKinley papers, LC.

41. Hay to McKinley, May 9, May 20, 1897, *ibid.*

42. Wolcott to Chandler, July 14, July 28, October 12, 1897, Chandler papers, LC; Hay to McKinley, July 30, 1897, Hay papers, LC.

43. Hay to McKinley, November 13, 1897, McKinley papers, LC; Jeremiah VI:30.

44. McKinley to Hay, July 27, 1897, Hay papers, LC.

45. Sherman to McKinley, June 22, 1897, McKinley papers, LC. The pencilled notation, "I would not give it out in any form or channel," in the President's hand is at the bottom of the page.

46. Washington *Post,* December 20, 1897; Chandler to McKinley, February 15, 1897, to Day, October 6, 1897, to Wolcott, June 21, 1897, Wolcott to Chandler, July 20, 28, August 6, 1897, all in Chandler papers, LC.

47. Wolcott to McKinley, November 22, 1897, McKinley papers, LC.

48. Chandler to Wolcott, October 10, 1897, Chandler papers, LC.

49. New York *Tribune,* July 28, 1897.

50. Richardson, *Messages and Papers,* X, 40–41.

51. Olcott, *William McKinley,* I, 344; Richardson, *Messages and Papers,* X, 11; Edwin Burritt Smith to McKinley, March 13, 1897, McKinley papers, LC.

52. New York *Tribune,* July 8, 1897; McKinley to Joseph Medill, January 20, 1897, Kohlsaat to McKinley, August 11, 1897, McKinley papers, LC.

53. Allison to W. W. Baldwin, July 15, 1897, Allison papers, ISDHA.

54. Gage, *Memoirs,* 124; Washington *Post,* May 29, 1897.

55. New York *Tribune,* November 16, 1897; Dawes, *Journal,* 128–129; Bynum to H. E. Fries, February 4, 1897, Bynum papers, LC; Gage to G. R. DeSaussure, June 7, 1898, Gage papers, LC.

56. Richardson, *Messages and Papers,* X, 28; Gage to Edward Atkinson, September 16, 1898, Gage papers, LC; Allison to Joseph Medill, November 13,

1897, Allison Papers, ISDHA; Lodge to W. S. Stuyvesant, December 8, 1896, to Charles [?], February 3, 1897, Lodge papers, MHS; B. F. Jones to Elkins, October 1, 1897, Elkins papers, WVU.

57. Dawes, *Journal*, 83; Cleveland *Leader*, January 5, 1897; White, *Autobiography*, 294–295; Foraker, *I Would Live It Again*, 216; Spooner to R. C. Heydlauff, March 24, 1897, Spooner papers, LC; Fairbanks to Day, September 10, 1897, Day papers; Beer, *Hanna*, 180.

58. Paul P. Van Riper, *The History of the Civil Service of the United States* (Evanston, Ill.: Row, Peterson, 1958), 173–174; Spooner to G. E. Mickelson, March 21, 1897, Spooner papers, LC.

59. Grosvenor to Chandler, February 14, 1897, Chandler papers, LX; Reid to Lodge, October 25, 1898, Lodge papers, MHS; Gallinger to Charles Marseilles, April 10, 1897, Gallinger papers, NHHS.

60. *Mr. Dooley's Philosophy*, 108; McKinley to Sherman, February 11, 1897, McKinley papers, LC.

61. Bristow, *Fraud and Politics*, 59; J. H. Claypool to McKinley, April 19, 1897, McKinley papers, LC.

62. Croly, *Marcus Alonzo Hanna*, 298; Bristow, *Fraud and Politics*, 36ff.

63. John J. McCook to J. H. Wilson, April 5, 1897, Wilson papers, LC; Gage, *Memoirs*, 149; Elizabeth Herring to Cortelyou, June 17, 1898, McKinley papers, LC; Hay to Reid, November 13, 1898, Reid papers, LC; Bristow, *Fraud and Politics*, 70; Thomas Byron to McKinley, August 11, 1898, McKinley papers, LC.

64. Teller to Gage, May 18, 1901, McKinley papers, LC.

65. Stewart to Frank Burk, May 7, 1900, Daniel papers, DUL.

66. Foraker to McKinley, November 7, 1896, Foraker papers, HPSO. "He is hunting for men who are utterly and entirely subservient to him, and a man who has any independence of character has not much show if he knows him to be such," Cullom wrote James Wilson, June 25, 1897, Wilson papers, LC, and Wilson apparently passed it on; see also, Cullom, *Fifty Years of Public Service*, 276–279; Bristow, *Fraud and Politics*, 31.

67. Platt to Chandler, December 26, 1896, Chandler papers, LC; Platt to McKinley, August 14, 1898, McKinley papers, LC; Platt, *Autobiography*, 397–398.

68. Richardson, *Messages and Papers*, X, 16; George McAneny to Schurz, April 2, July 14, 1897, Schurz papers, LC.

69. Lodge to Mr. Curtis, August 5, 1897, Lodge papers, MHS; Mem. dated April 11, 1899, McKinley papers, LC; Gage to R. M. Eastley, November 4, 1898, Gage papers, LC; Hanna to McKinley, May 15, 1899, McKinley papers, LC.

70. Leonard White, *The Republican Era 1869–1901* (New York: MacMillan and Co., 1958), 319–344; *Roosevelt–Lodge Correspondence*, I, 267, 405.

71. *Literary Digest*, 15 (August 7, 1897), 428; J. W. Pratt, "The Large Policy of 1898," *MVHR*, 19 (September, 1932), 219–242.

72. Carl M. Fuess, *Carl Schurz* (New York: Dodd, Mead and Co., 1932), 349; Pratt, *Expansionists of 1898*, 215.

73. *Ibid.*, 218, n87; Foster, *Diplomatic Memoirs*, II, 172–174.

74. *Ibid.*

75. T. A. Bailey, "Japan's Protest Against the Annexation of Hawaii," *JMH*, 3 (March, 1931), 46–61; Roosevelt to Mahan, May 3, 1897, Roosevelt papers, LC; *Roosevelt–Lodge Correspondence*, I, 276–277.

76. Hoar, *Autobiography*, II, 307–308.

77. C. D. Naylor to Morrill, March 15, 1897, Morrill papers, LC; Reid to McKinley, December 5, 1896, McKinley papers, LC; *Roosevelt–Lodge Correspondence*, I, 317.

78. Washington *Post*, June 16, 1896; Frye to Wilson, June 6, 1898, Wilson papers, LC; *Roosevelt–Lodge Correspondence*, I, 311, 330.

79. Olcott, *William McKinley*, II, 345–347.

80. Hanna to Foraker, February 25, 1897, Foraker papers, HPSO; McCook to Wilson, March 31, 1897, Wilson papers, LC; McKinley to Hanna, November 24, 1897, McKinley papers, LC; Croly, *Marcus Alonzo Hanna*, 272; Powers, *Portraits of Half a Century*, 168.

81. McKinley to Hanna, October 14, 1897, Dick papers, OHS.

82. McKinley to Hanna, November 4, 1897, Hanna Transcripts, Felt.

83. Dawes, *Journal*, 138; Hanna to Day, December 24, 1897, Day papers; Grosvenor to H. C. Corbin, January 8, 1898, *ibid.*

84. McKinley to Hanna, January 7, 1898, Dick papers, OHS; McKinley to Alger, January 13, 1898, Alger papers, WLCL.

85. *Roosevelt–Lodge Correspondence*, I, 267–268.

86. Dawes to McKinley, August 13, 1897, McKinley papers, LC; McKinley to Reid, July 19, 1897, Reid papers, LC.

XIV: *PRESIDENTIAL PROFILE*

1. Hobart, *Memories*, 7; Washington *Post*, April 27, 1897.

2. Edward Sanford Martin, *The Life of Joseph Hodges Choate*, 2 vols. (New York: Charles Scribner's Sons, 1920), II, 40.

3. Dunn, *From Harrison to Harding*, I, 207; Stoddard, *As I Knew Them*, 243–244.

4. Richardson, *Messages and Papers*, X, 143.

5. Leech, *In the Days of McKinley*, 126.

6. William E. Curtis to McKinley, January 12, 1897, McKinley papers, LC.

7. Ira Smith and Joe Morris, *Dear Mr. President* (New York: Julian Messner, 1949), 22; Porter to Fairbanks, March 20, 1897, McKinley papers. LC.

8. Henry Wilson to McKinley, November 22, 1899, McKinley papers, LC, box 212.

9. Smith to McKinley, January 29, 1899, McKinley papers, LC.

10. Bingham to Porter, May 18, 1898, *ibid.*

11. William DuBois to Cortelyou, September 13, 1898, *ibid.*

12. Porter to A. P. Miller, August 5, 1897, *ibid.*

13. Smith, *Dear Mr. President*, 35–38.

14. Hoover, *42 Years in the White House*, 14–15; Smith, *Dear Mr. President*, 38–39; O. L. Pruden to Cortelyou, August 10, 1900, McKinley papers, LC.

15. See Leech, *In the Days of McKinley*, 129ff.

16. Porter to Sherman, January 22, 1897, McKinley to Frye, February 6,

1901, McKinley papers, LC; McKinley to Hay, May 14, 1899, *ibid.;* Long, *America of Yesterday,* 153.

17. Washington *Post,* April 5, 1898; L. H. Kauffman to McKinley, April 25, 1898, McKinley papers, LC.

18. McKinley to Helen McKinley, December 15, 1899, *ibid.*

19. McKinley to Hanna, September 18, 1899, Hanna Transcripts, Felt; J. N Bishop to McKinley, January 15, 1897, McKinley papers, LC. See folder in box 216, *ibid.*

20. Beer, *Hanna,* 258.

21. Olcott, *William McKinley,* II, 433.

22. Hoover, *42 Years in the White House,* 279; Foraker, *I Would Live It Again,* 261; H. O. S. Heistand to McKinley, July 6, 1901, McKinley papers, LC.

23. Dunn, *From Harrison to Harding,* I, 208; Hobart, *Memories,* 29.

24. Hoover, *42 Years in the White House,* 21–22.

25. McKinley to Mrs. Myron Herrick, January 6, 1894, Herrick papers, WRHS.

26. New York *Tribune,* March 13, 1898; Diary of Whitelaw Reid, September 16, 1898, Reid papers, LC.

27. McKinley to Helen McKinley, June 2, 1900, McKinley papers, LC.

28. Cleveland *Plain Dealer,* August 31, 1897; New York *Times,* March 5, 1900; *Baltimore American,* May 2, 1897.

29. Will Rossiter, *McKinley Memoir* (Chicago: n.p., 1901), 5.

30. Dunn, *From Harrison to Harding,* I, 207; OAHS, *Publications,* 10 (1902), 243–249.

31. White, *Autobiography,* 333–334.

32. Hoover, *42 Years in the White House,* 238.

33. White, *Autobiography,* I, 245.

34. Hoover, *42 Years in the White House,* 290.

35. John J. McCook to J. H. Wilson, July 28, 1897, Wilson papers, LC.

36. White, *Autobiography,* 333.

37. Thompson, *Presidents I've Known,* 16.

38. William S. Hawk to McKinley, June 1, 1897, McKinley papers, LC.

39. Porter to Herrick, June 13, 1898, Herrick Papers, WRHS.

40. Beer, *Hanna,* 108.

41. Washington *Post,* June 17, 1900.

42. Ermine Winter to McKinley, March 18, 1898, box 216, McKinley papers, LC.

43. Otis to J. H. Woodard, June 21, 1898, *ibid.;* Hay to Henry White, March 18, 1901, Hay papers, LC.

44. Hanna to McKinley, n.d., filed at end of section on 1897, McKinley papers, LC.

45. Leech, *In the Days of McKinley,* 438.

46. Smith, *Dear Mr. President,* 42–45.

47. Martin, *Joseph H. Choate,* II, 75.

48. Art Young, *On My Way* (New York: H. Liveright, 1928), 90.

49. Stoddard, *As I Knew Them,* 231; Beer, *Hanna,* 217.

50. Gompers to Allison, December 6, 1898, Allison papers, ISDHA; Washington *Post,* April 7, 1897.

51. Stoddard, *As I Knew Them,* 232.

52. Beer, *Hanna*, 80.
53. McClellan, *The Gentleman and the Tiger*, 120.
54. Smith, *Dear Mr. President*, 37.
55. J. H. Walker to McKinley, November 13, 1897, McKinley papers, LC; Smith, *Dear Mr. President*, 35; New York *Tribune*, September 28, 1897.
56. *Mark Hanna: His Book*, 64.
57. *Ibid.*, 71; Dawes, *Journal*, 180.
58. Washington *Post*, March 25, 1900; McKinley to Ida Barber, September 25, 1899, McKinley papers, LC.
59. Dawes, *Journal*, 130, 134.
60. McKinley to Helen McKinley, November 20, 1899, McKinley papers, LC.
61. McKinley to W. B. Plunkett, May 7, 1900, *ibid.*; quoted in Leech, *In the Days of McKinley*, 238.
62. Thomas St. John to McKinley, December 17, 1898, McKinley papers, LC.
63. Herrick to McKinley, April 12, 1901, folder in box 217 labelled "Life Insurance," *ibid.*
64. Hoover, *42 Years in the White House*, 272; McKinley, *The Tariff*, 258ff; McKinley to Rhodes, October 24, 1899, McKinley papers, LC.
65. See Ida Tarbell, "President McKinley in War Time," *McClure's Magazine*, 11 (July, 1898), 209–224.
66. Beer, *Hanna*, 108–109.
67. Hoover, *42 Years in the White House*, 252.
68. Hay to McKinley, July 1, 1899, *ibid.*
69. *Mr. Dooley in Peace and War*, 83.
70. McKinley to Webb Hayes, August 10, 1897, Webb C. Hayes papers, HML.

XV: *CUBA LIBRE!*

1. Unfortunately there is no history of the Cuban rebellion in print, nor is there an adequate account of McKinley's diplomacy. John L. Offner, "President McKinley and the Origins of the Spanish-American War," unpublished doctoral thesis, Pennsylvania State University, 1957, is a sound and richly researched study on which I have leaned heavily. The most recent study in print is Ernest R. May, *Imperial Democracy* (New York: Harcourt, Brace and World, 1961). The work is something of a disappointment, since it offers little new information and analysis. Mr. May seems not to understand always how McKinley worked, and in general is unfriendly. He does show the pressures attendant upon diplomacy. He grants far too much influence to the newspapers and public opinion, however, in channeling the President's diplomacy. What information he does present on Spanish diplomacy confirms my own general view that Spain never intended to reform Cuba or grant her anything approaching autonomy, and that her policy was therefore never sincere.
2. H. B. Clarke, *Modern Spain* (Cambridge: Cambridge University Press, 1906), 454ff.
3. French Ensor Chadwick, *Relations of the United States and Spain: Diplomacy* (New York: Charles Scribner's Sons, 1909), 487, 492; W. H. Callcott, *The Caribbean Policy of the United States* (Baltimore: Johns Hopkins Press, 1942), 81.

4. Chadwick, *Relations: Diplomacy,* 430–431; Joseph Wisan, *The Cuban Crisis as Reflected in the New York Press 1895–1898* (New York: Columbia University Press, 1934), 88ff.

5. New York *Journal,* April 14, 1896; Chadwick, *Relations: Diplomacy,* 459.

6. Horatio Rubens, *Liberty* (New York: Brewer, Warren and Putnam, 1932), 123.

7. Wisan, *The Cuban Crisis,* 70ff.

8. Rubens, *Liberty,* 128; James Truslow Adams, *The Epic of America* (Boston: Little, Brown and Co., 1931), 335.

9. *Congressional Record,* 54th Congress, 1st Session, 2244–2248.

10. Olney to de Lome, April 14, 1896, *Papers Relating to the Foreign Relations of the United States* (Washington, 1897), 540–544; hereafter cited as *For. Rels.* See also Duc de Tetuan to de Lome, May 22, 1896, in *Spanish Diplomatic Correspondence and Documents 1896–1900* (Washington, 1905), 8–13; hereafter cited as *Sp. Corr.*

11. Richardson, *Messages and Papers,* IX, 719.

12. De Lome to Sherman, September 28, 1897, *For. Rels. 1897,* 533–534.

13. Chadwick, *Relations: Diplomacy,* 418; Washington *Post,* February 9, 1898; John Berryman, *Stephen Crane* (New York: Wm. Sloane, 1950), 167· Rubens, *Liberty,* 140ff.

14. Frederick H. Gillett, *George Frisbie Hoar* (Boston: Houghton-Mifflin Co. 1934), 195.

15. New York *Times,* February 27, 1895.

16. Frank L. Mott, *American Journalism* (New York, 1947), 537ff; New York *World,* May 17, 1896; Wisan, *The Cuban Crisis,* 459; New York *Journal,* February 23, October 13, 1897.

17. Charles Johnson Post, *The Little War of Private Post* (Boston: Little Brown, 1960), 5.

18. Day to Woodford, March 3, 1898, vol. 22, Instructions to Spain, Record Group 59, NA.

19. George W. Auxier, "The Propaganda Activities of the Cuban *Junta* in Precipitating the Spanish-American War, 1895–1898," *HAHR,* 19 (August, 1939), 286–305; Rubens, *Liberty,* 108, 204–205.

20. *Ibid.,* 105.

21. See Pratt, *Expansionists of 1898,* chap. vii.

22. New York *Journal,* June 1, 1897; Sacramento *Bee,* March 11, 1898.

23. Walter Millis, *The Martial Spirit* (New York: Houghton-Mifflin Co., 1939), 51.

24. Wisan, *The Cuban Crisis,* 102.

25. H. S. Burtt to Chandler, March 28, 1898, Chandler papers, NHHS.

26. Sam H. Acheson, *Joe Bailey: The Last Democrat* (New York: MacMillan Co., 1932), 85–86.

27. Washington *Post,* April 5, 1897.

28. *Ibid.,* May 13–21, 1897; Cleveland *Plain Dealer,* May 21, 1897.

29. Richardson, *William E. Chandler,* 583.

30. New York *Mail and Express,* June 15, 1896; New York *Sun,* February 9, 1897; New York *Journal,* November 6, 1896.

31. Quoted in S. F. Bemis, *The American Secretaries of State and Their Diplomacy,* IX (New York: Alfred Knopf, 1929), 29.

32. Whitelaw Reid to McKinley, December 5, 1896, McKinley papers, LC; *Roosevelt–Lodge Correspondence,* I, 240–241.

33. Long, *The New American Navy,* I, 127–128; John Bassett Moore, *Works,* III, 455–456.

34. Lodge to McKinley, March 21, 1898, McKinley papers, LC; de Lome to Minister of State, October 19, 1897, *Sp. Corr.,* 37.

35. *Roosevelt–Lodge Correspondence,* I, 277.

36. New York *World,* August 4–10, 1897.

37. Sherman to McKinley, February 15, 1897, McKinley papers, LC.

38. Foster to J. A. Porter, August 11, 1897, *ibid.*

39. Sherman to McKinley, August 21, 1897, *ibid.*

40. See the translation of a news clipping under date November 9, 1897, *ibid.* See also Charmion C. Shelby, "Mexico and the Spanish-American War: Some Contemporary Expressions of Opinion," in Thomas C. Cotner and Carlos Castaneda (eds.), *Essays in Mexican History* (Austin: Univ. of Texas Press, 1958), 209–228, for some interesting and infrequently cited examples of Latin press opinion on the Cuban problem and the war itself.

41. Cleveland, *Letters,* 488–449.

42. Frank Aldrich to Dawes, October 11, 1897, Day papers; *Mr. Dooley in Peace and War,* 12; Bristow, *Fraud and Politics,* 29; J. A. Porter to Sherman, March 15, 1898, McKinley papers, LC.

43. Nevins, *Henry White,* 122; Foster, *Diplomatic Memoirs,* II, 255; Dawes, *Journal,* 120; Washington *Post,* June 17, 1897.

44. New York *Tribune,* April 15, 1897; Washington *Post,* March 11, 1897; *Roosevelt–Lodge Correspondence,* I, 267; de Lome to Minister of State, February 13, 1897, *Sp. Corr.,* 24.

45. Washington *Post,* April 29, 1897.

46. *Ibid.,* May 12–15, 1897.

47. Richardson, *Messages and Papers,* X, 23–24.

48. Lee to Day, May 13, 14, 25, June 10, 1897, Consular Letters from Havana, RG 59, NA.

49. J. F. Rusling to McKinley, June 18, 1897, McKinley papers, LC.

50. John J. McCook to Day, September 14, 17, 1897, October 11, 1897, Dwight Braman to McKinley, October 15, 1897, Day papers.

51. Washington *Post,* May 25, 1897.

52. Lee to Sherman, March 17, 1898, vol. 129, Consular Letters from Havana, RG 59, NA.

53. Lee to Sherman, April 20, 1897, *ibid.*

54. Taylor to Sherman, June 6, 1897, vol. 131, Dispatches from Spain, RG 59, NA.

55. Taylor to Sherman, June 7, 1897, *ibid.*

56. Lee to Day, June 8, 1897, vol. 130, Consular Letters from Havana, RG 59, NA.

57. Lee to Day, June 12, July 14, 1897, *ibid.*

58. Sherman to de Lome, June 26, 1897, *For. Rels. 1897,* 507–508.

59. Minister of State to de Lome, August 24, 1897, *Sp. Corr.,* 32–35.

60. Woodford to McKinley, August 23, 1897, Dispatches from Spain, RG 59, NA; Adee to McKinley, August 21, 1897, McKinley papers, LC.

61. Porter to Bliss, August 10, 1897, Porter papers, LC.

62. Adee to Sherman, August 19, 1897, McKinley papers, LC.
63. Woodford to McKinley, September 6, 1897, vol. 131A, Dispatches from Spain, RG 59, NA.
64. See *Sp. Corr.*, 36, 127.
65. Woodford to Sherman, September 29, vol. 131, to McKinley, September 22, 1897, vol. 131A, Dispatches from Spain, RG 59, NA.
66. Woodford to McKinley, September 24, 1897, *ibid.*
67. Day to Woodford, October 1, 1897, vol. 22, Instructions to Spain, RG 59, NA.
68. Woodford to Day, October 6, 1897, vol. 132, Dispatches from Spain, *ibid.*
69. Woodford to Sherman, October 16, 1897, *ibid.*
70. Woodford to Sherman, October 26, 1897, *ibid.*
71. J. A. Springer to Day, November 4, 1897, Dispatches from Havana, RG 59, NA; Sherman to de Lome, November 6, 1897, *For. Rels. 1897*, 509–510.
72. Woodford to McKinley, November 7, 1897, vol. 131A, Dispatches from Spain, RG 59, NA.
73. De Lome to Sherman, November 10, 1897, *For. Rels. 1897*, 510–511; *Sp. Corr.*, 39.
74. Woodford to Sherman, November 13, 1897, vol. 132, Dispatches from Spain, RG 59, NA; Woodford to McKinley, November 14, 1897, *ibid.*
75. Woodford to Sherman, November 27, 1897, *ibid.*, encloses the royal decrees. See Wisan, *The Cuban Crisis*, 349ff, for press reaction to the plan.
76. Woodford to McKinley, November 27, 1897, vol. 131A, Dispatches from Spain.
77. Washington *Post*, November 24, 1897.
78. Lee to Day, November 23, 27, 1897, Consular Dispatches from Havana, RG 59, NA.
79. De Lome to Minister of State, December 16, 1897, *Sp. Corr.*, 52.
80. De Lome to Minister of State, December 2, 1897, *Sp. Corr.*, 43.
81. Richardson, *Messages and Papers*, X, 30–38.
82. Washington *Post*, December 7, 8, 1897; W. D. Sloan to Alger, December 8, 1897, Alger papers, WLCL.
83. Woodford to McKinley, December 11, 1897, vol. 131A, Dispatches from Spain, RG 59, NA; Captain Bliss to Major Wagner, January 3, 1898, Alger papers, WLCL.
84. Day to Lee, December 2, 1897, vol. 158, Instructions to Consuls, RG 59, NA; Lee to Day, December 7, 1897, Dispatches from Havana, *ibid.*
85. Woodford to Minister of State, December 20, 1897, *Sp. Corr.*, 52ff.
86. Lodge to Albert Griffin, December 31, 1897, Lodge papers, MHS.

XVI: *FROM PEACE TO WAR*

1. Lee to Day, January 8, 1898, Dispatches from Havana, RG 59, NA; Woodford to McKinley, January 8, 1898, vol. 131A, Dispatches from Spain, *ibid.*
2. Washington *Post*, January 13, 1898.
3. De Lome to Minister of State, January 14, 1898, *Sp. Corr.*, 64.
4. De Lome to Minister of State, January 14, 1898, *ibid.*, 64–65.

5. Woodford to McKinley, January 17, 1898, vol. 131A, Dispatches from Spain, RG 59, NA.

6. Quoted in Millis, *The Martial Spirit*, 35.

7. Lee to Day, January 18, 1898, Dispatches from Havana, RG 59, NA; de Lome to Minister of State, January 20, 1898, *Sp. Corr.*, 67.

8. De Lome to Minister of State, January 28, 1898, *ibid.*

9. The translation used here is from *For Rels. 1898*, 1007–1008, and is cited because of its official nature.

10. New York *Journal*, February 9, 1898.

11. New York *World*, February 15, 1898.

12. Rubens, *Liberty*, 387ff; see also *For. Rels. 1898*, 1018–1020.

13. Long, *America of Yesterday*, 162.

14. Chicago *Herald*, February 12, 1898.

15. Undated memo, Day papers.

16. Washington *Post*, February 12, 1898.

17. Woodford to Sherman, February 11, 14, 1898, vol. 133, Dispatches from Spain, RG 59, NA.

18. Woodford to McKinley, February 15, 1898, vol. 131A, *ibid.*

19. Woodford to Sherman, February 17, 1898, *ibid.;* Day to Woodford, February 18, March 3, 1898, Instructions to Spain, RG 59, NA.

20. Woodford to Sherman, February 3, 1898, to McKinley, January 18, 1898, vol. 131A, Dispatches from Spain, RG 59, NA.

21. Interview with the Spanish Minister, January 24, 1898, Day papers.

22. See Lee to Day, January 15, 1898, *ibid.;* Lee to Day, January 26, February 5, 1898, Dispatches from Havana, RG 59, NA.

23. Washington *Post*, January 25, 26, 1898.

24. C. D. Sigsbee, "Personal Narrative of the *Maine*," *Century Magazine*, 57 (November, 1898—January, 1899), 74–97, 241–263, 373–394.

25. Millis, *The Martial Spirit*, 102.

26. *Sp. Corr.*, 86.

27. Dingley, *Nelson Dingley*, 454.

28. Olcott, *William McKinley*, II, 12.

29. Long, *America of Yesterday*, 165.

30. Washington *Post*, February 16–18, 1898.

31. *Sp. Corr.*, 88.

32. Long, *America of Yesterday*, 171–172.

33. Quoted in Herman Hagedorn, *Leonard Wood*, 2 vols. (New York: Harper Bros., 1931), I, 141.

34. McKinley, *Speeches and Addresses* (1900), 77.

35. Boston *Transcript*, March 3, 1898.

36. New York *Tribune*, February 18, 1898.

37. *Sp. Corr.*, 88.

38. Day to Woodford, March 3, 1898, vol. 22, Instructions to Spain, RG 59, NA.

39. Busby, *Uncle Joe Cannon*, 186–198.

40. Washington *Post*, March 5–8, 1898.

41. Woodford to McKinley, March 9, 1898, vol. 131A, Dispatches from Spain, RG 59, NA.

42. Washington *Post*, March 12, 1898.

43. *Sp. Corr.*, 91.

44. *Congressional Record*, 55th Congress, 2nd Session, 2915ff.

45. New York *Times*, March 18–25, 1898; Dunn, *From Harrison to Harding*, I, 234; *Wall Street Journal*, March 19, 1898; *Sp. Corr.*, 93.

46. See Offner, "President McKinley and the Origins of the Spanish-American War," 276ff.

47. Woodford to McKinley, February 26, 1898, vol. 131A, Dispatches from Spain, RG 59, NA.

48. Woodford to Sherman, February 28, 1898, vol. 133, *ibid.*

49. Woodford to McKinley, March 17, 1898, vol 131A, *ibid.*; Day to Woodford, March 20, 1898, vol. 22, Instructions to Spain, *ibid.*

50. Acheson, *Joe Bailey*, 98–99; Oscar Straus to J. B. Angell, March 22, 1898, Straus papers, LC.

51. Long, *The New American Navy*, I, 141.

52. Lodge to Mr. Wright, February 28, 1898, Lodge papers, MHS.

53. See Young, *Life and Times of Art Young*, 195–196.

54. Washington *Post*, March 31, 1898; Rubens, *Liberty*, 336–337.

55. New York *Times*, February 19, 1898; Reid to Elkins, April 19, 1898, Reid papers, LC; A. W. Dunn, *Gridiron Nights* (New York: Frederick A. Stokes Co., 1915), 72.

56. Richardson, *Messages and Papers*, X, 52–55.

57. Chicago *Tribune*, February 27, 1898.

58. Day to Woodford, March 27, 1898, vol. 22, Instructions to Spain, RG 59, NA.

59. Day to Woodford, March 30, 1898, *ibid.*

60. Woodford to Sherman, Mar 21, 1898, vol. 133, to McKinley, March 24, 1898, vol. 131A, Dispatches from Spain, RG 59, NA.

61. Undated memo in McKinley's writing, Day papers.

62. Lodge to Henry [?], March 7, 1898, Lodge papers, MHS.

63. Chandler to Paul Dana, March 29, 1898, Chandler papers, LC.

64. Hobart, *Memories*, 61.

65. Olcott, *William McKinley*, II, 28; Dawes, *Journal*, 154; Acheson, *Joe Bailey*, 98–100; Hobart, *Memories*, 60.

66. Woodford to McKinley, March 17, 1898, vol. 131A, Dispatches from Spain.

67. Long, *America of Yesterday*, 184; Kohlsaat, *From McKinley to Harding*, 66–67.

68. Woodford to McKinley, March 25, 26, vol. 131A, Dispatches from Spain, RG 59, NA; Day to Woodford, March 26, 1898, vol. 22, Instructions to Spain, *ibid.*; Interview with Spanish Minister, March 29, 1898, Day papers.

69. Woodford to McKinley, March 29, 1898, vol. 131A, Dispatches from Spain, RG 59, NA.

70. New York *Tribune*, April 1, 1898.

71. Woodford to Day, March 31, 1898, *For. Rels. 1898*, 726–727.

72. *Sp. Corr.*, 107–108; Long, America of Yesterday, 165.

73. Woodford to McKinley, March 31, April 1, 1898, vol. 131A, Dispatches from Spain, RG 59, NA.

74. Day to Woodford, April 4, 1898, vol. 22, Instructions to Spain, *ibid.*

75. Woodford to Day, April 5, 1898, Dispatches from Spain, *ibid.*

76. Quoted in Acheson, *Joe Bailey*, 103.

77. Lee to Day, April 16, 1898, Consular Letters from Havana, RG 58, NA.

78. Olcott, *William McKinley*, II, 29.

79. Quoted in Leech, *In the Days of McKinley*, 190.

80. Woodford to Day, April 6, 1898, vol. 133, Dispatches from Spain, RG 59, NA.

81. Woodford to Day, April 8, 1898, Day papers; Washington *Post*, April 11, 1898; Woodford to McKinley, April 10, 1898, vol. 131A, Dispatches from Spain, RG 59, NA.

82. Elkins to A. B. White, April 9, 1898, White papers, WVU.

83. Offner, "President McKinley and the Origins of the Spanish-Amercan War," 336ff; Richardson, *Messages and Papers*, X, 85.

84. C. Parker to McKinley, August 6, 1900, McKinley papers, LC.

85. Filed under date July 19, 1899, *ibid.*

86. Henry S. Pritchett, "Some Recollections of President McKinley and the Cuban Intervention," *North American Review*, 189 (March, 1909), 397–403.

87. Long, *America of Yesterday*, 176.

88. Richardson, *Messages and Papers*, X, 560–567.

89. Acheson, *Joe Bailey*, 105; Chandler Diary, April 11, 1898, NHHS; Washington *Post*, April 12, 1898.

90. See Chandler to Paul Dana, April 13, 1898, Chandler papers, LC.

91. Washington *Post*, April 25, 1898.

XVII. *COMMANDER-IN-CHIEF*

1. There is no adequate account of the war. The most famous book is Millis, *The Martial Spirit*, which is readable and accurate, but which unfortunately makes the war seem small and comical. Frank Freidel, *Splendid Little War* (New York: Little, Brown Co., 1958), is largely a picture book and its text adds nothing new. The participant's view is best stated in C. J. Post, *The Little War of Private Post*.

2. Porter to G. M. Dodge, June 22, 1898, to Day, May 24, 1898, to E. A. Hitchcock, June 25, 1898, Porter papers, LC.

3. Carnegie to McKinley, April 27, 1898, McKinley papers, LC.

4. Day to Hay, July 14, 1898, Hay papers, LC; Nevins, *Henry White*, 133–134; Pauncefote to Day, August 15, 1898, copy McKinley papers, LC; Washington *Post*, January 3, 1899; Hay to McKinley, September 9, 1898, reprinted in Olcott, *William McKinley*, II, 135.

5. Chandler to Frank Jones, May 6, 1898, Chandler papers, LC; New York *Times*, April 24, 1898.

6. Helen M. Gould to McKinley, April 23, 1898, McKinley papers, LC; McKinley to Bryan, May 7, 1898, McKinley papers, LC.

7. Millis, *The Martial Spirit*, 214–215.

8. Boston *Journal*, May 12, 1898; Post, *The Little War of Private Post*, 812

9. Randall and Ryan, *History of Ohio*, IV, 419.

10. Alger to McKinley, May 26, 1898, McKinley papers, LC.

11. Dunn, *From Harrison to Harding*, I, 241; Leech, *In the Days of McKinley*, 236.

12. Olcott, *William McKinley,* II, 264; Post, *The Little War of Private Post,* 214–215.

13. Washington *Post,* May 6, 1898; Charles Eagan to F. J. Hecker, July 4, 1898, Hecker papers, WLCL.

14. McCook to Wilson, June 4, 1898, Wilson papers, LC.

15. *Roosevelt–Lodge Correspondence,* I, 303ff.

16. See vol. 34, n.d., McKinley papers, LC, apparently in answer to Alger's letter of December 28, 1899.

17. Olcott, *William McKinley,* II, 366–367.

18. Pringle, *Theodore Roosevelt,* 466.

19. Long, *The New American Navy,* I, 177.

20. *Ibid.,* I, 181–182; Long to Dewey, April 24, 1898, copy in McKinley papers, LC.

21. Millis, *The Martial Spirit,* 188.

22. Henry S. Pritchett, "Some Recollections of President McKinley and the Cuban Intervention," *North American Review,* 189 (March, 1909), 397–403.

23. Millis, *The Martial Spirit,* 181ff; Baltimore *American,* June 11, 1898; cf. New York *Tribune,* May 5, 1898, Cleveland *Plain Dealer,* May 5, 1898, Chicago *Inter-Ocean,* May 31, 1898.

24. Washington *Post,* May 6, 1898; Frye to Wilson, June 6, 1898, Wilson papers, LC; Leon Wolff, *Little Brown Brother* (New York: Doubleday, 1961), 159.

25. Mott, *Myron T. Herrick,* 325.

26. Kohlsaat, *From McKinley to Harding,* 68.

27. Dawes, *Journal,* 166; W. M. Laffan to Lodge, July 14, 1898, Lodge papers, MHS. Laffan was apparently a staff member for the New York *Sun.*

28. See James A. LeRoy, *The Americans in the Philippines,* 2 vols. (New York: Houghton Mifflin Co., 1914), I, 184; Millis, *The Martial Spirit,* 252; see dispatches dated June 22, July 20, 1898, in the B. F. Montgomery papers, HML; Long, *The New American Navy,* II, 107.

29. Montgomery papers, May 25, HML; McKinley's letter of instruction is dated May 19, reprinted in U.S. War Department, *Correspondence Relating to the War with Spain . . . ,* 2 vols. (Washington, 1902), II, 676–678, hereafter cited as *War with Spain.*

30. Alger, *The Spanish-American War,* 46; Alger to G. M. Dodge, May 21, 1898, Alger papers, WLCL.

31. U.S. War Department, *Report of the Commission Appointed by the President to Investigate the Conduct of the War Department in the War with Spain,* 8 vols. (Washington, 1899), II, 872–873, hereafter cited as *Dodge Comm. Rept.*

32. Alger to W. Livingstone, June 4, 1898, Alger papers, WLCL.

33. Millis, *The Martial Spirit,* 274.

34. Long, *The New American Navy,* I, 175–177; Alger, *The Spanish-American War,* 173; Foraker, *I Would Live It Again,* 220.

35. Hobart to Alger, July 4, 1898, Alger papers, WLCL; Shafter to Corbin, July 4, 5, 1898, Montgomery papers, HML.

36. Alger to Shafter, July 4, 1898, Corbin to Shafter, July 9, 1898, *ibid.;* Alger to Shafter, July 15, 1898, Montgomery papers, HML.

37. Washington *Post,* June 19, 1898.

38. Alger, *The Spanish-American War,* 48.

39. Porter to Kohlsaat, July 6, 1898, McKinley papers, LC.

40. Hanna to McKinley, May 2, 1898; Herrick to McKinley, July 30, 1898, in McKinley papers, LC; see Leech, *In the Days of McKinley,* 281, 292.

41. Long, *America of Yesterday,* 200; Alger to Miles, July 23, 1898, Alger papers, WLCL.

42. Miles to Alger, July 12, 1898, Shafter to Alger, August 4, 1898, Montgomery papers, HML; Shafter to Corbin, August 16, 1898, Corbin papers, LC.

43. McKinley to Shafter, August 5, 1898, Montgomery papers, HML; Alger to Charles Moore, August 6, 1898, Alger papers, WLCL.

44. McKinley to Alger, August 24, 1898, Montgomery papers, HML; see also Alger to Roger Woolcott, September 6, 1898, Montgomery papers, HML.

45. New York *Tribune,* September 4, 1898.

46. Alger, *The Spanish-American War,* 40.

47. Spencer Borden to McKinley, September 22, 1898, McKinley papers, LC; Dawes, *Journal,* 158.

48. Day to Hay, June 7, 1898, Hay papers, LC. Elbert J. Benton, *The International Law and Diplomacy of the Spanish-American War* (Baltimore; The Johns Hopkins Press, 1908), 220–221.

49. See Olcott, *William McKinley,* II, 57–75.

50. See U.S. Senate, 55th Congress, 3rd Session, Document No. 62, *A Treaty of Peace Between the United States and Spain . . .* (Washington, 1899), hereafter cited as *Treaty of Peace.*

51. *Sp. Corr.,* 216–217.

52. James Wilson to Allison, August 3, 1898, Allison papers, ISDHA; Olcott, *William McKinley,* II, 345; Diary of Whitelaw Reid, September 28, 1898, LC.

53. Philadelphia *Inquirer,* August 15, 1898.

54. Olcott, *William McKinley,* II, 64–66; the memo is filed under date July 26, McKinley papers, LC; *Sp. Corr.,* 208–209.

55. Porter to Hanna, August 2, 1898, Porter papers, LC; Proctor to Alger, August 15, 1898, Alger papers, WLCL; *Mr. Dooley in Peace and War,* 9.

XVIII: *MAKING PEACE*

1. Quoted in Olcott, *William McKinley,* II, 366.

2. Nevins, *Henry White,* 138–139; Dennis, *Adventures in American Diplomacy,* 82.

3. Hoar to J. W. Daniel, September 7, 1898, Daniel papers, DUL; Hoar to McKinley, September 14, 1898, McKinley papers, LC.

4. Lodge to Davis, August 11, 1898, Lodge papers, MHS; Allison to Aldrich, August 20, 1898, Aldrich papers, LC; Chandler to McKinley, August 17, 1898, McKinley papers, LC. McKinley approached several members of the Supreme Court for inclusion on the commission but they declined.

5. See Pratt, *Expansionists of 1898,* chapter VIII.

6. G. F. Seward to Hay, November 7, 1898, Hay papers, LC; J. F. Rhodes to McKinley, July 28, 1898, McKinley papers, LC.

7. Steiner Brothers to McKinley, August 31, 1898, I. M. Scott to J. B. Moore, August 4, 1898, *ibid.;* Pratt, *Expansionists of 1898,* 265–270.

8. Thomas A. Bailey, "Dewey and the Germans at Manila Bay," *AHR,* 45

(October, 1939), 59–81, disproves the old theory of German hostility, but Americans in 1898 thought otherwise.

9. Beer, *Hanna,* 212.

10. Adee to J. B. Moore with enclosure, November 9, 1898, Instructions to the Paris Peace Commission, RG 43, NA.

11. Undated memo, McKinley papers, LC, reprinted in Olcott, *William Mc-Kinley,* II, 165.

12. Long to McKinley, August 9, 1898, enclosed in Paris Peace Conference Records, RG 43, NA.

13. Beer, *Hanna,* 207; Spencer Borden to McKinley, June 10, 1898, McKinley papers, LC; Coolidge, *Orville H. Platt,* 287–290.

14. See Young, *Life and Times of Art Young,* 198; Joseph Medill to McKinley, October 17, 1898, McKinley papers, LC.

15. Long, *America of Yesterday,* 215; Dawes, *Journal,* 176.

16. *Roosevelt–Lodge Correspondence,* I, 299–300, 313, 232, 330.

17. Washington *Post,* September 14, 1898.

18. Otis to Corbin, October 19, 1898, Montgomery papers, HML; Adee to Moore, October 20, 1898, with enclosures, Instructions to the Paris Peace Commission, RG 43, NA.

19. See the remarkable letter from Wildman to Aquinaldo, July 25, 1898, in the J. R. Thomas, Jr. papers, LC; Dean C. Worcester, *The Philippines Past and Present* (New York: MacMillan and Co., 1930), 109.

20. Olcott, *William McKinley,* II, 146, 156; *Dodge Comm. Rept.,* II, 1337; *War with Spain,* II, 809.

21. Corbin to Merritt, August 17, 1898, reprinted in Richardson, *Messages and Papers,* X, 354.

22. Memo filed under date October 1, 1898, McKinley papers, LC.

23. September 16, 1898, Reid Diary, LC.

24. *For. Rels. 1898,* 904–908.

25. His speeches are reprinted in *Speeches and Addresses* (1900), 84–155.

26. Cole, *I Remember, I Remember,* 282–283; Washington *Post,* October 17, 1898; *Speeches and Addresses* (1900), 109.

27. McKinley to Reid, October 31, 1898, Reid papers, LC.

28. Millis, *The Martial Spirit,* 383; Lodge to Davis, November 18, 1898, Lodge papers, MHS; Hanna to McKinley, November 15, 1898, McKinley papers, LC.

29. Day to McKinley, September 30, 1898, McKinley papers, LC.

30. Reid to McKinley, October 4, 1898, McKinley papers, LC.

31. Day to Hay, October 12, 1898, McKinley papers, LC; Day to McKinley, October 14, 1898, *ibid.*

32. October 20, 1898, Reid Diary, LC.

33. Day to McKinley, October 23, 1898, McKinley papers, LC; Hay to Day, October 25, 1898, Instructions to the Paris Peace Commission, RG 43, NA; Day to Hay, October 27, 1898, Montgomery papers, HML.

34. October 1, 1898, Reid Diary, LC.

35. See *Treaty of Peace,* 319–677; October 3, 7, 14, Reid Diary, LC.

36. October 4, 1898, *ibid.*

37. Day to Hay, October 7, 1898, Reports from the Paris Peace Commission, RG 43, NA; Dewey to Long, October 13, 1898, Montgomery papers, HML.

38. Davis to Foraker, October 25, 1898, Foraker papers, LC; Day to Hay, October 25, 1898, McKinley papers, LC.

39. See Olcott, *William McKinley*, II, 107–108.

40. Day to Hay, October 25, 1898, Reports from the Paris Peace Commission, RG 43, NA.

41. See Olcott, *William McKinley*, II, 109–110.

42. John W. Foster, *American Diplomacy in the Orient* (New York: Houghton-Mifflin Co., 1903), 403, nl; Julius W. Pratt, "The 'Large Policy' of 1898," *MVHR*, 19 (September, 1932), 219–242.

43. Olcott, *William McKinley*, II, 308–309.

44. Day to Adee, October 27, 1898, Reports from the Paris Peace Commission, RG 43, NA.

45. Frye to McKinley, October 30, 1898, Hay to Frye, November 1, 1898, Montgomery papers, HML.

46. October 31–November 1, 1898, Reid Diary, LC.

47. *Sp. Corr.*, 309–311.

48. Day to McKinley, November 2, 1898, McKinley papers, LC.

49. Peace Commissioners to McKinley, November 11, 1898, *ibid.*; Hay to Day, November 13, 1898, Instructions to the Paris Peace Commission, RG 43, NA; Hay to Day, November 14, 1898, *ibid.*

50. Reid to McKinley, November 15, 1898, McKinley papers, LC.

51. Day to McKinley, November 19, 1898, *ibid.; Sp. Corr.*, 326.

52. November 28, 1898, Reid Diary, LC.

53. *Sp. Corr.*, 364.

54. Day to McKinley, December 12, 1898, McKinley papers, LC.

55. *Speeches and Addresses* (1900), 158–184.

56. Day to McKinley, November 19, 1898, McKinley papers, LC.

57. *Roosevelt–Lodge Correspondence*, I, 368.

58. Hoar, *Autobiography*, II, 315.

59. Roosevelt to Lodge, January 26, 1899, Roosevelt papers, LC.

60. Carnegie to McKinley, February 2, 1899, McKinley papers, LC.

61. New York *Times*, October 24, 1898.

62. Hay to Reid, November 29, 1898, Hay papers, LC.

63. Carnegie to Schurz, December 27, 1898, Carnegie papers, LC.

64. Fred H. Harrington, "The Anti-Imperialist Movement in the United States 1898–1900," *MVHR*, 22 (September, 1935), 211–230.

65. See Paolo Coletta, "Bryan, McKinley, and the Treaty of Paris," *PHR*, 26 (May, 1957), 131–146.

66. Omaha *World-Herald*, June 15, 1898, January 7, 1899; Washington *Post*, December 24, 1898.

67. Bryan to Carnegie, December 24, 30, 1898, Carnegie papers, LC.

68. Bryan to Carnegie, December 30, 1898, *ibid.*; W. J. Bryan, *Memoirs* (New York, 1925), 121–122.

69. Carnegie to Bryan, January 10 [1899], Bryan papers, LC; Gillett, *George Frisbie Hoar*, 225; Bryan to Carnegie, January 13, 30, 1899, Carnegie papers, LC.

70. *Congressional Record*, 55th Congress, 3rd Session, 502–503.

71. See Millis, *The Martial Spirit*, 394ff.

72. See Olcott, *William McKinley*, II, 138.

73. *Roosevelt–Lodge Correspondence*, I, 388, 391–392; New York *Journal*,

February 4, 1899; Pettigrew, *Imperial Washington,* 204–206; Morgan to Henry Watterson, December 10, 1903, Morgan papers, LC; W. Stull Holt, *Treaties Defeated by the Senate* (Baltimore: The Johns Hopkins Press, 1933), 172–173.

74. Hanna to McKinley, February 7, 9, 1899, McKinley papers, LC; Dunn, *From Harrison to Harding,* I, 282; Lodge to Paul Dana, January 25, 1899, Lodge papers, LHS.

75. Corbin to Merritt, August 17, 1898, Alger to Otis, December 20, 1898, *War with Spain,* II, 754, 864; Otis to Corbin, November 13, 1898, *ibid.,* 836; Otis to Corbin, November 27, 1898, to Alger, December 8, 1898, Montgomery papers, HML; Dewey to Long, January 30, 1899, McKinley papers, LC, copy.

76. *Literary Digest,* 18 (January 28, 1899), 93–94.

77. See Leech, *In the Days of McKinley,* 334.

78. *Ibid.,* 358; Dawes, *Journal,* 182; Washington *Post,* February 6, 1899.

79. *Speeches and Addresses* (1900), 216.

80. *Roosevelt–Lodge Correspondence,* I, 391–392.

81. Washington *Post,* February 7, 1899; Hay to Roosevelt, February 10, 1899, Roosevelt papers, LC; Lodge to Leonard Wood, February 7, 1899, Lodge papers, MHS.

82. February 6, 1899, Chandler Diary, NHHS; *Roosevelt–Lodge Correspondence,* I, 390–391.

83. Carnegie, *Autobiography,* 362; Carnegie to Schurz, February 10, 1899, Carnegie papers, LC; Gorman to Carnegie, February 9, 1899, *ibid.*

84. Gillett, *George Frisbie Hoar,* 228. A resolution introduced by Senator McEnery of Louisiana, favoring future local self-government for the Filipinos, though they were never to become U.S. citizens, passed by a vote of 26 to 22.

85. *Speeches and Addresses* (1900), 185–193; New York *Tribune,* February 17, 1899.

XIX: *PROBLEMS OF EMPIRE*

1. *Dodge Comm. Rept.,* I, 237.

2. Post, *Little War of Private Post,* 325ff.

3. Wilson to Allison, August 27, 1898, Allison papers, ISDHA.

4. See the long memo filed under date October 2, 1898, Alger papers, WLCL.

5. *Roosevelt–Lodge Correspondence,* I, 343.

6. Dodge to McKinley, September 10, 1898, McKinley papers, LC.

7. Dodge to H. V. Boynton, March 28, 1899, *ibid.*

8. *Dodge Comm. Rept.,* I, 156.

9. Alger to Hoar, February 8, 1902, Alger papers, WLCL.

10. Hanna to McKinley, April 1, 1899, McKinley papers, LC.

11. Leech, *In the Days of McKinley,* 383.

12. Hagedorn, *Leonard Wood,* I, 228–229.

13. *Dodge Comm. Rept.,* I, 121, 147–149; Dodge to H. J. Gallagher, February 15, 1899, Dodge papers, ISDHA.

14. Dodge to McKinley, April 20, 1899, McKinley papers, LC.

15. Dodge to General J. P. Sanger, February 24, 1899, Dodge papers, ISDHA.

16. Leech, *In the Days of McKinley,* 366–367.

17. Washington *Post,* September 22, 1898.

18. New York *Tribune*, February 18, 1899.

19. Dawes, *Journal*, 187–188.

20. *Roosevelt–Lodge Correspondence*, I, 399, 400; New York *Herald*, July 12, 1899.

21. See the memo filed under date July 19, 1899, McKinley papers, LC. There is no such message in the Alger papers, WLCL, which seems to indicate that the President did not send the text.

22. Washington *Post*, July 13, 1899; Hay to McKinley, July 13, 1899, McKinley papers, LC; Olcott, *William McKinley*, II, 90–91.

23. See the memo filed under date November 26, 1900, Alger papers, WLCL. There is no other record of the conversation and Alger may have magnified his harshness toward McKinley.

24. Olcott, *William McKinley*, II, 90–91.

25. McKinley to Alger, Alger to McKinley, July 19, 1899, McKinley papers, LC.

26. Hobart, *Memories*, 68–69.

27. Phillip Jessup, *Elihu Root*, 2 vols. (New York: Dodd, Mead Co., 1938), I, 215. Platt, *Autobiography*, 403ff., tells a slightly different and less creditable story.

28. Alger to Root, July 21, 1899, McKinley papers, LC.

29. Root to McKinley, July 24, 1899, *ibid.*

30. Leech, *In the Days of McKinley*, 380.

31. *Roosevelt–Lodge Correspondence*, I, 414.

32. Platt to Allison, July 26, 1899, Allison papers, ISDHA.

33. Proctor to McKinley, October 28, 1899, McKinley papers, LC.

34. Jessup, *Elihu Root*, I, 219.

35. Leech, *In the Days of McKinley*, 384.

36. Quoted in Thomas A. Bailey, *A Diplomatic History of the American People*, 6th edition (New York: Appleton-Century-Crofts, 1958), 478.

37. Quoted in G. A. Grunder and W. E. Livezey, *The Philippines and the United States* (Norman: Univ. of Oklahoma Press, 1951), 51.

38. *Mr. Dooley's Philosophy*, 133.

39. Millis, *The Martial Spirit*, 406.

40. *Ibid.*

41. Pettigrew to McKinley, April 17, 1899, McKinley papers, LC.

42. *Speeches and Addresses* (1900), 211–217.

43. *Ibid.*, 302.

44. *Ibid.*, 361–366.

45. Richardson, *Messages and Papers*, X, 240ff.

46. *Ibid.*, X, 160–172.

47. J. T. Dickman to W. T. Manning, May 16, 1900, Dickman papers, HML. See also, *War with Spain*, II, 1220–1221; Wolff, *Little Brown Brother*, 261–263.

48. *Ibid.*, 140–141.

49. McKinley to Root, August 19, 1899, McKinley papers, LC.

50. Otis to Corbin, April 20, 1899, *ibid.*

51. See LeRoy, *Americans in the Philippines*, II, 55.

52. Otis to Corbin, February 6, 1900, McKinley papers, LC.

53. Wheeler to McKinley, October 29, November 28, 1899, *ibid.*

54. Root to Abbott, December 13, 1899, Root papers, LC.

55. Dewey, *Autobiography*, 285; LeRoy, *Americans in the Philippines*, I, 418, n2.

56. Jacob G. Schurman, *Philippine Affairs* (New York: Charles Scribner's Sons, 1902), 1–2.

57. *Report of the United States Philippine Commission*, 4 vols. (Washington, 1899), I, *passim*.

58. Hay to Schurman, May 5, 1899, reprinted *ibid.*, I, 9.

59. Schurman to Hay, July 4, 1899, McKinley papers, LC.

60. *Report of the Philippine Commission*, I, 121.

61. Otis to Corbin, November 18, 1899, McKinley papers, LC.

62. McKinley to Day, January 30, 1900, *ibid.*

63. Henry F. Pringle, *The Life and Times of William Howard Taft*, 2 vols. (New York: Farrar and Rinehart, 1939), I, 158–160.

64. *Ibid.*, I, 165–166. The other commission members were: Luke Wright, Tennessee; Henry C. Ide, Vermont; Dean C. Worcester, Michigan; and Bernard Moses, California.

65. Olcott, *William McKinley*, II, 178.

66. See McKinley to Taft, May 26, 1900, Taft papers, LC.

67. Worcester, *The Philippines*, 272.

68. Taft to Roosevelt, June 27, 1900, Roosevelt papers, LC; to Charles P. Taft, October 2, December 13, 1900, Taft papers, LC; Pringle, *William Howard Taft*, I, 193–194.

69. Commission to Root, August 21, 1900, McKinley papers, LC.

70. Jose Ner to MacArthur, August 8, 1900, copy *ibid.*

71. Root to A. R. Chaffee, February 26, 1901, copy *ibid.*

72. Dunn, *From Harrison to Harding*, I, 257.

73. Taft to Root, April 3, 1901, Taft papers, LC.

74. Richardson, *Messages and Papers*, X, 97, 350ff; McKinley to General J. R. Brooke, December 22, 1898, McKinley papers, LC.

75. Root to Paul Dana, January 16, 1900, Root papers, LC.

76. *For. Rels., 1899*, xxxviii; Elihu Root, *The Military and Colonial Policy of the United States* (Cambridge, 1916), 171.

77. Hagedorn, *Leonard Wood*, I, 261.

78. *Ibid.*, 214–215, 251.

79. *Ibid.*, I, 266.

80. *Ibid.*, I, 213; Wood to Root, February 6, 1900, Root papers, LC.

81. Hagedorn, *Leonard Wood*, I, 270.

82. *Ibid.*, 272.

83. See Fitzgibbon, *Cuba and the United States*, 62ff.

84. Coolidge, *Orville H. Platt*, 326.

85. Bristow, *Fraud and Politics*, 100.

86. Hagedorn, *Leonard Wood*, I, 295.

87. *Ibid.*, I, 295.

88. *Ibid.*, I, 328.

89. Root to Hay, January 11, 1901, Hay papers, LC, cited also in Dennis, *Adventures in American Diplomacy*, 261–262.

90. Root to Wood, February 9, 1901, copy in McKinley papers, LC.

91. Wood to Roosevelt, April 12, 1902, cited in Hagedorn, *Leonard Wood*, I, 357.

92. Root to Wood, April 13, 1901, Montgomery papers, HML.

93. See Fitzgibbon, *The United States and Cuba,* 84–87; Dennis, *Adventures in American Diplomacy,* 263ff. The Platt Amendment was formally revoked in 1934.

94. Root, *Military and Colonial Policy,* 215.

95. Elisha Ely to McKinley, April 9, 1901, McKinley papers, LC.

XX: *THE DIPLOMACY OF POWER*

1. Thayer, *Life and Letters of John Hay,* II, 393.

2. *Ibid.,* 221.

3. *Speeches and Addresses* (1900), 102.

4. Foster, *Diplomatic Memoirs,* II, 184.

5. See Adee to Hay, May 4, 1897, Hay papers, LC.

6. Lionel M. Gelber, *The Rise of Anglo-American Friendship* (New York: Oxford Univ. Press, 1938), 37–38; Hay to Choate, May 22, 1899, Hay papers, LC; Hay to Roosevelt, July 14, 1899, Roosevelt papers, LC.

7. Dennis, *Adventures in American Diplomacy,* 140.

8. Hay to Choate, June 15, 1899, Hay papers, LC.

9. Hay to McKinley, August 19, 1899, *ibid.*

10. J. A. Porter to Adee, July 31, 1897, McKinley papers, LC; Sherman to Morgan, June 5, 1897, Hiram Hitchcock to Morgan, November 24, 1897, Morgan papers, LC.

11. See J. A. S. Grenville, "Great Britain and the Isthmian Canal," *AHR,* 51 (October, 1955), 48–69; Richard Olney to Hay, November 15, 1898, Hay papers, LC.

12. See Allan Nevins, *Henry White* (New York: Harper Bros., 1930), 144ff; Callcott, *The Caribbean Policy of the United States,* 119.

13. Dennis, *Adventures in American Diplomacy,* 158.

14. Leech, *In the Days of McKinley,* 508.

15. Holt, *Treaties Defeated by the Senate,* 184, n10, 188ff; Stewart to Hay, February 6, 1900, Hay papers, LC.

16. Nevins, *Henry White,* 150–151; Hay to J. J. McCook, April 22, 1900, Hay papers, LC.

17. The letters are reprinted in Thayer, *The Life and Letters of John Hay,* II, 226–228.

18. February 14, 1900, Roosevelt papers, LC; Roosevelt to William Cowles, February 16, *ibid.*

19. New York *Times,* March 4, 1900; Callcott, *American Policy in the Caribbean,* 121.

20. Leech, *In the Days of McKinley,* 512.

21. Elkins to Reid, March 2, 1900, Reid papers, LC.

22. Nevins, *Henry White,* 154–155.

23. McKinley to Hay, September 21, 1900, Hay papers, LC; Morgan to McKinley, August 9, 1897, Morgan papers, LC; Morgan to McKinley, September 22, 1900, McKinley papers, LC; Hay to McKinley, September 23, 1900, *ibid.*

24. Hay to Choate, December 21, 1900, Hay papers, LC; Hay to Henry Watterson, December 28, 1900, *ibid.*

25. Dennet, *John Hay*, 258; Morgan to Hay, February 9, 1901, McKinley papers, LC.

26. Carnegie, *Autobiography*, 359; Hoar to Lodge, May 31, 1901, Lodge papers, MHS.

27. Lyman Gage to W. T. Stead, December 30, 1898, Gage papers, LC.

28. Low to McKinley, June 13, 1899, McKinley papers, LC; White to Depew, July 25, 1899, Depew papers, LC.

29. See White to Hay, December 22, 1898, Montgomery papers, HML; Memorandum for Secretary James Wilson, January 4, 1900, Hay to McKinley, August 1, 1901, White to Hay, September 5, 1901, all in McKinley papers, LC.

30. C. D. Pierce to Hay, September 19, 1899, copy *ibid.;* Washington *Post,* October 12, 13, 1900; Richardson, *Messages and Papers,* X, 146.

31. J. H. Danskin to McKinley, January 12, 1900, McKinley papers, LC; Hay to White, March 10, 1900, *ibid.*

32. Cortelyou to McKinley, May 19, 1900, *ibid.;* Washington Post, May 18–21, 1900.

33. See John H. Ferguson, *American Diplomacy and the Boer War* (Phila.: Univ. of Pennsylvania Press, 1939), 148; Peck, *Twenty Years of the Republic,* 640–641; McKinley to Hay, August 20, 1900, Hay papers, LC.

34. Younger, *John A. Kasson,* 367–369.

35. See Cullom, *Fifty Years of Public Service,* 369; Holt, *Treaties Defeated by the Senate,* 196ff.

36. Cullom, *Fifty Years of Public Service,* 374.

37. Coolidge, *Orville H. Platt,* 258–259; Foster, *Diplomatic Memoirs,* II, 18; New York *Tribune,* February 8, 1900; see Allison to George Roberts, September 25, 1901, to Theodore Roosevelt, November 2, 1901, Allison papers, ISDHA.

38. Kasson to Allison, October 18, 1898, Allison papers, ISDHA; Wilbur F. Wakeman to Allison, July 12, 1901, *ibid.;* John A. Kasson, "Reciprocity," typescript of a speech before the Illinois Manufacturers' Association, Chicago, October 24, 1901, Kasson papers, ISDHA.

39. Leonard Wood to Lodge, January 12, 1901, Lodge papers, MHS; Lodge to Paul Dana, December 7, 1899, *ibid.;* Walters, *Joseph Benson Foraker,* 161–174.

40. *The Nation,* 70 (February 22, 1900), 137.

41. Kohlsaat, *From McKinley to Harding,* 69–71; Coolidge, *Orville H. Platt,* 359.

42. W. H. Hart to Beveridge, March 26, 1900, Beveridge papers, LC; Olcott, *William McKinley,* I, 217.

43. New York *World,* February 17, 1900; *The Nation,* 70 (March 6, 1900), 195.

44. Olcott, *William McKinley,* I, 218; John A. Kasson, "Impressions of President McKinley," *The Century Magazine,* 63 (December, 1901), 269–275.

45. New York *Times,* February 20, 1900.

46. Nevins, *Henry White,* 162–163; Gelber, *The Rise of Anglo American Friendship,* 12.

47. Dennett, *John Hay,* 285–286.

48. Foster, *Diplomatic Memoirs,* II, 257; Conger to Hay, November 3, 1898,

cited in A. Whitney Griswold, *The Far Eastern Policy of the United States* (New York: Harcourt, Brace Co., 1938), 59.

49. *Ibid.*, 30.

50. Hay to White, November 23, 1898, Hay papers, LC.

51. New York *Times*, August 16, 1899.

52. Griswold, *Far Eastern Policy*, 64ff; Dennis, *Adventures in American Diplomacy*, 185, 208ff.

53. Thayer, *Life and Letters of John Hay*, II, 241; *For. Rels.*, *1899*, 128–142.

54. *Ibid.*, 133–134; Hay to Wu Ting Fang, November 11, 1899, Hay papers, LC.

55. *For. Rels. 1899*, 77, 102; Conger to Hay, May 21, 1900, G. W. Ragsdale to Admiral Louis Kempff, May 29, 1900, copies in McKinley papers, LC; Dennis, *Adventures in American Diplomacy*, 218.

56. Kempff to Long, June 3, 1900, copy in McKinley papers, LC; Hay to Conger, June 10, 1900, Montgomery papers, HML.

57. Cortelyou to Perry Heath, September 4, 1900, McKinley papers, LC.

58. Hay to McKinley, July 6, August 20, September 3, 1900, McKinley papers, LC.

59. Jessup, *Elihu Root*, I, 382–383.

60. Olcott, *William McKinley*, II, 352.

61. Henry Adams, *The Education of Henry Adams* (Boston: Houghton-Mifflin Co., 1918), 392.

62. Olcott, *William McKinley*, II, 252.

63. Hay to McKinley, August 20, 1900, McKinley papers, LC.

64. Adee to McKinley, August 21, 1900, draft statement in Adee's hand, dated August 28, 1900, Root to McKinley, September 11, 1900, all *ibid.*

65. McKinley to Hay, September 14, 1900, Hay papers, LC.

66. Hay to McKinley, September 17, 1900, *ibid.*

67. Hay to Adee, September 14, 1900, McKinley papers, LC.

XXI: *PRESIDENT OF ALL THE PEOPLE*

1. Olcott, *William McKinley*, II, 304–306.

2. Long, *America of Yesterday*, 216.

3. Wilson to McKinley, July 19, 1899, McKinley papers, LC.

4. McKinley to Gordon, July 23, 1898, McKinley papers, LC.

5. Wilson to McKinley, August 21, 1899, *ibid.*; A. B. Cornell to Depew, July 10, 1899, Depew papers, LC; Peck, *Twenty Years of the Republic*, 628.

6. Porter to McKinley, November 14, 1899, McKinley papers, LC.

7. Adams, *Education*, 373–374.

8. Washington to McKinley, December 22, 1898, McKinley papers, LC.

9. Washington *Post*, July 16, 1899.

10. Hanna to McKinley, November 13, 1899, McKinley papers, LC.

11. Hanna to Hay, November 11, 1899, Hay papers, LC.

12. Stoddard, *As I Knew Them*, 261.

13. Gage to Holmes Hoge, April 17, 1899, Gage papers, LC.

14. Hanna to Chandler, March 25, 1899, Chandler papers, LC.

15. Roosevelt to Kohlsaat, August 7, 1899, Roosevelt papers, LC.

16. Chandler to P. E. Dow, August 17, 1899, Chandler papers, LC.

17. John A. Garraty, *Right Hand Man* (New York: Harper Bros., 1960), 160.

18. Leech, *In the Days of McKinley*, 547.

19. Chandler to Alger, July 22, 1899, Chandler papers, LC.

20. Dawes, *Journal*, 185–186.

21. Richardson, *Messages and Papers*, X, 135–136.

22. See Corbin to Alger, May 1, 1899, McKinley papers, LC; Corbin to General H. C. Merriam, May 26, 1899, Alger to Merriam, May 31, 1899, Merriam to Corbin, June 12, 1899, all in Montgomery papers, HML.

23. Brown, *The Leadership of Congress*, 11.

24. *Speeches and Addresses* (1900), 55.

25. *Ibid.*, 64.

26. Lodge to Henry [?], January 21, 1898, Lodge papers, MHS.

27. *Speeches and Addresses* (1900), 199.

28. Gage to Henderson, April 20, 1899, Gage papers, LC.

29. Gage to Henderson, March 23, 1899, *ibid.*

30. Dawes, *Journal*, 191.

31. Allison to Aldrich, May 11, 1899, Platt to Aldrich, May 13, 1899, Fairbanks to Aldrich, June 7, 1899, Aldrich papers, LC.

32. Washington *Post*, July 11, 1899; Dawes, *Journal*, 205; Richardson, *Messages and Papers*, X, 131ff; Gage to C. P. Jones, December 27, 1899, Gage papers, LC.

33. Lodge to Henry [?], December 20, 1899, Lodge papers, MHS.

34. Washington *Post*, January 16, 1900.

35. Gage to M. C. McDonald, March 16, 1900, Gage papers, LC; Gage to L. B. Sidway, March 23, 1900, *ibid.*

36. Murat Halstead to McKinley, October 1, 1899, McKinley papers, LC.

37. Hay to McKinley, August 28, 1899, *ibid.*

38. Washington *Post*, April 4, 5, May 2, 1900.

39. New York *Times*, April 6, 1900.

40. *Roosevelt–Lodge Correspondence*, I, 455; William Lamb to Dewey, April 9, 1900, Dewey papers, LC; H. C. Wallace to Dewey, June 2, 1900, *ibid.*

41. New York *Times*, April 5, 1900; Leech, *In the Days of McKinley*, 428; Dawes, *Journal*, 221.

42. Olcott, *William McKinley*, II, 307–308; Bristow, *Fraud and Politics*, 101.

43. Beer, *Hanna*, 180.

44. Washington *Post*, June 7, 1899.

45. Dawes, *Journal*, 229.

46. Hobart, *Memories*, 78.

47. Hay to McKinley, June 17, 1899, McKinley papers, LC.

48. New York *Times*, June 30, 1899.

49. C. C. Payne to McKinley, October 23, 1899, McKinley papers, LC; Washington *Post*, January 14, 1900.

50. *Roosevelt–Lodge Correspondence*, I, 423, 427, 416.

51. New York *Herald*, February 7, 1900; Kohlsaat, *From McKinley to Harding*, 86.

52. Pringle, *Theodore Roosevelt*, 219; *Roosevelt–Lodge Correspondence*, 219. See Roosevelt to Taft, August 6, 1900, Taft papers, LC.

53. Butler, *Across the Busy Years*, 226–231.

54. Washington *Post*, April 13, 1900; *ibid.*, May 10, 1900; Thayer, *Life and Letters of John Hay*, II, 342.

55. Quay to McKinley, May 21, 1900, copy in McKinley papers, LC.

56. Long to Alger, May 15, 1900, Alger papers, WLCL.

57. Dawes, *Journal*, 231.

58. Washington *Post*, April 11, 1900.

59. Murat Halstead to Reid, March 19, 1900, Reid papers, LC; Ross, *Jonathan Prentiss Dolliver*, 159.

60. Foraker, *Notes*, II, 90.

61. Washington *Post*, June 17, 1900.

62. New York *Times*, June 15, 1900; New York *Tribune*, June 14, 1900.

63. *Roosevelt–Lodge Correspondence*, I, 459–460; Olcott, *William McKinley*, II, 271; Platt, *Autobiography*, 384ff.

64. Olcott, *William McKinley*, II, 271ff.

65. *Ibid.*, 274.

66. *Ibid.*, 274–275. Roosevelt to Lodge, April 23, 1900, *Roosevelt–Lodge Correspondence*, I, 463: "By the way, I did *not* say that I would not under any circumstances accept the Vice-presidency."

67. Washington *Post*, June 18, 1900.

68. Dunn, *From Harrison to Harding*, I, 335.

69. *Official Proceedings of the Twelfth Republican National Convention* . . . (Philadelphia, 1900), 29; Pringle, *Theodore Roosevelt*, 220ff.

70. Olcott, *William McKinley*, II, 276–277. All the papers reprinted here by Olcott are in chronological order in the McKinley papers, LC.

71. New York *Tribune*, June 21, 1900; New York *Times*, June 12, 1900.

72. *Mark Hanna: His Book*, 16.

73. Ross, *Jonathan Prentiss Dolliver*, 161.

74. Olcott, *William McKinley*, II, 281–282; New York *Tribune*, June 22, 1900.

75. Lodge to Roosevelt, June 29, 1900, Roosevelt papers, LC.

76. Roosevelt to McKinley, June 21, 1900, McKinley papers, LC.

77. Butler, *Presidents I Have Seen and Known*, 39.

78. Hanna to McKinley, June 25, 1900, McKinley papers, LC.

79. McKinley to Hanna, June 22, 1900, Hanna Transcripts, Felt.

80. New York *Tribune*, July 12, 13, 1900.

81. Olcott, *William McKinley*, II, 286–287.

82. *Ibid.*, 288.

83. Leech, *In the Days of McKinley*, 553.

84. Dunn, *From Harrison to Harding*, I, 347–348.

85. *Mr. Dooley's Philosophy*, 229.

86. Cullom to Chandler, September 28, 1900, Chandler papers, LC; Root to Hay, September 2, 1900, Hay papers, LC; D. E. Rowe to McKinley, October 16, 1900, McKinley papers, LC.

87. Chandler to J. W. Babcock, September 13, 1900, Chandler papers, LC; Dawes, *Journal*, 240.

88. C. P. Taft to Taft, August 1, 1900, October 15, 1900, Taft papers, LC; *Ohio State Journal*, September 9, 1900; John Barrett to Cortelyou, September 3, 1900, Hanna to McKinley, October 14, 1900, McKinley papers, LC.

89. Washington *Post,* January 4, 1900; Heath to Cortelyou, October 31, 1900, Hanna to McKinley, August 10, 1900, McKinley papers, LC; Croly, *Marcus Alonzo Hanna,* 325.

90. New York *Tribune,* July 6, 1900; Chicago *Record,* July 12, 1900.

91. Hay to McKinley, September 3, 1900, McKinley papers, LC.

92. Unknown Addressee to McKinley, October 30, 1900, *ibid.,* box 208.

93. Wolcott to McKinley, August 22, 1900, *ibid.;* Hay to McKinley, July 2, 1900, *ibid.;* Stewart, *Reminiscences,* 319.

94. *Republican Campaign Textbook, 1900,* 78, 441–442; New York *Tribune,* September 18, 1900.

95. McKinley to Root, July 28, 1900, Root papers, LC.

96. T. A. Bailey, "Was the Presidential Election of 1900 a Mandate on Imperialism?" *MVHR,* 24 (June, 1937), 43–52.

97. Taft to Murat Halstead, June 30, 1900, Halstead papers, HPSO; Taft to C. P. Taft, August 11, 1900, Taft papers, LC.

98. The letter is reprinted in Croly, *Marcus Alonzo Hanna,* 329–330. Croly states that the letter was copied for the White House files and a future biographer. A search of the McKinley papers, LC, in 1958 failed to reveal such a copy or the letter cited above. The only text is that which Croly reprints, and which was presumably lost with the rest of Hanna's papers after Croly finished his biography.

99. Hanna to McKinley, August 28, 1900, McKinley papers, LC.

100. New York *Tribune,* September 20–27, 1900; see Dawes, *Journal,* 249, 252; New York *Tribune,* September 28, 30, 1900; Hanna to McKinley, July 27. 1900, McKinley papers, LC.

101. Croly, *Marcus Alonzo Hanna,* 333.

102. Beer, *Hanna,* 230.

103. C. A. Carlisle to McKinley, November 3, 1900, McKinley papers, LC; Grosvenor to McKinley, October 8, 1900, *ibid.*

104. Croly, *Marcus Alonzo Hanna,* 338; Washington *Post,* September 16. 1900.

105. *Ibid.,* September 19, October 21, 1900.

106. Roosevelt to Payne, September 29, 1900, Roosevelt papers, LC.

107. Cole, *I Remember, I Remember,* 293; Roosevelt to Lodge, November 9, 1900, Roosevelt papers, LC.

108. Washington *Post,* November 6, 1900.

109. Hanna to McKinley, November 7, 1900, McKinley to Hanna, November 16, 1900, McKinley papers, LC; Bryan to McKinley, November 8, 1900, *ibid.*

110. H. W. Taft to W. H. Taft, December 10, 1900, Taft papers, LC; Roosevelt to Hay, November 10, 1900, Roosevelt papers, LC.

111. Dawes, *Journal,* 253; New York *Tribune,* November 25, 1900; Olcott, *William McKinley,* II, 296.

XXII: *JOURNEY TO BUFFALO*

1. Julian Ralph, "McKinley as I Saw Him," Washington *Post,* April 7, 1901, p. 16.

2. Leech, *In the Days of McKinley,* 567.

3. Cortelyou to C. H. Grosvenor, May 11, 1899, McKinley papers, LC.
4. Hay to McKinley, January 9, 1901, *ibid.*
5. McKinley to M. C. Barber, January 31, 1901, *ibid.*
6. Hanna to McKinley, February 4, 1901, *ibid.*
7. Root to Wood, January 9, 1901, copy *ibid.*
8. McClure, *Recollections*, 152.
9. Bristow, *Fraud and Politics*, 109.
10. Washington *Post*, March 5, 1901.
11. Knox to McKinley, April 4, 1901, McKinley papers, LC.
12. Hay to McKinley, August 23, 1901, *ibid.*
13. T. D. Nicholls to McKinley, March 21, 1901, *ibid.*
14. Washington *Post*, August 3, 1901.
15. Roosevelt to Taft, July 15, 1901, Taft papers, LC.
16. Beer, *Hanna*, 245–246.
17. Washington *Post*, April 30, 1901.
18. *Ibid.*, May 8, 1901.
19. *Ibid.*, May 10, 1901.
20. *Ibid.*, May 11, 1901.
21. Henry Littlefield West, "The President's Recent Tour," *The Forum*, 31 (August, 1901), 661–669.
22. New York *Tribune*, May 19, 1901.
23. Olcott, *William McKinley*, II, 309–310; New York *Tribune*, June 11, 12, 1901.
24. McKinley to Hay, July 28, 1901, McKinley papers, LC.
25. Hay to McKinley, June 29, 1901, *ibid.*
26. Olcott, *William McKinley*, I, 126.
27. Pencilled notes in McKinley's hand, item 15765, vol. 80, McKinley papers, LC.
28. Leech, *In the Days of McKinley*, 582.
29. Kasson, "Impressions of President McKinley," 275.
30. Ross, *Jonathan Prentiss Dolliver*, 169.
31. Olcott, *William McKinley*, II, 300.
32. Lodge to Aldrich, June 20, 1901, Aldrich papers, LC.
33. Item 15755, vol. 80, McKinley papers, LC.
34. Butler, *Presidents I Have Seen and Known*, 40.
35. Dunn, *From Harrison to Harding*, I, 355.
36. The speech is reprinted in Olcott, *William McKinley*, II, 378–384. I have reconstructed the events of the assassination chiefly from the New York *Tribune* and Washington *Post*.
37. Olcott, *William McKinley*, II, 314.
38. *Ibid.*, 316.
39. Washington *Post*, September 7, 1901.
40. *Ibid.*, September 7, 1901.
41. *Ibid.*
42. The medical bulletins are arranged chronologically in McKinley papers, LC.
43. See Olcott, *William McKinley*, II, 320–321.
44. Washington *Post*, September 8, 1901.
45. *Ibid.*, September 10, 1901.

46. Hay to Morgan, September 13, 1901, Morgan papers, LC.
47. Olcott, *William McKinley,* II, 324–325.
48. Washington *Post,* September 14, 1901.
49. A fully documented autopsy was issued; see "Official Report of the Case of President William McKinley," *The American Journal of the Medical Sciences,* 122, number 5 (October 19, 1901).
50. Cortelyou to Day, September 17, 1901, McKinley papers, LC; Heald, *The McKinley Era,* 91. See Roosevelt to Lodge, September 23, 1901, *Roosevelt–Lodge Correspondence,* I, 506: "It is a dreadful thing to come into the Presidency this way; but it would be a far worse thing to be morbid about it."

XXIII: *EPILOGUE*

1. Ida McKinley to Webb C. Hayes, December 10, 1905, Webb C. Hayes papers, HML.
2. McClellan, *The Gentleman and the Tiger,* 121.
3. Gary to McKinley, July 31, 1900, McKinley papers, LC.
4. Chandler to Dawes, March 19, 1901, *ibid.*
5. *Speeches and Addresses* (1900), 326.
6. *Ibid.,* 129.
7. Leech, *In the Days of McKinley,* vi, frontispiece.

Index

Adams, Henry: on McKinley's cabinet in 1897, 269; and Boxer Rebellion, 472; on McKinley's career, 478

Adee, Alvee A.: 256; and de Lome letter, 357

Agoncillo, Felipe: 406, 420

Aguinaldo, Emilio: 388; as leader of Filipinos, 405; starts Philippine insurrection, 421; captured in 1901, 444; 503

Alaska Boundary Dispute: 451ff.

Aldrich, Nelson W.: manages McKinley Tariff in Senate in 1890, 136ff.; opposes higher tariff in 1897, 278ff.; helps manage Treaty of Paris, 419ff.

Alger, Russell: 111; 157; 206; accepts post in War Department, 260; on Roosevelt, 394; and post-war investigation of War Department, 425ff.

Allison, William B.: 6; 55; 111; 136; 165; as potential presidential candidate in 1896, 196–97; and treasury post in 1897, 254; and tariff reciprocity, 463; as vice-presidential possibility in 1900, 492

Altgeld, John P.: 221; 240

American Protective Association: 191–92

Antietam, Battle of: 24ff.

Armour, Philip: 174

Arthur, Chester Alan: 71; proposes tariff reform, 73; 305

Bacon, Augustus O.: 422

Bailey, Joe: 362; 377

Balser, Henry: 46

Bayne, William M.: 98

Beer, William C.: 236

Belden, George W.: 38

Beveridge, Albert: 435–36

Blackburn, J. C. S.: 68

Blaine, James G.: 55; 79; 95; favored by McKinley in GOP convention of 1884, 97; 108; in convention of 1888, 116ff.; and tariff reciprocity in 1890, 129ff.; 142ff.; 157

Blakelee, Miss E. M.: 11

Bland-Allison Act (1878): 57–60

Bland, Richard P.: 133

Bliss, Cornelius: 224; 265; 408

Boxer Rebellion: 469ff.

Bristow, Joseph L.: 447

Brooke, John R.: 445

Bryan, William Jennings: at Republican convention of 1896, 216; characterized, 222ff.; appeal of in 1896, 237–38; on Hawaiian annexation, 294; volunteers for War with Spain, 381; supports Treaty of Paris, 418ff.; as candidate in 1900, 502; and imperialism in 1900, 503

Buckner, Simon Bolivar: 241

Burrows, Julius Caesar: 260

Bushnell, Asa: 153; 181; 251; 255

Butler, Joseph G.: 498

Butler, Nicholas Murray: 490

Butterworth, Ben: 102; 112; 117

Bynum, William D.: 242

Calhoun, William J.: 339

Cambon, Jules: 396

Campbell, James E.: 102; 152; 156

Campos, Marshal: 327

Cannon, Frank: 216

Cannon, Joseph G.: 55; 123; 127; and sugar bounty, 132; 225; 363–64

Canovas del Castillo: 327; assassinated, 343

Carlisle, John G.: 55; 105; 125

Carnegie, Andrew: 119; 315; opposes Treaty of Paris, 416ff.; on results of Treaty of Paris, 422; on Philippine insurrection, 435

Carnifex Ferry, Battle of: 21–22

Carter, Thomas: 511

Chandler, William E.: 189; 199; 214; on Roosevelt, 262; and international bimetallism commission in 1897, 282ff.; 334; 377; 401; 480

Choate, Joseph H.: 317; 401; 454; 469

Clarkson, James S.: 134; 164; 224

Clay, Henry: McKinley's high regard for, 64

Clayton, Powell: 368

Cleveland, Grover: 79, 98, inaugurated as president in 1885, 105; 107; renominated for president in 1888, 111; 121; on tariff issue in 1890, 133; 220; during campaign of 1896, 241; inauguration-eve visit with McKinley in 1897, 270–

Cleveland, Grover (*continued*) 71; and Cuban issue, 328; as anti-imperialist, 417
Conger, Edward: 467
Conkling, Roscoe: 55; 202
Converse, George: 76
Cortelyou, George B.: 268; 296; 383; 395; 509; fears of McKinley's assassination, 518
Cox, George: 98
Coxey's "Army": 179
Cromwell, William Nelson: 453
Cullom, Shelby: as potential presidential candidate in 1896, 204–05; and treasury post in 1897, 257–58; 275; 462; 501
Czolgosz, Leon: 520

Danish West Indies: purchase plan, 460
Davis, Cushman K.: 206; 401; 408
Davis, Jefferson: 13
Dawes, Charles G.: 204ff.; as campaign manager in 1896, 225; 259; on Alger, 395; 480; 508
Day, William Rufus: 51; 252; as assistant secretary of state, 256; and Hawaiian annexation, 294–95; and yellow press, 331; 345–46; and de Lome letter, 357
de Lome, Enrique Dupuy: 336; 353
de Lome letter: 355ff.
Depew, Chauncey: 111; 116; 195; 203
Dewey, George: 385; on Philippine insurgency, 420; on First Philippine Commission, 441; as presidential timber in 1900, 285ff.
Dick, Charles: 189; 494
Dingley, Nelson: 277
Dingley Tariff (1897): 277ff.; and reciprocity provisions, 280–81; and reciprocity treaties negotiated under, 462ff.
Dodge Commission: 424–28
Dodge, Grenville M.: 424
Dolliver, Jonathan P.: as vice-presidential possibility in 1900, 492
Dudley, W. W.: 119; 134

Eagan, Charles P.: 427–28
Elkins, Stephen B.: 194; 374
Evans, Henry Clay: 501
Everett, Edward: 11

Fairbanks, Charles Warren: 194; 210
Federal Elections Bill (1890): 111; 135ff.
Floyd, John B.: 21
Folger, Charles: 75

Foraker, Joseph Benson: 78; enters Ohio politics, 93–94; senatorial ambitions, 101; at GOP convention in 1888, 114–17; 154; 160; 165; opposes Sherman in cabinet, 252ff.; and Cuba, 348; on McKinley's war declaration, 377; and tariff reciprocity for Porto Rico, 465; 492; nominates McKinley in 1900, 497
Foraker, Julia B.: 67
Foster, John W.: 294; 336
Frease, George: 149
Fremont, John C.: 16
Frick, Henry C.: 174
Frye, William P.: 142; 365; 401; suggests indemnity for Philippines, 413; 482
Fuller, Melville W.: 273

Gage, Lyman J.: accepts treasury post in 1897, 258–59; and international bimetallism, 285; and trust issue, 479; and gold standard legislation, 483
Gallinger, Jacob H.: 199; on civil service reform, 288; on McKinley, 199
Garfield, James A.: 6; socializes with McKinley as congressman, 57, 88; recommends McKinley to Ways and Means Committee, 69; assassinated, 70–72
Gary, James A.: 263; 527
Glidden, Charles: 15
Goff, Nathan B.: 263
Gold Standard Act: 482ff.
Gomez, Maximo: 327
Gordon, John B.: 477
Gorman, Arthur P.: 416
Gould, Helen: 380
Gowdy, John: 268
Grant, Ulysses S.: 41; 303
Gray, George: 401; as anti-expansionist at Paris Peace Conference, 409
Gresham, Walter Q.: 111
Griggs, John W.: 433; 440
Grosvenor, Charles: 112; 201; 506

Hague Conference: 459–60
Hahn, William M.: 154; 165
Hale, Eugene: 55; 226
Halstead, Murat: 102; 118
Hancock, Winfield Scott: 70
Hanna, Marcus Alonzo: 34; personality as younger man, 51–52; in Ohio politics, 93, 97–100; as Sherman manager in 1888, 111ff.; on Tariff of 1890, 145; after GOP convention of 1892, 167; as McKinley's campaign manager, chaps.

X and XI, *passim;* and proposed cabinet post in 1897, 250ff.; opposes exclusive tariff protection in 1897, 278; and civil service reform, 291; and relations with McKinley after 1897, 298ff.; elected to Senate in 1897–98, 299ff.; manages congressional elections of 1898, 402ff.; on vice-presidential nomination in 1900, 483ff.; and late relationship with McKinley, 488ff.; on GOP ticket of 1900, 498; as speaker in campaign of 1900, 505; on McKinley's assassination, 522
Harrison, Benjamin: 100–01; 111; nominated in 1888, 118ff.; and tariff reciprocity in 1890, 129; 164; as potential presidential candidate in 1896, 194ff.; in campaign of 1896, 230
Hastings, Daniel: 112
Hastings, Russell: 36; 220
Hawaiian annexation: 292ff.
Hay, John Milton: 174; and campaign advice to McKinley in 1895, 184; 227; on Bryan in 1896, 242; 266; and patronage, 289; and Anglo-American accord, 297; appointed secretary of state, 400–01; on Carnegie's anti-imperialism, 417; on Alger, 430; on Bryan's opposition to his diplomacy, 477; and partition of China, 468–70; on Roosevelt as vice-presidential candidate, 491; attacks Bryan in campaign of 1900, 502; 509
Hay-Pauncefote Treaty (first): 454ff.
Hay-Pauncefote Treaty (second): 458ff.
Hayes, Rutherford B.: 17; 18; 28–29; 30; advises McKinley on career, 33ff.; 45; 49; and disputed presidential election, 54; 57; 79; entertains McKinleys as president, 87; 120; 123–24; 150
Hayes, Webb C.: 378
Hearst, William Randolph: 326; 330
Henderson, David B.: 483
Henderson, John B.: 78
Herrick, Myron: 186–88; 206; and treasury post in 1897, 257; as manager of McKinley's income, 321
Hicks-Beach, Sir Michael: 283
Hill, David Bennett: 240
Hill, James J.: 227
Hippisley, Alfred: 468
Hitchcock, Ethan Allen: 268; 513
Hoadly, George: 95
Hoar, George F.: 142; 275; opposes Treaty of Paris, 416ff.; and McKinley after treaty fight, 422

Hobart, Garrett Augustus: as McKinley's choice for running mate in 1896, 220; as campaigner in 1896, 228; and McKinley in 1896, 237; characterized, 274; 303; as manager of McKinley's income, 321; asks Alger to resign, 430–31
Hobart, Jennie: 312

Ingalls, John: 142

Jones, A. W.: 101
Jones, John P.: 139

Kasson, John A.: 76; 281; 462ff.
Keifer, J. Warren: 55; 71
Kelley, William D.: 65–66; 126; 132
Kellogg, William P.: 206
Knox, Philander: 46; 174; 512
Kohlsaat, Herman H.: 166; 258; 370; 388

La Follette, Robert Marion: 60; on McKinley as a speaker, 86; 206; 263
Lamar, L. Q. C.: 55
Lauterbach, Edward: 267
Lee, Fitzhugh: 268; and Cuban problem, 340ff.; 359
Lincoln, Abraham: 30–31
Lodge, Henry Cabot: 125; 135; and gold standard platform plank in 1896, 211–12; 253; 294; on McKinley's Cuban policy in 1897, 349–50; on Alger, 384; and Philippines, 404; on Treaty of Paris, 419; opposes First Hay-Pauncefote Treaty, 457; and gold standard legislation, 483; on Roosevelt as vice-presidential candidate in 1900, 490; on Roosevelt's behavior as vice-presidential candidate, 498
Long, John Davis: as secretary of the Navy in 1897, 261; and sinking of the *Maine,* 360; on Dewey's promotion, 386; on retention of the Philippines, 404; as vice-presidential possibility in 1900, 491; 504
Low, Seth: 459
Lynch, William A.: 38

MacArthur, Arthur: 443
McBride, John: 177
McClellan, George B.: 22
McClellan, George B., Jr.: 526
McCook, John: 27; 264; 383
McKenna, Joseph: 133; 263–64
MacKinlay, James: 2
McKinley, Abner: 40; 189; 267; 270

McKinley, Anne: 37; 39

McKinley, David: 2

McKinley, Helen: 13; 320

McKinley, Ida Saxton (wife of president): personality as a young lady, 43–44; stricken by death of children, 47–49; precarious health as matron, 82–83; during husband's governorship, 163ff.; in campaign of 1896, 237; as first lady, 310ff.; illness in 1901, 513–16; last years, 526

McKinley, Ida (daughter of president): 47–48

McKinley, James: 245–46; 320

McKinley, Katherine (daughter of president): 47–48

McKinley, Mabel: 320

McKinley, Mary: 3

McKinley, Nancy Allison (mother of president): and family background, 4–5; and education, 7–8; 246; 269; death in 1897, 321

McKinley, Sarah: 12; 26; 39

McKinley, William, Jr.: (President U.S.): ancestors, 2–3; born, 6; childhood in Niles, Ohio, 6; youthful reserve and detachment, 7–8; life in Poland, Ohio, 9–10; cast of mind as youth, 11–12; and mother's hopes for in ministry, 12; and religion, 12; and slavery, 12–13; at college, 13–15; as teacher, 14; enlists in army, 15–16; trains as recruit, 16–17; as home-town correspondent at training camp, 17–18; and religion in army, 17; and patriotism in army, 18; on eve of first battle, 19; promoted to sergeant, 22–23; qualities as a soldier, 22–24; and Battle of Antietam, 24–26; promoted to lieutenant after Battle of Antietam, 26; and robust physical condition during war, 27; promoted to captain and major, 30; ideas on war, 31–32; joins Masons during war, 31; qualities of post-war personality, 34–36; at Albany Law School, 36–37; as a lawyer, 39–40; and first political speech, 40; runs for prosecuting attorney of Stark County, 42; married, 45; as temperance leader, 45–46; defends striking miners in 1876–77, 50–52; works with Hanna, 52; runs for Congress in 1876, 52ff.; arrives in Congress, 55; and Republican party of his congressional years, 56–58; and Bland-Allison Act, 57–59; and tariff philosophy, 59–64;

and "whiggish" doctrines, 64; and Negro rights, 67–68; on Southern obstructionism, 67–68; on regulation of interstate commerce, 69; fights and loses election contest, 73ff.; and idea of tariff commission, 73–74; loses congressional seat, 77; supports Blaine in 1884, 77–79; as temporary chairman in GOP convention of 1884, 78; and social life as congressman, 81–82; and living accommodations as congressman, 82; physical condition in middle age, 83; courtesy, 83–84; patience, 84; sense of humor, 85; as speaker in Congress, 85–87; and idea of democracy, 86; and income as congressman, 88; shaving habits, 89; vain about spectacles, 89; heavy smoker, 90; and Ohio politics as congressman, 92; and Ohio patronage as congressman, 98; and ballot box fraud case of 1888, 102–03; and regulation of interstate commerce, 105; opposes tariff changes 1887–88, 108ff.; as dark horse vice-presidential candidate in 1888, 111–13; formulates and reads GOP platform of 1888, 113–14; refuses dark horse presidential nomination in 1888, 116–20; as possible cabinet member in 1889, 121; as candidate for House speakership in 1889, 123ff.; as House majority leader, 126; on Reed rules in 1890, 128; and tariff hearings, 128–29; on Tariff of 1890, chapter VIII, *passim;* and relations with President Harrison, 136; and free silver in 1890, 139–40; on Federal Elections Bill in 1890, 141; and tariff reciprocity in 1890, 143–44; and congressional election of 1890, 148ff.; on defeat in 1890, 150; and idea of governorship of Ohio, 152–53; and silver question in 1891, 154–55; and anti-corporation legislation as governor of Ohio, 158; and labor as governor, 158; and Ohio legislature, 161; personal life as governor, 161ff.; in GOP presidential convention of 1892, 164ff.; as chairman of GOP convention of 1892, 166–67; and actions at GOP convention of 1892, 163ff.; and bankruptcy in 1893, 169ff.; and gubernatorial campaign of 1893, 175ff.; and relations with Hanna after 1895, 195–96; and GOP party bosses in 1895, 187–88; campaigns in South in 1895, 192–93; and gold standard plank in 1896, 211ff.; during nomination in 1896, 218–19; and tariff question in 1896, 224; and visiting delegations in 1896, 232ff.; and currency issue during campaign of 1896, 235–36; and nationalism in 1896, 235; thanks Hanna in 1896, 246; offers Hanna cabinet post in 1896, 253; inaugurated as president, 272ff.; and dealings with congressmen, 274–75; as cabinet administrator, 276; and international bimetallism, 281ff.; and fiscal reform after 1897, 286ff.; and civil service reform after 1897, 288ff.; on "manifest destiny," 296–97; and arbitration treaty with England, 297; helps Hanna in senatorial election of 1897, 299ff.; and confident America, 304–05; dislikes police guards, 307–08; and formal entertaining, 308ff.; and clothing as president, 314–15; and photographers, 315; and liquor as president, 315–16; patience, 316–17; forms of relaxation, 319–20; and newspapers, 322–23; as a speech-writer, 323ff.; public appearances, 324; and Congress on the Cuban question in 1897, 332–34; and ideas of foreign policy after 1897, 334–35; Cuban purchase plan, 340; and initial Cuban policy, 342ff.; and Cuban relief plan, 349; and riots in Havana in 1898, 352; and Dupuy de Lome, 354–55; and de Lome letter, 358ff.; and report on sinking of *Maine*, 367ff.; summation of Cuban policy, 375ff.; and wartime patronage, 382–83; on Alger during war, 384; early inclination to retain Philippines, 388; and cabinet debate on Philippines, 396ff.; and peace commission of 1898, 400–02; and final decision to retain Philippines, 410–13; and Southern tour of 1898, 415ff.; and ideas on Filipino liberty, 423; and Alger after war, 429ff.; and Alger's resignation, 431; dislikes Anglo-Saxon racists, 436; and executive rule in the dependencies, 437ff.; whole colonial policy strengthens presidency, 444; refuses Hay's resignation, 455–56; on Hay's diplomacy, 456; and Porto Rican tariff reciprocity, 463ff.; and Open Door policy, 466ff.; and Boxer Rebellion, 469ff.; and China policy, 473ff.; and sense of American destiny after 1898, 477ff.; and elections of 1899, 479; ideas on trusts and trust regulation, 480ff.; and gold standard legislation, 483ff.; on Dewey-for-President boom of 1900, 487; on vice-presidential nomination of 1900, 494ff.; on excessive use of patronage in campaign of 1900, 503–04; opposes Hanna campaign tour in 1900, 505; on re-election in 1900, 508; and second inauguration, 510–12; and western tour of 1901, 512ff.; and tariff reciprocity after 1900, 516ff.; visits Pan-American Exposition in Buffalo, 516ff.; assassinated, 521; last days, 522–23; death and funeral, 524–25; presidency and qualities summarized and analyzed, 527ff.

McKinley, William, Sr. (president's father): 3; on life in early Ohio, 6; and education, 7; 13

McKinley Tariff: 123–51 *passim*

McMillan, Benton: 127

Mahan, Alfred T.: 293; 332

Maine: dispatched to Havana, 359ff.

Manderson, Charles: 40–41

Manley, Joe: 210

Maria Christina, Queen Regent of Spain: 327, 347

Marti, Jose: 327

Mason, William: 195; 348

Matthews, Stanley: 17

Medill, Joseph: 255

Merritt, Wesley: 409

Michener, Louis T.: 119; 164

Miles, Nelson A.: 384; and Dodge Commission, 426–27

Mills Bill (1888): 121

Mills, Roger Q.: 55; 77; formulates tariff bill, 108; answers McKinley in tariff debate, 110–11; 130; 155

"Mongrel Tariff" (1883): 74–75

Montgomery, B. F.: 305

Moore, John Bassett: 401; 456

Moore, Opha: 162

Morgan, John Hunt: 28

Morgan, J. P.: 212

Morgan, John Tyler: 339; and isthmian canal, 453ff.

Morrill, Justin S.: 55; 136

Morrison, William: 76; 106

Morse, Leopold: 110

Morton, Levi Parsons: 119, 200–01; as possible presidential candidate in 1896, 202–03

Olney, Richard: 328–29

Osborne, William McKinley: 13, 15; 189; 251; 267

Otis, Elwell: characterized, 438
Otis, Harrison Gray: 264

Paine, Charles J.: 282
Palma, Estrada: 327
Palmer, John R.: 241
Pauncefote, Julian: 373
Payne, Henry C.: 213; 224; 262ff.
Payne, Sereno: 464
Perkins, George: 480; 496
Pingree, Hazen S:. 429
Platt Amendment: 447-49
Platt, Orville H.: 282; 370; on Philippine Islands, 403-04; favors Treaty of Paris, 419; 447; opposes tariff reciprocity, 462
Platt, Thomas Collier: 6; 194; placated by Hanna in 1896, 226; 267ff.; controlled by McKinley after 1897, 290ff.; and Root appointment, 431; on Roosevelt, 489
Porter, Horace: 268; 283; 399; on results of War with Spain, 477
Porter, John Addison: 198; 268
Porto Rican tariff controversy: 463ff.
Proctor, Redfield: 199; speech on Cuba, 365; 385
Pulitzer, Joseph: 330
Pullman, George: 174
Pullman Strike (1894): 178

Quay, Matthew Stanley: 6; characterized, 200; 231; 249; on vice-presidential nomination of 1900, 491
Quigg, Lemuel: 432

Randall, Samuel J.: 69; 108
Rathbone, Estes G.: 447
Reed rules: 127ff.
Reed, Thomas Brackett: 55; 85; 105; as candidate for House speakership in 1889, 123ff.; 164; 175; as potential presidential candidate in 1896, 197-98; in campaign of 1896, 230-31; elected Speaker in 1897, 277; opposes Hawaiian annexation, 296; 333; on Redfield Proctor's speech on Cuba, 365; as anti-imperialist, 417, 435
Reid, Whitelaw: 183; 196; 212; 249; as office-seeker in 1896, 265ff.; 313
Remington, Frederic: 330
Republican party: in McKinley's middle years, 56-58
Rhodes, James Ford: 322
Rockhill, W. W.: 468
Roosevelt, Theodore: on Hanna and Mc-
Kinley in 1896, 228-29; as candidate for assistant secretary of the Navy in 1896-97, 261ff.; on McKinley's foreign policy, 295; and Anglo-Saxon mission, 332; and "round robin" letter of 1898, 394; on anti-imperialists, 416-17; on vice-presidency, 489ff.; as campaigner in 1900, 507ff.; on McKinley's assassination, 522
Root, Elihu: 275; appointed secretary of war, 431ff.; on Insular Cases, 444; and Boxer Rebellion, 471; as vice-presidential possibility in 1900, 492
Rosecrans, William S.: 17
Rubens, Horatio: 355-56

Sagasta, Praxedes: 345
Salisbury, Lord: 284
Sampson, W. T.: 385
Sanford, Alva: 8
Sawyer, Philetus: 263
Schley, W. S.: 385
Schurman, Jacob Gould: heads First Philippine Commission, 441-42
Schurz, Carl: 294; as anti-imperialist, 417
Scott, H. T.: 514
Scott, Nathan B.: 229
Shafter, William: characterized, 385; and army in Cuba, 390-91; as negotiator, 391ff.
Sherman Anti-Trust Act (1890): 135
Sherman, John: in Ohio politics, 93; as candidate for GOP presidential nomination in 1888, 111ff.; 121; and sugar bounty, 132; on silver in 1890, 140; accepts post of secretary of state in 1897, 251ff.; and international bimetallism after 1897, 285; 335; leaves State Department, 380
Sherman Silver Purchase Act (1890): 137ff.
Smith, Charles Emory: 505
Smith, Joseph P.: 189; 260
Smithnight, Louis: 98
Spooner, John Coit: 142; 206
Springer, William: 75
Stevenson, Adlai: 282
Stewart, William M.: 138; 191; and lack of Republican patronage, 290; 502

Taft, Charles P.: 174; 501
Taft, William Howard: 262; heads Second Philippine Commission, 442ff.
Tariff Protection: McKinley's stand in early career, 59-63

Taylor, Hannis: 337; 348
Teller Amendment: 378
Teller, Henry Moore: 139; 214; leaves
    Republican party in 1896, 215–16; 239;
    opposes tariff reduction in 1897, 278;
    287; 290; 482
Thurston, John: 210
Tilden, Samuel J.: 53
Tillman, Benjamin: 274
Tower, Charlemagne: 268

Vest, George: 416

Wade, Benjamin: 9
Walker, Robert: 169
Wallace, Jonathan: unseats McKinley,
    72ff.
Warwick, John G.: 148
Washington, Booker T.: 479
Watterson, Henry: 256–57
Weaver, James B.: 221
West, William: 96
Weyler, Valeriano: 327, 346

Wheeler, Joseph: 383; 391
White, Andrew: 459
White, Henry: 337; 453
White, William Allen: 92; 230; 315
Wilson-Gorman Tariff (1894): 187
Wilson, James: 264; 425; 476
Wilson, William L.: 238
Windom, William: 138
Wolcott, Edward O.: as chairman of inter-
    national bimetallism commission in
    1897, 282ff.; on McKinley's attitude
    toward bimetallism in 1897, 285; 502
Wood, Fernando: 64–65
Wood, Leonard: 428; as civil governor of
    Cuba, 445ff.
Woodford, Stewart: 267; 343ff.; and au-
    tonomy idea for Cuba, 346; 353; after
    de Lome letter, 358ff.; 364; on ulti-
    matum to Spain, 370
Worcester, Dean C.: on First Philippine
    Commission, 441

Yellow press: and Cuban problem, 331–32